IRANICA

Herausgegeben von Alberto Cantera
und Maria Macuch

Band 33

2024
Harrassowitz Verlag · Wiesbaden

Deciphering the Illegible
Festschrift in Honour of Dieter Weber

Edited by
Maria Macuch and Arash Zeini

2024
Harrassowitz Verlag · Wiesbaden

Published with the financial support of the Bahari Fund at the Faculty of Asian and Middle Eastern Studies, University of Oxford, the Corpus Inscriptionum Iranicarum (CII), the Associazione Internazionale di Studi sul Mediterraneo e l'Oriente (ISMEO), and the Bita Daryabari Presidential Chair of Iranian Studies at the University of California, Berkeley.

Bibliografische Information der Deutschen Nationalbibliothek
Die Deutsche Nationalbibliothek verzeichnet diese Publikation in der Deutschen Nationalbibliografie; detaillierte bibliografische Daten sind im Internet über https://dnb.dnb.de abrufbar.

Bibliographic information published by the Deutsche Nationalbibliothek
The Deutsche Nationalbibliothek lists this publication in the Deutsche Nationalbibliografie; detailed bibliographic data are available in the Internet at https://dnb.dnb.de

For further information about our publishing program consult our website https://www.harrassowitz-verlag.de

Printed on permanent/durable paper.
Printing and binding: Hubert & Co., Göttingen
Printed in Germany

ISSN 0944-1271
ISBN 978-3-447-12269-6

Dieter Weber

Contents

Preface

It is with great pleasure that the authors and editors of this collection of essays present this volume to DIETER WEBER as a token of our appreciation and gratitude for the many scholarly contributions with which he has enhanced our field of studies. As one of the very few colleagues who have endeavoured to disentangle the extremely ambiguous Pahlavi cursive script he has indeed dedicated a large part of his scholarly work to "deciphering the illegible", hereby providing access to some of the most significant original documents of the late Sasanian and early Islamic era.

It is most regrettable and a cause for great sadness that our friend and colleague PHILIPPE GIGNOUX, the scholar with whom DIETER collaborated most closely on the decipherment of these texts, passed away before seeing the publication of the Festschrift. In his contribution to this volume, one of his last articles to be printed, he pays tribute to the many years of fruitful collaboration with the dedicatee, conducted in an atmosphere of mutual esteem despite many differences of opinion.

We would like to express our deep gratitude to all those who have made this volume possible: to DIETER's friends and colleagues for contributing so many excellent papers; to KIAN KAHROM for his meticulous typesetting, to YUHAN SOHRAB-DINSHAW VEVAINA and the Bahari Fund at the Faculty of Asian and Middle Eastern Studies, University of Oxford, to NICHOLAS SIMS-WILLIAMS and the Corpus Inscriptionum Iranicarum (CII), to ADRIANO ROSSI and the Associazione Internazionale di Studi sul Mediterraneo e l'Oriente (ISMEO), and to ADAM BENKATO and the Bita Daryabari Presidential Chair of Iranian Studies at the University of California, Berkeley, for providing generous subsidies toward the publication costs.

Berlin and Oxford, June 2024 — The Editors

Dieter Weber — A Scholarly Profile

MARIA MACUCH, Berlin*

DIETER WEBER was born on October 22, 1941 in Cologne (Köln), Germany, as the only child of DORA and WERNER WEBER. Since his father was tragically killed in the war in 1942, he was brought up by his mother alone, spending the first years of his life in Silesia (Schlesien) and later in Leverkusen, where he began school in 1948 and received his high-school diploma (Abitur) in 1961 at the Carl-Duisberg-Gymnasium. He is one of the very few specialists in Iranian Studies, who has focused his scholarly work of recent decades on deciphering the extremely challenging Pahlavi original texts and documents written on a variety of materials (papyri, ostraca, leather, parchment, linen, etc.) in the ambiguous cursive script. Taking up the work of OLAF HANSEN in the nineteen-thirties on the Middle Persian papyri from Egypt, DIETER has not only enhanced this field considerably, correcting many of HANSEN's readings, but has applied his growing experience in deciphering the papyri to other collections of original documents, which have come to light in increasing numbers in the past decades. As all those will know, who have attempted to tackle texts written in the Pahlavi cursive, the difficulties of deciphering the script and understanding the content are almost insurmountable due to the shortness and fragmentary state of many documents, on the one hand, and the equivocality of the script allowing various divergent readings, on the other. These primary sources from late antiquity offer first hand information on numerous economic and bureaucratic issues, are hence eminently important for recognizing and reconstructing significant administrative and legal institutions of pre-Islamic Iran, many of which continued to exist in the first centuries of Islam and had a significant impact on the development of many institutions of the Islamic era.

DIETER began his studies at the University of Cologne in 1961, choosing first Germanic Philology, but took up the fields of Comparative Philology and Iranian and Indian Studies at the University of Saarbrücken in 1962, continuing his studies at the University of Zürich in 1964. He spent a year, from 1965 to 1966,

* I am most grateful to my co-editor, ARASH ZEINI, for first suggesting this endeavour and for updating DIETER's list of publications and to CHRISTEL WEBER for providing supplementary information on his private life. Since the Festschrift is a surprise, I hope that DIETER will magnanimously pardon any inaccuracies, shortcomings or mistakes that may have been overlooked in this far too concise survey of his impressive scholarly work.

at the School of Oriental and African Studies in London, with a focus on Iranian Studies, visiting particularly courses on Middle Persian, Parthian, Classical New Persian, Avestan, Khotanese and Sogdian. After returning to Germany he continued his studies in Comparative Philology and Iranian and Indian Studies at the University of Saarbrücken, changing to the Georg-August-Universität zu Göttingen, in 1967, where he earned a Ph.D in 1970 with the thesis *Die Stellung der sog. Inchoativa im Mitteliranischen*, for which he collected and analysed material from Manichaean Middle Persian, Parthian, Sogdian and Khotanese under the supervision of WOLFGANG SCHMID, WALTER HINZ and HEINZ BECHERT. Besides these well-known experts, his teachers were some of the foremost scholars in the field of Indo-Iranian and Iranian Studies, MANFRED MAYRHOFER, MARY BOYCE, DAVID N. MACKENZIE and RONALD E. EMMERICK.

Due to his expertise in Iranian languages and his considerable philological skills WEBER held a readership in Middle Iranian languages at Harvard University in 1969. In his subsequent employments he worked in the Special Research Unit Oriental Studies (Sonderforschungsbereich Orientalistik) of the University of Göttingen in the project *Vergleichendes Wörterbuch der Iranischen Sprachen* (1970–1975), was assistant at the Linguistic Seminary (Sprachwissenschaftliches Seminar) of the same University from 1975 to 1982 and Hochschulassistent until the end of 1986. He intensified his work on texts in the cursive script in a project of the German Research Foundation (Deutsche Forschungsgemeinschaft, DFG) entitled *Pahlavi-Papyri* (1989–1991), an ambitious undertaking with the objective of editing the hitherto largely neglected Middle Persian papyri from Egypt. Focusing on the papyri at the Egyptian Museum in Berlin, he painstakingly separated the Pahlavi fragments from those in other languages for his edition and organised a special exhibition at the Egyptian Museum to present these texts to the general public. The convincing results of his research led to a second project (1994–1996) titled *Berliner Pahlavi Papyri* with the goal of editing all the Iranian papyri in the Egyptian Museum in Berlin. In the meantime texts in the Pahlavi cursive, written mainly on leather, parchment and linen, were also found in Iran and smuggled out of the land. Two spectacular finds consisting of documents from an archive in the vicinity of Qom (the so-called 'Pahlavi Archive') and longer legal documents from Tabarestān became known, providing enough material for a lifetime of intensive research. Since 1999 DIETER has continuously worked on these unique texts in projects financed by the DFG, continuing his research to this day, although he has officially retired in 2006.

Being aware of the fact that he is one of the very few scholars who has the experience of a lifetime in deciphering these difficult primary sources, DIETER has endeavoured to transmit his knowledge to the next generation not only in his regular courses at the University, but also in several Summer Schools on Pahlavi Papyrology. These he initiated in Vienna at the *Österreichische Nationalbibliothek* in 2009; in Rome at the *Sapienza* University in 2010; in Paris at the *École pratique des hautes études* in 2011 and in Berlin at the *Freie Universität Berlin* in 2012.

As an internationally renowned scholar he has been chosen as member of the *Corpus Inscriptionum Iranicarum* in 2002 and was elected to the Board of the *Societas Iranologica Europaea* in 2007. He is married since 1968 to CHRISTEL WEBER, née BECKMANN. They have a large family of three children and five grandchildren, who regularly spend time with them in their lovingly restored timber-framed house in Lower Saxony (Niedersachsen).

Iranian Philology

With his broad background in Indo-Iranian Studies and his intimate knowledge of Middle Iranian languages many of DIETER's early publications focus on the discussion of grammatical and philological problems in a variety of Iranian languages and texts. Besides his above mentioned thesis on the so-called inchoatives in Middle Iranian languages and an early contribution on Indo-European and Iranian morphology (1965)[1], his philological work consists of numerous studies on various grammatical peculiarities, etymological derivations of names and technical terms as well as other linguistic phenomena in Sogdian, Khotanese, Ossetic, Parthian and Pahlavi.

His work on Sogdian encompasses grammatical and etymological studies as well as text analyses. In his essay of 1971[2] he discusses the construction of direct speech, detecting a recurring pattern in all attestations. In 1975[3] he suggests several etymologies for the words (1) *tʾp-*, *tβt-* 'to seal' ("siegeln"), deriving it from the root *tap-* "heiß sein" against SZEMERÉNYI's Semitic explanation of the word; (2) *pšʾʾβr* 'provisions' ("Proviant") <**pasčābara-* "das, was hinter jemandem hergetragen wird", a technical term also attested as a loanword (*pacevara*) in the Niya documents from the 3rd century CE, and (3) the personal names *ʾstʾpsrʾk* ("Hartkopf, Trotzkopf") and *γʾwtws* ("Kuhbein"). WEBER 2000[4] focuses on the use of the Sogdian particle/conjunction *ʾty* and the two forms of the 3rd sg.pres., *ʾsty* and *xcy*, of the verb *x-* 'to be'. Another study of 2003[5] analyses the second part of the Sogdian text P3 containing a section on weather magic, which describes how to produce rain with the help of nine kinds of stones and

1 "Einige Verba mit langvokalischen Wurzeln im Indogermanischen". In: *Annali dell'Istituto Orientale di Napoli – Sezione Linguistica* 6, 1965, pp. 5–14.

2 "Also sprach Mandrī. (Bemerkungen zur direkten Rede im Sogdischen)". In: *Indogermanische Forschungen* 76, 1971, pp. 77–83.

3 "Sogdische Miszellen". In: *Indogermanische Forschungen* 80, 1975, pp. 90–97.

4 "Zur grammatisch-semantischen Bestimmung einiger Lemmata des sogdischen Lexikons". In: R.E. EMMERICK, W. SUNDERMANN, P. ZIEME (eds): *Studia Manichaica. IV. Internationaler Kongreß zum Manichäismus*, Berlin 14–18. Juli 1997. Berlin, 2000, pp. 639–647.

5 "Regen und Wind. Probleme um den sogdischen Regenzaubertext P 3". In: S. BRETFELD /J. WILKENS (eds.): *Indien und Zentralasien – Sprach- und Kulturkontakt, Vorträge des Göttinger Symposiums vom 7. Bis 10. Mai 2001.* Wiesbaden, 2003, pp. 227–237.

a magic incantation. In his scrutiny of the text he detects specific formulations and epitheta of the deity *w't*, 'Wind' and compares them to Avestan passages, in which Wind *(Vāta-)* is a rain bringer, concluding that although the correspondences between the vocabulary of the magic incantation and the Avestan passages demonstrate strong Zoroastrian traits, other features make it likely that the text is from the pre-Zoroastrian, common Indo-Iranian period.

WEBER's contributions on Khotanese include an analysis of the specific construction of the perfect of transitive verbs (1982)[6] and a meticulous linguistic discussion of the term *āṣaṇa-* "wert, würdig" in Khotanese Buddhist texts (1985)[7], explaining the word in comparison to the similar use of Tocharian A *āṣāṃ*, as a loanword from an Iranian dialect apart from Sogdian, possibly Bactrian, which had an impact on Buddhist traditions and their transfer to East Turkestan.

His publications on Ossetic focus mainly on etymological derivations and historical grammar, as in 1980 [1981][8] on (1) the Ossetic dative in *-än*, and (2) the reflexive forms of the personal pronoun, and in 1983[9] (3) on the forms of the verb 'to be' *(ŭyn)* in the present tense. WEBER 1988[10] discusses the Ossetic phonem /b/ and 1990[11] the provenance of the Ossetic word for 'beer', *bægæny/bægæni,* deriving it from a protoform **baganya-* "what is to be drunk, something to drink, drinkable" from the root **bag-* "drink" (+ compound suffix **-anya-).* In a contribution of 1993[12] he refutes ABAEV's explanation of both Ossetic *mœcyn* "sich wälzen" and Slavic *močiti* "befeuchten" from a root **mak-*, and suggests a derivation of the Ossetic word from the Ir. root **manϑ-* "rühren, quirlen, drehen, wälzen". In his study of 1997[13] he argues that the provenance of Ossetic *bæalon,* D *bælæu* 'dove' cannot be Iranian, but should rather be explained as a loanword from an Indo-European language related to Baltic and Germanic. The Ossetic word might reflect an old *n*-stem, also represented by Lith. *balañdis* and Latv. *baluodis* 'dove'. WEBER 1999[14] discusses the expression *murdtgun*

6 "Das Perfekt transitiver Verben im Khotansakischen". In: *Die Sprache* 28, 1982, pp. 165–170.

7 "Khotansakisch *āṣaṇa-* 'wert, würdig'". In: *Papers in Honour of Professor Mary Boyce II.* Leiden, 1985, pp. 675–681.

8 "Beiträge zur historischen Grammatik des Ossetischen". In: *Indogermanische Forschungen* 85, 1980 [1981], pp. 126–137.

9 "Beiträge zur historischen Grammatik des Ossetischen". In: *Indogermanische Forschungen* 88, 1983, pp. 84–91.

10 "Das Phonem /b/ im Ossetischen und seine Vorgeschichte". In: *Georgica,* fasc. 11. Jena/Tbilissi, 1988, pp. 25–28.

11 "An Ossetic query (Osset. *bægænyl/bægæni* 'beer')". In: GH. GNOLI/A. PANAINO (eds.): *Proceedings of the First European Conference of Iranian Studies (held in Turin, September 7th-11th, 1987 by the Societas Iranologica Europaea).* Part II: *Middle and New Iranian Studies.* Rome (Serie Orientale Roma LXVII, 2), 1990, pp. 585–591.

12 "Eine angeblich slavisch-ossetische lexikalische Übereinstimmung". In: *Indogermanische Forschungen* 98, 1993, pp. 100–107.

13 "Osset. *bælon,* D *bælæu* 'Taube' und lit. *balañdis*". In: *Res Balticae* 3, 1997, pp. 119–128.

14 "Ossetisch (D) *murdtgun (kærdæg)* 'gutes, saftiges (Gras)". In: E. EGGERS/J. BECKER/J. UDOLPH/D. WEBER (eds.): *Florilegium Linguisticum. Festschrift für Wolfgang P. Schmid*

(kærdæg) "gutes, saftiges (Gras)', besides the more frequently attested forms *murdtun/murttun (kærdæg),* deriving it from μύρτος "Myrtus communis L." + the element *-un*, a relict of **gauna-: *murta-gauna-* "myrtenähnlich".

DIETER's work on Parthian encompasses an analysis of theophoric and non-theophoric names from Nisā (2003)[15] and several articles on Parthian titles, names and loanwords in neighbouring languages as well as a new edition of all known Parthian texts in two extensive volumes dedicated to the history of the Parthian empire in collaboration with other scholars (2010)[16]. His work on Pahlavi includes, besides the edition of texts in the cursive script and numerous philological comments in these contributions, overviews of Pahlavi phonology (1997)[17] and morphology (2007)[18].

One of DIETER's specialities is the analysis of personal names and place names in a variety of sources (1967, 1972, 1988).[19] WEBER 1983[20] discusses the Iranian provenance of titles and personal names from the Achaemenid period in Central Asian sources; 1997[21] Iranian loanwords in the Niya documents from the third century CE, written in a northwestern Prakrit dialect in Kharoṣṭī script, found by Sir AUREL STEIN in the desert east of Khotan. In his scrutiny of names in Greek inscriptions from the colony Olbia, on the northern coast of the Black Sea, and from Tanais he suggests Iranian etymologies for the names Ιωδεσμαγος (<**yauda-aišma-* "Kampfeszorn" with *–ka*-suffix, from the root **yaud-* "kämpfen"), Σανδαρζιος (<**sāna-darzya-* "die Feinde bindend", from the root **darz-* "festbinden, fesseln") (1966)[22]; and Ασφωρουγος (arguing in favour of a suggestion

zum 70. Geburtstag. Frankfurt a.M., 1999, pp. 519–537.

15 "Notes on Some Parthian Names from Nisā". In: *Parthica* 5, 2003, pp. 127–129.

16 In: U. HACKL/B. JACOBS/D. WEBER (eds.): *Quellen zur Geschichte des Partherreiches*, Bd. I. Göttingen, 2010: "Anhang: Einige Titel (Kap. II.4.2.6.)", pp. 100–104; "Theophore Namen bei den Parthern (Kap. II.4.7.2.), pp. 154–164; "Parthische Entlehnungen in Nachbarsprachen (Kap. II.4.8.), pp. 165–168. In: *Quellen zur Geschichte des Partherreiches*. Bd. II. Göttingen, 2010 : "Parthische Texte (Kap. III.2), pp. 492–588; "Iranica auf arsakidischen Münzen (Kap. III.3.3.), pp. 633–639.

17 "Pahlavi Phonology". In: A.S. KAYE (ed.): *Phonologies of Asia and Africa (Including the Caucasus)*, Winona Lake, Indiana 1997, vol. II, pp. 601–636.

18 "Pahlavi Morphology". In: A.S. KAYE (ed.): *Morphologies of Asia and Africa*. Winona Lake (Indiana), 2007, pp. 941–973.

19 "Κερπατης". In: *Die Sprache* 13, 1967, pp. 65–66; "Zur sogdischen Personennamengebung". In: *Indogermanische Forschungen* 77, 1972, pp. 191–208; "Zu einigen iranischen Ortsnamen bei Ptolomaios". In: *A Green Leaf. Papers in Honour of Professor Jes. P. Asmussen*. Leiden, 1988, pp. 493–495.

20 "Sprachliches aus achämenidischer Zeit in Zentralasien". In: H. KOCH/D.N. MACKENZIE (eds.): *Kunst, Kultur und Geschichte der Achämenidenzeit und ihr Fortleben. Festschrift Prof. Dr. Walter Hinz*. Berlin (Archäologische Mitteilungen aus Iran, Ergänzungsband 10), 1983, pp. 91–100.

21 "Iranian Loans in the Niya Documents Re-examined". In: S. AKINER/N. SIMS-WILLIAMS (eds.): *Languages and Scripts of Central Asia*. London 1997, pp. 30–38.

22 "Zwei pontisch-iranische Namen". In: *Die Sprache* 12, 1966, pp. 90–93.

by HARMATTA) from **aspa-bāra-* "Reitersmann" + suffix **-uka-* (1986 [1988]).[23] WEBER 1988[24] argues *against* Iranian derivations for another range of personal names in the inscriptions of Greek cities on the northern coast of the Black Sea, assuming Germanic etymologies for most of the attested forms. His contribution of 2003[25] is another etymological study of a personal name transmitted from the Greek colony Olbia, Μανιαγος, which was recognized at an early period as Iranian and derived from the Ossetic word for 'man, husband', Iron *moj*, Digoron *mojnæ*. Arguing on phonetic grounds against the etymology by ABAEV from **man(u)ya-*, a **-ya-*derivative from Iranian **manu-* 'man', he supports an earlier suggestion by MILLER, deriving the word from <**mān(i)ya-*, which he combines with Avestan *nmāniia-* 'belonging to the house', translated by Pahlavi *mānbed* (Y. 19.18) 'master of the house', a meaning which fits in well with Μανιαγος, lit. "Hausmann" ('man/master of the house').

Papyri, Parchments, Linen and Leather Documents from Egypt

A large number of documents, consisting of economic texts, administrative records, legal documents and letters written mainly on papyrus and a few texts on parchment, leather and linen have survived from the short period of the Sasanian occupation of Egypt (619 to 629 CE) under Husraw II (Parwēz, 'The Victorious'). WEBER has dedicated numerous articles, besides two book editions to the decipherment of these challenging, largely fragmentary texts. In his contributions of 2005[26], 2007[27] and 2013[28] he outlines the history of the worldwide largest collection of papyri, originally in Vienna, and adds meticulous lists of the museums and libraries harbouring the dispersed fragments and collections. Although most of the items, encompassing, according to DIETER,

23 "Ασφωρουγος und Verwandtes". In: *Archäologische Mitteilungen aus Iran* 19 *(Festschrift Prof. Dr. W. Hinz)*, Berlin, 1986 [1988], pp. 171–175;

24 "Die ersten Germanen am Nordufer des Schwarzen Meeres". In: *Historische Sprachwissenschaft (Historical Linguistics)* 101, 1988, pp. 138–150.

25 "ΜΑΝΙΑΓΟΣ". In: C. CERETI/M. MAGGI /E. PROVASI (eds.): *Religious themes and texts of pre-Islamic Iran and Central Asia.* Studies in honour of Professor Gherardo Gnoli on the occasion of his 65th Birthday on 6 December 2002. Wiesbaden (Beiträge zur Iranistik 24), 2003, pp. 441–445.

26 "Pahlavi Papyri". In: *Encyclopaedia Iranica*, 2005.

27 "The Vienna Collection of Pahlavi Papyri". In: B. Palme (ed.): *Akten des 23. internationalen Papyrologenkongresses (Wien, 22.-28. Juli 2001).* Wien (Österreichische Akademie der Wissenschaften, Phil.-hist. Kl., Kommission für Antike Rechtsgeschichte), 2007, pp. 725–738.

28 "Die persische Besetzung Ägyptens 619–629 n. Chr. Fakten und Spekulationen". In: F. FEDER/A. LOHWASSER (eds.): *Ägypten und sein Umfeld in der Spätantike*, Wiesbaden (Philippika. Altertumswissenschaftliche Abhandlungen 61), 2013, pp. 221–246.

ca. one-thousand fragments have been known for a long time since their initial discovery together with Greek, Coptic and Arabic papyri in the late 19th century, these important first hand sources were largely neglected due mainly to two reasons: the fragmentary state of the texts and the difficulties involved in reading the ambiguous Pahlavi script, on the one hand, and the disappearance of the worldwide largest collection of papyri from Vienna after the second world war, on the other. This collection of the Austrian National Library (Österreichische Nationalbibliothek) had been almost completely transported to Berlin in 1936, where OLAF HANSEN was working at that time on the decipherment of the papyri in the Berlin museums.[29] It later became known that the Vienna papyri, the largest collection worldwide, had been taken from Berlin to the Hermitage in St. Petersburg after the war. Apart from this collection, comprising ca. 604 items, and the second largest collection of papyri in the Egyptian Museum in Berlin (ca. 219 items), the documents from Egypt are today dispersed in various museums and libraries, mainly in Europe and the USA.

DIETER's interest in the papyri was awakened at an early stage of his academic career. In one of his earliest publications he called the attention of the scholarly community to the Pahlavi fragments in the library of the University of Göttingen (Niedersächsische Staats- und Universitätsbibliothek zu Göttingen), written on papyrus and parchment, which had previously remained undetected (apart from one papyrus mentioned by OLAF HANSEN in 1938). WEBER's 1969[30] initial edition of the fragments in Göttingen was followed up in 1973[31] with a contribution on the specific features of the Pahlavi papyri. His article of 1983[32] assesses the papyri in the collection of Erzherzog Rainer in Vienna, and in 1984[33] he offers a survey of research work on the Pahlavi ostraca and papyri, describing the state of the art at that time.

In the meantime our access to these long neglected, but significant primary sources has been enhanced considerably thanks to DIETER's meticulous engagement in detecting the specific characteristics of the cursive script and deciphering even the most fragmentary pieces. WEBER's monograph of 1992[34] is an exemplary edition of a large number of Pahlavi papyri and parchments from Egypt

29 O. HANSEN: *Die mittelpersischen Papyri der Papyrussammling der Staatlichen Museen zu Berlin*. Berlin, 1938.

30 "Einige Göttinger Pahlavi-Fragmente". In: *Indogermanische Forschungen* 74, 1969, pp. 32–38.

31 "Einige Beobachtungen an Pahlavi Papyri". In: *Acta Orientalia* 35, 1973, pp. 83–88.

32 "Die Pehlevi-Papyri der Papyrussammlung Erzherzog Rainer zu Wien". In: *Festschrift Papyrus Erzherzog Rainer (P. Rainer Cent.)*. Wien, 1983, pp. 215–228.

33 "Pahlavi Papyri und Ostraca: Stand der Forschung". In: W. SKALMOWSKI/A. VAN TONGERLOO (eds.): *Middle Iranian Studies*. Proceedings of the International Symposium organized by the Katholieke Universiteit Leuven from the 17th to the 20th of May 1982. Leuven (Orientalia Lovaniensia Analecta 16), 1984, pp. 25–43.

34 *Pahlavi Papyri, Pergamente und Ostraca*. (Textband) *Corpus Inscriptionum Iranicarum*. London, 1992.

dating from the Persian occupation of the land (619–629 CE). The edition also includes Pahlavi ostraca, most of which are from one of the largest collections, unearthed by HERZFELD in 1926 in an excavation of the Varāmīn region near Ray (see below). As to the papyri and parchments, most of the pieces are fragmentary with many lacunae, often consisting of too little text to enable completely reliable readings or the reconstruction of a larger context with any certainty. In spite of these enormous difficulties, WEBER spares no effort to find the correct readings of names and words, discussing alternative readings extensively in his vast commentary to the texts in an attempt to reconstruct their content on the basis of the extant fragments. A comparison of the papyri, consisting largely of letters on different subjects, allows for a reconstruction of the recurring stylistic form of Middle Persian letters, which, as he elucidates, stereotypically consist of three parts: (A) introductory address with name(s) or title(s) of the addressee(s) and greeting formulae; (B) message of the letter; (C) repetition of the introductory address and the greeting formulae, often in a shortened form (pp. 233–236).

WEBER 2008[35] illustrates this recurring pattern, which is also confirmed by the letters of the so-called "Pahlavi Archive", with numerous examples from the letters on papyri and parchment from Egypt. One of his many significant findings in the edition of 1992 is the reading and interpretation of a comprised set of two characters, which occur regularly in the first section of a letter (part A). These characters were read ⟨nc⟩ by HANSEN, who interpreted them as an abbreviation for MP ⟨nmʾc⟩ *namāz* "Verehrung", a reading which was later revised by HARMATTA to ⟨nʾc⟩ *nāz* "plaisir, jouissance, cordialité". WEBER convincingly shows that the characters indeed represent the greeting *namāz*, as HANSEN had suggested, but are not an abbreviation of an eteographically written ⟨nmʾc⟩, as the latter assumed. They rather represent the ideogram ⟨ʿSGDH⟩, which renders the same word, *namāz* 'reverence' with *ʿain* as the first character in this abbreviation, followed by a shortened version of the rest of the word ⟨-SGDH⟩(pp. 212–214).

In his next monograph of 2003[36] DIETER takes up the subject of this greeting, elucidating that *namāz* always appears in this abbreviated form in texts written in the cursive script, but never as a full ideogram (p. 162, commentary on P.331, and p. 169 with further examples). This edition focuses on the objects in the Egyptian Museum (Ägyptisches Museum) in Berlin, several of which had been previously edited by HANSEN in 1938. As in his previous work, WEBER attempts to decipher all the available fragments, not only the longer texts, and is able to correct numerous readings of HANSEN, hereby enabling a far better understanding of the papyri and their administrative background. A remarkable example is the occurrence of the name Šahr-Ālānyōzān in several papyri (e.g. P. 136.7, p. 9;

35 "Sassanidische Briefe aus Ägypten". In: *Asiatische Studien/Études Asiatiques* LXII/3, 2008, pp. 803–826.

36 *Berliner Papyri, Pergamente und Leinenfragmente in mittelpersischer Sprache*. Unter Mitwirkung von W. BRASHEAR. Fotografien von MARGARETE BUSING und EVA MARIA BORGWALDT (*Corpus Inscriptionum Iranicarum)*. London, 2003.

P. 172.1, p. 60; P. 174.3, p. 63), which HANSEN 1938 had either left out or read falsely as ⟨štrwdʾrʾn⟩ (P. 58.1, p. 82), but was read correctly by PERIKHANIAN[37]. As WEBER 1991[38] elucidates, Šahr-Ālānyōzān is the name (not title!) of an important person, a high-ranking tax official within the Persian fiscal bureaucracy in charge of the Sasanian administration in Egypt between the years 619 and 629 CE, who also appears in Greek papyri as Σαραλανεοζαν (Saralaneozan).[39] He detects the name of this official in another legal document from Egypt written on leather (P.Pahl. 373a) in the papyrus collection of the Austrian National Library (Österreichische Nationalbibliothek). In his edition of this fragmentary text (2002)[40] DIETER identifies the document as an *ayādgār*, a 'memoir' — a recurring technical term in the records found later in Iran. Unfortunately the central message of the text is missing due to too many lacunae, but it is obvious that a bulla was attached to the document that was imprinted with the personal seal of the high official Šahr-Ālānyōzān *(pad muhr ī Šahr-Ālānyōzān āwišt* "sealed with the seal of Šahr-Ālānyōzān", pp. 187–188). In an interdisciplinary approach to these documents DIETER re-assesses together with PATRICK SÄNGER 2012[41] the Greek and Pahlavi papyri mentioning the name Saralaneozan/Šahr-Ālānyōzān, which occurs in two lists of groceries (BGU II 377 and P.140) and in a Pahlavi business letter, providing evidence on the everyday needs of the household of this high Persian official in Egypt.

In his two articles of 2007 and 2013 mentioned above,[42] besides offering a new survey of the extant Pahlavi papyri in museums and libraries, he returns to a few interesting texts containing details on military and economic matters, such as the rations given to specific troops and to high military officers[43] or lists of the troops stationed in various cities in Egypt.[44] Although most of the letters are fragmentary, they convey a range of titles of officials, who seem to have played in important role in the administration of Egypt, such as *awestwār* 'commissary' ("Kommissar"), *widarbed* 'transit officer' ("Transitbeamter") and *kārframān* 'commander' ("Befehlshaber").[45] An often attested title is that of *aswār* "horseman,

37 A. PERIKHANIAN: "Pexlevijskie papirusy sobranija GMII imeni A.S. PUŠKINA". In: *Vestnik drevnej istorii* 1961/2, pp. 78–93.

38 "Ein bisher unbekannter Titel aus spätsassanidischer Zeit?". In: R.E. EMMERICK/D. WEBER (eds.): *Corolla Iranica (Papers in honour of Prof. D.N. MacKenzie).* Frankfurt am Main/Bern/New York/Paris, 1991, pp. 228–236.

39 For an overview of the occurrences of the name see WEBER 2013, p. 230 (see fn. 28).

40 "Eine spätsassanidische Rechtsurkunde aus Ägypten". In: *TYCHE* 17, 2002 [2003], pp. 185–192.

41 "Der Lebensmittelhaushalt des Herrn Saralaneozan/Šahr-Ālānyōzān. Neuedition von zwei Speiselisten und einem Geschäftsbrief aus dem sasanidischen Ägypten". In: *Archiv für Papyrusforschung* 58/1 (2012), pp. 81–96.

42 See fn. 27 and 28 above.

43 WEBER 2007, p. 736.

44 WEBER 2013, pp. 223–224.

45 WEBER 2013, pp. 226 and 228 respectively.

rider", written usually with the heterogram ⟨PRŠY'⟩, which, as WEBER 2006–7[46] discloses, is the correct reading of a few hitherto misread words in military letters and other documents. In his contribution of 2019[47] he scrutinizes the occurrences of Jewish/Christian names in diverse original records of the 7th century, concluding that the readings of only two names can be confirmed with certainty, Samuel and Abraham, both attested in papyri from occupied Egypt.

A few unique texts have survived among the papyri. In 2005 [2009][48] DIETER discusses a letter, which was written *not* during the Sasanian occupation of Egypt, as the bulk of the papyri, but obviously in the early Islamic period (second half of the 7th or first half of the 8th century) by a Persian merchant living in Egypt. The letter contains presumably one of the earliest attestations of the *bismilllah*-formula in its adapted form in an original document, the greeting *pad nām ī yazd* "in the name of God" with the singular *yazd* instead of plural *yazdān* "gods" in the well-known original Zoroastrian formula. In his re-edition of this letter (2020)[49] WEBER assumes that the dispatcher, who does not mention his name, was in fact a Muslim, and corrects hereby his earlier assumption in the first edition that the sender had changed the formula in order to disguise his Zoroastrian religious affiliation. As DIETER is able to demonstrate in another context, the same formula with *yazd* occurs in documents of the "Pahlavi Archive" from the early Islamic period.[50]

WEBER 2009[51] introduces another remarkable text from Egypt written on parchment, which he identifies as P.Pehl. 371 of the Viennese Papyri collection and, following the description in the (unpublished) scholarly papers of OLAF HANSEN, as a fragment of the Alexander Romance. Although only a few lines have survived, the fragment demonstrates not only that, besides official documents and letters, literary texts were also produced during the Sasanian occupation of Egypt, but that there may in fact have been a Middle Persian version of the Alexander Romance, as THEODOR NÖLDEKE had surmised over a century

46 "On Middle Persian *aswār* 'horseman, rider' in Pahlavi Documents of the 7th Century". In: *Nāme-ye Irān-e Bāstān* 6/1&2, 2006–7 [2008], pp. 37–44.

47 "Christlich-jüdische Spuren in Pahlavi-Dokumenten des 7. Jhs. n. Chr.". In: J. RUBANOVICH AND G. HERMAN (eds.): *Irano-Judaica VII. Studies Relating to Jewish Contacts with Persian Culture Throughout the Ages.* Jerusalem, 2019, pp. 251–266.

48 "A Pahlavi Papyrus from Islamic Times". In: C.A. ALTMAN/N. SIMS-WILLIAMS/U. SIMS-WILLIAMS (eds.): *Iranian and Zoroastrian Studies in Honour of Prods Oktor Skjærvø, Bulletin of the Asia Institute* 19, 2005 [2009], pp. 225–231.

49 "Living together in Changing Iran. Pahlavi Documents on Arabs and Christians in Early Islamic Times". In: *Annales islamologiques* 54, 2020, pp. 139–164.

50 WEBER 2014, p. 180 (see fn. 81).

51 "Ein Pahlavi-Fragment des Alexanderromans aus Ägypten?". In: D. DURKIN-MEISTERERNST/CHR. RECK/D. WEBER (eds.): *Literarische Stoffe und ihre Gestaltung in mitteliranischer Zeit* (Kolloquium anlässlich des 70. Geburtstages von Werner Sundermann). Wiesbaden, 2009, pp. 307–318.

ago, even if the latter was wrong in assuming that the Syriac version was based on a Middle Persian *Vorlage*.

Due to the extreme ambiguity of the cursive script, new, previously unedited documents can lead to revised readings of terms and phrases in texts that have already been edited. DIETER has repeatedly corrected not only the interpretations of others, but previous readings in his own editions. In another article of 2009[52] he revises a Pahlavi letter from Egypt, already published in his monograph of 1992; three papyri are re-edited in another contribution.[53]

Pahlavi Ostraca and Dipinti

Despite the fact that a fairly large collection of Pahlavi ostraca had been discovered as far back as 1926 by HERZFELD in an excavation of the Varāmīn region near Ray, the content of these records written on potshards had remained largely unknown due to the same reading difficulties of the cursive script.[54] In an early article of 1974[55] WEBER discusses specifics of these records, which consist largely of notices on expenses and disbursements, and he includes a number of them in his above mentioned monograph of 1992. Thanks to DIETER's efforts, we can now establish that the ostraca contain short notices of an agricultural holding on its expenditures, consisting mainly of food, bread *(nān)*, wine *(may)*, meat *(gōšt)*, and some other objects, recording the date (usually only the day), the dispatched item(s) and usually the name(s) of the recipient(s).

Excavations in the year 1936 in Čāl Tarxān-Ešqābād, in the vicinity of ancient Ray, had brought to light a further number of ostraca in the Pahlavi cursive script (altogether ca. 19 items), besides others in Arabic script, in the debris of two palaces of the ʿUmmayad period, which were published in a facsimile edition in 1976.[56] WEBER 2003[57] presents the very first attempt to read a few of the best-preserved shards, which, similar to the ostraca he published in 1992, contain notes on the expenditure of wine *(may)* and bread *(nān)*. In a later

52 "A Pahlavi Letter from Egypt Re-visited (P. 44)". In: W. SUNDERMANN/A. HINTZE/F. DE BLOIS (eds.): *Exegisti monumenta, Festschrift in Honour of Nicholas Sims-Williams*. Wiesbaden (Iranica 17), 2009, pp. 537–550.

53 "Three Pahlavi Papyri Revisited". In: https://www.sasanika.org/wp-content/uploads/Sasanika_PS02_Weber.pdf

54 These were published as facsimile together with papyri from Egypt by JEAN DE MENASCE (ed.): *Corpus Inscriptionum Iranicarum*. Part III: *Pahlavi Inscriptions*. Vol. IV-V: *Ostraca and Papyri*. London, 1957.

55 "Zur Interpretation der Pahlavi-Ostraca". In: PH. GIGNOUX/ A. TAFAZZOLI (eds.): *Mémorial J. de Menasce*. Louvain, 1974, pp. 227–233.

56 THOMPSON: *Stucco from Chal Tarkhan-Eshqabad near Rayy*. Warminster, 1976.

57 "Die Pahlavi-Ostraca von Čāl Tarxān-Ešqābād". In: L. PAUL (ed.): *Persian Origins – Early Judaeo-Persian and the Emergence of New Persian*. Collected Papers of the Symposium, Göttingen 1999. Wiesbaden (Iranica 6), 2003, pp. 275–282.

publication of 2005[58], written after the documents of the so-called "Pahlavi Archive" came to light, he can show that the ostraca and the Pahlavi documents on linen and leather recording the distribution of food follow the same stereotype pattern, consisting of, first, a personal name, second, the date (usually only the day), third, the item (/food) to be dispatched, an indirect object (often the name of the recipient), and, finally, the verb *(dād)*. Given the reading difficulties of the cursive script and the lack of context, detecting a recurring pattern can be crucial for reaching a correct understanding of the document at hand. On the basis of this scheme he revises a few of his own earlier readings, in which he had wrongly assumed that the text begins with a "good luck phrase" ("Glücksfloskel") instead of a personal name (pp. 218–222). WEBER 2009[59] discusses a sign used repeatedly after the heterogram for "bread" ⟨LḤM'⟩ *nān* in numerous ostraca, which he explains as an abbreviation for the grain measure *kabīz* (one-tenth of a *grīw)*. He argues that the standard daily ration of bread pro person consisted of one *kabīz* of wheat, which could be baked into bread (pp. 387–388).

A substantial number of coins from the Sasanian period bear *dipinti,* often single words or phrases, written in ink, which was apparently a common way of marking coins with names (e.g. Māhwindād)[60] and other short remarks (such as *Astōg grawagān* "pledge of [the village of] Astōg").[61] In a contribution of 2014[62] together with other authors DIETER discusses several of these ink inscriptions on coins from a hoard from the time of Yazdegird III in Kirmān, including for comparison *dipinti* on coins minted under various Sasanian kings.

The "Pahlavi Archive"

The documents subsumed under the title "Pahlavi Archive" consist of original records from Iran written in the Pahlavi cursive script on leather, parchment and linen from an archive near the city of Qom, south of today's capital Teheran. The documents were smuggled to Europe and America in the nineteen-eighties of the 20th century and are now dispersed in two main collections: (1) the so-called "Pahlavi Archive" of the *Bancroft Library* in Berkeley, California (USA), consisting of more than 260 items (whole documents and fragments), and (2) the smaller collection of the Institute of Iranian Studies of the *Freie Universität*

58 "Kleine Nachlese zu einigen Pahlavi-Ostraca". In: D. WEBER (ed.): *Languages of Iran – Past and Present. Iranian Studies in memoriam David Neil MacKenzie.* Wiesbaden (Iranica 8), 2005, pp. 217–228.

59 "Zu den Brotrationen in den Pahlavi-Ostraka". In: PH. GIGNOUX/CHR. JULLIEN/FL. JULLIEN (eds.): *Trésors d'Orient – Mélanges offerts à Rika Gyselen.* Paris, 2009, pp. 379–389.

60 WEBER 2014 (see fn. 62), p. 115.

61 WEBER 2014 (see fn. 62), p. 114.

62 ST. HEIDEMANN/J. RIEDERER/D. WEBER: "A Hoard from the Time of Yazdgard III in Kirmān". In: *Iran* 52, 2014, pp. 79–124.

Berlin (Germany) with 30 items. A few documents are in the Los Angeles Museum of Art and dispersed in private collections in Europe and Iran. These texts consist mostly of receipts and letters referring to economic matters, lists of goods and records of transfer in kind. Since their discovery two scholars have predominantly worked on their decipherment, PHILIPPE GIGNOUX and DIETER WEBER, in a productive cooperation, which DIETER describes and comments impressively in his contribution to GIGNOUX's Festschrift in 2011[63].

In his attempt to date these documents WEBER 2008 [2012][64] takes up an earlier idea of GIGNOUX's, who had suggested that the dates recorded in the texts refer to the so-called Post-Yazdegird Era (PYE), beginning with the death of the last Sasanian king, Yazdegird III, in 651 CE. DIETER divides the documents according to their ductus into three groups, which he assigns to three distinctive periods, confirming the PYE dating in his discussion of a range of texts of the second group. These refer to a man with the unique name of Yazdānpādār, who played a prominent role in the region of Qom (in an estate called Yazdān-ābestān) and is also mentioned in the *Tārīkh-e Qom* as the leading local Zoroastrian Persian noble at the time when Arab tribes moved into this region (after 702 CE). He shows that the only coherent interpretation of the dates noted in these texts is that of the Post-Yazdegird Era, as noted above. In another article of 2010 [2014][65] he is able to locate the names of the villages and estates mentioned in the documents in the region of Qom *(Kom)* and in the vicinity of the city, which is also explicitly named in two texts (Berk. 34 and 136; p. 38).

His monograph of 2008[66] is the *editio princeps* of forty documents belonging to the same Archive, thirty of which are housed at the *Freie Universität Berlin* and ten further documents in private collections (an overview of the texts is on p. XIV). These are mainly economic documents, consisting of records called *čak* ('cheque'), **pădīrāy* ('receipt confirmation') and *ayādgār* ('memorandum'; pp. XV-XIX), besides seven administrative letters. Document no. 27 is unique in this group, as it seems to be a magical text, calling on Frēdōn in his function as healer and helper. Another remarkable document is no. 30, the only item of the whole group that still preserved its original bindings, held together with a bulla. All other documents of the Archive had already been opened before being offered for sale in the market after the bullae had been separated from the texts. DIETER's edition contains numerous insights into writing conventions and other

63 "Philippe Gignoux' Beitrag zur Interpretation der Dokumente des 'Pahlavi Archive' in Berkeley, Ca.". In: R. GYSELEN/CH. JULLIEN (eds.): *Florilège offert à Philippe Gignoux pour son 80 anniversaire*. Paris, 2011, pp. 283–303.

64 "New Arguments for Dating the Documents from the "Pahlavi Archive". In: *Bulletin of the Asia Institute* 22, 2008 [2012], pp. 215–222.

65 "Villages and Estates in the Documents from the Pahlavi Archive: The Geographical Background". In: *Bulletin of the Asia Institute* 24, 2010 [2014], pp. 39–67.

66 *Berliner Pahlavi-Dokumente. Zeugnisse spätsassaniischer Brief- und Rechtskultur aus frühislamischer Zeit.* Mit Beiträgen von MYRIAM KRUTZSCH und MARIA MACUCH. Wiesbaden (Iranica 15), 2008.

peculiarities, such as the abbreviation for *statēr* consisting of a small hook before the listed amount of money (e.g. ⟨NKSYʾ S-III⟩ *xwāstag s[tatēr] 3*, "three staters"; p. XXIV); or the use of the term *rōzīg* not only in its literal sense of 'daily ration', but as a general term for 'ration, sustenance' (pp. XXIX-XXXI). His discussion of other recurring terms enhances our knowledge of Sasanian bureaucratic terminology, such as *pădīrāy* 'receipt confirmation' ("Empfangsbestätigung", p. 20) or *gugāy-muhrīhā* 'witness seals' ("Zeugensiegel", pp. 21–23).

In the meantime Dieter has revised several of his own readings (often of rare words and names) in this edition, but he has also re-edited whole documents after gaining new insights in the course of deciphering other texts written in the Pahlavi cursive script (e.g. Berlin 10, 36 and 34 in 2015 [2019][67] and Berlin 6, 7, 8, 9 and 12 in 2020–2021[68]). Most significant is his 2022[69] revision of a recurring term in a large number of documents that he had read previously as *dārīg* 'manager' ("Verwalter", e.g. in Berlin 19 and 23, pp. 83, 99). Refuting this older interpretation he now proposes to read the term as *gālīg* "member of the household; belonging to the household" (< OP **garda-* + suffix *–īg*; p. 326), a word which is not only attested elsewhere in this sense, but fits in better with the content of the documents in which it is recorded.

Weber 2003 [2007][70] presents a remarkable interpretation of the Pahlavi document Berk. 27, in which for the first time the title of an officer appears, who was apparently engaged in the fiscal task of collecting the *xarāj* tax. He reads the title as *frašn-hargarīg*, a compound consisting of the two parts *frašn* "question" + *hargarīg* from **harg-gar-īg*, and explains the second part as *harg*, "duty, tribute; work, effort" (+ suffixes *–gar* and *–īg)*. The title designates a person engaged in (collecting) *harg*, the forerunner of NP and Arabic *xarāj*, and is presumably the title of a tax collector, who makes inquiries *(frašn)* on the amount (of items or persons) to be taxed. He discusses the topic of taxation in the documents of the early Islamic period in several contributions, presenting an overview in his article of 2013.[71] In his edition of financial texts (2012 [2016])[72] he detects a

67 "Studies in Some Documents from the 'Pahlavi Archive' (2)". In: *Bulletin of the Asia Institute* 29, 2015 [2019], pp. 79–116.

68 "Studies in Some Documents from the 'Pahlavi Archive (3)'". In: *Bulletin of the Asia Institute* 30, 2020–2021, pp. 29–65.

69 "Sasanian Festivals in the Documents from the 'Pahlavi Archive'". In: *Sasanian Studies/ Sasanidische Studien* I, 2022, pp. 323–345.

70 "The *xarāj* Taxation and the Pahlavi Document Berk. No. 27" Part III:2 (p. 27–29), in: G. Azarpay/K. Martin/M. Schwarz/D. Weber: "New Information on the Date and Function of the Berkeley MP Archive". In: *Bulletin of the Asia Institute* 17, 2003 [2007], pp. 17–19.

71 "Taxation in Pahlavi Documents from Early Islamic Times (late 7th Century CE)". In: S. Toxtas'ev/P. Lur'e (eds.): *Commentationes Iranicae. Sbornik statej k 90-letiju V.A. Livšica.* Sankt-Petersburg, 2013, pp. 171–181.

72 "Studies in Some Documents from the 'Pahlavi Archive'". In: *Bulletin of the Asia Institute* 26, 2012 [2016], pp. 61–95.

list of the amount of taxes to be paid in several cities ("fortified places", *dizīhā;* Berk. 37). Another noteworthy record (Berk. 81) contains a summary of the profit made by an entrepreneur called Windād-Burzmihr in the early Islamic period (12 PYE =663/664 CE), an apparently affluent man, whose name recurs in several other records from the year 11 PYE (=662/663 CE) to 48 PYE (=699/700 CE). In his edition and commentary of these texts (2014 [2018][73] and 2019[74]) he shows that the documents of the said entrepreneur reveal intense financial activities, including the erecting of a building, a pavilion *(kōšk)*, with the help of a carpenter *(durgar)* called Zādōy, whose income and investments are in turn registered in another surviving document (Berk. 231; WEBER 2013 [2017][75]). DIETER argues that Windād-Burzmihr's numerous activities culminated in the founding of a new village bearing his name, Windād-Burzmihr-ābād, a designation of the *fulānābād* place-name type, characterized by adding the element *–ābād* to a proper name (for an overview of these place-names in the documents see his above mentioned article of 2019,[76] pp. 373–375).

Among the numerous economic documents of the "Pahlavi Archive" also two fragmentary letters from the time of Hormizd V have survived (Berk. 129 and Berk. 212), which belong together, as WEBER 2010[77] concludes from the few legible lines, due to the mention of the said king and their similar content. WEBER 2011 [2015][78] discusses two previously unedited documents containing the title of the province governor, *ōstāndār*, of the province of Qom in the late 7th and early 8th centuries. Although the title of this important dignitary, who is described by a number of eminent epithets (such as *zād xrad-windād* "born with inherited/innate wisdom"), is omnipresent in the texts of the "Pahlavi Archive", none of the documents mentions a name. The two edited texts (Berk. 77 and 149) illustrate how various products, in the first case woolen garments, in the second goat meat, were tested before being delivered to the household of the *ōstāndār*, which, to judge by another list of expenses (Berk. 62), must have been enormous. The edited texts in WEBER 2015 [2019][79] include a guide to winemaking

73 "Pahlavi Documents of *Windādburzmihrābād*, the Estate of a Zoroastrian Entrepreneur in Early Islamic Times (With an Excursus on the Origin of the *Fulanabad*-Type of Village Names)". In: *Bulletin of the Asia Institute* 2014 [2018], pp. 127–147.

74 "The Story of Windād-Burzmihr. A Zoroastrian Entrepreneur in Early Islamic Times". In: A. HINTZE/D. DURKIN-MEISTERERNST/C. NAUMANN (eds.): *A Thousand Judgements. Festschrift for Maria Macuch*. Wiesbaden, 2019, pp. 373–384.

75 "Accountancy of a Zoroastrian Craftsman in Early Islamic Times (662–664 CE)". In: *Bulletin of the Asia Institute* 27, 2013 [2017], pp. 129–141.

76 See fn. 74.

77 "Two Pahlavi Letters from the Time of Hormizd V (A.D. 630–632)". In: *Bulletin of the Asia Institute* 20, 2010, pp. 55–63.

78 "Testing Food and Garment for the Ōstāndār (Two Unpublished Documents from the 'Pahlavi Archive' in Berkeley, (CA.)". In: *Bulletin of the Asia Institute* 25, 2011 [2015], pp. 31–37.

79 See fn. 67.

(Berk. 107), the financial settlement for a house that was burned down (Berk. 41) and livestock lists (Berk. 138, 230, 229). His above mentioned article of 2022[80] discusses several documents, in which Iranian festivals are referred to: *Nōg-rūz* (Berk. 142; Berlin 5) and *Mihragān* (Berlin 4; Berk. 24 and 88).

Changes brought about by the advent of Islam are reflected in several documents, as Dieter is able to show in a contribution of 2014[81] dedicated to this topic: the *bismillah*-formula *pad nām ī yazd* "in the name of God" replaces the older Zoroastrian formula with the plural *yazdān* in several texts (Berk. 187; 188; 197; as in the papyrus from Egypt mentioned above); the plural *mazgitān* "mosques" appears in Berk. 187 and the Arabic *amīr/Amīr* (either as the title of a high official or as a personal name) is attested in several text passages. Although he revises 2020[82] the latter reading in one case (in his renewed edition of Berk 93, p. 149), he retains *amīr/Amīr* in several other texts: Berk. 95 (pp. 151–153) in which the Arabs *(tāzīgān)* are expressly mentioned; Berk. 62 containing a list of goods to be delivered to the *amīr* (pp. 153–155); and Berk. 244 in which it appears in combination with a name *(Amīr Abdīn;* pp. 156–158). Another short document edited in this contribution mentions the Nestorian Christians *(dēn asūrīg)* (pp. 161–163). The texts presented in Weber 2015[83] (Berk. 108, 46 and 97 in chronological order) contain price lists for products in the very early Islamic period (651/2–669/670 CE). These unique records also enhance our knowledge of products and industries of this period: a Pahlavi letter from the late 7th century (Berk. 245) contains a rare word for "bottle (made of glass)" *(šīšag)*, confirming the art of glassmaking in the Sasanian and early Islamic period (Weber 2011[84]).

The Tabarestān Documents

In 2012 Philippe Gignoux[85] introduced the scholarly community to a large number of original legal documents, written on leather and linen in the Pahlavi cursive script from the region of Tabarestān, south of the Caspian sea, belonging to a private collector. Following the instructions of the proprietor, he did not

80 See fn. 69.

81 "Arabic Activities Reflected in the Documents of the 'Pahlavi Archive' (late 7th and early 8th centuries)". In: R. Gyselen (ed.): *Documents, argenteries et monnaies de tradition sassanide*, Bures-sur-Yvette (Res Orientales XXII), 2014, pp. 179–188.

82 See fn. 49.

83 "Spätsasanidische Preislisten im frühislamischen Iran". In: S. Farridnejad/R. Gyselen/A. Joisten-Pruschke (eds.): *Faszination Iran – Beiträge zu Religion, Geschichte und Kunst des Alten Iran. Gedenkschrift für Klaus Schippmann*. Wiesbaden (Göttinger Orientforschungen, III, Reihe: Iranica, n. F. 13), 2015, pp. 233–243.

84 "An Interesting Pahlavi Letter from Early Islamic Times (Berk. 245)". In: *Zeitschrift der Deutschen Morgenländischen Gesellschaft* 161, 2011, pp. 91–98.

85 Ph. Gignoux: "Une archive post-sassanide du Tabaristān (I)". In: R. Gyselen (ed.): *Objects et documents inscrits en* pārsīg. Bures-sur-Yvette (Res Orientales XXI), 2012, pp. 29–96.

convey any details on the circumstances of this spectacular find, but in the meantime we have been informed by a colleague from Iran that the documents were found in two hand-constructed and sealed troglodytic caves, called Dīv-tāgh ('demon-arc') and Tāgh-kheneh ('arc-house'), on Mount Serkhel, located in Do-āb in the region of Savādkūh in the province of Māzanderān, and sold by smugglers.[86] To date thirty-four documents from this archive have been made available, consisting of court records, transcripts of legal proceedings, administrative letters, contracts, records on leasehold, loan, compensation, inheritance and many other legal and administrative issues, all from the eighth century CE. After GIGNOUX's *editio princeps* of the documents (in 2012, 2014 and 2016)[87] they were studied by WEBER, who has suggested divergent readings of words and phrases as well as new interpretations of the documents in several recent studies.[88]

In his scrutiny of the shortest texts of the collection, the first ten documents (with the exception of Tab. 9, which had not been made available by the proprietor), WEBER 2016[89] recognizes correctly that these are records of legal proceedings, corresponding in language and content exactly to the details we are able to reconstruct on the Sasanian civil trial from other Pahlavi legal texts. The documents refer to three different civil cases, confirming not only step by step the formal procedure described (only incompletely) in other texts, but also the use of formulaic language and of specific technical terms, such as *dastwar* ('legal predecessor, *auctor*') and *dastwarīh* ('*auctor*-ship'), in this context. Other remarkable details are that the judge is a *hērbed*, a religious dignitary engaged in jurisdiction in the quarter *(tasūg)* of Dēl ī Dēlān in Tabarestān, and that a preliminary investigation is conducted by another official before the cases are brought to court. In another contribution in the same volume (2016)[90] DIETER re-opens the study of two other documents: Tab. 12 describes the measures

86 I am indebted to AHMAD BAVAND SAVADKOUHI from the *Foundation of Savadkouh Researches*, Center of Speleology in Savadkouh, for this invaluable information (per emails of Feb. 17 and 22, 2022). The circumstances of this find and many other details will be described in his forthcoming book (in Persian) on the Tabarestān documents.

87 GIGNOUX 2012 (see fn. 85 above); PH. GIGNOUX: "Une archive post-sassanide du Tabaristān (II)". In: R. GYSELEN (ed.): *Documents, argenterie et monnaies de tradition Sassanide.* Bures-sur-Yvette (Res Orientales XXII), 2014, pp. 29–71, and "Une archive post-sassanide du Tabaristān (III)". In: R. GYSELEN (ed.): *Words and Symbols: Sasanian Objects and the Tabarestān Archive.* Bures-sur-Yvette (Res Orientales XXIV), 2016, pp. 171–184.

88 It has been the privilege of the present author to collaborate with DIETER on these documents in an attempt to provide them with a legal background in Sasanian law.

89 "Court Records of Lawsuits in Tabarestān in the Year 86/7 PYE (737 CE): A Philological Examination". In: R. GYSELEN (ed.): *Words and Symbols: Sasanian Objects and the Tabarestān Archive.* Bures-sur-Yvette (Res Orientales XXIV), 2016, pp. 121–144.

90 "Two Documents from Tabarestān Reconsidered (Tab. 12 and 26)". In: R. GYSELEN (ed.): *Words and Symbols: Sasanian Objects and the Tabarestān Archive.* Bures-sur-Yvette (Res Orientales XXIV), 2016, pp. 185–192.

undertaken in a village, whose name repeatedly occurs in the documents, in the aftermath of a draught *(anābagīh)*; Tab. 26 records a complaint *(garzišn)* and the terms of a written (loan) contract *(paymān-nāmag)*. Reading the name of the recurring village, in whose archive the discovered documents were presumably kept, first as *Haspīn-raz, he corrects it in his later publications to *Asp-gurd (on this revised reading see WEBER 2020, p. 175).

Almost all the Tabarestān documents are from the above named village of *Asp-gurd (according to the revised reading), six of which DIETER re-edits in 2017.[91] Another article of 2017[92] is dedicated to reading the names in the documents. The texts in the first contribution grant insight into a large range of problems and controversies in the village, which were minutely recorded for later reference. Two of them are concerned with leasehold *(tāg)*: Tab. 13 records a dispute on the amount of produce that should be delivered as rent *(tāg)* for a leased vineyard *(razestān)*; Tab. 23 reveals another controversy on the amount of rent to be paid for the use of agricultural land on which wheat *(gandum)* was produced, after the tenants (or co-tenants) had received an abatement *(āsānīh)*. One document (Tab. 14) refers to a case of false testimony for which a compensation *(tāwān)* had to be paid to the complainant. Tab. 15 discloses the complaint *(garzišn)* of a scribe against a shield-maker *(spargar)* and registers the latter's self-commitment to deliver a specific shield to the claimant. Two loan contracts are among the legally most informative texts of the collection: Tab. 17 documents a loan without real security; Tab. 18 is a loan contract based on real security of the *antichresis* type *(grawagān)*, listing minutely the produce to be delivered to the creditor.

Two of the three documents re-edited in WEBER 2019[93] are administrative letters requesting a legal official to investigate claims: Tab. 21 involves the complaint of a father against his own son-in-law for cutting the maintenance of his daughter (= the defendant's wife) because of a false accusation *(mihōxt)* against her; Tab. 22 describes the unlawful seizure of valuable objects (ornaments and chalices) in a skin bag from the wife of the claimant, a case, which is — remarkably — taken up again two years later in another document, Tab. 22bis (published in WEBER 2022, see below), due to new evidence. One of the longest documents of the collection, Tab. 24, records meticulously the re-evaluation of crop yields of olive trees, mortgaged as security for a loan, after an earthquake *(wizandag)*.

91 "Pahlavi Legal Documents from Tabarestān on Lease, Loan and Compensation: A Philological Study (Tab. 13,14, 15, 17, 18, 23)". In: R. GYSELEN (ed.): *Sasanian Coins, Middle-Persian Etymology and the Tabarestān Archive*. Bures-sur-Yvette (Res Orientales XXVI), 2017, pp. 131–163.

92 "Bemerkungen zu einigen Personennamen in den neuen Dokumenten aus Tabaristan". In: E. MORANO/E. PROVASI/A.V. ROSSI (eds.): Studia Philologica Iranica Gherardo Gnoli Memorial Volume. Roma (Serie Orientale Roma, Nuova Serie 5), 2017, pp. 469–476.

93 "Pahlavi legal Documents from Tabarestān. Two Claims and a Re-evaluation of Crop Yields: A Philological Study of Tab. 21, 22 and 24". In: R. GYSELEN (ed.): *Sasanian Persia and the Tabarestān Archive*. Bures-sur-Yvette (Res Orientales XXVII), 2019, pp. 91–116.

The documents Tab. 11 and 28 in WEBER 2020[94] are unique in that they present two problematic, complex and controversial cases from the legal field of succession and inheritance, referring for the first time in a primary source to one of the central concepts of succession by proxy, using the technical term *stūrīh* ('substitute succession'). The third document (Tab. 27) is a written contract *(paymān-nāmag)* recording the commitment of a debtor to repay a loan he had taken up earlier by a fixed date. The texts in WEBER 2022[95] consist of loan contracts (Tab. 19 and 25), a contract for the loan of a plough animal (Tab. 16), a written confirmation *(čak)* specifying the amount of payment for a specific service (Tab. 20) and an administrative letter (Tab. 22bis) calling for the re-assessment of an earlier case of alleged appropriation of property, described in Tab. 22 (see above).

The Pahlavi Cursive Script

DIETER has included extensive lists of examples in the cursive script in many of his publications, particularly the monographs, not only in order to justify specific readings, but also to demonstrate how certain characters appear in various combinations (e.g. WEBER 1992, pp. 271–231; 2003, pp. 175–194; 2008, pp. 212–228; 2009, pp. 545–547). His study of 1993[96] is dedicated to discussing specific features of the cursive script in the ostraca and papyri, such as the use of two characters for /t/, which he transliterates as ⟨t⟩ and ⟨ṭ⟩, arguing that the ideogram ⟨PWN⟩ is in fact a pseudo-ideogram, as Hansen had assumed, to be read as ⟨pṭ⟩ *pad*, an interpretation which is underlined by its suffixed form ⟨pṭš⟩ *pad-iš*, and in fact renders the etymologically correct **pati* (however, he later seems to prefer ⟨PWN⟩, as in 2020, p. 154). He takes up this feature in his contribution of 2007[97] on the development of the Pahlavi script, assuming that a specific form of /t/ written with a stroke at the end of certain words, could be the origin of the Avestan *t̰*. The main part of this paper is dedicated to the discussion of a puzzling spelling of one the most frequent words in letters, the term for 'Lord, Sir', refer-

94 "Pahlavi Legal Documents from Tabarestān: the Documents Tab. 11, 28 and 27: A Philological Approach". In: R. GYSELEN (ed.): *Persia (552 BCE-758 CE): Primary Sources, Old and New*. Bures-sur-Yvette (Res Orientales XXVIII), 2020, pp. 171–188.

95 "Pahlavi Legal Documents from Tabarestān: The Documents Tab. 16, 19, 20, 22bis and 25. A Philological Approach". In: R. GYSELEN (ed.) *Sometimes Sasanian always ēr*. Bures-sur-Yvette (Res Orientales, XXIX), 2022, pp. 105–123.

96 "Kalligraphie und Kursive: Probleme der Pahlavi-Schrift in den Papyri und Ostraca". In: W. SKALMOWSKI/A. VAN TONGERLOO (eds.): *Medioiranica*. Proceedings of the International Colloquium organized by the Katholieke Universiteit Leuven from the 21st to the 23th of May 1990. Leuven (Orientalia Lovaniensia Analecta 48), 1993, pp. 183–192.

97 "Remarks on the Development of the Pahlavi Script in Sasanian Times". In: F. VAHMAN/C.V. PEDERSEN (eds.): *Religious Texts in Iranian Languages*. Symposium held in Copenhagen May 2002 (Det Kongelige Danske Videnskabernes Selskab). København 2007, pp. 185–195.

ring to the addressee(s) of a document or letter. The word had been previously read both by HANSEN and WEBER as ⟨hwṭ'k⟩, with final ⟨-k⟩, although the correct spelling would be ⟨hwt'y⟩ with final ⟨-y⟩. DIETER revises his earlier readings by showing that the noun 'Lord, Sir' is always written in these documents with the ideogram ⟨MRʿH(Y)⟩, never eteographically (as ⟨hwṭ'y⟩). Where an eteographic spelling occurs the word does not render the noun, but the adjective ⟨hwṭ'yk⟩ *xwadāyīg* 'lordly', a form which is also used in the Pahlavi text on "How to write letters" (*Nāmag-nibesišnīh),* confirming this interpretation.

Special features of the cursive script are discussed in all of DIETER's text editions and in separate contributions dedicated to elucidating distinct writing characteristics. On the basis of a comparison of the palaeographical features of certain characters WEBER 2007[98] corrects previously false readings of several terms and shows how the letter ⟨š⟩ is simplified almost beyond recognition in certain cases. WEBER 2008[99] continues this assessment of several hitherto illegible terms and phrases (such as *ǰāwēdān* "eternally, always" in the introductory formulae of letters or *uzēnišn ī dūdag* "expenses of the family" in economic texts and the formula *pad nēw xwarrah āzādīh sahēd* "by good fortune gratitude [may] seem [proper]") besides showing that the enclitic pronoun *–šān*, written ⟨-š'n⟩ in Book Pahlavi, is written without a *mater lectionis* as <-šn> in the papyri and other original documents. In his contribution of 2010[100] he solves another problem, showing on the basis of numerous examples that an additional small hook in front of a specific number in economic (and other texts) is in fact the abbreviation ⟨S⟩ for the term *satēr* "stater", indicating an amount of money in this currency. WEBER 2010[101] addresses another fascinating topic leading us directly into the daily practice of students learning to become scribes. He can identify several pieces as writing exercises due to several criteria, such as repetitions of words and phrases, the use of a written medium twice and sketches of letters.

In recent decades new finds, particularly the documents in the "Pahlavi Archive" and from Tabarestān, have considerably enlarged the material at our disposal on the cursive script, which still offers, despite WEBER's efforts, a true challenge to every decipherer. Taking all the available texts into consideration,

98 „Einige Bemerkungen zur Palaeographie des Pahlavi". In: M. MACUCH/ M. MAGGI/W. SUNDERMANN (eds.): *Iranian Languages and Texts from Iran and Turan.* Ronald E. Emmerick Memorial Volume (Iranica 13), Wiesbaden 2007, pp. 433–442.

99 "Minuscula Pahlavica (Pahlavi Notes)". In: *Bulletin of the Asia Institute* 18, 2008, pp. 135–142.

100 "The Pahlavi Script as a Medium of Iranian Identity. Some Palaeographical Notes". In: CARLO G. CERETI (ed.): *Iranian Identity in the Course of History.* Proceedings of the Conference Held in Rome, 21–24 September 2005 (Serie Orientale Roma CV; Orientalia Romana 9), Roma 2010, pp. 347–356.

101 "Writing Exercises in Late Sasanian Times. A Contribution to the Culture of Writing Pahlavi". In: M. MACUCH/D. WEBER/D. DURKIN-MEISTERERNST (eds.): *Ancient and Middle Iranian Studies.* Proceedings of the 6th European Conference of Iranian Studies, held in Vienna, 18–22 Sepember 2007 (Iranica 19), Wiesbaden 2010, pp. 255–263.

Dieter is now preparing another desideratum of Iranian Studies for publication: a monograph on the Pahlavi script with numerous examples from the original documents. Needless to say, this endeavour is eminently important not only for reading these first hand primary sources and understanding the development of the Pahlavi script, but also for resolving several fundamental, albeit still unsolved problems of Ancient and Middle Iranian Studies, such as the date of the invention of the Avestan script, based on the Pahlavi script, and subsequently the recording of the Avesta as a written text.

Publications of Dieter Weber

Monographs

Die Stellung der sog. Inchoativa im Mitteliranischen. Diss. Göttingen, 1970.

Pahlavi Papyri, Pergamente und Ostraca. (Textband.) *Corpus Inscriptionum Iranicarum*. London 1992. (Persian translation): Weber, Dieter: *Ostrākā, pāpīrūs wa pust-newešte*, CII. Tehrān, 1396.

Iranian Manichaean Turfan texts in publications since 1934. *Corpus Inscriptionum Iranicarum*, Supplementary Series IV. London 2000.

Berliner Papyri, Pergamente und Leinenfragmente in mittelpersischer Sprache. Unter Mitarbeit von W. Brashear. Fotografien von Margarete Busing und Eva Maria Borgwaldt. (Textband.) *Corpus Inscriptionum Iranicarum*. London, 2003.

Berliner Pahlavi-Dokumente. Zeugnisse spätsassanidischer Brief- und Rechtskultur aus frühislamischer Zeit. Mit Beiträgen von Myriam Krutzsch und Maria Macuch. Wiesbaden (Iranica 15), 2008.

Edited Books

(with R.E. Emmerick): *Corolla Iranica, Papers in honour of Prof. Dr. David Neil MacKenzie on the occasion of his 65th birthday on the eighth of April 1991*. Frankfurt am Main/Bern/New York/Paris, 1991.

(with J. Becker, E. Eggers, and J. Udolph): *Linguisticæ Scientiæ Collectanea, Ausgewählte Schriften von Wolfgang P. Schmid. anläßlich seines 65. Geburtstages*. Berlin/New York, 1994.

(with J. Becker, E. Eggers, and J. Udolph): *Florilegium Linguisticum, Festschrift für Wolfgang P. Schmid zum 70. Geburtstag*, Frankfurt/Main e.a., 1999.

(with C. Reck, C. Leurini, and A. Panaino): *Manichaica Iranica, Ausgewählte Schriften von Werner Sundermann*. 2 vols. Roma (Serie Orientale Roma LXXXIX, 1/2), 2001.

Languages of Iran: Past and Present. A Volume of Iranian Studies in memoriam David Neil MacKenzie. Wiesbaden (Iranica 8), 2005.

(with U. Hackl and B. Jacobs): *Quellen zur Geschichte des Partherreiches. Textsammlung mit Übersetzungen und Kommentaren*. 3 vols. Göttingen, 2010.

(with M. Macuch and D. Durkin-Meisterernst): *Ancient and Middle Iranian Studies. Proceedings of the 6th European Conference of Iranian Studies, held in Vienna, 18–22 September 2007*. Wiesbaden (Iranica 19), 2010.

Articles & Book Chapters

"Einige Verba mit langvokalischen Wurzeln im Indogermanischen". In: *Annali dell' Istituto Orientale di Napoli – Sezione Linguistica* 6, 1965, pp. 5–14.

"Zwei pontisch-iranische Eigennamen". In: *Die Sprache* 12, 1966, pp. 90–93.

"Κερπατης". In: *Die Sprache* 13, 1967, pp. 65–66.

"Einige Göttinger Pahlavi-Fragmente". In: *Indogermanische Forschungen* 74, 1969, pp. 32–38.

"Also sprach Mandrī. Bemerkungen zur direkten Rede im Sogdischen". In: *Indogermanische Forschungen* 76, 1971, pp. 77–83.

"Zur sogdischen Personennamengebung". In: *Indogermanische Forschungen* 77, 1972, pp. 191–208.

"Einige Beobachtungen an Pahlavi Papyri". In: *Acta Orientalia* (Copenhagen) 35, 1973, pp. 83–88.

"Zur Interpretation der Pahlavi-Ostraca". In: Ph. Gignoux/A. Tafazzoli (eds.): *Mémorial J. de Menasce*. Louvain, 1974, pp. 227–233.

"Sogdische Miszellen". In: *Indogermanische Forschungen* 80, 1975, pp. 90–97.

"Beiträge zur historischen Grammatik des Ossetischen: 1. Der sog. 'Dativ' auf *-æn*. 2. Die reflexiven Formen des Personalpronomens". In: *Indogermanische Forschungen* 85, 1980 [1981], pp. 126–137.

"Das Perfekt transitiver Verben im Khotansakischen". In: *Die Sprache* 28, 1982, pp. 165–170.

"Sprachliches aus achämenidischer Zeit in Zentralasien". In: H. Koch/D.N. MacKenzie (eds.): *Kunst, Kultur und Geschichte der Achämenidenzeit und ihr Fortleben. Festschrift Prof. Dr. W. Hinz*. Berlin, 1983 (Archäologische Mitteilungen aus Iran, Ergänzungsband 10), pp. 91–100.

"Die Pehlevi-Papyri der Papyrussammlung Erzherzog Rainer zu Wien". In: *Festschrift Papyrus Erzherzog Rainer (P. Rainer Cent.)*. Wien, 1983 (Textband), pp. 215–228.

"Beiträge zur historischen Grammatik des Ossetischen. 3. Das Präsens des Verbums *uyn* 'sein'". In: *Indogermanische Forschungen* 88, 1983, pp. 84–91.

"Pahlavi Papyri und Ostraca: Stand der Forschung". In: W. Skalmowski/A. van Tongerloo (eds.): *Middle Iranian Studies. Proceedings of the International Symposium organized by the Katholieke Universiteit Leuven from the 17th to the 20th of May 1982*. Leuven, 1984 (Orientalia Lovaniensia Analecta 16), pp. 25–43.

"Khotansakisch *āṣana-* 'wert, würdig'". In: *Papers in honour of Professor Mary Boyce* II. Leiden, 1985, pp. 675–681.

"Asfwrougoj und Verwandtes". In: *Archäologische Mitteilungen aus Iran* 19 (Festschrift Prof. Dr. W. Hinz. Berlin, 1986 [1988], pp. 171–175.

"Zu einigen iranischen Ortsnamen bei Ptolemaios". In: *A Green Leaf. Papers in Honour of Professor Jes P. Asmussen*. Leiden (Hommages et Opera Minora xii), 1988, pp. 493–495.

"Die ersten Germanen am Nordufer des Schwarzen Meeres". In: *Historische Sprachwissenschaft (Historical Linguistics)*, früher: *Kuhns Zeitschrift für Vergleichende Sprachforschung* 101 (1988), pp. 138–150.

"Das Phonem /b/ im Ossetischen und seine Vorgeschichte". In: *Georgica* 11 (Jena/ Tbilissi), 1988, pp. 25–28.

"Eine iranisch-baltische Parallele (parth. *rwmb* 'Mund')". In: *Indogermanische Forschungen* 94, 1989, pp. 94–100.

"Eine iranistische Kleinigkeit (zu lat. *zanca* 'Schuh')". In: *Historische Sprachwissenschaft (Historical Linguistics)*, früher: *Kuhns Zeitschrift für Vergleichende Sprachforschung* 102, 1989, pp. 127–128.

"An Ossetic query (Osset. *bægæny/bægæni* 'beer')". In: Gh. Gnoli/A. Panaino (eds.): *Proceedings of the First European Conference of Iranian Studies held in Turin, September 7th–11th, 1987 by the Societas Iranologica Europaea.* Part II, *Middle and New Iranian Studies.* Rome (Serie Orientale Roma, Vol. LXVII, 2), 1990, pp. 585–591.

"Ein bisher unbekannter Titel aus spätsassanidischer Zeit?" In: R.E. Emmerick/D. Weber (eds.): *Corolla Iranica. Papers in honour of Prof. Dr. D. N. MacKenzie.* Frankfurt am Main/Bern/New York/Paris, 1991, pp. 228–236.

"Lautgeschichte und Chronologie: Zu den Ordinalzahlen des Ossetischen". In: *Studia etymologica Indoeuropaea memoriae A. J. Van Windekens (1915–1989) dicata.* Leuven (Orientalia Lovaniensia Analecta 45), 1991, pp. 305–311.

"Pahlavi Papyri Revisited". In: A.H.S. El-Mosalamy (ed.): *Proceedings of the XIXth International Congress of Papyriologists, Cairo, 2–9 September 1989* (Ain Shams University, Center of Papyrological Studies). Cairo, 1992, vol. II, pp. 493–508.

"Kalligraphie und Kursive: Probleme der Pahlavi-Schrift in den Papyri und Ostraca". In: W. Skalmowski/A. van Tongerloo (eds.): *Medioiranica, Proceedings of the International Colloquium organized by the Katholieke Universiteit Leuven from the 21st to the 23rd of May 1990.* Leuven (Orientalia Lovaniensia Analecta 48), 1993, pp. 183–192.

"Eine angebliche slavisch-ossetische lexikalische Übereinstimmung". In: *Indogermanische Forschungen* 98, 1993, pp. 100–107.

"Zu einigen neuen Pahlavi Dokumenten". In: *Studia Iranica* 23, 1994, pp. 123–129.

"Zur Problematik eines Phonems /x^w/ im Pahlavi". In: *Studia Iranica, Mesopotamica et Anatolica* I. Praha, 1994 [1995], pp. 107–118.

"Iranian Loans in the Niya Documents Re-examined". In: S. Akiner/N. Sims-Williams (eds.): *Languages and Scripts of Central Asia.* London, 1997, pp. 30–38.

"Pahlavi Phonology". In: A.S. Kaye (ed.): *Phonologies of Asia and Africa (Including the Caucasus)* ii. Winona Lake (Indiana), 1997, pp. 601–636 [also as Private Printing 1996].

"Osset. *bælon*, D *bælæu* 'Taube' und lit. *balañdis*". In: *Res Balticae* 3, 1997, pp. 119–128.

"Ossetisch (D) *murdtgun* (*kærdæg*) ‚gutes, saftiges (Gras)'". In: E. Eggers/J. Becker/J. Udolph/D. Weber (eds.): *Florilegium Linguisticum, Festschrift für Wolfgang P. Schmid zum 70. Geburtstag.* Frankfurt am Main e.a., 1999, pp. 519–537.

"Zur grammatisch-semantischen Bestimmung einiger Lemmata des sogdischen Lexikons". In: R.E. Emmerick/W. Sundermann/P. Zieme (eds.): *Studia Manichaica. IV. Internationaler Kongreß zum Manichäismus, Berlin, 14.–18. Juli 1997.* Berlin, 2000, pp. 639–647.

"ΜΑΝΙΑΓΟΣ". In: C. Cereti/M. Maggi/E. Provasi (eds.): *Religious themes and texts of pre-Islamic Iran and Central Asia: studies in honour of Professor Gherardo*

Gnoli on the occasion of his 65th birthday on 6 December 2002. Wiesbaden, 2002, pp. 441–445.

"Regen und Wind. Probleme um den sogdischen Regenzaubertext P 3". In: S. Bretfeld/J. Wilkens (eds.): *Indien und Zentralasien – Sprach- und Kulturkontakt. Vorträge des Göttinger Symposiums vom 7. bis 10. Mai 2001*. Wiesbaden (Veröffentlichungen der Societas Uralo-Altaica 61), 2003, pp. 227–237.

"Die Pahlavi-Ostraca von Çāl Tarxān-Ešqābād". In: L. Paul (ed.): *Persian Origins – Early Judeo-Persian and the Emergence of New Persian. Collected Papers of the Symposium, Göttingen 1999*. Wiesbaden (Iranica 6), 2003, pp. 275–282.

"Notes on Some Parthian Names from Nisā". In: *Parthica* 5, 2003, pp. 127–129.

"Eine spätsassanidische Rechtsurkunde aus Ägypten". In: *TYCHE* 17, 2002 [2003], pp. 185–192.

"The Coin Legend *TANLISMAIDATES* and Related Problems". In: *Parthica* 6, 2004, pp. 247–250.

"Pahlavi Papyri". In: *Encyclopædia Iranica*, 2005. Available online: https://www.iranicaonline.org/articles/pahlavi-papyri (last accessed 25.10.2023).

"Kleine Nachlese zu einigen Pahlavi-Ostraca". In: D. Weber (ed.): *Languages of Iran – Past and Present. Iranian Studies in Memoriam David Neil MacKenzie*. Wiesbaden (Iranica 8), 2005, pp. 17–228.

"Remarks on the Development of the Pahlavi Script in Sasanian Times". In: F. Vahman /C.V. Pedersen (eds.): *Religious Texts in Iranian Languages* (Det Kongelige Danske Videnskabernes Selskab). København (Akten des Kongresses Kopenhagen 2002), 2007, pp. 185–195.

"The Vienna Collection of Pahlavi Papyri". In: B. Palme (ed.): *Akten des 23. Internationalen Papyrologenkongresses* (*Wien, 22.–28. Juli 2001*) [Österreichische Akademie der Wissenschaften, Phil.-Hist. Kl., Kommission für Antike Rechtsgeschichte]. Wien, 2007, pp. 725–738.

"Pahlavi Morphology". In: A.S. Kaye (ed.): *Morphologies of Asia and Africa*. Winona Lake (Indiana), 2007, pp. 941–973.

"The *xarāj* Taxation and the Pahlavi Document Berk. No. 27. Part III:2 (p. 27–29)". In: G. Azarpay/K. Martin/M. Schwartz/D. Weber (eds.): "New Information on the Date and Function of the Berkeley MP Archive". In: *Bulletin of the Asia Institute* 17, 2003 [2007], pp. 17–29.

"Einige Bemerkungen zur Palaeographie des Pahlavi". In: M. Macuch/M. Maggi /W. Sundermann (eds.): *Iranian Languages and Texts from Iran and Turan. Ronald E. Emmerick Memorial Volume*. Wiesbaden (Iranica 13), 2007, pp. 433–442.

"On Middle Persian *aswār* 'horseman, rider' in Pahlavi Documents of the 7th Century". In: *Nāme-ye Irān-e Bāstān* 6/1&2, 2006–7 [2008], pp. 37–44.

"Sassanidische Briefe aus Ägypten". In: *Asiatische Studien/Études Asiatiques* LXII/3, 2008, pp. 803–826.

"Minuscula Pahlavica (Pahlavi Notes)". In: *Bulletin of the Asia Institute* 18, 2008, pp. 135–142.

"Ein Pahlavi-Fragment des Alexanderromans aus Ägypten?" In: D. Durkin-Meisterernst/Chr. Reck/D. Weber (eds.): *Literarische Stoffe und ihre Gestaltung in mitteliranischer Zeit, Ehrencolloquium anlässlich des 70. Geburtstages von Prof. Dr. Werner Sundermann 30.–31. März 2006*. Wiesbaden, 2009, pp. 307–318.

"A Pahlavi Letter from Egypt Re-visited (P. 44)". In: W. SUNDERMANN/A. HINTZE/F. DE BLOIS (eds.): *Exegisti monumenta. Festschrift in Honour of Nicholas Sims-Williams.* Wiesbaden (Iranica 17), 2009, pp. 537–550.

"A Pahlavi Papyrus from Islamic Times". In: C.A. BROMBERG/N. SIMS-WILLIAMS/U. SIMS-WILLIAMS (eds.): *Bulletin of the Asia Institute* 19, 2005 [2009] (*Iranian and Zoroastrian Studies in Honour of Prods Oktor Skjærvø*), pp. 225–231.

"Zu den Brotrationen in den Pahlavi-Ostraka. In : PH. GIGNOUX/CHR. JULLIEN/FL. JULLIEN (eds.): *Trésors d'Orient – Mélanges offerts à Rika Gyselen.* Paris (Studia Iranica, Cahier 42), 2009, pp. 379–389.

"The Pahlavi Script as a Medium of Iranian Identity. Some Palaeographical Notes". In: C.G. CERETI (ed.): *Iranian Identity in the Course of History. Proceedings of the Conference Held in Rome, 21–24 September 2005.* Roma (Serie Orientale Roma CV, Orientalia Romana 9), 2010, pp. 347–356.

"Two Pahlavi Letters from the Time of Hormizd V (630–632 AD)". In: *Bulletin of the Asia Institute* 20, 2010, pp. 55–63.

"Writing Exercises in Late Sasanian Times. A Contribution to the Culture of Writing Pahlavi". In: M. MACUCH/D. WEBER/D. DURKIN-MEISTERERNST (eds.): *Ancient and Middle Iranian Studies. Proceedings of the 6th European Conference of Iranian Studies, held in Vienna, 18–22 September 2007.* Wiesbaden (Iranica 19), 2010, pp. 255–263.

"Anhang: Einige Titel (Kap. II.4.2.6.)". In: U. HACKL/B. JACOBS/D. WEBER (eds.): *Quellen zur Geschichte des Partherreiches. Textsammlung mit* Übersetzungen *und Kommentaren* I. Göttingen, 2010, pp. 100–104.

"Theophore Namen bei den Parthern (Kap. II.4.7.2.)". In: U. HACKL, B. JACOBS, and D. WEBER (eds.): *Quellen zur Geschichte des Partherreiches. Textsammlung mit* Übersetzungen *und Kommentaren.* Bd. I, Göttingen, 2010, pp. 154–164.

"Parthische Entlehnungen in Nachbarsprachen (Kap. II.4.8.)". In: U. HACKL/B. JACOBS/D. WEBER (eds.): *Quellen zur Geschichte des Partherreiches. Textsammlung mit* Übersetzungen *und Kommentaren* I. Göttingen, 2010, pp. 165–168.

"Parthische Texte (Kap. III.2.)". In: U. HACKL/B. JACOBS/D. WEBER (eds.): *Quellen zur Geschichte des Partherreiches. Textsammlung mit* Übersetzungen *und Kommentaren* II. Göttingen 2010, pp. 492–588.

"Iranica auf arsakidischen Münzen (Kap. III.3.3.)". In: U. HACKL/B. JACOBS/D. WEBER (eds.): *Quellen zur Geschichte des Partherreiches. Textsammlung mit* Übersetzungen *und Kommentaren* II. Göttingen, 2010, pp. 633–639.

"Philippe Gignoux' Beitrag zur Interpretation der Dokumente des 'Pahlavi Archive' in Berkeley, Ca". In: R. GYSELEN/CH. JULLIEN (eds.): *Florilège offert à Philippe Gignoux pour son 80e anniversaire.* Paris, 2011, pp. 283–303.

"An Interesting Pahlavi Letter from Early Islamic Times (Berk. 245)". In: *Zeitschrift der Deutschen Morgenländischen Gesellschaft* 161, 2011, pp. 91–98.

"Der Lebensmittelhaushalt des Herrn Saralaneozan/*Šahr-Ālānyōzān*. Neuedition von zwei Speiselisten und einem Geschäftsbrief aus dem sassanidischen Ägypten". (with PATRICK SÄNGER) In: *Archiv für Papyrusforschung* 58/1, 2012, pp. 81–96.

"New Arguments for Dating the Documents from the "Pahlavi Archive"". In: *Bulletin of the Asia Institute* 22, 2008 [2012], pp. 215–222.

"Die persische Besetzung Ägyptens 619–629 n. Chr. Fakten und Spekulationen". In: F. FEDER/A. LOHWASSER (eds.): *Ägypten und sein Umfeld in der Spätantike. Vom Regierungsantritt Diokletians 284/285 bis zur arabischen Eroberung des Vorderen Orients um 635–646; Akten der Tagung vom 7.–9.7.2011 in Münster.* Wiesbaden (Philippika 61), 2013, pp. 221–246.

"Taxation in Pahlavi Documents from Early Islamic Times (late 7th century CE)". In: S. TOXTAS'EV/P. LUR'E (eds.): *Commentationes Iranicae.* Sankt-Petersburg (*Sbornik statej k 90-letiju V.A. Livšica*), 2013, pp. 171–181.

"Villages and Estates in the Documents from the Pahlavi Archive: The Geographical Background". In: *Bulletin of the Asia Institute* 24, 2010 [2014], pp. 39–67.

(with ST. HEIDEMANN/J. RIEDERER): "A Hoard from the Time of Yazdgard III in Kirmān" (Chapters 5 and 13.6, pp. 87–89 and 114–121). In: *Iran* 52, 2014, pp. 79–124.

"Arabic Activities Reflected in the Documents of the 'Pahlavi Archive' (late 7th and early 8th centuries)". In: R. GYSELEN (ed.): *Documents, argenterie et monnaies de tradition sassanide.* Bures-sur-Yvette (Res Orientales XXII), 2014, pp. 179–188.

"Testing Food and Garment for the *Ōstāndār* (Two Unpublished Documents from the "Pahlavi Archive" in Berkeley, CA.)". In: *Bulletin of the Asia Institute* 25, 2011 [2015], pp. 31–37.

"Spätsasanidische Preislisten im frühislamischen Iran". In: S. FARRIDNEJAD/R. GYSELEN/A. JOISTEN-PRUSCHKE (eds.): *Faszination Iran – Beiträge zur Religion, Geschichte und Kunst des Alten Iran (Gedenkschrift für Klaus Schippmann).* Wiesbaden (Göttinger Orientforschungen III. Iranica, Neue Folge 13), 2015, pp. 233–243.

"Court Records of Lawsuits in Tabarestān in the Year 86/7 PYE (737 CE): A Philological Examination". In: R. GYSELEN (ed.): *Words and Symbols: Sasanian Objects and the Tabarestān Archive.* Bures-sur-Yvette (Res Orientales XXIV), 2016, pp. 121–142.

"Two Documents from Tabarestān Reconsidered (Tab. 12 and 26)". In: R. GYSELEN (ed.): *Words and Symbols: Sasanian Objects and the Tabarestān Archive.* Bures-sur-Yvette (Res Orientales XXIV), 2016, pp. 185–192.

"Studies in Some Documents from the "Pahlavi Archive"". In: *Bulletin of the Asia Institute* 26, 2012 [2016], pp. 61–95.

"Bemerkungen zu einigen Personennamen in den neuen Dokumenten aus Tabaristān". In: E. MORANO/E. PROVASI/A.V. ROSSI (eds.): *Studia Philologica Iranica (Gherardo Gnoli Memorial Volume).* Roma (Serie Orientale Roma, Nuova Serie 5), 2017, pp. 469–476.

"A Pahlavi Query". In: Team "Turfanforschung" (ed.): *Zur Lichten Heimat. Studien zu Manichäismus, Iranistik und Zentralasienkunde im Gedenken an Werner Sundermann.* Wiesbaden (Iranica 25), 2017, pp. 675–682.

"Accountancy of a Zoroastrian Craftsman in Early Islamic Times (662–664 CE)". In: *Bulletin of the Asia Institute* 27, 2013 [2017], pp. 129–141.

"Pahlavi Legal Documents from Tabarestān on Lease, Loan and Compensation: A Philological Study (Tab. 13, 14, 15, 17, 18 and 23)". In: R. GYSELEN (ed.): *Sasanian Coins, Middle-Persian Etymology and the Tabarestān Archive.* Bures-sur-Yvette (Res Orientales XXVI), 2017, pp. 131–163.

"The Pahlavi Letter Doc. 129 of the Khalili Collection. Appendix 2". In: N. Sims-Williams/F. de Blois (eds.): *Studies in the Chronology of the Bactrian Documents from Northern Afghanistan with contributions by Harry Falk and Dieter Weber.* Wien (Denkschriften der philosophisch-historischen Klasse 505; Veröffentlichungen zur Iranistik 83), 2018, pp. 99–108.

"Pahlavi Documents of *Windādburzmihrābād*, the Estate of a Zoroastrian Entrepreneur in Early Islamic Times (With an Excursus on the Origin of the *Fulanabad*-Type of Village Names)". In: *Bulletin of the Asia Institute* 28, 2014 [2018], pp. 127–147.

"Three Pahlavi Papyri Revisited". In: *Sasanika Papyrological Studies* 2, 2018, pp. 1–6. Availabe online: https://sites.uci.edu/sasanika/files/2020/02/Sasanika_PS02_Weber.pdf (last accessed 25.10.2023).

"The Story of *Windād-Burzmihr.* A Zoroastrian Entrepreneur in Early Islamic Times". In: A. Hintze/D. Durkin-Meisterernst/C. Naumann (eds.): *A Thousand Judgements. Festschrift for Maria Macuch.* Wiesbaden, 2019, pp. 373–384.

"Christlich-jüdische Spuren in Pahlavi-Dokumenten des 7. Jhs. n. Chr". In: J. Rubanovich/G. Herman (eds.): *Irano-Judaica* VII. *Studies relating to Jewish contacts with Persian culture throughout the ages.* Jerusalem, 2019, pp. 251–266.

"Studies in Some Documents from the 'Pahlavi Archive' (2)". In: *Bulletin of the Asia Institute* 29, 2015 [2019], pp. 79–116.

"Pahlavi Legal Documents from Tabarestān. Two Claims and a Re-evaluation of Crop Yields: A Philological Study of Tab. 21, 22 and 24". In: R. Gyselen (ed.): *Sasanian Persia and the Tabarestān Archive.* Bures-sur-Yvette (Res Orientales XXVII), 2019, pp. 91–115.

"Two Unknown Documents from the 'Pahlavi Archive'". In: *Sasanika Papyrological Studies* 3, 2019, pp. 1–6. Available online: https://sites.uci.edu/sasanika/files/2019/11/Sasanika_PS03_Weber-002.pdf (last accessed 25.10.2023).

"Living Together in Changing Iran. Pahlavi documents on Arabs and Christians in Early Islamic Times". In: *Annales Islamologiques* 54, 2020, pp. 139–164. Available online: https://doi.org/10.4000/anisl.8409.

"Studies in Some Documents from the 'Pahlavi Archive' (3): I. Breeding of Poultry II. *Aspbād*, the 'caretaker'". In: *Bulletin of the Asia Institute* 30, 2020/21, pp. 29–65.

"Sasanian Festivals in the Documents from the 'Pahlavi Archive'". In: *Sasanian Studies* I, 2022, pp. 323–345.

"Pahlavi Legal Documents from Tabarestān: the Documents Tab. 16, 19, 20, 22 bis and 25: A Philological Approach". In: R. Gyselen (ed.): *Sometimes Sasanian, always* ēr. Bures-sur-Yvette (Res Orientales XXIX), 2022, pp. 105–129.

"On the Formal Structure of Checks in Pahlavi Documents." In: A. Cantera/M. Macuch/N. Sims-Williams (eds.): *The Reward of the Righteous: Festschrift in Honour of Almut Hintze.* Wiesbaden (Iranica 30) 2022, pp. 515–548.

"Studies in Some Documents from the 'Pahlavi Archive' (4): The Meaning and Use of <splk> spārag 'Charging, Committing'". In: *Bulletin of the Asia Institute* 31, 2022/23, pp. 145–165.

"A Recently Found Pahlavi Document from Fars from the Time of Xusrō II", in cooperation with Khosro Roodani and Sahar Foroozanpour. In: R. Gyselen (ed.): *Reflets d'époques Sassanide et post-Sassanide (224–760 A.D.)* Bures-sur-Yvette (Res Orientales XXX), 2023, pp. 177–192.

"Cooking in 7th Century Iran". In: *Sasanian Studies* II, 2023, pp. 287–313.

Book Reviews

"F.F. Schwarz: Die Nala-Legende I und II. Text, Umschrift, Übersetzung und Kommentar (Arbeiten aus dem Institut für vergleichende Sprachwissenschaft, Graz 7.). Wien 1966". In: *Indogermanische Forschungen* 72, 1967, pp. 322–323.

"J. Gonda: A Concise Elementary Grammar of the Sanskrit Language. Leiden 1966". In: *Indogermanische Forschungen* 73, 1968, p. 164.

"A. Meillet: The Comparative Method in Historical Linguistics. Trsl. from the French by Gordon B. Ford jr. Paris 1967". In: *Indogermanische Forschungen* 73, 1968, p. 364.

(with W. Hinz): "W.B. Henning: Memorial Volume. London 1970". In: *Indogermanische Forschungen* 77, 1972, pp. 296–302.

"E.G. Domingo: Samdhi en Indoeuropeo. Burgos 1985". In: *Indogermanische Forschungen* 93, 1988, pp. 294–295.

"A. Etter: Annemarie. Die Fragesätze im Rgveda (Untersuchungen zur indogermanischen Sprach- und Kulturwissenschaft / Studies in Indo-European Language and Culture [= UISK], 1). Berlin/New York 1985". In: *Indogermanische Forschungen* 93, 1988, pp. 295–297.

"N. Rastegar/W. Slaje: Uto von Melzer (1881–1961). Werk und Nachlaß eines österreichischen Iranisten (Österreichische Akademie der Wissenschaften, Phil.-Hist. Kl., Sitzungsberichte, 477. Bd.; Veröffentlichungen der Iran. Komm., hrsg. von M. Mayrhofer 20). Wien 1987". In: *Indogermanische Forschungen* 96, 1991, pp. 311–312.

"A. Degener: Khotanische Suffixe (Alt- und Neu-Indische Studien, hrsg. vom Institut für Kultur und Geschichte Indiens und Tibets an der Universität Hamburg 39). Stuttgart 1989". In: *Zeitschrift der Deutschen Morgenländischen Gesellschaft* 143, 1993, pp. 421–425.

"W. Eilers: Die Mundart von S£vänd (Westiranische Mundarten aus der Sammlung Wilhelm Eilers III). Stuttgart 1988". In: *Bulletin of the School of Oriental and African Studies* 56/2, 1993, pp. 378–379.

"Sogdian and other Iranian Inscriptions of the Upper Indus. I. (Corpus Inscriptionum Iranicarum, Part II: Inscriptions of the Seleucid and Parthian Periods and of Eastern Iran and Central Asia III: Sogdian). London 1989". In: *Bulletin of the School of Oriental and African Studies* 56/3, 1993, pp. 599–600.

"M. Samadi: Das chwaresmische Verbum. Wiesbaden 1986". In: *Indogermanische Forschungen* 100, 1995, pp. 275–277.

"H. Lewis: Handbuch des Mittelkornischen. Dt. Bearbeitung von Stefan Zimmer. Mit einem bibliographischen Anhang von Andrew Hawke (Innsbrucker Beiträge zur Sprachwissenschaft 61). Innsbruck 1990. " and "H. Lewis/J.R.F. Piette: Handbuch des Mittelbretonischen. Dt. Bearbeitung von Wolfgang Meid (Innsbrucker

Beiträge zur Sprachwissenschaft 62). Innsbruck 1990". In: *Indogermanische Forschungen* 100, 1995, pp. 297–298.

"N. Sims-Williams: Corpus Inscriptionum Iranicarum. Vol. VI: Bactrian. Bactrian Documents from Northern Afghanistan. I: Legal and Economic Documents (Studies in the Khalili Collection III.). Oxford 2000". In: *Kratylos* 49, 2004, pp. 193–195.

"I.M. Diakonoff/V.A. Livshits: Corpus Inscriptionum Iranicarum. Part II: Inscriptions of the Seleucid and Parthian Periods and of Eastern Iran and Central Asia, vol. II: Parthian, Parthian Economic Documents from Nisa (Texts I pp. 161–215). Ed. by D.N. MacKenzie/A.N. Bader/N. Sims-Williams. London 2001". In: *Journal of the American Oriental Society* 125.3, 2005, pp. 410–415.

"N. Sims-Williams: Corpus Inscriptionum Iranicarum. Part II. Inscriptions of the Seleucid and Parthian Periods and of Eastern Iran and Central Asia.Vol. III: Bactrian. II: Letters and Buddhist Texts (Studies in the Khalili Collection III). Oxford 2007. " In: *Kratylos* 55, 2010, pp. 228–231.

Three Zoroastrian Manuscripts in Armenia

MIGUEL ÁNGEL ANDRÉS-TOLEDO, Toronto

Before the majority of the population converted to Christianity, Armenia was a stronghold of the Zoroastrian faith for many centuries.[1] Unfortunately, no manuscript written by Armenian Zoroastrian communities of late antiquity or later periods was known, until recently three Zoroastrian manuscripts were discovered in Armenia, which have so far remained unnoticed by specialists. In this contribution to honor DR. DIETER WEBER, one of the most important scholars of Middle Persian, I will present an analysis of these three manuscripts and their relevance for Old and Middle Iranian studies.

The largest collection of manuscripts in Armenia is preserved at the Library of the Mesrop Mashtots Institute of Ancient Manuscripts, generally known as Matenadaran, in Yerevan. In this library, KOSTIKYAN/MEHDI BAGHI (2017) identified some Pahlavi texts in three manuscripts (mss. 125, 129, and 130 of the Non-Armenian Manuscript Collection), which were donated by the Armenian poet and translator Mihrdat T'ireak'ean in 1970. He received them from his father Harut'iwn T'ireak'ean (1845–1919), who lived in Iran in 1896–1906, was the court physician of the Shāh, and also rendered into Armenian some Pahlavi and Classical New Persian texts.[2] It is unclear where or from whom he received them, but we know that he was in contact with Khodayar Dastur Shahriyar Irani, whom he had met in Shiraz.

KOSTIKYAN/MEHDI BAGHI (2017) already described the three Zoroastrian manuscripts at the Library of the Mesrop Mashtots Institute of Ancient Manuscripts. However, though highly meritorious, they did not correctly identify all the texts included in them and their description contains several inaccuracies. Therefore, after having examined all the pages, in the following I will fully describe each manuscript and comment on the most important details that are relevant for scholars of Zoroastrian texts.

1 See RUSSELL 1987.
2 For more information about Harut'iwn T'ireak'ean and his son, see RUSSELL 2011, p. 5, and KOSTIKYAN/MEHDI BAGHI 2017.

MMI 125

(Mesrop Mashtots Institute of Ancient Manuscripts, Non-Armenian Manuscript Collection, ms. 125): Composite manuscript with Avestan, Pahlavi, Pāzand and Zoroastrian New Persian texts

The manuscript contains 148ff., of which f. 1r, 125v–127r, 146r–148v are blank. 17,5 x 22,5 cm; 14 lines to the page. Black ink, with titles and ritual instructions in Pahlavi and New Persian in red ink. Depiction of the *baršnūm-gāh* (f. 124r). It includes three Pahlavi colophons, the first and third of which indicate that it was written by Marzbān Wahrom Marzbān Frēdōn Rostām. The first colophon bears the latest date (AY 1064 = CE 1695), and the third colophon is dated AY 1033 + 20 (= CE 1684). Nevertheless, the paper, the palaeography and the ink point to the quite likely possibility, confirmed by J. MARTÍNEZ PORRO (email of December 19, 2023) that this is a copy made by a 19th-century CE scribe, who eventually incorporated older materials from the 17th-century CE.

Contents:

- *Frahang ī pahlawīg* (f. 1v, l. 1 – f. 32v, l. 9), with Pāzand equivalent of each Pahlavi word, and including two Pahlavi–Avestan alphabets (1st alphabet in f. 28r, ll. 4–10; 2nd alphabet in f. 32v, ll. 1–9).

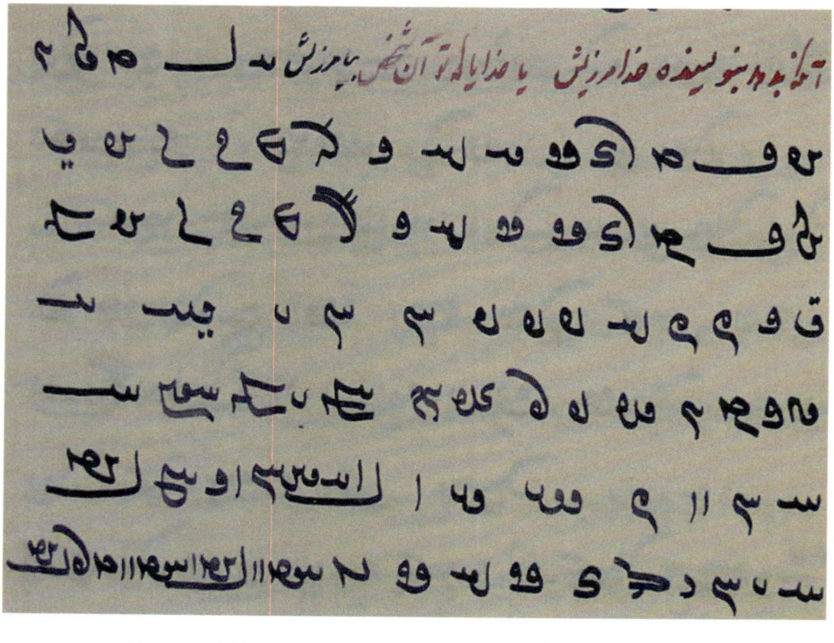

Fig. 1. 1st Pahlavi–Avestan alphabet (f. 28r, ll. 4–10)

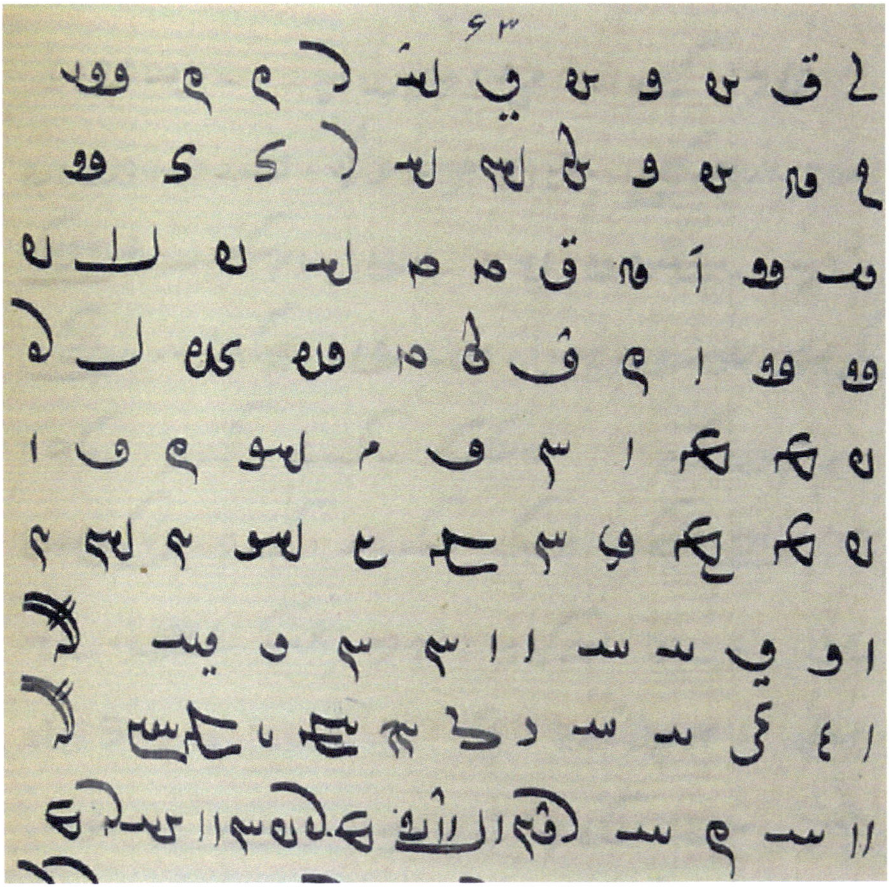

Fig. 2. 2nd Pahlavi–Avestan alphabet (f. 32v, ll. 1–9)

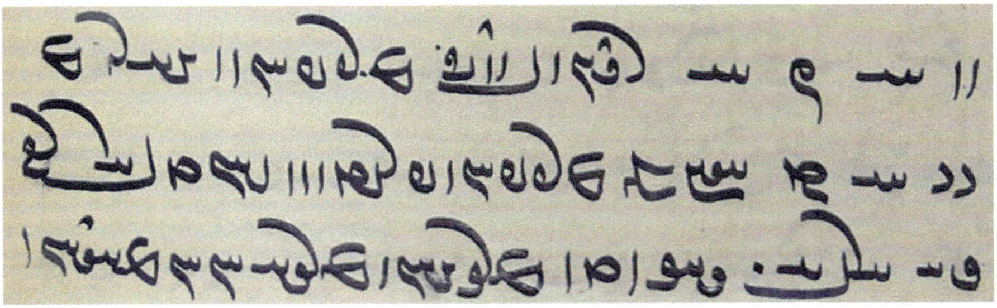

Fig. 3. 1st Pahlavi colophon (f. 32v, ll. 9–11)

L dyn' bnndk mlcp'n' w'hlwm mlcp'n' plytwn' ŠNT b'l 1000 60 ALBA . yẕdkrt'MLKA-'n' MLGA 'whrmẕdy'n'
man dēn bandag marzbān wahrom marzbān frēdōn sāl bār hazār šast cahār . yazdgird šāhān šāh ohrmazdyān
"I, the servant of the Religion, Marzbān Wahrom Marzbān Frēdōn, (have written it) in the year 1064 (= CE 1695) of the king of kings Yazdgird Ohrmazdyān."

- *Afsōn ī gubrāg cašm* "Incantation for the vigilant eye" ('pswn' *γubār cašm. īn.*; f. 32v, l. 12 – f. 33v, l. 7), in Pāzand and Pahlavi scripts.
- *Afsōn ī tab larz* "Incantation against shivering fever" ('pswn' tb llz; f. 33v, l. 8 – f. 35r, l. 14), in New Persian.
- *Paragṇā* in Pāzand:[3]

  1. *Nērang ī barsom cīdan* "Formula to cut the *barsom* (twigs)" (*auuistāi. barsəm. cīδən.* "Avestan text to cut the *barsom* (twigs)"; f. 35v, l. 1 – f. 37v, l. 14).
  2. *Nērang ī barsom bastan* "Formula to tie the *barsom* (twigs)" (*barsəm. bastin. durąn.* "Tying the *barsom* (twigs) around"; f. 38r, l. 1 – f. 40r, l. 5).
  3. *Nērang ī hōm cīdan* "Formula to cut the *hōm*" (*aβistāi. haōm. cīδən.* "Avestan text to cut the *hōm*"; f. 40r, l. 6 – f. 40v, l. 8).
  4. *Nērang ī urwarām cīdan* "Formula to cut the pomegranate (twigs)" (*uruuarąm. cīδən.* "(Formula) to cut the pomegranate (twigs)"; f. 40v, l. 8 – f. 41r, l. 6).
  5. *Nērang ī jīwan griftan* "Formula to collect the (goat's) milk" (*aβistāi. gąm. garəptin.* "Avestan text to collect the (goat's) milk"; f. 41r, l. 6 – f. 42v, l. 3).
  6. *Nērang ī zōhr griftan* "Formula to draw (water for) the libation" (*aβustāi. zaōr. girəptən.* "Avestan text to draw (water for) the libation"; f. 42v, l. 3 – f. 43v, l. 4).
  7. *Nērang ī hōm šustan* "Formula to wash the *hōm*" (*auustāi. hąm. šustin.* "Avestan text to wash the *hōm*"; f. 43v, l. 4 – f. 44r, l. 4).
  8. *Nērang ī barsom šustan* "Formula to wash the *barsom*" (*barsəm. šustin.* "(Avestan text) to wash the *barsom*"; f. 44r, l. 4 – f. 45r, l. 2).
  9. *Yašt sāxtan* "Preparing the Yasna" (*yašt sāx^{v}tin.*; f. 45r, l. 2 – f. 48v, l. 14).

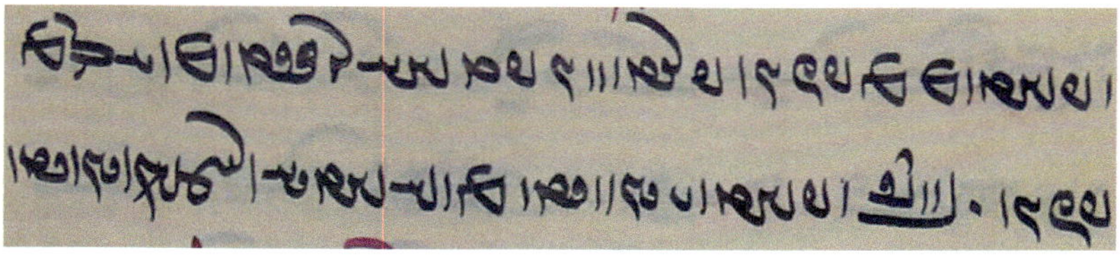

Fig. 4. 2nd Pahlavi colophon (f. 49r, ll. 1–2)

3 The *Paragṇā* is the prefatory ceremony required to prepare the *Yasna*, *Wīsperad* and *Wīdēwdād* ceremonies. See its description in ANKLESARIA 1888, DARMESTETER 1892, pp. LXX–LXXX, MODI 1922 [1937], pp. 266–329, KOTWAL/BOYD 1977; 1991, pp. 61–85, CANTERA 2020, REDARD/DARUWALLA 2021, and REDARD 2022.

npštwm MN pcyn' plytwn' gwptšh lwstwm *naō* MN pcyn' . bnndk npšt'y YY-WWN-yt' MNW-š štyh lymšn' YYWN-yt'
nibištom az paccēn frēdōn gōpatšah rōstom naō *az paccēn . bandag nibište bawēd kē-š šādīh rāmišn bawēd*
"I have written it from the manuscript of Frēdōn Gōpatšah Rōstom *naō*.[4] From the manuscript of X, he, who (may) have joy (and) pleasure, has written it."

10. *Nērang ī wars pōxtan* "Formula to wash (lit. 'cook') the bull's hair" (*naērəṇg. vars. puxtan.*; f. 49r, l. 3 – f. 50r, l. 10), in Pāzand script.
11. *Nērang ī parāhōm griftan* "Formula to take the *parāhōm*" (*ki. pirahaōm. gīrīṯ.* lit. "the one who takes the parāhōm"; f. 50r, l. 10 - 58v, l. 14), in Pāzand script.

- *Nērang ī āb ud pādyāb* "Formula for the water and ritual ablutions" (*naērəṇg. āβ. u. pāṯiiāβ. ẏaštin.*; f. 59r, l. 1 – f. 63v, l. 10), in Pāzand script.
- *Drōn ī frawardīn yašt* (f. 64r, l. 1 – f. 114v, l. 13), including Yt 13 in Avestan.

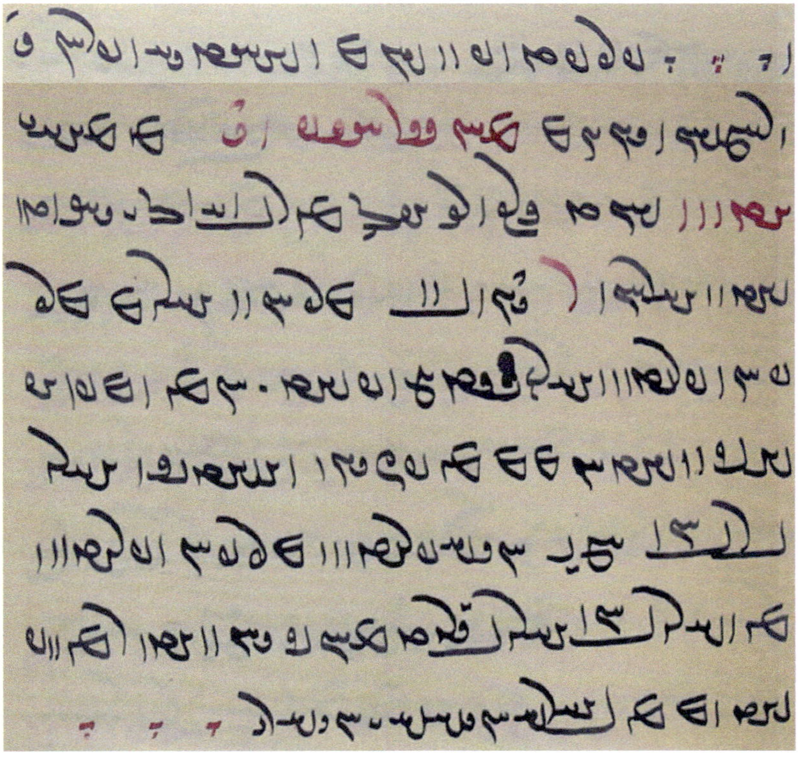

Fig. 5. 3rd Pahlavi colophon (f. 114v, l. 14 – f. 115r, l. 8)

4 In the sense of NP. نو "again", instead of repeating Frēdōn Gōpatšah Rōstom.

plcpt' PWN ŠRM W š'tyh W plhwy W l'mšn' ḆYN YWM m'nsr'spnd MN m'h y 'twr' ŠNT 1000 W LK *hō* MN 20 BRA OL y yz̲dkrt' štr'w'hl'n' L dyn' bnn<dk> mlc'wn w'hlwm mlcp'n' plytwn' w'hləst'm npšt . HWE'-m pr'c ŠḆKWN-št hwm m MN pcyyn' whštyk' 'hlwb-lb'n hmy hwyš plytwn' mlcp'n' plytwn' MNW-š lwb'n' 'hlwb glwtm'nyk YHWWN-'t' L MNW npštwm MN b'hlyh hwyšyh y hwyš L y

frazaft pad drōd ud šādīh ud farroxīh ud rāmišn andar rōz mānsraspand az māh ī ādur sāl hazār ud sīh hō[5] *az wīst bē ō ī*[6] *yazdgird šahwahrām man dēn bandag marzbān wahrom marzbān frēdōn rostām*[7] *nibišt hom frāz hišt hom az paccēn* <*ī*> *wahištīg ahlaw-ruwān hamē xwēš*[8] *frēdōn marzbān frēdōn*[9] *kē-š ruwān ahlaw garōdmānīg bawād man kē nibištom az bahrīh +ud xwēšīh ī xwēš man ī*

"Completed with peace, joy, happiness and pleasure. On the day Mānsraspand of the month Ādur, year 1033 after the (year) 20 of Yazdgird Šahwahrām, I, the servant of the Religion, Marzbān Wahrom Marzbān Frēdōn Rostām, have written (and) bequeathed it. From the manuscript of the glorious, righteous souled, always fortunate Frēdōn Marzbān Frēdōn, whose soul may be righteous in Paradise, I am the one who has written it from my own account and ownership."

- Beginning of the *Yasna* (f. 115v, l. 1 – f. 118v, l. 6), in Avestan with ritual instructions in Pahlavi and Pāzand.
- *Nērang ī pēšag sāmān* (f. 118v, l. 7 – f. 125r, l. 14), in Pāzand with ritual instructions in Pahlavi and New Persian, and with recitation of some Avestan texts. It includes a depiction of the *baršnūm-gāh* (f. 124r).
- Blank folios (ff. 125v – 127r).
- Fragment of the *Zand ī fragard ī Juddēwdād* (f. 127v, l. 4 – f. 137v, l. 6), corresponding to MOAZAMI's edition (2021, pp. 314–332) 36.19–37.15.
- *Yasna* 41.7–43.5 (f. 138r, l. 1 – f. 140v, l. 7), in Avestan.
- FrD 7 (f. 141r, ll. 1–14), in Avestan.
- *Nērang* dedicated to Srōš and Frēdōn (f. 141v, ll. 1–4), in Pāzand.
- *Sīh rōzag* 1 (f. 142r, l. 1 – f. 143r, l. 10), in Avestan.
- FrW 8.1–2 (f. 143v, ll. 1–14), in Avestan.
- *Afsōn ī zafar bastan* "Incantation to bind the mouth" (f. 144r, ll. 1–13) in Pahlavi, with some indications in New Persian at the end.
- *Yasna* 32.9 (f. 145v, ll. 14–15), in Avestan.
- *Yašt* 2.11–12 (f. 144v, l. 1 – f. 145r, l. 7), in Avestan.
- *Yasna* 32.1 (f. 145v, ll. 3–9), in Avestan.
- *Yasna* 32.15 (f. 145v, ll. 10–14), in Avestan.

5 Perhaps a Pāzand reinterpretation of Phl. hw, which might represent a wrongly written number 3.
6 Perhaps to be corrected as Phl. *bay ōy* "His Majesty" (?).
7 His father is mentioned in the colophon of the manuscript K4.
8 In the sense of NP. خوش "good, happy, fortunate".
9 The scribe of the manuscripts ML4050 and TU11263.

This manuscript contains some valuable information. It seems to have been copied from different sets of texts in different manuscripts, but it is unclear whether these sets can be divided according to the position of the colophons.

The first part until the first colophon, which strangely enough bears the latest date (AY 1064 = CE 1695), only contains the *Frahang ī pahlawīg*. Although the scribe Marzbān Wahrom Marzbān Frēdōn did not mention from which manuscript he copied it, the text very much resembles the one transmitted in the Pahlavi composite manuscript TD2, written by his uncle Frēdōn Marzbān Frēdōn in AY 978 + 20 (= CE 1629).[10] Like the latter, his nephew added in MMI 125 the Pāzand equivalent of each Pahlavi word below its corresponding line. However, unlike TD2, in which all the words after Phl. ⟨nym⟩ *nēm* and its equivalent Pāz. *nīm* are lost, MMI 125 preserves the full text, which continues up to ten more pages, and is therefore extremely important to reconstruct that lost part in TD2.

The second part, between the first and second colophon, includes two incantations (*Afsōn ī gubrāg cašm* and *Afsōn ī tab larz*) and the prefatory ritual of the *Paragṇā*. According to the scribe, who presumably is the very Marzbān Wahrom Marzbān Frēdōn, they were copied from a manuscript written by Frēdōn Gōpatšah Rōstom Frēdōn Gōpatšah Rōstom, copyist of the Iranian *Wīdēwdād Sāde* manuscript 4040 (CE 1632/1633).[11] From which manuscript the latter copied those texts is omitted in MMI 125. In any case, taking into account that, as underlined by CANTERA (2020, pp. 74–78, 101), descriptions of the Iranian performance of the *Paragṇā* before the 19th century CE are rarely preserved, this manuscript MMI 125 is very important for studying and editing this prefatory ceremony.

The third part, between the second and third colophon, transmits three *nērang* (*Nērang ī wars pōxtan*, *Nērang ī parāhōm griftan*, and *Nērang ī āb ud pādyāb*), and is followed by the *Drōn ī frawardīn yašt*, a ceremony that includes the complete Avestan text of the *Frawardīn Yašt* or Yt 13. The same scribe Marzbān Wahrom Marzbān Frēdōn copied it in AY 1033 + 20 (= CE 1684) from a manuscript written by his uncle Frēdōn Marzbān Frēdōn, copyist of the manuscript TD2 mentioned before. To my knowledge, no manuscript containing the *Drōn ī frawardīn yašt* that was written by the latter is preserved. Furthermore, it is curious that the scribe copied that text from his uncle's manuscript, but not from the manuscript of the *Drōn ī frawardīn yašt* known as VL1, copied by his own father Wahrom Marzbān Frēdōn in AY 976 + 20 (= CE 1627).

The fourth part, corresponding to all the texts after the third colophon, includes the beginning of the *Yasna*, and also several texts related to purifications

10 For the facsimile edition of TD2, see JAMASP ASA/MAHYAR NAWABI/TAVOUSI 1978 and 1979. Frēdōn Marzbān Frēdōn also copied the manuscripts of the *Wīsperad* 2010 (CE 1627, or + 20 = CE 1647), the two *Wīdēwdād Sāde* 4000 (CE 1607, or + 20 = CE 1627) and Jp1 (CE 1618, or + 20 = CE 1638), and the *Wištāsp Yašt* 5010 (CE 1627, or + 20 = CE 1647). For more information on these manuscripts, see CANTERA 2014, p. 94.

11 For the description of 4040, see ANDRÉS-TOLEDO/CANTERA 2012, p. 210.

and apotropaic rituals. The *Nērang ī pēšag sāmān*, recited in the purification ceremony of the *baršnūm*, is attested in its Pahlavi version in the manuscript TD2.[12] Its Pāzand text in MMI 125 may have been adapted therefrom. The next text is a fragment of the *Zand ī fragard ī Juddēwdād* referring to the *baršnūm* as described in PV 9, and this fragment clearly derives from TD2 (f. 621, l. 11 – f. 636, l. 5). Although MMI 125 is not necessary to supply TD2 in this regard, it is the oldest apograph known so far of this Pahlavi text.[13] The first folio of the fragment is numbered as 1 in New Persian numerals, which contributes to support the hypothesis that it might have been extracted from a different manuscript and bound together in the extant MMI 125. Its scribe must have made a conscious decision to interrupt the text, because there are several lines left blank on the last page of the fragment, in which more text could have been added.

The following text of this fourth part is *Yasna* 41.7 (from *ahū. vairiiō.* 4 gwptn') – 43.5 (until its first word *spəṇtəm*) in Avestan. Since the text of *Yasna* 41.7 is incomplete at the beginning of the page, it has most probably been detached from another manuscript and bound together with the rest of the pages of MMI 125 as well. The Persian numbering of each page was probably added after it was bound. Again, as there are some lines left blank in the page after the last word *spəṇtəm*, the scribe must have consciously interrupted the text.

The Avestan text of FrD 7, following *Yasna* 41.7–43.5 in this manuscript, is recited as an incantation to kill snakes, according to the New Persian *Revāyat* of Dārāb Hormazyār.[14] Because it is not frequently attested in our extant manuscripts, I reproduce here the transcription of its Avestan text as transmitted in MMI 125:

> *vərənahe. ϑβąm. aŋhō. uruš. jmā. duąma. ahē. puϑrahe. žuϑrəmca. apaitē.ynae. aŋhāi. ẏəm. dauuataṣ̌əš. apaiϑa. imō. pitī. āhəm. dąm. sāuuanəm. naōdat̰. aŋ̇āi. huuaztō. nōit̰. zānaiti. nōit̰. imāi. iranāi.* x^{v}*āiš. āitīe. ẏazana. caϑō. ānəm. sāiiete. ẏauuaēca. ẏauuaētā.taēšca. aṣ̌əm. vōhī.*

The following text is a *nērang* dedicated to Srōš and Frēdōn, which only contains the Pāzand text *pā. məm. dərəm. bušzāδə.*, and is followed by the Avestan text of *Sīh rōzag* 1.

The next one is the Avestan text of FrW 8.1–2 (from *sarəδahe. måŋhō.* to *auua. drūjō. auuō. ba.*),[15] which according to Antiā (1909, pp. 194–195), is recited as a *nērang* against witchcraft. Again, the scribe must have consciously interrupted the text, as there is space left in the last line of the page. Also because this text is not frequently attested in our extant manuscripts, I include the transcription of its Avestan text as found in MMI 125:

12 See its edition, translation and commentary in Filippone 2022.

13 For the list of other manuscripts of the *Zand ī fragard ī Juddēwdād*, all of them being apographs of TD2 written in the 19th century, see König 2010, pp. 119–120.

14 See Darmesteter 1893, pp. 152–153 and the manuscript Suppl. Pers. 46, f. 192r, ll. 1–7.

15 See Westergaard 1852–1854, I, p. 334.

FrW 8.1.

sarəδahe. måŋhō. auua.mīriiåite. mazdaiiasna. dəm. āfri.vanaēibiš. auua.janən. ẏō. hē. aošiṇtē. mōšucā. tī. duždå. āsuiiācā. auua.mīriiaēša.aēiti. drājąn. āhuuō. nōiṯ. zī. cīš. aŋ́hå. drujō. niiāsāitē.

FrW 8.2.

drī. snaϑəṇtē. snaϑahe. aēiti. hā. druxš. aṣ̌aōjasta. aŋhaṯ. hə̄cā. āϑaiti. zaraϑuštra. staxrahe. mərətō. ziia. auuaϑa. staxrō. ẏaṯ. hā. druxš. aēite. mərəzuuī. xšaϑrata. aŋhaṯ. mōi. rus. ẏaṯ. mahrkusō. auua. auua.mīriiāite. adāzī. auuadrījō. auuō. ba.

After the latter, a Pahlavi text not found elsewhere, but similar to the *Nērang ī zahr bastan*, is recorded. Its title does not appear in the text, but it is an incantation (Phl. *afsōn*) to bind the mouth of evil creatures with the help of heavenly beings. According to its contents and the use of the Pahlavi word *afsōn*, I call it *Afsōn ī zafar bastan* "Incantation to bind the mouth", and I provide the reader with its full text and the parallel texts of the *Nērang ī zahr bastan* in the manuscripts MK and K27 for comparison in the appendix to this article.

Finally, four fragments of the following Avestan texts are included, which probably were a sort of *nērang* with apotropaic function: *Yasna* 32.9, *Yašt* 2.11–12, *Yasna* 32.1, and *Yasna* 32.15. The latter is interrupted in *taō* (= OAv. *tōi.*) at the end of the page, but probably there were more pages in the manuscript that are lost. On the one hand, *Yašt* 2.11–14 is used as an apotropaic *nērang* in the *Tamām Xorde Avesta* manuscript E1 (= F4 at the Meherjirana Library).[16] On the other hand, the selected passages of *Yasna* 32 refer to enemies to be overcome, and, according to the Pahlavi text *Cim ī gāhān* 7 (= *Šāyist nē šāyist* 13.7),[17] *Yasna* 32 is associated with warriors and also protects from the 16 calamities mentioned in *Wīdēwdād* 1. Therefore, its apotropaic recitation after the *Afsōn ī zafar bastan* makes perfect sense.

MMI 129

(Mesrop Mashtots Institute of Ancient Manuscripts, Non-Armenian Manuscript Collection, ms. 129): *Frahang ī pahlawīg*

Ms. 129 is a Pahlavi manuscript of the *Frahang ī pahlawīg*, with interlinear New Persian translation. It contains 29ff., of which f. 1r, 29r–v are blank. 16,5 x 21 cm; 14 lines to the page. Black ink for the Pahlavi text, and red ink for the heading and the interlinear New Persian translation. No colophon. Unlike Kostikyan/Mehdi Baghi's (2017) description, the manuscript does not include the text of the *Frahang ī ōīm ēk*. Again, the paper, the palaeography and the ink indicate that it is a late copy to be dated in the 19th-century CE.

16 See its facsimile and analysis in Kotwal/Hintze 2008, p. 20.
17 See Kotwal 1969, pp. 42–43.

Contents:

- *Frahang ī pahlawīg* (f. 1v, l. 1 – f. 28v, l. 10), with New Persian equivalent under each Pahlavi word, and including a Pahlavi–Avestan alphabet (f. 28r, ll. 7–12).

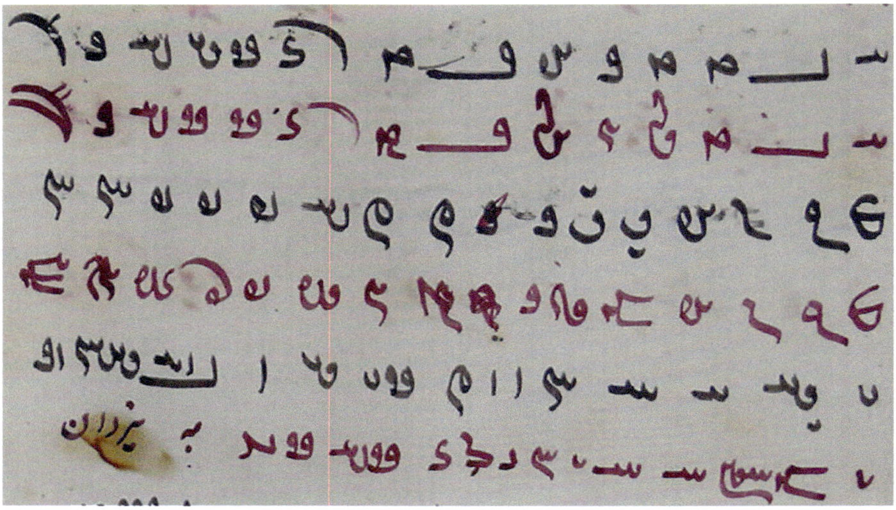

Fig. 6.

The Pahlavi–Avestan alphabet of MMI 129 reproduced here contains the same sequence as the one found in the *Frahang ī pahlawīg* manuscript K25 (f. 74r, ll. 1–6), preserved at the Royal Library of Copenhagen.[18]

MMI 130

(Mesrop Mashtots Institute of Ancient Manuscripts, Non-Armenian Manuscript Collection, ms. 130): *Paragṇā*

Ms. 130 is a Pāzand manuscript with the *Paragṇā*. It contains 9ff., of which f. 1 is missing. The manuscript, which is incomplete, finishes in *xšnaōϑrā. ahurahe. mazdå. aṣ̌əm. vohī. ẏak.* 17,5 x 22 cm; 14 lines to the page. Black ink, with titles and some ritual instructions in red ink. No colophon. Kostikyan/Mehdi Baghi (2017) wrongly described this manuscript as the *Frahang ī ōīm ēk*. The paper, the palaeography and the ink indicate that it is a late copy made in the 19th-century CE.

18 See the facsimile edition published by Barr 1944.

Contents:

1. *Nērang ī barsom čīdan* "Formula to cut the *barsom* (twigs)" (f. 2r, l. 1 – f. 3r, l. 12). The first folio is lost and second starts at *(barsə)m. rā. si. bār. nəmāj. burδən. u. bi. aṣ̌əm.*
2. *Nērang ī barsom bastan* "Formula to tie the *barsom* (twigs)" (*barsəm. bastin. durąn.* "Tying the *barsom* (twigs) around"; f. 3r, l. 13 – f. 5r, l. 4).
3. *Nērang ī hōm čīdan* "Formula to cut the *hōm*" (*aβistāi. haōm. čīδən.* "Avestan text to cut the *hōm*"; f. 5r, l. 4 – f. 5v, l. 1).
4. *Nērang ī urwarām čīdan* "Formula to cut the pomegranate (twigs)" (*uruuarąm. čīdən.* "(Formula) to cut the pomegranate (twigs)"; f. 5v, l. 1 – f. 6r, l. 1).
5. *Nērang ī jīwan griftan* "Formula to collect the (goat's) milk" (*aβustāi. jąm. garəftən.* "Avestan text to collect the (goat's) milk"; f. 6r, l. 1 – f. 7r, l. 1).
6. *Nērang ī zōhr griftan* "Formula to draw (water for) the libation" (*avustāi. zaōr. garəptən.* "Avestan text to draw (water for) the libation"; f. 7r, l. 1 – f. 7v, l. 8).
7. *Nērang ī hōm šustan* "Formula to wash the *hōm*" (*auustāi. hąm. šustin.* "Avestan text to wash the *hōm*"; f. 7v, l. 8 – f. 8r, l. 3).
8. *Nērang ī barsom šustan* "Formula to wash the *barsom*" (*barsəm. šusin.* "(Avestan text) to wash the *barsom*"; f. 8r, l. 3 – f. 8v, l. 9).
9. *Yašt sāxtan* "Preparing the Yasna" (*yašt. sāx̌tin.*; f. 8v, l. 9–14).

As we have observed, these three Zoroastrian manuscripts in Armenia are not only relevant to a better understanding of the written transmission, orthography, paleography, etc. of the specific Zoroastrian texts they contain and for reconstructing their *stemma codicum*. They are also important witnesses for retracing the circulation of Zoroastrian texts outside the sphere of the Zoroastrian communities that preserved and transmitted them, and have further implications beyond philology. Finally, they inevitably pose the question of how many of these manuscripts may still be hidden in libraries and private collections, and how we can contribute to making them known and available to scholars and the general public interested in Zoroastrianism.

Appendix

Nērang ī zahr bastan (MK, T) in comparison with *Afsōn ī zafar bastan* (MMI 125)

MK (f. 74v, l. 4–13)

PWN ŠM y yẕd’n
BYRH spndrmt W YWM spndrmt W YWM spndrmt W BYRH spndrmt W *spndrmt BYRH spndrmt YWM bst hm z’hl wšl W zpl y hm’k hlpstl’n PWN ŠM W nylwg y TḆ plytwn hdyb’lyh y wnnd <y> stl y ’whrmẕd w’plyk’n lwb’k b’t ’ywtwn YHWWN-’t . aṣ̌əm. byšz b’t*
pad nām ī yazdān
māh spandarmad ud rōz spandarmad ud rōz spandarmad ud māh spandarmad ud spandarmad māh spandarmad rōz bast ham zahr $^{+}$wiš ud zafar ī hamāg xrafstarān pad nām ud nērōg ī nēw frēdōn ayārīh ī wanand <ī> star ī ohrmazd wābarīgān rawāg bād ēdōn bawād . aṣ̌əm.bēšaz bād
“In the name of the deities.
(On) month Spandarmad and day Spandarmad, and day Spandarmad, and month Spandarmad, month of Spandarmad, day of Spandarmad, I have bound the poison, venom and mouth of all evil creatures. In the name and power of the brave Frēdōn, (with the) help of the star Wanand, star of Ohrmazd, may it be spread to the truthful ones. So may it be. May it be healing by Righteousness.”

K27 (f. 3r, ll. 5–13)[19]

BYRH spndrmt YWM spndrmt W YWM spndrmt BYRH spndrmt spndrmt BYRH spndrmt YWM bst HWE-m z’hl y wš W zw^{v}l[20] <y> hm’k hlpstl’n'PWN ŠM <W> nylwk y W TḆ plytwn' hdyb’lyh wnnd <y> stl <y> ’whrmẕd-d’t w’ply'g’n lwb’k YHWWN-’t ’ywtwn' YHWWN-’t *aṣ̌əm.baešaz.* YHWWN-’t . hlpstl ztn' KLYTWN-tn'
māh spandarmad rōz spandarmad ud rōz spandarmad māh spandarmad spandarmad māh spandarmad rōz bast ham zahr $^{+}$ud wiš ud zafar <ī> hamāg xrafstarān pad nām <ud> nērōg ī nēw frēdōn ayārīh <ī> wanand <ī> star <ī> ohrmazd-dād wābarīgān rawāg bawād ēdōn bawād aṣ̌əm.baešaz. bawād . xrafstar zadan xwāndan
“(On) month Spandarmad, day Spandarmad, and day Spandarmad, month Spandarmad, month of Spandarmad, day of Spandarmad, I have bound the poison, venom and mouth of all evil creatures. In the name (and) power of the brave Frēdōn, (with the) help of the star Wanand, created by Ohrmazd, may it be spread to the truthful ones. So may it be. May it be healing by Righteousness. Recite it to kill the evil creatures.”

19 See HAMPEL 1974, pp. 20–21.
20 Written ⟨zw^{v}l⟩ (with the Avestan grapheme *v* above the line), but corrected as ⟨zpl⟩ *zafar* on the right margin.

MMI 125 (f. 144r, ll. 1–10)

PWN ŠM y dʾtʾl ʾwhrmẕd
B̠YN YWM spndrmt' MN mʾh spndrmt' bstwm zpl y hmʾk' hlpstlʾn W dwcʾn W gwlgʾn W sthmkʾn ŠDYA-ʾn W dlwcʾn W yʾtykʾn W plykʾn W sʾstʾlʾn W wnʾskʾlʾn' PWN ŠM y yẕdt' W PWN ŠM y T'B̠ plytwn W PWN ŠM y yẕdt' W PWN ŠM y tyštl <y> stʾlk' W PWN ŠM y stkwys y stʾlk' W PWN ŠM y OLE-šʾn' stʾlk' hptwlng PWN ŠM y yẕdt' W PWN ŠM y T'B̠ plytwn' PWN ŠM y yẕdt' hpt bʾl gwptn' ʾšmhwk' ʾpsn

pad nām ī dādār ohrmazd
andar rōz spandarmad az māh spandarmad bastom zafar ī hamāg xrafstarān ud duzān ud gurgān ud stahmagān dēwān ud druzān ud +jādūgān ud parīgān ud sāstārān ud wināhgārān pad nām ī yazd ud pad nām ī nēw frēdōn ud pad nām ī yazd ud pad nām ī tištar <ī> stārag ud pad nām ī +sadwēs ī stārag ud pad nām ī awēšān stārag haftōring pad nām ī yazd ud pad nām ī nēw frēdōn pad nām ī yazd haft bār guftan +ašemwohū +afsōn

"In the name of the Maker Ohrmazd.
On day Spandarmad of the month Spandarmad, I have bound the mouth of all evil creatures, thieves, wolves, violent demons, lies, sorcerers, witches, tyrants, and sinners. In the name of the deity and in the name of the brave Frēdōn. In the name of the deity and in the name of the star Tištar, and in the name of the star Sadwēs, and in the name of those stars Haftōring. In the name of the deity and in the name of the brave Frēdōn. In the name of the deity. Say it seven times. *ašəmwohū.* Incantation."

Bibliography

ANDRÉS-TOLEDO, M. Á./A. CANTERA 2012: "Manuscripts of the Wīdēwdād". In: A. CANTERA (ed.): *The Transmission of the Avesta*. Wiesbaden, pp. 207–243.

ANKLESARIA, T.D. 1888: *Avesta. The sacred books of the Parsis.* Part I. *Yasna ba nirang*. Bombay.

ANTIĀ, E.K. 1909: *Pâzend Texts*. Bombay.

BARR, K. 1944: *Selections from Codices K7 and K25 (Vīspered and Frahang ī Pahlavīk) and Tracings of the Avesta Codex K1*. Copenhagen.

CANTERA, A. 2014: *Vers une édition de la liturgie longue zoroastrienne: pensées et travaux préliminaires*. Paris.

— 2020: "Avestan Texts in Context: Fragments Westergaard 6 and 7 and the Paragṇā". In: SH. FARRIDNEJAD (ed.): *zaraϑuštrōtəma. Zoroastrian and Iranian Studies in Honour of Philip G. Kreyenbroek*. Irvine, pp. 69–105.

DARMESTETER, J. 1892: *Le Zend-Avesta. Premier volume.* Paris.

— 1893: *Le Zend-Avesta. Troisième volume*. Paris.

FILIPPONE, E. 2022: "The Ablution of the Limbs in the *Baršnūm* Context: the *Nērang ī pēšag ud sāmān*." In: A. CANTERA/M. MACUCH/N. SIMS-WILLIAMS (eds.): *The Reward of the Righteous. Festschrift in Honour of Almut Hintze*. Wiesbaden, pp. 177–194.

HAMPEL, J. 1974: *Die Kopenhagener Handschrift Cod. 27.* Wiesbaden.

Jamasp Asa, K.M/Y. Mahyar Nawabi/M. Tavousi 1978: *Ms. TD2. Iranian Bundahišn & Rivāyat-i Ēmēt-i Ašawahištān, etc.* Part 1. Shiraz.

— 1979: *Ms. TD2. Iranian Bundahišn & Rivāyat-i Ēmēt-i Ašawahištān, etc.* Part 2. Shiraz.

König, G. 2010: "Der Pahlavi-Text *Zand ī Fragard ī Juddēvdād.*" In: M. Macuch/D. Weber/D. Durkin-Meisterernst (eds.): *Ancient and Middle Iranian Studies.* Wiesbaden, pp. 115–132.

Kostikyan, K./M. Mehdi Baghi 2017: "Three Pahlavi manuscripts in the Matenadaran." In: *ARAMAZD: Armenian Journal of Near Eastern Studies* 11 (1–2), pp. 293–305.

Kotwal, F.M. 1969: *The Supplementary Texts to the Šāyest nē-šāyest.* Copenhagen.

Kotwal, F.M./J.W. Boyd 1977: "The Zoroastrian *paragṇā* ritual." In: *The Journal of Mithraic Studies* 2, pp. 18–52.

Kotwal, F.M./A. Hintze 2008: *The Khorda Avesta and Yašt Codex E1. Facsimile Edition.* Wiesbaden.

Modi, J.J. 1922 [1937]: *The Religious Ceremonies and Customs of the Parsees.* Bombay.

Redard, C. 2022: *The Paragnā. Substitles of the Interactive Film.* Available online: https://muya.soas.ac.uk/tool/film-multimedia/Interactive film — MUYA (soas.ac.uk)

Redard, C./K. Daruwalla 2021: *The Gujarati Ritual Instructions of the Paragnā, Yasna and Visperad Ceremonies.* Leiden/Boston.

Russell, J.R. 1987: *Zoroastrianism in Armenia.* Cambridge, MA.

— 2011: "An Armenian magico-medical manuscript (bzhshkaran) in the NAASR Collection." In: *Journal of the Society for Armenian Studies* 20, pp. 1–20.

Westergaard, N.L. 1852–1854: *Zendavesta or the Religious Books of the Zoroastrians.* Copenhagen.

Windādag's Orders: Ten Unpublished Middle Persian Ostraca from Chāl Ṭarkhān-ʿEshqābād*

Thomas Benfey, Tübingen

I. Introduction

In this article, I offer *editiones principes* of ten Middle Persian ostraca from the site Chāl Ṭarkhān-ʿEshqābād, just south of Rayy and modern Tehran, which were excavated in 1936 by Erich Schmidt's Rayy Expedition.[1] Some thirty-six ostraca were found at Chāl Ṭarkhān-ʿEshqābād, which, along with the other materials found there (most notably, many carved stuccoes), are now dispersed across several museum collections, including the University of Pennsylvania's Penn Museum, the University of Chicago's ISAC Museum, the Boston Museum of Fine Arts, Harvard's Fogg Museum, and Tehran's National Museum

* I would like to thank the editors, Maria Macuch and Arash Zeini, for the opportunity to contribute to this Festschrift. I would also like to thank Eugenio Garosi for bringing these important materials to my attention, and for all his assistance and insights as we have tried to locate them, and discussed these materials' contents and importance. Many people have gone out of their way to help Eugenio and me to locate these ostraca, and secure high-quality images of them. Among these people I would like to single out Katherine Blanchard (Penn Museum, University of Pennsylvania) and Helen McDonald (ISAC Museum, University of Chicago) for special thanks, for working assiduously to locate these ostraca, and to provide us with the clear photographs without which this article would not have been possible. I would also like to thank Richard Payne, Theo van den Hout, and Jean Evans for helping to connect us to the right people at the University of Chicago; and Susan Allison, Servane Wetzel, and Lena Bull for their help with administrative matters. Eugenio Garosi and Adam Benkato read complete drafts and offered valuable suggestions. And I am grateful to Arezou Azad for her willingness to incorporate these "miserable scraps of pottery" into her Invisible East research program, which has supported my work here. This article is part of a project that has received funding from the European Research Council (ERC) under the European Union's Horizon 2020 research and innovation programme (Grant agreement No. 851607).

1 The site was referred to as Chāl Ṭarkhān in Schmidt and his team's initial publications (e.g., Miles 1938, p. ix), and continues to be referred to as such (in, e.g., Holod 2019). Thompson (1976, p. 1) in my view sensibly, refers to the site as Chāl Ṭarkhān-ʿEshqābād due to the site's proximity to the modern village of ʿEshqābād; the village of Chāl Ṭarkhān, though also close to the site, lies substantially further away than ʿEshqābād.

of Iran.[2] In an intriguing development, ostraca in both Arabic and Middle Persian are among the finds, although without more precise information about their findspots and the site's overall stratigraphy, it is difficult to say whether this constitutes rare material evidence for the co-occurrence, or at least close chronological proximity, of documentary production in Middle Persian and in Arabic.[3] RENATA HOLOD informs me that she and others at the Penn Museum are currently working on a publication based on SCHMIDT's unpublished excavation notes, which promises to be highly revealing on this score and otherwise; they could also inform us about where the ostraca were found with respect to Chāl Ṭarkhān-ʿEshqābād's three major components: a "citadel mound," and two buildings, both with a considerable amount of stucco decorations, which SCHMIDT and, following him, THOMPSON refer to as the "main palace" and the "subsidiary palace."[4] THOMPSON has posited that these buildings' origins by and large lie in the very late Sasanian era, with important elaborations in the first century or so of Muslim rule; a late Sasanian or early Islamic date can accordingly be posited for the Middle Persian ostraca presented here as well, although one hopes for more clarity and specificity as work on their contents and context proceeds.[5]

I learned about the Chāl Ṭarkhān-Eshqābād ostraca and their significance from EUGENIO GAROSI in May 2021, and since then the two of us have been working to establish their whereabouts. Although the plates in THOMPSON 1976 include images of twenty-nine distinct ostracon-surfaces, comprising some twenty-five items (several of which have writing on both sides), the locations of some of these ostraca continue to prove elusive, while our efforts have turned up several ostraca found at Chāl Ṭarkhān-Eshqābād that do not appear in THOMPSON's book. GAROSI has put together a concordance which details the current state of knowledge about these ostraca and their current locations, which is included as an appendix to this article. The ostraca published here include five now housed at the Penn Museum, images of three of which appear in THOMPSON

2 The stuccoes are comprehensively covered in THOMPSON 1976. The current locations of the finds are briefly and broadly discussed in THOMPSON 1965, p. 1.

3 As discussed in GAROSI 2022, pp. 98–99. GAROSI (2022, p. 99, n. 388) notes that one of these ostraca, CT-162/2 (THOMPSON 1976, pl. xxxvi, fig. 3), may be bilingual, containing Arabic text in addition to what is clearly Middle Persian. We have been unable to determine this ostracon's present whereabouts, and a better image may well clarify matters. Thanks to the clear images supplied by KATHERINE BLANCHARD at the Penn Museum, THOMPSON's (1976, pl. xxvi, fig. 1; pl. xxxvi, fig. 1) initial identification of CT-40's (PM 37-33-32) text as Arabic can be confirmed. As EUGENIO GAROSI has suggested, this is almost certainly a writing exercise, focused on the numerals 11–19 which present special difficulties in Arabic; the subsequent reidentifications of the text as Sogdian (RECK/SUNDERMANN *apud* WEBER 2003, p. 176) and a New Persian poem (HOLOD 2019, pp. 136–137), can accordingly be abandoned.

4 THOMPSON 1976, p. 1; see also KRÖGER 1990 The precise function of each structure continues to be debated; HARPER (1977) suggests the two buildings "perhaps had different functions," while HOLOD (2019, p. 335) calls SCHMIDT/THOMPSON's "main palace" and "subsidiary palace" a "vaulted reception hall" and "square fortified domestic building," respectively.

5 THOMPSON 1976.

1976 (CT-135/2 [PM 37-33-52], CT-135/4 [PM 37-33-50], and CT-135/5 [PM-37-33-21]) and two of which do not (CT-135/1 [PM 37-33-54] and CT-135/6 [PM 37-33-42]); four from the University of Chicago's ISAC Museum, which do not appear in THOMPSON's book (CT-205/1 [ISACM A154067], CT 205/3a [ISACM A154069], CT 205/3b [ISACM A154070)], and CT-205/4 [ISACM A154068]); and one more which does appear in THOMPSON, but whose whereabouts we have been unable to ascertain (CT-133/4). The proximity of most of the field numbers here (CT-135/1–6, CT-205/1–4) suggest that these ostraca were found very close to one another, which is consistent with the idea that they each involved the same person; and it is also conceivable that the remaining CT-133 ostraca (listed in the appendix; some have been published) likewise dealt with this same Windādag, a possibility that merits further investigation. I have listed and ordered the ten ostraca published here under their field numbers.

As DIETER WEBER's work has clarified for us, Middle Persian ostraca typically have to do with rather humble transactions: often, as is apparently the case with the ten ostraca presented here, dealing with the distribution of bread rations.[6] Despite the small scale of the business they attest to, they provide a vantage point on life on the western Iranian plateau, either shortly before or (more likely) just after the transition to Islamic rule, which is rare and precious. In this case, we have ten ostraca dealing with the distribution of bread that apparently involve the same man: a certain Windādag, who is being ordered to allocate certain amounts of bread to various parties.[7] Further advances in reading through the Chāl Ṭarkhān-ʿEshqābād ostraca, and integrating them with the other relevant material, archaeological, and literary evidence, promise to yield major contributions to the linguistic, social, economic, and administrative history of Sasanian and early Islamic Iran. It will be particularly important to undertake further comparisons between the Chāl Ṭarkhān-ʿEshqābād set and the much larger group of Middle Persian ostraca (190 items) discovered in 1925 and subsequently donated to the British Library by ERNST HERZFELD, which stem from a similar context — the Warāmīn Plain, south of Rayy and modern Tehran, and probably found in a late Sasanian structure — although their precise findspot remains unknown.[8]

6 WEBER 2009 is an exhaustive discussion of bread rations in ostraca; and see also the updated readings in WEBER 2022.

7 The correct reading for the final verb in each of these ostraca, "give" as opposed to "was given" or "[he] gave," is established in WEBER 2022. These six ostraca seem to follow the typical structure of a Middle Persian "check," according to which the person who is meant to distribute the given amount of bread (or another good) is named first, which has likewise been outlined in WEBER 2022, p. 515. Although I have been unable to find any other attestations of the name Windādag, Windād is relatively common, both as a freestanding name and as an element in compound names (GIGNOUX 1986, p. 184; JUSTI 1895, pp. 369–370; and, e.g., WEBER 2019); and *-ag* is a familiar hypocoristic suffix, frequently encountered in personal names (on this see, e.g., GIGNOUX 2011, p. 353).

8 For HERZFELD's description of the ostraca and the circumstances of their discovery, see HERZFELD 1926, p. 283, which is reproduced with helpful elaborations in DE MENASCE 1957 and WEBER 1974. WEBER (1992) discusses each of these ostraca individually, along

DIETER WEBER was the first to publish a reading of any Middle Persian ostracon, and what FRANÇOIS DE BLOIS noted in 1993 remains so today: "it is perfectly clear that any scholar who might in future venture to struggle with these miserable scraps of pottery... will take WEBER's meticulous work as his point of departure."[9] WEBER's work on Middle Persian ostraca spans nearly five decades, from his pioneering 1974 contribution to JEAN DE MENASCE's Festschrift, through his pathbreaking 1992 volume, to the important article "On the Formal Structure of Checks in Pahlavi Documents," published in summer 2022; and although the six ostraca presented here have hitherto remained unpublished, whatever progress on them I have made would not have been possible without frequent recourse to WEBER's work — on the Chāl Ṭarkhān-ʿEshqābād material and other ostraca, as well as on other kinds of Middle Persian documents.[10] I am accordingly honored to contribute to this volume, and I very much look forward to hearing DR. WEBER's thoughts (and, I would imagine, corrections) on the readings I have offered here.

II. Editions and Translations

CT-133/4

Transliteration

1. wn[d]ʾṭkʾ YWM
2. ... LHMA [?]
3. ...
4. ...***K*** #-I
5. lwn [?] ... YHBWN

Transcription

1. *Win[d]ādag rōz* [?]
2. ... *nān*
3. ...
4. ... *k[abīz]-1*
5. *rōn* [?] ... *dah*

Fig. 1. Field no. CT-133/4. Location unknown. THOMPSON 1974, pl. xxvi, fig. 2 [upside down].

with several others, and offers editions and translations of the vast majority of them, many of which have been updated in subsequent publications (e.g., WEBER 2005; 2022). Another group of ostraca from the Warāmīn Plain, found at Qalʿeh Īraj, have recently been published; these appeared too late to be substantially considered here, but should also certainly be brought into this comparison (CERETI/NEMATI/MOUSAVINIA 2022).

9 DE BLOIS 1993, p. 377.

10 WEBER 1974, WEBER 1992, AND WEBER 2022 are the works I have directly cited here. WEBER's other important publications on ostraca include WEBER 2003, the first publication to offer readings of any Chāl Ṭarkhān-ʿEshqābād ostracon, as well as WEBER 2005 and WEBER 2009.

Translation

Windādag, on the day...
give 1 *kabīz* of bread...

Commentary

As our only access to this object is a single black-and-white photograph in Thompson 1976, the reading is exceptionally uncertain; the text has largely been pieced together on the basis of its structural resemblance to the other ostraca in the Chāl Ṭarkhān-ʿEshqābād set published here.

Line 5: It is fairly clear that the first word here begins with ⟨l⟩, and then we have at least three of the characters that resemble a vertical line: most probably some combination of ⟨w⟩ and ⟨n⟩ although ⟨k⟩ or ⟨t⟩ are also possibilities, as is the word-final stroke ⟨'⟩. It is likely that the word extends beyond the four or so characters visible in the photograph, as there is a substantial amount of space between the last visible character and the closing ⟨YHBWN⟩, *dah*, "give."

CT-135/1 (PM 37-33-54)

Fig. 2. Field no. CT-135/1. Housed at the Penn Museum, Philadelphia. PM 37-33-54. Does not appear in Thompson 1974. Courtesy of the Near East Section, Penn Museum.

Transliteration

1. wnd'ṭk['] ...
2. LHMA ... OL l[syk'] [?]
3. ... l...'n
4. YHBWN

Transcription

1. *Windādag* ...
2. *nān ō ra[hīg]* [?]
3. ... ...*ān*
4. *dah*

Translation

Windādag ... give ... of bread to the servant ...

Commentary

The text here seems rather similar to what we have on CT-205/1 (ISACM A154067) and CT-205/3b (ISACM A154070), which are both somewhat better-preserved.

CT-135/2 (PM 37-33-52)

Fig. 3. Field no. CT-135/2. Housed at the Penn Museum, Philadelphia. PM 37-33-52. THOMPSON 1974, pl. xxxiii, fig. 3. Courtesy of the Near East Section, Penn Museum.

Transliteration

1. wn[dʾṭk'] [YWM]
2. ʾrṭw[hšṭ'] LHMA
3. ***K*** #-I OL ... Y [?]
4. mṭr... [YH]BWN

Transcription

1. *Win[dādag] rōz*
2. *Ardwahišt nān*
3. *k[abīz]-1 ō ... ī* [?]
4. *Mihr... dah*

Translation

Windādag, on the day Ardwahišt give 1 *kabīz* of bread to ... of [?] Mihr...v

Commentary

In l. 4 we seem to have the beginning of a personal name whose first element is the common Mihr. The *kabīz* of bread's intended recipient is most likely someone regarded as belonging to this individual; another possibility would be that in this Mihr... we have a patronymic.

CT-135/4 (PM 37-33-50)

Fig. 4. Field no. CT-135/4. Housed at the Penn Museum, Philadelphia. PM 37-33-50. THOMPSON 1974, pl. xxxiii, fig. 2. Courtesy of the Near East Section, Penn Museum.

Transliteration

1. wndʾṭk' YWM
2. mṭr' ... LHMA
3. ***K*** #-III II [?] OL ...ʾn
4. ...
5. ... YHBWN

Transcription

1. *Windādag rōz*
2. *Mihr ... nān*
3. *k[abīz]-5 ō ...ān*
4. ...
5. ... *dah*

Translation

Windādag, on the day Mihr … give five *kabīz* of bread to the …s.

Commentary

Line 2: it is unclear whether there is a word between the day-name Mihr and *nān*, "bread"; this conceivably could be a long space as well.

Line 3: I have been unable to make out the final word in the line, although the ending seems to be the animate plural marker ⟨-ʾn⟩, *-ān*.

CT-135/5 (PM 37-33-21)

Transliteration

Recto
1. wndʾṭk' YWM
2. sp̄n[drmṭ'] LHMA
3. *K* #-II OL gwlsk' [?] [or ⟨xwlšn'⟩?] Y
4. blcʾṭwr [?] YHBWN

Verso
1. kʾl Y YWM ʾmwrdṭ dʾn
2. …
3. …
4. …

Transcription

Recto
1. *Windādag rōz*
2. *Spandarmad nān*
3. *k*[*abīz*]*-2 ō gursag* [?] [or "*xwarišn*"?] *ī*
4. *Burzādur* [?] *dah*

Verso
1. *kār ī rōz Amurdād dān*
2. …
3. …
4. …

Fig. 5. Field no. CT-135/5 (r). Housed at the Penn Museum, Philadelphia. PM 37-33-21. THOMPSON 1974, pl. xxix, fig. 3. Courtesy of the Near East Section, Penn Museum.

Fig. 6. Field no. CT-135/4. Housed at the Penn Museum, Philadelphia. PM 37-33-21. THOMPSON 1974, pl. xxxi, fig. 1. Courtesy of the Near East Section, Penn Museum.

Translation

Recto
Windādag on the day Spandarmad give 2 *kabīz* of bread to the hungry one [?] [or "for the food"?] of Burzādur.

Verso
[For?] the work of the day Amurdād grain…

Commentary

It is somewhat unusual for a Middle Persian ostracon to have writing on both sides, as has happened here, although several more instances of the phenomenon are recorded in WEBER 1992 and later publications; there are, for instance, O. 115 and O. 114, each of which have a continuous text running from one side to the other (WEBER 2022, pp. 519–520, 528–529). The extent to which all the writing here fits into a single coherent document is not clear, given the uncertainties that remain in the reading, and it is possible, given the separation we have between the first and second two lines on the verso side, that we have as many as three distinct texts. At least one distinct calendar day seems to be mentioned on each side, Spandarmad (recto) and Amurdād (verso), although it is perhaps notable that these days are close to one another — the fifth and seventh day in the month, respectively.

Recto, line 3: I have been unable to find a satisfactory reading for the penultimate word here, despite the high likelihood that its third letter is the easily identifiable ⟨l⟩.

Verso, line 4: the elongated ⟨d⟩ in ⟨d'n⟩, *dān* resembles that in O. 110, l. 2 (WEBER 2022, p. 528).

CT-135/6 (PM 37-33-42)

Transliteration

1. wnd'ṭ[k'] …
2. … LHMA
3. …
4. …

Transcription

1. *Windād*[*ag*] …
2. … *nān*
3. …
4. …

Fig. 7. Field no. CT-135/6. Housed at the Penn Museum, Philadelphia. PM 37-33-42. Does not appear in THOMPSON 1974. Courtesy of the Near East Section, Penn Museum.

Translation

Windādag … bread …

Commentary

The text is very difficult to make out.

CT-205/1 (ISACM A154067)

Fig. 8. Field no. CT-205/1. Housed at the ISAC Museum, Chicago. ISACM A154067. Does not appear in THOMPSON 1974. Courtesy of the ISAC Museum.

Transliteration

1. wndʾṭkʾ Y[W]M ddw[ʿ PWN] mṭrʾ
2. LHMA [***K***-] … [O]L lsykʾn
3. LWṬE …ʾn
4. YHBWN

Transcription

1. *Windādag rōz Day [pad] Mihr*
2. *nān k[abīz]-… ō rahīgān*
3. *abāg …ān*
4. *dah*

Translation

Windādag on the day Day [pad] Mihr, give … *kabīz* of bread to the servants with the …s.

Commentary

A servant is otherwise attested as the recipient of a certain measure of bread in another ostracon from Chāl Ṭarkhān-ʿEshqābād, CT-133/1 (WEBER 2022, pp. 529-530).

Line 3: As in CT-135/4, l. 3, I have been unable to make out any part of the final word aside from the animate plural ending *-ān*.

CT-205/3a (ISACM A154069)

Fig. 9. Field no. CT-205/3a. Housed at the ISAC Museum, Chicago. ISACM A154069. Does not appear in THOMPSON 1974. Courtesy of the ISAC Museum.

Transliteration

1. wnd'ṭk' YW[M] [d]dw' PWN dyn
2. L[HMA] … [O]L [?]
3. l[syk'] [?]
4. …
5. …
6. YHBWN

Transcription

1. *Windādag rōz Day pad Dēn*
2. *nān … ō* [?]
3. *r*[*ahīg*] [?]
4. …
5. …
6. *dah*

Translation

Windādag, on the day Day pad Dēn give bread to [?] the servant [?] …

Commentary

The writing is difficult to make out, but it seems to have a similar structure to the rest of the ostraca presented here, although the portion designating the recipients of the bread ration appears to be unusually elaborate.

CT-205/3b (ISACM A154070)

Fig. 10. Field no. CT-205/3b. Housed at the ISAC Museum, Chicago. ISACM A154070. Does not appear in THOMPSON 1974. Courtesy of the ISAC Museum.

Transliteration

1. wnd'ṭk' YWM 'ṭwr'
2. LHMA ***K*** #-IIII [?] OL lsyk'n
3. Y … YHBWN
4. [l'sṭ] [?]

Transcription

1. *Windādag rōz Ādur*
2. *nān k*[*abīz*]*-4* [?] *ō rahīgān*
3. *ī … dah*
4. …

Translation

Windādag on the day Ādur give 4 [?] *kabīz* of bread to the servants of…

Commentary

There is an indistinct word or mark on the final line here; it may be a kind of scribal mark to show that the assigned task has been taken care of.

CT-205/4 (ISACM A154068)

Fig. 11. Field no. CT-205/4 (r). Housed at the ISAC Museum, Chicago. ISACM A154068. Does not appear in Thompson 1974. Courtesy of the ISAC Museum.

Fig. 12. Field no. CT-205/4 (v). Housed at the ISAC Museum, Chicago. ISACM A154068. Does not appear in Thompson 1974. Courtesy of the ISAC Museum.

Transliteration

Recto
1. wnd’ṭk' YWM [’ng]l’n [?]
2. LHMA K #-I OL
3. GB[RA] [?] …
4. YHBWN

Transcription

Recto
1. *Windādag rōz* [*Anag*]*rān* [?]
2. *nān k*[*abīz*] *1 ō*
3. *mard* [?] …
4. *dah*

Translation

Windādag, on the day Anagrān [?] give one kabīz of bread to the man [?] …

Commentary

There is some more writing on the verso — clearly two <l>’s — but I am unable to make out a single word. Further advances in deciphering the text here, on both sides, may help to clarify the text on the two sides of CT-135/5, and vice-versa.

Appendix. Concordance of Chāl Ṭarkhān-ʿEsqhābād Ostraca by EUGENIO GAROSI with Minor Adjustments by THOMAS BENFEY

Field no.	Language	THOMPSON 1976	WEBER Publications	BENFEY 2024	Location
CT-40 r	Arabic	pl. xxvii, fig. 1			PM (37-33-23 r)
CT-40 v	Arabic	pl. xxxvi, fig. 1			PM (37-33-22 v)
CT-42/2	Middle Persian	n.d.			PM (37-33-56)
CT-75	Middle Persian	pl. xxvi, fig. 3			?
CT-83	Middle Persian	n.d.			PM (37-33-9)
CT-85/1 r	Middle Persian	pl. xxvii, fig. 2			PM (37-33-20 r)
CT-85/1 v	Middle Persian	n.d.			PM (37-33-20 v)
CT-85/2 r	Middle Persian	pl. xxix, fig. 4			?
CT-85/2 v	Middle Persian	pl. xxxi, fig. 2			?
CT-92/1	Arabic?	pl. xxviii, fig. 1			?
CT-92/2	Middle Persian	n.d.			PM (37-33-46)
CT-94	Middle Persian	pl. xxxiv, fig. 1			?
CT-97	Middle Persian	pl. xxx, fig. 1	2003 (ČTE Pahl. 5)		?
CT-101	Middle Persian	pl. xxxiii, fig. 1			?
CT-102	Middle Persian	pl. xxxvi, fig. 2			?
CT-110	Middle Persian	pl. xxxv, fig. 2			?
CT-123	Arabic	pl. xxxv, fig. 1			?
CT-133/1	Middle Persian	pl. xxx, fig. 2	2003, 2005, 2009, 2022 (ČTE Pahl. 9)		?
CT-133/2	Middle Persian	pl. xxxiii, fig. 5	2003, 2005, 2009 (ČTE Pahl. 10)		PM (37-33-45)

Field no.	Language	Thompson 1976	Weber Publications	Benfey 2024	Location
CT-133/3	Middle Persian	pl. xxvi, fig. 1			PM (37-33-51)
CT-133/4	Middle Persian	pl. xxvi, fig. 2		pp. 18–19	?
CT-134	Uncertain	pl. xxix, fig. 1 (bottom)			?
CT-135/1	Middle Persian	n.d.		p. 19	PM (37-33-54)
CT-135/2	Middle Persian	pl. xxxiii, fig. 3		p. 20	PM (37-33-52)
CT-135/4	Middle Persian	pl. xxxiii, fig. 2		pp. 20–21	PM (37-33-50)
CT-135/5 r	Middle Persian	pl. xxix, fig. 3		pp. 21–22	PM (37-33-21 r)
CT-135/5 v	Middle Persian	pl. xxxi, fig. 1		pp. 21–22	PM (37-33-21 v)
CT-135/6	Middle Persian	n.d.		pp. 22–23	PM (37-33-42)
CT-139 r	Middle Persian	pl. xxviii, fig. 2			?
CT-139 v	Uncertain	pl. xxix, fig. 1 (top)			?
CT-140/1	Middle Persian	pl. xxvi, fig. 4			?
CT-140/2	Middle Persian	n.d.			PM (37-33-53)
CT-143	Middle Persian	n.d.			PM (37-33-47)
CT-161/2 r	Middle Persian?	n.d.			PM (37-33-48 r)
CT-161/2 v	Middle Persian?	n.d.			PM (37-33-48 v)
CT-162/2	Bilingual?	pl. xxxvi, fig. 3			?
CT-195	Arabic	pl. xxxiii, fig. 4			?
CT-205/1	Middle Persian	n.d.		p. 23	ISACM (A154067)
CT-205/3a	Middle Persian	n.d.		p. 24	ISACM (A154069)
CT-205/3b	Middle Persian	n.d.		pp. 24–25	ISACM (A154070)
CT-205/4	Middle Persian	n.d.		p. 25	ISACM (A154068)
n.d.	Arabic	pl. xxxii, fig. 1			?
n.d.	Middle Persian	pl. xxxii, fig. 2			?

Bibliography

DE BLOIS, F. 1993: "*Corpus Inscriptionum Iranicarum.* Part III: *Pahlavi Inscriptions.* Vol. IV. *Ostraca and* Vol. V. *Papyri. Texts I: Ostraca, Papyri und Pergamente: Textband.* Von Dieter Weber. x, 265 Pp., 42 Plates, 2 Maps. London: School of Oriental and African Studies for the CII, 1992. £30". In: *Bulletin of the School of Oriental and African Studies* 56 (2), pp. 377–378.

CERETI, C./M. NEMATI/M. MOUSAVINIA 2022: "Ostraca and bullae from Qal'eh Iraq" In: E.W. SAUER/J. NOKANDEH/H. O. REKAVANDI (eds.): *Ancient Arms Race: Antiquity's Largest Fortresses and Sasanian Military Networks of Northern Iran: A Joint Fieldwork Project by the Iranian Center for Archaeological Research, the Research Institute of Cultural Heritage and Tourism and the University of Edinburgh (2014–2016).* Oxford, pp. 461–473.

GAROSI, E. 2022: *Projecting a New Empire: Formats, Social Meaning, and Mediality of Imperial Arabic in the Umayyad and Early Abbasid Periods.* Berlin.

GIGNOUX, PH. 1986: *Noms propres sassanides en moyen-perse épigraphique.* Vienna.

— 2005: "On Syriac Proper Names of Iranian Origin". In: *The Harp* 18, pp. 351–356.

HARPER, P.O. 1977: "Stucco from Chal Tarkhan-Eshqabad near Rayy. By Deborah Thompson". In: *American Journal of Archaeology* 81 (3), pp. 407–408.

HERZFELD, E. 1926: "Reisebericht". In: *Zeitschriften Der Deutschen Morgenländischen Gesellschaft* 80, pp. 225–284.

HOLOD, R. 2019. "Chal Tarkhan". In: S. TINNEY/K. SONIK (eds.): *Journey to the City: A Companion to the Middle East Galleries at the Penn Museum.* Philadelphia, pp. 336–338.

JUSTI, F. 1895: *Iranisches Namenbuch.* Marburg.

KRÖGER, J. 1990: "Čāl Tarkān." In: E. Yarshater (ed.): *Encyclopædia Iranica IV.* London, pp. 654–655.

DE MENASCE, J. 1957: *Ostraca and Papyri. Corpus Inscriptionum Iranicarum,* Part III: *Pahlavi Inscriptions.* London.

MILES, G.C. 1938: *The Numismatic History of Rayy.* New York (Numismatic Studies 2).

THOMPSON, D. 1965: "A Discussion of Sasanian Stucco with Special Reference to the Material from Chal Tarkhan in the Philadelphia Museum of Art". Ph.D. diss., Columbia University.

— 1976. *Stucco from Chal Tarkhan-Eshqabad near Rayy.* Warminster.

WEBER, D. 1974: "Zur Interpretation der Pahlavi-Ostraca". In: P. GIGNOUX/A. TAFAZZOLI (eds.): *Mémorial Jean de Menasce.* Louvain, pp. 227–233.

— 1992: *Corpus Inscriptionum Iranicarum.* Part III: *Pahlavi Inscriptions.* Vol. IV. *Ostraca and* Vol. V. *Papyri. Texts I: Ostraca, Papyri und Pergamente: Textband.* London.

— 2003: "Die Pahlavi-Ostraca von Čāl Tarxān-Ešqābād". In: L. PAUL (ed.): *Persian Origins: Early Judaeo-Persian and the Emergence of New Persian: Collected Papers of the Symposium, Göttingen 1999.* Wiesbaden (Iranica 6), pp. 275–282.

— 2005: "Kleine Nachlese zu Einigen Pahlavi-Ostraca". In: D. WEBER (ed.): *Languages of Iran: Past and Present: Iranian Studies in Memoriam David Neil MacKenzie.* Wiesbaden (Iranica 8), pp. 217–228.

— 2009: "Zu den Brotrationen in den Pahlavi-Ostraka". In: P. GIGNOUX/C. JULLIEN/F. JULLIEN (eds.): *Trésors d'orient: mélanges offerts à Rika Gyselen*. Paris (Studia Iranica 42), pp. 378–389.
— 2019: "The Story of Windād Burzmihr: A Zoroastrian Entrepreneur in Early Islamic Times". In: A. HINTZE/D. DURKIN MEISTERERNST/C. NAUMANN (eds.): *A Thousand Judgements: Festschrift for Maria Macuch*. Wiesebaden, pp. 373–384.
— 2022: "On the Formal Structure of Checks in Pahlavi Documents". In: A. CANTERA/M. MACUCH/N. SIMS-WILLIAMS (eds.): *The Reward of the Righteous: Festschrift in Honour of Almut Hintze*. Wiesbaden (Iranica 30), pp. 515–548.

A Manichaean Remedy for Headaches*

ADAM BENKATO, Berkeley

Introduction

Medicinal or pharmacological texts are among the less common textual genres attested in Sogdian. While few texts have been identified as containing medicinal or pharmacological contents, even fewer have been edited, owing primarily to the fact that they typically contain many hapax legomena and names of unusual ingredients, besides being poorly preserved. The first such Sogdian text to come to light was the Paris fragment P19, originating from Dunhuang, a difficult text listing several remedies which has remained untranslated.[1] From Turfan, about two dozen fragments have now been identified as medicinal or pharmacological in content, most recently through the pioneering cataloguing work of CHRISTIANE RECK.[2] While a number remain unedited, in recent years, fortunately, there has been increased work on these texts, and several very interesting texts have been identified, including a Sogdian translation of part of Vāgbhaṭa's *Aṣṭāṅgahṛdayasaṃhitā* in Sanskrit (RECK/WILKENS 2015), a recipe for the restoration of virginity with close parallels in Sanskrit (RECK/BENKATO 2018), and a Sogdian translation of part of the Chinese medical treatise *Bingyuan lun* (BI 2021). The Sogdian texts written in Brāhmī script seem to be largely of pharmacological contents, though they have remained poorly understood.[3] These all seem to have been part of the Manichaean texts from Turfan or Buddhist texts

* In preparing this study, I benefited from Christiane Reck's knowledge of the pharmacological texts in Sogdian and am indebted to Nicholas Sims-Williams and Dieter Maue for several valuable comments and to Bi Bo for some keen suggestions and references. In addition, Sims-Williams kindly shared with me the unpublished notes of Ilya Gershevitch on M 568 and M 746c kept at the Ancient India and Iran Trust in Cambridge, UK; references to these are marked with 'IG'. Abbreviations: B, C, M before a Sogdian form indicate Buddhist, Christian, Manichaean writing traditions, respectively; Khot. = Khotanese; OTk. = Old Turkic/Uighur; Skt. = Sanskrit.

1 A transliteration with some commentary was given by BENVENISTE (1940, pp. 150, 231–232) with a later attempt at a partial translation by HENNING (1946, p. 713 n. 5).

2 See RECK 2018, p. 152. A descriptive list of the known pharmacological fragments is given in RECK/BENKATO (2018, pp. 83–86), while RECK (2018, pp. 165–166) provides a useful list of ingredients occuring in these fragments.

3 See MAUE/SIMS-WILLIAMS (1991) for Sogdian in Brāhmī script. Further work on these fragments can be found in MAUE (1996) and SIMS-WILLIAMS (1996).

from Turfan and Dunhuang. Two other fragments in Sogdian, and additional fragments in other languages including early New Persian and Syriac, stem from the remains of the Christian library at Bulayïq near Turfan.[4] Much work remains to be done in the area of Sogdian pharmacology, including identification of texts and of ingredients, editions of the remaining fragments, and studies of the sources of Sogdian pharmacological knowledge, which seem to be primarily Sanskrit or Prakrit, and with some Chinese as well. This paper is a humble attempt to contribute to a wider understanding of pharmacology in Sogdian through the edition of three fragments and discussion of their contents.

1. A Manichaean Medicinal Codex?

The only two known Sogdian pharmacological fragments in Manichaean script are M 568 and M 746c. M 568 is a fragment from the top inside corner, and M 746c is a fragment from the outside middle, of a single codex page: they join mostly without a gap to give ten lines of text, six of which are fully preserved.[5] The text is in black ink with the typical Manichaean punctuation of two black dots surrounded by red circles. The codicological features suggest that the text was produced by Manichaeans, but the uses to which they put the text and from where their knowledge of pharmacology might have come are unknown. The page gives parts of remedies for migraines (Sogdian *nymyy srxwyc*) and headaches (Sogdian *srxwyc*). The procedures, and several of the ingredients, are similar to those in the section on headaches given in both an Old Turkic book of remedies edited by RACHMATI (1985) and the Syriac *Book of Medicines* edited by BUDGE (1913), though an exact parallel does not seem to be attested in either tradition. In particular, the Old Turkic text contains the instruction to "pound (ingredients) finely, mix with butter, and smear/daub on the head".[6]

Recto		Translation
1	qpyy'tyy pṭwyš rwrt (n)[xw'y]	char fish-flesh, pound finely,

4 The two Sogdian fragments in Syriac script have now been edited by SIMS-WILLIAMS (2019, pp. 89–94). For the Syriac, see SIMS-WILLIAMS 2011, pp. 361–367 and MARÓTH 1984; most recently LIN (2020) shows that the Syriac fragments have parallels in Galenic texts.

5 A thin strip of paper glued to the right-hand edge of M 568 most likely is a reinforcement to the inner edge of the page, meaning that it must be the inner margin of the page. On this 'binding strip' in Manichaean manuscripts, see GULÁCSI (2005, pp. 67–71), for Christian Sogdian manuscripts see SIMS-WILLIAMS (1985, p. 16). It was NICHOLAS SIMS-WILLIAMS who first noticed that the two fragments could be joined together.

6 See RACHMATI (1985, lines 91ff. on p. 555 and lines 158ff. on p. 559) for an edition of the Old Turkic texts. In the Syriac text (BUDGE 1913, pp. 1–64), the lengthy chaper on ailments of the head, including both headaches and migraines, contains a number of overlap with the Manichaean remedy presented here, but no close parallels.

2	•• γ'wrwγ(n)y pryw pṭr[y]δ p(r)[7]	mix together with butter,
3	sryy δ'wt' (frtr) (β)wṭ •• ky'	daub on the head, it gets better. He who
4	nymyy srxw(y)c (β)'ṭ kwndpδy	has a migraine, (take?) *kwndpδy*,
5	xwšṭryy wyš(y) (t)xmy skpwndyy	seed of camel grass, scammony
6	wyx •• šnk mw(š)k' zyrṭyẖ	root, *šnk mwšk'*, yellow ...
7	[ ](.rxm.) s('ṭ) I mγwn β'ṭ	... all should be equal (?),
8	[s](ty)r XXXI styr	... staters, 31 staters
9	[s](t)yr šyr βyxš	... staters, boil well
10	*traces*	...

1 *pṭwyš* seems to correspond to C *ptwyš*, the meaning of which has to be assumed from the Syriac verb 'to cause to die' which it translates (Sims-Williams 1985, p. 222b). However, a slightly different meaning has to be assumed here as it makes little sense to 'kill off' fish meat. Sims-Williams (p.c.) suggested that *pṭwyš* could be related to Skt. *oṣ* 'to burn', meaning something like 'to char, burn'.

2 *γ'wrwγn* 'butter' (lit. 'cow-oil') appears frequently as an ingredient in medicinal recipes, such as those in M 7340. See also the similar phrasing in P14/5/ *ZY mw sršp' δ'wn γ'wrwγn pr'yw ptr'yδ't* 'when one mixes mustard together with butter'.

4 *srxwyc* is 'headache', lit. 'head-pain', also attested in So 20211/II/9/ as *srxwc*. For *nymyy srxw(y)c*, literally 'half head-pain', Gershevitch (IG) noted 'migraine', presumably on the basis of Greek ἡμικρανια lit. '(pain in) one side of the head', which has provided the basis for its name in other languages (e.g. Arabic *ṣudāʿ niṣfī* lit. 'half headache').

4 *kwndpδy* is a hapax. Since one expects here the name of an ingredient, the similarity of this word with B *kwnt'yk* 'pitcher' (< Skt. *kuṇḍikā*) or the unclear M *qwndyryẖ* in a wordlist M 614 (Henning 1940, p. 31) may not mean anything. Guesses from Sims-Williams (a shortened form of Skt. *kuñjara-pippalī*) and Maue (Skt. *goṇṭhāphala* 'betel nut') may prove to ultimately lead in the right direction.

5 *xwšṭryy wyš* may be interpreted as 'camel grass' (*Cymbopogon schoenanthus*), a plant appearing often in medieval medicine.

5 *skpwndyy* was compared by Gershevitch (1954, §352) with New Persian *saqmūniyā* 'scammonia' (cf. Greek σκαμμονια, Arabic *saqamūniyā*). Other Iranian cognates are unknown, and the change *p* > *m* is unusual. The root (Sogd. *wyx*) of scammony, *Convolvulus scammonia*, is either incised to yield a juice which is then dried, or dried and digested with alcohol to yield a resin.

7 A sg. verb restored on the basis of the preceding line, but the following impv. verb in /3/ is plural.

6 At first sight *šnk* reminds one of the measure word deriving from Chinese 升 *sheng* 'pint', a measure of about .84 liters.[8] But in view of the lack of numeral before it, Gershevitch's 'oyster' (IG), presumably based on Skt. *śaṅkha-* 'shell', is an interesting idea. Following this lead, Sims-Williams (p.c.) suggests the interpretation 'mussel', via a metaphor similar to that of English 'mussel' and 'muscle', both lit. 'little mouse' (cf. Latin *musculus*), and Khot. *mūla-* 'rat, muscle' < **mūša-* 'mouse'. šnk *mwšk'* 'mussel' might then be a synonymous hendiadys, a frequent enough occurrence in Sogdian, as well as Khot. and OTk., especially consisting of loan plus inherited word, see Gershevitch (1954, §1635–38)? Alternatively, *mwšk'* could represent Skt. *muṣkaka* "a species of tree (the ashes of which are used as a cautery)" (Monier-Williams 1899, p. 824), though the measurement of a *sheng* before it may be unusual.

6 *zyrṭyḇ* 'yellow' is probably the (partial) designation of an ingredient. Maue (p.c.) kindly draws my attention to the fact that some herbs and spices have names deriving from the word for 'yellow': Skt. *haridrā* 'turmeric (Curcuma longa)' lit. 'yellowish', Skt. *dāruharidrā* 'tree turmeric (Berberis aristata)', or OTk. *sarıg arire* 'yellow *harītakī*'; perhaps Sogdian ''ryry is to be restored in the gap at the beginning of **7**.

7 Does the end of the line mean that equal quantities of each ingredient are to be used?

9 *βyxš* is the same verb as *βy'xš* 'boil' in P19/6/, which Benveniste connected with B *βy'yš'ntk* 'boiling', going back to **abi-yaiša-* (Av. *yaēš-*, Yaghnobi *ēš-* without preverb). If this is the present stem, as Sims-Williams suggests (p.c.), it must have been influenced by its (hypothetical) past stem **βy'xšt*, similar to C present stem *spxš* beside *spyš* 'serve', past stem *spxšt-*.

	Verso	Translation
1	[. . .](.) k(w)n' srxwyc frtry'	... do [...] the headache gets better.
2	βwṭ •• •• ms ṭrypl δs'	Also (of) myrobalans 10
3	δr •• kw(δr)β XX δr rwrṭ nxw'y	drachms, (and of) kodo millet 20 drachms,
4	j'm ptw(y)c 'ngwpyn γ'w	pound finely, sift finely, mix honey
5	rwγnyy pryw šyr syγ pṭryδ	with butter very well,
6	I m'x ywy' cyndr xnsk	keep firmly inside one-month barley (?),
7	δ'rt' γyr(t)rk s(x)w'(y)[. . .]	lift out later, ...
8	δr pr ptm'[k]	drachms in measure ...
9	myδ myδ [ ]	daily ...
10	[. . .]ṭ[ ]	...

8 A detailed discussion of *sheng* in languages of Central Asia can be found in Sims-Williams/Hamilton (2015, pp. 38–39). Other attestations in Sogdian include Ch/U 7211/9/ *nymy* šnk 'half *sheng*', in the Khotan fragment 2 Bi/Sims-Williams (2010, pp. 500–501), and in the pharmacological fragment L47+L48 which mentions *'δw nym'k šnk* 'two-and-a-half *sheng*'.

2 *ṭrypl* most likely represents Skt. *triphala* 'three fruits', a formula consisting of the three myrobalan plants *Terminalia bellirica* 'beleric myrobalan', *Terminalia chebula* 'yellow myrobalan', and *Phyllanthus emblica* 'emblic myrobalan' known in Sanskrit as *harītakī*, *vibhītaka*, and āmala*ka*, respectively. These three are named individually in the Sogdian fragment So 10100k+ as ''r'yry, *βr'yr'y*, and ''mδ'y.[9] Maue & Sims-Williams (1991, p. 491), however, do not exclude the possibility that *ṭrypl* here could refer to 'turpeth' (Skt. *tripūṭa*), the plant *Operculina turpethum*. Though they are common in eye-related remedies, the myrobalans are also used for the treatment of headaches, migraines in particular, and are attested in other traditions, such as in the Cairo Genizah documents.[10] The 'three fruits' were well known in India and China since ancient times,[11] though, as Bi informs me (p.c.), it seems that in medieval China, it was mainly the yellow myrobalan (''r'yry / *harītakī*) which is used rather than the three collectively.

3 *kwδrβ* is likely from Skt. *kodrava* 'kodo millet', see Bi (2021, p. 475).

3 A parallel to this phrase is found in P19/16/ šyr 'rw'rt nxw'y. From the use of šyr and placement of 'rw'rt following it, I assume that there it must be an adverbial use of the adj. 'fine, small', hence 'pound very finely'. In So 10100k+, a similar phrase is attested (/6/ 'yny w'β'yδ rwr' ẓ'm nxw'y 'pound this remedy finely') where the word *rwr'* 'medical herb; remedy' comes before the adverb+verb combination meaning 'to pound finely'. Compare the syntax of **5** *šyr syγ pṭryδ* 'mix very finely' as well as that of P19/9/ *'yw my'wn šyr nxw'y* 'pound well at the same time'. Because of its position here and the fact that the ingredients to be pounded were just named, I assume that *rwrṭ* here means 'finely'.

4 *j'm ptw(y)c* is comparable with P19/9/ *z'm ptwyc*. One is tempted to draw a comparison with verbs such as B *wyc* 'to move, shake (itr.)', B *pw'yc* 'to shake, be agitated' deriving from **waič*, and even verbs such as C *žwyž* 'sift, winnow' < **uz-waija-* and C *'wyž* 'be shaken, agitated' < **ā-waija-* (on possible confusion of the roots **waij* 'shake' and **waič* 'sift' in Sogdian, see Sims-Williams (1985, pp. 84–85)). In any case, 'shaking' or 'sifting' makes good sense at this point of the recipe both here and in P19. Although Benveniste (1940, p. 232), commenting on P19/9/, noted that *j'm* 'fine' occurs often as an adverb in phrases meaning 'to cut finely', both here and there the verb *ptwyc* occurs *after* the verb *nxw'y* 'to pound, crush, press'. The act of cutting or chopping following pressing or pounding seems rather odd, but shaking or sifting an already pressed mixture makes more sense.

9 The Sogdian names correspond very well to those predicted by Maue in an overview of the names of the three myrobalans in Central Asian languages Maue (2009, pp. 299–304), though the third was already known from P10/3/ and the first from a Brahmi script fragment in the form <ā ri re>. The fragment So 10100k+ is edited in Reck & Benkato (2018).

10 Lev/Amar 2008, pp. 218–221, also Yoeli-Tlalim 2021, pp. 71–75.

11 See Yoeli-Tlalim 2021, pp. 63–84.

6 *ywy'* must be the loc.sg. of the infrequently attested *yw-* 'barley' (Yaghnobi *yaw*).[12] However, what one-month barley refers to remains unclear; perhaps barley which has been fermented for a month?[13] A parallel occurs in the Sanskrit *Siddhasāra* (28.9 in EMMERICK 1980), where ingredients are also to be placed inside barley: "... pours it into an iron vessel, and places it (in the midst of barley)."

6 *xnsk* could be an adverbial use of the adj. *xns* 'firm, strong' with *-ak* ending (cf. GERSHEVITCH [1954, §982–84]). Alternatively, GERSHEVITCH connected *xnsk* with New Persian *xasne* 'Galbanum' (IG). Galbanum (*Ferula galbaniflua*) is attested in OTk. as γasni, which MAUE (2009, pp. 298–299) suggests may be connected with the Sogdian adjective *γsn-* 'stinking' (metathesized variant B *γns-*), abstaining from deciding on whether or not *xnsk* belongs with these words. The word's placement in the phrase as well as its form (*x* for *γ* and *-i/e* written *k* in Manichaean script) seem obstacles to interpreting it as a word for Galbanum. The Persian form is nevertheless an enticing connection, though why the Sogdian text uses a form with *x-* remains to be explained.

7 Is *γyr(t)rk* also a previously unattested form of the adv. *γyrtr* 'later' with *-ak* ending, or yet another previously unknown ingredient?

2. From a Pustaka-Book of Remedies

So 10339 (find-signature T I α) is a roughly triangular fragment from the left-hand side of a long-line format pustaka leaf. Although the script, a style of Sogdian script similar to that used in Manichaean texts, is relatively clear, the fragment's surface has been abraded at points and several letters rubbed away. The use of long-line pustaka leaves is uncommon for Manichaean texts, though not unknown.[14] I give here the text with my own interpretation, in hopes of improving our understanding thereof in comparison with the medicinal text edited above.

12 The other two attestations being Mugh Б-10/3 *'δw kpc'kk yw'* 'two small-*kafch* of barley' and Mugh Б-10/1/ *X pδnyh yw'* 'ten measures of barley' (*yw'* is the numerative nom.-acc. form). See LIVSHITS (2015, p. 105 n. 236) for the measure word *pδn-* as well as an edition of Mugh Б-10. *kpc'kk* is the diminutive (in *-ak*) of *kpc*, for more on which see BI/SIMS-WILLIAMS (2010, p. 500).

13 SIMS-WILLIAMS suggests that line 6 could alternately mean 'keep galbanum (*xnsk*) inside barley for one month'. The context is unfortunately not enough to clarify how either interpretation fits into the overall remedy. An intriguing connection is the mention of soaking in barley in recipes in BUDGE (1913), see the text on verso, line 6.

14 See RECK (2013) for more on pustaka books from Turfan without an obvious Buddhist connection; this fragment was first edited there RECK (2013, pp. 170–172).

Side 1		Translation
1	](s βwt)	... is
2	ʾβ]ẓ-y βnt z-yrn	... are bad, yellow
3	]prsʾ ny(....)y	... ask(?) ...
4	](...)ky knp xcy •• ••	... is less.
5	](pr) kẓ-ʾr t(xmy wyspnʾc)	... on *kẓ-ʾr* seeds of all
6	ʾ]δw δr wyspw βrʾk xw(r)y[15]	... you should consume two drachms every morning

Side 2		
1	] cšmy ʾβẓ-y βy •• p(.s...)	... (if the) eye would be bad, ...
2	m]wrt βrʾy βwt (kδʾ)	... is myrtle-fruit. If
3	] kδʾ pr γrδʾ ʾβz-y	... If (it is) bad on the neck
4	ʾβ](z)-y βy β(r)z-wʾny β(wt)	... would be bad, will be long-lived
5	](k)βn (βwt)	... is little
6	](š) β(nt)	... they are

1.4 *knp* it may be used here as it is in some weight and measure inscriptions, meaning 'some quantity less (*knp*) some quantity'. For example, Weight No. 17 from Panjikent bears the inscription *ʾδry pʾtmnk ctβʾr mynt knp* '3 *batman* less 4 (drachms)' (Marshak/Raspopova 2005, pp. 46–47), and a silver omphalos dish from Samarkand the inscription *ʾyw knpy ʾYKZY 20 s* 'one less than 20 staters' (Livshits 2015, p. 236).

1.5 *kẓ-ʾr* is an unknown word, perhaps a body part on which the remedy is placed or a plant of which the seeds (following *txmy*) are used. No correspondence in Iranian is known to me.

2.2 Reck (2013, p. 171) suggests restoring [*m*]*wrt βrʾy* 'myrtle-fruit'. The myrtle tree is *mwrt* in Sogdian; it is attested as *mwrtʾ* in M 137, a poetical text, with the -ʾ added for metrical purposes, see now Morano (2017).

2.3 *γrδʾ* 'neck' is attested as M *γrδʾ* and S *γrδʾkh* (compare Yaghnobi *γurtak* 'nape of the neck'); the sentence may mean 'if there is pain in the neck'.

2.4 Reck (2013, p. 172) draws attention to the word *β(r)zwʾny* 'long-lived', until now only attested in Buddhist Sogdian texts.

2.5](*k*)*βn* an endlingless light-stem adjective, or part of another word?

15 I read thus instead of Reck's *γ/xw(n)y*. As the substance under preparation is unknown, it cannot be said whether it should be eaten or drunk (both *xwr-*).

3. *δr* is for Drachma

The three Sogdian fragments edited in the preceding sections share an interesting feature, namely the appearance of a two-letter word *δr*. Based on its context, that it is at least in M 568r7 preceded by a number, and that the measure word *styr* 'stater' also appears, *δr* must indicate a measurement. It seems quite likely, therefore, to be an abbreviation for 'drachma', Sogdian *δrxm*, or alternatively for Sogdian *δrxmδnk* 'drachm by weight', a measure which occurs in P19.

Fig. 1.
M 568v3

Fig. 2.
M 746cr2

Fig. 3.
M 746cr7

Fig. 4.
So 10339

Abbreviations for weight and measure words are known in Central Asian contexts, though most examples thereof so far occur on vessels, stone weights, or gold ingots, rather than in manuscripts. Among the Panjikent weights with Sogdian inscriptions, one comes across abbreviations such as *p't* seemingly for the large unit *p'tzmnk* (probably similar to OTk. *batman*, see (Marshak/Raspopova 2005, pp. 45–48; Sims-Williams 2016, p. 102), *C III δ* probably for '104 drachms' (Marshak & Raspopova 2005, p. 72), and *XI s* for '11 staters' (*ibid.*). A few Bactrian weight inscriptions on silver vessels are also preceded by the letters *υα* for *υαγγο* /hang/ 'weight'.[16] Furthermore, inscriptions in Kharoṣṭhī script on gold ingots include the abbreviations *sa* (for *sadera* 'stater') and *dra* (for *drakhma* 'drachm'), for example Sims-Williams 2016, p. 105. In manuscripts, the abbreviation *s* for 'stater' appears in So 14822/R/4/ (Bi 2021, pp. 464–465); in older texts, it is found also in two inscriptions from Sogdiana (Livshits 2015, pp. 236, 262).

Interestingly, in the fragments presented here, the abbreviation does not consist solely of the first letter of the word, as seems to have been the practice in Sogdiana, but of the first two letters. As for its value, it has recently been shown that the standard drachm weighed about 4.45 grams in Sogdiana (Marshak/Raspopova 2005; Sims-Williams 2016), though whether this was the case in Turfan cannot yet be shown. According to the system of weights used in Sogdiana, a *styr* 'stater' is the equivalent of four drachms, so about 17.8 grams. While one stater is not a large quantity, the 31 staters (which would equal to 558g according to the Sogdian drachm) of M 746c does seem to be, at least in the context of a medical prescription, quite large. Given the fragmentary context, however, we cannot at present assume a dramatically different value for either the drachm or stater.

16 *υαγγο* being the Bactrian equivalent of Sogdian *δnk* in *δrxmδnk* and Pahlavi *sang* (all from OIr. *ϑang-*), see Sims-Williams 2013.

Glossary of Pharmacological Terms

ʾngwpyn	n. 'honey' M 568V4
βyxš	v.2sg.impv. 'boil' M 568R9
δʾwtʾ	v.2pl.impv. 'daub' M 568R3
δr	abbreviation for 'drachma' M 568V3, V3, V8, 10339i6
γʾwrwγny	n.obl. 'butter' M 568R2, V4f.
qpyyʾtyy	n. 'fish-flesh' M 568R1
kwδrβ	n. 'kodo millet' M 568V3
kwndpδy	unknown ingredient M 568R4
[m]wrt βrʾy	n. 'myrtle-fruit (?)' 10339ii2
nymyy srxwyc	n. 'migraine' M 568R4
nxwʾy	v.2sg.impv. 'pound, crush' M 568R1*, V3
pṭryδ	v.2sg.impv. 'mix' M 568R2*, V5
pṭwyš	v.v2sg.impv. 'char (?)' M 568R1
ptwyc	v.2sg.impv. 'sift' M 568V4
skpwndyy	n. 'scammonia?' M 568R5
srxwyc	n. 'headache' M 568V1
styr	n. 'stater' M 568R8*, R8, R9*
šnk mwškʾ	n. 'mussel (?)' or another ingredient M 568R6
ṭrypl	n. 'myrobalan, turpeth (?)' M 568V2
txmy	n. 'seed' M 568R5, 10339i5
wyx	n. 'root' M 568R6
xnsk	adv.'firmly, strongly' or n. 'Galbanum' (?) M 568V6
xwry	v.2sg.opt. 'eat, drink' 10339i6
xwšṭryy-wyšy	n.obl. 'camel grass' M 568R5
ywyʾ	n.loc.sg. 'barley' M 568V6
zyrn	n. 'gold' 10339i2
zyrṭyẖ	adj. 'yellow' M 568R6

Bibliography

Benveniste, É. 1940: *Textes sogdiens*. Paris.

Bo, B. 2021: "A Sogdian Medical Text from Turfan." In: *Journal of the Royal Asiatic Society* 31(3), pp. 463–477.

Bo, B/N. Sims-Williams 2010: "Sogdian documents from Khotan, I: Four economic documents." In: *Journal of the American Oriental Society* 130(4), pp. 497–508.

Budge, E.A.W. 1913: *The Syriac Book of Medicines*. Vol. 2. Oxford.

Emmerick, R.E. 1980: *The Siddhasara of Ravigupta*. Vol. 1 *The Sanskrit Text*. Wiesbaden (Verzeichnis der Orientalischen Handschriften in Deutschland Supplement-Band 23,1).

Gershevitch, I. 1954: *A Grammar of Manichean Sogdian*. Oxford.

GULÁCSI, Z. 2005: *Medieval Manichaean Book Art. A Codicological Study of Iranian and Turkic Illuminated Book Fragments from 8th–11th Century East Central Asia*. Leiden (Nag Hammadi and Manichaean Studies 57).
HENNING, W.B. 1940: *Sogdica*. London.
— 1946: "The Sogdian texts of Paris." In: *Bulletin of the School of Oriental and African Studies* 11(4), pp. 713–740.
LEV, E/Z. AMAR 2008: *Practical Materia Medica of the Medieval Eastern Mediterranean According to the Cairo Genizah*. Leiden.
LIN, L. 2020: "Hippocrates and Galen in Turfan: Remarks on SyrHT 1 and SyrHT 388." In: *Aramaic Studies* 18(2), pp. 213–239.
LIVSHITS, V.A. 2015: *Sogdian epigraphy of Central Asia and Semirech'e*. London (Corpus Inscriptionum Iranicarum Part II, Vol. III).
MARÓTH, M. 1984: "Ein Fragment eines syrischen pharmazeutischen Rezeptbuches aus Turfan." In: *Altorientalische Forschungen* 11, pp. 115–125.
MARSHAK, B.I./V.I. RASPOPOVA 2005: *Согдийские гири из пенджикента*. St. Petersburg.
MAUE, D. 1996: "Zu den uighurischen und iranischen Brāhmī-Handschriften der Berliner Turfanfunde." In: RONALD E. EMMERICK (ed.): *Turfan, Khotan und Dunhuang. Vorträge der Tagung "Annemarie von Gabain und die Turfanforschung" veranstaltet von der Berlin-Brandenburgischen Akademie der Wissenschaften in Berlin (9.-12. 12. 1994)*. Berlin, pp. 211–220.
— 2009: "Einige uigurische Wörter indischen und iranischen Ursprungs." In: W. SUNDERMANN/A. HINTZE/F. DE BLOIS (eds.): *Exegisti monumenta: Festschrift in honour of Nicholas Sims-Williams*. Wiesbaden (Iranica 17), pp. 293–312.
MAUE, D./N. SIMS-WILLIAMS. 1991: "Eine sanskrit-sogdische Bilingue in Brāhmī." In: *Bulletin of the School of Oriental and African Studies* 54, pp. 486–495.
MONIER-WILLIAMS, M. 1899: *A Sanskrit-English Dictionary*. Oxford.
MORANO, E. 2017: Manichaean Sogdian Poems. In: S.N.C. LIEU/N.A. PEDERSEN/E. MORANO/E. HUNTER (eds.): *Manichaeism East and West*. Turnhout (Analecta Manichaica 1), pp. 171–184.
RACHMATI, G.R. 1985: "Zur Heilkunde der Uiguren [I]." In: *Sprachwissenschaftliche Ergebnisse der deutschen Turfanforschung* III. Leipzig, pp. 549–571.
RECK, C. 2013: "Nichtbuddhistische mitteliranische Pustakablätter." In: J.-P. LAUT/K. RÖHRBORN (eds.): *Vom Aramäischen zum Alttürkischen: Fragen zur Übersetzung von manichäischen Texten. Vorträge des Göttinger Symposiums vom 29./30. September 2011*. Berlin, pp. 167–178.
— 2018: *Berliner Turfanfragmente christlichen Inhalts und Varia in soghdischer Schrift*. Stuttgart (Verzeichnis der Orientalischen Handschriften in Deutschland 18.4 Mitteliranische Handschriften 3).
RECK, C./A. BENKATO 2018: "'Like a Virgin': A Sogdian recipe for restoring virginity and the Sanskrit background of Sogdian medicine." In: *Written Monuments of the Orient* 6(2), pp. 67–91.
RECK, C./J. WILKENS 2015: "Eine soghdische Version von Vāgbhaṭas Aṣṭāṅgahṛdayasaṃhitā." In: E. RAGAGNIN/J. WILKENS (eds.): *Kutadgu Nom Bitig. Festschrift für Jens Peter Laut zum 60. Geburtstag*. Wiesbaden, pp. 431–452.
SIMS-WILLIAMS, N. 1985: *The Christian Sogdian manuscript C2*. Berlin (Berliner Turfantexte 12).

— 1996: "The Sogdian Manuscripts in Brāhmī Script as Evidence for Sogdian Phonology." In: Ronald E. Emmerick (ed.): *Turfan, Khotan und Dunhuang. Vorträge der Tagung "Annemarie von Gabain und die Turfanforschung" veranstaltet von der Berlin-Brandenburgischen Akademie der Wissenschaften in Berlin (9.-12.12.1994)*. Berlin, pp. 307–315.

— 2011: "Early New Persian in Syriac script: Two texts from Turfan." In: *Bulletin of the School of Oriental and African Studies* 74(3), pp. 353–374.

— 2013: Some Bactrian inscriptions on silver vessels. In: *Bulletin of the Asia Institute* 23, pp. 191–198.

— 2016: "'Stater' and 'drachm' in Sogdian and Bactrian weight inscriptions." In: 吐鲁番学研究院/吐鲁番博物馆 (eds.): 吐鲁番与丝绸之路经济带高峰论坛暨第五届吐鲁番学国际学术研讨会论文集. Shanghai, pp. 102–108.

— 2019: *From Liturgy to Pharmacology. Christian Sogdian texts from the Turfan Collection*. Turnhout (Berliner Turfantexte 45).

Sims-Williams, N./J. Hamilton 2015: *Turco-Sogdian Documents from 9th–10th century Dunhuang*. London.

Yoeli-Tlalim, R. 2021: *ReOrienting Histories of Medicine: Encounters along the Silk Roads*. London.

The Passive Suffix *-ī̆h-* in Middle Persian[1]

Alberto Cantera, Berlin

The origin and exact shape of the suffix *-ī̆h-* in Middle Persian is controversial. On the one hand, the functional identity appears to indicate that the origin of this suffix is the Old Iranian passive-intransitive and also denominative[2] suffix *i̯a-* (Henning 1933, p. 211; Sundermann 1989, p. 151). However, the presence of the *h* raises problems, so the link between the Old Iranian and the Middle Persian suffix has been frequently questioned. Accordingly, its origin is presented as unclear (Henning 1933, p. 210) or alternative solutions have been sought (Bartholomae 1915, pp. 45f.; Skjærvø 1997, p. 178). On the other hand, the quantity of the vowel is problematic. The systematic spelling as *-yh-* seems to point to a reading as *-īh-* and this is, indeed, the almost universally adopted reading. However, some pieces of evidence in Judeo-Persian and a singular form in Parthian rather presuppose a reading *-ih-* that in turn would fit better with a derivation from the Old Iranian suffix *-i̯a-*.

The shape of the suffix alternates between *-ī̆h-* and *-ī̆y-*. The first is regular in Pahlavi, Manichaean Middle Persian, and Judeo-Persian. However, in the Psalter the denominative and passive forms show the suffix *-ī̆y-* ⟨-yd-⟩: *afsōsiyēnd* "they are mocked" ⟨ʼpswsydyndy⟩, denominative from *afsōs* (Andreas 1933, p. 35; Henning 1933, p. 211; Skjærvø 1997, p. 177) and *wizandiyēnd* ⟨wcndydyndy⟩ "they are made to tremble" (Andreas/Barr 1933, p. 128; Henning 1933, p. 211; Skjærvø 1997, p. 177). Henning (*ibid.*) surprisingly doubts the reality of this spelling and mentions the possibility that these two forms might be read as *-īh-*. Skjærvø takes them, however, seriously and attempts an explanation of this variation. He derives both suffixes from passive stems of verbs in dental. Thus, *-ī̆y-* would be the result of the reanalysis of some passive stems like **sidi̯a-* > **sī̆y-* and **skadi̯a-* > **škīy-* and *-ī̆h-* to stems such as **miϑi̯a-* > *mīh-*. As he admits, he has no examples of passive stems ending in ϑ in Middle Persian. Nonetheless, the descendants of **sidi̯a-* and **skadi̯a-* are in Middle Persian *°sīh-* and *ških-* (sic!). He explains this alternation between *h* and *y* as the result of an occasional change of intervocalic *d (δ)* to ϑ in Middle Persian, as in Phl. *dah-* vs. Manichaean Middle Persian *day-*. However, the latter example might be better explained as

1 The redaction of this paper has been accompanied by numerous conversations and discussions with Benedikt Peschl, Thomas Jügel, and Juan José Ferrer Losilla that have enriched it. My gratitude to them.

2 The denominative forms are less frequent than the passive ones, but not rare, e.g. *agārī̆histan, agārīh-* "to become powerless", *paydāgīhistan, paydāgīh-* "to appear, be revealed", *čērihistan, čērih-* "be victorious", etc.

deriving either from the present stem **daδa-* (secondarily thematized, cf. Av. *daδāiti*) or *daϑa-* (cf. Av. *daϑat̰* and even *daϑaiti* VytS7.6). SKJÆRVØ's assumption of a reanalysis of *škīh-* and *sīh-* (or its variants **škīy-, sīy-*) is unlikely, even more so if we take into account that *škadi̯a-* would hardly have led to **škīh-* or *škīy*. The expected result of the form **škaϑi̯a-* is rather *škeh-*, cf. Phl. *meh-* < **maϑiah-*. Similarly, we might also suppose a reading **škey-* < **škadi̯a-*. As assumed by KORN (2021, p. 113), any ⟨y⟩ where we expect an *a* in syllables preceding another syllable with *i, y* should be explained as an *Umlaut* effect[3]. In any case, an evolution to *škīy-* that might have served as a model for the creation of a passive suffix *-īy-* in the Psalter is rather unlikely.

There is, however, a more likely alternative explanation. The alternation *y/h* is not only found in the passive suffix *-ĭh-* but also in other verbal stems ending in Proto-Iranian *i̯*. The closest parallel is offered by some combinations of the verb **ai̯-* "to go" with preverbs such as *uzīdan* "to go out," whose present stem goes back to **uz-i̯a-*[4]. In this case, Pahlavi shows forms with *y*, but Manichaean Middle Persian with *h*: Phl. *uz(iy)ēd*[5] ⟨ʾwzyt⟩ (e.g. WZ30.52) < **uz-i̯-ai̯ati, uziyēnd* ⟨ʾwzydynd⟩ (e.g. WZ35.23, 24) < **uz-i̯-ai̯anti*, but MMP *uzihēd* ⟨ʾwzyhyd⟩, *uzihēnd* ⟨ʾwzyhynd⟩. The verb *adih-* "to enter, to approach" (< **ati-i̯a-*, cf. OP *atiyaiš*) shows again in Manichaean Middle Persian an *h* between the stem and the endings: MMP *adihēd* ⟨ʾdyhyd⟩ <**ati-i̯-ai̯a-ti*. The same alternation is seen in other groups appearing at the end of the stem and even in some nouns:

ai̯	**čai̯a-*[6] "to mourn"	MMP *čey-* ⟨cy-⟩	Phl. *čeh-* ⟨cyh-⟩
	**u̯i-šaHi̯a-* "to untie"	Phl. *wišāy-*[7], NP *gušāy-*.	MMP *wišāhēd*[8] ⟨wyšʾhyd⟩; Parth. *wišāh-*
āi̯	**u̯i-kāi̯am* "witness"	MMP *gugāy* ⟨gwgʾy⟩, Psalter *hugāyīh* ⟨gwkʾdyhy⟩, Pāz. *guyāī*, Arm. (loan) *vkay-*	Phl. *gugāh* ⟨gwgʾs⟩[9], Parth. *wigāh* ⟨wygʾh⟩ , NP *guvāh*

3 The comparable **madi̯āna-* appears in Phl. as ⟨myyʾn⟩ or ⟨mdyʾn⟩ (with historical spelling) and in Manichaean Middle Persian as ⟨myʾn⟩. These forms may be read as *meyān* instead of *ma(y)yān*.

4 This is a thematization of the old zero degree of the plural forms.

5 The 3p.sg. *uzēd* could be derived from **uz-ai̯-a-ti*. However, the preservation of the old apophonic alternation is not very likely. MMP shows *uzihēd* <**uz-i̯-ai̯a-ti*. For the evolution **uziyēd* > *uzēd*, see below.

6 Kind indication by B. Peschl.

7 FīP21.7 records for the heterogram ŠLYTWN- the present forms *wšyt, wšym* for *wišēd* and *wišēm*, but, according to NYBERG (1974, p. 215), the codices U2, U4 show *wšʾyt, wšʾym*, probably for *wišāyēd, wišāyēm*. The latter is also confirmed by Pāzand, see ZWY4.57 *vāšāit̰* (ANTIA 1909, p. 344) for *wišāyēd /wišāʾēd*.

8 Beside a present stem *wiš-* see (GHILAIN 1939, p. 88; DURKIN-MEISTERERNST 2004, p. 359a; CHEUNG 2007, p. 136).

9 The Phl. form is usually read as *gugāy* and transliterated as ⟨gwkʾdy⟩. However, the final *-āy* is mostly spelt as ⟨ʾy⟩ or ⟨-ʾy̆⟩, but I do not know other cases of ⟨-ʾdy⟩.

īi̯	*_j́iH-i̯a-_ "to disappear, to be removed"[10]	[Phl. _zyān_ ⟨zyd'n'⟩ "harm"; MMP ⟨zy'n⟩]	MMP _zīh_- "to disappear, to be removed" ⟨zyh-⟩ (_zīhānd_ 3.p.sg. subj.)

The same evolution also takes place when the _i̯_ is not original, but goes back to Proto-Iranian _d_ or even to a _d_ resulting from an old primary palatal _j́_ in Southwestern Iranian:

d	_škad-i̯a-_ "to be broken"		MMP ških- ⟨škyh-⟩, Judeo-Persian škyh-, škh-
	sid-i̯a- "to be destroyed"	NP _gusel-_[11] < *_wi-siδ-_ < *_u̯i-sid-i̯a-_	Phl. _abesih-_ ⟨'p̄sh-⟩, ⟨'p̄sh⟩, MMP ⟨'bysyh-⟩
_d_ < _j́_	*_xu̯ādai̯a-_ < *x_u̯āj́ai̯a-_[12] "to want, desire"	_xwāyišn_ ⟨hw'dšn'⟩[13]	Phl. _xwāh-_[14], MMP _xwāh-_ ⟨xw'h-⟩, NP _ḫ^{v}āh-_

Such alternations never happen, however, when the stem goes back to $\vartheta > h$ (e.g. _gāh, padifrāh._ etc.).

At least in some positions, the _y_ of the stem would have been menaced by this disappearance. Thus, *_wišāi̯ati_ should have evolved to *_wišād_ (cf. OP _xšāyaϑiya-_ > _šāh_). The expected evolution of *_ati-i̯-ai̯ati_ would have been *_adiyēd_ > _adēd._ Thus, the present _wiš-_ "untie" goes back to *_wišiyēd_ < *_u̯i-šH-i̯a-_. Similarly, we find a form _nišēd_ ⟨nyšyt⟩ "he sits" (PV7.12) instead of the standard _nišiyēd_ (Cantera 2023). This is also the most likely explanation for the 3.p.sg. _uzēd_ ⟨'wzyt⟩ "he goes out" < *_uziyēd._

These evolutions were prevented at the end of the verbal stem through the preservation of the morphological boundaries, so the stem remains unchanged through the addition of the endings. The result was a hiatus between the stem and the ending, e.g. /_wišā'ēd_ (see Pāzand _vāšāit̰_) resolved through either a glide _y_ or a hiatus preventing consonant _h_. The distribution between the two does not follow a clear pattern. Apparently, both forms alternate quite freely and there were just lexical preferences that did not fall identically in all variants.

The same explanation applies to the passive suffix -_ĭh_-. Some archaic passive forms preserved in the Middle Persian Inscriptions give us some clues for the reconstruction and understanding of the history of this suffix. The forms in question are the following (Skjærvø 1997, p. 177):

10 See OP _vi-dīya-_ in _vidītu_ "let it not damage" (A^{2}Sa, A^{2}Ha), Bactr. οιζιιανο (1st.p.sg.subj.) < *_u̯i-jíHi̯āni_ (Fattori 2022, p. 386ff.).

11 It is used transitively ("to break off") like the present stem _wisinn-_. It functions as present stem of _gusestan_ and _guselidan_ (Steingass _et al._ 1930, p. 1089).

12 *_hu̯ādai̯a-_ < *_hu̯āj́ai̯a-_.

13 Mackenzie reads it _as xwāhišn._

14 In FīP21.14 the heterogram BOYHWN- is read as _hw'stn'_, _hw'hyt'_ and _hw'hym_ for _xwāstan, xwāhēd_ and _xwāhēm._

- *kylyt, klyty*: 3.p.sg. present of the verb *kar-* "to do", see also Psalter *klyty*; cf. Av. *kiriieiti*
- *ʾkylydy*[15]: 3.p.sg. imperfect of the same verb, cf. OP *akar̯iya*
- *gwgʾnyhy* "was destroyed": 3.p.sg. injunctive <**u̯i-kāni̯a(t)*, cf. OP *viyakanam*
- *ʾpzʾyhy* "was increased": 3.p.sg. injunctive <**abi-jāu̯ai̯am*, cf. OP *abijavayam*
- *wyšwpyhy* "was disturbed": 3.p.sg. imperfect <**u̯ii̯-a-xšau̯bi̯a(t)*

According to HUYSE (2003, p. 92), the difference between the two attested endings of the 3.p.sg. imperfect (⟨-ydy⟩ and ⟨-yhy⟩) is purely graphical and both represent -*ī*. However, the coincidence of the ending ⟨-yhy⟩ with the passive suffixe of Book Pahlavi makes this assumption unlikely. SKJÆRVØ links, indeed, this ending with the latter suffix. He explains the difference between the first three forms (without ⟨-yhy-⟩) and the last three (with ⟨-yhy⟩) postulating an original suffix -*iya-* that would behave differently after heavy and light syllables. The underlying assumption is that Old Iranian -*i̯a-* resulted in Proto-Middle Persian -*iya-* as it does in Old Persian, following HOFFMANN's idea (HOFFMANN 1976, pp. 636ff.). Like HOFFMANN, SKJÆRVØ also hypothesises that the group -*iya-* would have known a different treatment after a light or heavy syllable. After a light syllable it evolves into *ī*, e.g. *anī* "other"[16] < **anii̯a-*, but after heavy it disappears completely without a trace, e.g. *mard* "human" < **martii̯a*. Accordingly, the passive suffix -*iya-* would have appeared as *ī* after a light syllable as in *akarī(y)*. By contrast, in forms with -*yhy*, the suffix follows a heavy syllable. Thus, it should have disappeared, leading to forms identical to the indicative. Then he adds: "The passive function of these forms therefore needed to be clarified, and for reasons no longer clear to us the suffix -*yhy* was chosen." (SKJÆRVØ 1997, p. 178).

KORN's analysis of the treatment of -*i̯a-* in Middle Persian has shed new light on the problem of analysis of the forms of the verb *kar-* (KORN 2021). Firstly, the suffix -*i̯a-* does not evolve to -*iya-* in Middle Persian, as SKJÆRVØ supposed. Furthermore, and more importantly, **kəri̯a-* would not regularly evolve to *akirī*, but to *akīr*, exactly like *məri̯a-* appears as *mīr-* (KORN 2021, pp. 104f.). The same metathesis is also found in *mērag* < **mai̯raka-* < **mari̯aka*, cf. OP *marīka-*. This evolution is shown to be likely by the 3.p.sg. ⟨kylyt⟩ that should then be read as *kīrēd* (see already HÜBSCHMANN 1895, p. 131; HENNING 1933, pp. 205f.; SKJÆRVØ 1989, p. 339; HUYSE 2003, p. 91). The reading with *ī* is, however, unlikely for *ʾkylydy* and *klyty*. In the first case, *kīr-* would be justified if there is a metathesis, but there is not[17]. Accordingly, *y* likely represents the short vowel *i*. In the latter,

15 SKJÆRVØ writes in his paper systematically ⟨ʾklydy⟩, but the right spelling seems to be ⟨ʾkylydy⟩.

16 For a reading *any* see KORN (2021, p. 22, n. 59).

17 The alternative would be that there is hypercharacterisation of the passive stem *kīr-* < **kəri̯a-* with the passive suffix -*iia-* (HENNING 1958, p. 102, n. 2).

the absence of *y* prevents a reading *kīr*-. Both forms likely do not represent the regular evolution, but rather the form with a morphological boundary that has led to a hiatus, similar to the one assumed for *uziyēnd/uzihēnd*. Then, it develops a glide: **akərʾa* > *akiriya* with emphatical preservation of the ending -*a*. The present form ⟨klyty⟩ requires a similar explanation and would be a variant (and not simply a different spelling) of *kīrēd* ⟨kylyt⟩: **əriʾad* > *kiryad*. Accordingly, I assume that in the flexion of the stem **kəri̯a*- in Inscriptional Middle Persian two different groups of forms coexist: 1. forms of a stem *kīr*- with the regular metathesis of the *i̯* after *r*, with the present *kīrēd* being the only attested example; 2. forms in which the metathesis of *i̯* after *r* has been prevented through a morphological boundary that has led to a present stem *kiriy*- (*akiriya, kiriyad*) from which the form *kirihēd* attested isolated in Parthian is a further example.

The other three imperfect forms ending with -*yhy* have to be explained exactly like *akạriya*, but the consonant preventing the hiatus is now *h* instead of *y*, exactly as it happens in the suffix -*ĭh*- in Pahlavi and Manichaean Middle Persian. Thus, ⟨gwgʾnyhy⟩ derives from **gugāniʾa*, again with emphatical preservation of the ending and must be read as *gugāniha*. Against Henning (1933, p. 206), MMP ⟨qyryh-⟩ is not secondarily hypercharacterised with the passive suffix -*ĭh*-, but rather continues exactly the same form as IMP ⟨klyty⟩. The only difference is that we see the hiatus preventing *h* instead of the glide *y*, and that the endings attached are now the set of -*ē*-endings, as is regular in Manichaean Middle Persian. This is the evolution that has been generalized in Pahlavi and Manichaean Middle Persian and has led to the creation of the productive suffix -*ĭh*- in these two variants of Middle Persian, whereas the Psalter regularly shows the form with the glide -*ĭy*.

The derivation from the Old Iranian suffix -*i̯a*- with morphological boundary and a following glide or hiatus preventing consonant *h* implies reading the suffix as -*ih*- and not as -*īh*-. The latter is the current reading with very rare exceptions (Henning 1933, pp. 210, 222; Korn 2021, p. 22, n. 59). However, some indications point to a reading -*ih*-. It was noticed early on that Pāzand -*ih*- and the alternation in Judeo-Persian between the spellings -*yh*- and -*h*- invite a reading as -*ih*- (Bartholomae 1906, pp. 71f; Henning 1933, p. 210; Korn 2021, p. 21, n. 55). The Pāzand is, indeed, irrelevant, since Pāzand does not distinguish the quantity of *ī/i* as happens with these letters in the Avestan manuscripts. More significant is the evidence from Judeo-Persian, since Paul's explanation of the form as a shortening of -*īh*- is purely *ad hoc* (Paul 2013, p. 136, §171). The Parthian translation of IMP *kiryad* ⟨klyty⟩ in ŠKZ 35 is ⟨krḥyd⟩ *kirihēd*,[18] thus confirming the suffix as -*ih*-. In Pahlavi, we also find occasional spellings of the passive suffix without *y*: *ayābihē* (3.p.sg.opt.) ⟨ʾyʾp̄hyḏ⟩ (NM I.4.4; kind indication from I. Colditz).

18 See Huyse (1999, p. 48, §35).

Summing up, the old passive (and denominative) suffix *-i̯a-* was preserved in the inherited stems because the morphological boundary prevented the expected evolutions. The resulting hiatus between suffix and ending lead to the introduction of a glide *y* or a consonant *h* for preventing the hiatus, a phenomenon well known from other forms. The resulting *-ih-* (or *-iy-*) was then analysed as a passive marker that can be attached to any present stem. Most varieties of Middle Persian generalized the suffix *-ih-*, but the Psalter preserves the variant *-iy-*.

Bibliography

ANDREAS, F.C. 1933: *Bruchstücke Einer Pehlevi-Übersetzung Der Psalmen*. Berlin.

ANDREAS, F.C./K. Barr 1933: *Bruchstückte Einer Pehlevi-Übersetzung Der Psalmen Aus Dem Nachlass Nerausgegeben von Kaj Barr*. Phil.-Hist.Klasse. Berlin.

ANTIA, E.K. 1909: *Pâzend texts*. Bombay.

BARTHOLOMAE, CH. 1906: *Zum Altiranischen Wörterbuch. Nacharbeiten Und Vorarbeiten*. Beihefte Indorgermanische Forschungen. Strassburg.

— 1915: "Mitteliranische Studien V. Die mit *st* gebildeten Präterita der mittel- und neuiranischen Dialekte. Ein Versuch zur Lösung des Problems." In: *Wiener Zeitschrift für die Kunde des Morgenlandes* 29, pp. 1–47.

CANTERA, A. 2023: "The Interpretatio Iranica of the Heterograms in Book Pahlavi: The Case of YTYBWN- 'to Sit down, to Dwell and to Set' and Some Related Problems." In: *Estudios Iranios y Turanios* 5, pp. 7–22.

CHEUNG, J. 2007: *Etymological Dictionary of the Iranian Verb*. Leiden/Boston (Leiden Indo-European Etymological Dictionary Series 2).

DURKIN-MEISTERERNST, D. 2004: *Dictionary of Manichean Middle Persian and Parthian (Dictionary of Manichaean Texts.* Vol. III *Texts from Central Asia and China*, Part 1*)*. Turnhout.

FATTORI, M. 2022: "The Elamite Version of A2Ha and the Verb *Vidiyā-* in Old Persian." In: *Iran and the Caucasus* 26 (4), p. 376.

GHILAIN, A. 1939: *Essai Sur La Langue Parthe Son Système Verbal d'après Les Textes Manichéens Du Turkestan Oriental*. Louvain.

HENNING, W.B. 1933: "Das Verbum Des Mittelpersischen Der Turfanfragemente." In: *Zeitschrift Für Indologie Und Iranistik* 9, pp. 158–253.

— 1958: "Mitteliranisch." In: *Handbuch Der Orientalistik* IV. *Iranistik. Linguistik*, pp. 20–130.

HOFFMANN, K. 1976: 'Zur Altpersischen Schrift'. In: *Aufsätze Zur Indoiranistik* 2, pp. 620–645.

HÜBSCHMANN, H. 1895: *Persische Studien*. Straßburg.

HUYSE, PH. 1999: *Die dreisprachige Inschrift Šābuhrs I. an der Kaʿba-i Zardušt (ŠKZ)*. 2 vols. *Corpus Inscriptionum Iranicarum*. Pt. 3: *Pahlavi inscriptions*. Vol. 1: *Royal inscriptions, with their Parthian and Greek versions, texts* I. London.

— 2003: *Le y Final Dans Les Inscriptions Moyen-Perses et La Loi Rythmique Proto-Moyen-Perse*. Paris (Studia Iranica. Cahier, 29).

KORN, A. 2021: "Contributions to a Relative Chronology of Persian. The Non-Change of Postconsonantal *y* and *w* in Middle Persian in Context." In: *Indo-European*

Linguistics 9, pp. 85–127. Available online: https://doi.org/10.1163/22125892-bja10009.
NYBERG, H.S. 1974: *A Manual of Pahlavi*. Part II: *Glossary*. Wiesbaden.
PAUL, L. 2013: *A Grammar of Early Judeo-Persian*. Wiesbaden.
SKJÆRVØ, P.O. 1989: "Verbal Ideograms and the Imperfect in Middle Persian and Parthian." In: *Études Irano-Aryennes Offertes à Gilbert Lazard* (Studia Iranica Cahier 7), pp. 333–354.
— 1997: "On the Middle Persian Imperfect." In: *Syntaxe Des Langues Indo-Iraniennes Anciennes. Colloque International, Sitges (Barcelona), 4–5 Mai 1993*. Ed. by ÉRIC PIRART. Barcelona (Aula Orientalis, Supplementa 6), pp. 161–188.
STEINGASS, F.J./J. RICHARDSON/CH. WILKINS/F. JOHNSON 1930: *A Comprehensive Persian-English Dictionary, Including the Arabic Words and Phrases to Be Met with in Persian Literature*. London.
SUNDERMANN, W. 1989: "Mittelpersisch." In: *Compendium Linguarum Iranicarum*. Ed. by RÜDIGER SCHMITT, pp. 138–164.

From the *Zamyād Yašt* to the Seventh Book of the *Dēnkard*: Some Notes on Sistan and Zoroastrian Eschatology

CARLO G. CERETI, Rome

Sistan holds a very special place in Iranian religious history and in the national history of Iran. In this paper, dedicated to DIETER WEBER, a friend and colleague whom I know since the years I spent in Göttingen and whose work I have always read and appreciated, I shall try to outline the genesis of the Zoroastrian eschatological narrative in Sistan, which determined the birth of a very specific *geographia sacra* in the region, a landscape centering on the Hamun lake, Kuh-i Khwaja and the Karkuy fire. Some of the elements belonging to this narrative are attested already in the Younger Avesta but it only reached its present shape in the Pahlavi tradition. The eschatological narrative is closely connected to Zoroaster's legend and must be kept separate from the more specifically apocalyptic storyline that will only develop in late Sasanian and early Islamic times. Moreover, to better understand the interplay between the Iranian doctrine about the eschaton and other religious traditions dealing with the end time it is important to build a relative chronology of existing Zoroastrian narrations about the last days.

In an important article dedicated to politics and royalty in Sasanian times, GHERARDO GNOLI (1971, p. 231) underlines that the Zoroastrian clergy made a deliberate effort to adapt ancient traditions to the needs of the monarchy and contemporary society. In my opinion, the developments correctly identified by GNOLI did not take place only in the west of the Empire, as he himself seems to believe (1971, p. 232f.), but also in areas such as Sistan that was the home of a version of Zoroaster's hagiography connected to national history. In fact, I agree with MATTHEW CANEPA (2013; 2018, pp. 272, 281) who has shown that the sanctuary of Kuh-i Khwaja represents one of the earliest attempts of the Sasanian dynasty to integrate eastern Iranian traditions into a shared Iranian national history that culminated in the reign of the Sasanian kings themselves.

What is peculiar about our knowledge of pre-Islamic Sistan is that archeological data integrate well with what we learn from Zoroastrian texts, as already noted by GNOLI in his *Ricerche storiche sul Sīstān antico* (1967). Moreover, the *Zamyād Yašt* and the *Dēnkard* attest two stages in the evolution of the same narrative theme, the Middle Persian one being the product of Sasanian priestly circles. Kuh-i Khwaja was not the sole Sasanian shrine that laid a claim to being Zoroaster's homeland, since similar assertions were done by major temples in other regions, such as Khorasan and Azerbaijan (Terribili 2020 and 2021). The Sistanian narrative of Late Antique times, however, focused on events that took place on the shores of the Hamun, namely, the birth of Zoroaster's future sons. This specific belief is not attested as such in the Avesta but derives from the exegesis of the *Zamyād Yašt.*

Zoroaster's legendary biography reached its full maturity under the Sasanian kings, and we have reason to believe that the narration attested by the seventh book of the *Dēnkard* achieved its present form towards the end of the Sasanian period. In its established form the events associated with Zoroaster's life are repeated in the millennia of his future sons, giving birth to a threefold eschatological narration. This whole process builds on an earlier narration of mythical Iranian national history that is found in its most complete version in the Avestan *Zamyād Yašt*, having at its center Fraŋrasiian's quest for the *x*^{v}*arənah.* In his edition of the Pahlavi texts containing different versions of Zoroaster's hagiography, Marijan Molé (1967, pp. 230–233) rightly underlines the parallel between the final *karde*s of the *Zamyād Yašt* and chapter 11 of the seventh book of the *Dēnkard*, showing that the latter derives from *Yašt* 19. Reading Yt 19, 91–96 and Dk 7.11 in parallel, the similarities between the two texts are immediately apparent. Moreover, the Middle Persian texts also contain information, names and words, that derive from *karde* 13 of the *Zamyād Yašt*. However, the narrative form and setting of the Middle Persian text differs deeply from what is attested in Young Avestan and must derive from the Zand, possibly rearranging it for the author's purpose.

The geographical horizon of both texts is that of Sistan, and more specifically the Hamun lake and Kuh-i Khwaja, where the rulers and clergy of Sasanian and perhaps already Arsacid times built an impressive religious complex. The "Mountain of the Lord" must have attracted pilgrims not only from Drangiana itself, but also from areas as far apart as Arachosia, Gandhara, Areia and Carmania (Boyce/Grenet 1991, p. 150f.), probably already being a pilgrimage spot before Sistan became Zoroastrian. Remarkably, the *Opus imperfectum in Matthaeum*, a commentary on Matthew likely dating to the 5th century and a few later Syriac works such as the *Chronicle of Zuqnin* preserve the memory of Mons Victorialis and of a Zoroastrian tradition according to which the Magi waited there for a future savior from Zoroaster's lineage that some may have identified with the Messiah himself (Monneret de Villard 1952, Boyce/Grenet 1991, pp. 447–453). The possible identification of Mons Victorialis with Avestan mount Usaδā Ušidarəna and of the latter with modern Kuh-i Khwaja (Kuhn 1893, p. 218) speaks in favour of the prestige of the sacred geography centering on the Hamun basin in late Sasanian times but cannot throw much light on earlier periods.

Looking at the texts themselves, the parallels between the *Zamyād Yašt* and the *Dēnkard* are clear. Moreover, the prose of the Pahlavi text shows that it is based on the Zand, since some sentences and words can only be understood by assuming an Avestan original:

Yt 19, 91–96 — Karde 15

91) Uγrəm kauuaēm x^{v}arənō – mazdaδātəm yazamaide – aš.vaṇdrəm uparō.kairīm – ϑamnaŋ^{v}haṇtəm varəcaŋ^{v}haṇtəm yaoxštiuuaṇtəm – taraδātəm aṅiiāiš dāmąn
92) yat̰ astuuat̰.ərətō fraxštāite – haca apat̰ kąsaoiiāt̰ – aštō mazdå ahurahe – ^{x}vīspa.tauruuariiå puϑrō – vaēδəm vaējō yim vārəϑraγnəm – yim barat̰ taxmō ϑraētaonō – yat̰ ažiš dahākō jaini
93) yim barat̰ fraŋrase turō – yat̰ druuå zainigauš jaini – yim barat̰ kauua haosrauua – yat̰ turō jaini fraŋrase – yim barat̰ kauua vīštāspō – aṣ̌ahe ^{x}haēnå $^{+}$jaēšəmnō – ^{x}tā auuaδa drujəm nižbarāt̰ – aṣ̌ahe haca gaēϑābiiō
94) hō diδāt̰ xratāuš $^{+}$dōiϑrābiia – vīspa dāmąn paiti vaēnāt̰ – $^{+}$pasca ^{x}išō dušciϑraiiå – hō vīspəm ahum astuuaṇtəm – ižaiiå vaēnāt̰ dōiϑrābiia – ^{x}darəšca daϑat̰ ^{x}amarəxšiiaṇtīm – vīspąm yąm astuuaitīm gaēϑąm
95) aŋhe haxaiiō ^{x}frāiieiṇti – astuuat̰.ərətahe vərəϑraγnō – humanaŋhō huuacaŋhō – huš́iiaoϑnåŋhō huδaēna – naēδa.cit̰ ^{x}miϑō.vaox^{v}åŋhō – aēšąm x^{v}aēpaiϑiia hizuuō – aēšu parō frānāmaite – aēšmō ^{x}xruii.druš dušx^{v}arənå – vanāt̰ aṣ̌a akąm drujim – yąm dušciϑrąm təmaŋhaēnīm
96) ^{x}vanaite akəmcit̰ manō – vohu manō tat̰ vanaiti – ^{x}vanaite miϑaoxtō ^{x}vāxš – ərəžuxδō vāxš təm vanaiti – vanāt̰ hauruuåsca amərətåsca-uua šuδəmca taršnəmca – vanāt̰ hauruuåsca amərətåsca – aγəm šuδəmca taršnəmca – ^{x}frānāmāite dužuuarštāuuarš – aŋrō maṅiiuš ^{x}axšaiiamnō …

Dēnkard 7, ch. 11

1) [524, 15] abar abdīh ī pas az hazangrōzem ī ūšēdarmāhān sar ud <pēš az>rasišn ī sūdōmand pērōzgar tā panǰāh ud haft sāl $^{+}$ī sōšāns sar ud Frašgird dahišnīh ī andar axwān
2) abar abdīh ī sōšāns pad tan warz ud xwarrah rāy gōwēd kū ka az awēšān āwām wardišnīh ī ūšēdarmāhān ān ī abdom wardišn rasišn ān mard ul zāyēd sōšāns ī mēnōg-xwarišn <ud> xwaršēd-karb {kū-š tan ēdōn rōšn čiyōn xwaršēd} ēn-iz kū **_ān nigerēd pad šeš dōisrīh az harwisp nēmag abar wēnēd ān ī druz bēš čārag ∴_**
3) ēn-iz kū-š abāg bawēd kayān xwarrah ī pērōzgar kē-š $^{+}$burd tagīg frēdōn ka-š azi-dahāg $^{+}$zad u-š burd kay-husraw ka-š tūr $^{+}$zad frangrāsiyāg u-š burd frangrāsiyāg ka-š $^{+}$druwand *zayinīgāg zad <u-š> burd kay-wištāsp ka ō ahlāyīh *hēn bē *hāxtēd pad ān druz bē burd az ēn ī ahlāyīh gēhān ∴
4) ud ēn-iz kū andar panǰāh ud haft sāl <ī> ōy bawēd abēsīhišn ī dō-zang-tōhmag ud abārīg drūzīh ud ānābišn ī wēmārīh ud zarmānīh <ud> margīh ud bēš ud hammis anāgīh ud sāstārīh ud ahlamōyīh ud wattarīh <ī> bawēd hamēšag urwar zargōn-waxšišn ud *hamāg dahišn urwāhman[īh] bawēnd haftdah sāl urwar-xwarišn <ud> sīh sāl āb-xwarišn <ud> dah sāl mēnōg-xwarišn ∴
5) ud hamāg warz ud xwarrah ud ōz ī abar har warzāwandān <ud> xwarrōmandān <ud> ōzōmandān būd pad ōy [ī] abar ō ham rasēd ud ō ān ī ōy ka-š was kay <ud> wīr ī warzāwand <ud> ōzōmand hangēzīhistēnd pad ān ī awēšān ōz ud xwarrah hamāg druz [ud] gurd[īh] wānīhēd 6) ud wisp mardōm abar ēk

*hamīh [ī] pad ān ī ohrmazd dēn ēstēnd az dādār kām ud framān [ō] u-š hambāgān <ud> abzār[īh] 7) pad frazām ī panǰāh ud haft sāl druz ī ahreman *abesīhēd frašgird ud tan ī pasēn bawēd hamāg [ī] weh dahišn pad abēzagīh ud +purr-šēdāyīh +winnārīhēnd 8) čiyōn dēn gōwēd kū ka ān hazangrōzem bē sazēd ī sidīgar pad dēn ī mazdēsnān* ***ēg ān mazdēsn frāz rawēd az āb ī kānmāsāy kē ast [ud] pērōzgar nām abāg hazār hamxāk *be *rawēd *ud *ahlomoγ *ī *anahlaw <ud> mardōm <ī> druwand ī sāstār +zanēd. u-šān abesīhēnēd*** *9) ēg awēšān mazdēsn zanēnd u-šān nē zadār hēnd 10) ēg awēšān mazdēsn frašgird andar axwān <pad> kāmag dahēnd hamē zīndag ud hamē sūd ud hamē [ud] kāmag-xwadāy (10) ēg man kē ohrmazd hom frašgird pad kāmag andar axwān daham hamē zīndag ud hamē sūd ud <hamē> kāmag-xwadāy*

91) We worship the mighty x^{v}*arənah* of the Kavi, created by Mazdā, the highly praised, supreme worker, determined, energetic, skillful, overcoming the other creatures. 92) **When Astuuat̰.ərəta steps forth from lake Kąsaoiia, the messenger of Ahura Mazdā, the son of Vīspa. tauruuairī, brandishing the victorious weapon that brave Θraētaona bore when Āžī Dahāka was slain** 93) **which Fraŋrasiian Tura bore when deceitful Zainigau was slain, which Kauui Haosrauuah bore when Fraŋrasiian Tura was slain, which Kauui Vīštāspa bore when he was to defeat the armies of the enemies of truth. There, by means of this, he will drive out Falsehood from the world of Truth.** 94) **He will gaze with eyes of insight . He will look at all creatures belonging to the one of evil origin, then attack. At all corporeal life he will gaze with eyes**

1)About the marvels that <will take place> after the end of Ušēdarmāh's millennium and before the coming of Sūdōmand Pērōzgar until the end of Sōšān's fifty-seven years and the accomplishment of the Renovation among beings 2) About the mirabilia of Sōšāns in the body, in power, and in the *xwarrah* it says: when the last revolution of the days of Ušēdārmāh will come, that man will be born, Sōšāns, eating (only) *mēnōg* and having a body similar to the sun, {i.e. his body was as luminous as the sun}. **This also, he observes through (his) six eyes, he sees in all directions, he (will be) a remedy against the hostility of the demons.** 3) **This also, the victorious xwarrah of the Kays will be with him, (the xwarrah) that bore mighty Frēdōn when he smote Azi-Dahāg, that Frangrāsiyāg bore when he smote evil *Zayinīgāg, that Kay**

that render strength, and his gaze will render the whole corporeal world indestructible. 95) Advancing are the companions of Victorious Astuuaṯ.ərəta, whose thought are good, whose words are good, whose deeds are good, whose faith is good, having never spoken in Falsehood because of control over their own tongues. And before them will flee Aēšma (Rage) whose attack is cruel, luckless. He will overcome by Truth the wicked Falsehood of evil origin, which consists of darkness. 96) Evil Thought is overcome, Good Thought overcomes it. The falsely spoken Word is overcome, the rightly spoken Word overcomes it. Wholeness and Immortality will overcome both Hunger and Thirst. Wholeness and Immortality will overcome evil Hunger and Thirst. The worker of evil deeds, the Evil Spirit will retreat, powerless. (Text and translation follow HINTZE 1994b, p. 39f., with minor variants, for §95 *miϑō vaox^{v}ą̊ŋhō* see HUMBACH/ICHAPORIA 1990, p. 169, who follow SKJÆRVØ 1997)

Wištāsp bore when he led the army to Righteousness; with that he will chase away the demons from the world of righteousness. 3) And this also, in his fifty-seven years the destruction of the stock of the two-legged (wolves) and of the other demons (will take place) and warding off sickness, old age, death, pain and all harm, tyranny, heresy, and evil that will exist. Plants will always grow green; all creatures will be joyous. For seventeen years they will eat (only) vegetables, (then) for thirty years they will drink (only) water, and (finally) for ten years they will eat (only) the spirit. And all the power and *xwarrah* and strength of all those who were powerful, blessed by the *xwarrah* and strong, will merge in him and with the one that belongs to him. When enough Kay and powerful and strong men will have been awakened by him, the heroes, by their strength and *xwarrah*, will destroy all the demons. All men will be united in the Religion of Ohrmazd, by the Creator's will and command (they will be) his companions and instrument. 7) At the end of the fifty-seven years Ahriman's demons will be destroyed, Renovation and the Future Body will take place, all good creatures will *prosper in purity and fullness of bliss. 8) **Since in the religion it says: when the third millennium of the Mazdean religion will pass, the Mazdean one, who is called Victorious (one) will go forth from the *Kayānsē water. Together with one thousand companions he will go (forth) and will smite the unrighteous heretic and the sinful tyrannical men and will destroy them.** 9) And the Mazdeans will smite and not be smitten, 10) then those Mazdeans will accomplish the Renovation among beings according to wish, forever living, forever gaining, forever ruling by will.

11) Then I who am Ohrmazd will accomplish Renovation among beings, forever living, forever gaining, (forever) ruling by will.
(Cf. Cereti 1995a, pp. 69–71 and Molé 1967, pp. 102–105)

Yt 19.89 — Dk 7.11.2: Middle Persian *sūdōmand pērōzgar* corresponds to Av. *vərəϑrajan-saošiiaṇt-*, showing that for the author of the *Dēnkard* and possibly already for the Zandist, the protagonists of Kardes 14 and 15 of the *Zamyād Yašt* had been identified one with the other.

Yt 19.92a–d and Yt 19.a–c — Dk 7.11.7–8: Here the Avestan and Middle Persian texts correspond very loosely one to the other. Molé's (1967, p. 232) attempt to reconstruct a precise Avestan original is unconvincing.

Yt 19.92–93 — Dk 7.11.3: The *Dēnkard* presents a correct translation of the Avestan passage, with an inversion between Kay Husraw and Frangrāsiyāg (Molé 1967, p. 231). More interesting is the interpretation of the Avestan sentence *vaēδəm vaējō yim vārəϑraγnəm . yim barat̰ …* "brandishing the victorious weapon, which … bore …" that the author of the *Dēnkard* understood as a reference to the *xwarrah*: *ēn-iz kū-š abāg bawēd kayān xwarrah ī pērōzgar kē-š burd* "and this also that with him was the victorious *xwarrah* of the Kayanids, that … bore …", an interpretation that presupposes knowledge of the subject matter of *Yašt* 19 and more specifically of the introductory paragraph found *i. a.* in Yt 19.91.

Yt 19.94 — Dk 7.11.2: According to Molé (1967, p. 231), the original Avestan text should have been: ***hō dīδāt̰ xšuuaš-dōiϑrābiiō vispaēbiiō naēmaeibiiō pairi.vaēnat̰ aŋhe drujō-tbaēšaŋhō čarəm*. However, considering that MSS F1 and L18 read *x(…)š* with 14 and 7 mm. space between the two letters, while H3 and R115 read *xš* without any space between the letters, for the *xratəuš* of the edited text, and moreover that MS Pt1 reads outrightly *xšaš* (Hintze 1994a, p. 381) there is no need to suppose a different source for the Avestan *Zand* that stands behind our passage, rather it seems that a reading **xšuuaš* "six" must have crept rather early in the manuscript tradition, since it has influenced the text found in the *Dēnkard*.

Dk. 7.11.10: Molé (1967, p. 232f.) suggests a parallel with a passage similar in content to Yt 19.89 but shorter: *yat̰ upaŋhacat̰ saošiiaṇtąm – vərəϑrājanəm – uta aṅiiåscit̰ haxaiiō – yat̰ kərənauuat̰ frašəm ahum – ⁺azarəsəṇtəm ˣamarəšaṇtēm – afriϑiiaṇtəm apuiiaṇtəm – yauuaējīm yauuaēsūm – vasō.xšaϑrəm – yat̰ irista paiti ˣusəhištąn – jasāt̰ juaaiiō amərəxtiš – daϑaite frašəm vasna aŋhuš* "Which will accompany the Victorious one among the Saviours and also his other comanions, so that he will make life excellent, ageless, without decay, not rotting, not putrefying, living forever, thriving forever, ruling as it wishes. When the dead will rise (then) will come the one without decay revving (the dead and) life will create excellent things according to its own wish" (Hintze 1994b, p. 38). Probably, however, the shortening took place either in the Zand or else in the *Dēnkard* itself, and there is no need to imagine a different source for the Middle Persian passage.

The Pahlavi text ultimately derives from the Avestan one, but the context is completely different. While the *Zamyād Yašt* relates the deeds of ancient civilization heroes and kings, being so-to-say at the root of later Iranian epics, *Dēnkard* 7 is a hagiographic text, belonging to the religious tradition. Context and unfolding of the two narrations are far apart, the older one depicting the deeds of heroes and foes competing to conquer the *x^varənah*, the younger one narrating Zoroaster's legend inscribed in the 12,000 years of Limited Time. The founder of the Good Religion was born 3000 years after Gayōmard and 3000 years before Sōšāns, central to human history in the *gētīg* world.

The *Zamyād Yašt*[1] can be divided in two very dissimilar parts, one consisting of a list of mountains (Yt 19.1–8) the other (Yt 19.9–97) describing the deeds of divinities, heroes, foes, and kings that were either accompanied by the *x^{v}arənah* or strove to conquer it. As a matter of fact, the latter part presents a mythical history of humanity, that contains *in nuce* some of the epic themes that will be fully developed in much later literary texts, the most famous being Firdausi's *Šāhnāma* (Pirart 1992, p. 9). Considering the importance that cliffs and mountains have always had in Zoroastrian religious imagery, it comes as no surprise that the two parts were eventually joined in one only hymn. *Yašt* 19 is one of the great hymns of Zoroastrian tradition, belonging to the more ancient layer of young Avestan texts. According to Almut Hintze (1994a, p. 43) it should be dated around the 6th century BCE, being therefore slightly younger than the oldest Young Avestan texts. Hintze's opinion is to some extent shared by another editor of this text, Eric Pirart (1992, p. 9), who also considers it to be a relatively late text, though his wary suggestion to assign it to the Sasanian period seems to be too farfetched,[2] though the Zoroastrian clergy of Sasanian times used it to bolster the prestige of Sistan's sacred landscape. Hintze correctly recognized that the main part of the *Zamyād Yašt* is a ring composition having at its center two episodes, each one narrating a contest to conquer the *ax^{v}arətəm x^{v}arēnah*, embedded in the longer narration of the deeds of those who carried the *kauaēm x^{v}arənah*, the Glory of the Kavi.[3] The second episode relates the efforts of the civilization hero Fraŋrasiian (Yt 19.55–64) to obtain his prize. Here Fraŋrasiian (MP Frāsyāg, NP Afrāsyāb) is described as being a *tuiriia-* "Turanian" though in the early stages of Iranian history the *tuiriia-* were part of the

1 Recent editions of this texts are Pirart 1992, Hintze 1994a and 1994b and Humbach/Ichaporia 1998.

2 Two other editors of the text, Helmut Humbach and Pallan Ichaporia, are less straightforward on the subject, stating: "the connection found in Yasht 19 between the mountains of the Geographical Fragment (§§1–8) and the Kavyan Glory of the Kayān Yasn (§§9–96), appear to be relatively old but, looking at the matter from a different point of view, the two pieces give the impression of having been joined together at a relatively recent time" (Humbach/Ichaporia 1998, p. 12).

3 "Der Aufbau des Hauptteils des Zamyād-Yašt ist eine Ringkomposition: im Zentrum steht der Preis des *ax^{v}arətəm x^{v}arənō*, eingerahmt von dem des *kauuaēm x^{v}arənō*. Auch die Beschreibung von *Frašō.kərəti* steht am Anfang und am Ende des Hymnus, wobei dieses Ereignis am Ende ausführlicher dargestellt wird" (Hintze 1994a, p. 14f.).

airiia- people or at least closely related to them. Three times does Fraŋrasiian dive into the *Vouru.kaṣ̌a* in search of the *x*^{v}*arēnah* and each time a new gulf is created (Yt 19.55–64)[4] by his deed, in a pattern specular to Yima's triple enlargement of the earth. Kardes 7 and 8, respectively dedicated to the contest between the Good and the Evil Spirit for the *x*^{v}*arənah*, and to Fraŋrasiian's quest for the *ax*^{v}*arətəm x*^{v}*arēnah* are immediately followed by a detailed description of the endorheic basin of the *Haētumaṇt* river feeding the *Kąsaoiia* lake and of the nine rivers (Karde 9, Yt 19.65–69) that form the Hamun basin in Sistan.

HINTZE (1994a, p. 38f.) rightly emphasizes that the most ancient nucleus of the *Zamyād Yašt* is to be found in the three central Kardes of the hymn that praise the *ax*^{v}*arətəm x*^{v}*arēnah*. Interestingly, Karde 9 mentions the *ax*^{v}*arətəm x*^{v}*arēnah*, in Yt 19,65a, and the *kauuēm x*^{v}*arēnah*, in Yt.19.68d. In fact, one may envisage the possibility that Karde 9 was composed by an early diaskeuast, who identified the *Vouru.kaṣ̌a* with lake *Kąsaoiia* in Sistan.[5] Looking at things from a formal point of view, one should also underline that in Karde 8 the metric is less regular than in other parts of the Yašts, such as Yt 19.92–96 dealing with the final days, where the octosyllabic verse prevails.[6] Moreover, according to Pahlavi texts (MX 8.27–30) Fraŋrasiian was originally immortal and therefore may play a role in the Final Battle (ZWY 7.32), this notion, likely old, may have influenced the narration of the *Zamyād Yašt* setting a narrative nucleus, possibly of non-Zoroastrian origin, dedicated to this hero in the wider framework of world history, culminating in Zoroaster's revelation and future salvation. Furthermore, it is a well-known fact that Fraŋrasiian's activity is closely connected with waters, and he is shown to be the cause of drought and the consequent famine. Considering Afrāsyāb's character in later Persian epics, where he is depicted as a formidable foe, wicked but at the same time mighty and proud (YARSHATER 1982), one wonders whether the Zoroastrian clergy of Sistan did not deliberately substitute the older cult with a ritual cycle centering on Zoroaster's life and

4 The narrative theme was already known in one of the most important and ancient Avestan hymns, the *Ābān Yašt*. According to Yt 5.41–44 Fraŋrasiian offers sacrifice to Ardvī Sūrā Anāhitā asking her to help him in his quest for the *x*^{v}*arēnah* found in the *Vouru.kaṣ̌a* sea.

5 HINTZE (1994a, p. 41) considers the Sistanic context to be strictly Mazdaic: "Die Verschiedenheit der Gewässer, mit denen das *x*^{v}*arənah-* in Verbindung gebracht wird, erklärt sich möglicherweise dadurch, daß es bei dem *x*^{v}*arənah-* im See Vourukaṣ̌a um das *ax*^{v}*arətəm xvarənō* handelt, bei demjenigen im Kąsaoiia-See und dem Haētumaṇt-Gebiet dagegen um das *kauuaēm xvarənō*. Im Unterschied zu dem See Vourukaṣ̌a, der auch in anderen Yašts und in mythologischen Kontexten eine Rolle spielt, wird der See Kąsaoiia im Avesta nur in der geographischen Beschreibung von Yašt 19,66–67 sowie in Yt 19,92 und Vd 19,5 genannt. Im Vergleich zu den Textstellen, die von den See Vourukaṣ̌a nennen, steht der See Kąsaoiia im Licht geographischer Identität und zugleich in stark religiös-mazdayasnisch geprägtem Kontext".

6 On metrics in the *Zamyād Yašt* see HINTZE 1994a, p. 52f., with reference to LAZARD 1990.

the deeds of his future son, identified with the Victorious Savior. In its turn, this idea brings one back to JOSEPH MARQUART's pioneering intuition about the role played by the god Zūn/Zūr (MARQUART/DE GROOT 1915) in Zabul, now outdated in many of its elements but revitalized by GIANROBERTO SCARCIA in a number of sharp articles on the religion of Zabul (SCARCIA 1965, 1966, 1967, 1973, 2002, 2010 and, with plenty bibliographical information, COMPARETI/ SCARCIA 2013), showing the existence of two rival divinities in the Sistan area, one of whom certainly identifiable with Aži-Dahāka, who also plays a role in the *Zamyād Yašt*, the other possibly to be seen in the god Zūn/Zūr, possibly related to the Sistanic hero Zāl. In the given context, one may wonder whether Fraŋrasiian and Astvaṯ.ərəta do not represent here the "zoroastrianized" version of the older pair, established once the new religion had gained the upper hand, taking hold of the sanctuaries of the Hilmand basin. Moreover, SCARCIA (1971; 2013, p. 227) has shown that still in Islamic times the memory of a competition between rival cults survived in Sistan, though in Islamicate garb.

In the *Zamyād Yašt* the Victorious Saošiiaṇt appears in the final part of the Yašt,[7] where the events that are foretold to happen at the end of times are narrated in some detail. After the central Kardes dedicated to Fraŋrasiian (Karde 8) and to the Haētumaṇt's fluvial basin (Karde 9),[8] the narration resumes telling the mythical history of the Kavi dynasty, first listing seven princes, from Aipi. vohu to Siiāuuaršan (Karde 10), then describing in some detail Kauui Haosrauuah's deeds, the hero who slew Fraŋrasiian and defeated Kərəsauuazdah in the famous chariot race (Karde 11).

Karde 12 sings Zoroaster's deeds, the best of all material beings, who thinks, speaks, and acts in accordance with the religion and is accompanied by the *kauuaēm xvarənō* (Yt 19.78a). He destroys the demons, who previously walked about free in the world, by reciting one *Ahuna Vairiia*. Fraŋrasiian storms through the seven continents seeking Zoroaster's *x^{v}arənah (xvarənō zaraϑuštrāi)*[9] but cannot conquer it. Karde 13 speaks about Kauui Vīštāspa, who thinks, speaks, and acts according to the Good Religion, and is accompanied by the *x^{v}arənah* of the Kauuis. This veritable paladin stands up for the Religion, fights and triumphs over Tąϑriiāuuaṇt, Pəṣ̌ana, Arəjaṯ.aspa and the other evil X́iiaona. These two Kardes tell two aspects of the same story: Zarathustra promoting the Good Religion through ritual acts, Kauui Vīštāspa defending it in the war against Arə-

7 On the parallel with Yt 19.86, HUMBACH and ICHAPORIA (1998, p. 141f.) restore the name of the Victorious Saviour *(Saošiiaṇt Vərətrajan)* at the beginning of the short geographical passage describing the Haētumaṇt basin in Karde 9, Yt 19.66. However, I share HINTZE's (1994, p. 307) opinion that here the *x^{v}arənah* accompanies the river Haetumaṇt, rather than the future savior.

8 Where the focus is on the life-giving and glorious river itself.

9 On the use of the dative instead of the genitive, see HINTZE 1994a, pp. 347 and 317f.

jaṯ.aspa. Remarkably, this brief description of Zoroaster's life includes episodes that were later fully developed in the religious tradition, while not being wholly unknown to Firdousi, such as the part where Zarathustra destroys the demons' corporality by pronouncing an Ahuna Vairiio. This narration is closer to Zoros aster's epic legend as attested in the *Ayādgar ī Zarērān* and in the *Šāhnāma* than to the description of the prophet's life transmitted in religious works such as the seventh book of the *Dēnkard* and the *Zarātušt-nāma*. Here, as is appropriate in a *yašt* dedicated to the transmission of the *x^varənah* of the Kavi, the focus is on the actions of Vīštāspa and the heroes that will defend the Good Religion, rather than on the episodes of Zoroaster's hagiography.

Karde 14, describing the deeds of the Victoriuous Saošiiaṇt and Karde 15, dealing with Astuuaṯ.ərəta form a similar couple. The Victorious one among the *Saošiiaṇt*s *(vərəϑrājanəm saošiiaṇtąm)*, will make existence imperishable and unsullied, living forever, forever thriving. When the dead will rise, the one without decay will come reviving life. A belief which is not fully expanded in the *Zamyād Yašt* but was to develop in the full-blown doctrine of the Sōšāns bringing about the Renovation and the Future Body, the *Frašgird* and *Tan ī Pasēn* of the Pahlavi writings. The karde dealing with Astuuaṯ.ərəta is much more martial in character, when he rises from lake Kąsaoiia gazing with eyes of insight he brandishes the weapon that Thraetaona, the great dragon-slayer of Iranian tradition, held when he smote Aži Dahāka, and which the other great Iranian and Turanian heroes bore when each smote his enemy.[10] Remarkably, *Vərəϑrajan* is also an attribute of Astuuaṯ.ərəta (Yt 19.95b; HINTZE 1994a, p. 366; KELLENS 1974, pp. 204f.; 207–209), though according to KELLENS "Tout suggère que, si *saošiiaṇt-* et le nom propre *astuuaṯ.ərəta-* tendent à devenir inséparables, la function de *saošiiaṇt-* et celle de sauveur n'ont pas encore fusionné dans l'Avesta". In fact, in his reconstruction the Saošiiaṇt originally is basically a human being who by performing sacrifices obtains vital and concrete benefits for the human community (KELLENS 1974, p. 203). HINTZE takes a different position, stating that if the *Gatha*s are not read as a ritual text but as a fully religious one, to use her terminology, Saošiiaṇt, not attested in the *Yasna Haptaŋhāiti*, may have acquired the meaning of "saviour" already in the Old Avestan period (HINTZE 1995, pp. 79–89). On the other hand, KELLENS rightly underlines that Yt 19.22 *zātanąmca azātanąmca frašō.carəϑrąm saošiiaṇtąmca* "les saošiiaṇts nés et à naître, qui rendent vigoreux" (*id.* 1974, p. 207) shows that the *saošiiaṇts* are beings that may indifferently belong to past, present or future. This phrase allows for a better and more precise understanding of clauses such

10 *Frawardīn Yašt* (Yt 13) is one of the great Yašts going back to early Young Avestan times, but its repetitive structure allows for later interpolations, especially in its second part. While the occurrence of Astuuaṯ.ərəta in Yt 13.110 is in line with the evidence of Yt 19, Yt 13.128–129 and 141–142 show a later stage of development. Interestingly, Yt 13.129 explicitly says that Astuuaṯ.ərəta is the Saošiiaṇt *vərəϑrājan* and Yt 13.142 overtly identifies ʒrədaṯ.fəδrī with Vispa.tauruuairī as if confirming a new creed.

as Y 24.4 and Yt 13.17 (KELLENS 1974, p. 207) an interpretation that may also be applied to Yt 19.89 *yat̰ upaŋhacat̰ saošiiaṇtąm vərəθrājanəm* "which will accompany the victorious one among the *saošiiaṇts*" a passage that might have later contributed to the rise of a belief in multiple future saviours. On the other hand, HINTZE (1995, p. 92) is right in suggesting that the *saošiiaṇt-* qualified by the epithet *vərəθrājan-* attested in Y 26.10 (= Y 59.27) must refer to the end of human history, which begins with Gaiiō Marətan, and she is also right in seeing in the actions of "Victorious Saošiiaṇt" a reference to the Indo-European dragon-slayer myth, setting the *saošiiaṇt-* at the crossroads of the national and religious traditions (HINTZE 1995, pp. 93–95; 1999, pp. 76–78). Again, what we are looking at in the Young Avesta is the progressive birth of a belief, which will reach its maturity only in later times. Remarkably, Astuuat̰.ərəta is not an inherited name being the creation of learned priests and theological speculation.[11] Though this may seem to some extent an exaggeration, phonetics shows that Astuuat.ərəta became part of the tradition once the Avestan people had come in contact with the Arachotic adstratum. Again, this speaks in favour of a secondary, progressive innovation, though it is often difficult to identify different layers of tradition — which may or may not be identical with linguistical strata — in the Avesta. KELLENS closes his article by saying "Il faudra un jour établir si elle résulte d'un développement secondaire ou de la réapparition d'une vieille croyance" (*id.* 1974, p. 209). HINTZE (1995, p. 95) goes one step further, stating that not only the name but probably the entire eschatological myth of Astuuat̰.ərəta may have become part of Zoroastrian doctrine in that same period. Though Young Avestan passages such as Y 26.10 and Wd 19.5 (HINTZE 1994a, p. 366) suggest the existence of a belief in a future Saošiiaṇt (cf. HINTZE 1994a, pp. 151–157 and 366; 1995, p. 95), they may at best stand at the root of the later developments in the eschatological narration that is only attested much later.[12]

In the Middle Persian literature of the Zoroastrians different layers of tradition about the Final Days coexist one next to the other. One belongs to the realm of historical apocalypses, characterized by the presence of *ex eventu* prophecies, another is more cosmological in nature, focusing on the eschatological actions of the three unborn sons of Zoroaster. The first genre is most clearly represented by books such as the *Zand ī Wahman Yasn* (CERETI 1995b) and the

11 Thus KELLENS 1974, p. 209. HOFFMAN (1986, p. 167) and BOYCE (1975, p. 293) suggest that Astuuat̰.ərəta may in its second member attest an Arachosian form parallel with Ved. *ṛtá-*. They consider this form to be Arachosian because the *Zamyād Yašt* clearly identifies the Kąsaoiia with the Hamun basin (HINTZE 1994a, p. 371f.). The presence of a form belonging to a linguistic adstratum may suggest assigning this part of the *yašt* to a relatively later date.

12 This is not the place to discuss the contacts between Zoroastrism and other religious traditions, I personally agree with the horizontal model of contact as proposed in our field by PANAINO (2004, p. 220f.) and HINTZE (2019, p. 47f.).

Bundahišn (AGOSTINI/THROPE 2020, PAKZAD 2005), which both belong to one and the same manuscript tradition, and by the later and composite *Ayādgār ī Jamāspīg* (AGOSTINI 2013) and needs not concern us here.

The seventh book of the *Dēnkard* begins by describing the events that lead to Zoroaster's birth and ends with a description of the Sōšāns's fifty-seven years. In other words, it presents the religious history of the second half of human history. Late Sasanian times are seen as the beginning of the millenary crisis and the description of what will happen when Ērānšahr will tremble and fall belongs to the realm of apocalyptic literature. However, the narrative structure focuses comparatively more on eschatological events. Remarkably, Zoroaster's hagiography, though profoundly different from the Avestan *yašt*, preserves the intimate connection between Zoroaster and the Sōšans.

Chapters 7, on the events that will take place between the end of Wištāsp's reign and the fall of the Iranian empire, and 8, on the period going from the fall of the Empire to the rise of Ušēdar, are dedicated to the events that have taken place or will take place in Zoroaster's millennium. The largest portion of the two chapters, Dk 7.29–8.45, describes the grim situation in Ērānšahr between the end of Husraw Anōšagruwān's reign and the coming of Čihrōmehān, who will come accompanied by one hundred and fifty disciples to usher in the new age. This part needs not concern us here, since it mainly belongs to the realm of apocalyptic imagery.

Chapter 9, on the events from Ušēdar to Ušēdarmāh, and chapter 10, from Ušēdarmāh to Sōšāns are very similar one to the other. Both begin with a description of the deeds of Ušēdar/Ušēdarmāh, both talk about dietary laws: in Ušēdar's millennium Ašwahišt will teach humankind piety towards cattle, while when fifty-three years are left of Ušedarmāh's millennium, mankind will renounce meat and when only three years are left humans will become vegetarians, and finally both chapters describe the events that led to the birth of Ušēdar/Ušēdarmāh that took place thirty years before the end of their predecessor's millennium, and the first thirty years of life of the two future saviors. The only structural difference between the two chapters is to be observed in the major crisis caused by Markūs/Malkōs in the fifth century of Ušēdar's millennium, which corresponds to Ardašīr's rising to power in Zoroaster's millennium. Finally, chapter 11 describes the events that will take place in Sōšāns' short millennium, developing a narration the must already have been present in the *zand* of the *Zamyād Yašt* as we have seen above. This narrative is devoid of references to historical events, focusing instead on the ritual actions of Sōšāns.

Observing with some attention the structure of the eschatological narration as it is found in Pahlavi texts, it is immediately clear that the biography of the saviors coming at the end of each future millennium repeats episodes known to be part of Zoroaster's hagiographic life and that the narration of the events due to take place in the last millennia is also quite repetitive, multiplying by three the events of the life of the founder of the Good Religion (CERETI 1995a, pp. 46–50). Interestingly, number three comes forth often in the *Zamyād Yašt*. Thrice does Yima lose the *xvarənah*, the first time it is taken by Mithra of wide pastures, the second time by Θraētaona of the House of the Āϑβiia, who slew Aži Dahāka, the third time it was caught by Kərəsāspa, another character that will play a role in the final days. Much like Θraētaona, Kərəsāspa, a persona intimately bound to Sistanic Sām, slays a dragon, Aži Sruuara. Moreover, he also defeats Gandarəβa, Arəzō.šamana and Snauuiδka the latter being so mighty that he could only be defeated because of young age. The Good Spirit and the Evil Spirit are now set one against the other, each flanked by three impressive creatures, and compete to capture the *axᵛarətəm xᵛarənō* that finally takes refuge in the sea Vouru.kaṣ̌a, to be protected by Apąm Napāt. Forth comes Fraŋrasiian (Yt 19.55–64). Three times does the Turanian try to conquer the *xᵛarənah* "welcher den arischen Landesbewohnern gehört, den geborenen und ungeborenen, und welcher dem wahrhaften Zarathustra gehört".[13] Each time he dives in the sea Vouru.kaṣ̌a and causes the opening of a new inlet, each time he pronounces mischievous words.[14]

Here again, the need to add three millennia after Zoroaster is determined by a scholastic desire to place the founder of the Good Religion at the center of human history, halfway between Gayōmard and Sōšāns, while fitting this schema in the 12,000 years of the world's duration. However, a skilled Zandist may have used the numerous triplets found in the *Zamyād Yašt* to justify the triplication of future saviours.

An important late Sasanian work, the *Šahrestānīhā ī Ērānšahr*[15] may provide a clue to better understand the development of the legend about Zoroaster and his three sons in Sistan. While describing the cities belonging to the Southern Quarter of Ērānšahr, its author writes:

> 38) *šahrestān <ī> zarang naxust gizistag frāsiyāg ī tūr kard u-š warzāwand ātaxš karkōy ānōh nišāst u-š manūčihr andar ō padišxwārgar kard u-š spandarmad pad zanīh xwāst ud spandarmad andar ō zamīg gumēxt, šahrestān awērān kard. u-š ātaxš afsārd ud pas kay husraw [ī] siyāwaxšān šahrestān abāz kard. u-š ātaxš karkōy abāz nišāst ud ardaxšīr [ī] pābagān šahrestān be pad frazāmēnīd.*
>
> "38) The city *(šahrestān)* of Zarang was first made by Frāsiyāg ī Tūr, he placed there the miraculous fire Karkōy. He made Manuščihr (captive) in Padišxwārgar, he asked Spandarmad in marriage and Spandarmad mingled herself in the earth (and) made the country *(šahrestān)* desolated.[16] He extinguished the Fire and later Kay Husraw ī Siyāwaxšān renovated the city *(šahrestān)*. He re-established the fire Kārkōy and Ardašīr ī Pābagān completed it." (Cereti 2020, p. 85f.)

13 Yt 19.64, in Hintze's (1994a, p. 304) translation, slightly different according to Humbach/ Ichaporia 1998, p. 46 and Pirart 1992, p. 86.

14 See Panaino 1998.

15 Markwart 1931, Daryaee 2002. For a recent reassessment of this work, see Cereti 2020.

16 On my reading of this passage, see further Cereti 2020, p. 86, n. 23.

Three different stages of foundation are here represented. Frāsiyāg may represent a pre-Zoroastrian tradition, attested also in the older layer of *Zamyād Yašt*. Kay Husraw embodies the moment in which Zarang became Zoroastrian and finally Ardašīr witnesses the moment in which the Sasanian dynasty appropriated Avestan mythologic and epic themes.

Furthermore, the Middle Persian literature of the Zoroastrians attests that Sistan has always been proud of its intimate link with the legend of Zoroaster and his three future sons. In fact, the *Abdīh ud sahīgīhā ī Sēstān* praises the glory of Sistan by extolling its religious merits:

> MK 26r, r 7–26v, r. 1
> *pad nām ī yazdān abdīh ud sahīgīh ī zamīg ī (sēstān) az abārīg šahrīhā ēd rāy abērtar ud weh ēk ēn kū rōd ī hēdmand ud war ī frazdān ud zrēh ī kayānsē ud gar <ī> ōšīhdāštār andar zamīg ī sēst‹ān›. zāyišn ud parwarišn ī ušēdar ud ušēdarmāh <ud> sōšāns ī zarduštān ī spitāmān aziš ristāxēz kardan.*
> "In the name of God. The marvels and wonders of the land of Sistan. It is superior and better than other provinces on account of (the following): one, that the river Hilmand and lake Frazdān and the sea Kayānsē and mount Ōšīhdāštār are in the land of Sistan. (And on account) of the birth and fostering of Ušēdar, Ušēdarmāh and Sōšāns (son) of Zarduxšt of the Spitama, by whom Ristāxēz is accomplished."[17]

So far, we have been able to recognize several different layers of traditions. A pre-Zoroastrian one, attested by the centrality of Franrasiian's actions in the *Zamyād Yašt*, that was later to be "zoroastrianized" and included in Yt 19. A second layer of tradition which is still affected by the influence of the Indo-European dragon-slayer myth, is attested by the *Zamyād Yašt* itself, dating to the early Achaemenid period with possible interpolations of a later date. Two layers may be assigned to the Sasanian period. The most recent one, attested by the *Dēnkard* can with some confidence be dated to the 6th-century CE. Its narrative most probably relies on the lost Zand of the *Zamyād Yašt* that must therefore predate it, though we are in no position to date it more precisely.

Turning to archaeological evidence for some help, the most recent assessments have identified three different layers in the construction of the great monumental complex at Kuh-i Khwaja. The oldest one probably dates to the early Parthian era, but the evidence is too scanty to fully understand the extent and relevance of the site in that period. A second and monumental one has been dated by radiocarbon testing to the period 80–240 CE (+/– 50) and a third one, mainly consisting in renovation and restoration activities on the old buildings, can be assigned to the years 540–650 CE (+/– 50) (CANEPA 2013

17 The memory of Afrāsyāb's hydraulic deeds around the Hamun is still found in the *Tārīḫ-e Sīstān* where it is said that the source of part of this information is the "*Bundahišn* of the Zoroastrians" (BAHAR 1935, pp. 13–18; GOLD 1976, pp. 11–14). Here I wish to thank my colleague, Prof. ALMUT HINTZE, for allowing me to use manuscript MK and my PhD student, CARLO MARCHETTI, for discussing with me contents and nature of the *Abdīh ud sahīgīhā ī Sēstān*.

and 2018, pp. 271–283; Ghanimati 2000 and 2015). Probably the site hosted a temple and a Hērbedestān, proving that it was a pilgrimage spot and a primary religious center. Furthermore, Canepa has strongly argued in favour of its representing "one of the first major attempts of the Sasanian dynasty to take control of the powerful Avestan tradition and create a monumental focus for it" (*id.* 2018, p. 281). Would it be too bold to theorize that the exegetical work on *Yašt* 19 took place in Sistan, starting at the beginning of the Sasanian period, or possibly even in the Parthian period, and that it gradually led to the development of the legend as we know it in Pahlavi literature and through New Persian works such as the *Sad dar Bundeheš*? Possible witness of this gradual evolution may be found in *Widēwdād* 19.5 that perhaps attests a slightly later stage of the legend, while the evidence of the *Frawardīn Yašt* that knew of the existence of three future saviours and their respective mothers may be read as a witness throwing a ray of light on the evolution that took place between the middle of the 1st millennium BCE, when the *Zamyād Yašt* was composed and the early centuries of the 1st millennium CE, when Kuh-i Khwaja became the major Zoroastrian cultic complex in Sistan. Or again, the passages in *Yašt* 13 may be late interpolations added by Zoroastrian theologians once the myth was fully developed. Similarly, I wonder whether karde 9 of the *Zamyād Yašt* may not have been a product of the Zoroastrian clergy of Sistan. To conclude, the textual evidence shows that the eschatological myth of the three future sons of Zoroaster developed in eastern Iran and was an essential element of the religious narrative relative to the sanctuary of Kuh-i Khwaja and, more extensively, of Sistan's *geographia sacra*. For once, literary texts and archaeological evidence do not contradict one another, but contribute to a better understanding of the development of Zoroastrian eschatology.

Abbreviations

Av.	Avestan	Ved.	Vedic
Dk	*Dēnkard*	Wd	*Widēwdād*
MP	Middle Persian	Y	*Yasna*
MX	*Mēnōg ī Xrad*	Yt	*Yašt*
NP	New Persian	ZWY	*Zand ī Wahman Yasn*

AION	*Annali dell'Istituto Universitario Orientale di Napoli* [NS]
EIr	*Encyclopædia Iranica*. Ed. by E. Yarshater. London/Boston/New York Online edition available at https://www.iranicaonline.org/
HdO	*Handbuch der Orientalistik*
JAOS	*Journal of the American Oriental Society*
SOR	Serie Orientale Roma
StIr	*Studia Iranica*

Bibliography

AGOSTINI, D. 2013: *Ayādgār ī Jāmāspīg. Un texte eschatologique zoroastrien*. Rome.

AGOSTINI, D./S. THROPE 2020: *The Bundahišn. The Zoroastrian Book of Creation*. Oxford.

BAHĀR, M. 1935: *Tāriḫ-e Sistān*. Teherān [1314 š.]

BOYCE, M. 1975: *A History of Zoroastrianism*. Vol. I: *The Early Period*. Leiden/Köln (HdO I.8.1.2.2A).

BOYCE, M./F. GRENET 1991: *A History of Zoroastrianism*. Vol. III, with a contribution by R. BECK: *Zoroastrianism under Macedonian and Roman Rule*. Leiden/Köln (HdO I.8.1.2.2.III).

CANEPA, M. P. 2013: "Building a New Vision of the Past in the Sasanian Empire: The Sanctuaries of Kayānsīh and the Great Fires of Iran." In: *Journal of Persianate Studies* 6, pp. 64–90.

— 2018: *The Iranian Expanse. Transforming Royal Identity through Architecture, Landscape, and the Built Environment, 550 BCE – 642 CE*. Oakland, Ca.

CERETI, C. G. 1995a: "La figura del redentore futuro nei testi iranici zoroastriani, aspetti dell'evoluzione di un mito." In: *Annali dell'Istituto Universitario Orientale di Napoli* 55, pp. 33–81.

— 1995b: *The Zand ī Wahman Yasn. A Zoroastrian Apocalypse*. Rome (SOR 75).

— 2020: "Remarks on The cities of Ērānšahr and its date in the light of the Xwadāy-nāmag and Sasanian primary sources." In: M. ASHTIANY/M. MAGGI (eds.): *A turquoise coronet. Studies in Persian language and literature in honour of Paola Orsatti*. Wiesbaden, pp. 79–96.

COMPARETI, M./G. SCARCIA 2012: "Zone d'ombra nell'est iranico alla vigilia dell'islamizzazione." In: *Parthica: incontri di culture nel mondo antico* 14 [= *Essays in Memory of Boris Anatol'evich Litvinsky*], pp. 207–254.

DARYAEE, T. 2002: *Šahrestānīhā ī Ērānšahr. A Middle Persian Text on Late Antique Geography, Epic and History, with English and Persian Translations, and Commentary*. Costa Mesa, Cal.

GHANIMATI, S. 2000: "New Perspectives on the Chronological and Functional Horizons of Kuh-e Khwaja in Sistan." In: *Iran* 38, pp. 137–150.

— 2015: "Kuh-e Ḵᵛāja." In: EIr, online edition, available at http://www.iranicaonline.org/articles/kuh-e-khvaja (accessed on 28 September 2015).

GOLD, M. 1976: *The Tārikh-e Sistān*. Rome.

GNOLI, GH. 1967: *Ricerche storiche sul Sīstān antico*. Rome.

— 1971: "Politica e concezione della regalità sotto i Sassanidi." In: *La Persia nel Medioevo: Atti del convegno internazionale sul tema (Roma, 31 marzo – 5 aprile 1970)*. Rome, pp. 225–253.

HINTZE, A. 1994a: *Der Zamyād-Yašt. Edition, Übersetzung, Kommentar*. Wiesbaden (Beiträge zur Iranistik 15).

— 1994b: *Zamyād Yašt. Introduction, Avestan Text, Translation and Glossary*. Wiesbaden (Beiträge zur Iranistik 17).

— 1995: "The Rise of the Saviour in the Avesta." In: CH. RECK/P. ZIEME (eds.): *Iran und Turfan. Beitrage Berliner Wissenschaftler, Werner Sundermann zum 60. Geburtstag gewidmet*. Wiesbaden (Iranica 2), pp. 77–97.

— 1999: "The Saviour and the Dragon in Iranian and Jewish/Christian Eschatology." In: SH. SHAKED/A. NETZER (eds.): *Irano-Judaica IV. Studies Relating to Jewish Contacts with Persian Culture Throughout the Ages.* Jerusalem, pp. 72–90.

— 2019: "Defeating Death: Eschatology in Zoroastrianism, Judaism and Christianity." In: J. RUBANOVICH/G. HERMAN (eds.): *Irano-Judaica VII. Studies Relating to Jewish Contacts with Persian Culture Throughout the Ages.* Jerusalem, pp. 23–72.

HOFFMANN, K. 1986: "Avestisch ṣ̌." In: R. SCHMITT/P.O. SKJÆRVØ (eds.): *Studia Grammatica Iranica. Festschrift für Helmut Humbach.* München, pp. 163–183.

HUMBACH, H./P.R. ICHAPORIA 1998: *Zamyād Yasht. Yasht 19 of the Younger Avesta: Text, Translation, Commentary.* Wiesbaden.

KELLENS, J. 1974: "Saošiiaṇt-." In: StIr 3.2, pp. 187–209.

KUHN, E. 1893: "Eine zoroastrische Prophezeiung in christlichem Gewande." In: E. KUHN (ed.): *Festgruss an Rudolf von Roth zum Doktor-Jubiläum 24. August 1893: von seinen Freunden und Schülern.* Stuttgart, pp. 217–221.

LAZARD, G. 1990: "Composition et métrique dans le Yasht de l'Avesta." In: GH. GNOLI/A. PANAINO (eds.): *Proceedings of the First Conference of Iranian Studies held in Turin, September 7th–11th, 1987.* Rome (SOR 67), pp. 217–228.

MARKWART, J. 1931: *A Catalogue of the Provincial Capitals of Ērānšahr.* Ed. by G. MESSINA. Rome.

MARQUART J./J.J.M. DE GROOT 1915: "Das Reich Zâbul und der Gott Žûn vom 6–9 Hundert." In: G. WEIL (ed.): *Festschrift Edward Sachau, zum siebzigsten Geburtstage gewidmet von Freunden und Schülern.* Berlin, pp. 248–292.

MOLÉ, M. 1967: *La légende de Zoroastre selon les textes pehlevies.* Paris.

MONNERET DE VILLARD, U. 1952: *Le leggende orientali sui magi evangelici.* Città del Vaticano.

PAKZAD, F. 2005: *Bundahišn. Zoroastrische Kosmogonie und Kosmologie.* Tehran.

PANAINO, A. 1998: "A Daevic Speech (Yt. 19.57, 69, 63)." In: N. SIMS-WILLIAMS (ed.): *Proceedings of the Third Conference of Iranian Studies held in Cambridge 11–15 September 1995.* Pt. 1: *Old and Middle Iranian Studies.* Cambridge, pp. 71–78.

— 2004: "Trends and Problems concerning the Mutual Relations between Iranian pre-Islamic and Jewish Cultures." In: A. PANAINO/A. PIRAS with collaboration of G.P. BASELLO (eds.): *Schools of Oriental Studies and the Development of Modern Historiography. Proceedings of the Fourth Annual Symposium of the Assyrian and Babylonian Intellectual Heritage Project, held in Ravenna, Italy, October 13–17, 2001.* Milano, pp. 209–236.

PIRART, E.V. 1992: *Kayân Yasn (Yasht 10.9–96). L'origine avestiques des dynasties mythiques d'Iran.* Barcelona.

SCARCIA G. 1965: "Sulla religione di Zâbul." In: AION 15, pp. 119–165.

— 1966: "Ancora su 'Znbyl'." In: AION 16, pp. 201–205.

— 1967: "Epica iranica e motivo turanico. Considerazioni sui 'Turchi di Zâbul' e sulla leggenda di Afrâsyâb-Alp Är Tonga." In: AION 17, pp. 1–34.

— 1973: "Kûh-e Khwâgè: forme attuali del mahdismo iranico." In: *Oriente Moderno* 9, pp. 755–764.

— 2002: "Ripensare Zâbul." In: C. SILVI ANTONINI/B.M. ALFIERI/A. SANTORO (eds.): *Oriente e Occidente. Convegno in ricordo di Mario Bussagli. Roma, 31 maggio–1 giugno 1999.* Pisa/Roma, pp. 236–241.

— 2010: "Montagne sacre d'Iran." In J. RIES (ed.): *Montagna Sacra*. Milano, pp. 103–121.

SKJÆRVØ, P.O. 1997: "Avestica I: A Perfect participle: *vaox^{v}ą̊ŋhō*." In: JAOS 117, pp. 145–147.

TERRIBILI, G. 2020: "Relocating the Prophet's Image: Narrative Motifs and Local Appropriation of the Zarathustra Legend in Pre- and Early Islamic Iran (Part I – East Iran)." In: *Iran and the Caucasus* 24, pp. 1–16.

— 2021: "Relocating the Prophet's Image: Narrative Motifs and Local Appropriation of the Zarathustra Legend in Pre- and Early Islamic Iran (Part II – North-West Iran)." In: *Iran and the Caucasus* 25/3, pp. 225–245.

YARSHATER, E. 1982: "Afrāsyāb." In: EIr I, pp. 570–576; an updated version is available online at http://www.iranicaonline.org/articles/afrasiab-turanian-king (accessed on 14 March 2014).

How to Make Clarified Butter in Sogdian

Iris Colditz, Bochum

Clarified butter or *ghee* (Chin. 醍醐 *ti hu*; Skt. *ghṛta* or *sarpirmaṇḍa*) plays an important role in Indian medicine and is considered as one of the best medications. It is also often mentioned in Buddhist texts in this context. The five stages of *ghee*-making are mentioned in the *Mahāyāna Mahāparinirvāṇasūtra*. Moreover, clarified butter is used as a symbol of the purity of the Buddhist teachings and of the Buddha-nature. The Mahāyāna Tiantai school (Chin. 天台宗 *tian tai zong*) relates these five stages or 'five flavours' (Chin. 五味 *wu wei*, Skt. *pañcarasa*, *pañcarasāḥ*) of the respective dairy products metaphorically to the five periods of Buddha's teachings. These correspondences can be shown as follows (see Table 1, based on SH, pp. 115f.; *PDB*, p. 1005):

Table 1

Stage of *ghee* making or 'flavour'	Teachings of the Buddha
Fresh milk (Chin. 乳 *ru*; Skt. *kṣīra*)	Avataṃsaka (Chin. 華嚴經 *hua yan jing*), for śrāvakas and pratyeka-buddhas
Coagulated milk, cream (Chin. 酪 *luo*; Skt. *dadhi*)	Āgamas (Chin. 阿含經 *a han jing*), for Hīnayāna generally
Curdled milk, *i. e.*, fresh butter or buttermilk (Chin. 生酥 *sheng su*; Skt. *navanīta*)	Vaipulyas (Chin. 方等經 *fang deng jing*), for the Mahāyāna
Butter (Chin. 酥 *su*; Skt. *ghola*)	Prajñā (Chin. 般若經 *bo re jing*), for the Mahāyāna
Clarified butter, *ghee* (Chin. 醍醐 *ti hu*; Skt. *ghṛta*, *sarpirmaṇḍa*)	Lotus-sūtra (Chin. 法華經 *fa hua jing*) and Nirvāṇa-sūtra (涅槃經 *nie pan jing*), for the Mahāyāna

During the editorial work on a Sogdian version[1] of the Northern edition of Dharmakṣema's Chinese translation of the *Mahāyāna Mahāparinirvāṇa-sūtra* (MPNS), *Taishō Tripiṭaka* (T. T.) no. 374, vol. 12, 365a3–604a31 (largely cor-

1 For the identification of this text see Utz 1976, pp. 4f.; Sundermann 2010, pp. 77–79. It is ms. 2 (MPNS 2) of the three (or four?) Sogdian mss. of this version identified so far

responding to the Southern edition, T. T. 375, vol. 12), I came across some examples of a metaphorical use of clarified butter. They are of special interest because of the Sogdian terms that designate the dairy products of the individual steps of its fabrication process. While some terms are already known in Sogdian, the meaning of others can now be defined by their Chinese equivalents. In the following, first the respective passages will be presented in which they occur. Then, the terms will be discussed with reference to their Chinese equivalents and within the context of the production process of clarified butter.

I am pleased to dedicate this paper to DIETER WEBER, whose rich and inspiring scholarly work covers such a broad range of subjects from Pahlavi papyri from Egypt and Pahlavi documents in cursive script from Iran to Sogdian proper names from Central Asia. Since he already addressed this topic briefly on another occasion (WEBER 1970, p. 54), and especially the Pahlavi documents often deal with food products, I hope that this paper will be of interest for him.

So 15289 [no finding siglum]

This hitherto unpublished large fragment consists of two joining parts and preserves twenty-one lines on the recto and twenty lines on the verso side as well as parts of the lower (recto) or upper (verso) margin of the *pustaka* (for a detailed description see RECK 2016, no. 755). The extant text on the recto side corresponds to T. T. 374, vol. 12, 394c16–26, that on the verso side to 395a9–19; transl. BLUM 2013, pp. 157f. (= T. T. no. 375, vol. 12, 635a10–21, 635b4–15; transl. YAMAMOTO 1973–1975, I, pp. 126f.; the indication of the correspondence with the Chinese text as given in RECK 2016, no. 755 based on SUNDERMANN, *Materials*, differs slightly). SUNDERMANN *(ibid.)* refers to the leaf as fragments 60 and 61 or as leaf IV respectively (2010, p. 79). In the forthcoming edition it will be designated as leaf 4, which is folio 11 or 12 of the passage corresponding to scroll (Chin. 巻 *juan*) 5 of the Chinese version of MPNS.

Passage 1:

Chin. T. T. no. 374, vol. 12, 394c16–18
又解脱者抜諸因縁。譬如因乳得酪因酪得酥因酥得醍醐眞解脱中都無是因。無是因者即眞解脱。眞解脱者即是如來 *you jie tuo zhe ba zhu yin yuan pi ru yin ru de luo yin*

(see YOSHIDA 2015, p. 171, no. 10; RECK 2017, pp. 597f.), consisting of more than ninety fragments. It is in *pustaka* format while the other mss. are written on scrolls. WERNER SUNDERMANN had prepared a draft of its edition in cooperation with KOGI KUDARA (in the following referred to as SUNDERMANN, *Materials*), which did not reach a final, publication-ready state. The present article is an excursus to the edition of MPNS 2 that will be published in *Berliner Turfantexte* (COLDITZ [forthcoming]). Since it will be in English, this paper is also provided in this language. We thank the colleagues of the Turfan Research Project at the Berlin-Brandenburg Academy of Science for granting us access to this material.

luo de su yin su de ti hu zhen jie tuo zhong du wu shi yin wu shi yin zhe ji zhen jie tuo zhen jie tuo zhe ji shi ru lai

"In addition, liberation abolishes causality. The usual pattern of milk yielding sour milk, sour milk yielding butter, and butter yielding clarified butter would be a disanalogy, for within liberation such forms of causality do not exist. Not having any causality is precisely what true liberation is, and true liberation is what the Tathāgata is." (Blum 2013, pp. 156f. but cf. Yamamoto 1973–1975, I, p. 126: For example, from milk we get cream; from cream, we get butter; and from butter, we get sarpirmanda. The true emancipation has none of these causes. The causelessness is the true emancipation. The true emancipation is the Tathagata.)

Sogd. /r/1–5/

*/1/ [12–14](2–3)[16–28] /2/ [9–11](.) ʾP(ZY c)nn cšt*ʾ*[18–20] /3/ [*ʾʾ*mtyc xwy](c)k[*ʾ*](w)k myδ*ʾ*(n)y γ(wn*ʾ*k)[*ʾ*nβ*ʾ*nt nyst rty n]wkr k(δ*ʾ*) /4/ [2–3] (Z)K[*ʾ*n](β)[*ʾ*n](t)(?) L*ʾ* βwt rty *ʾʾ*(m)[t](yc) x(w)yck*ʾ*(wk) (x)w(nyty)(?)*[2] *ʾ*(P)[Z]Y Z(K) — /5/ [*ʾʾ*mty](c)(?) x(w)y(c)k*ʾ*(wk p)wty (xyδ) …*

"[For example, from milk one gets cream,] and from cream [one gets butter, from butter one gets *sarpirmaṇḍa*.] In [the true libe]ration [there is not this cause. And] now when there is not the [cause] that is called the true liberation. And the [true] liberation is the Buddha."

The fabrication of clarified butter[3] serves here as an example for causality (Chin. 因 *yin*). The terms in question are Chin. 乳 *ru* 'milk', 酪 *luo* 'coagulated milk, cream' (but Blum: 'sour milk'), 酥 *su* 'butter', and 醍醐 *ti hu* 'clarified butter'. These dairy products must therefore also occur in the Sogdian version. The text is very fragmentary but many words can be restored according to the Chinese text and the repetitive character. The only preserved term for a dairy product is /r/2/ *cšt*ʾ rendering Chin. 酪 *luo* 'coagulated milk, cream'.[4] It is translated here as 'cream' according to its position within the fabrication process of clarified butter (see below). One may also compare it with a similar list Sogd. *rty cntn ZY mrʾynckʾ nβrʾytk ryz-ʾkh βwt ZY šywšpδn ZY cšth ZY ʾnkwpyn ZY γʾwrwγn cnn wyspnʾc mγʾwn wʾβʾyδ wnʾy rtšy ptrʾ(y)δʾy* 'and of sandalwood and pepper (gloss:) *i.e.*, pounded rice and mustard-seed and *cšth* and honey and butter let him make like amounts of all and mix them' (*Padm.* 39–41, ed. MacKenzie 1976, I, pp. 14–17, II, p. 11, n. on 39). Since it is consecrated to the fire, this mixture should not be too liquid. *cšt-* may therefore also rather mean 'cream' or 'curdled milk' here than 'koumiss' (thus translated by MacKenzie).

2 Misspelling of *xwynty* (thus Reck 2016, no. 755)? The letters are faded.

3 For a useful graphic representation of dairy products and how they are produced see "Milk products and production relationships" at *Wikimedia Commons*, online available at https://commons.wikimedia.org/w/index.php?curid=9879413 (Last Accessed 26 March 2021).

4 To be distinguished from Sogd. *cšth* for *cštyh* 'terror' in So 14080(1)c [T II D 89]/v/6/ as translation of (T.T. no. 374, vol. 12, 457a28) Chin. 怖 *bu* 'fear; afraid' (ed. Colditz [forthcoming], as leaf 14/v/39/). Cf. also B *ʾcštyh*, Av. *taršti-* (Benveniste 1940, pp. 179 on 785, 242; *GMS*, §§ 150, 277, 948; Gharib 1995, pp. 24, 130; *EWA*, I, pp. 678f., *s.v. TRAS*); MPth. *tyštjd* 'hit by fear', *tyštyn* 'terrible' (*DMT III/1*, p. 333).

Passage 2:

Chin. T.T. no. 374, vol. 12, 394c22–25
又解脱者能除無明。如上妙酥除諸滓穢乃名醍醐解脱亦爾除無明滓生於眞明。如是眞明即眞解脱。眞解脱者即是如來 *you jie tuo zhe neng chu wu ming ru shang miao su chu zhu zi hui nai ming ti hu jie tuo yi er chu wu ming zi sheng yu zhen ming ru shi zhen ming ji zhen jie tuo zhen jie tuo zhe zhi shi ru lai*
"In addition, liberation eliminates the darkness of ignorance. It is like when you take the best quality butter and remove its impurities, yielding what is then called 'clarified butter'. Liberation is like this: removing the dregs of ignorance produces true light. This true light is what true liberation is, and true liberation is what the Tathāgata is." (BLUM 2013, p. 157)

Sogd. /r/13–19/
/13/ ZK rty(m)[s ZK](x)wyc[kʾwk wʾ](γ)wnʾk m[ʾ](δ) [Z](Y) /14/ [Z](K)w (mnt...)yʾkyh (pxʾ)ršt wn(ty) m(ʾ)yδ ʾYKZY ZK š(y)[rʾ](k(?) zpʾ)[rt(?)] /15/ [rwγ](n)[ʾYK](ʾ) ZK pysʾ (Lʾ βwt)[rt]y prw k(r)krwγn (xw)[ynty ʾPZY ZK] /16/ [xwyckʾw](k) ʾy(wγw)ncyδ prʾw ʾP(ZY my)[2–3 ʾ](pw r)wxš[ny](ʾ)[kh 8–10] /17/ [3–5](h) ʾPZYšy ZK ʾʾmtyc r(w)xšny(ʾkh)[2–3](t rty y)[wnʾk wkry rwxš-] /18/ [nyʾk](y(?) ʾʾmtyc) xw(y)[ckʾw](y) x(w)[yn](t)y ʾPZ(Y ZK ʾʾmtyc)[xwyckʾwk] /19/ [pwty xyδ] ...
"And [the] liberation is so that it can *exclude [ignorance], it is like fine, pure [butter when] there is no *defilement(?)[5], and then it is called *sarpirmaṇḍa*. [And the liberation] is like that. Then also this [dreg of ig]noran[ce is removed] and from it the true brightness [comes(?).] And [this kind of brightness] is called the true liberation. And the true [liberation is the Buddha]."

Clarified butter is used here as a symbol of the highest purity of true enlightment (Chin. 眞明 *zhen ming*). The dairy products mentioned in this passage are Chin. 上妙酥 *shang miao su* 'best quality butter' and 醍醐 *ti hu* 'clarified butter, *ghee*' which is its purified essence. As Sogdian equivalent of Chin. 酥 *su* 'curd, butter; crisp', SUNDERMANN *(Materials)* restores /r/15/ *rwγn* 'fat, oil; butter'. Chin. 醍醐 *ti hu* 'clarified butter, *ghee*' is translated /r/15/ as Sogd. *krkrwγn /karakrōγan/* '(lit.) butter-fat'.[6]

So 15512 [T III D 261 K]

This hitherto unpublished fragment from the left part of a *pustaka* follows immediately So 15289. It preserves the upper (recto) or lower (verso) margin

5 SUNDERMANN *(Materials)* reads and translates *pysʾ* '*scum'. The word corresponds to Chin. 穢 *hui* 'foul, filthy, unclear, impure' (SH, p. 466b; *BCSD*, p. 906b), cf. maybe OIr. **pais-*, **pis-* 'to adorn; to pockmark', Av. *paēs-* 'to colour' (on the lexical family of this verb see ROSSI 2013, pp. 373f.). One could alternatively read *pymʾ* for *pymʾkh* 'froth, foam' used also for 'foam at the mouth, sputum' (REICHELT 1928, p. 213 on 323; MACKENZIE 1970, pp. 18f., 68; 1976, II, p. 128).

6 SUNDERMANN (2010, pp. 79, 83, n. 41) considers alternatively a reading *kβkrwγn* 'creamy butter', cf. Av. *kafa-*, NP *kaf* 'foam', *kafk* 'froth, scum'.

respectively and nine incomplete lines on each side (for a detailed description see Reck 2016, no. 765). The extant text corresponds to T.T. no. 374, vol. 12, 395a26–b1 (recto) and 395b17–20 (verso); transl. Blum 2013, pp. 159f. (= T.T. no. 375, vol. 12, 635b21/22(?)–25, 635c13/14(?)–17; transl. Yamamoto 1973–1975, I, pp. 128f.; slightly different in Reck 2016, no. 765 based on Sundermann, *Materials*). Sundermann *(ibid.)* refers to the leaf as fragment 46 or as leaf V respectively (2010, p. 79). In the forthcoming edition it will be designated as leaf 5, which is folio 12 or 13 of the passage corresponding to scroll (Chin. 卷 *juan*) 5 of the Chinese version of MPNS.

Passage 3:

> Chin. T.T. no. 374, vol. 12, 395b19–20
> 如水酒酪酥蜜等瓶。雖無水酒酪酥蜜時。猶故得名爲水等瓶 *ru shui jiu lou su mi deng ping sui wu shui jiu luo su mi shi you gu de ming wei shui deng ping*
> "It is like jars for water, wine, yogurt, butter, honey, and the like: even when they have no water, wine, yogurt, butter, or honey inside them, they are still called water jars, wine jars, and so on." (Blum 2013, p. 160)
>
> Sogd. /v/5–8/
> */5/ [ʾYKZY ZK γwδʾk pr ʾʾp ʾWZY zwty ktʾr cš](t)ʾ ʾWZY rwγn ktʾr /6/ [ʾnkwpyn ZYms ʾnyw-znkʾn 6–8 Lʾ] ʾʾp βwt Lʾ zwty /7/ [Lʾ cštʾ Lʾ rwγn Lʾ ʾnkwpy](n)[Lʾ](Z)Yms ʾnyw-znkʾn /8/ [30–32](.) pcʾyt wγty*
> "[For example, when there are pots for water, liquor, cre]am or butter or [honey] or other kinds (of drinks), then even if there is no] water, no liquor, [no cream, no butter, no honey] or any other kind (of drinks) [in the pots,] it is still right to call [them water pots and other pots.]"

The passage is about the not-emptiness-and-emptiness (Chin. 不空空 *bu kong kong*) of worldly phenomena as shown by the example of specified jars for various products. As dairy products the text mentions Chin. 酪 *luo* 'coagulated milk, cream' and 酥 *su* 'curd, butter'. Blum translates the first term as 'yogurt', but Yamamoto (1973–1975, I, p. 129) as 'cream'. For 酪 *luo* one can restore here again Sogd. *cštʾ* (see passage 1), Chin. 酥 *su* 'curd, butter' is translated as Sogd. *rwγn* 'fat, oil; butter'.

So 14216 [T II D 96]

The hitherto unpublished fragment from the interior of a *pustaka* right from the binding circle preserves the upper (verso: lower) margin and about half of the width of twelve lines both on the recto and verso side (for a detailed description see Reck 2016, no. 648). The extant text corresponds to T.T. no. 374, vol. 12, 531b26–c1 (recto) and 531c12/13(?)–17 (verso) (= T.T. no. 375, vol. 12, 776b11–15, 777b27/28(?)–c2; transl. Yamamoto 1973–1975, II, pp. 690f.; the identification slightly differs in Reck 2016, no. 648 based on a proposal by Yutaka Yoshida). Sundermann *(Materials)* refers to the leaf as fragment 32 or leaf XVII respectively (2010, p. 79). In the forthcoming edition it will be designated as leaf 20, which is folio 7 or 8 of the passage corresponding to scroll (Chin. 卷 *juan*) 28 of the Chinese version of MPNS.

Passage 4:

> Chin. T.T. no. 374, vol. 12, 531c15–16
> 世尊。若了因無者。云何得名有乳有酪 *shi zun ruo liao yin wu zhe yun he de ming you ru you luo*
> "<O World-Honoured One!>[7] If there is no revealed cause, how can one say that there is milk or cream?" (YAMAMOTO 1973–1975, II, p. 691, who translates 酪 *luo* as 'butter', but this would be 酥 *su*).
>
> Sogd. /v/8–10/
> */8/ (ʾ)[βcʾnpδy xwyštrʾ*[8] *kδwty ZK] /9/ wy(c)ʾγtk ʾnβʾnt Lʾ ʾstʾ[t 18–20] /10/ ʾxš(yβ)ty ZY ʾsty ʾPZY cš(t)[h]*
> "O m[aster of the world, if there were] no wise cause, [how could one say: There is] milk and there is cream."

The passage is about the uniqueness of the nature of things (cf. Chin. 一法 *yi fa* 'one *dharma*'). The text lists the dairy products Chin. 乳 *ru* 'milk' and 酪 *luo* 'coagulated milk, cream'. The first term is translated as Sogd *ʾxšyβty* 'milk', while the latter is rendered again as Sogd. *cšth*.

We will now return to the five stages of *ghee* making (see Table 1). In comparing the Sogdian with the Chinese terms it will be possible to define the exact meaning of the Sogdian equivalents of the specific dairy products within the fabrication process. Furthermore, we will refer to the Zoroastrian Avestan-Pahlavi text *Nērangestān* (N) that contains some passages on offerings to the water and the fire, among them several kinds of dairy products.

1. Milk

Clarified butter is rendered from butter. The whole production starts therefore with fresh milk (Chin. 乳 *ru*, Skt. *kṣīra*, *dughda* etc., see SH, p. 248a; *BCSD*, p. 78b), the Sogdian equivalent is n.m. *ʾxšyβt-* /ᵊxšīft/ (see passage 4: nom.sg. *ʾxšyβty*; cf. BENVENISTE 1946, p. 103; MACKENZIE 1976, II, p. 78; *DMT III/2*, p. 217), < Av. *xšuuipta-* (*GMS*, §§ 157, 243).

2. Cream

Milk contains butterfat in a fat-in-water emulsion. When it is allowed to stand for a while, the milk coagulates and the fat concentrates at its surface (it can also be yielded by centrifugation). This fat layer, the cream (Chin. 酪 *luo* 'coagulated milk, cream', 'a thick, sour milk which is highly esteemed as a food and as a remedy or preventive'; Skt. *dadhi*, see SH, p. 115b, *s.v.* 五同緣意識, p. 417b; *BCSD*, p. 1175b),

7 Translation skipped by YAMAMOTO.
8 Or *xwštr(ʾ)/xwyštr*?

is skimmed from the milk and used for the fabrication of butter. What remains from the milk is whey, a liquid of low fat content that can be taken for the fabrication of some kinds of fresh cheese. The Sogdian designation of 'cream' is here n.f. *cšt-* /*cašt-*/ (see passage 1: acc. sg. *cšt'* for abl. sg. *cšty'*?; passage 3: acc. sg. *cšt'*; passage 4: nom. sg. *cšth*). Sogd. *cšt-* has been hitherto translated as 'koumiss', a fermented dairy product with low alcoholic content traditionally made in Central Asia from mare's milk (Henning 1946, p. 724, n. on 1017; *Padm.* 40, ed. MacKenzie 1976, I, pp. 16f., II, p. 97; Gharib 1995, p. 130). In the *Nērangestān*, this kind of beverage occurs as Av. *xšāudri- paiiah-* 'alcoholic beverage made from milk, koumiss', 'fermented milk' (*AiW*, col. 553) and is rendered as Pahl. *šusar pēm* 'liquid milk' (N 48.1, §66; 49.1, §67, ed. Kotwal/Kreyenbroek 2003, pp. 218–221). As Sundermann (*Materials*, n. 1 on translation) rightly states for the respective passage in MPNS, "*cšt'* [...] cannot be an alcoholic drink produced from milk, in this context". But he continues: "It must be that milky substance which develops from milk. It does not produce butter, but it is what of the milk remains when butter is materialized." He translates the term as 'whey'. Although one may also produce whey butter from sweet whey, this product is not used for the fabrication of clarified butter. Moreover, from the liquid that remains from the cream after butter is churned, buttermilk is produced, not whey.

The term is also recorded in a Christian Sogdian text, a homily on fasting: *zwty n' xwr' y'ty ZY n' qpy n' γ'wrwyn n' cšt' n' xšybty n' pyn n' rxpyn* "Do not consume neither liquor nor meat nor fish nor butter nor *cšt'* nor milk nor cream nor yoghurt!" (n 196/r/1–2/, quoted Sims-Williams 2012, p. 167, E29/5). Sims-Williams (2016, p. 63) translates the term as 'koumiss' too. Weber (1970, p. 54) also quotes this sentence (by skipping *zwty*) and translates: "Iss kein Fleisch, keinen Fisch, keine Butter, keinen Apéritif(?), keine Milch, keinen Quark und keinen frischen Käse!" The meanings *γ'wrwyn* 'butter' and *xšybty* 'milk' are clear in this passage. For *cšt'*, Weber (*ibid.*, n. 13) assumes a meaning 'Apéritif(?) (*i. e.*, aperitif)' with reference to Henning's translation (see above) and relates the term with NP *čašte* 'taste, whet; breakfast' (Steingass 1892, p. 392). It may belong to OIr. **čaš-* 'to drip; to drink, eat(?)', cf. MMP, NP *čašīdan*, *čaš-* 'to taste, sip', (+ **pati-*) B *ptcš-*, C *pcš-* 'to drink', B *'pc'š-*, M *pcš-* 'to taste', cf. *cš'nt* 'drink', *cš'ntk* 'thirsty', *cšn-* 'thirst', Khwar. *'cnk-* 'thirst', etc. (Benveniste 1940, p. 251; Henning 1940, p. 37 on 24; MacKenzie 1976, II, p. 97; *EWA*, III, pp. 183f.; *DMT III/1*, p. 128; Cheung 2007, pp. 35f.). Furthermore, we can refer to IAr. *chacchikā-* 'buttermilk' from **chāśī-*, **chācchī-*, cf. Pkt. *chāsī-*, Hi. *chāc(h)* '*idem*' (*EWA*, III, p. 200).

The other two terms mentioned in this passage are *pyn* and *rxpyn*: Sims-Williams (2016, p. 162) translates *pyn* as 'cream', but Weber (1970, p. 54, with n. 14) as 'Quark (*i. e.*, quark, curd, curd cheese)' with reference to NP. پینو *pīnū*, پینوک *pīnūk* 'new cheese, cream-cheese; butter-milk' (Steingass 1892, p. 270) and Av. *paiiah-* 'milk' (*AiW*, cols. 848–849). It seems that Sogd. *pyn* therefore designates a fermented dairy product resulting from coagulation of milk or whey. Sogd. *rxpyn*, probably a compound formed with *pyn*, is translated by SIMS-WILLIAMS (2016, p. 168) as 'yoghurt', but by WEBER (1970, p. 54, with n. 15) as 'frischer Käse (*i. e.*, fresh cheese, cottage cheese)' with reference to NP. رخبین *rihbīn*, *ruhbīn* 'sour milk; butter-milk, or anything dressed with it; a dish made of sour and fresh milk with flour; new cheese' (STEINGASS 1892, p. 571), cf. also NP. ریخبین *rehbīn* 'a dark-coloured acid preparation of sheep's milk and flour' (*ibid.*, p. 601). It seems that this is a dish based on a dairy product such as sour milk, but not necessarily yoghurt or cheese.

It becomes obvious that C *cšt-* is listed in this passage with other dairy products and dishes that are prohibited during fasting, and not with *zwty* 'alcoholic beverage, liquor'[9]. Another possible record of *cšt-* is in the medical-magical text So 20168/A/4/ (unpublished, quoted RECK 2018, no. 1060, as *(ʾ)štʾ* 'eight', but a reading *(c)štʾ* seems possible) where also *rwyn* 'oil, fat; butter' and *zwtk* 'alcoholic beverage, liquor' are mentioned. None of the contexts of these records of Sogd. *cšt-* necessarily requires an alcoholic beverage. Since passage 1 (see above) clearly says that butter is made from it, *cšt-* should mean 'cream' there. Butter can be made from sweet cream or from soured cream. The latter is fermented with lactic acid bacteria such as *lactobacillus* and is used to produce cultured butter. But the fabrication of clarified butter is usually from sweet cream butter. But when milk stands or is gathered for days (especially in warm climate), a natural fermentation takes place. Of course we do not know the exact fabrication process in the 5th century when the text was translated into Chinese or around the 10th century when the ms. of MPNS 2 was written.[10] Did the Sogdians really have the knowledge of the production of clarified butter, and if so, did they use the same manner of fabrication like the Chinese did centuries before? If *cšt-* can be related to IAr. *chacchikā-* 'buttermilk', this seems unlikely. From buttermilk one cannot produce butter since it is a by-product of butter-making. Either the Sogdian translator did not use the correct equivalent for Chin. 酪 *luo* but the term of a dairy product that was familiar to him in connection with butter-making, *i. e.*, 'buttermilk'. Or, he used the correct term, *i. e.*, *cšt-* really means 'cream', maybe besides other meanings.

There is no corresponding term for *cšt-* /*čašt-*/ 'cream' in other Iranian languages since other designations are used, cf. for example NP *tūy-e šīr*, *čarābe*, *čarbak*, *čarbe*, *dumāye*, *sar-e šīr* (STEINGASS 1892, pp. 338, 389–390, 535, 666). A meaning 'cream(?)' has been assumed for MPth. *pymʾdg* /*pēmādag(?)*/ (HENNING 1937, p. 87; *DMT III/1*, p. 289). The term occurs in the Manichaean

9 In MPNS 2 (So 15512 [T III D 261 K]/v/6/, ed. COLDITZ [forthcoming], as leaf 5), Sogd. *zwty* 'alcoholic beverage, liquor' renders (T.T. no. 374, vol. 12, 395b19) Chin. 酒 *jiu* 'alcoholic beverages in general, *beer, liquor, wine, intoxicant', Skt. *surā*, *maireya*, *madya* (SH, p. 340b; *BCSD*, pp. 1174f.). The term is also attested as Sogd. *zwtʾk*, *zwtk* elsewhere (HENNING 1946, pp. 719f., n. on 388; *SCE* 412, ed. MACKENZIE 1970, pp. 24f., 77; 1976, II, p. 200; GHARIB 1995, p. 469).

10 On the dating see SUNDERMANN 2010, pp. 80f.

Sermon on the Living Soul as designation of something that gives the milk stability and substance *(pym'dg pd šyft)* like the bones to the body *('stg pd tnb'r)* (SUNDERMANN 1997, pp. 65, 78–79, 122, §67,2). SUNDERMANN relates it to Pahl. *pēm* 'milk', *pēmēnīdan*, *pēmēn-* 'cause to well up, swell up' (*CPD*, p. 68) and Av. *pay-* '*idem*', *paēman-* 'breast milk' (*AiW*, cols. 817, 848). A very similar word is Sogd. *ptmδ'k* that renders in the Manichaean *Speech of the Living Soul* MMP *frwšg* /*frōšag*/, also as *prwšg*, 1) 'a dish, a kind of sweetmeats', 2) 'a curdling substance' (HENNING 1937, p. 86 and 1943, p. 63; SUNDERMANN 1985, p. 640, n. 64; *DMT III/1*, p. 281). The passage reads MMP *'wd 'gr frwšg wynd'n ky pdyš m'syh'n* = Sogd. *[rty kt]('r ZK)w (ptm)δ'k βyr'n [ ]* 'And if I will find some *frwšg*/*ptmδ'k* in which I will coagulate' (M 717/v/3/ = So 14791/16/, ed. SUNDERMANN 2012, pp. 58, 97, 112–115, 181, as 1.57) Cf. the similar passage MMP *c'wn myrd ky prwšg [š](y)yr 'bgnd ° hwstyg'n bwd* 'is like unto a man that threw *prwšg* [into] milk(?). It became hard [ ]' (M 101f/r/6–7/, ed. HENNING 1943, p. 63, frgm. A, ll. 179–180). We may also refer to Phl. *frušag* 'beestings' (*CPD*, p. 34) that is recorded in N 49.11, §67: *frušag pad pādyāb ul stānēd* 'if one offers up beestings with consecrated water' (KOTWAL/KREYENBROEK 2003, pp. 222f.). These terms designate a substance that makes the milk coagulate or curdle, MMP, MPth. *m's-*, < **mad-* (CHEUNG 2007, pp. 253f.), *i. e.*, it initiates the fermentation process. DURKIN-MEISTERERNST (*apud* SUNDERMANN 2012, p. 181, following SIMS-WILLIAMS *apud ibid.*, p. 168, n. 57,1) also translates 'beestings', *i. e.*, the colostrum or foremilk of the mother in the first hours after having given birth to a child, cf. NP فرشه *furše*, *firše* (STEINGASS 1892, p. 919). Beestings of mammals is used for the coagulation of milk to make cheese. But often rennet is applied for this purpose. Thus one may translate MMP *frwšg* and Sogd. *ptmδ'k* also as 'rennet' (cf. COLDITZ *apud* SUNDERMANN 2012, p. 168, n. 57,1). MPth. *pym'dg* could have the same meaning if one assumes that it is a MP loanword in Pth. (against MPth. **pdm'dg*) and that it goes back to **pati-mad-* like Sogd. *ptmδ'k*. All three terms cannot mean 'cream' but designate that substance that is added to the milk to ferment it and produce soured milk, *i. e.*, beestings or rennet.

Actually, the list of five stages of *ghee*-making corresponding to the 'five flavours' and the teachings of Buddha (see Table 1) mentions in third place 'curdled milk, soured milk' (Chin. 生酥 *sheng su*; Skt. *navanīta*, but cf. MW, p. 530, *s. v. náva*: 'fresh butter'). But this dairy product is usually the basis for the fabrication of cheese curd, quark, and cheese, and not of butter. In the *Nērangestān*, Av. *tūiriia-* means 'curdled, curdled milk', the Pahlavi text gives as equivalent *tēr* 'solid (food)', the gloss *panīr* 'cheese' rather points to 'solid (milk)' (N 48.2, §66, 49.3, §67, ed. KOTWAL/KREYENBROEK 2003, pp. 218–221 with n. 869, 878; cf. *AiW*, col. 656; DHABHAR 1963, p. 304, n. 8). Passage 1 (see above) mentions only four stages of butter-making, while 'curdled milk, soured milk' is missing. Maybe one could assume for Sogd. *cšt-* a meaning 'soured cream' instead from which cultured butter can be produced. Probably no difference is made here between '(sweet) cream' and 'soured cream' since fermentation could naturally happen at this stage of fabrication. Both dairy products may have been called *cšt-* in Sogdian.

3. Butter

Having been skimmed from the milk, the cream is churned, that means by agitating it the membranes of the fat globules are raptured enabling them to join with each other. A water-in-fat emulsion emerges, and the cream is separated into buttermilk and butter (Chin. 酥 *su*; Skt. *ghola*, see SH, p. 392b; *BCSD*, p. 1175a). The Sogdian equivalent is n. *rwγn* 'fat, oil; butter' (see passages 1, 3), the product is also called *γ'wrwγn* 'butter, (lit.) cow-oil' elsewhere (BENVENISTE 1940, pp. 253, 270; MACKENZIE 1976, II, pp. 101, 130); cf. also MS, C, CS *rwγn*, M, C *γ'wrwγn* (*DMT III/2*, pp. 85, 169; SIMS-WILLIAMS 2016, p. 167). But *γ'wrwγn* is not used in the passages cited above.

4. Clarified butter

Clarified butter is pure milk fat, which is produced by melting and simmering butter (usually sweet cream butter) to remove any impurities from it. The water evaporates, and the milk solids (protein and sugar) sink to the bottom or float to the surface as foam. The description of *ghee* production in passage 1 does not refer to such a defilement, but cf. passage 2. The foam is skimmed from it and the separated fat is poured off from the solids. The result is clarified butter or *ghee*, Chin. 醍醐 *ti hu*; Skt. *ghr̥ta*, *sarpirmaṇḍa* (SH, p. 451b; *BCSD*, p. 1176a). The Sogdian equivalent is n. *krkrwγn* /*karakrōγan*/ '(lit.) butter-fat' (see passage 2), cf. Av. *kāra-* 'butter' in *kārauuant*, NP *kare* 'butter' < OIr. **karaka-* (BAILEY 1955, p. 71). The word occurs also in a Sogdian medical text (So 10100k + So 18249 + So 18250 + So 18251/v/3/, ed. RECK/BENKATO 2018, text 1, pp. 70f., 72 on 3) and as a loanword in OUyg. in *U 9224 [no finding siglum]/r/3/ *kakrugun* (RACHMATI 1932, p. 432, text 5.3, as *kakruγun*) and possibly also in *U 9216 [T II Y 18]/v/11/ (*ibid*., p. 408, text 1.61, p. 435 n., as *karγučïγun(?)*) and *U 9220 [T II D 53]/15/ (*ibid*., p. 422, text 3.73, as *kakruqa(?)*; see also KNÜPPEL 2013, nos. 3, 33, 38). BLUM (2013, pp. 346f., n. 56) refers to the fact that "this sutra at times distinguishes between cooled, solid clarified butter (*ghr̥ta*) and the froth that forms on top of heated, liquid clarified butter (*sarpis* or *sarpirmaṇḍa*), based on a comparison with the Sanskrit fragments and Tibetan translations" (ed. HABATA 2007), but that Chin. 醍醐 *ti hu* is used for both although it "corresponds to the Middle Indic form *gr̥ta*, which is the equivalent of the Sanskrit *ghr̥ta*", cf. LMChin. *tɦiaj xɦuə̆*, EMChin. *dɛj γɔ* (PULLEYBLANK 1991, pp. 127, 305). It is not clear whether Sogd. *krkrwγn* has this double meaning as well.

We can now summarize the four stages of the fabrication of clarified butter as described in the passages of MPNS 2 cited above (see Table 2):

Table 2

Stage of *ghee* making	Sanskrit	Chinese	Sogdian
Fresh milk	*kṣīra*	乳 *ru*	*ʾxšyβt-*
Coagulated milk, (sweet or soured) cream	*dadhi*	酪 *luo*	*cšt-*
Butter	*ghola*	酥 *su*	*rwγn*
Clarified butter, *ghee*	*ghṛta*, *sarpirmaṇḍa*	醍醐 *ti hu*	*krkrwγn*

Abbreviations

General Abbreviations

abl.	ablative
acc.	accusative
Av.	Avestan
B	Buddhist Sogdian
C	Christian Sogdian
Chin.	Chinese
EMChin.	Early Middle Chinese
f.	feminine
Hi.	Hindi
IAr.	Indo-Aryan
Khwar.	Khwaresmian
LMChin.	Late Middle Chinese
M	Manichaean Sogdian in Manichaean script
m.	masculine
MMP	Manichaean Middle Persian in Manichaean script
MPth.	Manichaean Parthian in Manichaean script
MS	Manichaean Sogdian in Sogdian script
ms(s).	manuscript(s)
n.	noun; also (foot)note
nom.	nominative
NP	New Persian
OIr.	Old Iranian
Phl.	Pahlavi
Pkt.	Prākrit
sg.	singular
Skt.	Sanskrit
Sogd.	Sogdian
OUygh.	Old Uyghur

Bibliographical abbreviations

AcIr	Acta Iranica
BSO(A)S	*Bulletin of the School of Oriental (and African) Studies*
BTT	Berliner Turfantexte
CFM	Corpus Fontium Manichaeorum
MPNS	*Mahāyāna Mahāparinirvāṇa-sūtra*
MPNS 2	Manuscript 2 of the *Mahāyāna Mahāparinirvāṇa-sūtra*
N	*Nērangestān*
Padm.	*Padmacintāmaṇidhāraṇīsūtra*
SCE	*Sūtra of the causes and effects of actions*

SPAW	*Sitzungsberichte der Preußischen Akademie der Wissenschaften zu Berlin, Philosophisch-Historische Klasse*
StIr	Studia Iranica
TPS	*Transactions of the Philological Society*
VOHD	Verzeichnis der Orientalischen Handschriften in Deutschland
WMO	*Written Monuments of the Orient*
ZII	*Zeitschrift für Indologie und Iranistik*

Bibliography

AiW = BARTHOLOMAE, CH. 1904: *Altiranisches Wörterbuch.* Strassburg [repr. Berlin 1961].

BAILEY, H.W. 1955: "Indo-Iranian Studies III." In: *TPS* 54/1, pp. 55–82.

BCSD = HIRAKAWA, A. 1997: *Buddhist Chinese-Sanskrit Dictionary.* Tokyo.

BENVENISTE, E. 1940. *Textes sogdiens, edites, traduits et commentes par E. Benveniste.* Paris (Mission Pelliot en Asie Centrale; serie in-quarto 3).

— 1946: *Vessantara Jātaka: texte sogdien edite, traduit et commente par E. Benveniste.* Paris (Mission Pelliot en Asie Centrale; serie in-quarto 4).

BLUM, M.L. 2013: *The Nirvana Sutra (Mahāparinirvāṇa-sūtra).* Vol. 1 *(Taishō volume 12, number 374).* Transl. from the Chinese by MARK L. BLUM. Berkeley, Cal. (BDK English Tripiṭaka series).

CHEUNG, J. 2007: *Etymological Dictionary of the Iranian Verb.* Leiden/Boston (Leiden Indo-European Etymological Dictionary Series 2).

COLDITZ, I. (forthcoming): *A Sogdian Version of the* Mahāyāna-Mahāparinirvāṇasūtra *in* pustaka *Format.* Turnhout (BTT).

CPD = MACKENZIE, D.N. 1971: *A Concise Pahlavi Dictionary.* London.

DHABHAR, B.N. 1963: *Translation of Zand-î Khûrtak Avistâk.* Bombay.

DMT III/1 = DURKIN-MEISTERERNST, D. 2004: *Dictionary of Manichaean Middle Persian and Parthian.* Vol. III: *Texts from Central Asia and China.* Pt. 1: *Texts in Middle Persian and Parthian.* Turnhout (CFM. Subsidia. Dictionary of Manichaean Texts).

DMT III/2 = SIMS-WILLIAMS, N./D. DURKIN-MEISTERERNST 2012: *Dictionary of Manichaean Sogdian and Bactrian.* Vol. II: *Texts from Central Asia and China.* Pt. 2: *Texts in Sogdian and Bactrian.* Turnhout (CFM. Subsidia. Dictionary of Manichaean Texts).

EWA, I–III = MAYRHOFER, M. 1992–2001: *Etymologisches Wörterbuch des Altindoarischen.* 3 vols. Heidelberg (Indogermanische Bibliothek, Reihe 2: Wörterbücher).

GHARIB, B. 1995: *Sogdian Dictionary: Sogdian-Persian-English.* Tehran.

GMS = GERSHEVITCH, I. 1954: *A Grammar of Manichaean Sogdian.* Oxford.

HABATA, H. 2007: *Die zentralasiatischen Sanskrit-Fragmente des Mahāparinirvāṇa-Mahāsūtra. Kritische Ausgabe des Sanskrittextes und seiner tibetischen Übertragung im Vergleich mit den chinesischen Übersetzungen.* Marburg (Indica et Tibetica. Monographien zu den Sprachen und Literaturen des indo-tibetischen Kulturraumes 51).

Henning, W.B. 1937: "A List of Middle Persian and Parthian Words." In: *BSOS* 9 (1937–1939), pp. 79–92 [= Henning 1977, I, pp. 559–572].
— 1940: *Sogdica*. London (James G. Forlong Fund 21) [= Henning 1977, II, pp. 1–67].
— 1943: "The Book of the Giants." In: *BSOAS* 11, pp. 52–74 [= Henning 1977, II, pp. 115–137].
— 1946: "The Sogdian Texts of Paris." In: *BSOAS* 11, pp. 713–740 [= Henning 1977, II, pp. 231–258].
— 1977: *W. B. Henning Selected Papers*. 2 vols. Leiden/Téhéran/Liege (AcIr 14–15).
Knüppel, M. 2013: *Alttürkische Handschriften*. T. 17: *Heilkundliche, volksreligiöse und Ritualtexte*. Stuttgart (VOHD XIII, 25).
Kotwal, F.M./Ph.G. Kreyenbroek 2003: *The Hērbedestān and Nērangestān*. Vol. III: *Nērangestān, Fragard 2*. Paris (StIr, Cahier 30).
MacKenzie, D.N. 1970: *The 'Sūtra of the causes and effects of actions' in Sogdian*. London (London Oriental Series 22).
— 1976: *The Buddhist Sogdian Texts of the British Library*. Téhéran-Liège (AcIr 10).
MW = Monier-Williams, M. 1899: *A Sanskrit-English dictionary, etymologically and philologically arranged with special reference to cognate Indo-European languages*. Oxford [repr., new ed., greatly enl. and improved, with the collaboration of E. Leumann. Oxford 1960].
PDB = Buswell Jr., R.E./D.S. Lopez Jr. (eds.) 2014: *The Princeton Dictionary of Buddhism*. Princeton.
Pulleyblank, E. 1991: *Lexicon of reconstructed pronunciation in early Middle Chinese, late Middle Chinese, and early Mandarin*. Vancouver.
Rachmati, G.R. 1932: "Zur Heilkunde der Uiguren II." In: *SPAW* 1932, no. XXII Berlin, pp. 401–448.
Reck, Ch. 2016: *Mitteliranische Handschriften*. T. 2: *Berliner Turfanfragmente buddhistischen Inhalts in soghdischer Schrift*. Stuttgart (VOHD XVIII,2).
— 2017: "Zwei weitere kleine Bruchstücke soghdischer Versionen des *Mahāyāna Mahāparinirvāṇa-sūtras* in der Berliner Turfansammlung." In: Team "Turfanforschung" (ed.): *Zur lichten Heimat: Studien zu Manichäismus, Iranistik und Zentralasienkunde im Gedenken an Werner Sundermann*. Wiesbaden (Iranica 25), pp. 597–604.
— 2018: *Berliner Turfanfragmente christlichen Inhalts und Varia in soghdischer Schrift*. Stuttgart (VOHD XVIII, 3).
Reck, Ch./A. Benkato 2018: "'Like a virgin': A Sogdian Recipe for Restoring Virginity and the Sanskrit Background of Sogdian Medicine." In: *WMO* 8/2, pp. 67–91.
Reichelt, H. 1928: "Soghdisches II." In: *ZII* 6, pp. 206–214.
Rossi, A.V. 2013: "Perception of unevenness and the lexical family of sogdian *Pēsak* ~ *Pesē̆* ~ *Pisē*." In: S.R. Tochtas'ev/P.B. Lurje (eds.): *Commentationes Iranicae: sbornik statej k 90-letju V.A. Livšica*. St. Petersburg, pp. 367–377.
SH = Soothill, W.E./L. Hodous 1937: *A Dictionary of Chinese Buddhist Terms*. London [repr. Delhi 2003].
Sims-Williams, N. 2012: *Mitteliranische Handschriften*. T. 4: *Iranian Manuscripts in Syriac Script in the Berlin Turfan Collection*. Stuttgart (VOHD XVIII,4).
— 2016: *A Dictionary: Christian Sogdian, Syriac and English*. Wiesbaden (Beiträge zur Iranistik 41).

STEINGASS, F.J. 1892: *A comprehensive Persian-English dictionary: including the Arabic words and phrases to be met with in persian literature. Being Johnson and Richardson's Persian, Arabic and English dictionary. Revised, enlarged, and entirely reconstructed.* London [repr. 1963].

SUNDERMANN, W. 1985: "Der Gōwišn ī grīw zīndag-Zyklus." In: *Papers in Honour of Professor Mary Boyce.* Vol. II. Leiden (AcIr 25), pp. 629–650.

— 1997: *Der Sermon von der Seele: Eine Lehrschrift des östlichen Manichäismus. Edition der parthischen und soghdischen Version mit einem Anhang von Peter Zieme: Die türkischen Fragmente des "Sermons von der Seele".* Turnhout (BTT XIX).

— 2010: "A Sogdian *Mahāyānamahāparinirvāṇasūtra* manuscript." In: T. IRISAWA (ed.): *"The Way of Buddha" 2003: The 100th Anniversary of the Otani Mission and the 50th of the Research Society for Central Asian Cultures.* Kyoto (Cultures of the Silk Road and Modern Science 1), pp. 75–83.

— 2012: *Die Rede der Lebendigen Seele. Ein manichäischer Hymnenzyklus in mittelpersischer und soghdischer Sprache.* Turnhout (BTT XXX).

— [unpublished]: *Materials and preliminary manuscripts of an edition of the Sogdian version of the Mahāyāna Mahāparinirvāṇa-sūtra in pustaka format.* Unpublished drafts.

T. T. = *Taishō Tripiṭaka. The SAT Daizōkyō Text Database.* Online edition, available at https://21dzk.l.u-tokyo.ac.jp/SAT/satdb2015.php?lang=en (accessed 10. April 2021).

UTZ, D. 1976: *An Unpublished Sogdian Version of the Mahāyāna Mahāparinirvāṇa-sūtra in the German Turfan Collection.* Unpublished Ph.D. thesis. Harvard University.

WEBER, D. 1970: *Die Stellung der sogenannten Inchoativa im Mitteliranischen.* Göttingen.

YAMAMOTO, K. 1973–1975: *The Mahayana Mahaparinirvana-sutra: A Complete Translation from the Classical Chinese Language in 3 volumes, annotated and with Full Glossary, Index, and Concordance.* Tokyo.

YOSHIDA, Y. 2015: "A handlist of Buddhist Sogdian texts." In: 京都大學文學部研究紀要 *Kyōto daigaku bungakubu kenkyū kiyō* 54, pp. 167–180.

The Owl in the Zoroastrian Tradition: Contribution to Iranian Bestiary I

Touraj Daryaee, Irvine

One of the earliest and well-known modern novels in Persian literature is the *Blind Owl,* written in 1930 by Sadeq Hedayat, in which the protagonist in the story is in dialogue with his shadow in the form of an owl. While the interpretation of the story is open to discussion,[1] one of its effects was the popularization of the term *būf* "owl" in contemporary Persian at the cost of *joγd* which is Sogdian in origin.[2] The nocturnal character of the owl makes it susceptible to ill omen and desolation in the Iranian tradition. This is made amply apparent in Persian poetry where the owl nests among ruins of buildings. It is interesting that the house of the protagonist in Hedayat's novel is just outside the confines of the desolate city of Rayy which had been brought into ruin by the Mongol invasion in the thirteenth century. It is of note that while where the owl resides is in a place of ruin, for the people of Rayy and Marv in the medieval period, the presence of this bird was considered an auspicious sign.[3] This, I believe is the vestige of an older belief in the importance and benevolence of the owl. In Hedayat's own study of Iranian folklore, however, the owl was shown to be considered as a bad omen, hence appearing in the darkest novel of modern Persian literature.[4]

In the world of Zoroastrian animals and beasts, it appears that the owl has a curious position, where it is believed that it (*būf*) is classified as an evil creature,[5] and in other places under the term *joγd*, it is thought of as a beneficent bird. This divergent view of the owl in Zoroastrian literature has not been adequately explained and in this essay in honor of my colleague, Dieter Weber, I will attempt to clarify the matter and demonstrate the reason for such a discrepancy regarding the supposed dualistic view of the owl. By stripping the Islamic view of the owl which has impacted the Iranian notions of the bird, I will try to show that the owl in the Zoroastrian tradition was always considered benevolent, in many ways similar to the Greek tradition.

1 Ajudani 2006, p. 90.
2 Henning 1939, p. 96.
3 Emil Homerin 1985, p. 166; A'lam 1989.
4 Hedayat 1342, p. 131.
5 Moazami 2005, p. 313.

Let us look at the general conception of the owl in world religions. While the owl has both benevolent and malevolent characteristics, in most traditions such as that of the Judeo-Christian tradition, the bird is a sign and symbol of evil. This negative view of the owl in the Judaic tradition is apparent where for example the destroyed city of Babylon becomes the abode of wild and evil creatures in the book of Isaiah (13:21–22):

"Wildcats will lie there,
And owls will fill their homes,
And there will be the young ostriches,
And demons will dance there,
And hyenas will howl in their palaces,
And jackals in their palaces of delight"

This ruin of places, where the owl resides, is repeated in the book of Isaiah and has been thought to make the bird the agents of Yahweh to provide divine lessons for human discretion.[6] It is of note that in the Christian tradition the owl continues to be disdained, from the time of Physiologus, where the Latin rendition of his work invokes similar Biblical passages. The notable addition to Physiologus is the anti-Semitic turn, where there is the association of the owl with the Jewish people, connecting them with darkness, versus the Christian choice of Jesus and the light.[7]

This negative view is in contrast, for example, with the positive image of the owl in Greece and American Indian religions.[8] Thus, the owl is not viewed universally as negative. In the pre-Islamic Arabic tradition which continued into the Islamic period the owl was one of the attendants of the *jinns*, and its presence signaled death and destruction.[9] This negative view has probably impacted the post-Sasanian world of Iran as well, with the exception of the *Shāhnāmeh*.[10] Recently an Iranian scholar has suggested that the discrepancy regarding the owl has to do with the differences between the birds in the species of owl, where the large one, which hunted animals, was deemed evil, while the small one was considered as beneficent.[11] While this suggestion seems most interesting, I believe the ambivalent nature of the owl is due to another reason all-together. We already have birds of prey in the Zoroastrian tradition which are hunters, such as the eagle, but they are still classified as beneficent animals.

In the *Manāfi' Haywān*, one of the most important medieval Persian bestiary books, the owl again has the same ambivalent position, where it is considered as a bad omen,[12] but it is also seen as the strongest of all birds and the hunter

6 NOEGEL 2019, pp. 108–109.
7 PHYSIOLOGUS 2009, p. 10.
8 DUNNIGAN 1987, pp. 6936–6937.
9 EMIL HOMERIN 1985, p. 166.
10 SOLTANI 1389, pp. 388–390 ; MOTEVASELI/NADAFI 1394, p. 167.
11 SOLTANI 1389, p. 381.
12 ROSHAN 2009 [1388], p. 46.

of snakes and deadly creatures, with the best eyesight at night.[13] Certainly this Xrafstar-killing nature would be considered as most positive in the Zoroastrian world-view, and would surely make it a beneficent bird. However, in the Persian book of bestiary, its association with bad omen and with ruins is suggested to originate from the notion that it is a bird which in fact protects desolate places from evil residence.[14] Alas, in Medieval Persian literature, colored by the Arabic and Islamic view of the owl, the animal is not regarded in such a positive light with such poets as Khaqānī, Nezāmī, and specially Sa'dī.[15]

Fig. 1. Manāfi' Haywān (Morgan Library)

13 Roshan 2009 [1388], p. 135.
14 Soltani 1389, p. 383.
15 Motevaseli/Nadafi 1394, pp. 171–175.

Long ago, the Zoroastrian savant, J.J. MODI attempted to provide a different view of the owl, in comparing both the Zoroastrian and world traditions, but in fact showed the inauspiciousness of the bird in Persian literature.[16] This fact has also been shown in the meticulous study of the owl, under the entry "*Būf*," by the late Houchang Aʿlam, who traced all the evidence for the owl, from the Zoroastrian and non-Zoroastrian tradition in the Iranian world. However, he does point out that the earlier term *joγd* is better represented than *būf* and that Arabic *būm*, and also *būf*, only became popular with HEDAYAT's novel in the twentieth century.[17] This matter is consequential and important as a clue to understanding the reason why the owl has this ambivalent character in the Iranian tradition.

Let us look at the *Avesta* to find the earliest evidence for the place of the owl in the Zoroastrian bestiary. In the seventeenth chapter of the *Wīdēwdād*, there is an important section on the disposal of nails which in the Zoroastrian and in the Iranian tradition till today, needs special care. If the proper ritual and covering of the nails are not taken into consideration, then demons and noxious creatures will spring and they will use them as a weapon.[18] In the *Wīdēwdād* there is the mention of a specific bird with regard to taking care of nails (WD 17.9):

paiti tē mərəγa aṣ̌ō.zušta
imą̊ sruuą̊ vaēδaiiemi
imą̊ sruuą̊ āuuaēδaiiemi
imą̊ sə tē sruuą̊
mərəγa aṣ̌ō.zušta hiiārə
arštaiiasca karətaiiasca
θanuuarəca iṣ̌auuasca ərəzifiiō.parəna
asanasca fradaxṣ̌aniia
paiti daēuuō māzaniiąn
"To you, O bird, Ašōzušt,
these nails I announce and consecrate unto you.
May these nails be for you, O bird, Ašōzušt,
spears and knives,
bows and falcon-feathered arrows,
and sling-stones against the Maznīyan Daivas."

In this passage, the bird (*mərəγa*) which uses the nails against the Maznīyan Daivas is called the Ašōzušt. While in the *Avesta*, the Ašōzušt is not given a specific identity, it is in the Middle Persian texts that we find the first associations with the owl. The association of this bird in the Zoroastrian Middle Persian and

16 MODI 1924, pp. 51–60.
17 AʿLAM 1981: Thanks to Ali Ashraf Sadeghi I had access to the mention of the owl in Persian literature. There were twenty five texts in which the *būf* is invoked, usually with a negative connotation. Only in the *Bāz-nāme-ye Naserī*, one kind of owl, the Shāh-būf "King of owls," is considered beneficent, HESAM UD-DOWLEH 1391, p. 107.
18 LINCOLN 1977, p. 360; BUYANER 2019, pp. 25–31.

Persian texts is amply clear to be identified with the owl.[19] In the *Bundahišn* it is stated that (XXVII.46):

> *murw ī Ašōzušt kē murw ī zōrbarag Wahman murw šuyd*
> *rāy gōwēnd kē abestāg pad uzwān dād ēstēd, ka gōwēd dēwān az-iš wirēzēnd ānōh bun nē kunēnd.*
> "The Ašōzušt bird which is called the Zōrbarag Wahman bird,
> they say it is the owl who spoke the *Avesta*, when it speaks (the *Avesta*), the demons flee from it and will not stay there."[20]

It is in the Iranian *Bundahišn* that this connection is given a full treatment (24.28):

> *murw ī ašōzušt kē murw ī zōhrbarag ud Wahman murw ī* ***šugzag****-iz xwānēnd rāy gōwēd kū-š Abestāg-ē(w) pad uzwān dād ēstēd ka gōwēd dēwān aziš wirēzēnd ud ānōh bunag nē dārēnd ēd rāy bunag pad wiyābān kunēd ud andar Anērānestān bawēd tā dēwān ānōh bunag nē kunēnd*[21]
> "It says about the Ašōzušt bird, which they also call the righteous libation-bearing bird, the bird of Wahman, and also the owl. It says: 'The *Avesta* was created on its tongue. When it recites, the demons flee from it and do not dwell there. This is the reason why it builds its home in the desert and in non-Iranian lands, so that the demons will not dwell there."[22]

A few observations are in order for this passage. First is the important identification of the habitation of the owl in desolate places (*wiyābān*), which may give an alternative, and not all-together negative reason, for this residence. As we mentioned above, the reason for the existence of the owl in such places would be to keep the demons and evil away. Secondly, we find the term *šugzag* for the owl, Sogdian *cywt-* which has entered into the Persian language as *joyd or čuyd*.[23] In the sixteenth chapter of Saddar Nasr the bird is again described as follows:

> که اورمزد به افزونی مرغی بیافریده است که او را اشو زشت خوانند و بهمن مرغ نیز خوانند کوف نیز خوانند ناخن خورد
> That Ohrmazd has created a bird who is called Ašōzušt and also is called Bahman bird, it is also called Kūf, it eats nails.[24]

Likewise in the *Persian Rivayats of Hormazyar Framarz*, we find a general classification of Ohrmazdian animals which includes the owl (*joyd*), who, curiously, when dead is said not to be considered as carrion (*nasā*).[25] The *joyd* or "owl" then is on a different plain of sanctity and is placed among some of the holiest animals of the Zoroastrian world. It should be mentioned that as a rule in

19 Moazami 2014, p. 395, ft. 3.
20 Behzadi 1990, p. 101.
21 Pakzad 2005, pp. 275–276.
22 Agostini/Thrope 2020, p. 123.
23 Henning 1939, p. 96.
24 Dhabhar 1909, ch. 14.
25 Dhabhar 1932, p. 256.

the Zoroastrian tradition, birds are beneficent animals and are created for a clear function, and according to the *Bundahišn* all are opponents of noxious creatures (*hamēstārīh xrafstarān*).[26] Then one must conclude that it must be the Islamic and the Abrahamic tradition which has imposed this negative view of the owl, as a bird associated with dead, ruin and as a bad omen. This hypothesis could be accepted if it were not for the alleged appearance of the owl in the *Bundahišn*. In Chapter V regarding the opposition of the two spirits we read that for every beneficent creation of Ohrmazd, the Evil Spirit made a counter creation (Bd. 5.3):

> *šagr ud gurg sardagān duzān ō sagān ud gōspandān wazag*
> *ō māhīgān* ***būg*** *abāg abārīg xrafstar ī parrwar ō murwān*[27]
> "Lions, wolf species, and cheetahs against dogs and cattle; frogs against fish; owls and other winged vermin against birds."[28]

The late Mehrdād Bahār in his translation of the passage remarked that all the three manuscripts, TD1, TD2 and DH, have *bwk* (*būg*) and wondered why the owl would be considered as a winged *xrafstar*![29] The second passage where the supposed word for owl appears is in the chapter on the nature of the wolf species, where the Evil Spirit fabricated fifteen species against the Ohrmazdian ones. Some of these include (Bd. 23.2):

> *yōz ud haftār ud tōrag kē ušgāl-iz xwānēnd gār-kan*
> *garzag ud gurbag ud ān ī parrwar čiyōn* ***būg***[30]
> Cheetahs, hyenas, jackals — which they also call *ušgāl*;
> cave digger *garzag*, cats, winged ones such as owls"[31]

In this passage TD2 and DH have *bwk*, while TD1 supplies *bwp*.[32]

It is interesting that in the same chapter later the *joγd* is mentioned as a beneficent animal. Then how can we explain such a discrepancy regarding the owl in the same chapter of the *Bundahišn*? I would like to suggest that in fact none of the two passages above are about the owl and that the owl only appears as the beneficent *joγd* in this unique Middle Persian encyclopedic text. Thus, *būf* does not appear in any Middle Persian texts as far as we know and D.N. MacKenzie's *būf, *būg* in his dictionary obviously relies on the passages quoted above.[33] Long ago Hanns-Peter Schmidt suggested that *bwk*, which is the main winged creature opposing the birds in the *Bundahišn*, and also in the list of wolf species, should be a kind of mythical serpent, perhaps a loanword from Sanskrit, *bhoga*.[34]

26 Behzadi 1368, p. 101.
27 Pakzad 2005, p. 72.
28 Agostini/Thrope 2020, p. 36.
29 Bahar 167, no. 3.
30 Pakzad 2005, pp. 263–264.
31 Agostini/Thrope 202, p. 117.
32 Pakzad 2005, p. 264.
33 MacKenzie 1990, p. 20.
34 Schmidt 1980a, p. 210.

There are indeed references in the Iranian tradition to a winged/flying/gliding snake (*mār ī pad parr*). Arash Zeini (per personal correspondence) suggests that the term *būg* in the two *Bundahišn* passages is not to be equated with *būf*, as other editors have suggested, but rather with MP *karbūg* 'lizard', seemingly designating a species of winged lizard: ***būg*** *abāg abārīg xrafstar ī parrwar* (Bd. 5.3) "the lizard together with other winged vermin"; *ān ī parrwar čiyōn* ***būg*** (Bd. 23.2) "winged ones such as the lizard". If this explanation is correct, we are facing in the quoted passages a (possibly mythical) winged creature, a snake or lizard, opposing in the Zoroastrian world the beneficent bird species, created by Ohrmazd.

I believe what needs to be done is a much more detailed study of Zoroastrian bestiary to better understand and distinguish the fabulous animals and creatures from those real and corporeal. In the Medieval period a number of books on animals, including the fabulous ones (*ʿAjāʾīb al-makhlughāt*),[35] came to be written, which draws on the Zoroastrian tradition. From the Avesta to the Middle Persian Zoroastrian texts, there are classifications and divisions which present a native Zoroastrian view of the animal world. However, this is only an initial inquiry into the animal world of the rich Zoroastrian tradition and the identity and function of certain animals remains vague at best. What can be said here is that in the world of Zoroastrian bestiary, while such mythical birds as Čamrūš[36] and Sēnmurw[37] personify the beneficent creation, Būg (and the Kamak bird)[38] represent the evil and fabulous winged creatures. Consequently, the owl was not considered evil in the Zoroastrian classification of animals, as all corporeal birds were beneficent and created by Ohrmazd.[39] Only with the influence of the Islamic tradition did the owl lose its status, where in the twentieth century Hedayat provided a negative connotation for it, both in the Persian novel and Perso-Islamicate folklore.

Bibliography

Ajudani, M. 2006: *Hedāyat, Būf-e Kūr va Nacionalism.* London.

A'lam, H. 1989: "Būf." In: E. Yarshater (ed.): *Encyclopaedia Iranica.* Available online: https://www.iranicaonline.org/articles/buf-owl-commonly-called-jogd (last accessed: 02.12.23).

Bahar, M. 1990: *Bundaheš.* Tehran.

Behzadi, R. 1991: *Bundaheš-e hendī.* Tehran.

Buyaner, D.B. 2019: "Zur Haar- und Nagelpflege im Zoroastrismus Beiträge zur Erklärung mittelpersischer Rechts- und Religionsterminologie III." In: A.

35 Compareti 2018, p. 126.
36 Williams 1990.
37 Schmidt 2002; Compareti 2018.
38 Schmidt 1980b, pp. 1–85.
39 Bahar 1369, p. 102.

Hintze/D. Durkin-Meisterernst/C. Naumann (eds.): *A Thousand Judgements: Festschrift for Maria Macuch.* Wiesbaden, pp. 25–42.

COMPARETI, M. 2018: *Fabulous Creatures and Spirits in Ancient Iranian Culture.* Bologna.

CURLY, M.J. (tr.) 2009: Physiologus, *A Medieval Book of Nature Lore.* Chicago.

DUNNIGAN, H. 2005: "Owls." In: L. JONES (ed.): *Encyclopedia of Religion* 10. Oakland, pp. 6936–6397.

HEDĀYAT, S. 1963 [1342]: *Neyrangestān.* Tehran.

HENNING, W.B. 1939: "Sogdian Loan-Words in New Persian." In: *Bulletin of the School of Oriental Studies* 10, 1, pp. 93–106.

EMIL HOMERIN, T. 1985: "Echoes of a Thirsty Owl: Death and Afterlife in Pre-Islamic Arabic Poetry." In: *Journal of Near Eastern Studies* 44, 3, pp. 165–184

LINCOLN, B. 1977: "Treatment of Hair and Fingernails among the Indo-Europeans." In: *History of Religions* 16, 4, pp. 351–362.

MACKENZIE, D.N. 1990: *A Concise Pahlavi Dictionary.* Oxford.

MOAZAMI, M. 2005: "Evil Animals in the Zoroastrian Religion." In: *History of Religions* 44/4, pp. 300–317.

MODI, J.J. 1924: "The Owl in Folklore." In: *Journal and Proceedings of the Asiatic Society of Bengal* 19, pp. 51–60.

MOTEVASELI, N./M. NADAFI 2006: "Vīrāneh nešīn-e mēnō-ye khojastegī va gojastegī joghd dar Asār-e sarāmadān-e sabkha-ye mokhtalef-e še'r-e fārsī." In: *Dehkhoda* 7, 26, pp. 155–178.

NOEGEL, S.B. 2019: "From Ape to Zebra. On Wild Animals and Taxonomy in Ancient Israel." In: R. MATTILA/S. ITO/S. FINK (eds.): *Animals and their Relation to Gods, Humans and Things in the Ancient World*, pp. 95–133.

PAKZAD, F. 2005: *Bundahishn: Zoroastrische Kosmologie und Kosmogonie.* Tehran.

ROSHAN, M. 2009 [1388]: 'A-H. M.M. Ibrahim Marāghe'ī, *Manāfi' Haywān.* Tehran.

SCHMIDT, H.-P. 1980a: "Ancient Iranian Animal Classification." In: *Studien zur Indologie und Iranistik* 5/6, pp. 209–244.

— 1980b: "The Sēmurw. Of Birds and Dogs and Bats." In: *Persica* 9, pp. 1–85.

— 2002: "Simorḡ". In: *Encyclopædia Iranica.* Available online: https://www.iranicaonline.org/articles/simorg (last accessed 20.06.24).

SOLTANI, S. 2011: "Joghd dar gozar-e rūzegārān." In: *Bukhara* 75, pp. 373–393. Available online: https://bukharamag.com/1389.04.2111.html (last accessed: 02.12.23).

WILLIAMS, A.V. 1990: "Čamrūš." In: E Yarshater (ed): Encyclopaedia Iranica. Available online: https://www.iranicaonline.org/articles/camrus-or-cinamrus-menog-i-xrad-chap (last accessed: 02.12.23).

Hübschmann and the Middle Iranian Part on Armenian Loanwords

DESMOND DURKIN-MEISTERERNST, Berlin

To DIETER WEBER in high esteem

In HÜBSCHMANN's *Armenische Grammatik* 1897 (AG in the following), as is well known, there is a section on 'Persische Wörter' from pages 91–259. He numbers the entries from 1–686. Most of these are words of the middle Iranian period, but of course at his time only Middle Persian and Modern Persian were attested. What was entirely remarkable about these words in Armenian, is that they sometimes had a different form from Middle Persian words. For HÜBSCHMANN they were Parthian words, of which at the time only a few were attested. Only in 1904 when the results of the First Turfan Expedition were being made known in Berlin was it possible to see attestations of these Parthian words. HÜBSCHMANN was ahead of his time, and this was because of his strict observance of the sound laws.

I would like to draw attention to two aspects of HÜBSCHMANN's work. One is the form of his catalogue of 686 words and the other is the amount of genuine Middle Persian words he counted as loanwords. He considered a large number of words as Middle Persian, but most of them are actually (unattested at the time) Parthian words; I will scrutinize the genuine Middle Persian words he had come across in the anonymous work entitled 'History of Sebeos'.

On the form of the catalogue of 686 words, we can see that the entries are standardised. First is the Armenian source, then a Persian word, then a commentary on that, and some further notes. The Persian cognates are indicated by '='. But occasionally this is different, where he could have used the sign '≠' to indicate a mismatch. However it was not his intention to point out mismatches. He also has cross references. So we are looking at a well-kept numbered note-book.

This is the common case:

<AG>[1] 29 (p. 99) "անդոհական *andohakan* 'beängstigend, schrecklich' Sargis 12. Jhd., Grig. Mask. 13. Jhd., *andohil* 'Angst bekommen' Axtark̔, abgeleitet von *andoh*, das nicht belegt ist

= np. *andōh* 'Kummer, Betrübniss', *andōhgīn* 'bekümmert, betrübt', phl. *andōh* 'sorrow, grief, mourning' P.N. p. 68."

1 The entries are prefixed by numbers in HÜBSCHMANN's *Armenische Grammatik* (AG).

The second paragraph is regularly introduced by a '='. However, there are exceptions.

The following case is less common:

<AG> 19 (p. 96). "անանուխ *ananux* ἡδύοσμον 'Minze' (nur Mt. 23, 23, Luc. 11, 42 und Med. Schr.)
zu syr. נגעא *nānʿā* (für *naʿnəā*, arab. *naʿnaʿ* 'Minze' oder np. *nān-x*^{v}*āh* A.M. 260, Achund. Nr. 551 = *nānūxēh* 'Ammi' (νανοῦχα 'Ammi' du Cange, vgl. A.St. Nr. 1418)? Über Ammi und Minze vgl. Löw, Aram. Pflanzennamen p. 259ff. Phl. *nānā nānūkspram* Bdh. S. 66, z. 21 nach Justi = 'Minze zur Brotwürze', nach West, PT.1, 104: 'the bread-baker's basil' ??"

Here he inexplicably uses 'zu' instead of '='. There are also other cases where the sign '=' does not open the second paragraph. For example:

<AG> 99 (p. 117). "բան *ban* MGg. 612 = np. *bān* 'Moringa aptera' (Myrobalane) Achund. 213."

The usual way is that '=' is the starter for the second paragraph. But here the first entry is so short, that the second paragraph is simply placed with the first.

<AG> 639 (p. 251). "տակառ *takaṙ* 'Tonne' Arist. = np. *taγ*ār 'Krug', davon *takaṙapet* 'Mundschenk, Obermundschenk' Gen. 40, 1,2, MX.93,5etc., als persischer Titel FB. 157 = np. **taγārbaδ*. Modern arm. *t́aγar* 'Blumenvase'."

The same here:

<AG> 100 (S. 117). "բանուկ *banuk* = np. *bānū* 'Herrin', phl. *bānūk*, bal. *bānuk* 'Herrin, Frau' (Horn, Grdr. Nr. 178) ist nach A. Carrière (briefl. Mittheilung) für *banak* zu lesen bei Sb. 27: »sie nahmen das ganze Lager (*z banakn*) sammt den königlichen Schätzen und nahmen die Königin und *z banakn* (lies *z banuksn* = 'die (königlichen) Frauen' ?)«, vgl. FB. 189: »sie nahmen die Königin (*tiknanç tikin*) sammt den andern Frauen (*kanambkͨn*) gefangen«, ähnlich FB. 55. Auch für *banskan* FB. 56: »sie nahmen die Frauen (*z kanais*) des Königs und die Königin (*bambišn*) und die *banskan* mit ihnen« will Carrière '*banokan*' lesen mit Rücksicht auf georg. (aus dem Persischen entlehntes) *banogani* (TCHOUBINOF p. 48) 'dame', das aber doch *banowani* (vgl. g. *bānewān* 'Königin', Horn, Grdr. Nr. 178) zu lesen ist.
Ueber die Frauen und Kebsen der pers. Könige vgl. Tab.353, Sb. 45, Thom. 94, 95, Mos. Kal. I, 252.
Unsicher. War im Armenischen *banuk* — phl. *bānūk* vorhanden, so musste der Plural *banukkͨ* oder collectivisch *bankani* (vgl. *avagani* 'Magnaten' von *avag* u. s. w.) lauten."

<AG> 109 (p. 119). "բդեաշխ *bdeašx* (gen. *bdešxi*) hiessen die Fürsten einiger armenischen Grenzprovinzen, an Rang die höchsten nach dem armenischen König, in der ältesten Zeit vier an der Zahl, FB. 21, Ag. 650; der *Bdeašx*

von Ałdznik̃, »der grosse *Bdeašx*«, Ag. 596, FB. 21, z. 4, 5; 211, z. 2 v. u.; der *Bdeašx* von Ałdznik̃ und der *Bdeašx* von Norširakan und Mahkertun und Nihorakan und Dassəntrē FB. 159; Bakur, genannt *Bdeašx* von Ałdznik̃ MX. 190; der Statthalter von Norširakan, erster *Bdeašx* Ag. 650; der *Bdeašx* von Gugark') FB. 159, 211; Ašušay, der *Bdeašx* der Gugarer (var. Gargarer; MX. 258 = Ašušay, der *Bdeašx* von Georgien Laz. 134; der *Bdeašx* des Landes der Gargarer) Ag. 597; die vier *Bdeašx* von Norširakan, Asorestan, Arvastan (? *Arvestakan kołmn*) und der Mask̃ut) Ag- 650; *p̃oxanak bdešxin* Proconsul (= ἀνθύπατος) Apg. 13, 7, 8, 12

= lat. *vitaxa* des Ammian, syr. *aptaxšā* (= ὕπαρχος des Königs), gr. βιτάξης, älter Πιτιάξης (Πητιάξης) de Lagarde, Ges. Abh. 187, Arm. Stud. p. 29, Nöldeke, ZDMG. 33, 159 Anm. (hier ein *Bdeašx* von Arzen), gr. Ag. p. 144 und 161, Inǰiǰean, Alterthumskunde II, 74, 75, georg. *pitiaxši* (mit *xš*?), *patiašxi* nach Brosset, Histoire de la Siunie II, p. 6, Description géogr. de la Géorgie (Petersburg 1842) p. 118, arm. georg. *Patiašx* Gesch. Georg. 86, z. 5. Arm. *bdeašx* geht nach armenischen Gesetzen auf älteres **bidiaxš* zurück, das, nach syr. *aptaxšā*, gr. Πιτιάξης und den georgischen Formen zu urtheilen, aus **pitiaxša-* entstellt ist. Es liegt nahe, für das Wort persischen Ursprung zu vermuthen, doch kann ich das Wort aus dem Persischen nicht deuten."

The last quotation is a famous one, where HÜBSCHMANN exhibits the correct intuition but also the correct caution. Not until the word was attested in Parthian *bdyg*[2] 'second; other' (*bdyg* + *xšʾh* 'the second king') years after HÜBSCHMANN, the case was clear. HÜBSCHMANN did not live long enough to see it though since he died in January 1908.

<AG> 612 (p. 245). "վարձ *varj* (u-St.) 'Lohn, Sold' Mt. 20, 2 u.s.w., *varjkan* 'Tagelöhner, Söldner, Dirne, feil', *varjim* 'dingen' Richter 9, 4 u. s. w.

= np. *varzīdan* 'erwerben, verdienen', *varza* 'Gewinn'.

Echt oder entlehnt? — Dazu *varjak* 'Sängerin, Tänzerin' MX. 141, z. 2 v. u., 2 Kg. 19,35, Michael 314 etc. ? Vgl. βάρζα des Suidas = ψάλτρια, de Lagarde Symm. 91."

<AG> 355 (p. 183). "[հրաշք *hraš-k̕* (i-St.) 'Wunder', alt und in vielen Comp.,z. B. *hrašakert* 'wunderbar' A. T., El. 12, 22 [(*hrašakert yarut̃iun* 'die wunderbare Auferstehung'), *hrašačar tar* 'mit wunderbarer Kunst' (einmal bei Steph. Orb.) etc.

gehört nicht zu zd. *fraša-* 'vorwärts, neu' (von der Welt am jüngsten Tage), *frašōkərəiti-* 'Neu-machung' (der Welt am jüngsten Tage = Auferstehung), *frašōčarətar-* 'Neu-macher' (der Welt etc.), da die Bedeutung durchaus verschieden ist. Vgl. ZDMG. 35, 173.]"

2 C. SALEMANN, *Manichaeische Studien I. Die mittelpersischen Texte in revidierter Transcription, mit Glossar und grammatischen Bemerkungen.* C. Petersburg, 1908. This includes the first published dictionary of the new material. On p. 59 he has bdyg 'zweit, zweitens'.

In the last example he has a negative and could have used the symbol '≠' for 'gehört nicht zu', if it was available to him. He was wrong in his judgement at least in the sense that *hraš-* and *fraša-* are the same lexeme, though used in different ways.

In the age of digitised books HÜBSCHMANN's list of Iranian loanwords is an interesting example of how to organise a word list. It has of course been followed by B. OLSEN, who updated the list with words actually attested in Parthian and Middle Persian.[3]

HÜBSCHMANN saw the Armenian 'History of Sebeos' as an important source of late Middle Persian because this work deals with the late phase of the Sasanian empire and the Arabic wars which spelt the end of the Sasanian empire.[4] It is eminently placed. HÜBSCHMANN translated part of it, the Arab invasion, as his Habilitation thesis in 1875 (chapter 42ff.). In the English translation it is noted that 'It was written at the end of the first phase of the Islamic conquest, where there was a perceptible faltering in the hitherto irresistible advance of Arab forces and hope rose among Christians that they might awaken from the nightmare, ..'[5] The date is from the middle of the 7th century, after 661.[6]

The MS of the anonymous history dates to the 17th century and was published as the 'history of bishop Sebeos on Heraclius' by Mihrdataean in 1851.[7] The first (part) translation into German followed soon after by HÜBSCHMANN in 1875. The attribution to 'Sebeos (Eusebios), bischop of Begratunik' who is recorded in 645 as one of the participants of a council of Dvin held in that year, was no more than a whim.[8] The modern edition knows more manuscripts. On the date of the history, THOMSON remarks 'Nonetheless, the author's personal knowledge of the circumstances of the time, and especially of details of Iranian culture, would be surprising in one who lives two centuries after the demise of the Sasanian dynasty'.[9]

The following examples will concentrate on the Iranian, specifically Middle Persian, words:

> Chapter 8: Vardan's defeat by Khosrov.
> 'They captured the queen (*z-bambišn*[10]) and the women (*z-⁺banouk-n*[11]) and appropriated the entire [royal] pavilion (*z-mašaperčan-n*[12]), and the golden carriage

3 B. OLSEN. *The Noun in Biblical Armenian*. Berlin/New York, 1999. Appendix I The Iranian Element. Nr. 1–728, 857–920.

4 Edition of the Armenian text: G.V. ABGARIAN. *Sebēosi. Patmut'iwn Sebeosi*. Erevan, 1979.

5 *The Armenian History attributed to Sebeos,* Translated, with notes, by R.W. THOMSON. Historical commentary by J. HOWARD-JOHNSTON. Assistance from T. GREENWOOD. Part I. Translation and notes. Liverpool, 1999, xi.

6 THOMSON 1999, (see note 1), lxi.

7 THOMSON 1999, xxxii.

8 THOMSON 1999, xxxiv.

9 THOMSON 1999, xxxix.

10 *bāmbišn* Parth. and MP.

11 For *z-banakn* of the manuscripts (THOMSON 1999, 8, ft. 50), s. AG 100, above; *banugān* MP.

12 AG 394, *maškā-parzēn* MP.

(*despag*[13]) of great value, which was set with precious stones and pearls and was called by them the 'glorious (*p'arac'*[14])' carriage (*despak*[15]).'

This is a good source of five Middle Persian words in close vicinity. In fact they are so dense and without Armenian equivalents that it shows that there must have been a knowledge of Middle Persian at the court in Armenia. The sentence is not clear without an understanding of these words. Possibly it belongs to the tales reported in the History of Armenia by Moses of Khoren. His history is supposed to be of the 5th cent., but it could have been written in the 6th or even the 7th century.[16] Either date would fit this text.

Chapter 10: the death of Ormizd.
'There gathered at the royal hall (*dahlic*[17]) all the nobles, generals, and troops who were present at that time.[18] Entering the royal chamber (*seneak*[19]) they seized king Ormizd; immediately they put out his eyes on the spot and then killed him.'

These are two words giving an air of authenticity to the tale of the king's murder. Again, they are not glossed.

Chapter 12 Khosrov's letter
'At the same time he ordered a letter (*yetkar*) to be written. .... Mushel took the letter tʿułtʿ.'

See AG 423 on this:

<AG> 423 (pp. 198–199). "յետկար *yetkar* (i-St.) 'Brief' Sb. 41, 14, 'Bericht' Sb.122, 21 = Steph. Asol. 97, z. 5 v.u., 'handschriftliche Urkunde' Joh. Kath.
= np. *yādgār* 'Andenken, Erinnerungszeichen' Fird. I, 16, v. 56, phl. *ayātkār* 'a writing, book, treatise, pamphlet' Ganj. Gl. S. 1, 'a memorandum, memorial, record, register' Gl. and Ind. 23, pāz. *ayādagar* 'memorandum' Shk. 235, vgl. *ayādkārāt* 'Memoiren' Hoffmann S. 294.
Man sollte im Arm. **ayatkar* erwarten. Hat volksetymologische Anlehnung an die Comp, mit *yet-* 'nach' stattgefunden?"

13 AG 190, *dēspaçg* MP.
14 AG 659, p'aŕ-*kʿ* = *wrarrah* MP.
15 See note 13 above.
16 Movsēs Xorenacʿi: Hayocʿ Patmowtʿiwn. *Histoire de l'Arménie par Moïse de Khorène.* Nouvelle traduction .. par ANNIE et JEAN.PIERRE MAHÉ. Gallimard, 1993, S. 222–223: 70 Les légendes sur les Pahlavik.
17 AG 160, *dahlič.* OLSEN 159. S. 874. S(outh) W(estern) Iranian development of *-*rϑ*-, so MP.
18 *naxarar-kʿ* 'nobles' (see S. 514 AG. = ap. **naxaδara*-, Andreas), ***zawra****glowx-kʿ* and *zawr-kʿ* 'generals', and 'troops', are all Old Iranian or Parthian loanwords in this sentence.
19 Not in AG; *seneak* OLSEN 601, p. 906. Is this a Parth. or a MP loanword? Not in D.N. MACKENZIE's *A Concise Pahlavi Dictionary*, London 1971.

The meaning of the word in Ferdawsi is 'Andenken, Erinnerung, Erinnerungszeichen, Freundschaftsgabe, Erbe'[20] rather than just a 'letter'. But in this case the item is more banal. The Pahlavi Form is *ayādgār* 'memoir'[21]. This would give the meaning 'He ordered a memorandum to be written'. Or to pick up the meaning HÜBSCHMANN has for the Armenian: 'He ordered a hand written document to be written'.

The form in Armenian is unusual, we would not expect *-e-*. This is why HÜBSCHMANN added his last note. The two other authors, Steph(annos) von Taraun, gen Asołik and Joh(annes) Kath(olikos), are, according to HÜBSCHMANN[22], from the 10th century and quote Sebeos.

The meaning of the MP word fits very well in the passage. The Armenian word for the item is tułt the normal word for 'letter', as THOMPSON pointed out.[23] The interesting thing is that *yetkar* is not glossed in any way, so its original form must have been known. Again this text uses a number of words that must have been known to (educated) Armenians from other texts. The other attestion of *yetkar* in Sebeos 46 is without a gloss. The word was corrupted somewhere along the line. Maybe the Syr. *eggartā* 'letter' had a role to play in the initial *e-*.

This leads to the question about how well attested the loanwords are. In the case of Sebeos with just a small number of manuscripts available, we can only say that the loanwords are usually very clear, despite small differences. However the manuscript is in places corrupt. See, for example, above 'women (*z-+banoukn*)'.

Interestingly, HÜBSCHMANN notes a gloss in Turkish *wêrki* 'tax' (*vergi*[24]) on Armenian *sak* 'tax'[25]. Since Turkish was known since the middle of the 6th century (and prominent in Menander's history of the late sixth century) this is not a problem, but in fact it does indicate a possible later addition to the manuscript.

20 F. WOLFF.*Glossar zu Firdosis Schahname*. Berlin, 1935 (rep. Hildesheim, 2000); *yādgār*, p. 873.
21 D.N. MACKENZIE 1971, p. 15.
22 HÜBSCHMANN 1897, pp. 5 and 7.
23 THOMSON 25, note 171: 'Just below it is referred to by the common word tułt.
24 H.C. HONY. *A Turkish-English dictionary*. Oxford, 1947, p. 369.
25 HÜBSCHMANN 1875, S. 30. The passage is in the newer edition of R.W. THOMSON 1999, p. 136, without mentioning the Turkish gloss. It is mentioned by ABRAPYAN, p. 164. G.V. ABGARYAN: *Sebeos. Patmut'iwn Sebēosi*. Erevan, 1979.

“Who Will Protect the Cattle”?

On Dogs and the Sin of Meat Consumption in Zoroastrianism

Shervin Farridnejad, Hamburg/Arash Zeini, Oxford

In the millennia that the Zoroastrian texts cover, the attitudes towards animal sacrifice and consuming meat has undergone various changes, be that in the ritual or in daily consumption.[1] This evolution is evident in both the context of rituals and everyday dietary practices.[2] For instance, if the animal sacrifice belonged traditionally to the core of the performance of the Zoroastrian high rituals, its usage had completely disappeared from the tradition of the liturgical manuscripts sometime in the first Islamic century.[3] However, meat has continued to play an important role within the Zoroastrian lay rituals up to the 19th and 20th centuries, even though it has either been completely abandoned or has gradually lost its importance.[4] The restrictions on the consumption of meat and slaughter of animals are still observed in the living Zoroastrian tradition on the so-called four *nābor* (“no cut/slaughter”) days, which are the days under the custody of the deity Wahman (2nd day), presiding over the animal kingdom and his collaborators (MP *hamkār*) Māh, Gōšurwan and Rām (which are respectively 12th, 14th and 21st of each month in the Zoroastrian calendar), as well as during the first three days after the death of a member of the household (ŠnŠ 17.1-2; ṢdN 78).[5] Again, among the Iranian community, it was until

1 We dedicate this paper to our teacher Dieter Weber, from whose knowledge and experience in reading the Pahlavi documents we benefited over many years in the summer schools convened by him between 2009 and 2012.

2 Cf. Farridnejad 2022a for an overview on ritual food and sacrificial meat in Zoroastrianism. For a discussion of the meat consumption in Iranian mythology and the Zoroastrian tradition cf. furthermore Daryaee 2022. For insights into how Zoroastrianism views food as a means of distinguishing and identifying individuals cf. Daryaee 2012.

3 Cf. Cantera 2014; Farridnejad 2022a, p. 91.

4 Regarding the presence of the animal sacrifice among Iranian Zoroastrians till the 20th century, cf. Boyce 1977, among others pp. 244–246. Cow sacrifice was abandoned in the Zoroastrian lay rituals under pressure from the Pārsīs in the 19th century; cf. Farridnejad 2020. It is noteworthy that even in mid-20th century, a lay Zoroastrian animal slaughter could only be lawfully done in the presence of a priest.

5 Cf. Kotwal 1969, p. 70; Dhabhar 1909, p. 54.

recently the custom to sacrifice a sheep on the first Mehrīzad (i.e. the festival of *Mehragān*) directly after a person's death.

Eating Meat as a Zoroastrian

Examining the earliest linguistic evidence might shed light on the significant place of meat in early Zoroastrianism. The Avestan term *pitau-* "meat" overtook the semantic field of all types of "food", especially solid "meat dish"[6] and terms such as *arəm-piϑwā* "noon, midday" (Y. 44.5) referring to time for meat preparation. Zoroastrian teachings emphasise the vital role of eating to sustain life, specifically pointing out that consuming meat enhances human mental acuity and physical strength. This harmony ensures the optimal functioning of the body, empowering the soul to effectively confront evil (Vd. 4.48).[7]

There are also traces of the Zoroastrian precautious and ambiguous attitudes towards eating meat within the narratives attested in the later Zoroastrian traditions. Three narratives among others play an essential role, marking the beginning and end of human history. First, the narrative of the first human couple, second, the narrative of the last great apocalyptic sacrifice marking the end of the material history of the world, and the third, the narrative of the primordial first king Yima; all three are connected to the notion of animal sacrifice and the consumption of meat.

The First Human's Animal Sacrifice

The 14th chapter of the *Bundahišn* provides an account of the first human couple, Mašyā and Mašyāne, and their first animal sacrifice, when they were assisted by spirits to make fire and prepare the sacrificial meat. They roast the meat of a sheep for the first time on the fire and present their first offering:[8]

GrBd. 14.21[9]
*pas pad sī rōz šabān ī didīgar ō gōspand-ēw mad hēnd ī dabr ī spēd-ērwārag u-šān bē kušt u-šān az dār ī kunār ud šimšār pad nimūdārīh ī mēnōyān ātaxš abgand čē awēšān harw dō dār ātaxš-dādārtar bawēnd u-šān pad-iz dahan ātaxš abrōxt u-šān nazdist ēzm ī *kahenz ud dār ī kundur ud pēš ī muy sōzēnīd u-šān*

6 AirWb, col. 905.
7 AirWb, col. 189; BOYCE 1975a, pp. 214–215.
8 Some scholars consider the roasting and its offering a sinful act of worship cf. DE JONG 2002; FARRIDNEJAD 2022a.
9 This and following passages of the *Bundahišn* are quoted from SKJÆRVØ's unpublished critical transcription with modifications.

ān gōspand wardānāg kerd u-šān sē mušt masā gōšt andar ātaxš bē hišt ud guft kū bahr ī ātaxš ud az ān pārag-ēw ō āsmān wist u-š guft kū ēn bahr ī yazadān.
"Then, after another thirty days and nights, they came upon a dark sheep with white cheeks, and they killed it. From the wood of the Jujube and box trees, they made a fire by the guidance of the spirits, for these two trees produce the best fire. (Then) they kindled the fire (by blowing on it) with their mouths and burned first the firewood of **kahenz* (?), and frankincense, and the date palm [lit., in the presence of the date palm]. And they grilled that sheep on a spit. Then they put three handfuls from the meat of the sheep into the fire and said: 'This is the share of the fire.' Then they threw one part to the heaven and said: 'This is the share of the gods.'"

Their first transgression in the narrative is that after preparing the meat, it is clumsily, and perhaps sinfully, offered to the fire and the divine beings by throwing it in the air.[10] This seems to reflect the recurring theme of misguided and sinful offerings to divine beings.[11] The passage suggests that neither the slaughtering nor the preparation of the sacrificial meat, but the incorrect way of performing the sacrifice, categorises their sacrificial ritual as a sinful act. In this way, the parallel position of their original ritual of animal sacrifice equates it with their first sin.[12]

The Last Human's Animal Sacrifice

The very moment of the first animal sacrifice and the cooking of the meat as an offering and for self-consumption flanks the narratives surrounding the last animal sacrifice and consumption of meat by humans in the context of the eschatological events, which are characterised by the coming of the three redeemers (MP *Sōšāns*), each at the beginning of the last three millennia of cosmic history. Each of the saviours will pave the way for the next to achieve the final victory of good over evil, ensuring the restoration and renewal of the world to its original state of perfection (Av. *frašō. kərəti-*; MP *frašgird* "making wonderful"). Both narratives depict a world where dietary imperfection unfolds gradually from a so-called water-fasting, to vegetarian and finally meat diet. At the outset, the initial couple solely consumed water. Subsequently, they progressed to incorporating plants into their diet, then embraced the consumption of milk, and ultimately delved into the realm of eating meat. Much like the initial phase when the first couple exclusively consumed water and later incorporated vegetables into

10 The phrase is briefly discussed by de Jong 1995, p. 217. See also DD 34:3; Dk 7:10:2 and WZ 34:39.
11 For the failed rituals and their demonic power in the Zoroastrian tradition, cf. Farridnejad 2022b.
12 For an interpretation of animal sacrifice in this passage as a divine or heroic concept, cf. de Jong 2002, p. 146.

their diet before introducing meat, a parallel pattern is foreseen in the distant future. In the third and final millennium, humans are envisioned to renounce meat once again, opting for a diet centred solely on plants and sheep milk. Even the consumption of milk, the last remaining animal product, will eventually cease, giving way to a diet restricted to the consumption of vegetables. In the ultimate stage, humans will return to exclusively drinking water. In the penultimate decade leading up to the arrival of the final saviour, Sōšāns, a profound transformation will unfold within humanity. During this pivotal period, the cessation of both eating and drinking will become a universal phenomenon, ushering in an extraordinary era where mortality is suspended, and no individual will experience death. This extraordinary shift in the human condition marks a prelude to the imminent arrival of Sōšāns, promising a radical departure from the customary cycles of sustenance and mortality that have defined human existence:

> GrBd. 34.1-3
> *gōwēd pad dēn kū az ān čiyōn Mašyā ud Mašyāne ka az zamīg abar rust hēnd nazdist āb pas urwar ud pas šīr pas gōšt xward hēnd. mardōm-iz ka-šān murdan nazdist gōšt ud šīr ud pas az nān xwardan bē estēnd. ud ēwāz tā bē murdan āb xwarēnd. ēdōn-iz pad hazārag ī Ušīdarmāh nērōg ī abāyīdan bē kāhēd kū mardōm pad ēk pih xwarišnīh sē šab rōz pad sagrīh estēnd. pas az ān az gōšt xwarišnīh estēnd. urwar ud pēm gōspandān xwarēnd. ud pas az ān (az pēm-xwarišnīh-iz estēnd. pas az urwar-xwarišnīh-iz estēnd ud āb-xwarišn bawēnd. pēš pad dah sāl ka Sōšāns āyēd ō a-xwarišnīh estēnd ud nē mīrēnd. pas Sōšāns rist ul hangēzēnēd.*
>
> "It says in the *dēn*: 'When Mašyā and Mašyāne had grown from the earth, first they only drank water, then they ate plants, then consumed milk, and finally they ate meat. So, for the people, when death comes close, they first stop eating meat, [then they stop drinking] milk, then stop eating bread too, and from then to the time until they die, they only will drink water.' The same will happen during the millennium of Ušīdarmāh, the strength of longing will weaken so that people will be content to eat one meal every three days and nights. Then they will stop eating meat. Next, they will eat only vegetables and the milk of the sheep (beneficent domestic animal). Soon after this they will stop drinking milk and then they will stop eating plants too, and then they will just drink water. Ten years before the advent of Sōšāns, they will also stop eating and they will not die. Then Sōšāns will raise the dead."

In a symmetrical reflection of its inception, the grand narrative of the universe will culminate in a climactic finale. At this conclusive stage, the curtain will fall on cosmic history through the ultimate animal sacrifice – an offering of the sacred bull, Hadayōš (*gāw ī Hadayānš*). This solemn act will be orchestrated by the last Sōšāns and their devoted assistants (*hadayanš pad ān yazišn kušēnd*, GrBd. 34.23), mirroring the profound spiritual and cosmogonic sacrifice undertaken by Ohrmazd at the dawn of the creation (GrBd. 3.23).

This apocalyptic sacrifice serves as the *magnum opus*, concluding the material world's narrative with a deliberate nod to Ohrmazd's primordial sacrifice, a pivotal event that set the stage for the entire cosmic order (GrBd. 26.27). The ceremonial offering of Hadayōš becomes the culminating chapter, not merely an end but a transformative passage, as it prepares the elixir of immortality, a transcendent libation destined for the salvation of humankind. This intricate tapestry of sacrifice, referencing both the genesis and the ultimate resolution, weaves together the threads of spiritual resonance and cosmic closure, casting the grand narrative into eternal significance. The narrative also contains another important aspect, which subliminally reflects the paradoxical aversion to eating meat among mankind, namely in the fact that at the time, at the last cosmic sacrifice, mankind has already stopped eating, so that meat is no longer consumed. This leads to the fact that the communal act of eating sacrificed animals cannot be performed. Thus, the meat sacrifice is dedicated solely to the gods. This is strongly reminiscent of the third important narrative, in which the meat-eating behaviour of humanity is recounted, namely Yima's sin of distributing meat.

Yima's Sin of Distributing Meat

Yima (Av. *yima-xšaēta-*, MP J̌amšēd), the primordial legendary king who ruled over all living beings during the cherished Golden Age, occupies a central place in the Iranian cultural lore. This iconic figure is woven into the rich fabric of the Zoroastrian tradition, leaving an indelible mark that continues in later literary expressions, including Ferdōsī's *Šāhnāme* and various works in the broader spectrum of (Muslim) Persian literature.[13] Yima's legacy is not confined to a singular myth but rather extends across a myriad of narratives within the Zoroastrian tradition. His reign embodies an era of prosperity and harmony, symbolising the zenith of virtuous governance. This epoch is characterised by a utopian existence, echoing the paradisiacal ideals of the Iranian cultural ethos. Centuries later, in Ferdōsī's *Šāhnāme* and other Persian literary works, shaped by Islamic influences, Yima's narrative undergoes reinterpretation and embellishment. HUMBACH has already astutely noted the connection in *Šāhnāme* between the ritual slaughter of animals and the legendary serpent king Żaḥāk. However, a curious observation arises as this narrative finds its place within the chapter dedicated to Ǧamšīd (Yima).[14]

The enigmatic appearance of Yima permeates the ancient Zoroastrian tradition. In the *Gāϑās* (Y. 32.8), he is condemned for a mysterious transgression — he allowed people to eat sacrificial animal flesh:

Y. 32.8
aēšą̄m aēnaŋhą̄m / vīuuaŋhušō srāuuī yimascīt̰

13 Cf. HUMBACH 2002; HUMBACH 2004.
14 Cf. HUMBACH 2002, p. 73, fn. 17. For an in-depth exploration of Yima's myth, its origins, and the scholarly discourse surrounding this topic, cf. SKJÆRVØ 2012.

yə maṣ̌iiəṇg cixšnušō / ahmākəṇg gāuš bagā xᵛārəmnō
aēšąmcīṯ ā aŋ́ī / ϑβaŋ́ī mazdā vīciϑōi aipī
"(Particularly) Yima, the son of Vivanghan, has become infamous (for being guilty) among these sinners, who tried to satisfy the mortals, our (people), by giving them portions of meat to eat; as for me, I submit to your decision regarding such (crimes), o Mazdā."[15]

Zoroastrian sources ascribe different sins to Yima, most prominently his lie (Yt. 19.33–34; Y. 32.8), the rejection of Ohrmazd's offer to serve the religion (Vd. 2.1–4) as well as claiming to be the creator of the world (PRivDd. 31.10; DD. 38.19–21). Yet, certain renditions of the Yima myth narrate a different perspective, suggesting that Yima's purported transgression was introducing humanity to the practice of slaughtering animals and partaking in the consumption of oxen meat:

PY. 32.8[16]
kē-š ō mardōmān čāšīd kū amāgān gōšt pad bazišn xwarēd
"who taught people: 'Our people! Eat meat in appropriate portions!"

As a result of Yima's transgression, he faced the loss of his kingship and divine fortune (Av. *xᵛarənah-*, MP *xwarrah*). The traditional interpretation of the ancient Pahlavi scholars, which underlies the Pahlavi translation of Y. 32.8, triggered extensive contemporary scholarly deliberation to decipher the enigmatic passage, which gave rise to a variety of interpretations in modern discourse. The Zand's interpretation of *gāuš* as *gōšt* "meat", *bagā* as *bazišn* "portion, sharing" and *xᵛārəmnō* as *xwarēd* "to eat" requires comprehensive discussions that are beyond the scope of this paper.[17]

Nevertheless, the Pahlavi Zoroastrian tradition has a discernible inclination to acknowledge a potential connection between the consumption of meat and the commission of a sinful act. This inclination becomes more conspicuous when the Avestan strophe is subjected to further layers of interpretation. A passage in the ninth book of *Dēnkard* provides evidence of its development into a theological-legal matter:

Dk. 9.32.12 [DkM 838.2ff.][18]
ud ān ī wiwanghānan jam ā-š šnāyēnīd mardōm u-š šnāyēnīd gōspand ī hudahāg ēdōn pad gōwišn Zardušt ka-š guft ō mardōmān kū ašmā gōspand mardōm-ēd kū ašmāh xwēš pad bazišn mardōm-ēd gōšt xwarēd u-tān pad bazišn gōšt sagr bawišn

15 To revisit previous discussions, cf. GERSHEVITCH 1987; HUMBACH 2002; HUMBACH 2004, and most recently DARYAEE 2022, p. 237 and FARRIDNEJAD 2022a, pp. 87–88.
16 MALANDRA/ICHAPORIA 2013, p. 42. For further discussions cf. HUMBACH 2002, p. 74.
17 Cf. HUMBACH 2002, p. 75; HUMBACH 2004, p. 48. Cf. also SKJÆRVØ 2012.
18 For previous discussions cf. CHRISTENSEN 1934, p. 20; HUMBACH 2002, p. 75; HUMBACH 2004, pp. 48–49. HUMBACH states that *mardōm-ēd* must be a scribal mistake corrupting *hušnūdag* ⟨hwšnwdk'⟩ to *mardōm* ⟨ANŠWTA⟩, which made the passage incomprehensible; *ibid.*, pp. 47–48.

ast mardōm-ēd ma āz rāy ud ma arešk rāy ud ma bē abgand-pid ī rōdīg ud ma bē abgand-pid ī ⟨wpyšk'⟩ rāy pad kušišn kušēd kū-tān ēdōn nēk u-tān bowandag ∴
And Jam, son of Wiwanghān, then satisfied the humans, and he gratified the beneficent animal in this manner, O Zardušt, when he told people: "You have cattle. You are humans, that is, they are your own through apportionment. You are humans, eat meat, and you will be satisfied [lit., you will be full] by the apportionment of meat. You are humans, do not eat meat out of greed, nor out of envy. And do not throw (away) the meat of the entrails, and do not throw away the meat of ⟨wpyšk'⟩ (which) you slay in the slaughter, so that in this manner it may be good for you, (so that it may be) complete for you".

It is unclear whether the passage is an admonition by Yima "to be moderate in consuming meat" as HUMBACH suggested[19], or whether the passage describes Yima's sin which would be permitting humans to consume meat. Perhaps the Pahlavi translation of *Hōm Yašt* is an allusion to Yima's sin, which could be reflected in Y. 32.8 and its interpretation in Dk. 9.32.12. PY. 9.1 seems to suggest that Yima's offering meat to humans was a sin, as a result of which they became mortal:[20]

PY. 9.1[21]
*hād ā-š tan pad frārōnīh amarg kard ēstēd ud nē ēdōn ciyōn awēšān kē gōšt ī jam jūd u-šān andar tan *marg kard ēstēd.*
That is, his body [Hōm's] is made immortal by means of goodness and not thus like those who chew Jam's meat. And in body they may have been made *mortal.

In a narrative reminiscent of the primordial human couple's tale, Yima's defiance against Ohrmazd and the subsequent transgression unfold as a rich tapestry of cosmogonic and eschatological significance. This account not only delves into the personal journey of Yima but resonates with broader themes, symbolising an epoch marked by the interweaving (MP *gumēzišn*) of good and evil within the fabric of the world. This pivotal moment serves as a profound turning point, encapsulating the loss of paradise and the introduction of mortality to humankind. The repercussions of Yima's actions ripple through the cosmic narrative, painting a vivid picture of a world where the delicate balance between virtue and vice becomes an enduring feature of the human experience.

Zoroastrian Unease with Meat Consumption

Although offering meat as an important sacrificial requisite still plays a role within Zoroastrian lay rituals, mostly restricted to rural life, the disappearance

19 HUMBACH 2004, p. 49. Elsewhere in PRivDd. 31.1–3, it is said that Yima tried to prevent humans from slaughtering animals.
20 Note the use of the daevic verb *jūdan* "to chew; devour" in this passage.
21 DHABHAR 1949, p. 56. The passage is discussed by HUMBACH 2002, pp. 72–73; HUMBACH 2004, pp. 49f.; ZEINI 2020, p. 53.

of the animal sacrifice and meat offering from the core of the Zoroastrian high liturgies remains enigmatic. However, the unease of consuming meat seems to have a long history in Zoroastrianism, which may explain the disappearance of the animal sacrifice from the high liturgies. The Gāϑic well-known lament of the cow in Y. 29,[22] where the cow's soul complains to the gods about its bad treatment (MP *a-paymān kušēd* "slaughters falsely"),[23] is a particularly fitting example as it reflects the ambiguous relationship to the killing of an animal in a text of antiquity. These notions, however, also find reflections in later Middle as well as New Persian Zoroastrian literature. For instance in the following passage where the torment of animals, especially cattle, is directly linked to the torment of Wahman:

> Bd 26.18–20
> (18) *az hamāg yazdān wahuman ō dādār nazdīktar* (19) *u-š gētīy gōspand ud wastarg ī spēd xwēš kē awēšān rāmēnēd ayāb bēšēd ēg-iš wahuman rāmēnīd ayāb bēšīd bawēd* (20) *u-š ham-kār māh ud gōšurwan ud rām*
> Of all divine beings, Wahman is closer to the creator. (19) And his are the tangible world, the cattle and the white garment. Whoever comforts or harms them, comforts or harms Wahman too. His assistants are Māh, and Gōšurwan, and Rām.

Similar notions emerge from later periods reflected in the corpus of the New Persian *Revāyāt*. In a letter dated 928 AY/1559 CE and signed by the priests of Torkābād, Šarifābād, Khorāsān and Sīstān, which Kāmdīn Šāpūr took to the Zoroastrians of India, the community leaders are voicing their despair and worries about the promised rescue by the eschatological saviour Šāh Bahrām Varjāvand, also known as King Bahrām, the Glorious (MP Wahrām ī Warzāwand). In the larger context of the unstable situation of Zoroastrian communities after the Mongol conquest of Iran and the centuries that followed, one of the recurring themes from time to time is the expression of doubt that the promised redemption will not come anytime soon, leading to the notion that there is also no foreseeable possibility for them to leave their homeland for a better future.[24] The priests try to explain this situation, by putting their misery into the context of the creation and eschatological narratives, in which the age of *gumēzišn*, characterised by the coexistence of good and evil, serves as the backdrop for the profound suffering and significant setbacks experienced by the Zoroastrian community. Within the context of this era, a central and distinctive theme emerges — namely, the improper consumption of meat. The narrative unfolds as this dietary practice is expounded upon, revealing its role in bestowing strength for the commission of sins and engaging in various sinful actions:

22 The core of Y. 29 is the question of theodicy, in which Mazdā, in response to the cow's lament, declares that his plan for the 'cow' (i.e. humanity at large) is perfect, though a human leader with divine support is needed to realise this plan in the world, and god's choice for a protector in this world is Zaraϑuštra; On this passage cf. most recently KREYENBROEK 2023, pp. 71, 181–182, for a new translation, pp. 193–194.

23 Cf. HUMBACH 2015, p. 40.

24 Cf. FARRIDNEJAD, *forthcoming*.

Per.Rev. Kāmdīn Šāpūr (MU. I. 60–61)

اندر دین پیداست که چون دادار اورمزد این جهان آفرید و هر چیز بگیتی خواست فرستاد، سه چیز گفتند که ما بگیتی نشویم، یکی مردم و یکی آتش و یکی گوسفند [...] پس گوشورنگ ایزد که موکل گوسفندان و چهارپایانست برپای ایستاد و گفت: ای دادار اورمزد، من بگیتی نشوم چه بعد از هزاره زرتشت اسفنتمان، گوسفند را بسیار کشند به بیداد، چون گاو و ورزا و اسپ کارزاری و بره و بزغاله و چون گوشت ایشان خورند، بدان قوت گناه بسیار کنند. این بگفت پس خاموش شد. دادار اورمزد گفت که ایشان هر سه راست می‌گویند [...] وگوشورنگ را گفت که گوسفند سردکان بگیتی فرست چه هر گناهی که حیوانان کنند بگردن آن کس باشد که چهارپایان را به بیداد کشند و چون گوشت بخورد، بگناه کردن مشغول شود. گوشورنگ خرسند شد و گوسفند سردکان بگیتی فرستاد [...]

In religion, it is evident that when Ohrmazd, the Creator, created this world and wanted to settle everything in the tangible world, three said that we will not enter the world, one is man, one is fire and one is cattle [...] So, Gušūrang (i.e. Gōšurwan), the divine shepherd, the custodian of cattle and quadrupeds, stood up and said, "O Creator Ohrmazd, I will not enter the tangible world, for after the millennium of Zardušt Sfantmān, (people) will unjustly slaughter many animals such as cows, oxen, horses for warfare and lambs and calves, they will commit many sins by getting strength after eating their flesh." After saying this, he fell silent. Ohrmazd the Creator said that they are all speaking the truth [...] And then he told Gušūrang to let the cattle species enter the tangible world, for whatever sins the animals commit, let the responsibility fall on the one who unjustly slaughters the quadrupeds, eats their flesh and bears the burden of sin. Gušūrang was pleased and sent the cattle species into the tangible world [...]

In addition to the aforementioned *nābor* days, on which the slaughter of animals and the consumption of meat is prohibited, there are also other occasions, on which meat consumption should be avoided, namely during the first three days after a person's death, a time of the separation of the soul from the body and when the Nasuš, the demon of carrion takes possession of the corpse. Many passages in Pahlavi and New Persian literature prescribe the renunciation of meat consumption for family members during this period:

ṢdN 78[25]

اینکه در هر سرایی کسی از دنیا ودیران شود، نخست سه روز دران باید کوشیدن که گوشت تازه نخورند و نپزند، چه بیم باشد که کسی دیگر ودیران شود و خویشاوندان آن کس سه روز گوشت نخورند.

In a house from which a person departs from the world, initially, for three days, they should strive not to consume raw or cooked meat. The concern is that someone else might pass away, and the relatives of that person should also refrain from eating meat for three days.

This prohibition, along with the prohibition of weeping and wailing during funeral ceremonies, seems to be among the important prescriptions that have been repeated and handed down over a long period of time and are also found in various Persian *Revāyāt*:

Per.Rev. Kāma Bohra (MU. I. 145–146)

در سرایی که کسی از دنیا برود سه روز در آن سرای آن بباید که گوشت تازه نیاورند و نپزند، چه بیم باشد که دیگر کسی در پی آن برود و بر ماست و پنیر و ماهی و خایه و ریچال قناعت بباید کردن و خویشاوندان ایشان سه روز گوشت نشاید خوردن.

25 Also cf. MU. I. 146.

> In a house from which a person departs from the world, it is necessary that they do not bring fresh meat nor cook it for the (first) three days; for the danger is that another person will follow him (i.e. will die). They should be content with yoghurt, cheese, fish, eggs and confectionery, and the relatives (of the deceased) should not eat meat during these three days.

With all these passages, one might wonder what could be behind this regulation. Again, it seems that the renunciation of meat consumption by the family members of the deceased makes them prone to committing sins, due to the very prominent presence of the greatest polluter of the world of Ohrmazd, namely the demon of carrion, which recalls the eschatological view of the unstable state of *gumēzišn*, during which the unjust slaughter of the quadrupeds and the consumption of their flesh enables mankind to commit sins.

The complexities of this ambivalence pose a nuanced challenge that requires further examination and analysis. However, and in order to leave the discussion open for future studies, one key to this problem might be the likeness of humans and animals in the tangible creation. In *Bundahišn* 1a.3, for instance, we read that the seed of humans and the cattle (*gōspand*) came from fire and not water like the rest of the creation: *čiyōn gōwēd pad dēn kū fradom dām hamāg āb-ēw srešk-ēw būd kū hamāg az āb būd ǰud tōhm ī mardōmān gōspandān čē ān tōhm ātaxš-tōhm* "As it says in the *dēn*: At first, the entire creation was a drop of water. (It says) that everything was from water except the seed of humans (and) the cattle, for that seed (was) the fire-seed". Moreover, in GrBd. 1a we also find out that the sole-created cow (*gāw ī ēk-dād*, Ohrmazd's fifth creation in GrBd. 1a.14) and Gayōmard (Ohrmazd's sixth creation in GrBd. 1a.15) were both created next to the river Dāitī in Ērānwēz. According to these passages, the shared origin of humans and cattle (or beneficent animals) is undeniable. In the cow's complaint, as reflected in GrBd. 4a, we find another key to the ambivalence towards meat consumption. After the death of the sole-created cow and Gayōmard, the soul of the cow, Gōšurwan, complains to Ohrmazd and demands the promised protection: *kū ast ān mard kē-t guft kū daham tā pahrēz*[26] *bē gōwēd* "Where is that man, who you promised to create so that he would sooth (us) with words?" (GrBd. 4a.2). Gōšurwan agrees to be created as cattle in the tangible world (*gētīy*), only after Ohrmazd shows Gōšurwan the Frawahr of Zardušt: *hunsand būd gōšurwan ud padīrift dām bē parwāram kū pad gōspand abāz ō gētīy dahišnīh ham-dādestān būd* "Gōšurwan was pleased and accepted: 'I will nourish the creation[27]'. It agreed to be re-created in the tangible world as cattle" (GrBd. 4a.6). The soul of the cow thus only agrees to be re-created after negotiating for its kind's protection by humans. It seems plausible to conclude that the uneasy relationship

26 It is the reflection of this care, *pahrēz*, that we find in the *Zand* of Y. 35.6b: *ud ān-iz ī gōspandān kār kū az kār ī gētīy pahrēz ī gōspandān pahlom menom* "and also that, which is the care for the cattle, that is, of the worldly matters I consider the care for the cattle (to be) best". Cf. ZEINI 2020, especially p. 132.

27 Here, *dām* can easily be translated as "livestock".

of Zoroastrianism with animal slaughter, even in the case of animal sacrifice, is tightly connected with the story of the creation and the care and protection that Ohrmazd promised to the sole-created cow. This notion of protection by humans is reflected in another passage in the *Bundahišn*, namely in the story of the creation of the dog. In GrBd. 13.28 we read that the dog was created from the mixture of humans and cattle and that one third of a dog is human:

> GrBd. 13.28
> *sag rāy gōwēd kū az star-pāyag kū az ān kustag ī star ī haftōring ā-š az mardōmān pad yuǰyast frāz dād pānagīh ī gōspandān rāy čiyōn gumēzag az gōspandān ud mardōmān ēd rāy sag xwānīhēd čē-š 3 ēk-ēw az mardōmān*
> About dogs, it says that (they are) from the star station, that (they are) from that region of the star of Haftōring. Then he created (the dog) for the protection of the cattle a Yuǰyast (away) from humans. As (the dog) is a mixture of cattle and humans, for that reason it is called dog (*sag*). For one third of it is human'.

This passage alludes to GrBd. 4a, the complaint of the soul of the cow, and seems to confirm the suggestion that the primordial promise to protect the cow and cattle is of utmost importance to Zoroastrianism. The need to protect the cattle (*gōspand*) in the tangible world is so paramount that one third of a dog is cattle and the other human,[28] namely that archetypal human whose pre-existing soul Ohrmazd showed to Gōšurwan before it agreed to be re-created in the tangible world.

Concluding Remarks

In this paper, we have sought to note some of the reasons for the Zoroastrian ambivalence towards animal slaughter and the subsequent consumption of meat. Unravelling the layers of this complex perspective demands a much larger exploration of socio-historical, cultural, and religious contexts that shape the Zoroastrian stance on the treatment of animals and the ethical considerations woven into their attitudes towards meat consumption. Certain episodes from the universal history of the world contain moments of doubt (see the passages from the *Bundahišn*), sometimes directly and at times subliminally associating the consumption of meat with a sin. It seems, producing meat for dietary needs is lawfully protected with the frame of ritual sacrifice, to be performed solely by the priests. The legal framework restricting the slaughter of animals and the consumption of meat is extended to monthly recurring days of prohibition of meat consumption and to specific times of burial ceremonies.

28 This is a brilliant play with the Middle Persian term *sag* 'dog', which is here read as a derivation from Middle Persian *3 ēk* or *sĕ ēk* 'one third'.

Abbreviations

AirWb	= BARTHOLOMAE 1961
Av.	Avestan
DD	*Dādestān ī Dēnīg*
Dk.	*Dēnkard*
DkM	= MADAN 1911
GrBd.	Greater *Bundahišn*
MP	Middle Persian
MU	Ervad Manockji Rustamji Unvala's lithographed edition of *Revāyāt Dārāb Hormazdyār* = UNVALA 1922
NP	New Persian
Per.Rev.	Persian *Revāyat*
PRivDd.	*Pahlavi Rivāyat* accompanying the *Dādestān ī Dēnīg*
ṢdN	*Ṣad dar Naṣr* = DHABHAR 1909
ŠnŠ	Šāyest nē-Šāyest
Vd.	*Vīdēvdād*
Y.	*Yasna*
Yt.	*Yašt*
Vd.	*Vīdēvdād*
WZ	*Wizīdagīhā ī Zādspram*

Bibliography

BARTHOLOMAE, CHR. 1961: *Altiranisches Wörterbuch*. Strassburg.

BOYCE, M. 1975: "Mihragān among the Irani Zoroastrians." In: J.R. HINNELLS (ed.): *Mithraic Studies. Proceedings of the First International Congress of Mithraic Studies* 1. Manchester, pp. 106–118.

CANTERA, A. 2014: "Repetitions of the Ahuna Vairiia and animal sacrifice in the Zoroastrian long liturgy." In: *Estudios Iranios y Turanios* 1, pp. 25–29.

CHRISTENSEN, A. 1934: *Les types du premier homme et du premier roi dans l'histoire légendaire des Iraniens.* IIe parties: *Jim*. Leiden (Archives d'Études Orientales 14, 2).

DARYAEE, T. 2012: "Food, Purity and Pollution: Zoroastrian Views on the Eating Habits of Others." In: *Iranian Studies* 45, 2, pp. 229–242.

— 2022: "Eaing Meat: The Sin of Zoroastrian Primordial Heroes and Villains." In: B. CASEAU/H. MONCHOT (eds.): *Religion et interdits alimentaires. Archéozoologie et sources littéraires*. Leuven (Orient & Méditerranée 38), pp. 237–242.

DHABHAR, B.N. 1909: *Saddar Nasṛ and Saddar Bundehesh*. Bombay.

— (ed.) 1932: *The Persian Rivayats of Hormazyar Framarz and Others: Their Version with Introdoction and Notes*. Bombay.

— 1949: *Pahlavi Yasna and Visperad: With an Introduction and Glossary of Select Terms*. Bombay (Pahlavi Text Series 8).

FARRIDNEJAD, S. 2020: "Cow Sacrifice and the Hataria's Dedicatory Inscription at the Zoroastrian Shrine of Bānū-Pārs." In: *Dabir. The Digital Archive of Brief Notes & Iran Review* 7, pp. 101–111.

– 2022a: "The Banquet for the Gods: Sacrificial Meat and Bread as the Main Ritual Foods in Zoroastrian Liturgies." In: S. Farridnejad/T. Daryaee (eds.): *Food for Gods, Food for Mortals. Culinary and Dining Practices in the Greater Iranian World*. Irvine (ČISTĀ. Studies in the History, Cultures and Religions of the Iranian World), pp. 77–131.

– 2022b: "Demonic Gifts and Counter-Gifts in Ancient Zoroastrianism." In: T. Sala (ed.): *The Dangers of Gifts from Antiquity to the Digital Age*. New York (Studies in Cultural History 120).

– Forthcoming: "Death and Destruction: Zoroastrians during Turco-Mongol Invasions and in the Aftermath." In: F. Fiaschetti/B. De Nicola (eds.): *Central Asiatic Journal*. Wiesbaden (Special Issue: The Mongols and Religions 63).

Gershevitch, I. 1987: "Yima's Beef-Plea." In: G. Gnoli/L. Lanciotti (eds.): *Orientalia Iosephi Tucci Memoriae Dicata*. Roma (Serie Orientale Roma 56, 2), pp. 487–499.

Humbach, H. 1977: "Zarathustra und die Rinderschlachtung." In: B. Benzing/O. Böcher/G. Mayer (eds.): *Wort und Wirklichkeit: Studien zur Afrikanistik u. Orientalistik; [Eugen Ludwig Rapp zum 70. Geburtstag]*. Meisenheim am Glan, pp. 17–29.

– 2002: "Yama/Yima/Jamšed, King of Paradise of the Iranians." In: *Jerusalem Studies in Arabic and Islam* 22, pp. 68–77.

– 2004: "Yima/Jamšēd." In: C.G. Cereti/B. Melasecchi/F. Vajifdar (eds.): *Varia Iranica*. Roma (Orientalia Romana 7), pp. 45–58.

Humbach, H. 2015: "The Gāthās." In: M. Stausberg/Y.S.-D. Vevaina (eds.): *The Wiley-Blackwell Companion to Zoroastrianism*. Hoboken, pp. 39–43.

Kotwal, F.M.P. (ed.) 1969: *The Supplementary Texts to the Šāyest nē-Šāyest*. København (Historisk-filosofiske meddelelser: HfM; Det Kongelige Danske Videnskabernes Selskab 44, 2).

Kreyenbroek, Ph.G. 2023: *Early Zoroastrianism and Orality*. Wiesbaden (Iranica, GOF III/NF 20).

Madan, D.M. 1911: *The Complete Text of the Pahlavi Dinkard*. Bombay.

Malandra, W.W./P. Ichaporia 2013: *The Pahlavi Yasna of the Gathas and Yasna Haptanghaiti*. 2nd rev. ed. Wiesbaden.

Mirfaḫrāī, M. 2011 [1390]: *Revāyat-e pahlavi [Pahlavi Riwāyat]*. Tehran.

Skjærvø, P.O. 2012: "S.v. Jamšid. i. Myth of Jamšid." In: E. Yarshater (ed.): *Encyclopædia Iranica* XIV, Fasc. 5. New York, pp. 501–522.

Unvala, M.R. (ed.) 1922: *Dârâb Hormazyâr's Rivâyat*. 2 vols. Bombay.

Zeini, A. 2020: *Zoroastrian Scholasticism in Late Antiquity: The Pahlavi Version of the Yasna Haptaŋhāiti*. Edinburgh.

A Contribution to Pahlavi Lexicography: The Case of ⟨twk(')⟩ and ⟨twp(')⟩ in the Pahlavi Corpus and their Possible Cognates in Modern Iranian Languages*

Ela Filippone, Tuscia University

The aim of the following notes, offered as a small tribute to Dieter Weber, a very prominent scholar of Pahlavi and Iranian philology, is to shed some light on two Pahlavi words, spelt, respectively, (1) ⟨twp(')⟩ and (2) ⟨twk(')⟩. These words, whose number of occurrences is not very high but still not negligible, deserve in my opinion more attention than that they have received. Their range of uses have not been sufficiently specified so far, as a quick overview of dictionaries and glossaries citing them testifies:

(Dictionaries) MacKenzie 1986: (1) **tōf* 'layer',[1] (2) unrecorded; Farahvaši 1967: (1) *tōp* 'fold, layer [tā, lā]'; (2) *tōk* 'fold, layer [tāh, tā, lā]'; Mansuri 2015–2021: (1) *tōf* 'layer; eyelid; (tree) bark'; (2) *tōg* 'leaf (paper), folio; inside; bottom'.

(Glossaries) Kapadia 1953: (1) *tôp* 'rind, bark, outer skin; cover, lid'; (2) *tûk* 'plait, fold'; Tavadia 1930: (1) *tōp* 'fold'; (2) *tōk* 'fold'; Tavusi 1986: (1) *tōb* 'bark of wood, wood [pust-e čub, čub]'; (2) *tōg* 'inside; fold, layer [tu, tuy, lā, lāye]'; Bahār 1972: (1) *tōp, tōv* 'portion, layer, peel, crust [baxš, lāye, qešr, puste]'; Gignoux/Tafazzoli 1993: (1) *tōf* 'couche, niveau'; Jaafari-Dehaghi 1998: (1) *tōf* 'fold'; Moazami 2014, 2021: (1) *tōf* 'layer'.

To capture the full range of application of ⟨twk(')⟩ and ⟨twp(')⟩, that here will be conventionally transcribed *tōg and tōf*, all their attestations in the whole Pahlavi documentation I am aware of, have been taken into consideration and commented on.[2] Since the passages in which they occur often present critical

* This research has been conducted within the framework of the PRIN 2020PLEBK4 Project *Cultural interactions and language contacts: Iranian and non-Iranian languages in contact from the past to the present,* by me directed at the Tuscia University, Viterbo.

1 Here the asterisk marking **tōf* is ambiguous, as the asterisk always is in that work, signalling both doubt in the transcription and meaning.

2 This operation was facilitated by the fact that I had the possibility to consult the database produced by Prods Oktor Skjærvø and containing a new edition of most of the known Pahlavi texts (hereinafter Skj.). I warmly thank Oktor for his generosity in making such highly valuable material available to other scholars and for his useful remarks to this paper. I also take the opportunity to thank Salman Aliyari

elements and ambiguities, suggestions for possible new readings of single words or interpretations of specific passages from different Pahlavi texts have occasionally been advanced. At the end of the analysis, possible cognates to Phl. *tōg and tōf* in Modern Iranian languages have been briefly discussed.

The occurrences of *tōf* in the Pahlavi documentation

I have parenthetically dealt with Phl. *tōf* many years ago, commenting on a passage in the *Škand Gumānīg Wizār* (ŠGW) where the various eye components are listed, in association with the functions performed by them.[3] The sequence that interests us on this particular occasion is given below in the transliteration from Pāzand (a) and in the transcription from Pahlavi (b):[4]

(1a) ŠGW 5.66–67[5]
čuṇ čašm i əž vas āinaa ǰaδ nām u ǰaδ
kār čuṇ mazg u tōw, spədaa u xāēaa,
sāēaa u ϑəidaa

(1b) ŠGW 5.66–67[6]
čiyōn čašm az was ēwēnag ǰud-nām ud
ǰud-kār čiyōn mazg ud tōf, spēdag ud
xāyig, sahīg ud tītak[7]

"So the eye, that is made up of many components with different names and different functions, such as the eyelash and the eyelid, the white and the eyeball, the iris and the pupil."

That *tōw/tōf* could be intended as 'eyelid' was first assumed by JÂMÂSP-ÂSÂNÂ/WEST;[8] this proposal, however, was discarded by DE MENASCE, according to whom, "*tuf*: litt. salive" in that specific context would rather refer to the lachrymal liquid (1945, pp. 68, 69).[9]

In fact, *tōf* as a designation for 'eyelid' is not found in other Phl. texts nor I am able to cite a direct outcome in Persian or other Iranian languages. Nevertheless,

---

BABOLGHANI and ADRIANO ROSSI, with whom I have discussed single parts of this paper. Thanks are also due to GARNIK ASATRIAN, who made available to me the relevant Persian headwords of his Persian etymological dictionary in progress, to be published soon.

3 More details on this passage and a comparison with its Sanskrit translation made by Nēryōsang are given in FILIPPONE 1995, pp. 57–64.

4 As is well known, the ŠGW has come down to us in full in a Pāzand version together with a Sanskrit translation; we also have the first five chapters of the Phl. version, but all MSS containing them are secondary and the Phl. version is generally considered as a recent conversion from the Pāzand one. On the manuscript tradition see CERETI 2014.

5 Cf. JÂMÂSP-ÂSÂNÂ/WEST 1887, p. 38.

6 Cf. JÂMÂSP-ÂSÂNÂ/WEST 1887, p. 212; DE MENASCE 1945, p. 68.

7 For Phl. *tītak* 'pupil of the eye' instead of **tīdag*, as in MACKENZIE 1986, p. 83, see FILIPPONE 2020, pp. 125, 127 (despite the fact that the Pāzand spelling does not support this claim).

8 JÂMÂSP-ÂSÂNÂ/WEST 1887, p. 269 "*tôw*, 𐭲𐭥𐭯, *puta* eyelid". See also WEST 1885, p. 145; FILIPPONE 1995, p. 59; ASHA 2015, p. 77.

9 Cf. also *tuf* 'salive; humeur' in DE MENASCE 1945, p. 286.

from the perspective of cognitive onomasiology, being a term used to designate concepts like 'layer', 'skin', 'coating' etc., *tōf* is a good candidate for a lexical innovation producing a designation for 'eyelid', that may be perfectly understood in terms of metaphorical similarity.[10]

If this review of occurrences of *tōf* begins with an instance of metaphorical extension it is simply because the ŠGW passage in (1a–b) has been the starting point of the present investigation. But 'eyelid' may not be considered as one of the core senses of this word.

Chapter 30 in the *Wizīdagīhā ī Zadsprām* (WZ) focuses on the structure of the human body. This consists of more components, among which the corporeal, that in turn is structured as follows:

(2) WZ 30.4
tanīgardīg pad haft tōf *+*uspurrīgīhēd ī ast ān ī andartom mazg pēramōn mazg ast ud pēramōn ast gōšt ud pēramōn gōšt pay ud pēramōn pay rāg*[11] *ud pēramōn rāg pōst ⟨ud⟩ pēramōn pōst mōy*[12]
"The corporeal consists in its totality of seven layers which are: the innermost, the marrow; around the marrow the bones, around the bones the flesh, around the flesh the nerves, around the nerves the veins, around the veins the skin, around the skin the hair."

What is meant by *tōf* in (2) is clear; it refers to any concentric layer of the corporeal, which overlaps the previous one, covering it. Still in the WZ we find a slightly different sense of *tōf*. In 34.36 we are told that Āz, Greed, has divided its powers *(zōrān)* into three (*ō sē baxt* "has divided into three") and these three divisions are, respectively, natural, unnatural and outside-nature. How these divisions relate to each other is not specified; they generally seem to be different parts of a unified whole. Each portion, which in turn forks into two, may be referred to as *tōf*:[13]

(3) WZ 34.37
har tōf-ēw ō dō baxt
"Each portion is divided into two."

In different contexts, Phl. *tōf* is variously used to indicate one of the elements of a larger structural unit. For this reason, it occurs with a certain frequency in those Zoroastrian texts based on the Pahlavi translations and commentaries of the Avesta that treat questions of ritual and practice and contain prescriptions on purity and consequently require accuracy in detail.

10 The data I have collected for a paper in preparation *(The Iranian names of the 'eyelid' and 'eyelash': lexical conceptualisations and procedures of lexical creation)* proves that this is one of the preferred cognitive solutions to create designations for 'eyelid' in the Iranian languages.

11 Perhaps better *rahag*; cf. also *rag* and *rahag* (two headwords) in MacKenzie 1986.

12 Gignoux/Tafazzoli 1993, p. 98.

13 Zaehner 1955, pp. 346, 352 ("each part"); cf. also 1955, p. 474 *tōβ* 'part'.

In 17.3 of the *Zand ī Fragard ī ǰud-dēw-dād* (ZFJD), the late important commentary on the *Wīdēvdād* recently edited by Moazami 2021, the focus is on the possibility to restore a city ossuary that is in ruin *(awērān)* and inside which there are corpses. Among the various recommendations that are made about the ossuary wall, we read:

(4) ZFJD 17.3
ān ī dēwār tōf-ēw pad gōmēz bē handūdan
"A layer of that wall should be smeared with bull's urine."

In my proposal,[14] *tōf* should refer to the thin plaster surface covering the wall.[15]

When speaking of the configuration of vegetal elements, such as trees, fruits or pieces of wood and the like, *tōf* is in general the outer covering; in the case of a tree or wood it is the bark. In fact, *tōf* is not the most usual term to designate this concept, which is instead *pōst* (as *pust* is in Persian), but it seems to have been a possible alternative to *pōst*, as proved by the two very similar following passages from the *Šāyest-nē-šāyest* (ŠnŠ) and the Supplementary texts to the ŠnŠ (Suppl.ŠnŠ) concerning tooth-picks:[16]

(5a) ŠnŠ 10.20
ēk ēn kū dandān-parišn pōst pāk bē tāšišn čē dastwarān čāšt kū ka dandān-parišn pad pōst ō dahan kard ud bē ōbadēd ud zan ī ābustan ka-š pāy abar nihēd pad nisēy[17] *būdan bīmōmand*

"One is this, that the bark *(pōst)* of the tooth-pick should be clearly scraped off, because authorities have taught, that when a tooth-pick with bark *(pōst)* is applied to the mouth and it falls down, and if a pregnant woman sets foot upon it, she is fearful of abortion."

(5b) Suppl.ŠnŠ 12.13
ēk ēn dandān-parišn tōf xūb aziš bē tāšišn čē pōryōtkēšān ast kē guft kū kē-š tōf abar ō dandān kunēd ud bē abganēd zan ī ābustan kē-š pāy abar nihēd pad nisēy būdan gumān

"One is this, that the bark *(tōf)* of the tooth-pick should be well scraped off from it, because there are ancient sages who have said that whoever applies its bark *(tōf)* on the teeth and throws it away, if a pregnant woman sets foot upon it, (there is) doubt of abortion."

14 Cf. instead Moazami 2021, p. 137 ("That wall should be plastered with a layer of bull's urin").
15 See for instance Sistāni *tuf* below.
16 On the reading and the etymology of the Phl. word for 'tooth-pick', there are different positions, all commented on by Buyaner 2019, pp. 38–39 (Appendix 2: phl. KKA-pl(y)š(n')/ *dandān-parišn* ‚Zahnstocher') who also takes into account the several Prs. variants and suggests a new etymology. For the sake of brevity, I do not go into detail and quote the word according to Buyaner's transcription, as it is the most recent proposal, without taking a position on my part.
17 On *nisēy*, referring specifically to dead fetuses and abortions, see Skjærvø 2014, p. 16. This word has been recorded as *nasāk* 'miscarried or still-born child' in Tavadia 1930, pp. 136, 163 ("Thus or 'miscarriage', not 'dead matter'"). For a different reading *nasā(y)* 'corpse, dead matter', see Kotwal 1969, pp. 31, 99(15); Mazdāpur 2011, pp. 128, 156; Buyaner 2019, p. 35.

The content and the almost identical structure of these two passages points to a single source from which both have been drawn; we have no clue as to the question of what has triggered the choice of different lexical items in the case of *tōf* and *pōst* (for example, a different dialectal background?).[18]

Purity and pollution of elements of different nature (such as textiles, earth, plants, fruits, vegetables, utensils, etc.) in case of direct or indirect contact with dead matter, and ritual treatment of any kind of pollution may be listed among the major concerns of the Zoroastrian scriptures. The different cases presented in the frame of a scholastic discourse are usually detailed; the possibility is often taken into account of various degrees of pollution, involving both dead matter *(nasā)* and dry dead matter *(hixr)*, the latter being responsible of a less polluting state. The question is also of how dead matter might affect their surroundings with pollution. Notably, as it has been already remarked elsewhere,[19] the Zoroastrian exegetical tradition was not uniform throughout the centuries and there have been disagreements in various fields among priests belonging to different schools, from the same and different generations. This caused the presence of different visions transmitted (and consequently statements somewhat conflicting and/or confusing in the texts).

In a long comment in the Pahlavi *Wīdēvdād* (PVd 5.4 G–Q), instructions are given on how to intervene to limit the contamination of firewood *(ēsm)* in case of contact with *nasā* and *hixr*. Here we read:

(6) PVd 5.4 O
ka-š hixr abar rasēd ka hamāg[20] *ān and gyāg ka nē hamāg pērāmōn tōf ēw be tāšišn*
"When dry died matter comes on it, if all [is polluted], that much place, if not, all the bark all around should be cut."[21]

18 Buyaner 2019, p. 35, proposes two different German translations: "die Basthaut des Zahnstochers" (for *dandān-parišn pōst*), "die (Ober)schicht des Zahnstochers" (for *dandān-parišn tōf*). Note that in a passage of the Persian Saddar Nasr (Dhabhar 1909, p. 15 [§17 15]), where the focus is similarly on a tooth-pick (*xelāl*), the same concept is referred to as *pust*.

19 See for instance Skjærvø/Elman 2014.

20 Anklesaria 1949, p. 96 emends *hamāg* into *paydāg* (and translates: "when dry-dead-matter comes on it, if manifest, that much portion, if not, the entire surrounding skin shall-be-scraped.") We may justify his intervention by analogy with other similar passages, where visibility is taken into account as one of the parameters determining the degree of pollution. In particular, cf. the passage that slightly anticipates (6): PVd 5.4 Q *ka ō tāg-ē nasā rasēd ka paydāg ān and tāg ka nē hamāg* vitasti drājō frārāθni drājō "when dead matter comes to a branch, if it is visible, that much of the branch (should be cut), if not, the whole (should be cut) *vitasti drājō frārāθni drājō*" (Moazami 2014, pp. 126–127). However, though it cannot be definitively excluded, Anklesaria's proposal remains a mere hypothesis.

21 Cf. Moazami 2014, p. 25: "When dry died matter comes on it [firewood], that portion, if not the entire surrounding layer, should be cut/scraped."

In (6), *tōf* is evidently referring to the wood outer covering. The ZFJD probably provides us with a further occurrence of *tōf* in the sense of 'bark', so far gone unnoticed. SKJÆRVØ/ELMAN 2014, p. 23ff. comment some cases of pollution due to a dead object, highlighting how the determination of degree of pollution is made from a variety of parameters whose possible combinations give places to different scenarios. Among these cases, there is the one of a dead object on a branch of a tree, with the concern for pollution of the earth; this case has been treated with some differences in PVd 6.5, ŠnŠ 2.25–29 and ZFJD 13.5–8. The parameters involved are: wetness versus dryness, fear (of the dead object's falling down) versus no fear, contact with the trunk versus non-contact, variously combined.

Let us consider here the involved passages in ZFJD. First of all, 13.5–7, concerning a dead object on a dry tree *(dār-ēw tarr)*:

(7) ZFJD 13.5–7
ka abar dār-ēw tarr murd estēd čiyōn.
ka pad azg-ēw murd ast u-š tis-iz handām abāz ō stūnag ī mayān nē estēd frōd nē barišn.
ka handām-ēw abāz ō stūnag mayān estēd tan-masāy frōd barišn.
"If something dies on a moist tree, how is it?
If something died on a branch, and no limb reaches the central column (= the trunk), there is no carrying down (of pollution).
If one limb reaches the central column, there is carrying down (of pollution) (in the measure of) the size of a body."

A little below the case concerning a dead object on a dry tree *(dār-ēw hušk)* is dwelt upon:

(8) ZFJD 13.8
pas ka abar dār-ēw hušk murd estēd čiyōn.
*ka-š az ōbastan bīm nēst u-š handām abāz *ō mādagwar nē estēd frōd nē barišn.*
*ka-š az ōbastan bīm ayāb handām-ēw abāz *ō mādagwar frōd barišn.*
"Then if it has died on a dry tree, how is it?
If there is no fear of its falling and no limb reaches the central column, there is no carrying down.
If there is fear of its falling or a limb reaches the central column, there is carrying down."

In between the two passages (7) and (8), the author of the ZFJD inserts a comment from an unspecified authority that might interest us here:

(9a) ZFJD 13.7
pad čāštag ān handām ka [illegible] *hušk ayāb nasāy abāz ō hušk-ēw estēd ān hušk ō zamīg paywastag ēnyā agar draxt az ān ī pōst tarr ka handām-iz abāz ō stūnag mayān estēd pas-iz rēman*

Both Skjærvø/Elman 2014, p. 25 and Moazami 2021, p. 98 read *tan-iz* (as if it were spelt ⟨tnc'⟩[22] and translate as follows:

(9b) "According to the teaching: That limb (is important only) when the body too [*tan-iz*] is dry [i.e., *hixr*] or a *nasāy* reaches a dry (something), unless that dry (something) is connected with the earth. If the tree is of the moist-bark kind, and if the limb reaches the trunk, then too it is polluted." (Skjærvø/Elman 2014, p. 25)

(9c) "According to a teaching, that limb (is important only) when the *body too is dry (i.e., it has become *hixr*) or dead matter (i.e., *nasāy*) reaches (something) dry and that dry (thing) is connected with the earth; otherwise, if the tree is of the moist-bark kind, and if the limb reaches the trunk, then, in that case there is pollution." (Moazami 2021, p. 99)

My tentative hypothesis is that in (9a) ⟨twp'⟩ should be considered as a further occurrence of *tōf* in the sense of 'bark', alternating with *pōst* 'bark'; that the reported comment, inspired by the mention of the limb reaching the trunk, is wedged in the text and somehow cuts the thread of discourse: it summarizes the whole question in a very succinct but perhaps not very clear way, including both the cases of a dry-bark and a moist-bark tree, thus anticipating what will be said later in (8); that (9a) should be translated as follows:

(9d) "According to the teaching: That limb (is relevant), when the bark *(tōf)* is dry or dead matter reaches (something) dry and that dry (thing) is connected with the earth. Moreover, if the tree is of the moist-bark *(pōst)* kind, when the limb reaches the trunk, then too there is pollution."

Admittedly, this is only a proposal, though supported by the fact that in ŠnŠ the reference is also to a moist-bark tree *(draxt [...] ka-š pōst tarun)* and to a dry-bark tree *(ka draxt pōst hušk)* and not simply to a moist or dry tree,[23] as it is in ZFJD, foreshadowing the existence of different scholastic traditions with different formulas.

Another possible occurrence of *tōf*, with an *-ag* extension and reference to vegetable products, could be recognized in a passage from the ZFJD where the concern is for the behavior one should assume in case of contamination of a pomegranate and the rules for its purification:

(10) ZFJD 23.9
anār dādestān čiyōn. harw-iš tis-ēw rēman ud tōfag astag šōyišn ēdōn čiyōn dār
"What is the decision about pomegranate? Every part of it is polluted and the washing of its rind and stones is like that of wood."

22 In fact, Moazami has **tan-iz*.
23 See also Unvala 1922, p. 127 (ll. 15–18), (ll. 8–16) treating the cases of a dead object on a tree with moist bark *(pust-e tar)* and dry bark *(pust-e xošk)*.

Instead of *tōfag*, MOAZAMI 2021, p. 164 proposes reading *tōzag* (as if it were written ⟨twck'⟩, and not ⟨twpk'⟩) and translating "skin."[24] The connection is obviously with *tōz* 'bark, skin' in MACKENZIE 1986, that, however, does not seem to be really documented in Middle Persian.[25] But in fact, the whole passage focusing on pomegranate (ZFJD 23.9) is ambiguous on some points. After (10) the text proceeds as follows:

(11) ZFJD 23.9
u-š pid mazg ēdōn čiyōn ǰōrdāy. u-š anārag ī pōst ud pid ēdōn čiyōn ǰōrdāy. u-š dānag ēdōn čiyōn anār. (MOAZAMI 2021, p. 166)
"And its marrow seeds are like barley. And the skin of pomegranate and flesh are like barley. And its aril is like the pomegranate." (*ibid.*, p. 167)

In ZFJD 23.9 [here (10) and (11)] the elements that make up the pomegranate, a fruit with a very complex configuration, are listed in detail, with a tendential progression from the outside to the inside. Seemingly, we find in (10) the smooth hard outer skin *(tōfag)* and the white seeds inside any grains *(astag)*; in (11) the pulp (*pid* 'flesh, pulp') and pith (*mazg* 'marrow, brain'), i.e., the spongy, white albedo; again the pulp *(pid)* and the white membrana *(pōst)* covering pomegranate grain clusters (*anārag*?), and at the end the aril (*dānag*, cf. Prs. *dāne-ye anār*). In fact, the correspondence between these terms, sometimes listed twice, as is the case with *pid*, and the proper referents is not always certain.[26] And what would mean that the pomegranate aril is like the pomegranate? Probably, looking for absolute precision in this type of texts leads us nowhere.

A substantial part of Zoroastrian scriptures is devoted to the topic of menstruation and the precautions to be taken at the period of menstrual discharge.[27] To prevent pollution through direct contact and avoid the negative effect on people exposed to their glance, women are obliged to remain secluded in a special place during the whole period. This place may be a small hut intended for that purpose *(daštānestān)* and set at some distance from the house or a separate room inside the house. Among the many questions raised on it, there is that on whether the seclusion place may be restored or not and how to do that:

(12) ZFJD 33.29
daštānestān ka awērān[28] *bē bawēd bīm wirāstan pādixsāy ayāb nē.*

24 See also *tōzag* 'bark, skin' in her *Glossary* (MOAZAMI 2021, p. 427).

25 This spelling would also require a justification as the coalescence of ⟨p⟩ and ⟨c⟩ occurs in case of ligature, not after a sign that cannot be connected to the preceding one, as is the case of ⟨w⟩.

26 Metaphorical applications adapt time to time to the configuration of the various vegetable products. In the case of a walnut, for instance, *pōst* and *mazg* seem to denote, respectively, the shell and the kernel; see, for instance, ŠnŠ 2.120–121.

27 For the strict rules regulating the seclusion of women during menstruation, see in particular PVd 16, ŠnŠ 3, ZFJD 33.

28 MOAZAMI 2021, p. 244 reads *an-ērān* ("If there is fear that the secluded place is of non-Iranians", p. 245). The reading *awērān* is supported by other contexts where referents said

bērōn pad āb pādixšāy wirāstan. andarrōn ka kand ayāb ǰud šāyēd.
ān tōf-ēw bārīk ā-š pad gōmēz ayāb pad āb tan-tōmag ǰud bē kardan ud ān ī abārīg pad āb pādixšāy.
"If there is fear[29] that the *daštānestān* is in ruin, is it permitted to restore it or not?
Outside it is permitted to restore it with water. Inside, when it is dug or (made) separate, it is permitted.
That narrow part should be made separate with bull's urine or *tan-tōmag* liquid[30] and it is permitted (to restore) the rest with water."

Seemingly, in (12) *tōf* could refer to the portion inside a house that has been demarcated in order to be used for seclusion, not unlike in (13) below, where the isolated portion inside a building that is not identified as *daštānestān* is equated to all purposes to a *daštānestān*. The ZFJD passage reads as follows:

(13) ZFJD 33.33
ka nē pad daštānestān paydāgenīd estēd ēg-iš dādestān čiyōn. ka-š daštān aziš āmad pad gyāg pāk. ka tōf[31]*-ēw pad ēd kār kard estēd čiyōn. ka-š daštān andar nišast ēdōn bawēd čiyōn daštānestān*
"If it has not been revealed to be a *daštānestān*, then what is the judgement? When a menstruating woman comes out from it,[32] it is immediately pure. If a part[33] has been made for this purpose, how is it? If the woman in menses has dwelled in it[34], it becomes like a *daštānestān*."

Contact of textiles with a corpse is another threat to be grappled with unceasingly.
A large number of situations are examined in the commentaries. As usual, different parameters are taken into account, with possibility of cross-over, and the proper ritual treatment for any situation is pointed out.

to be *awērān* are expected to be restored (*wirāy-*, *wirāstan*; cf. ZFJD 5.6 *ka wēšag awērān kē pad-iz nasāy ud warōmand pad ātaxš bē wirāyēnd* "If there is a desolate forest that [...] they (want to) restore with fire." ZFJD 17.3 *ka hazzān bē awērān bawēd u-š wirāyišn abāyēd kardan čiyōn kunišn* "if the ossuary is ruined and must be restored, how should it be done?"

29 'Fear' in the sense of 'probability' or 'risk' of being in ruin (Skjærvø/Elman 2014, p. 24).

30 The spelling ⟨°twmk'⟩ (also in FZJD 33.42) alternates with ⟨°twhmk'⟩ (FZJD 33.67 [twice]). This juice, obtained from herbs and leaves and called *āb-e tamtume* in the Persian *Revāyats* (Vitalone 1996, pp. 173, 255), may on specific occasions replace the *gōmēz* as a purifying substance; for more details see Chacha 1936, pp. 70–71 (with interesting textual and bibliographic references and the original proposal to identify with sumaq the herbs used for the preparation of this liquid). Note that Moazami is not consistent in the translation of *āb tan-tō(h)mag*; cf. "(*)agricultural water", "(sap of) plants/agriculture", "water used for agriculture"(2021, pp. 47, 213, 245, 267, 365).

31 ⟨tp'⟩.

32 Differently Skjærvø/Elman 2014, p. 42 ("When the menstruant woman has come (home) from it."

33 Perhaps better than "If a *layer has been made for this purpose (to catch the flow)", as in Skjærvø/Elman 2014, p. 42 and fn. 38 [*tōb* "*layer"].

34 Cf. "has sat down on it" in Moazami 2021, p. 247 and Skjærvø/Elman 2014, p. 42. In fact, *andar nišastan (nišīn-)* means 'to live, to remain, to dwell', and not simply 'to sit down'.

Here I have to make something clear. There are several general terms for 'cloth, clothing, garment' in Pahlavi. One of these is spelt ⟨wstlg⟩. It is generally transcribed as *wastarg* or *wastarag*,[35] and obviously referred to Avestan *vastra-*.[36] However, when the notion evoked is that of cloth spread on the floor at bedtime, that same spelling is read *wistarg* or *wistarag* by most scholars and translated 'bedding, cover'; reference is to Prs. *bestar, bastar* 'bed, mattress'.[37] Contrary to this current view,[38] I assume that ⟨wstlg⟩ does not record two (homographic) words, but one single word (*wistarg* or *wastarg*),[39] with the general sense of 'cloth', that may assume different senses according to the contexts in which it is used: bed cloth, dresses or other kinds of cloth covering. Its modern outcomes, however, have mostly assumed the sense of 'bedding'.[40]

Generally, when speaking of cloth, *tōf* may be intended as 'layer', as clarified by the following passages, though the wording of some of them is not clear and unequivocal:

(14) ZFJD 19.1
wistarg bālišn kē sag ud mard padiš bē widerēd rēmanīh čiyōn. ān ī azabar ud ān ī azēr ān tōf-ēw hamāg rēman
"Bedding and pillows on which men or dogs have passed away, how is the impurity? The one above and the one below, those layers are all impure." [41]

(15) ZFJD 20.5
wistarg kē nasāy abar barēnd ān ⟨ī⟩ abar wišōbēnd. ān kē hixr ī murdagān padiš ud ān kē mard padiš ō dār kunēnd [...] dādestān čiyōn.
ān kē nasāy barēnd ud ān kē padiš ō dār kunēnd a-kār. ān kē padiš wišōbēnd tōf-ēw. ān kē hixr ī murdagān padiš ān and gyāg

35 Cf. MacKenzie 1986, p. 88 (*wastar, wastarag* 'clothing, garment'), etc.
36 Referred to IE **u̯es-* 'to wear'; see also Andrés-Toledo 2017, p. 399, Ciancaglini 2017, p. 54.
37 Cf. MacKenzie 1986, p. 91 (*wistar(ag)* 'bedding, cover'), etc. The current etymology for Phl. *wistar* (as well as Prs. *bestar, bastar* and cognates) refers it to the Phl. verb *wistar-* 'to spread'; cf. Cheung 2007, p. 364 *starH^1, Hasandust 2016, pp. 482–483, Ciancaglini 2017, p. 54.
38 This view, however, is shared by Western scholars only. For a different position see Kotwal 1969, p. 180 *wistarg* 'clothes, garment; carpet, bedding'; Bahār 1961, p. 321 *wistarg* 'cloth [ǰāme]'; Mansuri 2015–2021 *wastar* 'bedding, clothing, garment [bastar, ǰāme, pušāk]', *wastarg* 'cloth, clothing, bedding [bastar, pušāk, ǰāme, pušeš]'; *wistar* 'bedding, cover [bastar, pušeš (pušāk)]', *wistarag* 'bedding, clothes' (with cross-references between these headwords).
39 In the following I will conventionally transcribe it as *wistarg*. Since /-ag/ is generally spelt ⟨-k⟩, for a spelling ⟨-lg⟩, /°rg/ is preferable to /°rag/. On this matter, see Ciancaglini 2017.
40 This hypothesis could also explain why *wastar* (allegedly other than *wistar*) is not continued in New Persian. To accept it, one may assume that the Pahlavi translators, who systematically rendered Av. *vastra-* by Phl. *wistar(g)/wastar(g)*, have chosen it among other general terms for 'cloth' because of its phonetical similarity to the Av. one.
41 On this matter, see also PVd 7.9–15.

"Cloth on which they carry dead bodies, that on which (dead bodies) decompose, that on which there is excrement of dead bodies, that with which they hang a man, [...] what is the judgement?
That on which they carry a dead body and that on which they hang a man are unfit for use; that on which (dead bodies) decompose, a layer (is polluted); that on which there is dry dead matter of dead bodies, that much place (is polluted)."

(16) ZFJD (Summary)
wistarg kē padiš bē kešēnd agar hazār-tōf ast hamāg a-kār
"The cloth that they pull [the corpse] with, even if it is made of one thousand layers it is completely unfit for use."

(17) ZFJD 20.4
ka jāmag hamāg ān dārēd ī ēč abāg tan nē bast estēd čiyōn.
ān tōf-ēw rēman ī ham-karzag bawēd
"If all he wears is a clothing and nothing is tied onto his body, how is it? That one layer that is in direct contact[42] is polluted."

(18) Dk 5.15.2
wastarg ān ī a-wizīrišnīg čiyōn ēbyāstišnīh ī ast šabīg tōf-ēw pad garzag[43] *ud kustīg azabar ham šabīg bastan* (Amouzgar/Tafazzoli 2000, p. 52)
"Les vêtements indispensables sont ceux que l'on porte (selon les règles religieuses), à savoir une seule chemise dont une couche est en contact (avec le corps) et la ceinture (sacrée) attachée sur cette même chemise." (*ibid.*, p. 53)

As is well known, the religious outfit of traditional Zoroastrians is made up of a sacred shirt, that is a thin, white under-shirt made of cotton, worn in contact with the skin, and a sacred girdle, generally made up of lamb's wool, tied around the waist. These two elements may be regarded as symbols of faith and emblems of Zoroastrian identity. The fact that Phl. *ēbyāstišnīh* (a noun derived from an adjective adapted from Av. *aiβiiāstō* 'girded with the sacred girdle' (see also Stausberg 2004, pp. 11–12), and connected to the notion of girdling (Av. *yāh-* 'to girdle') is used to indicate the correct outfit with reference to both the shirt and belt, shows that, though both articles are mandatory, the latter is to be considered as the really essential one.[44] This is also testified by the fact that numerous passages and even entire texts are reserved to explain in a more or less elaborated way the meaning and symbolism of the girdle,[45] as well as by the fact that while for the sacred girdle there is in Pahlavi a specific term, *kustīg*, used

42 Phl. *ham-karzag* is one of the technical terms used to refer to direct contact with polluted persons or things. See Moazami 2014, p. 12 and fn. 41, also quoting the translation 'having a part in common' by Skjærvø 2009, p. 481.

43 Madan 1911, p. 447 ⟨klpk'⟩.

44 The same conceptual extension is recorded in Avestan. Cf. Av. *aiβi* + *yāh-* as 'to put something on' (Stausberg 2004, p. 12). According to *Nērangestān* (Nēr. 77.5–6), for instance, only not wearing the girdle may be considered as a sin.

45 Cf. Stausberg 2004; Choksy/Kotwal 2014.

consistently[46] which has survived over times (Prs. *kosti*, *košti* and cognates), various terms are reserved for the shirt, although the most widespread is *šabīg*,[47] the one also occurring in (18).

The reading *garzag* for ⟨klpk⟩ in (18) is an emendation by the editors Amouzgar/Tafazzoli (2000, pp. 52 and 120), who refer to *ham-karzag* in ŠnŠ 2.67 and 3.31; to their references we can add (17) above. However, this emendation is far from being certain. The main objection towards it is the initial voiced /g/, while °*karzag*, that is always attested in the compound *ham-karzag* has an initial unvoiced /k/. This reading might be replaced with *pad kirbag*, that does not require any emendation but is not satisfactory from the semantic point of view ('virtuously'?, 'with merit'?), unless one tries to somehow connect this expression (i. e., *pad kirbag*) to that pocket over the chest that is a typical element of the Zoroastrian sacred shirt, symbolic of the place where the good deeds done during the day are kept and called in Persian *geribān*[48] or *kisse-ye kerfe*[49] (i. e., 'the purse of the good deeds').[50] An explicit textual reference to this element is found in the *Wizirgerd ī Dēnīg* (WD) 114.1–2[51] (Sanjana 1848, pp. 180–181), where the shirt and the pocket are repeatedly mentioned and variously denominated: *stahr-pēsanghem abāg grībān* 'the sacred shirt with the pocket', with *stahr-pēsanghem* that is the rendering in Phl. script of the Av. adjectival compound *stəhrpaēsaŋhəm* 'star-studded (acc.)', generally adapted in Pahlavi as *star-pēsīd*;[52] *wastarg star-pēsīd kū taškanag* 'the star-studded cloth, i. e., the *taškanag*'; *pas ōy ēbyāghān abar ōy stahr ī ō mayān čiyōn kamarband bandēd* 'then they tie the sacred girdle *(ēbyāghān)* on the shirt *(= stahr)* around the waist like a girdle'; *abāg wurrōyišn-bān kū grībān* 'with the Protector of the faith, i. e., the *gribān*', *čiyōn ōy wurrōyišn-bān kū grībān* 'like the Protector of the faith, i. e., the *gribān*',[53] etc.

That *pad kirbag* may be considered as an elliptic expression for the pocket on the frontal side of the sacred shirt is a mere conjuncture to be proved. The im-

46 Only rarely replaced by *ēbyānghan* (MacKenzie 1986; from Av. *aiβiiāŋhana*).

47 Besides *šabīg*, the other terms are *pērāhan* and *taškanag*; to these also add *stahr-pēsanghem* and the 'shortened' form *stahr* (lit. 'star'), to my knowledge, only in WD (see below). Several terms are also attested in the Persian *Revāyats* (*zir-kusti* or *šib-kusti*, *nimak, nime*), although today among the Parsis *sedre/sudre* is predominant (see also Dhabhar 1932, p. 29, fn. 10). On Prs. *šib* 'under, below', see Filippone 2022.

48 'Collar; a pocket (which in old times was the opening or breast of a garment)' (Haim 1992).

49 Note that Prs. *kerfe* is the outcome of Phl. *kirbag* (Hasandust 2016, no. 3944).

50 For the '*giriban*' as the element of recognition of the *sudre*, see Modi 1937, p. 173; Cama/Liloawala 2014, Kotwal/Boyd 1982, p. 41.

51 Paragraphing is that of Daniel Sheffield, also followed in Skj.

52 Most frequently used as an adjective in collocation with one of terms for the sacred belt. See, for instance, DD 38.15 *ēbiyānghan ī star-pēsīd* "the girdle adorned with stars" or (21) and (22) below.

53 The form *gribān* (⟨gryp'n'⟩) instead of *grīwbān* (⟨grywp'n'⟩, cf. MacKenzie 1986 'neck-guard, gorget') points to a NPrs. interference.

portant aspect for our topic is the presence of *tōf* in (18) and its clear connection with a shirt. I have not understood well the editors' interpretation of this point. Translating "dont une couche est en contact" do they mean that the shirt has two (or more) layers and one of these should be in contact with the skin? Differently, I assume that *šabīg tōf-ēw* intends to denote "the shirt (of) one layer", i. e., a one-fold shirt.[54]

Failure to respect the rules of proper clothing gives rise, depending on the combinations, to sins of various kinds. One of these is that referred to with the technical term *wišād-dwārišnīh* 'going about open', often cited in the texts containing regulations:

(19) DD 39.3
ka wišādag ayāb brahnag ayāb pad ǰāmag [ī] 2-tōf rawēd ēg-iš wišād-dwārišnīh andar bun nēst[55]
"If one goes open (= untied) or naked or with a two-layered clothing, then the sin of 'going around open' is not in his account."

In (19) three conditions considered as inappropriate while walking are mentioned: being without girdle wrapped around the waist *(wišādag)*, being naked *(brahnag)*, wearing a two-fold *(2-tōf)* garment *(ǰāmag)*, here probably referring to the inner shirt, that is instead expected to be made of one layer.[56]

In DD 39.1 the question is raised about what is good and bad with regard to the sacred shirt *(pērāhan)* and the sacred belt *(kustīg)*. The answer reads as follows:

(20) DD 39.2
pad dēn-parwandīh ī drust ī dō-tāg ī dō-tōf ī čiyōn ān-iz ī dō-tōf ī dēnīg xrad parwandīhēd āgāhīhān kārān
"As for the right religious girdling, it is with two folds and two layers, just as the two layers of the religious wisdom are girdled around the works of those who have awareness."[57]

The two layers of the religious wisdom would be, respectively, the 'inborn' *(āsnīg)* and the 'heard by the ear, learnt' *(gōšōšrūdīg)*. It remains to define what it exactly means that a girdle should have two *tōf* to be proper. West (1882, p. 133 and fn. 4) tried to advance an explanation: proper girdling is double in the sense

54 Cf. also (26) and (29) below.

55 ⟨LOYT'⟩. Jaafari-Dehaghi 1998, p. 164 emends into **ast*. Cf. however also the negative particle in ŠnŠ 4.6 (below (28)), also emended by Tavadia 1930, p. 88 ("višātakīh <nē> bavēt") and in Nēr. 73.5.

56 See also (26) and (27) below.

57 For the general interpretation of this passage, I follow that proposed in Skjærvø 2011, pp. 208–209, with the phrase *pad dēn-parwandīh* at the opening of the sentence. As an alternative, see Jaafari-Dehaghi 1998, pp. 164–165: *[...] pad dēn. parwandīh ī drust ī dō-tāg ī dō-tōf* "[...] in the religion. The proper girdle is of two folds and double layered, which is like the double layer of the wisdom of the religion which encloses the works of knowledge themselves."

that "it is passed twice round the waist before it is tied the first time, but then it is passed a third time round the waist". Is this really the correct interpretation?

As rightly underlined by WEST, the girdle has to be wrapped three times around the waist; it is also tied twice in a double knot in the front and back, its ends hanging on the back. Then we have three turns and four knots in all, as also stressed in the *Bundahišn* (Bd):[58]

(21) Bd 6j.1
ēbyānghan homānāg ī ast kustīg homānāg star-pēsīd ī mēnōyān-tāšīd 3 tāg pad 4 grih
"like a girdle — that is, like the *kustīg*, adorned with stars and fashioned by spirits in three folds and four knots."

(22) Bd 28.15
kustīg [...] ī star-pēsīd ī mēnōyān-tāšīd [...] 3 tāg andar 4 grih-ēw [...] mardōm-iz [...] kustīg pad mayān dārēnd 3 tāg andar 4 grih čiyōn humad hūxt huwaršt
"the *kustīg* [...], adorned with stars and fashioned by spirits [...] in three folds and four knots [...] the people, too, [...] wear the sacred girdle of three folds and four knots around their waist."

However, as we have seen in (21) and (22), in the relevant Bd passages the number of times the girdle has to be winded around the waist is defined by *tāg*,[59] and not by *tōf*. Unless we want to consider *dō-tōf* and *dō-tāg* as redundant, we have to explain their co-occurrence in the specific context of (20). Since we know that the sacred girdle should be strictly *ēw-tāg* ('in one piece'),[60] what meaning should we attribute to *dō-tāg* here? A possibility is that it refers to the numbers of encirclements around the waist, despite the strangeness of the number 'two' in place of the usual 'three'. In this case *dō-tōf* would not refer to the encirclements, as suggested by WEST, but to the fact that the sacred girdle actually has two layers, with a hollow middle, that in recent Zoroastrian commentaries is said to symbolize the space between this world and the other, the sky and the earth.[61]

58 Quoted according to PAKZAD 2005 and, for translation, AGOSTINI/THROPE 2020. As remarked by STAUSBERG 2004, p. 23, the *Bundahišn* stands out among the older Pahlavi texts, "in that it connects a technical aspect of the *kusti*, the three folds, and the tying of it with four knots, to the question of its significance."

59 Phl. *tāg* is a polysemous word, with several functions ('item, unit; -fold, made of X pieces (after numbers); alone, single'). It is the precursor of Persian *tā*, that however also works as a (unmarked) numerative classifier. Though Middle Persian cannot be considered as a numeral classifier language, it seems likely that the grammaticalization process of *tāg* towards the development of a classifier has already started during Middle Persian times, when classifier-like uses of *tāg* were on the rise (CATHCART *et al.* 2021, pp. 279–280). The issue is interesting and deserves further in-depth studies.

60 Cf. for instance Nēr. 3.67.6, 9, 10, where we are told that the girdle should be *ēw-tāg* ('in one piece').

61 MODI 1937, p. 176, KOTWAL/BOYD 1982, p. 43; CAMA/LILOAWALA 2014. One should note that Zoroastrian traditional scriptures do not pay much attention to the technical

The occurrences of *tōg* in the Pahlavi documentation

Chapter 7 of PVd provides instructions about how to contrast contamination of cloth due to contact with dead matter. One of the questions concerns the extension of contamination of beddings and pillows over which persons have passed away. In the course of Ohrmazd's answer, one reads as follows:

(23) PVd 7.11A
ān ī abardom awēšān wistarg ud ān ī andardom abarnihumb [*ēd*[62] *tōg ī azēr ud ēk azabar*]
"Their superior bedding cloth and the inferior cover [that is, the lower layer and the upper one] ..."

(24) PVd 7.11C–E
ka-š mōy ēw-tāg abar ēstēd ā juttar nēst ud tōg ī azēr ud ēk ī azabar rēman. har abāg ān ēw-kardag rēman
"If one of his/her hair(s) remains on it (= bedding), then it is not otherwise, and the lower layer and the upper one (are) impure. Everything (that is) in direct contact with it (is) impure."[63]

It seems clear to me that (23) and (24) may be easily connected to (14) above, a passage drawn from FZJD, where, however, the lower and the upper layer are referred to as *tōf* and not *tōg*. It is for this reason, I suppose, that MOAZAMI 2014, p. 188 has emended in both cases *tōg* into **tōf*, only signalling in footnote 5 that K1 & L4 (i.e., the two MSS the author declares to have used) have in fact ⟨twk⟩. But this emendation is, in my opinion, unjustified.[64] There are other attestations of *tōg* in contexts in which seemingly *tōf* could also be found.

Another possible occurrence of *tōg* 'layer' used with reference to cloth but unnoticed so far is in ZFJD 27.2:

(25) ZFJD 27.1–2
kē jāmag abar nasāy abganēd u-š padiš bē barēd jāmag čiyōn. ān jāmag kē-iz hazār-tōg[65] *ast hamāg a-kār*
"If one throws a cloth on a corpse and carries it with it, the cloth, how is it? That cloth even if it is made of one thousand layers is totally useless."

fabric of the sacred girdle, at least up to the 19th century. According to STAUSBERG 2004, p. 29, one may interpret this fact in two different ways: "Either the authors did not attach any importance to it, or the kusti did only in recent centuries take on the complex shape and fabrication mentioned in recent interpretations — such as the 72 threads, 12 strands, 6 tassels, the hollow inside, the twisting, doubling, etc."

62 So according to MOAZAMI 2014, p. 188. However, it could also be read *ēw* (*ēw tōg*); for HDA as a possible spelling for *ē(w)* see below.

63 See also ANKLESARIA 1949, p. 156, MOAZAMI 2014, p. 189; a slightly different translation is in ANDRÉS-TOLEDO 2016, p. 131 ("If a hair is over him / her in direct contact [...]."

64 See ANKLESARIA 1949, pp. 155–156 (*tô*); ANDRÉS-TOLEDO 2016, p. 131 (*tōg*).

65 Ms. ⟨1000 twwk'⟩.

Instead of *hazār-tōg*, MOAZAMI (2021, p. 184) and Skj. read *hazār-tanag*.[66] In my opinion, similarly to *hazār-tōf* in (16), *hazār-tōg* ('thousand-layered') is used here as a rhetoric tool (hyperbole) to assert that under the mentioned conditions (i. e., cloth thrown on a corpse) the contamination of the cloth in its entirety, however it may be, cannot be questioned.

On the proper way of wearing the Zoroastrian sacred shirt we may read in the ŠnŠ the following:

(26) ŠnŠ 4.7
ka šabīg-ēw ī ēw-tōg paymōxt frēg[67] *harw dō kust nihuft estēd ā-š kustīg abar bast estēd šāyēd*
"When a sacred shirt of one layer is put on, the shoulders on both sides are covered, and then the sacred girdle is tied on it, it is proper."

The sacred shirt is then expected to be one-folded *(ēw-tōg)*; when two-folded, it would be considered as unfit, as we have already learned from (19):

(27) ŠnŠ 4.6
ka dō-tōg ayāb ast (ī) brīd[68] *estēd nē šāyēd*
"If it (= the shirt) is two-folded or torn, it is improper."

Shortly after in the same passage, the unsuitability of being double-folded is reaffirmed, although we have difficulty in understanding that statement because of a still unidentified word and the presence of an unclear negative particle:

(28) ŠnŠ 4.6
ka az kust-ēw pad ⟨ywlm'wk⟩[69] *ī dō-tōg paymōxt estēd ka-iz kustīg dārēd ud ka kustīg nē dārēd ēg-iz wišādagīh nē*[70] *bawēd*
"If from one side one is clothed with a two-folded ⟨ywlm'wk⟩, whether he/she wears a belt or not, even then it is not (the state of) being open."

As already noted above, levels of inappropriateness with respect to proper clothing (i. e., one-folded shirt in direct contact with the skin and a girdle, aptly tied on the shirt), may vary depending on the possible combinations; for instance, proper shirt associated with (unproper) lack of girdle:

66 Cf. MOAZAMI 2021, p. 185: "That garment even (if it accommodates) one thousand bodies is completely unfit for use."
67 I agree here with the reading *frēg* ('shoulder') proposed in Skj. TAVADIA 1930 read *parīk* 'hip'; "When a *šapīk* of one fold is put on, [whereby] the hips are covered on both sides, and the *kustīk* is tied on it, it is allowed"; similarly MAZDĀPUR 2011 and MANSURI 2015–2021, s. v. *ēw-tūg*. See also DHABHAR 1932, p. 30 fn.: "When a shirt of one fold is put on and the skirts fit (*lit.* are worn) on both sides."
68 So MAZDĀPUR 2011, p. 72, Skj. Differently TAVADIA 1930, p. 87: *ka 2-tōk aδāp āstarit ēstēt, nē šāyēt* (though advancing, as a second hypothesis, the reading *ast brit* in footnote).
69 Reading and meaning uncertain. Cf. TAVADIA 1930, p. 87 (note to 6^2) *garmānak*, 'warm-clothing', name of an article of dress, connected to *garm* 'warm'; MAZDĀPUR 2011, p. 72, 75(7) *gawr-mānāg* '[pušāk-e] gabr-mānand'.
70 ⟨L'⟩. Considered as a mistake by TAVADIA 1930 "it may be rāδ."

(29) PhlRDD 11.1
mardōmān ka-šān kustīg wišād ud pērāhan ī ēw-tōg paymōxt estēd [...]
"If men have untied their sacred girdle and have put on the shirt of one fold [...]"

Although the sequence ⟨HD twk'⟩ is clearly legible in the MSS,[71] Alain Williams opts for a reading *ēw-tāg*.[72] Similarly, Yaakov Elman suggested to emend *dō-tōg* in *dō-tāg* in ŠnŠ 4.6 (= 27 above).[73] The reason behind their position should be that elsewhere, as in *Dādestān ī dēnīg* (DD) 39.2, 'being *ēw-tāg*' is listed among the requirements for a shirt to be proper (*niyābag ast* "it is fitting":[74]

(30) DD 39.2
niyābag ast pad drust spēd ī pāk ī ēw-tāg ī ēw-kard [...]

Let us consider now how different scholars have translated the adjectives used to refer to the four conditions listed in (30), and in particular Dhabhar 1932, p. 29, fn. 10 [D], Jaafari-Dehaghi 1998, p. 165 [JD], Skjærvø 2011, p. 208 [Sk]:

(a) *pad drust spēd*	(b) *pāk*	(c) *ēw-tāg*	(d) *ēw-kard*
"proper, white"[D]; "completely white" [JD, Sk]	"pure"[D]; "clean"[JD]; left untranslated [Sk]	"of one fold"[D]; "single"[JD];[75] "made whole"[Sk]	"made of one substance (only)"[D]; "of one piece"[JD];[76] "in one piece (without seams)"[Sk]

In his Commentary, Williams (1990, II, p. 143) mentions this DD passage ("The shirt should be all of one piece, according to DD 39.2"), also comparing the Zoroastrian shirt to the seamless garment of Jesus and making reference to its symbolic value. But there is something about this issue that seems to escape us. Judging at least from the recent literature and without entering into detail, one should say that the Zoroastrian shirt cannot be called 'seamless' (in fact, it has nine seams[77]) and even the fact that it should made up of a single piece of cloth can be somehow questioned.[78]

71 See Williams 1990, I, p. 242.
72 Williams 1990, I, p. 73. See also "*ēw-tāg* [HDt'k] adj. 'of one piece': *11.1" in *ibid.*, p. 301.
73 Cf. Skjærvø/Elman 2014, p. 40, fn. 32: "We should probably also read *dō-tāg* in *Šāyist nē šāyist* 4.6, 7, where the mss. have ⟨2-twk⟩."
74 See also Nēr. 67.9, 10, 69.4 etc. (though sometimes with a spelling requiring emendation); see Kotwal/Kreyenbroek 2009.
75 "Of one piece" in Jaafari-Dehaghi 1998, p. 256 (Glossary).
76 "United" in Jaafari-Dehaghi 1998, p. 256 (Glossary).
77 "The sudreh has nine seams, including the two side seams, two sleeve seams, one neck seam, one girdo (the storehouse of potential good), one gireban (the pocket of good deeds), one straight tiri or line (a reminder of imperfection in the physical world) and a triangular tiri" (Cama/Liloawala 2014).
78 According to Modi 1937, p. 173, "the shirt must not be made up of one continuous piece of cloth but of two pieces sewn together on the sides". Doubts are expressed

What we can only take for granted is that the shirt is a type of garment that must not consist of overlapping layers. In any case, the interpretation of *ēw-tāg* and *ēw-kard* in (30) remains somehow puzzling. Generally, *ēw-kard*, more frequently *ēw-kardag*, means 'in contact, united, joined', as opposed to *ǰud-kardag* 'separated, not in contact'; it is a technical term widely used in the religious discourse about purity and pollution.[79] One might assume that here it also could mean 'in contact' (with the skin) or, as an alternative 'in one piece'. As for *ēw-tāg*, one might think of different possibilities: 1) 'single,'[80] i. e., one should wear only one shirt, not two, or more, one above the other';[81] 2) 'in one piece'; 3) 'one-folded.'[82] In the latter case, one should admit that *ēw-tāg* and *ēw-tōg* on some occasions may convey the same meaning and can be used interchangeably in specific contexts.

Question 33 of the *Rivāyat ī Ēmēd ī Ašwahištān* (REA) involves the possibility of ablution of a menstruous woman after nine days from the start of menstruation and the proper treatment of menstruation clothing. From the related answer we learn that treatment is differentiated depending on whether the material is stained with blood or other impurities or not. Casuistry, as usual, is rich. For instance, it is not proper to expose a cloak (?)[83] to rainfall. In fact, it would be a sin and for the following reason:

(31) REA 33.7
tōg ī azērīn ēdōn bawēd čiyōn ka-š āb awiš rasid
"The lower layer would be in such a condition that water would get to it."

In the same text the question is treated whether it would be proper leaving menstruation clothing in open air before a rainfall and then letting rain fall upon it. The answer reads:[84]

in Nēr. 69.4, according to which "there is one who says" that as far as shirt "made of two pieces" is concerned, "it is not clear (whether it is permissible); made from three pieces it is not permissible if it causes discomfort" (Kotwal/Kreyenbroek 2009, p. 33).

79 Cf. Moazami 2014, pp. 12, 522 ('connected, united; joined; close contact; made one'); MacKenzie 1986 ('united, joined'). For another instance, see (24) above.

80 Cf. MacKenzie 1986, p. 31 ('alone, single, individual').

81 Cf. for instance ŠnŠ 4.8 *ka šabīg 2 paymōxt estēd ud kustīg abar ān ī azabar bandēd [...]* "if one has worn two shirts and has tied the sacred girdle on that above [...]."

82 Cf. Prs. *yektā* 'a garment without a lining' (Steingass 1963).

83 ⟨kbw'k⟩. It could be considered as a variant of the spelling ⟨kp'k⟩ for *kabāh* 'garment, cloth', an Arabic word penetrated into Pahlavi. See also Mansuri 2015–2021 s. v.

84 Similar concerns are treated in ZFJD 31.2.

(32) REA 33.9
ān šāyēd ka-š hixrōmandīh ēwāz az ham-karzagīh ī zan ī daštān ayāb[85] *kas kē pad pišag abāyēd šustan u-š hixrīh ēw paydāgīg padiš nēst ēw-tōg* (⟨HNA twk'⟩) *abganēd čiyōn čādur ud sarband ud wāšāmag*[86]
"That is permitted if the defilement had only been the result of direct contact with a menstruating woman or with a person who should be washed ritually *(pad pišag)* and no filth on it is visible (and) it is left lying one-folded, like a veil, a turban, a curtain."[87]

Some readings in and/or the interpretation of this passage may be matter of debate. One of the crucial points is how to read ⟨HNA⟩ preceding ⟨twk'⟩. HNA is the logogram of the demonstrative *ēd* 'this' that at the time when the manuscripts were written, had probably lost its final *-d* and become *ē*.[88] As the result of this phonetic change, *ēd* has become homophone with the verbal particle *ē*, used with the present to express exhortation to other than 2nd person. The particle *ē*, currently spelled ⟨'y⟩, is frequently also spelled ⟨HNA⟩ in the manuscripts, as reported, among others by Skjærvø 2020, p. 90).[89] A similar phenomenon may have favoured the use of ⟨HNA⟩ to write *ē(w)* 'a, one', more currently written ⟨HD⟩ or with the sign of number ⟨I⟩.[90] As also stated by Nyberg 1974, p. 70 (s.v. *ē, ēt*), "*ē* as the normal equivalent of ḤN' [...] would best explain the widely spread use of ḤN' as the ideogr. for homonyms."

The ambiguity of the spelling ⟨HNA⟩ for *ē(w)*, appearing with some frequency in the MSS and requiring a strong interpretive intervention by the editors, may sometimes be a source of disagreement in the editions of the texts. In the *Zand ī Wahman Yasn*, for instance, a possible *ē(w)* has been written HNA on some occasions (see e.g., 2.1 and 7.16). Cereti transcribes it as **ēw*, commenting "Here HNA must be read **ēw*" (1995, p. 80, fn. 7 to Ch. 2) and "Better HD" (1995, p. 117, fn. 122). With his words, he leads one to think that this should be considered as a copyist's mistake, which is not the case. Rāšed Mohassel recognizes ⟨HNA⟩ as possible spelling for *ē(w)* in that specific text ("*dar in ketāb*" (1991, p. 79, n. 1, 93), but he transcribes *ēd* in all the relevant passages (*ibid.*, pp. 50, 55).

85 ⟨'ywp'⟩ (so also Skj.); *ēg-iz* in Safa-Isfehani 1980, p. 224.
86 Ms. ⟨w'š'mk⟩; *wāšmag* in Safa-Isfehani 1980, p. 224. Cf. Prs. *bāšāma* 'veil, curtain' and cognates in Hasandust 2016 s.v.
87 Quite different from Safa-Isfehani's (1980, p. 224) interpretation ("As for the question regarding the necessary steps that should be taken when the menstruation clothing is left in open air prior to rainfall and later rain falls upon it. If the only defilement had been the result of direct contact with a menstruating woman, it should be washed by a professional person [of the rite of purification]. When this defilement is no longer visible it can be worn like a veil or scarf or *wāšmag* [a type of head garment]").
88 See Bahār 1966, p. 57, Nyberg 1974, pp. 69–70 (s.v. *ē, ēt*), "it would seem to be most advisable simply to give *ē* as the normal equivalent of ḤN'".
89 See also Kotwal 1969, p. 140 [345].
90 Bahār 1966, p. 57, Tafazzoli 1969, p. 48.

As for (32), one may note that ⟨HNA twk'⟩ is read *ēd tōg* in SAFA-ISFEHANI 1980, p. 223,[91] while it is not clear what the function of the demonstrative would be in the relevant phrase;[92] *ēd tōg* 'this fold [in lā]' in MANSURI 2015–2021, p. 1037. In the present paper, ⟨HNA twk'⟩ has been considered as a possible spelling for *ēw-tōg*, equivalent to ⟨HD twk⟩ in (29) above.[93]

To conclude this survey of occurrences of *tōg* in Pahlavi, I just mention two other passages, in particular ZFJD 14.8[94] and PhlRDD 55.3,[95] which however have not been satisfactorily explained by the editors, nor am I able to present more convincing alternative proposals to explain them, and for this reason I am not going to dwell on them on the present occasion.

The semantic range of Phl. *tōf* and *tōg*

A thorough analysis of the occurrences of *tōf* shows that it can be associated with multiple related meanings. In general, one may note that *tōf* is used to denote a layer or one of the elements of a larger structural unit, in particular a layer that overlaps and covers a surface, the surface coating or enveloping of different elements, such as wood ('bark'),[96] fruit ('skin, peel, rind'), wall ('plaster'), eye ('eyelid'), etc., and that these senses may be determined by the context of the discourse. When speaking of cloth, *tōf* is identified with its single thickness, i. e., the sheet of fabric; in these cases, its sense is that of 'layer, fold'. By conceptual extension, *tōf* is also used in the sense of 'part, portion'.

If we compare *tōf* and *tōg*, the typology of referents to which the latter can be associated is very limited. Excluding the two unexplained passages mentioned above, we only find *tōg* in connection with cloth, with the sense of 'layer, fold'.[97] Seemingly, in some of the contexts examined, *tōg* seems to be semantically equivalent to and interchangeable with *tōf*.[98]

All this considered, one might raise this question: Are the meaning(s) of these two words close enough for one to try to connect them etymologically? Is it

91 Note that in the same passage (= 32 above) SAFA-ISFEHANI (1980, p. 223) reads ⟨HNA⟩ as *ē(w)* in two other occurrences (⟨gyw'k' HNA⟩ / *gyāg-ēw*; ⟨hyhlyh HNA⟩ / *hixrīh-ē*).

92 Cf. SAFA-ISFEHANI 1980, p. 224, fn. 1, quoting the idiom *pad tōg abganēd* 'lay down upon'.

93 Similarly, in MOAZAMI 2014, p. 190 (PVd 7.15) *mōy ēd tāg* should be emended to *mōy ēw tāg*.

94 See MOAZAMI 2021, p. 104 where, however, ⟨twk'⟩ is read *did* ('again').

95 See WILLIAMS 1990, I, pp. 196–197; II, p. 92. Doubts about the reading of some words and interpretation of this passage are in WILLIAMS 1990, I, p. 266 (note 11 to Ch. 55); II, p. 246.

96 As for the sense of 'wood [čub]' in TAVUSI 1986 s. v. *tōb*, this has probably been inspired by the Prs. gloss *čub* in PVd 5.4O (see JAMASP 1907, I, p. 145, fn. 89, who however does not mention the MS(S) where this gloss would appear).

97 The senses 'inside' and 'bottom' for *tōg* in MANSURI 2015–2021 are to be discarded.

98 Compare above (14) and (23)–(24), (16) and (25), (19) and (26).

possible, for instance, to think of a single root with different morphological developments? In general, it is not impossible to occasionally find pairs of variants in Middle Persian or Modern Iranian that could support some relation between these two words. One of these is the Phl. term for 'owl', that in the *Bundahišn* occurs in the forms *būg* ⟨bwk⟩ and *būf* ⟨bwp⟩.[99] As for the etymology of *tōf* and *tōg*, no explicit proposal has been advanced so far, but only a connection to Prs. *tu* ('fold, ply'), as a possible outcome in a later linguistic stage. Notably, Prs. *tu* is hinted at as the continuation of Phl. *tōf* by MacKenzie 1986[100] and Bahār 1972; of Phl. *tōg* by Tavadia 1930, Tavusi 1986 and Andrés-Toledo 2016, p. 131, fn. 4.[101] A review of the certain or possible cognates to Phl. *tōf* and/or *tōg*, that may be attributed to language internal development in any single variety or contact induced effects, does not simplify the picture, as we will see below. It can however contribute to a better understanding of the semantic ranges of *tōf* and *tōg*, with a confirmation of the regularity in the semantic change and lexical creation, and possibly offer hints for the interpretation of a couple of passages containing *tōg* not yet fully understood.

Possible cognates to Phl. *tōf* and/or *tōg*

In Modern Western Iranian one may find a set of lexical items belonging to different semantic fields that could be recognized as outcomes of earlier forms cognate to Phl. *tōf* or *tōg*.[102] One may recognize in these words the effects of sound-changes, processes of word-formation (such as suffixation or the like), semantic changes based on different kinds of cognitive relations (metaphorical similarity, contiguity, etc.) starting from an initial concept, probably that of 'coating surface', and also grammaticalization processes.

Let us start with Prs. *tu*, already called into question by other scholars. It is recorded in dictionaries with the senses of 'layer, stratum [lāye va tabaqe; rešte, lā]'

99 See Bd 5.3 (all MSS ⟨bwk⟩), 23.2 (TD1 ⟨bwp⟩, TD2, DH ⟨bwk⟩) in Pakzad 2005, pp. 72, 264. Cf. *būf* [bwp'] [and **būg* [bwk'] 'owl' in MacKenzie 1986, most probably of phono-symbolic origin. Cognates of Phl. *būf* and *būk*, such as Prs. *buf*, *bum*, *boh* (also *guf*) are numerous in Modern Iranian. For the sake of convenience, I refer to the forms quoted in Hasandust 2016, nos. 928, 933, 941, to which other could be easily added as, for instance, Abdui *bok-e kur* (Salāmi 2004, p. 132).

100 In MacKenzie 1986, the phonetic rendering *tōf* (instead of *tōb*) for the spelling ⟨twp'⟩ is probably due to this assumed connection: Phl. *tōf* is one of the words that in a later linguistic stage maintained the final bilabial fricative or weakened it (as is the case of *kaf* ⟨kp⟩ 'foam', *kōf* ⟨kwp⟩ 'mountain', *kulāf* ⟨kwl'p̣⟩ 'cap', etc.; cf. Prs. *kaf*, *kuh*, *kulāh*, etc.)

101 See also Mo'in 1992 s.v. *tuh*, where reference is made to Phl. *tōk*.

102 No cognates of these words are found in Eastern Iranian.

(ANVARI 2002, s. v. *tu*²), (also *tuh*) 'curtain, coating, layer [parde, lā]' (MOʿIN 1992, s. v. *tu*²). Traditional dictionaries record other senses as well, as for instance that of 'wall' (see DEHXODĀ 1946–1981, s. v.), that finds parallels in Sistāni (*tuf* 'very thin layer [lāye], covering [parde], coating [rukeš], such as a thin layer of cement smeared on a wall' [MOHAMMADI XOMAK 2000]) and Kurdish (*tôf* 'wall around the garden'; *tôfa* a layer of a mud wall [čin-e divār-e geli]' [HAŽĀR 1990][103]).

Prs. *tu* 'layer' does not belong to the lexicon of Colloquial Persian, where it mainly survives in phraseology; consider *tu-be-tu*, *tu-dar-tu* 'complicate, intricated, etc.' *hazār-tu(y)* 'a thing having many layers [lāye], or bends [pič-o-xam] or cavities [hofre] or a place with many passages and cells, a labyrinth'[104] (NAJAFI 1999).

Probably from *tu* 'layer, fold', a semantic change based on a metonymical relation ('fold' > 'enveloping fold' > 'inner part of a fold') has produced in Persian a designation for inner part (of any objects), i. e., 'the inside'. At this stage, the content item *tu*, as relational noun has been considered as fit to appropriately describe spatial relationships, in particular containment, and in fact it is extensively used (at first mainly in colloquial language) as a functional word marking spatial relations ('in, inside, between'). In Colloquial Persian it also acts as a preposition (ANVARI 2002 s. v. *tu*¹, MOʿIN 1992, s. v. *tu*¹).[105] The path of this grammaticalization process is similar to that through which Prs. *lā(y)* 'layer, fold, stratum', a word whose semantic range partially overlaps with that of *tu* (being, however, much more frequent than the latter), has acquired spatial meanings and has given rise to a grammatical noun ('inside, within, between, etc.'). This case is an instance of regularity in semantic change.

Outcomes of this grammaticalization process, which seems to have started after Middle Persian times and may be considered therefore as a relatively recent phenomenon, are widely attested in most varieties spoken in Iran, especially Central and Southern Iran, where a grammatical item of the *tu*-type ('inside') is in use. I shall mention here just Lāri, Gerāši *tuf* 'the inside, inside something; inner part' (EQTEDĀRI 1955)[106] for its interesting final voiceless labiodental fricative *-f*, to be compared however with Gerāši *tek* (SALĀMI 2007, p. 221), Lāri *tek* (KAMIOKA/RAHBAR/HAMIDI 1986), Evazi *tek* (besides *tu*) (JĀNFEDĀ 2019), Hormozgāni *teke* (besides *tu*) (NAʿIMI 2008), but also Xonǰi *te:v* and *teg* (XONJI 2015), [107] all meaning 'in, inside, in the middle, etc.' Worth noting is also Kelhuri

103 HAŽĀR 1990 primarily collects Sorani Kurdish material but it also contains lexical items from other Kurdish varieties.
104 Also used in the sense of 'omasum'; it is synonymous with *hazār-lā* and *hazār-xāne*.
105 Note that Tajik *tū* 'layer; inside' is not used commonly and is recorded in dictionaries as 'literary [ketobi]' (NAZARZODE et al. 2010).
106 See also ADIB TUSI 1963, p. 473.
107 IN XONJI 2015, attention is drawn to the fact that the two forms do not always match and the difference of meaning of the two compounds *tegdār* ('capacious (of container)') and *tēvdār* ('secretive') is evidenced.

Kurdish *tuv* 'inside' (also 'valley', see below) as well as Balochi *tōkā* (mainly Southern Bal.) 'in, between, inside' (FILIPPONE 1996, pp. 203; 340–341), related to *tōk, tōx* 'inner part; valley', 'inside; the middle part of something; inside of the body, abdomen, body cage'. To these, Bal. items clearly conveying the notion of 'wrapping' are also connected (*tōxō* 'the cloth or fabric in which babies are wrapped with; being wrapped'; *tōkā deag* 'to wrap something inside something else' [DAŠTI 2017, DASHTI 2019]; [108] Eastern Balochi *tox* 'a blanket wound around the head' [ELFENBEIN 1990, II]; *tōx dēaγ* 'to clothe, wrap' [DAMES 1907, II, p. 199][109]).

In many varieties, particularly in the areas where Lori and Fārs dialects are spoken, from *tu* as 'inner part', words for 'room', 'home' or 'shelters' for animals of various species have been produced and commonly used; cf. *tu* 'room, etc.' in Lori, Baxtiāri, Šuštari, Dezfuli, Davāni, etc. In Daštestāni, a subsequent conceptual association, in this case that of contiguity, is responsible for *tu* 'roof, roof of the house or similar' (BORĀZJĀNI 2003).

Classical Prs. dictionaries also attest the usage of *tu* as 'skin formed on the surface of boiled milk or yoghurt'. Though *saršir* (*sarmāst* in case of yoghurt), or *xāme* are more commonly used in Modern Persian as a designation of this special referent,[110] we find a long list of cognates of Prs. *tu* with this (or a very close) sense widespread in Western Iranian:

Lori Area

Lori *tuž* (IZADPANĀH 2001); (Malāyer) *tu* (AMIN MADANI 2018); (Boyer Ahmadi) *tūk* (TĀHERI 2016); Baxtiāri *tu-šir* (MADDADI 1996); (Čahār Lang) *tu* (SARLAK 2002); (Kuhrang) *tū* (TĀHERI 2010) 'layer of cream on milk (or yoghurt)'; (Kuhrang) *tuf* 'yoghurt [duγ] from which liquid has been removed that is used to prepare *kašk*' (TĀHERI 2010), etc.

Kurdish Speaking Areas

Kurmanji Krd. *to, tok, tûk* [(fig.) 'le meilleur'], *toxav, toxavk* (NEZAN *et al.* 2017);[111] Sorani Krd. *töž, töžâḷ* (HAKEM 2012); Solemaniye Krd. *töjaḷ* (WAHBY/EDMONDS 1966); Kelhuri (Kermanšāhi) Krd. *tuž, tužik* (KARIMPUR 2001); Lakki *tuž* (KIĀNI KULIVAND 2011), etc. 'layer of cream on milk (or yoghurt)'

108 See also Brahui *tōk* 'inner part of a fold, etc.', *tōk kanning* 'to fold up' (ROSSI 1979, no. I331).

109 Cf. *Dāī, šoδ manī malgōrā/ā / mā burzā tōx-deā/ā čūniyā/ā* DAMES 1907, II, p. 119 "Nurse, wash my hair and I will put on a red chadar."(DAMES 1907, I, p. 118).

110 Similarly in Tajik, where *tū* as '*saršir*' is marked as "literary [kitobi]."(NAZARZODE *et al.* 2010)

111 NEZAN *et al.* 2017 mainly contains Kurmanji items; other varieties of Kurdish are also represented (in these cases generally with the dialectal indication).

Central Dialects

Xunsāri *tu* (AŠRAFI XĀNSĀRI 2004); Deliǰāni *tū* (SAFARI 1994); Abiānei *tūq*, Jusqāni *tū* (ASATRIAN 2011);[112] Amorei *tuak* (ʿĀDELXĀNI 2000), Moškenāni *tu* (SADRI 2007); Jarquyei *touveh* (KARIMI 2009), etc. 'layer of cream on milk (or yoghurt)'

Dialects of North Iran

Gilaki *tūk* ('foam [kaf] of milk or *dušāb* when boiling') (ADIB TUSI 1964); Sorxei *tü*, Semnāni *tui*, Sangesari *tük*, etc. (SOTUDE 1963); Tāleqāni *tūk* (FALLĀHI/SĀDEQIĀN 2011); Demāvandi *tü* (ʿALAMDĀRI 2005); Tāleši *tü* (MILLER 1930); Ir.Azāri (Lerdi) *tu* (MEʿRĀJI LERD 2009), Tāti *tuq* (ADIB TUSI 1964), etc. 'layer of cream on milk (or yoghurt)'.

To this group of words also belong Balochi *tukk* 'skinned cream, scum on boiled cream' (ELFENBEIN 1990, II; DASHTI 2017), and probably Pašto *tə́va* 'dregs of milk' (PASHTOON 2009), apparently an isolated recording in Eastern Iranian.

In EWA I, p. 684, MAYRHOFER refers to a convincing proposal by MACKENZIE to connect to Sanskrit *tvác-* ('Haut, Fell'),[113] Iranian words such as Kurd. *töž* ("Auf iran. *tauka-/*tauča-* sind Wörter wie kurd. *töž* ‚skin' (on boiled milk, etc.)' zurückzuführen"). Notably, this Sanskrit word with a large range of uses[114] does not seem to have been continued consistently in later Indo-Aryan and appears rather isolated (cf. TURNER 1966, no. 6087 and Addenda).

To find the plurality of senses that in Pahlavi texts appear associated especially with *tōf* (i. e.,'(general) coating', 'skin', 'hide', 'peel', 'bark', but also 'thin layer', 'fold', 'piece', 'slice', etc.), we should look at the Lori and Kurdish linguistic areas, and this survey can also be interesting for those who raise the complex question of the dialectal stratification that characterizes the Pahlavi lexicon. Considering the phonetic structure of the words listed below, their antecedents appear to be forms connected to Phl. *tōg* rather than *tōf*, but there are also signs that go in another direction, as demonstrated by the coexistence of forms such as *tofil, towil, tokil* in Kurmanǰi Kurdish:

Lori Area

Lori *tuk* 'coating [pust] such as bark of a tree or skin of human body etc.' (IZADPANĀH 2001); (Xorram Ābādi) *tuk* 'skin', *tuk šomi* 'watermelon rind';

112 Here a possible connection with Prs. *duγ* is hinted at.

113 Skt. *tvác-* is generally referred to IE **tu̯éks-* 'skin'. According to MALLORY/ADAMS 1997, p. 522, this IE root, "[t]hough sparsely attested, […] would appear to be the oldest word reconstructible for ‚skin' in PIE". In fact, considering the items really attested and associated to it (apart from Skt. *tvác-*), one could even question the need to posit it.

114 Cf. MONIER-WILLIAMS 1899 'skin (of men, serpents, etc.), hide (of goats, cows etc.; a cow's hide (used in pressing out the Soma); a leather bag; (fig. a cloud); bark, rind, peel; cinnamon, cinnamon tree; a cover (of a horse); surface (of the earth)'.

tuž 'thin layer of snow; dust and the like' (NĀDERI 2011);[115] (Darre-ye Juzāni) *tu*, (Sagvand, Delfāni) *tük* 'skin of the body [pust-e badan]' (ALIĀRI BĀBOLĪĀNI 2017); (Boyer Ahmadi) *tūk* 'crust [puste]' (TĀHERI 2016); Baxtiāri *tu* 'skin [pust], layer [lāye]; (figurative) offspring, seed [nasl]'); *tu-wâl* 'dried peel of pomegranate' (MADDADI 1996); (Kuhrang) *tū* 'skin, layer [pust, lāye]' (TĀHERI 2010).

Kurdish speaking areas and surroundings

Kurmanji Krd. *tox* 'couverture, enveloppe'; *tovil, tîvil, tîvkil* 'peau très fine, membrane; pelure; peau; enveloppe'; *tovilî* '(anat.) membrane', *tîvilê hêkê* 'membrane de l'œuf', *tîvilê mar* 'peau de serpent', *tîvilên pivazê* 'peaux d'oignon', etc. (NEZAN *et al.* 2017); *to* 'thin layer, film, skin'; *tîvil, tofil, towil* 'skin (of fruit), shell, rind' (CHYET 2020); *towil, tokil* 'écorce, cosse, enveloppe de certains legumes' (JABA/JUSTI 1879); *tûkil* 'Schale, Rinde, Schuppe' (OMAR 2016);

Sorani Krd. *tö* 'couverture; tranche'; *töx* 'croûte de fromage'; *töž* 'croûte, callosité', *töž î ṛaq* 'carapece'; *töžâḷ* 'couche'; *töžamâr* 'peau du serpent'; *tökiḷ* 'peau, épluchure, pelure, brou, écorce'; *tökiḷa göz* 'coque de noix', etc. (HAKEM 2012);

Mukri Krd. *têkul* 'Borke' (HOUTUM-SCHINDLER 1884);

Solemaniye Krd. *tö* 'slice, layer'; *töǰ* 'thin layer, film, skin on liquid' (WAHBY/EDMONDS 1966);

SouthKrd. *tô* 'fold'; *tôk* 'bark of tree'; *tôfil* 'strato, incrostazione [qešr, puste]' (HAŽĀR 1990); Kelhuri (Kermānšāhi) Krd. *tük* 'skin [pust]'; *tükdar* 'with peel (said of fruit)', *tukiḻ* 'skin [pust]', *tukiḻāš* 'dried bark of tree', *tukiḻ anār* 'peel of pomegranate'; *tuž* 'the healing of the wound after a layer of red blood has thickened on it'; etc.; *tuv* 'valley between high mountains; the inside of a valley [darun-e darre]' (also *tuv* 'inside [darun, dāxel]') (KARIMPUR 2001); Lakki *tuk* 'bark of the tree or skin of the body' (IZADPANĀH 1989); 'skin, outer layer [pust, lāye-ye xāreǰi] that covers plant and living beings; external stratum [parde] and protective peel [qešr] of fruit; foreskin; covering and sheat [ǰeld va γelāf]; outer and protective layer [lāye] of most elements on the earth, like wheat, tree, snail, snake, earth, kid, etc.'; (as a separate headword) *tuk* '(sometimes used as) covering of shame and spiritual veil; veil, curtain, covering [parde va heǰāb, pušeš]; *tukel* 'dried tree bark, suitable for burning'; *tužâl, tužâleng, tužek* 'thin layer of snow; any type of thin layer or lining with which a surface is coated' (KIĀNI KULIVAND 2011);

Gorāni (Awromāni) *tokıḻ* 'skin, shell' (MACKENZIE 1966).

To conclude, Classical Persian dictionaries record *tōz* (also *tōza*), *tōž* and the Arabicized form *tuǰ* as 'a thin bark, generally used as a coating of saddles or

115 See also below.

bow handles.'[116] With this sense, Prs. *tōz/tuz* is attested in classical poetry (cf. Dehxodā 1946–1981 s.v.). On its origin there is an open debate. According to Doerfer 1965, no. 960 and Clauson 1972, p. 571, Prs. *tōz* is a loanword from Turkish. An Iranian origin is claimed by Hasandust 2016, no. 1599[117] and Monchi-Zadeh 1990, no. 565. As its antecedent, Hasandust points to Middle Persian *tōz* 'bark, skin', mentioned by MacKenzie 1986 (with a reference to Prs. *tōz*), that, however, as I have stated above, does not seem to have a real attestation in the Phl. documentation. Monchi-Zadeh points to "av. *taozya-* (Adj. zu *+taoza-* 'einer Völkerschaft, die dem Volk des Av. bekannt war', mp. *tōz/ž*, des öfteren *Šn twr* geschrieben). *tōz* 'Birke' ist der Baum par excellence jenes Volks und jener Gegend gewesen". I do not enter into this debate here. It would also require, in fact, an investigation into the relationships between the concept 'bark' and the names of the trees from which a specific bark is removed, as indicated by Doerfer and also by Monchi-Zadeh, and this would take us too far. Whatever the origin of Prs. *tōz/tuz*, it seems to me that for words like this, whose areal dimension is evident, one may also think of contamination phenomena as contact-induced effects. Probably a phenomenon of lexical contamination gives account of the polysemy of Xorasāni (Tuni) *tuz* 'thin crust/coating [puste] or layer [lāye] of anything; fine dust [gerd] that settles on containers or other objects' (Yāhaqi 2017), or Lori (Xorram Ābādi) *tuž* 'thin layer of snow, of dust or the like' besides *tuz* 'dust' (Nāderi 2011). In these two cases, the concepts of 'surface layer' and 'dust', that generally settle on a surface, originally associated with two distinct but phonetically close items, seem to converge into a single lexical element. As for *tuz* 'dust', the source is Turk. *toz* 'dust' (Clauson 1972, pp. 463, 570–571, s.v. *to:ğ* and *to:z* 'dust') that has entered the lexicon of Kurdish and other surrounding linguistic areas, as well as that of Xorāsāni.

Bibliography

Adib Tusi, M.A. 1963: "Farhang-e loɣāt-e bāzyāfte (mostadarak)." In: *Našre-ye Dāneškade-ye Adabiāt-e Tabriz* 15/4 (1342), pp. 467–518.

Agostini, D./S. Thrope 2020: *The Bundahišn. The Zoroastrian Book of Creation.* Oxford.

ʿAlamdāri, M. 2005: *Guyeš-e demāvandi.* Tehrān.

Aliāri Bābolɣāni, S. 2017: *Ganǰine-ye guyeshā-ye irāni. Haft guyeš az hāšie-ye Zāgros.* Tehrān [1396].

Amouzgar, J./A. Tafazzoli 2000: *Le cinquième livre du Denkard.* Paris.

Amin Madani, S. 2018: *Guyeš-e Malāyer.* Tehrān [1397].

116 Cf. Dehxodā 1946–1981 s.v. Taj. *tūz* is marked as "literary [kitobi]" in Nazarzode *et al.* 2010. As a Prs. loanword, this word also entered Urdu, cf. *toz, tūz* 'The thin bark of a species of birch (used for wrap round bows, saddles, etc. and, in Kashmir, for writing upon in lieu of paper)' (Platts 1930).

117 The same position is held by Garnik Asatrian (p.c.).

ANDRÉS-TOLEDO, M. A. 2016: "Shrouds in Ancient Zoroastrian Funerary Practices." In: J. ORTIS *et al.* (eds.): *Textiles, Basketry and Dyes in the Ancient Mediterranean World/Textiles, Cestería y Tintes en el mundo mediterráneo antiguo*. Valencia, pp. 129–136.

— 2017: "Sasanian Exegesis of Avestan Textile Terms." In: S. GASPA/C. MICHEL/M.-L. NOSCH (eds.): *Textile Terminologies from the Orient to the Mediterranean and Europe, 1000 BC to 1000 AD*. Lincoln, Nebraska.

ANKLESARIA, B.T. 1949: *Pahlavi Vendīdād*. Bombay.

ANVARI, H. 2002: *Farhang-e bozorg-e Soxan*. 9 vols. Tehrān.

ASATRIAN, G.S. 2011: *A Comparative Vocabulary of Central Iranian Dialects*. Tehrān.

ASHA, R. 2015: *Šak-ud-Gumānīh-Vizār: the Doubt-removing Book of Mardānfarrox*. Paris.

AŠRAFI XĀNSĀRI, M. 2004: *Guyeš-e xānsāri*. Tehrān [1383].

BAHĀR, M. 1961: *Vāženāme-ye Bondaheš*. Tehrān.

— 1966: *Vāženāme-ye Bondaheš*. Tehrān [1345].

— 1972: *Vāženāme-ye Gazidehā-ye Zādspram*. Tehrān [1351].

BORĀZJĀNI, T. 2003: *Sir-i dar guyeš-e daštestāni*. Širāz [1382].

BUYANER, D.R. 2019: "Zur Haar- und Nagelpflege im Zoroastrism. Beiträge zur Erklärung mittelpersischer Rechts- und Religionsterminologie III." In: A. HINTZE/D. DURKIN-MEISTERERNST/C. NAUMANN (eds.): *A Thousand Judgements. Festschrift for Maria Macuch*. Wiesbaden, pp. 25–42.

CAMA, SH./A.Z. LILAOWALA 2014: "Sacred Armour: Ritual Garments of the Parsi Zoroastrians." In: *Marg: A Magazine of the Arts* (June 1, 2014), pp. 39–49.

CATHCART, CH. *et al.* 2021: "Numeral classifiers and number marking in Indo-Iranian: A phylogenetic approach." In: *Language Dynamics and Change* 11, pp. 273–325.

CERETI, C.G. 1995: *The Zand ī Wahman Yasn. A Zoroastrian Apocalypse*. Roma.

— 2014: "Škand gumānīg Wizār." In: *Encyclopædia Iranica*, online edition, available at http://www.iranicaonline.org/articles/shkand-gumanig-wizar (accessed on 03 February 2023).

CHACHA, H.F. 1936: *Gajastak Abâlish. Pahlavi Text with Transliteration, English Translation, Notes and Glossary*. Bombay.

CHEUNG, J. 2007: *Etymological Dictionary of the Iranian Verb*. Leiden.

CHOKSY, J.K./F.M. KOTWAL 2014: "Kustīg." In: *Encyclopædia Iranica*, online edition 2014, available at http://www.iranicaonline.org/articles/kustig (accessed on 3rd February 2023).

CHYET, M.L. 2020: *Ferhenga birûskî. Kurmancî – Înglîzî. Kurmanji – English Dictionary*. 2 vols. 2nd ed. London.

CIANCAGLINI, C.A. 2017: "Phonology, Etymology and Transcription. Issues of Middle Persian Final Sequences <-lg> and <-lk'>." In: E. MORANO *et al.* (eds.): *Studia Philologica Iranica. Gherardo Gnoli Memorial Volume*. Roma, pp. 51–62.

CLAUSON, G. 1972: *An Etymological Dictionary of Pre-Thirteenth-Century Turkish*. Oxford.

DAMES, M.L. 1907: *Popular Poetry of the Balochees*. 2 vols. Glasgow.

DASHTI, N. 2019: *Balōčī angrīzī labz balad / Balochi English Dictionary*. Quetta.

DAŠTI, J.M. 2017: *Balōčī labzbalad* (dōmī čāp). Koeṭṭa.

DEHXODĀ, ʿA. A. 1946–1981: *Loγātnāme*. Tehrān [1325–1360].
DHABHAR, E. B. N. 1909: *Saddar Nasr and Saddar Bundehesh*. Bombay.
— 1932: *The Persian Rivayats of Hormazyar Framarz and others*. Bombay.
DOERFER, G. 1965: *Türkische und mongolische Elemente im Neupersischen*. Vol. II: *Türkische Elemente im Neupersischen alif bis tā*. Wiesbaden.
ELFENBEIN, J. 1990 *An Anthology of Classical and Modern Balochi Literature*. Vol. I: *Anthology*. Vol. II: *Glossary*. Wiesbaden.
EQTEDĀRI, A. 1955: *Farhang-e lārestāni*. Tehrān [1334].
FALLĀHI, K./F. SĀDEQIĀN 2011: *Dar āmadi bar guyeš va farhang-e Tāleqān*. Tehrān [1390].
FARAHVAŠI, B. 1967: *Farhang-e Pahlavi*. Tehrān [1346].
FILIPPONE, E. 1995: *The "Pupil of the eye." in the Iranian Languages*. Napoli.
— 1996: *Spatial Models and Locative Expressions in Baluchi*. Naples.
— 2020: "The Sound-Symbolic Component of the Iranian Lexicon of the Body Parts: Some Case Studies (‚Pupil', ‚Cheek', ‚Buttock')." In: M. C. BENVENUTO *et al.* (eds.): *Word Formation, Grammar and Lexicology. Contrastive, multilingual and comparative-historical Perspectives*. Amburgo, pp. 121–147.
— 2022: "Along the Path of a Grammaticalization Process: Prs. *šib* and *nešib* 'Slope' and Their Cognates in the Iranian Languages." In: E. FILIPPONE/S. BELELLI/M. DE CHIARA (eds.): *Studi di linguistica e filologia iranica / Studies in Iranian Linguistics and Philology*. Roma, pp. 9–41.
GIGNOUX, PH./A. TAFAZZOLI 1993: *Anthologie de Zādspram*. Paris.
HAIM, S. 1991: *Farhang-e bozorg-e fārsi-englisi*. Tehrān [1371].
HAKEM, H. 2012: *Dictionnaire kurde-français (sorani)*. Paris.
HASANDUST, M. 2016: *Farhang-e rišešenāxti-ye zabān-e fārsi*. 5 vols. 2nd ed. Tehrān [1395].
HAŽĀR 1990: *Farhang-e kordi-fārsi*. Tehrān [1369].
HOUTUM-SCHINDLER, A. 1884: "Beiträge zum kurdischen Wortschätze." In: *Zeitschrift der Deutschen Morgenländischen Gesellschaft* 38, pp. 43–116.
IZADPANĀH, H. 1989: *Farhang-e lakki*. Tehrān [1368].
— 2001: *Farhang-e lori*. Tehrān [1380, 1st ed. 1343].
JABA, A./F. JUSTI 1879: *Dictionnaire kurde – français*. St. Pétersbourg.
JAAFARI-DEHAGHI M. 1998: *Dādestān ī dēnīg*. Part I. Paris.
JAMASP, H. 1907: *Vendidâd. Avesta Text with Pahlavi Translation and Commentary, and Glossarial Index*. 2 vols. Bombay.
JÂMÂSP-ÂSÂNÂ, H. J./E. W. WEST 1887: *Shikand-Gûmânîk Vijâr. The Pazand-Sanskrit Text Together with a Fragment of the Pahlavi*. Bombay.
JĀNFEDĀ, ʿA. 2019: *Farhang-e bozorg-e guyeš-e evazi*. 2 vols. *Širāz* [1398].
KAMIOKA K./A. RAHBAR/A. A. HAMIDI 1986: *Comparative Basic Vocabulary of Khonjī and Lārī. Lārestānī Studies* 2. Tokyo.
KAPADIA, D. D. 1953: *Glossary of Pahlavi Vendidad*. Bombay.
KARIMI, A. 2009: *Ādāb o rosum o farhang-e ʿāme-ye Ahmad Ābād-e Jarquiye*. Tehrān [1388].
KARIMPUR, K. 2001: *Farhang-e guyeš-e kordi-ye kalhori (kermānšāhi). Kordi – fārsi*. Kermānšāh [1380].
KIĀNI KULIVAND, K. 2011: *Farhang va vāženāme-ye lakki*. 2 vols. Xorramābād [1390].

KOTWAL, F. M. P. 1969: *The Supplementary Texts to the Šāyest nē-šāyest.* København.

KOTWAL, F. M./J. W. BOYD 1982: *A Guide to the Zoroastrian Religion. A Nineteenth Century Catechism with Modern Commentary.* Chico.

KOTWAL, F. M./PH. G. KREYENBROEK 2009: *The Hērbedestān and Nērangestān.* Vol. IV: *Nērangestān, Fragard 3.* Paris.

MADDADI, Z. 1996: *Vāženāme-ye zabān-e baxtiāri.* Ahvāz [1375].

MALLORY, J./D. Q. ADAMS 1997: *Encyclopedia of Indo-European Culture.* London.

MACKENZIE, D. N. 1966: *The dialect of Awroman (Hawrāmān-ī luhōn). Grammatical sketch, texts, and vocabulary.* København.

— 1986: *A Concise Pahlavi Dictionary.* 2nd ed. Oxford.

MADAN, D. M. 1911: *The Complete Text of the Pahlavi Dinkard.* Part I: *Books III–V.* Bombay.

MANSURI, Y. 2015–2021: *Farhang-e zabān-e pahlavi (pahlavi – fārsi – englisi).* Vol. I: *ā-a* [1394/2015]. Vol. II: *b-g* [1396/2017]. Vol. III: *h-n* [1398/2019]. Vol. IV: *o-t* [1400/2021]. Vol. V: *u-z* [1400/2021]. Tehrān.

MAZDĀPUR, K. 2011: *Šāyest nā šāyest. Matn-i be zabān-e fārsi-ye miyāne (pahlavi-ye sāsāni).* 2nd ed. Tehrān [1390].

DE MENASCE, J. 1945: *Une apologétique mazdéenne du IXe siécle: Škand-gumānīk vičār. La solution décisive des doutes.* Fribourg en Suisse.

MEʿRĀJI LERD, J. 2009: *Farhang-e mauzuʿi-ye tāti be fārsi. Guyeš-e tāti-ye rustā-ye Lerd-e baxš-e Šāhrud va Xalxāl.* Rašt [1388].

MILLER, B. V. 1930: *Talyšskie teksty. Teksty, russkij perevod i talyšsko-russko-francuzskij slovar'.* Moskva.

MOAZAMI, M. 2014: *Wrestling with the Demons of the Pahlavi Widēwdād.* Leiden/Boston.

— 2021: *Laws of the Ritual Purity. Zand ī Fragard ī Jud-Dēw-Dād. A Commentary on the Chapters of the Widēwdād.* Leiden/Boston.

MODI, J. J. 1937: *The religious ceremonies and the customs of the Parsees.* 2nd ed. Bombay.

MOʿIN, M. 1992: *Farhang-e fārsi (motavasset).* 6 vols. Tehrān [1371 (8th ed.)].

MOHAMMADI XOMAK, J. 2000: *Vāženāme-ye sakzi (Farhang-e loγāt-e sistāni).* Tehrān [1379].

MONCHI-ZADEH, D. 1990: *Wörter aus Xurāsān und ihre Herkunft.* Leiden.

MONIER-WILLIAMS, M. 1899: *A Sanskrit-English dictionary. Etymologically and philologically arranged with special reference to cognate Indo-European languages.* Oxford.

NĀDERI, ʿA. 2011: *Farhang-e loγat-e lori.* Xorramābād [1390].

NAʿIMI, M. 2008: *Farhang-e ǰāmʿe-ye Hormozgān-e yekǰaldi.* Bandar ʿAbbās [1386].

NAJAFI, A. 1999: *Farhang-e fārsi-e ʿāmiāne.* 2 vols. Tehrān [1378].

NAZARZODE, S. *et al.* 2010: *Farhang-i tafsir-i zabon-i toǰiki.* 2 vols. Dušanbe.

NEZAN, K. *et al.* 2017: *Dictionnaire kurde–français. Ferhenga kurdî–fransizî.* Paris.

NYBERG H. S. 1974: *A Manual of Pahlavi.* Part II: *Glossary.* Wiesbaden.

OMAR, F. F. 2016: *Kurdisch-Deutsches Wörterbuch (Kurmancî).* Berlin.

PAKZAD, F. 2005: *Bundahišn. Zoroastrische Kosmogonie und Kosmologie.* Vol. I: *Kritische Edition.* Tehran.

PASHTOON, Z. A. 2009: *Pashto-English Dictionary.* Hayttsville, MD.

PLATTS, J. T. 1930: *A Dictionary of Urdū, Classical Hindī, and English*. London (5th ed.).
RĀŠED MOHASSEL, M. T. 1991: *Zand-e Bahman Yasn*. Tehrān [1370].
ROSSI, A. V. 1979: *Iranian Lexical Elements in Brāhūī*. Naples.
SADRI, J. 2007: *Guyeš-e Moškenān*. Tehrān [1386].
SAFA-ISFEHANI, N. 1980: *Rivāyat-i Hēmīt-i Ašawahistān. A Study in Zoroastrian Law*. Harvard.
SAFARI, H. 1994: *Vāženāme-ye rāǰi. Guyeš-e Deliǰān*. Tehrān [1373].
SALĀMI, ʿA. 2004: *Ganǰine-ye guyeš-šenāsi-ye Fārs*. Vol. II. Tehrān [1383].
— 2007: *Ganǰine-ye guyeš-šenāsi-ye Fārs*. Vol. IV. Tehrān [1386].
SANJANA, P. B. 1848: *Vajarkard Dini*. Mumbai.
SARLAK, R. 2002: *Vāženāme-ye guyeš-e baxtiāri-ye Čahār Lang*. Tehrān [1381].
SKJÆRVØ, P. O. 2011: *The Spirit of Zoroastrianism*. New Haven/London.
— 2014: "Philological Gleanings from the Pahlavi Videvdad." In: *Iran Name* 29/2, pp. 6–21.
— 2020: *Pahlavi Primer*. Unpublished paper, available at https://www.academia.edu/72410048/Pahlavi_Primer_2020_1_.
SKJÆRVØ, P. O./Y. ELMAN 2014: "Concepts of Pollution in Late Sasanian Iran. Does Pollution Need Stairs, and Does It Fill Space?" In: *Aram* 26/1–2, pp. 21–45.
SOTUDE, M. 1963: *Farhang-e semnāni, sorxei, lāsgardi, sangsari, šahmerzādi*. Tehrān [1342].
STAUSBERG, M. 2004: "The Significance of the „kusti": A History of Its Zoroastrian Interpretations." In: *East and West* 54, No. 1/4, pp. 9–29.
STEINGASS, F. 1963: *A comprehensive Persian-English dictionary*. London (5th ed., 1st ed. 1892).
TĀHERI, E. 2010: *Guyeš-e baxtiāri-ye Kuhrang*. Tehrān [1379].
— 2016: *Guyeš-e lori-ye boyer ahmadi*. Tehrān [1395].
TAFAZZOLI, A. 1969: *Vāženāme-ye Minu-ye xerad*. Tehrān.
TAVADIA, J. C. 1930: *Šāyast-nē-šāyast. A Pahlavi Text on Religious Customs*. Hamburg.
TAVUSI, M. 1986: *Vāženāme-ye Šāyest-na-šāyest*. Tehrān.
TURNER, R. L. 1966: *A Comparative Dictionary of the Indo-Aryan Languages*. London.
UNVALA, E. M. R. 1922: *Dârâb Hormazdyâr's Rivâyat*. Vol. I. Bombay.
VITALONE, M. 1996: *The Persian Revāyat "Ithoter." Zoroastrian Rituals in the Eighteenth Century*. Napoli.
WAHBY, T./C. J. EDMONDS 1966: *A Kurdish-English dictionary*. Oxford.
WILLIAMS, A. V. 1990: *The Pahlavi Rivāyat Accompanying the Dādestān ī Dēnīg*. 2 vols. Copenhagen.
WEST, E. W. 1882: *Pahlavi Texts*. Pt. III: *Dînâ-î Maînôg-î Khirad. Sikand-gûmânîk Vigâr. Sad Dar*. Oxford.
— 1885: *Pahlavi Texts*. Pt. II: *The Dâdistân-î dînîk and the Epistles of Mânûskîhar*. Oxford.
XONJI, A. H. 2015: *Guyeš-e lārestāni*. Širāz [1394].
YĀHAQI, M. J. 2017: *Vāženāme-ye guyeš-e Tun (Ferdows)*. Tehrān [1396].
ZAEHNER, R. C. 1955: *Zurvan. A Zoroastrian Dilemma*. Oxford.

Sur l'argenterie sassanide, relectures et nouveautés

PHILIPPE GIGNOUX †

DIETER WEBER est incontestablement un remarquable chercheur non seulement dans le domaine de la linguistique du moyen-iranien mais aussi par ses nombreux travaux conduisant à la lecture et à l'interprétation des textes écrits en moyen-perse tardif sur les ostraca, papyri et parchemins, jusqu'au pehlevi des livres (Book Pahlavi).

D'une maîtrise parfaite de l'informatique au service de la recherche fondamentale, et d'un amical esprit de coopération avec moi-même, assez peu fréquent dans le passé chez les Iranistes occidentaux, nous avons partagé les résultats de nos recherches durant la période 2000–2010, grâce à une correspondance avec D. WEBER que j'ai précieusement conservée, un travail commun témoignant de notre bonne entente. À ce sujet je me permets de reproduire ici dans le long article qu'il m'a offert dans le volume édité par RIKA GYSELEN et CHRISTELLE JULLIEN à l'occasion de mon anniversaire (2011), ce qu'il pensait de cette amitié :

> « Welche Veränderungen sich in den Lesungen der Dokumente im Laufe der Zeit ergaben, dokumentieren am besten die zahlreichen Publikationen sowie der konstante Briefaustausch zwischen Ph. Gignoux und mir. Es ist diese intensive Zusammenarbeit, die es erlaubte, immer weiter in die Geheimnisse der früh-islamischen, mittelpersisch geschriebenen Dokumente einzudringen. » (GYSELEN/JULLIEN 2011, p. 285).

Parmi les différentes sources primaires, épigraphiques et textuelles, d'époque sassanide et post-sassanide — numismatiques, sigillographiques, argenterie —, cette dernière à ma connaissance n'a pas été exploitée par D. WEBER. En effet sur les vaisselles en argent, des inscriptions en pointillé portent soit le nom d'un possesseur (avec ou sans ⟨NPŠH⟩) assorti d'une indication de poids, soit seulement celle-ci. RIKA GYSELEN a eu l'excellente idée de faire un catalogue de 58 pièces en argent qui avaient fait l'objet de plusieurs publications en y ajoutant toutes les données matérielles, métrologiques et iconographiques. Ces objets proviennent de collections publiques (musées) ou privées. Les publications, y compris les miennes, péchaient sous deux aspects : on a essayé de lire des noms propres sans faire assez attention à leur graphie, et en proposant des lectures qui n'étaient pas justifiables sur le plan sémantique, de même que les évaluations de poids calculées approximativement pour obtenir une valeur de la drachme de 4 grs environ (16 pour le *stēr*). R. GYSELEN a montré à juste titre en 2014 que celle-ci était comprise entre 3,60 et 4,35 grs.

En ce qui me concerne, étant toujours intéressé par l'onomastique, j'ai repris les données du Catalogue GYSELEN publié dans le volume XXII des *Res Orientales*, dans le but d'améliorer la lecture des inscriptions grâce à une concordance plus rigoureuse entre la graphie et la sémantique. De plus, je publierai dans cet article quelques objets non encore lus ou édités. La première partie sera ainsi consacrée à une relecture des objets du Catalogue GYSELEN. C'est d'après celui-ci que j'emprunte les numéros des documents dont je crois avoir amélioré les lectures ou les interprétations. On voudra bien se reporter au travail de GYSELEN pour les photos ou facsimiles.

N°5 : Il faut supprimer ma lecture Farrbag (1984 n°7) et lire Farroxānān, la suite a été bien lue par GYSELEN (2014) : Dēldēlān Xwārāsān (p. 111).

N°6 : Il faut lire : ⟨lmyk S 2 ZWZN 2⟩ : *Rāmīg s<tēr> 2 drahm 2*. Ce nom est un hypocoristique formé sur *rām* « paix » (IPNB II/2 n°792 et CPD 70). Cf. ci-dessous n°B.

N°7 : ma lecture du nom propre est sûre, le poids serait à lire selon GYSELEN 59 (50-3-3-3 = 236 drachmes).

N°8 : toutes les lectures sont peu crédibles, y compris la mienne de 1984 n°5. On peut lire comme suit : ⟨bwlcswl Y hwslw'n NPŠH MN⟩ (mention du poids lue correctement par BRUNNER 1974/75) = *Burz-sūr ī Husrawān xwēš az* « Honoré (et) fort » (CPD 78 : strong). Voir ci-dessous p. 114.

N°11 : le nom lu Dām est à corriger en dhm = Dahm, cf. CPD 24 « virtuous, pious », hypocoristique non encore attesté. Il faut corriger ma lecture dans le IPNB II/2, n°300, p. 74, car on ne peut pas appeler quelqu'un « créature ».

N°20 : aucune lecture n'est satisfaisante car ⟨'nwš⟩ ne peut s'écrire de cette façon car ⟨'n-⟩ est impossible et il n'y a pas seulement deux lettres, d'où peut-être : ⟨yzd'nwyh⟩ = Yazdānweh, nom propre.

N°21 : j'ai compris cette inscription difficile, mais très intéressante car elle est à la fois nouvelle, originale et unique. On peut lire comme suit : (1) ⟨ZNH 'bzn ...... NPŠH (2) hncyt zryn 200 [s] W ZWZN 3⟩ = *ēn ābzan .... xwēs hanjīd zarrēn 200 [stēr] ud drahm 3.*

Traduction : « Ce bol (pour le bain) appartient à ...(pour) puiser (de l'eau), doré, [poids] 200 *s<tērs>* et trois drachmes. »

Commentaire

ābzan : GIGNOUX 1984, n°19, ⟨'bcny⟩ est impossible car le /c/ ne peut se lier à la lettre suivante, et la lecture de Brunner est correcte. Le mot est traduit dans

CPD 4 par « bath ». Lazard p. 217a traduit *āb zadan* par « arroser, prendre », et p. 217b « jeter de l'eau, plonger ». STEINGASS p. 8 : « a particular kind of bathing-vessel made of copper or iron ».

hanjīd est la lecture proposée par GYSELEN (p. 127), d'où ma traduction de « bol servant à puiser de l'eau ».

Enfin *hanjīdan* est à rapprocher de *hixtan* (CPD 42) avec le sens de « tirer (de l'eau) ».

Il serait tentant de comprendre que cet objet servait à puiser de l'eau dans une salle de bains privée ou collective pour la jeter sur le corps, mais je n'ai pas trouvé de parallèle dans les thermes romains, mais que l'on peut supputer comme existant dans les bains (collectifs) des pays musulmans (?). Le qualificatif 'doré' de ce récipient pourrait convenir s'il appartenait à un riche personnage, et il n'est pas dirimant à mon avis. Quoi qu'il en soit, la paléographie est respectée puisqu'en MMP (Manichean Middle-Persian) cette lecture est attestée : CPD 98.

N°25 : Je ne sais pourquoi la transcription retenue pour le nom propre a été translittérée ⟨thmk'd't⟩ = *Tahmag-dād, dans BRUNNER (1978), mais transcrite par tous Tagmag, inexplicable sémantiquement pour le premier membre de ce composé. C'est bien Tahmag-dād qu'il faut retenir. Mais la translittération sera : ⟨thmk' d't⟩, même si l'intrusion du trait final entre les deux éléments n'est pas du tout fréquente. Mais aussi bien les trois lettres de la seconde ligne sont indéchiffrables, et je ne peux en proposer une lecture. Le t initial de cette inscription est tout à fait semblable à celui du n°F de GYSELEN (p. 164).

Commentaire

le premier élément du composé est à rapprocher du nom persan bien connu comme le surnom de Rostam Tahm-tan « au corps puissant » (LAZARD 1990, p.115). STEINGASS (1947, 339a) : *tahm/taham* « brave, warlike », mais *tahmak* « naked, empty » ?

N°32 : la deuxième lecture de GYSELEN n'est guère plausible, car le deuxième élément du composé devrait être écrit ⟨*wyc⟩, et de toutes façons cela n'aurait guère de sens. Le poids correspond bien à la lecture de GYSELEN.

N°33 : toutes les lectures, y compris la mienne (1984, n°20) de Panāh-veh sont très conjecturales. Je voudrais proposer une lecture très différente d'un nom propre inconnu jusqu'à présent, mais qui tient compte rigoureusement de la paléographie. Ainsi mon déchiffrement sera-t-il : ⟨zyb'-'hwyh⟩ = Zībā-huīh « (qui a) une belle bonté », qui tient compte de la succession de deux alefs au milieu du nom propre.

Commentaire

le premier mot de ce composé est bien connu en persan, cf. LAZARD (1990, p. 223) : ⟨zyb'⟩, *zibā* « beau, joli » et le second terme de ce composé existe en moyen-perse, CPD 44 : **huīh*. Voir aussi dans STEINGASS (1947, p. 632) : *zībā-khū*

« of good disposition ». L'attestation du premier élément du composé inconnu en moyen-perse mais récurrent en persan pourrait indiquer une date très tardive pour cette inscription.

N°36 : Les propositions de FRYE (1973) et BRUNNER (1975) semblent fantaisistes pour la lecture du nom propre initial. La mienne est aussi déficiente car il manquerait le p final de Gušnasp. Je n'ai pas trouvé de lecture alternative. Toutefois je me risque à lire : ⟨s'sn gwšnyn' Y kpk'n' ...⟩ Sāsān-Gušnēn ī Kabagān, le premier terme étant le nom d'une divinité (cf. SCHWARTZ 1996).

N°40 : il faut corriger la mention du poids, car il y a trois 3 à la suite, et lire 89 et non 86.

N°41 : le nom propre initial est difficile à interpréter mais BRUNNER (1975) a lu à peu près correctement le patronyme qui peut se transcrire Ardā-kōf, mais il le lit *Ardānaf* qui ne peut se comprendre. Il faut sans doute accepter STEINGASS (p. 1062) et traduire le composé « (qui est) juste (et) estimé », *kōf* = estime, honneur, refuge ». Le CPD 51 ne signale pas ce mot à côté de plusieurs homophones.

N°42 : ma lecture (dans GUNTER/JETT 1992) semble correcte mais le /p/ devrait être remplacé par un /w/. De plus le nom du dieu est attesté comme nom propre : IPNB II/2, n°1089 à 1092.

N°46 : on peut renvoyer à Erān-Gušnasp, IPNB II/2, n°335.

N°55 : ma lecture du nom propre n'est pas possible. On peut penser à un hypocoristique formé sur **Sug-wār*, d'où *Sugwārēn*, cf. STEINGASS (1947, p. 691b) : « mournful, afflicted », ce qui est exclu pour un nom de personne, ou encore on peut lire *Sōg-wār/war*, CPD 75.1 : « profitable » ?, en assumant que le graveur ait oublié les deux voyelles longues ou bien lire **Sag-warēn*, le premier élément désignant l'ethnonyme *saka-* ?, voir IPNB II/2, n° 821 p.154. Une meilleure lecture est la suivante : ⟨škwlyn⟩ = *Sakurēn*, cf. STEINGASS (1947, p. 755) « arabe grateful, one of the names of God », où il n'y a pas à supposer une absence de voyelles longues. Si cette interprétation est possible, il s'agirait comme ci-dessus pour le n°33 d'une inscription très tardive, de la période islamique.

N°56 : GYSELEN (p. 158) a lu « 40-3-3 ou 4-3 » mais cela est impossible car le nombre supérieur 4 doit être placé avant le 3, d'où il faut lire peut-être 4 et 4. ». Or dans tous les nombres de poids, on ne peut avoir un petit nombre (3) suivi d'un plus grand (4). Il faut donc admettre qu'il y a ici une erreur du graveur, et restituer 3-3 = 6.

N°57 : le déchiffrement de SIMS-WILLIAMS (1990) est tout à fait correct, mais le premier mot de l'inscription demeure énigmatique. Toutefois la lecture *mp/(myp)-yk* pourrait se justifier si une transcription plausible était sémantiquement intelligible. La finale ⟨-yk⟩ (*-īg*) semble lisible.

N°58 : le sens du mot *nizan* très rare, s'il ne peut se lire autrement, demeure une croix ! Dans l'article de GYSELEN (p. 160) il faut corriger ⟨*nycyny⟩ (avec un iod en trop).

N°B : Dans un article d'AKBARZADEH *et al.* (2001), l'interprétation de l'inscription sur deux bols en argent de *Qurī Qal'eh*, que GYSELEN (2014, p. 161) n'a pas commentés, mérite un long commentaire. L'un d'eux ne contient qu'une formule, ce qui est assez rare sur un tel récipient. L'autre a fait l'objet par l'archéologue d'une explication fantaisiste : en effet, la lecture correcte ⟨MALE pyh⟩ « full of fat » indiquerait que la mention de la graisse désigne une *fonction rituelle* puisque celle-ci servait à allumer le feu sacré. D'une part, il serait étrange de noter la fonction d'un tel objet . D'autre part, il faut oublier, i.e. annuler un usage religieux affecté à des bols, l'exemple des *Anahitas* dévolu à des danseuses ayant été déjà rejeté depuis longtemps.

Assiette en argent de la collection de la David Aaron Gallery, n°D1163, publié par FRANÇOIS DE BLOIS (2009, pp. 13–16, 2 fig., repr. 2020).

Cette belle pièce d'argenterie sassanide a fait l'objet d'une minutieuse et excellente description iconographique par DE BLOIS. C'est pourquoi on regrettera que celle-ci ait été assortie d'une lecture et d'une interprétation peu plausible de l'inscription. Je rappelle les exigences de compréhension des inscriptions sur ce genre d'objets. La cohérence de toute lecture s'obtient par l'harmonisation de deux paradigmes : d'une part le strict respect de la paléographie dans la lecture difficile d'une écriture cursive en pointillé et d'autre part la crédibilité de la sémantique par une juste interprétation du nom propre qui marque le début de l'inscription de manière assez générale. L'abondance des noms de personnes qui continue de s'accroître (cf. IPNB II/2, 3 et VII/5) ne doit pas conduire à rechercher systématiquement un nom déjà connu, mais si la lecture est correcte, le sens du nom personnel doit aussi être compréhensible. Il y a juste un exemple de mon affirmation dans le nom que FR. DE BLOIS a lu correctement : ⟨lmyk⟩, mais un hypocoristique formé sur le nom abrégé de Ramīg signifiant « herd, flock » n'a pas de sens, sans raison suffisante pour que l'on suppose que « Ramīg might mean 'herdsman' » (p. 14), tout à fait absent de l'onomastique moyen-perse (cf. ci-dessus n°6). Aussi bien mon interprétation de Rāmīg (cf. n°6), malgré l'absence de l'aleph qui est fréquente en moyen-perse/pehlevi, se justifie par le sens.

Venons-en au nom du possesseur au début de l'inscription : les difficultés ici sont très nombreuses. En effet l'auteur note à juste titre que la lettre du milieu de ce mot ne peut se lire /n/ qui n'est jamais lié à ce qui suit, mais par contre il propose de lire un /c/ puisque cette lettre également ne peut se lier à ce qui suit, mais cela lui permet de lire le nom comme **āzād* ! De fait ce /c/ serait fort mal écrit puisqu'il lui manquerait une boucle vers l'avant. Le désir de trouver un nom connu a entraîné l'auteur à une incohérence, ce qui invite à trouver une alternative plausible. Les deux aleph lus par DE BLOIS ne sont pas semblables, et de plus le premier est précédé d'une lettre. À mon avis, le premier aleph est plutôt un /š/ comme dans une écriture lapidaire et la lettre précédente peut être le début d'un /b/ qui est noté par un long trait, appelé par l'auteur 'baseline' qui n'existe nulle part ailleurs. Ainsi le long trait coupe simplement toutes les lettres du mot, et le /n/ a la forme connue en écriture lapidaire, comme d'ailleurs le /m/ dans le mot Rāmīg. En bref, je propose la lecture suivante : ⟨bsn't lmwk⟩ = Basnād Rāmōg. Cf. *basn* « stature, height » (STEINGASS 1947, p. 189 ; CPD 17). Le deuxième nom, peut-être le patronymique, n'a pas la terminaison en *-īg*, mais en *-ōg*, car l'avant-dernière lettre n'a pas la forme d'un yod. La seconde ligne présente aussi quelques difficultés : certes la mention du nombre (71) a été bien lue par DE BLOIS, mais il est précédé d'un ⟨S⟩ = *s<tēr>*. Le dernier mot pose problème. La lecture de DE BLOIS est à rejeter non pas pour la lecture mais pour des raisons de sémantique. Si *mizd* désigne l'assiette comme cela paraît normal, comment un objet précieux en argent servirait-il de salaire ? Ce serait en effet plutôt un cadeau, un présent.

La seconde ligne se lira : S-70-1 M-2-1. Comme on le sait, la valeur de ⟨M⟩/⟨MC(y)⟩ demeure encore aujourd'hui problématique. Sorte d'idéogramme pour *dāng*, il est étrange que les drachmes (⟨ZWZN⟩) ne soient pas mentionnées également. On remarquera enfin que ce ⟨M⟩ est différent de celui de Rāmōg, ce qui peut faire douter de la lecture d'un /m/ dans ce nom, qui ressemble davantage à un /s/ dans la grande boucle, peut-être précédé d'un aleph.

Assiette en argent, non répertorié dans GYSELEN 1914.
Provenance : Tenri Sankoukan Museum in Nara, Japon. Diamètre 24,5 cm ; hauteur 4,5 cm. Poids de l'objet inconnu.
Publication : TANABE 1987, fig. 7, p. 84.
Scène d'un roi sassanide chassant à l'arc un lion ou un léopard, doré à l'origine. L'auteur propose de l'identifier avec Ardashir III. À l'extérieur, une inscription en pointillé, en moyen-perse, qui dans une correspondance de 1982 à TANABE, a été estimée par GIGNOUX comme un nom propre, mais ceci est à rejeter, car il s'agit seulement d'une mention du poids de l'objet, à lire dubitativement : 50 [*stēr*] (W) ZWZN 1 = 201 drahms.

Glossaire
(les lectures et transcriptions erronées ne sont pas répertoriées)

ābzan	21
āb zadan	21
Anōš-veh	20
Ardākōf	41
Bundōg	K
Dahm	11
Dām	11
Dēl Dēlān	5
ēn	21
Erān-Gušnasp	46
Farrbag	5
Farroxānān	5
hanjīd	21
hanjīdan	21
hixtan	21
Husrawān	8
Kabagān	36
kōf	41

**nizan*	58	Tahmag-dād	25
Panāh-veh	33	Tahmtan	25
Rāmīg	6	Wyhyh	20
Rāmōg	K	Xwarāsān	5
Rostam	25	*xwēš*	21
Sāsān-Gusnēn	36	*zarrēn*	21
Spurrag	A392	Zibā	33
Sakurēn	55	Zibā-huīh	33
Tahm/Taham	25	Zibā-xū	33

Bibliographie

AKBARZADEH D./T. DARYAEE/J. LERNER 2001: "Two Recently Discovered Inscribed Sasanian Silver Bowls". In: *Bulletin of the Asia Institute*, NS 15, pp. 71–75.

AMIRANACHVILI, CH. 1959: "Une coupe en argent du début de l'époque sassanide provenant des fouilles d'Armasiskheri". In: *Rivista di studi orientali* 34, pp. 149–162.

G. AZARPAY/W.B. HENNING 1967: "A Hunting Scene on an Inscribed Sassanian Silver Vessel". In: *Iranica Antiqua* VII, pp. 145–152, pl. XXXI-XXXIII.

DE BLOIS, F. 2009: "A Sasanian Silver Bowl". In: W. SUNDERMANN/A. HINTZE/F. DE BLOIS (eds.): *Exegisti monumenta, Festschrift in Honour of Nicholas Sims-Williams*. Wiesbaden (Iranica 17), pp. 13–16 [repr. 2020].

BRUNNER, C.J. 1975: "Middle Persian Inscriptions on Sasanian Silverware". In: *Metropolitan Museum Journal* 9/1974, pp. 109–121.

CPD: D.N. MACKENZIE 1971: *A Concise Pahlavi Dictionary*. London [repr. 1986].

FRYE 1973: "Sasanian Silver Plates". In: *Journal of the K.R. Cama Oriental Institute* 44, pp. 81–86.

GIGNOUX, PH. 1975: "Coupes inscrites de la collection Mohsen Foroughi". In: *Monumentum H.S. Nyberg (*Acta Iranica 4), pp. 269–276/509–510.

— 1975–1976: "Sur quelques noms propres iraniens transcrits en syriaque". In: *Mélanges offerts au R.P. François Graffin, S.J., Parole de l'Orient* VI/VII, pp. 515–523.

— 1984: "Eléments de prosopographie : II. Les possesseurs de coupes sasanides". In: *Studia Iranica* 13, pp. 19–40, pl. VII–IX.

— 1986: *Noms propres sassanides en moyen-perse épigraphique, Iranisches Personennamenbuch.* Band II/2. Wien.

— 1990: "Noms d'ustensiles (Aegenterie et Poterie) en moyen-iranien". In: Akira Haneda (ed.): *Documents et Archives provenant de l'Asie Centrale* (Actes du Colloque Franco-Japonais). Kyoto, pp. 71–86.

— 2003: *Noms propres sassanides en moyen-perse épigraphique*, Supplément [1986-2001], *Iranisches Personennamenbuch*, Band II/3. Wien.

GIGNOUX PH./L. KALUS 1982: "Les formules des sceaux sasanides et islamiques : continuité ou mutation ?" In: *Studia Iranica* 11, pp. 123–153.

GIGNOUX PH./C. JULLIEN/F. JULLIEN 2009: *Noms propres syriaques d'origine iranienne, Iranisches Personennamenbuch.* Band VII/5. Wien.

GRENET, F. 1983: "Un plat sasanide d'Ardasir II (379-363) au bazar de Kabul." In: *Studia Iranica* 12, pp. 195–205.

GUNTER, A.C./P. JETT 1992: *Ancient Iranian Metalwork in the Arthur M. Sackler Gallery and the Freer Gallery of Art*. Washington.

GYSELEN, R. 1989: "Note de métrologie sassanide : les drahms de Khusro II." In: *revue belge de Numismatique et de Sigillographie* CXXXV, pp. 5–23.

— 2014: "Inscriptions en moyen-perse sur la vaisselle d'argent sassanide : Quelques nouvelles données." In: *Res Orientales* XXII, pp. 73–178.

GYSELEN, R./CH. JULIEN 2011: *Rabbo l'olmyn 'Maître pour l'éternité': Florilège offert à Philippe Gignoux pour son 80e anniversaire*. Paris (Cahiers de Studia Iranica 43).

HARMATTA, J. 1973: "Inscriptions de vaisselle de l'époque sassanide et post-sassanide." In: *Acta Antiqua Academiae Scientiarum Hungaricae* 21, pp. 245–267.

— 1974: "Remarques sur les inscriptions de vaisselles sassanides." In: PH. GIGNOUX/A. TAFAZZOLI (eds.): *Mémorial Jean de Menasce*. Louvain, pp. 189–198.

HARPER, P.O. 1978: "The Royal Hunter, Art of the Sasanian Empire." In: *The Cleveland Museum of Art* 23, pp. 69–71.

HENNING, W.B. 1953: "New Pahlavi Inscriptions on Silver Vessels." In: *BSOAS* 22, pp. 132–134.

— 1961: "A Sassanian Silver Bowl from Georgia." In: *BSOAS* 24, pp. 353–356.

JUSTI, F. 1963: *Iranisches Namenbuch*. Hildesheim [Marburg, 1895].

LAZARD, G. 1990: *Dictionnaire Persan-Français*. Leiden/New York/Kobenhavn/ Köln.

LIVSHITS V.A./V.G. LUKONIN 1964: "Srednepersidskie i sogdijskie nadpisi na serebryanykh posudakh". In: *Vestnik drevnej istorii* 3, pp. 155–176.

ORBELI, I.A./K.V. TREVER 1935: *Sasanidskij Metall*. pl. XII.

Petit Palais (Paris) *Sept mille ans d'art en Iran*, 1961-1962.

SCHWARTZ, M. 1996 : "*Sasm, Sesen, St. Sisinnios, Sesengen Barpharangês, and ... 'Semanglof', Shorter Notices". In: *Bulletin of the Asia Institute*, N.S. 10, p. 253–257.

SIMS-WILLIAMS, N. 1990 : D. VON BOTHMER (ed.): *Glories of the Past, Ancient Art from the Shelby White and Leon Levy Collection*. New York [1990–1991].

SMIRNOV, J.I. 1909: *Vostovcnoe Serebro*. St-Petersburg.

STEINGASS, F. 1947: *Persian-English Dictionary,* Third Impression. London.

TANABE, K. 1981: *Silk Road Gold and Silver in Japan*, Ancient Orient Museum. Tokyo.

— 198: "A Sasanian Silver Plate with Leopard Hunt". In: *Bulletin of the Asia Institute* 1, pp. 81–94.

WEBER, D. 2007: "Remarks on the development of the Pahlavi Script". In: F. VAHMAN/C.V. PEDERSEN (eds.): *Religious Texts in Iranian Languages*. Kobenhaven (Akten des Kongresses Kopenhagen 2002), pp. 185–195.

Les articles de Herzfeld et de Ghirshman (cf. GYSELEN 2014) entre autres, sont aujourd'hui obsolètes. Cette bibliographie déjà longue peut être complétée par celle de R. GYSELEN 2014.

Le *y* final et le trait final en moyen-perse : le cas des sceaux des administrations territoriales

Rika Gyselen, Paris

Le *y* final et le trait final en moyen-perse sont deux phénomènes graphiques bien attestés[1]. Le premier est associé à l'écriture lapidaire comme en témoignent les inscriptions rupestres et monumentales des IIIe et IVe siècles, et quelques rares inscriptions plus tardives. Le trait final est propre à l'écriture cursive des livres en moyen-perse (communément désigné comme 'Book Pahlavi'). Toutefois une relation entre les deux ne fait aucun doute[2].

Dès la découverte des inscriptions du premier siècle sassanide, les philologues ont relevé qu'à la fin de nombreux mots figurait un signe qui ressemblait à la lettre *yod* tournée de 90° dans le sens contraire du cadran horaire. Récemment, une étude détaillée a été consacrée à ce phénomène et a confirmé que la valeur phonétique de cet *y final* est ø et ne constitue donc pas une syllabe autonome. En revanche, la présence de ce *y* final muet s'explique dans le cadre d'une 'loi rythmique'[3]. En écriture cursive le trait final de certains mots est représenté par le même signe que les lettres cursives w, n, r et ʾ. Ce trait est également muet et n'apparaît qu'à la fin des mots qui se terminent par une consonne qui ne peut être liée à la lettre qui suit.

En 2005, Huyse revenait sur la question de la transition du *y* final vers le trait final dans le but de pouvoir dater le phénomène[4]. Quelque temps après, Cereti abordait en termes chronologiques la question du début de l'écriture cursive dans le but de pouvoir dater les plus anciens écrits de l'Avesta[5]. Dans leurs articles respectifs, les deux auteurs ont mis à contribution des sceaux sassanides dont certains venaient d'apparaître comme par exemple ceux des quatre Ērān-spāhbed datant du VIe siècle[6]. Cereti a également intégré dans sa démonstration des inscriptions

1 Notre reconnaissance va au professeur Rüdiger Schmitt qui a accepté de relire cet article et qui a formulé plusieurs suggestions.

2 Pour l'état de la question, voir Huyse 2003, pp. 19–28.

3 Huyse 2003, *passim* et particulièrement p. 97–98 : … on peut reformuler comme suit la 'loi rythmique' … "En proto-moyen-iranien, le *y* final des noms — restant muet d'une désinence ayant subi l'effet de l'intonation — tombe à la fin des noms polysyllabiques qui ne sont ni composés ni dérivés (ceux-ci se conformant aux mots simples resp. mots-base), après une syllabe finale tonique à voyelle longue, à condition que cette dernière ne se trouve pas en fin absolue du mot ; dans tous les autres noms, le *y* se maintient".

4 Huyse 2005.

5 Cereti 2008.

6 Gyselen 2001.

monumentales et monétaires des Ve et VIe siècles. À ma connaissance, aucune étude n'a été publiée prenant en compte la documentation fournie par les sceaux des administrations territoriales. Avec cet article nous espérons combler cette lacune.

Corpus examiné

Les sceaux des administrations territoriales sont des sceaux purement épigraphiques qui portent le nom d'une administration et le nom de la circonscription territoriale qu'elle gère[7]. Dans le texte qui suit, ce type de sceau sera souvent désigné simplement comme 'sceau administratif' sauf si le contexte exige d'être plus explicite et d'y ajouter 'des administrations territoriales'. À part une bonne trentaine de sceaux-matrices, ce sont essentiellement les empreintes de sceau sur des bulles d'argile qui fournissent les informations. Si beaucoup d'autres sceaux et bulles sont conservés dans des collections privées qui sont restées fermées à toute étude, le corpus actuellement accessible peut être considéré comme un échantillon représentatif du système administratif du territoire bien qu'il soit loin de couvrir l'ensemble des régions et des administrations. Presque deux-cent cinquante sceaux administratifs ont été réunis dans GAES 2[8]. S'y ajoutent dix nouveaux sceaux administratifs dont la grande majorité provient d'empreintes sur des bulles trouvées dans des fouilles officielles[9]. Ce corpus a permis d'établir les modèles des sceaux administratifs d'après le contenu de l'inscription, sa formulation, sa disposition[10] et sa graphie. Parmi les différents aspects de la graphie, seules les occurrences du *y* final et du trait final dans les inscriptions sigillaires seront examinées ici.

Datation des sceaux administratifs

Il est coutume de considérer que les sceaux administratifs sont d'apparition récente dans l'histoire sassanide contrairement aux sceaux officiels des respon-

7 Si cette définition est exacte elle est aussi minimaliste parce que de nombreux sceaux portent le nom de la circonscription ET le nom de la province dans laquelle elle s'inscrit, ou deux fois le nom de la même circonscription, ou encore l'abréviation du nom de la circonscription et le nom entier. Voir à ce propos GYSELEN (sous presse 1).

8 Les numéros des sceaux mentionnés dans cet article sont ceux utilisés dans GAES 2, pp. 415–446.

9 ATb950a (bulle dont l'étude a été remise pour publication en novembre 2019 (GYSELEN, sous presse 2)) et des empreintes de neuf sceaux administratifs provenant des fouilles de Tappe Bardnakoon (KHOSROWZADEH/NOROUZI/GYSELEN/HABIBI 2020, pp. 106–111) : ATb951a (= TB B6-3a), ATb 952a (= TB BB39-15a), ATb954a (= TB B44-4a), ATb956a (= TB B19-11a), ATb962a (= TB B47-4a), ATb966a (= TB B16-6a), ATb967a (= TB B47-12a), ATb968a (= TB B6-5a), ATb969a (= TB B33-17a).

10 Ces aspects ont été traités par GYSELEN (sous presse 1).

sables des administrations territoriales qui ont été produits depuis le premier siècle de l'époque sassanide. Ces derniers portent un motif iconographique entouré d'une inscription qui mentionne le nom du responsable ainsi que ceux de l'administration et de la circonscription qu'il gère. Quelques mentions analogues figurent aussi dans des inscriptions monumentales des IIIe et IVe siècles qui comportent les noms de responsables d'administrations territoriales comme les *dādwar*, les *handarzbed* et les *šahrab*[11].

La création des sceaux administratifs purement épigraphiques serait liée aux réformes administratives du VIe siècle, attribuées à Kawād Ier lors de son 2e règne (499–531) et poursuivies par son fils Husraw Ier (531–579). Si un consensus s'est fait autour de cette datation, il n'existe aucune preuve explicite que cette réforme ait été appliquée à l'ensemble des administrations territoriales.

La seule source moyen-perse qui évoque la création des sceaux administratifs est le *Mādayān-i-hazār dādestān* (ci-après MHD) « Le recueil des mille jugements » où est écrit que certaines administrations, comme par exemple celle du *dādwar*, n'auront pas eu de sceau administratif avant le règne de Husraw Ier[12]. En réalité sur une bonne dizaine d'administrations provinciales attestées par les sceaux administratifs seules quatre sont mentionnées dans le MHD et le contexte dans lequel sont nommés le *mowbed* et le *driyōšān-jādaggōw(-ud-dādwar)* reste confus. N'empêche qu'il est peut-être exact que l'idée de créer des sceaux administratifs anonymes, purement épigraphiques, appartienne au VIe siècle et qu'auparavant seuls des sceaux officiels de hauts dignitaires territoriaux avaient cours.

Si le VIe siècle peut être désigné comme celui de l'invention des sceaux administratifs sassanides, l'usage de ces sceaux ne s'arrête pas à la chute de la dynastie sassanide. Bien qu'on puisse supposer qu'après l'éviction de la dynastie sassanide par les Arabes, plusieurs administrations territoriales ont été éliminées ou ont changé de nom, il semble sensé de penser que l'appareil judiciaire qui appliquait la loi coutumière était resté en place et que ces administrations continuaient d'utiliser leurs sceaux. C'est certainement le cas des offices juridico-religieux de proximité comme l'administration du *mowūh* « bureau des mages » dont la juridiction se limite à la superficie d'un canton. Reste à savoir dans quelle mesure les administrations territoriales 'civiles' et 'fiscales' sont restées en place au début de l'époque islamique et ont continué d'utiliser leurs sceaux. Quoiqu'il en soit, ces sceaux inscrits en moyen-perse disparaîtront à partir de 77H (± 696 de notre ère) suite à la réforme administrative arabo-islamique qui a lieu sous le règne du calife omeyyade ʿAbd el-Malek. Le moyen-perse comme langue administrative sera alors remplacé par l'arabe et le canevas de l'administration territoriale modifié. Seule la région au sud de la mer Caspienne échappera aux suites immédiates de cette réforme comme le prouvent les documents de l'archive du Tabarestān. Ceux-ci sont écrits en moyen-perse et datent de la première moitié

11 Voir à ce propos : GAES 2 sous les rubriques correspondantes.
12 Voir Macuch 1993, p. 596, MHD93.5–9 et Macuch 1997, p. 83.

du VIIIe siècle, le plus récent étant de l'an 107 P.Y., c'est-à-dire 758 de notre ère[13]. Plusieurs de ces documents sont scellés par des sceaux administratifs de *mowūh* ce qui prouve la continuité dans l'usage de sceaux par cette administration[14].

La graphie moyen-perse sur les sceaux administratifs

Sur l'échantillon disponible[15], plus de 90% des sceaux administratifs sont gravés dans une écriture lapidaire[16], environ 2% en pure écriture cursive[17] et ± 5% dans une écriture mixte[18]. Il faut y ajouter qu'un certain nombre de sceaux (6 à 7%) inscrits en écriture lapidaire comportent des erreurs de graphie pour des lettres qui sont écrites de la même façon en écriture cursive[19].

Aux IIIe–IVe siècles, il semblerait que l'écriture lapidaire était la seule graphie pour le moyen-perse[20]. Elle n'était pas seulement celle des inscriptions sur pierre, mais elle était aussi utilisée sur d'autres supports comme des parchemins ou des ostraca[21]. D'une manière générale, les sceaux administratifs sassanides sont gravés dans une écriture lapidaire du moyen-perse proche de celle des inscriptions monumentales des IIIe et IVe siècles. Toutefois la forme de certaines lettres n'est déjà plus la même que celle qu'elles avaient dans ces inscriptions. Un phénomène similaire avait été observé par Henning lors de son étude de l'inscription de Mihr-Narseh à Fīrūzābād qui date de la première moitié du Ve siècle. Henning attirait l'attention sur la transformation des lettres m, t et l par rapport à leur graphie dans les inscriptions des IIIe–IVe siècles[22]. Mais à la même époque, d'autres inscriptions privées sont encore gravées en pure écriture lapidaire comme par exemple celles sur du stuc trouvées sur le tépé A de Bandiān[23]. Quoiqu'il en soit, cette graphie lapidaire avec quelques lettres modifiées semble être la règle dès la deuxième moitié du Ve siècle comme l'illustre le sceau royal de Pērōz (459–484)[24].

13 Pour l'archive du Tabarestān, on trouvera toutes les références bibliographiques mentionnées dans GYSELEN (ed.) 2020, p. 170.
14 ATb901a et ATb902a.
15 Sur les deux cent soixante sceaux administratifs connus, une bonne trentaine n'a pas été intégrée car leurs inscriptions ne sont conservées que très partiellement.
16 Voir Appendice, tableau, première colonne à gauche.
17 *Ibid.*, deuxième colonne à gauche.
18 Souvent désigné sous le terme "écriture intermédiaire" (voir CERETI 2008). Voir Appendice, tableau, troisième colonne à gauche.
19 *Ibid.*, première colonne à gauche, les numéros de sceaux suivis d'un astérisque.
20 Appelée par HUYSE 2003, pp. 26–27 'proto-moyen-perse'.
21 On en trouvera les références chez CERETI 2008, p. 187.
22 HENNING 1954, p. 99. CERETI (2008, p. 186) est quelque peu sceptique considérant que cela peut provenir aussi de l'exécution de la gravure sur un support plus rugueux.
23 RAHBAR 1998.
24 GYSELEN dans BARATTE/BOPEARACHCHI/GYSELEN/SIMS-WILLIAMS 2012.

Étant des instruments de l'administration, les sceaux administratifs sont censés suivre un modèle graphique établi par l'État. La majorité des sceaux administratifs sont, en effet, gravés en écriture 'lapidaire modifié', mais, comme on l'a fait remarquer auparavant, ce n'est pas le cas de tous les sceaux. Faut-il en déduire qu'un certain nombre de modèles pour les inscriptions n'émanait pas d'un organisme central, mais était produit localement ? Bien que robustes grâce à leur forme de dactyloïde, ces objets en pierre semi-précieuse comme la calcédoine ou l'agate ont pu se casser suite à un usage intensif. Non seulement des sceaux administratifs ont pu se casser, mais ils ont aussi pu s'égarer. Que se passe-t-il alors ? Le graveur du nouveau sceau avait-il la possibilité de copier l'ancien modèle du sceau ? Si le modèle n'avait pas été préservé, il a bien fallu en établir un nouveau. Devait-on faire appel pour ce modèle à un office central ou le modèle pouvait-il être exécuté localement ? Jusqu'à présent l'archéologie n'a pas encore découvert des 'modèles' pour les sceaux administratifs et on ne sait pas sur quel support ce modèle était procuré au lapicide : sur un bout de cuir ou de tissu, ou sur un tesson ? Celui qui était chargé d'établir le modèle appartenait-il à la classe des scribes et a-t-il pu être influencé par les graphies utilisées pour rédiger les documents et les textes, c'est-à-dire l'écriture cursive ? Il faut y ajouter aussi qu'on ne sait pas si le modèle était fourni en négatif c'est-à-dire de la manière dont le lapicide devait graver l'inscription, ou en positif comme le texte s'affichait sur l'empreinte du sceau. Ces différentes situations peuvent expliquer les graphies 'non conformes' d'un certain nombre de sceaux.

Le *y* final et le trait final dans les inscriptions des sceaux administratifs

Le *y* final dans les inscriptions du premier siècle sassanide est un élément pseudo-historique et s'inscrit dans un système de 'loi rythmique'[25]. À partir du Ve siècle cette marque graphique sera peu à peu abandonnée. Au début du VIe siècle le *y* final s'écrit dans les cas où il est nécessaire pour la 'loi rythmique' ET en même temps après des lettres qui ne se lient pas à gauche[26]. Vers la fin du VIe siècle le *y* final subit une évolution paléographique et est remplacé par le trait final[27].

Est-ce que ces conclusions s'appliquent aussi aux sceaux administratifs ? La confrontation entre le système général que Huyse a étudié et celui sur les sceaux administratifs est certes biaisée puisque il ne s'agit pas du même type de vocabulaire, celui des sceaux administratif étant limité à des toponymes et des noms d'administrations. Toutefois, il nous a semblé utile de pouvoir disposer d'un inventaire mettant en évidence la présence (ou l'absence) du *y* final et du trait final dans la graphie des inscriptions sigillaires sur les sceaux administratifs. Ces

25 Voir note 2.
26 Ceci est le système appliqué en écriture cursive pour le trait final.
27 Pour plus de détails, voir Huyse 2005.

données ont été réunies sur des bases purement formelles et visuelles[28] et ont été regroupées dans un tableau (Appendice). Si la présentation ici suit vaguement celle de Huyse 2003, la nature même des matériaux incite à la simplifier. Pour tous les commentaires philologiques on se reportera aux trois articles déjà cités[29].

A. Le *y* final dans les inscriptions sigillaires en écriture lapidaire

L'objectif ici est de signaler dans les inscriptions sigillaires les mots en écriture lapidaire qui se terminent par un *y* final, ou les mots où on pourrait s'attendre à trouver un *y* final et qui ne l'ont pas. Le schéma général suit plus ou moins celui proposé par Huyse qui a formulé les règles — et les exceptions — qui régissent la présence du *y* final[30].

a) De nombreux mots monosyllabiques ayant l'accent sur leur unique syllabe se terminent par le *y final*[31] :

> *āb* : ʾpy (ATs24) ; *Bost* : bsty (ATb936a) ; *dar* : dly (ATb901a); *Cašn* : cšny (ATb944a) ; *gund* : gwndy (ATb369a) ; *Hūb* : hwby (ATb236a) ; *Īg* : ygy (ATb937a)[32] ; *Kar* : kly (ATb264a) ; *Kēn* : kyny (ATb82a) ; *marz* : mlcy (ATb367a) ; *Marw* : mlwy (ATb372a) ; *nōg* : nwky (ATb90a) ; *Raz* : lcy (ATb32a) ; *Saz* : scy (ATb895a) ; *Staxr* : sthly (ATb87a, ATb232a) ; *šahr* : štly (ATb27a, ATb481a, ATb947a) ; *Tūs* : twsy (ATb558a) ; *xwāst* : hwʾsty (ATb555a) ; *Yazd* : yzdy (ATb950a).

Dans de nombreux cas, des mots monosyllabiques peuvent porter un *y* final ou ne pas en porter :

> *Gay* : gdy (ATb876a, ATb952a) et gd (ATb956a, ATb962a) ; *kust* : kwsty (ATb8a, ATb29a, ATb30a, ATb33a, ATb34a, ATb204a, ATb221a, ATb222a, ATb302a, ATb481a, ATb555a, ATb760a, ATb968a) et kwst (ATs18, ATb7a, ATb32a, ATb205a, ATb229a, ATb285a, ATb286a, ATb288a, ATb547a, ATb886a, ATb889a, ATb948a) ; *Mād* : mʾdy (ATb29a, ATb204a, ATb222a, ATb302a) et mʾd (ATb34a, ATb289a, ATb555a, ATb879a, ATb898a) ; *Ray* : ldy (ATb43a, ATb152a, ATb550a, ATb868a) et ld (ATb45a, ATb46a, ATb48a ATb54a, ATb72a, ATb261a, ATb264a, ATb346a, ATb357a, ATb900a).

Dans quelques cas des mots monosyllabiques ne sont attestés que dans une graphie sans *y* final :

> *Kaš* : kš (ATb936a), *Šūš* : šwš (ATb15a).

28 Il n'a été tenu compte que du signe proprement dit. Par exemple, la mention de la lettre -d- ne tient pas compte de sa valeur qui peut simplement être la consonne -d- mais aussi représenter un -y- archaïque.

29 HUYSE 2003, 2005 et CERETI 2008.

30 HUYSE 2003.

31 HUYSE 2003, p. 96 et aussi, pour plus de détail, pp. 29–33.

32 Corrigé de *Gī* (gy/yb) en *Īg* (ygy) par GYSELEN dans KHOSROWZADEH / NOROUZI / GYSELEN / HABIBI 2020, pp. 108–109.

b-1) Un *y* final peut figurer aussi à la fin de mots di- et polysyllabiques dont la dernière syllabe est atone[33] :

Abāward : (ʾ)pʾwlty (ATb924a); *Armen* : ʾlmny (ATb367a, ATb369a, ATb481a, ATb490a); *Bānardan* : bʾnltny (ATb33a); *Dārābgerd* : dʾlpkly (ATb232a); *Dāzad* (?) : dʾ(c)dy (ATb222a) ; *Frawaxt* : plwhty (ATs15) ; *Ganzag* : gncky (ATb355a) ; *Guhgand* : gwhgndy (ATb760a) ; *Gušnasp* : gwšnspy (ATb111a) ; *Nēmar* : nymly (ATb251a) ; *Nēmāwand* : nymʾwndy (ATb29a, ATb32a, ATb33a, ATb34a, ATb222a, ATb229a, ATb879a) ; *Nēsawan* : nyswny (ATb367a); *Sarag* : slky (ATs13) ; *Saraxs* : slhsy (ATb924a) ; *Sardag* : sltky (ATs21) ; *Xwābag* : hwʾpky (ATb879a) ; *Yazdgerd* : yzdklty (ATs19, ATb406a) ; *Zarang* : zlngy (ATs31).

Le *y* final peut aussi s'ajouter à des toponymes non-iraniens[34] :

Nahr-malk : nhlmlky (ATs55).

La règle énoncée ci-dessus d'ajouter un *y final* n'est pas toujours appliquée et il y a de nombreux cas où l'on trouve le mot soit avec *y final*, soit sans :

Abaršahr : ʾplštly (ATs32) et ʾplštl (ATs16, ATs22, ATb1a, ATb2, ATb42a, ATb256a, ATb370a) ; *Abhar* : ʾphly (ATb842a, ATb843a) et ʾphl (ATs18, ATb7a, ATb8a, ATb889a, ATb895a); *āmārgar* : ʾmʾlkly (ATs8, ATb13a, ATb27a, ATb92a, ATb94a, ATb223a, ATb225a, ATb232a, ATb270a, ATb271a, ATb275b, ATb372a, ATb403a, ATb415a, ATb457a, ATb468a, ATb474a, ATb490a, ATb511a, ATb550a, ATb695a, ATb874a) – et ʾmʾlkl (ATb16a, ATb237a, ATb361a, ATb363a, ATb370a, ATb373a, ATb380a, ATb401a, ATb406a, ATb481a) — et les graphies déviantes: hmʾlkly (ATs1, ATb12a), ʾmhlkly (ATb217a), ʾmhlkl (ATb258a, ATb358a) et [y?] ʾmʾlkly ; *Ardašīr* : ʾlthštly (ATs5, ATb110a, ATb967a) et ʾlthštl (ATs4) ; *dādwar* : dʾtwbly (ATb6a, ATb9a, ATb24a, ATb25a, ATb42a, ATb75a, ATb87a, ATb91a, ATb110a, ATb162a, ATb204a, ATb950a, ATb952a), et dʾtwbl (ATb41a) et dtwbl (ATb43a) ; dnbʾwndy (ATb236a) ; *Kōmiš* : kwmšy (ATb275b, ATb365a, ATb370a) et kwmš (ATb363a); *Ohrmazd* : ʾwhlmzdy (ATb284a) et ʾwhlmzd (ATb954a) et dans la graphie déviante hwhlmzdy (ATs6); *Nēmāwand* (erreur graphique) : wymʾnwdy (ATb30a, ATb38a) et wymʾwndy (ATb555a), et wymʾnwd (ATb221); *šahrab* : štlpy (ATb29a, ATb155a, ATb242a, ATb312a, ATb354a, ATb718a, ATb876a, ATb877a) et štlp (ATb74a, ATb109a, ATb368a).

Les mots se terminant sur -pt prennent la plupart du temps un *y* final[35] :

andarzbed : ʾndlcpty (ATb100a, ATb947a) ; *darīgbed* (?) : dlnkpty (ATb366a) ; *ēwēnbed* : ʾdwynpty (ATb11a) ; *zarrbed* : zlpty (ATb367a).

Un seul ne comporte pas systématiquement un *y* final :

mowbed : mgwpty (ATs6, ATs10a, ATb10a, ATb34a, ATb95b, ATb365a), mgwptw (ATb1a) et mgwpt (ATb111a).

33 Plus de détails : Huyse 2003, p. 33–45.
34 Je dois à Samra Azarnouche la suggestion qu'il pourrait en réalité s'agir d'un toponyme syriaque qui a été assimilé dans l'iranien.
35 Huyse 2003, pp. 79–81.

b-2) Un *y* final peut figurer aussi à la fin de mots di- et polysyllabiques dont la dernière syllabe n'est pas brève. Plusieurs cas évoqués par Huyse se retrouvent aussi dans le vocabulaire des sceaux[36] :

- un *y* final peut figurer, ou pas, après une syllabe devenue 'lourde' suite à une voyelle brève placée devant deux consonnes :

  Bayšābuhr : bgšhpwhly / byšhpwhly / bgšhpwhry (ATs21, ATb83a, ATb97a, ATb162a, ATb938a, ATb942a, ATb943a, ATb944a, ATb945a, ATb949a), mais aussi byš'pwhl (ATb94a) ; *Šābuhr* : šhpwhly (ATb11a, ATb23a, ATb42a, ATb76a, ATb938a) et š'pwhly (ATb10a), et šhpwhl (ATb76a, ATb256a), šhpwhr (ATb15a) et š'pwhl (ATb13a) ; *Wanānd* : wn'nty (ATb558a).

- un *y* final peut apparaître après une voyelle longue[37] :

  Bāzāhā : b'c'h'y (ATb481a) ; mais aussi sur l'idéogramme pour kadag : BYTAy (ATb111a) et BYTA (ATs20, ATb271a, ATb946a)[38].

- un *y* final se trouve aussi dans la graphie *ydy* qui exprime la voyelle longue ē[39] :

  Harē : hlydy (ATb358a, ATb400a) et hlyd (ATb372a) ; *mowūh* : dans la graphie déviante mgwydy (ATs31, ATb89a) et mgwyd (ATb26a).

- un *y* final peut aussi se trouver dans la graphie -wdy[40] :

  Husraw : hwslwdy (ATb361a, ATb375a) et hwslwd (ATs9, ATb386a).

- un *y* final peut figurer, ou pas, après une syllabe longue, lorsque le mot se termine sur b, c (s), k, n [w et r], p et t (et remplacerait donc le trait final attesté dans l'écriture cursive) :

  Asprāyēn : 'spl'dyny (ATs22) ; *driyōšān* : dlgwš'ny (ATb6a, ATb25a, ATb75a, ATb87a, ATb91a, ATb110a, ATb162a) et dlgwš'n (ATb24a, ATb43a, ATb952a) et aussi dlgwš'nw (ATb9a) ; *Gūrān* (?) : gwl'ny (ATb30a) ; *jādaggōw* : y'tkgwby / y'tngwby (ATb6a, ATb9a, ATb25a, ATb75a, ATb87a, ATb91a, ATb110a, ATb162a, ATb952a) ; *Kawād* : kw'ty (ATs26, ATb82a, ATb244a, ATb270a, ATb279a, ATb281a, ATb282a, ATb290a, ATb368a) et kw't (ATb283a, ATb718a, ATb898a) ; *Kāzrūn* : k'clwny (ATb943a) ; *Marw-rōd* : mlwlwt (ATs28) ; *Māyēn* : m'yny (ATb852a) ; *Mēšūn* : myšwny (ATs11) et myšwn (ATs17) ; *Pērōz* : pylwcy (ATb26a, ATb238a, ATb245a, ATb275b, ATb370a) et pylwc (ATb139a, ATb247a, ATb274a, ATb380a, ATb490a, ATb886a, ATb900a, ATb948a) ; *Sīrāz* : syl'cy (ATb85a) ; *Siyāg* : syd'ky (ATb83a) ; *tasōg* : tswky (ATs31) ; *Walaxšābād*: wldhšp'ty (ATs5).

36 HUYSE 2003, pp. 35, 82–83.
37 HUYSE 2003, pp. 38–39.
38 Un parallèle est l'idéogramme LBA « grand » qui est écrit LBAy sur plusieurs sceaux d'Ērān-spāhbed (GYSELEN 2001).
39 HUYSE 2003, p. 84.
40 HUYSE 2003, p. 41, note 51

– un *y* final peut aussi figurer, ou pas, après une syllabe longue, lorsque le mot se termine sur une autre lettre que b, c (s), k, n [w et r], p et t :

> *ādur* : ʾtwly (ATb111a) ; *framādār* : plmʾtʾly (ATs2) et plmʾtʾl (ATs20, ATb108a, ATb364a) ; *Syārazūr* : sydʾlcwly (ATb74a).

B. Le trait final dans les inscriptions sigillaires en écriture cursive

Selon plusieurs philologues, l'écriture cursive apparaît dans sa forme définitive au VIe siècle[41]. La graphie cursive 'normalisée' est censée être celle des textes zoroastriens post-sassanides, le 'pahlavi des livres' ou 'Book Pahlavi'[42]. Bien sûr l'écriture cursive est d'abord celle des scribes et n'est, *a priori*, pas destinée à la gravure sur pierre ou métal. Néanmoins son influence sur les inscriptions monétaires et lapidaires est bien attestée.

Les sceaux administratifs en pure écriture cursive sont extrêmement rares (2%). D'après les règles de l'écriture cursive, le trait final devait figurer après les lettres — b, c (s), k, n [w et r], p et t — sur les quatre[43] sceaux en écriture cursive. C'est le cas sur certains :

> *Kawād* : kwʾtˡ (ATs3, ATb278a) ; *kust* : kwstˡ (ATb845a, ATb866a) ; *pērōz* : pywlcˡ (ATb845a, ATb866a) ; *Wēdand* : wytʾntˡ (ATb866a).

mais pas après les mots se terminant sur -n et -r dont le signe graphique en cursif est le même que celui du trait final :

> *Arbān*: ʾlpʾn (ATb278a) ; *Bayšābuhr* : byšʾpwhr (ATs3) ; *šahrestān* : štrstn (ATb845a).

C. Le trait final dans l'écriture mixte

Dans l'introduction sur les graphies du moyen-perse on a évoqué que l'écriture lapidaire sur les sceaux administratifs a parfois été contaminée par l'écriture cursive. Cette contamination se situe à plusieurs niveaux. Certains ne s'expriment pas graphiquement, c'est-à-dire toute la légende est écrite en lapidaire mais comporte des erreurs qui sont dues à l'écriture cursive. En effet, dans cette dernière les lettres ʾ et h sont rendues par le même signe, ainsi que n, w et r. En transposant en écriture lapidaire — très probablement d'après un modèle en écriture cursive — le graveur s'est trompé de signe en mettant par exemple un h au lieu d'un ʾ. Une des conséquences peut être une haplologie, c'est-à-dire que deux mêmes lettres se suivent. Ainsi on peut passer de -ʾh- (forme exacte) à un passage -hh- qui peut devenir simplement -h-. Les sceaux qui comportent ces

41 Huyse 2005 ; Cereti 2008, p. 191.
42 Cf. CPD, p. xi.
43 Sur ATb866a, seul le mot mgwh est écrit en lapidaire.

deux types d'erreurs mais qui sont gravés en écriture lapidaire sont notés dans la première colonne à gauche par un astérisque après le numéro[44].

Un autre aspect de cette contamination est l'introduction dans une légende en écriture lapidaire du trait final en écriture cursive. Ces sceaux ont été rangés dans la colonne cursive/lapidaire et portent un astérisque après le numéro.

Puis il y a les sceaux administratifs qui comportent des parties gravées en écriture lapidaire et d'autres en écriture cursive. Dans quelques rares cas le trait final de l'écriture cursive suit un mot gravé en lapidaire :

> *Arūb* : ʾlwp' (ATs10) ; *Kawād* : kwʾt' (ATb283a) ; *kust* : kwst' (ATs10, ATb956a et ATs24a ?) ; *rōd* : lwt' (ATb286a, ATb956a) ; *Marw-rōd* : mlwlwt' (ATb373a).

Mais un mot peut aussi se terminer sur un -w ou un -n lapidaire, ce qui est dû à la polyvalence du trait final qui présente la même graphie que les lettres w et n en écriture cursive, et on trouvera ainsi un -w ou un -n au lieu d'un trait final :

> *mowbed* : mgwptw (ATb1), *rōd* : lwtn (ATb285a) ; *tasōg* : tswkw (ATb42a).

D. Quelques remarques sur l'utilisation du *y* final et du trait final dans les inscriptions sigillaires

Les sceaux administratifs montrent bien la complexité et l'incohérence dans l'utilisation du *y* final et du trait final aux VIe–VIIe siècles et les confusions qui en résultent. Son utilisation appelle à quelques observations d'ordre général.

On trouve parfois sur un même sceau en écriture lapidaire deux mots dont l'un porte un *y* final et pas l'autre, pourtant aussi susceptible de le porter. On peut citer par exemple bwsty et kš (ATb936a), ʾmʾlkly, mais mlwlwt et hlyd (ATb372), hlydy, mais ʾmhlkl (ATb358a), etc. À première vue aucune raison graphique ne semble justifier ce manque d'uniformité dans l'usage ou le non-usage du *y* final.

Lorsqu'il s'agit de mots composés, c'est uniquement le dernier terme qui porte un *y* final[45]. Ce principe s'applique à tous les toponymes composés sur les sceaux administratifs. D'une manière générale les mots devant ZY suivent le système général des mots isolés et peuvent éventuellement porter un *y* final[46]. Les noms de cantons formés avec le terme šahrestān « capitale provinciale » ne sont apparemment pas considérés par les Sassanides comme des noms composés

44 Voir Appendice.

45 HUYSE 2003, p. 41.

46 ʾtwly ZY gwšnpy ʻādur-ī-gušnaspʼ « Feu de Gušnasp » (dans la marge : BYTAy ZY ʾtwly ZY gwšnpy ʻkadag-ī-ādur-ī-gušnaspʼ « Maison du Feu de Gušnasp » (ATb111a). D'autres exemples avec *y* final : ATs5, ATs15, ATs24, ATs31, ATb27a. et sans *y* final : ATb15a, ATb90a, ATb282a. Voir aussi kwsty et kwst avant ZY.

puisque le terme précédant le terme štrdst'n porte parfois un *y* final[47]. C'est aussi parfois le cas de termes avant kwst 'kust' (ATb760a).

Dans la plupart des cas les noms des administrations que nous avons interprétés comme des noms composés, ainsi *gund-ī-kadag-xwadāyān-framādār* et *wāspuhragān-framādār* semblent bien être considérés aussi par les Sassanides comme des noms composés puisqu'on n'y trouve un *y* final qu'après le dernier mot ou celui avant ZY. Il en va autrement pour le nom de l'administration du *driyōšān-jādaggōw-ud-dādwar* « juge et avocat des pauvres » puisque les trois termes peuvent porter le *y* final.

Si le trait final est censé figurer, comme le *y* final, à la fin d'un terme composé et pas après le premier terme, sur les sceaux administratifs il faut mentionner une exception : alors que le mot composé de *rōd* et de *bār* est écrit en graphie lapidaire, un trait final figure après le premier terme : *rōdbār* : lwtˡbʾl (ATb956a).

Épilogue

Si l'ajout du *y* final semble souvent suivre les mêmes règles sur les sceaux administratifs inscrits en écriture lapidaire que dans les inscriptions des IIIᵉ–IVᵉ siècles[48], ce n'est pas toujours le cas. Si quelques très rares sceaux administratifs sont gravés en écriture cursive dans laquelle un trait final suit les mots se terminant sur une des six consonnes — b, c (s), k, n [w et r], p et t — dans le moyen-perse cursif des livres, ce n'est pas le cas systématiquement[49]. Dans les inscriptions en écriture lapidaire montrant d'une manière ou d'une autre l'influence de l'écriture cursive, des mots qui ne porteraient probablement pas de *y* final dans les inscriptions anciennes se terminent par un *y* final. La raison est très probablement que le trait final qui est de règle dans l'écriture cursive après des mots se terminant sur b, c (s), k, n [w et r], p ou t semblait difficile à ajouter à un mot en écriture lapidaire[50] et qu'on a eu recours à un phénomène graphique du lapidaire — le *y* final — sans que les règles inhérentes à ce phénomène graphique soient respectées.

47 ATs31, ATb76a, ATb355a, ATb367a, ATb369a mais aussi sans *y* final : ATs4, ATb78a, ATb290a, ATb900a.

48 On trouvera toutes les attestations : Huyse 2003.

49 Il ne faut toutefois pas considérer que le trait final y est aussi systématiquement appliqué qu'on peut l'entendre dire. Beaucoup de négligences dans la notation du trait final peuvent se remarquer dans certains ouvrages moyen-perses. Un bel exemple en est le *Husraw ī Kawādān ud rēdag-e* « Husraw fils de Kawād et un page » dont une édition récente rend compte (Azarnouche 2013). Nous remercions Samra Azarnouche pour son commentaire qui a conforté notre observation de ce phénomène.

50 Du moins sur les sceaux administratifs. En revanche sur les sceaux officiels des quatre Ērān-spāhbed, l'ajout du trait final à un mot écrit en graphie lapidaire ne pose pas problème. Voir Huyse 2005 à ce propos : le trait final remplace le -*y* final sur les sceaux des Ērān-spāhbed sous Ohrmazd IV.

Les données issues du vocabulaire des sceaux administratifs pourraient peut-être compléter ou nuancer certaines analyses du phénomène du *y* final et du trait final auxquelles ont procédé les philologues. Mais l'objectif principal de passer en revue le vocabulaire des sceaux administratifs est évidemment d'y trouver des critères pour dater ces sceaux. Ayant été en utilisation pendant deux siècles, il serait bien utile de pouvoir mettre un sceau administratif en relation avec un règne d'un souverain sassanide ou de pouvoir l'attribuer à l'époque post-sassanide. Reste à savoir si dans cette perspective la présence du *y* final et du trait final peut présenter une donnée intéressante.

Dans l'état actuel de la documentation, un début de réponse ne peut être apporté que par des sceaux dont les empreintes figurent sur des bulles trouvées dans un contexte archéologique à condition que les fouilleurs puissent en fournir une datation. Si l'on examine des bulles trouvées dans un même contexte archéologique comme celles de TQS (Tol-e Qaleh Seyfabad) ou de TB (Tappe Bardnakoon)[51], le résultat de l'analyse n'est pourtant guère concluant. En ce qui concerne les neuf sceaux administratifs de TQS[52], le *y* final est présent sur la plupart des termes auxquels on peut s'attendre à trouver un *y*, par exemple pour Bayšābyhr : en général byšʾpwhry mais aussi byšʾpwhl sans *y* [53]. En revanche les onze empreintes de sceaux à peu près lisibles sur les bulles trouvées à TB sont beaucoup moins homogènes : on y trouve par exemple gd et gdy, ʾwhmzd et ʾlthštly, mais aussi le trait final sur des sceaux où figure le terme gd « Gay ».

D'une manière générale, le pourcentage des empreintes de sceaux trouvées dans des fouilles officielles est faible (± 17%) et pour seulement la moitié de ces sceaux administratifs le contexte archéologique est réellement connu. L'image de ce 9% des sceaux administratifs est loin d'être homogène, et toute interprétation définitive du phénomène de la présence (ou l'absence) du *y* final ou du trait final ne peut se reposer sur une si petite quantité de données. On doit espérer qu'un jour prochain d'autres archives de bulles seront découvertes et qu'elles pourraient être datées avec précision. Jusque-là il faudrait être très prudent dans l'attribution des sceaux administratifs des VIe–VIIe siècles sur des critères graphiques comme l'écriture (lapidaire, cursive et 'intermédiaire'), ou la présence ou l'absence d'un *y* final. Le tableau que nous avons brossé ici ne permet certainement pas encore de déterminer des critères qui pourraient servir à la datation des sceaux administratifs. Dans le cas où les différentes consignes, qui définissent la graphie des sceaux administratifs, n'émanent pas d'une instance centrale, mais ont été régies par des circonstances, les différences graphiques ne peuvent pas constituer des critères de datation.

51 On ne possède pas de références pour les lieux où ont été trouvées les bulles à QAN (Qasr-i Abu Nasr). Pour les autres fouilles, réelles ou présumées, trop peu d'empreintes de sceaux administratifs sont attestées pour qu'elles puissent fournir une trame.

52 GHASEMI/GYSELEN 2018.

53 L'état de conservation des bulles avec l'empreinte du sceau de šahrab de Bayšābuhr trouvées à TQS (TQS26 et 27) et à QAN ne permet pas de trancher sur la présence du *-y* final à *šahrab*.

Appendice

Ce tableau comporte de gauche à droite :

a) Les sceaux inscrits en écriture lapidaire ; * après la référence indique la présence dans l'écriture lapidaire d'erreurs de lettres qui sont dans l'écriture cursive rendues par le même signe ;
b) Les sceaux inscrits en écriture cursive ;
c) Les sceaux inscrits en écriture 'mixte' ;
d) La provenance des sceaux ou bulles (pour les abréviations des sites voir GAES 2, p. 381–382) ;
e-f) Mots monosyllabiques avec un *y* final et sans *y* final ;
g-h) Mots di- et polysyllabiques avec un *y* final et sans *y* final ;
i) Mots avec un trait final.
Rien n'est noté dans les colonnes pour les sceaux dont la graphie des termes est conforme au système général.

Graphie			Prov.	Mots mono-syllabiques		Mots di- et poly-syllabiques		Trait final
lapidaire	cursive	cursive / lapidaire		avec *y*	sans *y*	avec *y*	sans *y*	
Sceaux								
ATs1*			—			hm'lkly		
ATs2*			—			plm't'ly		
	ATs3		—					kw't'
ATs4			—				'lthštl	
ATs5*			—			nhlmlky wyh<'>lthštly wldhšp'ty		
ATs6*			—			hwhlmzdy mgwpty		
ATs7 = ATb225a			—			[y ?]'m'lkly		
ATs8*			—			'm'lkly		
ATs9			—				hwslwd	

Graphie			Prov.	Mots mono-syllabiques		Mots di- et poly-syllabiques		Trait final
lapidaire	cursive	cursive / lapidaire		avec *y*	sans *y*	avec *y*	sans *y*	
		ATs10*	—			mgwpty		ʾlwp' k<w>st'
ATs11			—			myšwny		
ATs12			—				gwbl	
ATs13			—			slky		
ATs14			—					
ATs15			—			plwhty		
		ATs16	—				ʾplštl	
ATs17*			—				myswn ʾmʾlkl	
ATs18			—		kwst		ʾphl	
ATs19			—			yzdklty		
ATs20			—				plmʾtʾl BYTA	
ATs21			—			sltky bgšhpwhry		
ATs22			—			ʾsplʾdyny	ʾplštl	
ATs23			—					
		ATs24*	—	ʾpy				kwst[' / y]
ATs25= ATb941a			—					
ATs26			—			kwʾty		
ATs27			—					
ATs28			—				mlw[lw]t	
ATs29			—					
ATs30			—					

Graphie			Prov.	Mots mono-syllabiques		Mots di- et poly-syllabiques		Trait final
lapidaire	cursive	cursive / lapidaire		avec *y*	sans *y*	avec *y*	sans *y*	
ATs31			—			zlngy tswky mgwydy		
ATs32			—			ʾplštly		
Empreintes								
ATb1a*			—				ʾplštl	mgwptw (sic)
ATb2a			—				ʾplštl	
ATb6a						dlgwšʾny yʾtngwby dʾtwbly		
ATb7a			—		kwst		ʾphl	
ATb8a			—	kwsty			ʾphl	
ATb9a			—			dlgwšʾnw yʾt[kgw]by dʾtwbly		
ATb10a			Suse			šʾpwhly mgwpty		
ATb11a			Suse			šhpwhry ʾdwynpty		
ATb12a*			Suse			hmʾlkly		
ATb13a			Suse			ʾm[ʾ]lkly	šʾpwhl	
ATb15a			Suse		šwš		šhpwhr	
ATb16a			Suse				ʾmʾlkl	
ATb23a			Suse			šhpwh[l]y		
ATb24a			—			dʾt[w]b[l]y	dlgwšʾn	

Graphie			Prov.	Mots mono-syllabiques		Mots di- et poly-syllabiques		Trait final
lapidaire	cursive	cursive / lapidaire		avec *y*	sans *y*	avec *y*	sans *y*	
ATb25a			–			dlgwš’ny y’tngwby d’twbly		
ATb26a			–			pylwcy	mgwyd	
ATb27a			–	štly		’m’lkly		
ATb29a			–	m’dy kwsty		nym’wndy štlpy		
ATb30a*			–	kwsty		wym’nwdy gwl’ny		
ATb32a			–	lcy	kwst	nym’wndy		
ATb33a			–	kwsty		b’nltny nym’wndy		
ATb34a			–	kwsty	m’d	nym’wndy mgwpty		
ATb38a*			–			wym’nwdy		
ATb41a			–				dlgwš’n d’twbl	
		ATb42a	–				’plštl	tswkw (sic)
ATb43a			–	ldy			dlgwš’n y’tkgwb dtwbl	
ATb45a			–		ld			
ATb46a			–		ld			
ATb48a			–		ld			
ATb54a			–		ld			
ATb72a			–		ld			
ATb74a			–			syd’lcwly	štlp	

Graphie			Prov.	Mots mono-syllabiques		Mots di- et poly-syllabiques		Trait final
lapidaire	cursive	cursive / lapidaire		avec *y*	sans *y*	avec *y*	sans *y*	
ATb75a*			–			dlgwš'ny y'tngwby d'twbly		
ATb76a			–			[šh]pwhly	šhpwhl	
ATb78a			–				zlng (?)	
ATb79a			–					
ATb82a			–	kyny		kw'ty		
ATb83a			QAN			syd'ky bgšhpwhly		
ATb85a			QAN			syl'cy		
ATb87a			QAN	sthly		dlgwš'ny y'tngwby d'twbly		
ATb89a			QAN			mgwydy		
ATb90a			QAN	nwky				
ATb91a			QAN			dlgwš'ny y'tngwby d'twbly		
ATb92a			QAN			'm'lkly		
ATb94a			QAN TQS			'm'lkly	byš'pwhl	
ATb95a			QAN			mgwpty		
ATb97a			QAN TQS			byšhpwhly		
ATb100a			QAN			'ndlcpty		
ATb108a			TS				plm(')t'l	
ATb109a			TS				štlp	

Graphie			Prov.	Mots mono-syllabiques		Mots di- et poly-syllabiques		Trait final
lapidaire	cursive	cursive / lapidaire		avec *y*	sans *y*	avec *y*	sans *y*	
ATb110a			TS			ʾlthštly dlgwšʾny yʾtngwby dʾtwbly		
ATb111a			TS			ʾtwly gwšnspy BYTAy	mgwpt	
ATb139a			—				pylwc	
ATb152a			—	ldy				
ATb153a			—					
ATb155a			—			štlpy		
ATb162a			QAN TQS			dʾtwbly dlgwšʾny byšhpwhly yʾtngwby		
ATb204a			—	mʾdy kwsty		dʾtwbly		
ATb205a			—		kwst			
ATb210a			—					
ATb212a			—					
ATb217a*			—			ʾmhlk[l]y		
ATb221a*			—	kwsty			wymʾnwd	
(ATb222a)			—	mʾdy kwsty		dʾ(c)dy [nymʾwn]dy		
ATb223a			—			ʾmʾlkly		
ATb225a =ATs7			—			ʾmʾlkly		

Graphie			Prov.	Mots mono-syllabiques		Mots di- et poly-syllabiques		Trait final
lapidaire	cursive	cursive / lapidaire		avec *y*	sans *y*	avec *y*	sans *y*	
ATb229a					kwst	nym'wndy		
ATb232a			—	sthly		d'lpkly 'm'lkly		
ATb235a			—					
		ATb236a	—	hwby		dnb'wndy		
ATb237a			—				'm'lkl	
ATb238a			—			pylwcy		
ATb242a			—			štlpy		
ATb244a			Š			kw'ty		
ATb245a			Š			pylwcy		
ATb247a			TT				pylwc	
ATb250a			—					
ATb251a			—			nymly		
ATb256a			(TK)				'plštl šhpwhl	
ATb258a*			(TK)				'mhlkl	
ATb261a			—		ld			
ATb264a			—	kly	ld			
ATb267a			—					
ATb268a			—	ldy				
ATb270a			—			'm'lkly kw'ty		
ATb271a			—			'm'lkly	BYTA	
ATb273a			—					
ATb274a			—				pylwc	

Graphie			Prov.	Mots mono-syllabiques		Mots di- et poly-syllabiques		Trait final
lapidaire	cursive	cursive / lapidaire		avec *y*	sans *y*	avec *y*	sans *y*	
ATb275a			–			ʾmʾlkly kwmšy pylwcy		
ATb277a			–					
	ATb278a		–					kwʾtʹ
ATb279a			–			kwʾty		
ATb281a			–			kwʾty		
ATb282a			–			kwʾty		
		ATb283a	–				kwʾt	kwʾtʹ
ATb284a			–			ʾwhlmzdy		
		ATb285a	–	kwsty				lwtn (sic)
		ATb286a	–		kwst			lwtʹ
ATb288a			–		kwst			
ATb289a			–		mʾd			
ATb290a			(TK)			kwʾty		
ATb302a			–	mʾdy kwsty				
ATb312a			–			štlpy		
ATb346a			–		ld			
ATb354a			–			štlpy		
ATb355a			–			gncky		
ATb357a			–		ld			
ATb358a			B			hlydy	ʾmhlkl	
ATb361a			–			hwslwdy	ʾmʾlkl	
ATb363a			–				ʾmʾlkl kwmš	

Graphie			Prov.	Mots mono-syllabiques		Mots di- et poly-syllabiques		Trait final
lapidaire	cursive	cursive / lapidaire		avec *y*	sans *y*	avec *y*	sans *y*	
ATb364a			–				plm'ṭ'l	
ATb365a						kwmšy mgwpty		
ATb366a						dlnkpty		
ATb367a				mlcy		'lmny nyswny zlpty		
ATb368a			–			kw'ty	štlp	
ATb369a			–	gwndy		'lmny plm'ṭ'ly		
ATb370a			–			kwmšy pylwcy	'm'lkl 'plštl	
ATb372a			–	mlwy		'm'lkly	hlyd mlwlwt	
		ATb373a	–				'm'lkl	mlwlwt'
ATb374a			–					
ATb375a			–			hwslwdy		
ATb377a			–					
ATb378a			–					
ATb379a			–					
ATb380a			–				'm'lkl pylwc	
ATb385a			–					
ATb386a			–				hwslwd	
ATb387a			–					
ATb388a			–					

Graphie			Prov.	Mots mono-syllabiques		Mots di- et poly-syllabiques		Trait final
lapidaire	cursive	cursive / lapidaire		avec *y*	sans *y*	avec *y*	sans *y*	
ATb400a						hlydy		
ATb401a							’m’lkl	
ATb403a						’m’lkly		
ATb406a						hwslkdy yzdklty	’m’lkl	
ATb415a						’m’lkly		
ATb449a								
ATb457a						’m’lkly		
ATb468a						’m’lkly		
ATb474a						’m’lkly		
ATb481a				štly kwsty		’lmny b’c’h’y	’m’lkl	
ATb490						’lmny ’m’lkly	pylwc	
ATb511a						’m’lkly		
ATb547a					m’d kwst			
ATb550a				ldy		’m’lkly		
ATb551a								
ATb555a				hw’sty kwsty	m’d	wym’wndy		
ATb558a				twsy		wn’nty		
ATb636a								
ATb695a						’m’lkly		
ATb718a						štlpy	kw’t	
ATb755a								
ATb756a								

Graphie			Prov.	Mots mono-syllabiques		Mots di- et poly-syllabiques		Trait final
lapidaire	cursive	cursive / lapidaire		avec *y*	sans *y*	avec *y*	sans *y*	
ATb760a			–	kwsty		gwhgndy		
ATb842a			–			[’]phly		
ATb843a			–			’phly		
	ATb845a		–					kwst' pywlc'
		ATb852a	–			m’yny		
	ATb866a		–					kwst' pywlc' wyt’nt'
ATb868a			–	ldy				
ATb869a			–					
ATb874a			–			’m’lkly		
ATb876a			TB	gdy		štlpy		
ATb877a			–			štlpy		
ATb879a			–		m’d	nym’wndy hw’pky		
ATb886a			–		kwst		pylwc	
ATb889a			–		kwst		’phl	
ATb895a			–	scy			’phl	
ATb898a			–		m’d		kw’t	
ATb900a			–		ld		pylwc	
ATb901a			–	dly				
ATb902a								
ATb924a			AT			(’)p’wlty slhsy		
ATb936a			–	bsty	kš			

Graphie			Prov.	Mots mono-syllabiques		Mots di- et poly-syllabiques		Trait final
lapidaire	cursive	cursive / lapidaire		avec *y*	sans *y*	avec *y*	sans *y*	
ATb937a			TB	ygy				
ATb938a			TQS			šhpwhly byšhpwhly		
ATb941a =ATs25			TQS					
ATb942a			TQS			byšhpwhly		
ATb943a			TQS			byšhpwhly k'clwny		
ATb944a			TQS	cšny		byšhpwhly		
ATb945a			TQS			byšhpwhly		
ATb946a			TS				BYTA	
ATb947a			EQL ? KA ?	štly		'ndlcpty		
ATb948a			K		kwst		pylwc	
ATb949a			TQS			byšhpwhly		
ATb950a			–	yzdy		d'twbly		
ATb952a			TB	gdy		y'tngwby d'twbly	dlgwš'n	
ATb954a			TB				'whlmzd	
		ATb956a	TB		gd			kwst' lwt'b'l
		ATb962a	TB		gd			kl(wn ?)'
ATb966a			TB					
ATb967a			TB			'lthštly		
ATb968a			TB	kwsty				
ATb969a			TB					

Bibliography

AZARNOUCHE, S. 2013 : *Husraw ī Kawādān ud Rēdag-ē* « Khosrow fils de Kawād et un page ». Paris (Studia Iranica, Cahier 49).

BARATTE, F./O. BOPEARACHCHI/R. GYSELEN/ N. SIMS-WILLIAMS 2012 : "Un plat romain inscrit en bactrien et *pārsīg*." In : R. Gyselen (ed.) : *Objets et documents inscrits en* pārsīg. Bures-sur-Yvette (Res Orientales XXI), pp. 9–28.

CERETI, C.G. 2008 : "On the Pahlavi cursive script and the Sasanian Avesta." In : *Studia Iranica* 37, pp. 175–195.

CPD: *A Concise Pahlavi Dictionary* : MACKENZIE 1971.

GAES 2: *La géographie administrative de l'empire sassanide, d'après les sources épigraphiques en moyen-perse* : GYSELEN 2019.

GHASEMI P./R. GYSELEN 2018 : "Bulles administratives sassanides trouvées à Tole Qaleh Seyfabad (Fārs)." In : S. Gondet/E. Haerinck (eds.) : *L'Orient est son jardin. Hommage à Rémy Boucharlat*. Leuven (Acta Iranica 58), pp. 179–184.

GYSELEN, R. 2001 : *The Four Generals of the Sasanian Empire: some Sigillographic Evidence*. Rome (Conferenze 14).

— 2019 : *La géographie administrative de l'empire sassanide. Les témoignages épigraphiques en moyen-perse*. Bures-sur-Yvette (Res Orientales XXV).

— (ed.) 2020 : *Persia (552 BCE – 758 CE): Primary Sources, Old and New*. Bures-sur-Yvette (Res Orientales XXVIII).

— [sous presse 1] : "Sceaux sassanides épigraphiques : Contenu, formulation et emplacement des inscriptions en moyen-perse".

— [sous presse 2] : "Yazd, une province de l'empire sassanide".

HENNING, W.B. 1954 : "The Inscription of Firuzabad." In : *Asia Major* N.S.t. IV, pp. 98–102.

HUYSE, PH. 2003 : *Le* y *final dans les inscriptions moyen-perses et la 'loi rythmique' proto-moyen-perse*. Paris (Studia Iranica, Cahier 29).

— 2005 : "Ein erneuter Datierungsversuch für den Übergang vom Schluß-y der mittelpersischen Inschriften zum Endstrich im Buchpahlavi (6.–7. Jh.)." In : D. WEBER (ed.) : *Languages of Iran: Past and Present. A Volume of Iranian Studies in Memoriam David Neil MacKenzie*. Wiesbaden (Iranica 8), pp. 51–68.

KHOSROWZADEH, A./A. NOROUZI/R. GYSELEN/H. HABIBI 2020 : "Administrative Seal Impressions on Bullae Discovered on Tappe Bardnakoon." In : R. GYSELEN (ed.) : *Persia (552 BCE - 758 CE): Primary Sources, Old and New*, pp. 83–112.

MACUCH, M. 1993 : *Rechtskasuistik in Iran. Die Rechtssammlung des Farroḫmard i Wahrāmān*. Wiesbaden (Iranica 1).

— 1997 : "The use of Seals in Sasanian Jurisprudence." In : R. GYSELEN (ed.) : *Sceaux d'Orient et leur emploi*. Bures-sur-Yvette (Res Orientales X), pp. 79–87.

MHD: *Madayān-e hazār dādestān* : MACUCH 1993.

RAHBAR, M. 1998 : "Découverte d'un monument d'époque sassanide à Bandian, Dargaz (Nord-Khorassan). Fouilles 1994 et 1995." In : *Studia Iranica* 27, pp. 213–250.

The Pahlavi Psalter in its Historical Context

ALMUT HINTZE, London

The[1] Pahlavi Psalter constitutes one of the most remarkable documents to be unearthed in the Turfan oasis in eastern Turkistan, the present-day Xinjiang Uyghur Autonomous Region of the People's Republic of China. Its exceptional status rests on the fact that it is the only Middle Persian version of a biblical text known so far. It is also the oldest extant paper manuscript in the Pahlavi script.[2] Moreover, the Pahlavi Psalter bears witness to a style of writing that is more archaic than the Book-Pahlavi script and the Pahlavi cursive script, of which Dieter Weber is the world's leading expert. The archaic form of the Psalter's script agrees with the more archaic form of its language, which, as PRODS OKTOR SKJÆRVØ (1983) has demonstrated, still distinguishes direct and oblique cases in the plural of certain categories of nouns and adjectives.

The form of the Psalter script is also attested in an 8th-century CE Iranian Christian artefact from Herāt but is found nowhere else. However, the fact that some letters of the Pahlavi Psalter script were employed in the creation of the Avestan alphabet indicates that the script must also still have been known in the province of Pārs in Western Iran around 600 CE. Pārs was the power centre of the Zoroastrian priesthood during the Sasanian period and presumably the area in which priests developed the Avestan script to create a phonetic written representation of the words they recite in their rituals.[3]

Considering the significance of the Pahlavi Psalter and the relatively little scholarly attention it has so far found, I am hoping to provide a useful contribution here by surveying the Psalter's main features and points of debate. The question of the date of the Pahlavi Psalter is discussed not only regarding its script and language but also from the point of view of the paper on which it is written. After a review of the history of paper in the context of the discoveries of the documents from Central Asia in the early 20th century, the detailed results of the radiocarbon C14 analysis of the paper of the Pahlavi Psalter which DIETER WEBER initiated in 2008 are presented here for the first time with his kind and generous permission, anticipating his own publication of the result in the context of his

1 For helpful comments and corrections, I am grateful to Erica Hunter, Mark Dickens and Nicholas Sims-Williams. I am of course responsible for any remaining shortcomings.

2 GIGNOUX 2002. On the Pahlavi Psalter, see ANDREAS 1910; ANDREAS/BARR 1933; ASMUSSEN 1964; GIGNOUX 1969; SKJÆRVØ 1983.

3 On the development of the Avestan alphabet, see the research survey in HINTZE 2014, pp. 2–7.

forthcoming work on the history of the Pahlavi script. In a separate contribution to this volume, the paper conservator Dr ANNA-GRETHE RISCHEL (Environmental Archaeology and Materials Science, National Museum of Denmark) presents details of her microscopic and macroscopic examination of the paper of the Pahlavi Psalter and of other Central Asian documents. The Herāt Cross, which bears a Middle Persian inscription written in the same archaic script as the Pahlavi Psalter and which can be dated to the 8th century CE, is also discussed as part of the debate on the historical context of the Pahlavi Psalter.

I am delighted to dedicate this article to DIETER WEBER, who has elucidated many documents written in the most difficult cursive Pahlavi script in a masterly fashion and who has thrown unparalleled light on the historical development of the Pahlavi script.

1. Discovery and Studies of the Psalter

The Pahlavi Psalter was found in 1905 at Xipang near Bulayïq, a site situated about ten km north of Turfan, during the Second German Turfan expedition led by Albert von Le Coq. It was buried in what must have once been the library of a monastery of the Church of the East. The Psalter was one of many other fragmentary documents found there. Most of them are thought to date from the 9th–14th centuries and are written in a range of scripts and languages, including Syriac, Sogdian, New Persian, and Old Turkic.[4] Apart from the Pahlavi Psalter, a second text written in the Pahlavi script found at this site is a single leaf of a *Farhang ī Pahlavīg*. Written in the cursive form of the Pahlavi script, the *Farhang ī Pahlavīg* could indicate the use of the Pahlavi script and language by the Christians of Turfan, unless it was left behind by a visitor.[5]

The Turfan oasis has yielded the largest corpus of Psalmic material from Central Asia. The recitation of the psalms played a central role in the daily liturgical practice of the Church of the East, and especially in its monastic life. This is borne out by the fact that no other Biblical text found at Turfan was translated into more languages than the psalms.[6] While most Turfan psalter fragments are in Syriac,

4 On Bulayïq, see SIMS-WILLIAMS 1990, on the expeditions to Central Asia by different countries and the Berlin Turfan collection, see DICKENS 2013b, pp.4–5 and pp.18–19 notes 8 and 9. DURKIN-MEISTERERNST (2011) discusses the importance of the Middle Persian texts from Turfan. Some Old Turkish manuscripts were also found in Hami, which is located east of Turfan. The second Turfan expedition immediately passed over to the third expedition in December 1905 when Grünwedel, together with H. Pohrt, arrived in Kashghar. Grünwedel took over leadership and headed the final part of the campaign as the third expedition, which ended on July 6, 1907. This was by far the longest of all four German expeditions. Theodor Bartus (1858–1941) was a technical crew member on all four German Turfan expeditions between 1902 and 1914, headed by Albert von Le Coq and Albert Grünwedel.

5 DURKIN-MEISTERERNST 2014, pp. 22–23 and fn.52; MACKENZIE 2000.

6 For a survey, see SCHWARTZ/SIMS-WILLIAMS 2014, pp. 10–11 and DICKENS 2013b, p. 6.

including six leaves of the psalter in Syriac transliterated in Uyghur script,[7] there are also remnants in several other Iranian languages apart from Middle Persian, in particular Sogdian in Sogdian script[8] and New Persian written in a modified Syriac script.[9] As DICKENS (2013a, p. 358 fn.5) notes, the only other text whose popularity comes close to that of the psalms is the Legend of St. George, which is found in Syriac (MARÓTH 1991; Lin 2020 and 2021), in Sogdian in Syriac script (HANSEN 1941; SIMS-WILLIAMS 2019) and in Uyghur Turkic (BANG 1926).

The extant remnants of the Pahlavi Psalter consist of eleven leaves measuring 11.1×9.6 cm and two smaller fragments (fols. 10 and 13). Two of the folios are consecutive (fols. 1, 2), two are single (fols. 3, 4), and eight folios form a quire (fols. 5–12). The small fragment which constitutes fol. 13 cannot be placed.[10] Many of these folios are deteriorated in the centre of the leaf and have gaps. In the estimation of DURKIN-MEISTERERNST, they represent the remaining 10% of the complete codex. The folios are written on both sides with 18–21 lines per page in black ink in a clear and careful manner. They provide the Middle Persian text of most of Psalms 94–99, Psalm 118, and Psalms 121–136. The numbering of the psalms agrees with that of the Syriac Bible rather than with the Hebrew Bible.[11] Headings written in red ink indicate the number of the psalm and Syriac punctuation is employed.

In 1910 FRIEDRICH CARL ANDREAS presented the Pahlavi Psalter to the scholarly world in a short article but failed to publish the edition before his death in 1930. This task fell on KAJ BARR, who completed ANDREAS's work and published the *editio princeps* under both authors' names in 1933 (ANDREAS/BARR 1933). The work includes a brief introduction, the edition of the Pahlavi text transcribed in Hebrew characters, a German translation, a glossary, and facsimiles of the thirteen folios (plates 1–11). It also provides the Syriac text of the psalms according to BARNES's edition of *The Peshitta Psalter According to the West Syrian Text* (1904). The Syriac text of the canons is taken from the third part of the *Breviarium Chaldaicum* (1887). In the German translation of the Pahlavi text, gaps are filled in according to the Syriac version, thus providing the literary context of the fragments. The glossary (pp. 117–150) contains all the Pahlavi words and forms with their Syriac equivalents. ANDREAS and BARR's edition has remained the only one of this text to the present day.

Despite its significance, an up-to-date edition of the Pahlavi Psalter, the absence of which SHAKED (1989) rightly deplores, is still a desideratum. DESMOND DURKIN-MEISTERERNST prepared what comes close to an edition for the Fourth Summer School on Pahlavi Papyrology at the Institute of Iranian Studies of the Freie Universität Berlin, September 24–28, 2012 (session on 27th Sept. at the Berlin Brandenburg

7 The Syriac psalter in Uyghur script was published by DICKENS/ZIEME (2014). HUNTER (2017, p. 79 and fn. 8) surveys the various translations of the Syriac psalter.

8 Edited by SCHWARTZ/SIMS-WILLIAMS 2014; SIMS-WILLIAMS 2004 and 2011a.

9 Edited by SUNDERMANN 1974; SIMS-WILLIAMS 2011b.

10 ANDREAS 1910, p. 869; ANDREAS/BARR 1933, plates 1–11; DURKIN-MEISTERERNST 2006, p. 3.

11 ANDREAS/BARR 1933, p. 5 fn.1; DURKIN-MEISTERERNST 2006, pp. 3–4.

Academy of Science and Humanities, Turfanforschung) and has made it freely available online (DURKIN-MEISTERERNST 2012). His work provides a Romanised transliteration of the Pahlavi text from the manuscript, together with the interlinear Syriac and Greek versions, and the English translation of the King James Bible (i.e., not a translation of the Middle Persian text). The work also includes indices of the transliterated and transcribed words and a glossary of the transcribed words with the reference, for each word, to ANDREAS/BARR's edition of 1933.

Only a few philological studies have been devoted to this text. In his 1933 edition, BARR promised a detailed study of the Psalter language and script, but, sadly, this was never published. The few published studies on individual problems include ESSABALIAN's article (in Armenian, 1942) on Armenian–Persian loanwords in the Pahlavi Psalter, ASMUSSEN's (1964) translation of Psalm 122, MACKENZIE's (1966) study of the ideograms for 'sheep' and for the verb *nimūdan* 'to show' (ideogram MḤWḤYT, Syr. *ḥawwī*), and FRYE's (1967) discussion of the reading of some heterograms. GIGNOUX (1969) examines the translation technique with a view to establishing the mother tongue of the translator. He concludes that the translator knew Middle Persian but was not a native Persian speaker. JOSEPHSON (2017) also discusses the translation technique but with a view to establishing how the translator rendered the Semitic syntactic constructions of Syriac in Middle Persian. The most detailed studies of the language of the Pahlavi Psalter are the articles by SKJÆRVØ's 1983 on case in Inscriptional Middle Persian and Parthian and in the Pahlavi Psalter and by CANTERA (1999), who argues that the grammar of the Pahlavi translation of the Avesta represents a stage of linguistic development comparable to that of the Pahlavi Psalter. SIMS-WILLIAMS (2001) established the meaning of MP *padisāy* as 'on account of, for the sake of' on the basis of the Psalter, where it translates the Syr. *mṭl* at its five attestations. He argues that *padisāy* is a calque on the Akkadian phrase *ina ṣilli ša* 'in the shadow of, under the protection of' and thus attributes a long history to the Pahlavi word. The preposition is rare in Book Pahlavi[12] and in Manichaean Middle Persian[13] and mostly occurs in older texts. It could thus be another archaic feature of the language of the Pahlavi Psalter. DURKIN-MEISTERERNST (2006) studies the relationship between the language of the Pahlavi Psalter and its Syriac sources, and FERRER LOSILLA (2012) discusses the translation of Psalm 128 on folios 7v–8r of the Pahlavi Psalter.

2. The Canons and Mār Abā

Those who used the Pahlavi Psalter were in all probability Iranians who had (or whose ancestors had) converted to Christianity from one of the religions

12 In Book Pahlavi, *padisāy*, spelt ⟨pts'y⟩, is attested, for example, in the law-book "Book of a Thousand Judgements" (MHDA 26.1), MACUCH 1981, pp. 50 (text), 188 (translation).

13 DURKIN-MEISTERERNST (2006, p.17 fn. 22) adds three further, but unpublished, Manichaean Middle Persian attestations to the eleven known to SIMS-WILLIAMS.

practised in Iran, especially Zoroastrianism. This is true, for example, of the patriarch Mār Ābā I himself, whose canons play an important role in the debate on the date of the Pahlavi Psalter. Born into a Zoroastrian family around 490 CE in the Sasanian province of Garamēgān in northern Mesopotamia east of the Tigris River,[14] Mār Ābā was fully educated in the Zoroastrian tradition and well versed in Pahlavi literature.[15] His Iranian name, however, seems to be unknown. Widely travelled to places such as Nisibis, Edessa, Antioch, Egypt, and Constantinople and highly respected by his contemporaries, he held an important position in the Zoroastrian Sasanian society of his time and continued to enjoy good relations with the King of Kings even after his conversion to Christianity.[16]

According to the Syriac Acts of the Persian Martyrs, Mār Ābā was appointed *arzabed*, a high-ranking position in the public service of the Sasanian state.[17] After his conversion, which is described in terms like that of St Paul, he entered the theological school at Nisibis, where he first learned the Psalms of David by heart before turning to the study of the other scriptures.[18] Having previously been a Zoroastrian persecutor of the Christians, he later became a Christian who was then persecuted by the Zoroastrian priests. In 540 CE Mār Ābā was appointed Catholicos of the Church of the East at Ctesiphon and held this office until his death in 552 CE.

The Pahlavi Psalter includes liturgical additions, referred to as canons, which are ascribed to Mār Ābā. The attribution of the canons to the Patriarch is based on statements found in his Syriac vita, such as the one that "he made firm the canons of the apostles in the orient" ("Er befestigte die Kanonen der Apostel im Orient").[19] The term 'canon' derives from the Syriac word *qānonā*, (pl. *qānonē*), 'canon' or 'farcing'. Of the many uses which the term has, in connection with the Pahlavi Psalter it refers to sentences which are usually inserted after the first verse of each psalm. Originally composed in Syriac and translated into Middle Persian in the Pahlavi Psalter, the canons usually give the psalm a Christian application.[20]

14 On *Garmēgān*, see MORONY 1989. The toponym is also attested on Sasanian administrative seals; see GYSELEN 2019, p.81.

15 LIEU 1992, p. 52. HUTTER (2003) discusses two Zoroastrian customs that lived on among Iranian Christians and Mār Ābā's opposition against these customs. On the legal proceedings against the Catholicos and the accusations of the Zoroastrian priesthood see MACUCH 2014.

16 BROCK 1982, p. 5.

17 BRAUN 1915, p. 188; HUTTER 2003, p. 167 and fn.5. On this title see MACUCH 2014, pp. 47–49, with further references.

18 BRAUN 1915, p. 191. HUNTER (2017, p. 79 fn. 7) quotes a similar story reported in another Syriac source according to which converted "Magians" were taught "the psalms and hymns".

19 BRAUN 1915, p. 195; BAUMSTARK 1922, p. 120 and fn. 7. Two types of canons are attributed to Mār Ābā: one is the insertions at the beginning of each of the psalms. The other, edited and translated by CHABOT (1902, pp. 318–351) consists of 40 canons Mār Ābā issued during an itinerant synod in 544 CE when he visited several dioceses, see VAN ROMPAY 2011.

20 MACLEAN 1894, p. xvii. On the Syriac text of the canons see DICKENS 2013a, p. 359 and fn. 13.

The headings of the psalms and the canons are written in red ink while the text of the psalms is written in black ink. The headings usually consist of the psalm number written in Pahlavi numerals. For example, on fol. 5 verso, which provides the Pahlavi version of Psalm 122.4–124.1, line 2 gives the heading of Psalm 123 and line 18 that of Psalm 124 in red ink. The canons are also written in red ink in lines 5–6 and inserted into verse 2 of Psalm 123. Verse 2 and the canon at the beginning of Psalm 123 read as illustrated in Figure 1.

Fig. 1. Pahlavi Psalter fol. 5v lines 4–6.

4 ʾdyl[y][21]. (Ps. 123.2:) ḤT-mṅ Lʾ MH MRWḤY YKʿY̤MWN-t
5 ḤWH-[d.] (Canon in red ink): ʾplyny ʾYTy kwnʾkl-mn MNW bwcẏt
6 ʿL-š [nm](ʾ)cblʾn MN bcklʾn (Ps. 123.2 contd.:) ʾMT-mʾn

4 *i(srā)yēl* (Ps. 123.2:) *agar-mān nē čē xwadāy ēstād*
5 *hād* (Canon in red ink): *āfrīn ast kōnāgar-mān kē bōzēd*
6 *ō-š namāzbarān az bazzakkarān* (Ps. 123.2 contd.:) *ka-mān*

4 Israel. (Ps. 123.2:) If it had not been the Lord who was on our side,
5 (Canon in red ink:) Praise belongs to our maker who saves
6 those who honour him from their sins. (Ps. 123.2 cont.:) When (against) us …

3. Middle Persian Translations of Biblical Texts

As already noted by ANDREAS in 1910, the presence of the canons in the Psalter warrants that the text in its present form post-dates Mār Ābā's death in 552 CE. While DICKENS (2013a, pp. 365–37) has identified at least six Syriac Turfan psalters which include the canons, of all the non-Syriac psalters found at Turfan, the Pahlavi Psalter is the only one that includes the psalm canons, translated from Syriac into Middle Persian. This has been interpreted as indicating that the Middle Persian translation was made in a Syriac-Persian community in Persia. At any rate, considering his grounding in the Zoroastrian tradition, Mār Ābā

21 SCHAEDER (1935, p. 374) regards the spelling ⟨ʾdyly⟩ as a transcription of a Syriac equivalent of the Greek abbreviation $\overline{\iota\eta\lambda}$, for Ἰσραήλ (reference kindly provided by NICHOLAS SIMS-WILLIAMS).

himself must have been a Persian speaker. The connection between the Pahlavi Psalter and Syriac Christianity is beyond question and is reinforced by the observation of DURKIN-MEISTERERNST (2006, p. 2) that there are indications suggesting that the Pahlavi translation of the psalter was meant to be read in conjunction with the Syriac original.

However, the Middle Persian translation of the psalms and that of the canons are not necessarily of the same date, since the canons could have been added to an already existing Pahlavi version. It is thus possible that the Pahlavi translation of the psalter is much older than the canons and that the canons are later additions to the Pahlavi text. According to SKJÆRVØ, the Pahlavi of the canons bears traces of a later language stage. This would be indicated by plurals ending in *-ān*, which are a later development and which, apart from two instances, all occur in the canons. He opts for a fourth century CE date for the translation of the Pahlavi Psalter, based on extensive agreement between the grammar and orthography of it and the Middle Persian inscriptions of the 3rd century CE.[22] In SKJÆRVØ's view, the psalter was translated from Syriac into Middle Persian in the 3rd–4th century CE, when the text was written down in the form of the Pahlavi script current at that time. The text would then have been copied and re-copied in the form of that script, which over the centuries became archaic. The surviving text from Turfan would be a sixth century copy, written in the (by then) archaic script of the early Sasanian period. In the view of SKJÆRVØ (1983, p. 179), the translator of the Pahlavi Psalter was a native Persian speaker. He disagrees on this point with GIGNOUX (1969, p. 244), according to whom the translator was a member of the Church of the East whose mother tongue was not Middle Persian.

On the basis of Greek and other literary sources, ASMUSSEN and PAPER (1977, p. 5) argue for an early Sasanian date of Middle Persian versions of biblical texts. One of the earliest witnesses is found in the writings of the Antiochian theologian Theodoret of Cyrrhus, who lived in the fifth century CE, about a hundred years before Mār Ābā. Theodoret mentions a translation of the Bible into the language of the Persians alongside translations into the languages of the Romans, Egyptians, Armenians, Scythians, and Sauromatians.[23] Moreover, the existence of Sasanian versions of biblical texts may be inferred from quotations contained in the Middle Persian apologetic work *Škand-gumānīg Wizār*, or 'Doubt-dispelling exposition' by the ninth-century author Mardān Farrox, son of Ohrmazddād, who, in his criticism of Judaism and Christianity, quotes extensively from the Bible. Unfortunately, these quotations contain few clues to allow further identification of the translations which the Middle Persian Zoroastrian theologian used.[24]

22 SKJÆRVØ 1983, pp. 48, 178–179.
23 ASMUSSEN/PAPER (1977, p. 5) referring to Migne, Patrologia Graeca 83, Paris 1859, cols. 947f.
24 See DE MENASCE 1945, pp. 177f. SIMS-WILLIAMS (2009, pp. 266–270) provides a survey, with references, of translations of biblical texts into Middle Persian.

4. The Paper of the Pahlavi Psalter

Apart from the *terminus post quem* for the date of the Pahlavi Psalter, provided by the presence of the canons of Mār Ābā, a second *terminus post quem* comes from the material on which the text is written: paper. Paper was invented in China in the second century BCE, possibly earlier.[25] Chinese paper was principally made from bast fibres collected directly from semi-tropical plants and shrubs, especially from the paper mulberry tree, whose inner bark yields a fibre suitable for papermaking.[26] This was particularly the technology used to produce paper in the north-western province of Gansu at the eastern end of the Silk Road, which linked China to the western countries. Paper was one of many commodities that were traded along the Central Asian Silk Roads,[27] whose rise coincided with the Han dynasty (206 BCE–220 CE) in China and with the appearance of paper as a new writing material.[28] HELMAN-WAŻNY (2021, p. 425) suggests that the increase of paper production could have coincided with the increase of the production of silk, since both commodities required the cultivation of the mulberry tree. Although the paper mulberry could also grow in the desert oases of Central Asia, it was used there for silk production, which was more profitable, rather than papermaking.[29] In general, in the arid climate of Central Asia, paper was predominantly made out of fibres that had already been processed and bleached in the sun, in particular from the cellulose in linen and cotton rags, old rope, and other textile waste.[30]

Up to the early twentieth century, the history of papermaking was chiefly based on literary sources, predominantly Arab accounts. According to one of these accounts, first reported by the court encyclopaedist and anthologist ʿAbd-al-Malek Moḥammad Ṯaʿālebi (died 1038 CE),[31] the Arabs learned the technology of papermaking from two Chinese prisoners of war captured in the battle at the Talas river in 751 CE.[32] It would have been the Arabs who invented the production of paper from rags,[33] i.e. the technology which spread westwards to the Arab world via Samarkand, with the first paper mill built in Baghdad in 793, making it current in Central Asia, Sasanian Iran and all over the Middle East, North Africa and Europe.

25 LOVEDAY 2001, pp. 17, 27 n.1; BLOOM 2017a, p. 54.
26 TSIEN 1985, pp. 52–64; 2004, pp. 145–148; BLOOM 2017a, p. 58.
27 HOERNLE 1903, pp. 675–676.
28 HELMAN-WAŻNY 2021, p. 425 and fig.1 (map).
29 HELMAN-WAŻNY 2021, p. 431.
30 BLOOM 2017a, pp. 52, 58.
31 BLOOM 2017b.
32 HUNTER 1947, pp. 60, 139, 233–234; DICKENS 2013b, p .7; TSIEN 1985, pp. 296 and fn. c, 297 and fn. e, critically evaluates that story and points out that Chinese sources record several prisoners who were craftsmen, but no papermakers. RUSTOW (2020, p. 116–117 and p. 472 notes 12–18) discusses the Arabic source in detail.
33 TSIEN 1985, pp. 11, 293; 2004, p. 154.

However, the scholarly account of the transmission of the papermaking technology from China to Central Asia changed with the British, German, French and Chinese expeditions to Central Asia in the early twentieth century and the discovery of vast numbers of documents written on paper, birch bark, and wood. Christian, Manichaean, Buddhist, and other communities used paper to write texts in languages including Sogdian, Middle Persian, Turkic and Tocharian. These documents date from the third to the thirteenth century CE.[34] They include the Pahlavi Psalter and the Sogdian Ancient Letters. The latter date from the early 4th century CE and were discovered in 1907 in the ruined watchtower T.XII.a of the Chinese Wall west of Dunhuang in Gansu Province, China.[35]

These discoveries enabled scholars to examine the paper of Central Asian documents directly, and this has led to a picture that is quite different from the one given in the Arabic accounts. One of the pioneers in the study of Central Asian paper was the botanist JULIUS RITTER VON WIESNER. Sir MARC AUREL STEIN, who had led the British excavations, provided VON WIESNER with specimens of documents whose language ROBERT GAUTHIOT identified as Sogdian in 1911.[36] VON WIESNER examined the signatures T.XII.a.ii.1, T.XII.a.ii.1a and T.XII.a.ii.4, which are the signatures of the Sogdian Ancient Letters no.1 and no.4, in his seminal study of 1911.[37] He concluded that their paper was made from both pure plant and rag pulp, and he pointedly noted, "We doubtless have the Chinese to thank for the original use of rags in the production of paper between the fourth and eighth century".[38] His work has demonstrated that the Chinese already used rags as well as pure plants to produce paper.

A small number of European and Chinese scholars subsequently studied the Dunhuang papers preserved at the British Museum and in Peking.[39] It was, however, not until more recent decades that research on the materiality of written artefacts from Central Asia and further East was resumed in a way that drew on expertise from different disciplines, including the humanities, conservation studies, technology, statistics, and the natural sciences. Thus, the project *Khartasia*

34 HELMAN-WAŻNY 2021, p. 424.

35 SIMS-WILLIAMS 2023, p. 25.

36 GAUTHIOT 1911. STEIN (1921, 5, pp. 675–676) describes the history of the identification of the script and language of the Ancient Letters.

37 RISCHEL 2014, pp. 33–37. Of T.XII.a.ii.1a, which VON WIESNER describes as the oldest of these documents, Sir AUREL STEIN had sent him a paper strip of 10 x 4 cm with no writing on it (VON WIESNER 1911, p. 13). REICHELT (1931, p. 1) shows awareness of the results of VON WIESNER's studies when he refers to the paper of the Ancient Letters as Chinese "Hadernpapier" (rag paper), although VON WIESNER's work is not referenced.

38 VON WIESNER 1911, p. 9, transl. RISCHEL 2020, p. 373. GRENET/SIMS-WILLIAMS 1987, pp. 104–106 refer to VON WIESNER's work and quote the result of an examination of the paper of Ancient Letters 1 and 4 by JEAN-PIERRE DRÈGE of the École française d'Extrême-Orient in Paris. They confirm HENNING's dating of the Sogdian Ancient Letters to shortly after 311 CE (p.115).

39 For references, see TSIEN 1985, p. 11.

under CLAUDE LAROQUE at the Centre de Recherche sur la Conservation des Collections (2010) and, later, with funding from Paris I Panthéon-Sorbonne University, examined paper manufacture in China, Korea, and Japan. At about the same time, MICHAEL FRIEDRICH of the Centre for the Study of Manuscript Cultures, University of Hamburg directed the project "History and typology of paper in Central Asia during the first millennium AD: Analysis of Chinese paper manuscripts" (2010–2013) in cooperation with the Turfan Project at the Berlin Brandenburg Academy of Sciences and Humanities and the International Dunhuang Project, British Library (London). The fourth cooperation partner was the Federal Institute for Materials Research and Testing (BAM, Berlin), where scholars examined "The Writing Materials of the Silk Road Cultures in Turfan: An Analysis of Inks and Pigments" (Das Schreibmaterial der Seidenstraßenkulturen in Turfan: Analyse von Tuschen und Pigmenten).[40] Moreover, in 2018–2023, GEORGES PINAULT and his team analysed the paper of Tocharian manuscripts in the project "History of the Tocharian texts of the Pelliot Collection" (HisTochText).

These and other projects have changed our understanding of papermaking in Central Asia and thus of the history of paper. It has emerged that the Chinese were making paper from recycled rag fibres as well as from pure plant fibres already in the early centuries of the Christian era. The Arabs thus learned a technology that had already been fully developed and widely practised in Central Asia for many centuries by the time they arrived there.[41] While paper was widely used by merchants and missionaries throughout Central Asia in pre-Islamic times, there is, however, hardly any evidence that papermaking technology was available in the Sasanian heartlands and the royal power centres, where parchment and (in Egypt) papyrus were the main writing materials. It was only after the arrival of the Arabs that papermaking technology spread from Central Asia to Iran, and from there throughout the Abbasid Empire and later to other lands.[42]

In 2009, in connection with the research of the Turfan Project in Berlin, ANNA-GRETHE RISCHEL examined, both macroscopically and microscopically, the paper of 314 Turfan fragments kept at the Turfan collection. These fragments included specimens from folios 6 and 7 of the Pahlavi Psalter. While the results of the complete analysis of all 314 fragments currently only exist in the form of an unpublished Excel file, RISCHEL presents the results of her analysis of the Pahlavi Psalter in her contribution to this volume. She concludes that the paper of the two folios of the Pahlavi Psalter consists of recycled hemp and flax fibres (Fibre material Ps 6: Recycled hemp/flax fibres, Ps 7: Recycled hemp/flax fibres).[43]

40 NÖLLER/HELMAN-WAŻNY 2013; DURKIN-MEISTERERNST *et al.* 2016b; DICKENS 2013b, p. 8 and p. 21, n. 39.

41 STEIN 1921, 2, pp. 672–673 and fn. 17; BLOOM 2001, pp. 38, 42–45; RUSTOW 2020, p. 117.

42 BLOOM 2017b; LOVEDAY 2001, p. 20.

43 The abbreviation Ps, which stands for "psalter", is here equivalent to folio. I am grateful to SIMONE-CHRISTIANE RASCHMANN for drawing my attention to ANNA-GRETHE RISCHEL's work.

In other words, the paper was made of rags. Of the 314 Turfan paper documents examined, RISCHEL (2012) published the results of 62 Old Turkish manuscripts. She concludes that mixtures "of two or more types of recycled ramie-, hemp- and flax fibres, sometimes with addition of new mulberry and grass-fibres, are characteristic of the early Central Asian paper production". She also notes that "from the 5th century, Chinese papermakers concentrated their production on new bast fibres from local plants as fibre material. This technological development was naturally spread eastwards to the local production of paper in Korea and Japan and westwards along the Silk Road. However, characteristic for the paper in the Turfan Collection is a dominance of recycled textile fibres compared to the presence of pure new plant fibres."[44]

Thus, in principle, the composition of the paper suggests that the Pahlavi Psalter could have been copied as early as the 4th century CE, which is the date of the earliest documents found in the Turfan oasis. In 2008 DIETER WEBER arranged for a radiocarbon C14 analysis of the paper of the Pahlavi Psalter to obtain a more precise date for the paper. For this purpose, a small portion of paper bearing no writing was taken from folio 7 of the manuscript. The investigation was carried out by Professor PIETER M. GROOTES of the Institute for Ecosystem Research in the University of Kiel. I am very grateful to DIETER WEBER for giving me permission to publish here the report, which includes the graph reproduced below in Fig. 2 together with its interpretation by PIETER M. GROOTES and DIETER WEBER's own conclusion. The graph and explanation comes from DIETER WEBER's work, currently in preparation, on the history of the Pahlavi script. According to GROOTES's explanation, the graph shows the relative probability of the date when the fibres of the paper could have been formed by photosynthesis from atmospheric CO_2. There is a probability at the points where the curve rises from the base line (x-axis). The greatest probability is at the three peaks, although this remains only a possibility. The third, lower, peak in 921–944 CE is also a possibility, but only has a 5.7% probability.[45]

On the basis of this C14 analysis, DIETER WEBER concludes:

> "Regarding this information it seems safe to say that the paper of the Psalter must have been manufactured by the end of the 9th century (with a small possibility of having been made even somewhat later). Therefore, the Psalter itself could have been written only afterwards, i.e. in the 10th century."

44 RISCHEL 2012, p. 267.

45 The German wording of Professor GROOTES's explanation is as follows: "Die Kurve stellt die relative Wahrscheinlichkeit dar, daß das Grundmaterial des datierten Papiers in einem bestimmten Jahr durch Photosynthese aus atmosphärischem CO_2 gebildet wurde. Überall wo die Kurve sich von der X-Achse anhebt, gibt es also eine Wahrscheinlichkeit. Am größten ist diese während der drei „peak" Intervalle. Man kann aber nicht kategorisch sagen, daß das Material aus dieser Zeit stammt. Die Ausbuchtung AD 921–944 ist eben auch eine Periode, wann das Material gewachsen sein kann; es hat allerdings nur 5,7% Wahrscheinlichkeit."

Papier - Turfan

KIA37517

Papier, Buyaliq, Oase Turfan (Uigurisches Autonomes Gebiet Xinjiang im Westen der Volksrepublik China), sampled by submitter.

Fraktion	PMC (korrigiert)†	Radiokarbonalter	$d^{13}C$(‰)p̄
Papier, Laugenrückstand, 2.5 mg C	86.34 ± 0.28	1180 ± 25 BP	-21.40 ± 0.20

Radiocarbon Age:	BP	1180 ± 26
One Sigma Range:	cal AD	782 - 789 (Probability 6.8 %)
(Probability 68,3 %)		810 - 848 (Probability 32.1 %)
		853 - 887 (Probability 29.4 %)
Two Sigma Range:	cal AD	774 - 898 (Probability 89.7 %)
(Probability 95,4 %)		921 - 944 (Probability 5.7 %)

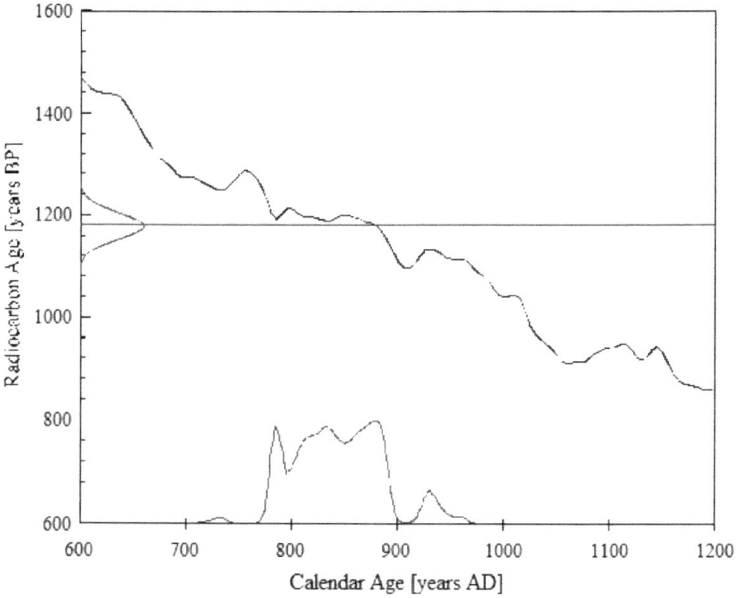

Fig. 2. Result of the C14 analysis of the Pahlavi psalter initiated by WEBER in 2008

Thus, the C14 dating suggests that the paper of the Pahlavi Psalter was manufactured in the ninth century CE, or in the late 8th century at the earliest.[46] Its language and script, however, are much older, as suggested by SKJÆRVØ's linguistic studies (1983).

46 SIMS-WILLIAMS (2022, p. 60 and fn. 19) also suggests these dates with reference to a personal communication by DIETER WEBER.

5. The Processional Cross from Herāt

In contrast to the Manichaean script, which has remained unchanged since its invention, the Pahlavi script continued to develop during the Middle Iranian period. The shapes of the letters of the Pahlavi script allow us to distinguish three phases: inscriptional, Psalter and Book Pahlavi. The Pahlavi script of the Psalter is more like the script of the inscriptions than like the cursive ductus of the Pahlavi books. Thus, the alphabet of the Psalter contains 18 distinct characters as compared to Book Pahlavi, which has only 14. The Psalter script distinguishes ⟨d⟩, ⟨g⟩ and ⟨y⟩; ⟨ḥ⟩/⟨h⟩ and ⟨ʾ⟩; ⟨w⟩ and ⟨n⟩; and *tsāde* ⟨c⟩ has a special shape. As in the Middle Persian inscriptions, in Persian words the character *ḥēth* is used for both the voiceless velar fricative [x] and the voiceless glottal fricative [h], e.g. fol. 6r line 9 ⟨ḥwhly⟩ / xwahl/ 'bent, crooked' (Fig. 3). The character is transliterated here as ⟨ḥ⟩ or ⟨h⟩ according to the expected value.

Fig. 3.

Throughout the twentieth century, the Pahlavi Psalter was the only witness for this form of the script. The situation changed in 2000, when MICHEL VAN ESBROECK, the distinguished scholar of Eastern Christianity, drew the attention of PHILIPPE GIGNOUX to an inscribed cross in the private possession of the collector of Byzantine art Dr CHRISTIAN SCHMIDT in Munich.[47] The cross measures 18.3×14.1 cm. The upper vertical arm of the cross was broken off and lost, leaving the lower three arms and a base with an inverted cup with holes for attaching a wooden pole or a stand with nails. The upper vertical arm has now been restored. The cross is inscribed on both sides in the same type of writing as the Pahlavi Psalter, as already recognised by MICHEL VAN ESBROECK (GIGNOUX 2001a, pp. 291–292). In 2001, GIGNOUX published images and drawings of the cross and the inscription with a commentary. I am grateful to the late Professor GIGNOUX for kindly providing me with high-resolution images of the cross when I was first working on it in 2015 and to Dr IGLESIA Y NIKOLAUS of the Diözesanmuseum Freising for sending me new photographs in 2023. The latter images, taken by MICHAEL HOPF of the Diözesanmuseum Freising, are reproduced below with the kind permission of the museum. For while the letters are clear in the tracings published by GIGNOUX (2001, p. 304, reproduced below, Fig. 6), the letters are less clear in the photographs on pp. 302–303.

47 In 2023 Dr CHRISTIAN SCHMIDT donated the Herāt cross together with other parts of his substantial collection of Byzantine art to the Diözesanmuseum Freising, which now houses the cross. Dr SCHMIDT passed away on 20 September 2023. I am grateful to Dr ANNA-LAURA DE LA IGLESIA Y NIKOLAUS of the Diözesanmuseum Freising for providing this information.

Fig. 4. Herāt Cross recto. Diözesanmuseum Freising, photo: MICHAEL HOPF.

Fig. 5. Herāt Cross verso. Diözesanmuseum Freising, photo: MICHAEL HOPF.

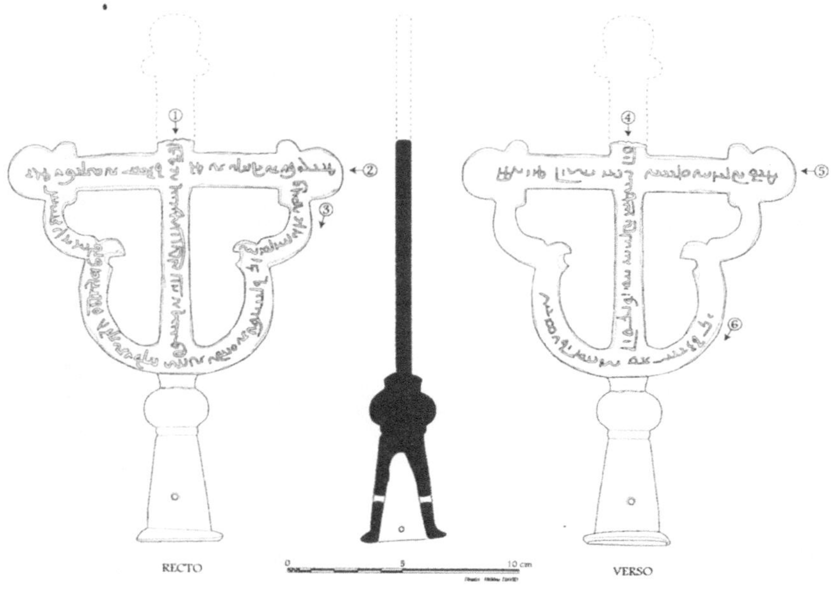

Fig. 6. Drawings of the cross from Herāt in GIGNOUX 2001a, p.304 (© PH. GIGNOUX)

The inscription mentions a date of an unspecified era, which GIGNOUX (2001a: 292–293, 297) reads as 507 or 517. He suggests that the date could refer to the Bactrian era. In the most recent discussion of the extensive debate on the beginning of the Bactrian era, SIMS-WILLIAMS/DE BLOIS (2018, pp. 9–11 and 30–44) reaffirm DE BLOIS's (2006) conclusion that the beginning of the Bactrian era coincides with that of the Sasanian era, marked by the accession to the throne of Ardašir I on Nowruz on 2 October 223. Considering that Herāt was counted among the provincial capital towns of the Sasanian Empire,[48] it is also conceivable that the era referred to on the cross is actually the Sasanian era. Since the beginning of the Bactrian and Sasanian eras coincides, the date on the Herāt Cross would be 730 or 740 CE.

Although the text contains several words that have not yet been fully understood, some aspects of the content is clear. The front side records that a certain Mārē from the church of Herāt, donated (*dād*) an object[49] to the Church[50] in the year 507 or 517 CE of that unspecified era. The back of the object presents a theological formula affirming that there are not three 'creators' and

48 Herāt is mentioned alongside Merw in §12 of the Pahlavi text *Šahrestānīhā ī Ērānšahr* as one of the provincial capitals located in the eastern part of the empire; see DARYAEE 2002, pp. 13, 18, 37.
49 The reading and interpretation of this word is unclear; see below, fn. 55.
50 See below, fn. 56.

concludes with a wish for the prosperity of this church. GIGNOUX's edition of this inscription has much facilitated the text provided below. Words which are here interpreted differently are discussed in the footnotes.

Recto

Fig. 7. Herāt Cross, recto, line 1. Diözesanmuseum Freising, photo: MICHAEL HOPF.

(1) ⟨... bd]k ZY nšyymy bwrcly BRH ZY n'yzdp⟩
(1) /... bad]ag ī nišēm-burzar pus ī ⁺nāypazd(?)/
(1) ...bad]ag, son of Nišēm-burzar[51], the flute-player(?).[52]

Fig. 8. Herāt Cross, recto, line 2. Diözesanmuseum Freising, photo: MICHAEL HOPF.

51 GIGNOUX (2003, p. 52 no. 255) comments that there is no clear etymology of the two parts of this name.

52 GIGNOUX (2001a, pp. 293–294) transliterates the last word of line 1 as ⟨nyšyd-c⟩ and transcribes it as /nīšēd-iz/. He translates this line as '... badag, fils de Nišēm-burzar, qui (voit/écrit) aussi.' Pointing out the difficulties with reading the last word, he considers it to be a verbal form which, however, should be spelt with the ending ⟨yt⟩ in Pahlavi. He therefore suggests an early New Persian, rather than Middle Persian, spelling. Commenting that a form of the verb *nīš-* 'to see' makes little sense in the context of this line, he suggests that it would be preferable to read /nibēsēd-iz/, from the verb *nibištan*, *nibēs-* 'to write', but admits that there is little support for such a reading in the way the word is written. Considering these difficulties, a different reading emerges if the second letter is read as *aleph* and the third letter as *yōd*, which seems to be followed by a very small *zayin*. The following letter is clearly a *dāleth* and the last letter could possibly be a *pē* rather than *tsāde* as GIGNOUX suggests. This would result in the reading ⟨n'yzdp⟩, a word which makes no sense. The only way to give meaning to such a reading is if one assumes a spelling error for ⟨n'ypzd⟩ /nāypazd/ 'flute-player' (DURKIN-MEISTERERNST 2004, p. 238; NYBERG 1974, p. 135). The assumption of a spelling error could explain the rather awkwardly written ⟨p⟩ at the end of the word, where is appears to have been added as an afterthought. One would have to assume that the engraver first wrote ⟨n'yzd⟩ and then realised that he had made a mistake and added the letter ⟨p⟩ at the end of the word rather than before ⟨zd⟩. Furthermore, one must assume that the first term of the compound is spelt phonetically rather than in the historical Pahlavi spelling ⟨n'd⟩ /nāy/ 'tube, flute'. While there are also other instances of phonetic rather than historical spellings in this inscription (in particular ⟨'prydgl⟩ /āfrīdgar/ 'creator'), the assumption of a spelling error remains hypothetical.

(2) ⟨m'lydy ZY gn'ly (or yn'ly) ZY MN knš'[53] ZY hlydy MNW⟩
(2) / Mārē ī gn'ly (or yn'ly) ī az kenšā ī Harēy kē/
(2) Mārē[54] son of (?) gn'ly (or yn'ly), who (is) of the congregation of Herāt, who

Fig. 9. Herāt Cross, recto, line 3 part 1. Diözesanmuseum Freising, photo: MICHAEL HOPF.

(3 part 1) ⟨d'ty ZNH lyywlmyh 'L klysydy ZY p'ky ZY⟩
(3 part 1) /dād ēn lyywlmyh ō karisē ī pāk ī/
(3 part 1) gave this lyywlmyh[55] to the Church,[56] the holy,

53 GIGNOUX (2001a, p. 293–294) transliterates this word as ⟨knyšy⟩ in line 2 and as ⟨knšyy⟩ in line 6 on the verso side of the cross. He transcribes /kanīš/ in line 2, but /kaniš/ in line 6 and translates both attestations as 'l'Eglise'. On p.295 he comments that an alternative reading would be ⟨knšy⟩. The letter after ⟨kn⟩ looks indeed more like ⟨š⟩ than ⟨y⟩. As NICHOLAS SIMS-WILLIAMS kindly points out to me, both words are best read as ⟨knš'⟩, a loanword from Syriac ⟨knš'⟩ */kenšā/* 'assembly, community', on which see SIMS-WILLIAMS 2021, pp. 35, 303.

54 GIGNOUX (2001a, p. 295) notes that the spelling ⟨m'lydy⟩ of this name has previously been recognised by SHAKED (1995, pp. 248–249 no. 28) on a Christian seal.

55 GIGNOUX (2001a, p. 293) transliterates this and the preceding word as ⟨ZNH 'ywlmyḥ⟩ and transcribes and translates them as /ēn ēw-ramīh/ 'ce (même) troupeaux'. On p. 296 he comments that the reading ⟨'ywlmyḥ⟩ appears to be certain to him, although a compound *ēw-ramīh* is not found elsewhere. It would refer to the Christian community of Herāt. However, it appears that the reading proposed by GIGNOUX is not the only possibility. The first character could also be read as *lāmed* and the second letter as *aleph* or as two *yōd* or as *sāmekh*. Accordingly, one could read ⟨l'wlmyh⟩, ⟨lyywlmyh⟩ or ⟨lswlmyh⟩, but there is no clear interpretation for any of these readings. I therefore prefer to leave this word without an interpretation. Considering the context, one would expect a reference to the cross which bears this inscription, as NICHOLAS SIMS-WILLIAMS suggested to me. One could perhaps read /rēwramīh/ with *rēw* < OIr. **raiu̯a-* 'splendent', Av. *raēuua-* (BARTHOLOMAE 1904, col. 1484; NYBERG 1974, p. 169), which also forms the first term of Middle Persian personal names. The word /rēwīh/ 'wealth', spelt ⟨lywyh⟩, is found in line 5.

56 GIGNOUX (2001a, p.293) transliterates and transcribes this word as ⟨klssdy⟩ /karisisē/. On p. 296 he comments that he regards this as a personal name of Syriac origin and compares Syriac *kryss*, which is the name of a martyr and which has been interpreted as *Charisius*. However, more plausible is the proposal of SIMS-WILLIAMS (personal communication), who suggests reading the word as ⟨klysydy⟩ and interpreting it as a rendering, via Syriac, of Greek *ecclesia* 'Church'. MARK DICKENS (personal communication) reminded me of New Persian كليسا for 'church'.

Fig. 10. Herāt Cross, recto, line 3 part 2. Diözesanmuseum Freising, photo: MICHAEL HOPF.

(3 part 2) ⟨'ḥ'lky ZY zlnyn[57] PWN ŠNT-dyk 507 (or 517)⟩
(3 part 2) / 'ḥ'lky ī zarnēn pad sālīg 507 (or 517)/
(3 part 2) the 'ḥ'lky[58], the golden, in the year 507 (or 517).

Verso

Fig. 11. Herāt Cross, verso, line 4. Diözesanmuseum Freising, photo: MICHAEL HOPF.

(4)) ⟨ ...] PWN 'sm'n-c L' 3 'prydgl PWN⟩
(4) / ...] pad asmān-iz nē sē āfrīdgar pad/
(4) in heaven (there are) not three creators, (and) on

Fig. 12. Herāt Cross, verso, line 5. Diözesanmuseum Freising, photo: MICHAEL HOPF.

57 GIGNOUX (2001a, pp. 293, 296) transliterates this word as ⟨zln(yn)⟩ but omits it in his transcription (p. 294) and refrains from translating it. In his commentary (p. 296), however, he suggests a connection with Middle Persian *zarrēn* 'golden'. The reading of the last two characters of this word is uncertain, but if the transliteration ⟨zlnyn⟩ is correct, then this word would be identical with Parthian *zarnēn* 'golden', on which see DURKIN-MEISTERERNST 2004, p. 384; BOYCE 1977, p. 104.

58 As GIGNOUX (2001a, p. 296) notes, the word is probably a further attribute of *karisē*. Reading the first letter as *aleph*, he suggests that the word could be formed with a privative *a-* at the beginning, but refrains from a further analysis. The first letter could possibly also be read as *sāmekh*, but no interpretation emerges.

(5) ⟨zmyk-c lywyh plšh ʾy YḤWWN myyhmn⟩
(5) /zamīg-iz rēwīh frašīh ē baw mehmān/
(5) earth wealth and perfection may be the dwelling

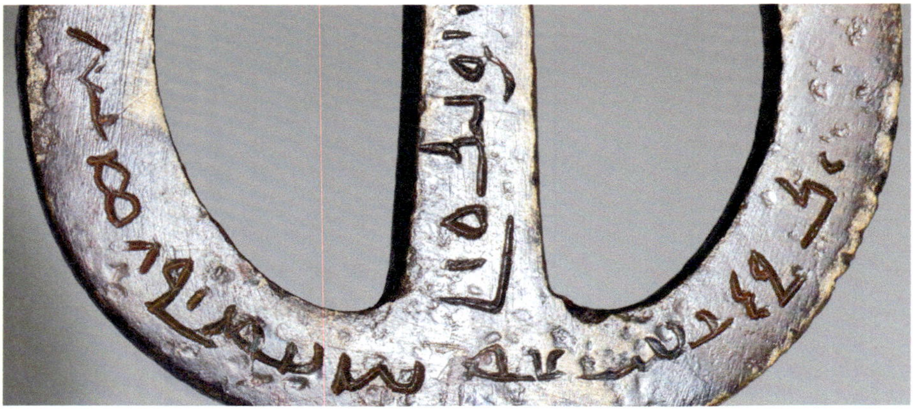

Fig. 13. Herāt Cross, verso, line 6. Diözesanmuseum Freising, photo: MICHAEL HOPF.

(6) ⟨ʿL knšʾ ZY-m hw ʾmwk ∧ pt ∧∧⟩
(6) /ō kenšā ī-m hu-ammōg ∧ pt ∧∧
(6) for the congregation of my good teaching ∧ pt ∧∧[59].

As GIGNOUX (2001a, p. 291–292 and 2001b) notes, the script of the Processional Cross from Herāt shows the same characteristics as that of the Pahlavi Psalter:

1. the letter ⟨d⟩ has not merged with ⟨g⟩ and ⟨y⟩ but has the same form as the ⟨d⟩ of the Pahlavi Psalter and of the Avestan script.
2. The letter ⟨k⟩ is distinct, with a line towards the right at the bottom.
3. The letter ⟨n⟩ is distinctly characterised by a line to the right at the bottom, although it occasionally has the same form as the ⟨n⟩ of the inscriptions. The latter ⟨n⟩ is similar to the character ⟨ń⟩ of the Avestan script.
4. The character *tsāde* ⟨c⟩ has the same form as in the Psalter and is identical with the letter ⟨j⟩ of the Avestan script.
5. The letter ⟨ḥ⟩ (*ḥēth*) has the same form as in the Psalter. It is used for both /x/ and /h/ and has not merged with aleph.

GIGNOUX (2001a, p. 291 and 2001b) describes the cross as a considerable source for the very poorly documented Christian history of Herāt. The city was represented by a bishop at synods in 424, 486 and 497 CE alongside Merw, and

59 The characters ⟨pt⟩ are legible. They appear to be preceded and followed by graphic signs. GIGNOUX (2001a, p. 297) suggests that they represent a sort of monogram.

some of the names of Herāt's bishops and clergymen are Iranian.[60] GIGNOUX (2001a, p. 297) notes that the way faith in a single god is expressed echoes a passage in the Acts of Mār Mārī. Regarding the theological affiliation of the Herāt community, JULLIEN (2011, pp. 182–186) discusses the historical context of the Herāt cross and proposes that theological teachings expressed in the short inscription point to a Melkite Christian community, whose presence in Herāt would result from two deportations of Christians, one of them in 609 CE from Edessa to Herāt.[61] On the basis of the little evidence available, it is, however, difficult to be sure to which denomination the Christian community which used the Processional Cross from Herāt belonged. That the cross is a local production is indicated by the name of Herāt, which occurs in line 2 of the inscription.

6. Concluding Remarks

The Processional Cross from Herāt and the Pahlavi Psalter provide evidence that the more archaic ductus of the Pahlavi script was still in use in the eighth and tenth centuries and well into the time when the Pahlavi cursive script was common among Persian speakers. We thus have evidence that the Christians of the East adhered to the archaic style of the Pahlavi script at least up to the tenth century. That the archaic ductus was also known in Western Iran during the late Sasanian period is indicated by the Avestan script, which includes some of the same characters. However, the presence of the *Farhang-ī Pahlavīg* in Turfan shows that the cursive form of the Pahlavi script was also known, and possibly used, in Central Asia.

During the Sasanian period, Middle Iranian and Syriac speaking Manichaeans and Christians of Syria, Mesopotamia and Western Iran mainly used parchment in their book cultures and copies must have been expensive and rare until the Arabs spread the use of paper from Central Asia to Western Iran and beyond. The ancestor manuscript of our Pahlavi Psalter, whose language and script points towards the third or fourth century CE, is likely to have existed in the form of a valuable parchment manuscript in a Persian speaking Christian community of Sasanian Western Iran. That the Pahlavi Psalter has its origins in Western Iran among Iranians of the East Syrian Christian tradition is indicated by the Syriac punctuation, the canons of Mār Ābā and by Syriac characters inserted in the manuscript before the Middle Persian version, possibly indicating the points where the Syriac version should be read, as DURKIN-MEISTERERNST (2006a) has suggested. It is conceivable that the ancestor manuscript made its way to Eastern Iran with the deportation of Christians, as JULLIEN suggests. When paper became more widely available the Pahlavi Psalter was copied in the late ninth or tenth century on Central Asian or Chinese paper, but in the ancient

60 GIGNOUX 2021a, pp. 299–300; FIEY 1973, pp. 89–90; HUNTER 1992, p. 364.
61 On the deportation, see KETTENHOFEN 1994, p. 300; GIGNOUX 2001a, p. 300 and fn. 37.

script, the scribe imitating the ductus of the original which he was copying. The Herāt Cross shows that the archaic script was still in use in Christian communities of the eighth century CE.

DURKIN-MEISTERERNST (2016b) suggests that the manuscript of the extant Pahlavi Psalter may have been copied in Herāt and taken from there to Turfan, possibly as the personal copy of a priest or of a merchant. Although the postulated origin of the manuscript in Herāt remains hypothetical, that manuscripts were taken from one place to another has also been suggested for other texts. Thus, according to HUNTER/COAKLEY (2017, p. 16) the Syriac codex MIK III 45, which is the manuscript of a service book of the Church of the East, was likely taken from Merw to Turfan. There the Pahlavi Psalter was eventually buried and remained so until it was unearthed in 1905 by the team of the Turfan expedition.

Bilbliography

ANDREAS, F.C. 1910: "Bruchstücke einer Pehlevi-Übersetzung der Psalmen aus der Sasanidenzeit." In: *Sitzungsberichte der Preussischen Akademie der Wissenschaften*, pp. 869–872.

ANDREAS, F.C./K. BARR 1933: *Bruchstücke einer Pehlevi-Übersetzung der Psalmen.* Berlin (Preussische Akademie der Wissenschaften, Sitz.-Ber. d. Phil.-hist. Kl. 1933/1), pp. 1–64, Taf. 1–11.

ASMUSSEN, J.P. 1964: "The Pahlavi Psalm 122 in English". In: *Dr. Unvala Memorial Volume.* Bombay, pp. 123–126.

ASMUSSEN, J.P./H. PAPER 1977: *The Song of Songs in Judeo-Persian.* Copenhagen

BANG, W. 1926: "Türkische Bruchstücke einer nestorianische Georgspassion." In: *Le Muséon* 39, pp. 41–75.

BARNES, W.E. 1904: *The Peshitta Psalter According to the West Syrian Text.* Cambridge.

BARTHOLOMAE, CHR. 1904: *Altiranisches Wörterbuch.* Strassburg.

BAUMSTARK, A. 1922: *Geschichte der syrischen Literatur mit Ausschluß der christlich-palästinensischen Texte.* Bonn.

DE BLOIS, F. 2006 [2008]: "Du nouveau sur la chronologie bactrienne post-hellénistique: l'ère de 223/224 ap. J.-C.". In: *Comptes rendus de l'Académie des Inscriptions et Belles-Lettres*, pp. 991–997.

BLOOM, J.M. 2001: *Paper Before Print: The History and Impact of Paper in the Islamic Lands.* New Haven/London.

— 2017a: "Papermaking: The Historical Diffusion of an Ancient Technique." In: H. JÖNS/P. MEUSBURGER/M. HEFFERNAN (eds.): *Mobilities of Knowledge.* Cham, pp. 51–66.

— 2017b: "PAPER i. Paper in the Iranian World Prior to Printing." In: E. YARSHATER (ed.): *Encyclopædia Iranica*, online edition. Available online: http://www.iranicaonline.org/articles/paper-iran-prior-printing (last accessed 25.01.2024).

BOYCE, M. 1977: *A word-list of Manichaean Middle Persian and Parthian.* With a reverse index by R. ZWANZIGER. Leiden (Acta Iranica 9a).

BRAUN, O. 1915: *Ausgewählte Akten persischer Märtyrer.* Mit einem Anhang: Ostsyrisches Mönchsleben. Aus dem Syrischen übersetzt von Oskar Braun. Kempten/München (Bibliothek der Kirchenväter 1, 22).

Breviarium Chaldaicum. Pars tertia: A pentecoste ad dedicationem. Paris, 1887.

BROCK, S. 1982: "Christians in the Sasanian Empire: A case of divided loyalties." In: *Studies in Church History* 18: Religion and National Identity, pp. 1–19.

CANTERA, A. 1999: "Die Stellung der Sprache der Pahlavi-Übersetzung des Avesta innerhalb des Mittelpersischen." In: *Studia Iranica* 28, pp. 173–204.

CHABOT, J.-B. 1902: *Synodicon Orientale ou Receuil des synods nestoriens.* Publié, traduit et annoté. Paris.

DARYAEE, T. 2002: *Šahrestānīhā ī Ērānšahr.* A Middle Persian Text on Late Antique Geography, Epic, and History. With English and Persian Translations, and Commentary. Costa Mesa, CA. (Bibliotheca Iranica, Intellectual Traditions Series 7).

DICKENS, M. 2013a: "The Importance of the Psalter at Turfan." In: L. TANG/D.W. WINKLER (eds.): *From the Oxus River to the Chinese Shores.* Studies on East Syriac Christianity in China and Central Asia. Zürich/Berlin (Orientalia – Patristica – Oecumenica 5), pp. 357–380.

— 2013b: "Scribal Practices in the Turfan Christian Community." In: *Journal of the Canadian Society for Syriac Studies* 13, pp. 3–28.

DICKENS, M./P. ZIEME 2014: "Syro-Uigurica I: A Syriac Psalter in Uyghur Script from Turfan." In: J. DEN HEIJER,/A.B. SCHMIDT/T. PATARIDZE (eds.): *Scripts Beyond Borders. A Survey of Allographic Traditions in the Euro-Mediterranean World.* Leuven (Publications de l'Institut Orientaliste de Louvain, Vol. 62), pp. 291–328.

DURKIN-MEISTERERNST, D. 2004: *Dictionary of Manichaean Middle Persian and Parthian.* Turnhoutm (*Dictionary of Manichaean Texts* 3, part 1).

— 2006: "The Pahlavi Psalter fragment in relation to its source." In: *Studies in the Inner Asian Languages* 21, pp. 1–20.

— 2011: "The importance of the Middle Persian Texts from Turfan." In: M. MAGGI/P. ORSATTI (eds.): *The Persian Language in History.* Wiesbaden, pp. 97–104.

— 2012: The Pahlavi Psalter arranged according to units of the text, glossary and index. Version for the Fourth Summer school on Pahlavi Papyrology. Berlin (PDF available online on the website of the Berlin-Brandenburgische Akademie der Wissenschaften).

— 2014: *Grammatik des Westmitteliranischen (Parthisch und Mittelpersisch).* Wien (SbÖAW 850; Grammatica Iranica 1).

— 2016a: "Ein mittelalterliches Pahlavi-Psalter-Fragment aus der Berliner Turfansammlung |A Middle Persian Pahlavi Psalter-Fragment in the Berlin Turfan Collection." In: M. PEHLIVANIAN/C. RAUCH/R. VOLLANDT (eds.): *Orientalische Bibelhandschriften aus der Staatsbibliothek zu Berlin – PK. Eine illustrierte Geschichte / Oriental Bible Manuscripts from the Staatsbibliothek zu Berlin – PK. An Illustrated History.* Wiesbaden, pp. 114–116.

DURKIN-MEISTERERNST, D./M. FRIEDRICH/O. HAHN/A. HELMAN-WAŻNY/R. NÖLLER/S.-C. RASCHMANN 2016b: "Scientific methods for philological scholarship: Pigment and paper analyses in the field of manuscriptology." In: *Journal of Cultural Heritage* 17, pp. 7–13.

ESSABALIAN, P.P. 1942: "Armenisch-persische Lehnwörter im Pahlavi-Psalter." In: *Handes Amsorya* 56, pp. 61–69 [in Armenian].

FERRER LOSILLA, J.J. 2012: "La traducción de los Salmos en persa medio: comentarios al Salmo 128." In: A. AGUD *et al.* (eds.): *Séptimo centenario de los estudios orientales en Salamanca.* Salamanca (Estudios filológicos 337), pp. 533–541.

FIEY, J.M. 1973: "Chrétiens syriaques du Ḫorāsān et du Ségestān." In: *Le Muséon* 86, pp. 75–104.

FRYE, R.N. 1967: "A Brief Note on the Pahlavi Psalter and Bare Ideogramms." In: *Sir J. J. Zarthoshti Madressa Centenary Volume.* Bombay, pp. 70–74.

GIGNOUX, PH. 1969: "L'auteur de la version Pehlevie du Psautier serait-il nestorien?" In: *Mémorial Mgr Gabriel Khouri-Sarkis* (1898–1968). Louvain, pp. 233–244.

— 2001a: "Une croix de procession de Hérat inscrite en pehlevi." In: *Le Muséon* 114, fasc. 3–4, pp. 291–304.

— 2001b: "Prozessionskreuz aus Herāt." In: Chr. STIEGEMANN (ed.): *Byzanz. Das Licht aus dem Osten.* Mainz (Katalog der Ausstellung im Erzbischöflichen Diözesanmuseum Paderborn), pp. 150–151.

— 2002: "Pahlavi Psalter". In: *Encyclopaedia Iranica Online.* Available online: https://www.iranicaonline.org/articles/pahlavi-psalter (last accessed 07.02.2024).

GRENET, F./N. SIMS-WILLIAMS 1987: "The historical context of the Sogdian Ancient Letters". In: *Transition periods in Iranian history, Actes du Symposium de Fribourg-en-Brisgau (22-24 Mai 1985).* Leuven, pp. 101–122.

GYSELEN, R. 2019: *La géographie administrative de l'Empire sassanide: Les témoignages épigraphiques en moyen-perse.* Bures-sur-Yvette (Res Orientales 25).

HANSEN, O. 1941: *Berliner soghdische Texte I, Bruchstücke einer soghdischen Version der Georgspassion (C1).* Berlin (Abhandlungen der Preussischen Akademie der Wissenschaften, Phil.-hist. Klasse, 1941 (10).

HELMAN-WAŻNY, A. 2021: "A Tale of Papermaking along the Silk Road". In: J.B. QUENZER (ed.): *Exploring Written Artefacts. Objects, Methods, and Concepts* 1. Berlin & Boston (Studies in Manuscript Cultures, vol. 25), p. 424–440.

HINTZE, A. 2014: "Avestan Research 1991–2014. Part 1: Sources and Phonology". In: *Kratylos* 59, p. 1–52.

HOERNLE, A.F.R. 1903: "Who was the inventor of rag-paper?" In: *Journal of the Royal Asiatic Society* 43, pp. 663–684.

HUNTER, D. 1947: *Papermaking: The History and Technique of an Ancient Craft.* Second, revised and enlarged edition. New York.

HUNTER, E.C.D. 1992: "Syriac Christianity in Central Asia". In: *Zeitschrift für Religions- und Geistesgeschichte* 44 (4), pp. 362–368.

— 1996: "The Church of the East in Central Asia". In: *Bulletin of the John Rylands Library* 78 (3), pp. 129–142.

— 2017: "Syriac Manuscripts from Turfan: Public Worship and Private Devotion". In: T. LI/K. DYER (eds.): *From Ancient Manuscripts to Modern Dictionaries: Select Studies in Aramaic, Hebrew, and Greek.* Piscataway, NJ (Perspectives on Linguistics and Ancient Languages 9), pp. 77–96.

HUNTER, E.C.D./J.-F. COAKLEY 2017: *A Syriac Service-Book from Turfan.* Museum für asiatische Kunst, Berlin MS MIK III 45. Turnhout (Berliner Turfantexte XXXIX).

Hutter, M. 2003: "Mār Abā and the Impact of Zoroastrianism on Christianity in the 6th Century". In: C.G. Cereti/M. Maggi/E. Provasi (eds.): *Religious Themes and Texts of Pre-Islamic Iran and Central Asia*. Wiesbaden, pp. 167–173.

Josephson, J. 2019: "The Pahlavi Psalter as a Translation". In : E. Morano/E. Provasi/A.V. Rossi (eds.): *Studia Philologica Iranica. Gherardo Gnoli Memorial Volume*. Roma, pp. 187–197.

Jullien, C. 2011: "Chrétiens d'Iran entre hagiographie et histoire. Avec une nouvelle proposition sur la croix de Hérat". In: R. Gyselen/C. Jullien (eds.): *Florilège Ph. Gignoux pour son 80e anniversaire*. Paris (Studia Iranica. Cahier 43), pp. 175–192.

Kettenhofen, E. 1994: "Deportations. ii. In the Parthian and Sasanian periods". In: *Encyclopaedia Iranica* VII, Fasc. 3, pp. 297–308.

Lieu, S.N.C. 1992: *Manichaeism in the Later Roman Empire and Medieval China*. 2. edition, revised and expanded. Tübingen (Wissenschaftliche Untersuchungen zum Neuen Testament 63).

Lin, L. 2020: "The First Round of Tortures in the Legend of St. George: Remarks on the Turfan Syriac Fragments SyrHT 359 and SyrHT 360". In: *Oriens Christianus* 103, pp. 115–143.

— 2021: "Preliminary Notes on the Syriac Version of the Legend of Saint George Found in Turfan". In: Ch. Barbati/V. Berti (eds.): *Iranianate and Syriac Christianity in Late Antiquity and the Early Islamic Period*. Vienna (Veröffentlichungen zur Iranistik 87), pp. 245–277.

Loveday, H. 2001: *Islamic Paper. A Study of the Ancient Craft*. London.

Maróth, M. 1991: "Eine unbekannte Version der Georgios-Legende aus Turfan". In: *Altorientalische Forschungen* 18(1), pp. 86–108.

MacKenzie, D.N. 1966: "'Sheep' and 'show': Two Pahlavi Ideograms. In: J.P. Asmussen/J. Læssøe (eds.): *Iranian Studies. Presented to Kaj Barr on his Seventieth Birthday June 26, 1966*. Copenhagen (*Acta Orientalia* 30), pp. 151–157.

— 2000: "Frahang ī Pahlawīg". In: *Encyclopaedia Iranica* X, Fasc. 2, pp. 123–125.

MacLean, A.J. 1894: *East Syrian Daily Offices*. Translated from the Syriac with introduction, notes and indices, and an appendix containing the lectionary and glossary. London.

Macuch, M. 1981: *Das sasanidische Rechtsbuch 'Mātakdān i hazār dātistān' (Teil II)*. Wiesbaden.

— 2014: "The Case against Mār Abā, the Catholicos, in the Light of Sasanian Law". In: *ARAM. Zoroastrianism in the Levant and the Amorites* 26/1&2. Oxford, pp. 47–58.

de Menasce, P.J. 1945: *Škand-Gumānīk Vičār: la solution décisive des doubtes*. Texte pazand-pehlevi transcrit, traduit et commenté. Fribourg en Suisse.

Morony, M. 1989: "Bēṯ Garmē". In: *Encylopaedia Iranica* IV, Fasc. 2, p. 187.

Nöller, R./A. Helman-Ważny 2013: "The Materials of Turfan and Dunhuang Manuscripts: Analysis of Paper, Pigments and Dyes". In: *International Dunhuang Project News* 41, pp. 6–7.

Nyberg, H.S. 1974: *A Manual of Pahlavi*. Part II: Glossary. Wiesbaden.

Raschmann, S.-C. 2012: *Buddhica aus der Berliner Turfansammlung*. Teil 1: *Das apokryphe Sutra Säkiz Yükmäk Yaruk*. Mit einem Appendix von

Anna-Grethe Rischel. Stuttgart (Verzeichnis der Orientalischen Handschriften in Deutschland 18.26.1).

Reichelt, H. 1931: *Die soghdischen Handschriftenreste des Britischen Museums,* in Umschrift und mit Übersetzung. II. Teil: *Die nicht-buddhistischen Texte.* Heidelberg.

Rischel, A.-G. 2012: "Old Turkish Fragments from the Berlin Turfan Collection. Paper analysis of 62 manuscripts and block prints". In: S.-Ch. Raschmann (ed.): *Buddhica aus der Berliner Turfansammlung.* Teil 1: *Das apokryphe Sutra Säkiz Yükmäk Yaruk.* Stuttgart (Verzeichnis der Orientalischen Handschriften in Deutschland 18.26.1), pp. 265–311.

— 2014: "Julius von Wiesner and his importance for scientific research and analysis of paper". In: *Paper History. Journal of the International Association of Paper Historians* 18 (1), pp. 31–39.

— 2019: "The provenance of Paper analysis of Syriac Service book and other Syriac Manuscripts in the Turfan Collection". In: *IPH Paper History* 23, 1, pp. 8–13.

— 2020: "English translation of Julius von Wiesner, Über die ältesten bis jetzt aufgefundenen Hadernpapiere; ein neuer Beitrag zur Geschichte des Papiers. Wien: In Kommission bei A. Hölder, 1911". In: *Z Badań nad Książką i Księgozbiorami Historycznymi* (The Studies into the History of the Book and Book Collections) 14, no. 3, pp. 367–383.

van Rompay, L. 2011: "Aba I." In: S.P. Brock/A.M. Butts/G.A. Kiraz/Lucas van Rompay (eds.): *Gorgias Encyclopedic Dictionary of the Syriac Heritage.* Piscataway, N.J., p. 1.

Rustow, M. 2020: *The Lost Archive: Traces of a Caliphate in a Cairo Synagogue.* Princeton.

Schaeder, H.H. 1935: "Beiträge zur iranischen Sprachgeschichte". In: *Ungarische Jahrbücher* 15, pp. 560–588.

Schwartz, M./N. Sims-Williams 2014: "A Sogdian Psalter". In: N. Sims-Williams (ed.): *Biblical and other Christian Sogdian texts from the Turfan Collection.* Turnhout, pp. 7–53.

Shaked, Sh. 1989: "BIBLE iv. Middle Persian Translations". In: E. Yarshater (ed.): *Encyclopaedia Iranica* IV, Fasc. 2, pp. 206–207.

— 1995: "Jewish Sasanian Sigillography". In: R. Gyselen (ed.): *Au carrefour des religions: Mélanges offerts à Philippe Gignoux.* Bures-sur-Yvette, pp. 239–256.

Sims-Williams, N. 1990: "Bulayïg". In: E. Yarshater (ed.): *Encyclopaedia Iranica* IV, Fasc. 5, p. 545.

— 2001: "Middle Persian *padisāy* and Old Persian *vašnā*". In: A.A. Ṣādeqi (ed.): *Tafazzoli Memorial Volume.* Tehran, pp. 59–65.

— 2004: "A Greek-Sogdian bilingual from Bulayïq". In: *La Persia e Bisanzio.* Roma (Atti dei convegni Lincei, 201), pp. 623–631.

— 2009: "Christian literature in Middle Iranian languages". In: R.E. Emmerick/M. Macuch (eds.): *The Literature of Pre-Islamic Iran.* Companion Volume I to A History of Persian Literature. London (A History of Persian Literature XVII, general editor E. Yarshater), pp. 266–287.

— 2011a: "A new fragment of the Book of Psalms in Sogdian". In: D. Bumazhnov et al. (eds.): *Bibel, Byzanz und Christlicher Orient. Festschrift für Stephen Gerö.* Leuven (Orientalia Lovaniensia Analecta 187), pp. 461–465.

— 2011b: "Early New Persian in Syriac script: Two texts from Turfan". In: *Bulletin of the School of Oriental and African Studies* 74, pp. 353–374.

— 2019: "A Newly Identified Sogdian Fragment from the Legend of Saint George". In: *Dabir* 6, pp. 110–115.

— 2021: *A Dictionary: Christian Sogdian, Syriac and English.* Wiesbaden [2nd edition] (Beiträge zur Iranistik 41).

— 2022: "Langue sacrée, écriture sacrée? Le syriaque et ses rivaux dans les textes chrétiens et manichéens de Tourfan". In: J.-N. Robert (ed.): *Hiéroglossie III: Persan, syro-araméen et les relations avec la langue arabe.* Paris (Collège de France 25 Juin 2018), pp. 55–71.

— 2023: *The 'Ancient Letters' and other Early Sogdian documents and inscriptions.* With contributions by Frantz Grenet. London (Corpus Inscriptionum Iranicarum 2, Volume 3/5).

Sims-Williams, N./M. Schwartz 2014: "A Sogdian Psalter". In: N. Sims-Williams (ed.): *Biblical and other Christian Sogdian texts from the Turfan Collection.* With contributions by M. Schwartz and W.P. Pittard. Turnhout, pp. 7–53.

Sims-Williams, N./F. de Blois 2018: *Studies in the Chronology of the Bactrian Documents from Northern Afghanistan.* With contributions by Harry Falk and Dieter Weber. Wien.

Skjærvø, P.O. 1983: Case in Inscriptional Middle Persian, Inscriptional Parthian and the Pahlavi Psalter. *Studia Iranica* 12, pp. 47–62, 151–181.

Stein, M.A. 1921: *Serindia.* Detailed report of explorations in Central Asia and Westernmost China. 5 vols., Oxford.

Sundermann, W. 1974: "Einige Bemerkungen zum syrisch-neupersischen Psalmenbruchstück aus Chinesisch-Turkestan". In: P. Gignoux/A. Tafazzoli (eds.): *Mémorial Jean de Menasce.* Louvain, pp. 441–452.

Tsien, T.-H. 1985: *Paper and Printing. Science and Civilisation in China*, ed. by Joseph Needham, vol. 5: *Chemistry and Chemical Technology*, Part 1. Cambridge.

— 2004: *Written on Bamboo & Silk. The beginnings of Chinese books & inscriptions.* With an Afterword by L. Edward. Shaughnessy. Chicago/London [2nd edition].

von Wiesner, J. 1911: *Über die ältesten bis jetzt aufgefundenen Hadernpapiere; ein neuer Beitrag zur Geschichte des Papiers.* Wien.

Klimawandel und die spätantike Pest im sasanidischen Reich

PHILIP HUYSE, Paris

Über ein halbes Jahrhundert ist mittlerweile vergangen, seitdem der Arzt und Demograph JEAN-NOËL BIRABEN zusammen mit dem Mittelalter-Historiker JACQUES LE GOFF einen für ihre Zeit bahnbrechenden Aufsatz zur Pest im Frühmittelalter veröffentlichten (BIRABEN/LE GOFF 1969). Aufgrund jener ersten ernstzunehmenden historischen Analyse der literarischen Quellen hatten die beiden Forscher auf eine langwierige Pandemie der Beulenpest[1] geschlossen, die von 541 bis etwa 750 N.CHR.[2] in fünfzehn aufeinander folgenden, alle neun bis zwölf Jahre wiederkehrenden ‚Wellen' im westlichen und östlichen Mittelmeerbecken bis nach Mesopotamien und darüber hinaus gewütet haben soll,[3] bis sie für knapp sechs Jahrhunderte ebenso plötzlich wieder ‚verschwand', wie sie aufgetaucht war. Diese Pandemie wird heute gemeinhin als die ‚justinianische Pest' bezeichnet, obwohl der Terminus sich streng genommen nur auf den ersten Ausbruch (*ca.* 541–544 N.CHR.) bezieht und daher ein neutralerer Ausdruck wie ‚spätantike Pandemie' demgegenüber den Vorzug verdient.[4]

Bereits damals hatten die beiden französischen Autoren die Hoffnung ausgesprochen, dass die fortschreitende Wissenschaft künftighin noch so manches Rätsel zu lösen vermögen würde,[5] und ihnen war es in erster Linie auch eher darum gegangen, die historischen Probleme in den dürftigen schriftlichen Quellen anzusprechen und weniger darum, diese mit dem ihnen zur Verfügung

1 S. BIRABEN/LE GOFF 1969, S. 1491.

2 Der Anfang der Pandemie wird für gewöhnlich im Jahr 541 angesetzt, als sie wohl rund Mitte Juli (dazu s. STATHAKOPOULOS 2004, S. 113) die ägyptische Hafenstadt Pelousion an der Nilmündung befiel. Das ungefähre Enddatum von 750 gilt insbesondere für den östlichen Mittelmeerraum und bezieht sich auf den letzten, von den schriftlichen Quellen gesicherten Ausbruch in Syrien von 740 bis 750; die letzte Erwähnung der Pest im Westen ist für den Ausbruch in Italien südlich von Neapel im Jahr 767 belegt. Für weitere Alternativvorschläge zum ‚Ende' der ersten Pandemie, s. EISENBERG/MORDECHAI 2019, S. 159–160; EISENBERG/MORDECHAI 2020, S. 1642–1643.

3 S. BIRABEN/LE GOFF 1969, S. 1492–1493; dagegen ging STATHAKOPOULOS 2004, S. 113–124 unter Berücksichtigung weiterer Quellen von achtzehn ‚Wellen' aus (zum Zeitabstand zwischen den verschiedenen Infektionsausbrüchen, s. STATHAKOPOULOS 2004, S. 123–124).

4 S. in diesem Sinne auch EISENBERG/MORDECHAI 2020, S. 1633.

5 BIRABEN/LE GOFF 1969, S. 1484 Anm. 2: „Peut-on espérer que l'histoire de la peste dans le Haut Moyen Age soit un jour éclairée par les progrès de l'archéologie, de l'anthropologie physique et de la préhistoire démographique?".

stehenden epidemiologischen Wissen lösen zu wollen. Sehr vieles von dem, was ihnen und ihren Nachfolgern aufgrund ihrer Prüfung der literarischen Quellen[6] noch als wahrscheinlich oder gesichert erschienen war, ist seither in der Tat infrage gestellt worden oder hat sich als der weiteren Diskussion bedürftig erwiesen, und umgekehrt konnten Fragen, die in den antiken Texten naturgemäß keine Antwort fanden, inzwischen befriedigend geklärt werden.

So konnte unterdessen dank immer feineren Methoden der Genomanalyse eindeutig geklärt werden, dass die drei großen Pestpandemien der Geschichte (541–*ca.* 750, 1347–1771, 2. Hälfte des 19. Jh.s – Anfang des 20. Jh.s) nicht einfach auf drei — *antiqua*, *mediaevalis*, *orientalis* genannte — Varianten desselben, 1894 vom schweizerisch-französischen Arzt Alexandre Yersin (1863–1943) identifizierten Bakteriums *Yersinia pestis* zurückzuführen sind, wie anfangs noch gemutmaßt wurde.[7] Vielmehr liegt ihnen ein weitaus komplexeres phylogenetisches Modell mit mehreren unterschiedlichen Stämmen dieses Pathogens zugrunde, das sich im Laufe der Geschichte immer wieder von neuem entwickelt und verzweigt hat.[8] Erst als das Pestbakterium dank vermehrter *aDNA*-Funde (‚ancient DNA') seit etwa Mitte der 1990er Jahre aus den Knochen und Zähnen menschlicher Überreste gewonnen werden konnte, wurde es möglich, einen über jeglichen Zweifel erhabenen ursächlichen Verband mit der spätantiken Pest nachzuweisen.[9] Nach neuesten Erkenntnissen soll der Krankheitserreger bereits in der späten Bronzezeit (d.h., ± 3 800 BP), wenn nicht sogar noch über ein Jahrtausend früher, mit allen genetischen Merkmalen ausgestattet gewesen sein, die ihn dazu befähigten, von Flöhen übertragen zu werden.[10]

Des Weiteren sind die literarischen Quellen zu wenig zahlreich und zu ungenau, als dass sie es uns zweifelsfrei erlaubten, die spätantike Pandemie als ein einheitliches und kontinuierliches Ereignis mit periodischen Aufschwüngen

6 Für einen allgemeinen Überblick über die griechischen, syrischen, arabischen (und weiteren) literarischen Quellen zur spätantiken Pandemie, s. etwa STATHAKOPOULOS 2004, S. 113–124; MORDECHAI/EISENBERG 2019, S. 8–20; MEIER 2020, S. 175–178; SARRIS 2022, S. 324–328. Für einen Überblick über die dokumentarischen (juristischen, numismatischen, epigraphischen, papyrologischen) und archäologischen Quellen, s. MORDECHAI/EISENBERG 2019, S. 20–35; MEIER 2020, S. 178–184; SARRIS 2022, S. 328–337.

7 So hatten es noch BIRABEN/LE GOFF 1969, S. 1486 nach der damals gängigen Meinung formuliert (vgl. dazu auch EISENBERG/MORDECHAI 2019, S. 171). EISENBERG/MORDECHAI 2020, S. 1637–1640 zeichnen detailliert nach, wie sich allmählich das Konzept drei verschiedener Pandemien entwickeln konnte, die jeweils durch einen spezifischen pathogenen Erreger verursacht wurden.

8 S. KELLER *et al.* 2019a; MORDECHAI/EISENBERG 2019, S. 40; SARRIS 2022, S. 319 mit Anm. 14.

9 S. EISENBERG/MORDECHAI 2019, S. 169–170; MEIER 2020, S. 185–186; SARRIS 2022, S. 320–321.

10 S. SPYROU *et al.* 2018, s. auch EISENBERG/MORDECHAI 2019, S. 176–177, sowie hier unten Anm. 141. Auch ohne so weit in die Zeit zurückzugehen, hatte der Arzt Rufus von Ephesos bereits über eine Krankheit mit Pestbeulen-ähnlichen Symptomen berichtet, die um 100 n. Chr. in Libyen, Ägypten und Syrien gewütet haben soll, s. EISENBERG/MORDECHAI 2020, S. 1640, 1663.

einer und derselben Seuche zu betrachten.[11] Nicht immer ist es auf deren Grundlage möglich, eindeutig die Art der Infektionskrankheit (Beulen- oder Lungenpest?),[12] die Infektionsanfälligkeit (möglichen Zusammenhang mit einer unterernährten oder immungeschwächten Bevölkerung?),[13] den Übertragungsweg und die Verbreitungsgeschwindigkeit (genaue Rolle von schwarzen Ratten und Flöhen, falls maßgeblich involviert),[14] oder noch den Grad der demographischen Auswirkungen der Pandemie (lokal und zeitlich begrenzte Ausbruchsherde oder flächendeckenden Zusammenbruch?)[15] zu bestimmen. In letzterer Frage stehen sich daher die sogenannten ‚Minimalisten' den ‚Maximalisten' unversöhnlich gegenüber:[16] während Erstgenannte für die spätantike Pandemie eine hohe Sterblichkeitsrate mit katastrophalen demographischen Auswirkungen und nachhaltigen kulturellen und sozialen Folgen kategorisch verneinen, nehmen Letztere dagegen an, dass die todbringende Krankheit zwischen 25 und 60 Prozent (etwa 15 bis 100 Millionen Individuen) der eurasiatischen Bevölkerung dahingerafft haben könnte.[17]

11 Statt ‚Wellen' verwendeten Biraben/Le Goff (1969, S. 1492) dafür den Begriff von ‚Schüben' (frz. *poussées*). Zur leicht verständlichen, aber etwas unglücklich gewählten Metapher der ‚Welle', s. Mordechai/Eisenberg 2019, S. 37–46 (mit einer Warnung vor übereilten Schlussfolgerungen aufgrund eines Vergleichs mit der dritten großen Pandemie), sowie Eisenberg/Mordechai 2020, S. 1650–1653.

12 S. Mordechai/Eisenberg 2019, S. 33; Eisenberg/Mordechai 2019, S. 164–166; White/Mordechai 2020, S. 13–15. Während die Beulenpest (auch: bubonische Pest) auf indirektem Weg über den Biss infizierter Flöhe übertragen wird, die sich im Fell eines sich in menschlicher Nähe aufhaltenden Wirtstiers — im Fall der spätantiken Pandemie mutmaßlich der schwarzen Ratte (*Rattus rattus*) — eingenistet haben, ist die Lungenpest (auch: pneumonische Pest) eine Tröpcheninfektion, die durch Husten und Niesen oder auch einfach durch Sprechen und Ausatmen, direkt von Mensch zu Mensch übertragen wird.

13 S. Morony 2007, S. 84–85; Schamiloglu 2016, S. 295 (und Anm. 11); Newfield 2018a, S. 100–109; Eisenberg/Mordechai 2019, S. 169–171.

14 S. Mordechai/Eisenberg 2019, S. 32–33; Eisenberg/Mordechai 2019, S. 165; Eisenberg/Mordechai 2020, S. 1653–1655; White/Mordechai 2020.

15 S. Dols 1974, S. 372; Mordechai/Eisenberg 2019, S. 34–38; Eisenberg/Mordechai 2019, S. 173–174; Eisenberg/Mordechai 2020, S. 1664–1665; Sarris 2022, S. 340.

16 Zu den ‚Minimalisten' gehören etwa Eisenberg/Mordechai 2019 (s. die Schlussfolgerung, S. 179–180); Mordechai/Eisenberg 2019 (s. die Schlussfolgerung, S. 48–50); Mordechai/Eisenberg/Newfield/Izdebski/Kay/Poinar 2019; Mordechai/Eisenberg/Newfield/Izdebski/Kay 2020 (in Antwort auf Meier 2020). Zu den ‚Maximalisten' gehören — neben Biraben/Le Goff 1969, S. 1499 — Meier 2016 und 2020 (s. die Schlussfolgerung [S. 186–192], in Widerrede auf Mordechai/Eisenberg/Newfield/Izdebski/Kay/Poinar 2019). Eine Mittelposition nimmt etwa Sarris (2022, S. 341–342) ein, der Todeszahlen, wenn isoliert betrachtet, für nicht aussagekräftig hält, sondern es vorzieht, die Auswirkung der Sterblichkeit auf die Gesellschaft von Fall zu Fall zu studieren. Ähnlich hatten bereits Eisenberg/Mordechai (2020) argumentiert, die es bedauern, dass „almost no work has been done on the post-540s outbreaks as distinct historical events" (S. 1643); vgl. auch die Schlussfolgerung: „Future research (…) should focus on the effects of late antique plague *on humans* by investigating the outbreaks circa 541–570 c.e. in their local contexts" (S. 1665).

17 S. Eisenberg/Mordechai 2020, S. 1634.

Neben der Archäologie sind es vor allem die Naturwissenschaften gewesen, die uns in den vergangenen Jahrzehnten diesbezüglich wesentliche Erkenntnisfortschritte gebracht haben: zunächst wurden ab 1980 wegen eines besonderen Naturereignisses um 536 herum,[18] auf das im Nachfolgenden noch genauer einzugehen sein wird, verstärkt Fragen zu Klima und Umwelt in der (Spät-)Antike berücksichtigt;[19] insbesondere die Frage nach einem möglichen Zusammenhang zwischen Klima(wandel), wiederholten Hungersnöten und Pestausbrüchen war hier von unmittelbarem Interesse.[20] Seit der Jahrtausendwende kamen dann noch die Molekularbiologie und die Paläogenetik dazu, die ihrerseits in den letzten zehn Jahren mit weiterentwickelten Verfahren noch einmal einen kräftigen Vorschub erhielten.[21]

War man anfangs aufgrund einer knappen Bemerkung des syrischen Kirchenhistorikers Euagrios Scholastikos[22] noch davon ausgegangen, dass die Krankheit, die 541 in der ägyptischen Hafenstadt Pelousion am äußersten östlichen Rand des Nildeltas ausgebrochen war, ihren Ursprung in Äthiopien oder einer anderen, an der ostafrikanischen Küste gelegenen Region gefunden hatte,[23] so legen die neuesten Ergebnisse der Paläogenetik nunmehr nahe, dass der Erreger vielmehr in (Zentral-)Asien gesucht werden muss.[24] Diese

18 S. zuletzt zusammenfassend Newfield 2018a/b (und außerdem noch Helama *et al.* 2018).

19 S. auch Haldon *et al.* 2017a/c.

20 S. Morony 2007, S. 84 (Hungersnot und Pest) sowie Stathakopoulos 2004, und die Kritik dazu von Eisenberg/Mordechai 2019, S. 158–159, 171–173; Stathakopoulos 2012 (Bedeutung paläopathologischer Untersuchungen menschlicher Überreste); Schamiloglu 2016, S. 295; Eisenberg/Mordechai 2019, S. 171–173; Meier 2020, S. 184–185 (palynologische Daten); Eisenberg/Mordechai 2020, S. 1655–1658.

21 S. Eisenberg/Mordechai 2019, S. 169–171; Keller *et al.* 2019a/b; Meier 2020, S. 185–186; Eisenberg/Mordechai 2020, S. 1658–1664; Sarris 2022, S. 337–340.

22 S. Euagrios, *Hist. Eccl.* 4.29 (tr. Whitby 2000, S. 229): „Es wurde gesagt, und das gilt bis jetzt noch, dass es [d.h., das Pestleiden, gr. πάθος (…) λοιμῶδες] in Äthiopien angefangen haben soll".

23 Als einer der Ersten hatte bereits Dols (1974, S. 372) die Vermutung geäußert, Euagrios könnte hier womöglich Thukydides (2.48) zum literarischen Vorbild genommen haben. In seiner kenntnisreichen Schilderung der attischen Seuche im Jahr 430 v.Chr. war der athenische Stratege und Geschichtsschreiber nämlich ebenfalls von einem Infektionsausbruch in Äthiopien ausgegangen (allerdings dürfte es sich bei der attischen Pandemie im 5. Jh. v.Chr. wohl kaum um die bubonische Pest gehandelt haben, auch wenn die genaue Krankheitsbestimmung bis heute umstritten bleibt). Weitere literarische Parallelen für einen afrikanischen Ursprung späterer Epidemien werden von Whitby (2000, S. 229–230 Anm. 78) in seinem Kommentar zur betreffenden Stelle bei Euagrios angeführt, s. dort auch für weitere Ähnlichkeiten zwischen den Darstellungen des spätantiken Kirchenhistorikers und Thuk. 2.47–54.

24 Zur primären Herkunft des Pathogens *Y. pestis* s. neuerdings Keller *et al.* 2019a (insbes. die Schlussfolgerung auf S. 12368: „The most parsimonious location for the divergence event that give rise to the First Pandemic lineage is Central Asia"), sowie Eisenberg/Mordechai 2019, S. 166–167 mit Anm. 48–49. Vgl. daneben noch Schamiloglu 2016, S. 298–301 („(…) plague may have originated in or near the Qinghai-Tibet-Plateau and was transmitted between rodent populations by human travel along the ancient trade

erst in den letzten Jahren hinzugewonnene Erkenntnis zieht daher sofort die doppelte Fragestellung nach sich, ob sich zum einen in dem riesigen vorderasiatischen Raum zwischen der Levante und Zentralasien, insbesondere in Mesopotamien und dem iranischen Hochland, direkte oder indirekte Spuren einer Pandemie finden lassen,[25] und zum anderen auf welchem Weg (Land- oder Seeweg?) der Krankheitserreger vom Fernen Osten zum Mittelmeerbecken gelangt sein könnte.

Bevor wir uns diesen beiden Fragen zuwenden können, ist jedoch zunächst noch auf die vorangehenden Naturereignisse um 536 einzugehen, da sie offensichtlich mit klimatischen Veränderungen einhergingen und ein möglicher Zusammenhang mit dem Ausbruch der Pest in Erwägung gezogen wurde.[26] Die Quellen für die außergewöhnlichen Vorkommnisse sind zur Genüge bekannt[27] und brauchen hier nicht noch einmal im Einzelnen aufgeführt zu werden.[28] Mögen die Details auch etwas von einander abweichen,[29] so sind sich die Quellen jedoch darin einig, dass die Sonne für knapp anderthalb Jahre — wohl etwa in der Zeit vom März 536 bis zum Juni 537?[30] — verschleiert war. Ihre strahlende Leuchtkraft wurde zu einem weichen, blauartigen Schimmer gedämpft, wodurch sich der Himmel Tag und Nacht verdunkelte.[31] Außerdem kühlten die sommerlichen Temperaturen im darauffolgenden Jahrzehnt bis etwa 545–550 merklich

routes" [S. 299]; „(...) we should not exclude the equally strong possibility that bubonic plague spread rapidly to Central Asia in the 6th century, too, just as it did in the 14th century" [p. 301]). S. noch Newfield 2018a, S. 99 („Genomic evidence, however, refutes the idea that plague comes from Africa") mit Anm. 101–102, sowie Newfield 2018b, S. 472 („ultimately (...) from northwestern China") mit S. 482 Anm. 155; Jackson Bonner 2020, S. 191 Anm. 111; Sarris 2022, S. 319 mit Anm. 14.

25 Diese Frage zu beantworten wäre umso wichtiger, als die Auswirkungen der Pest auf Vorderasien im Allgemeinen (etwa auf Syrien, die arabische Halbinsel, die Kaukasus und Armenien, Mesopotamien, usw.) und auf Persien im Besonderen von der Forschung weitestgehend vernachlässigt wurden, gemessen an der Aufmerksamkeit, die der Krankheit in Byzanz und Europa zuteilwurde, s. Eisenberg/Mordechai 2019, S. 163, sowie Eisenberg/Mordechai 2020, S. 1650 Anm. 87.

26 Vgl. die bereits oben in Anm. 20 erwähnte Literatur.

27 Proc., *Vand.* 4.14.4 (ed./tr. Dewing 1916, S. 328–329); Cassiod., *Var.* 12.25 (tr. Hodgkin 1886, S. 518–520); Joh. Lyd., *De Ost.* 9c (ed. Wachsmuth 1897, S. 25); Joh. Ephes. *apud* Ps.-Dion. von Tell-Maḥrē = *Chronik von Zuqnīn* III (tr. Witakowski 1996, S. 65; tr. Harrak 1999, S. 87); Ps.-Zach. Rhet. 9.19d (tr. Phenix/Horn 2011, S. 370), für weitere Einzelheiten s. Arjava 2005, S. 78–80; Newfield 2018a, S. 94 n. 52; sowie Newfield 2018b, S. 449–452).

28 Zwar waren Althistoriker und Byzantinisten bereits vor den 1980er Jahren auf die betreffenden Zeugnisse einer rätselhaften Trübung des Himmels aufmerksam geworden, doch nahmen sich erst von da an auch Naturwissenschaftler das Phänomen zu Herzen, s. Newfield 2018b, S. 475 Anm. 1 für weitere Einzelheiten.

29 So datiert Pseudo-Dionysios von Tell Maḥrē die Ereignisse irrtümlicherweise in die Jahre 530–531, dazu s. Arjava 2005, S. 79: „not unusual in this author's work".

30 S. Newfield 2018a, S. 94.

31 Nach Joh. Ephes. *apud* Ps.-Dion. von Tell-Maḥrē = *Chronik von Zuqnīn* III (tr. Witakowski 1996, S. 65; tr. Harrak 1999, S. 87) schien die blasse Sonne nur wenige Stunden am Tag.

ab,[32] wie vor allem die Dendroklimatologie dank Baumringuntersuchungen gezeigt hat.[33] Wiederholte Dürren in den frischen Sommermonaten, wie in den frostigen aber sturmfreien Wintern führten zu Missernten mit anschließenden Hungersnöten[34] und weiteren Folgen für die Gesundheit der Bevölkerung.[35] Nachdem lange nach der Ursache des ‚Staubschleiers' — manchmal auch als eine Art ‚Nebel' dargestellt[36] — gerätselt wurde, scheint die Wissenschaft sie nun auf mindestens zwei größere vulkanische Eruptionen um die Jahre 535/536 und 539/540 zurückführen zu können (eher als auf die Einwirkung von Asteroiden oder Kometen).[37] Bleibt noch die Frage nach den tatsächlichen, mittel- oder

32 Im Schnitt dürften die Sommer etwa um 1,5°C kühler gewesen sein, s. BÜNTGEN *et al.* 2020. Unter Berücksichtigung einer Fehlermarge mag die Abweichung zwischen etwa -1°C und knapp -3°C gelegen haben; vgl. diesbezüglich auch NEWFIELD 2018a, S. 96: „June–August 536 was about 2.5 Celsius and June–August 541 2.7 Celsius below the preceding 30 year average". Von den 16 kühlsten Sommern seit 500 v.CHR. (im Vergleich zur Referenzperiode 1901–2000) ereigneten sich allein deren sechs zwischen 536 und 550, s. NEWFIELD 2018b, S. 448, 459–462.

33 S. NEWFIELD 2018b, S. 452–459.

34 Ob die Hungersnöte allgemein verbreitet, oder doch eher lokal und zeitlich beschränkt waren, steht zur Debatte, vgl. NEWFIELD 2018b, S. 467–469.

35 Dazu s. HELAMA *et al.* 2018. So erwähnt der Continuator des Chronisten Marcellinus Comes (*MGH AA* 11 [ed. MOMMSEN], S. 105; tr. CROKE 1995, S. 46, Komm. S. 130) etwa, dass eine schlimme Dürre (*ob nimiam siccitatem*) im Jahr 536 riesige Weideflächen im persischen Reich — genauer: im lakhmidischen Südarabien, das unter dem Vasallentum der Sasaniden stand — ausgetrocknet hatte und somit 15 000 Beduinen (*circiter quindecim milia Saracenorum*) vom Stamm der Kinda nach Syrien (*limitem Eufratesiae ingressa*) vertrieben hatte, s. STATHAKOPOULOS 2004, S. 80, 162, 269 [Nr. 93]; NEWFIELD 2018a, S. 98; NEWFIELD 2018b, S. 450, 472.

36 Dazu s. ARJAVA 2005, S. 81–83; NEWFIELD 2018a, S. 94 Anm. 48, 95. Ein hochauflösendes Multi-Proxy-Verfahren zur Rekonstruktion des äolischen Eintrags und der Veränderungen der paläohydrologischen Bedingungen auf der Grundlage einer 13 000 Jahre alten Aufzeichnung aus dem peripheren Torf des Neor-Sees im Nordwesten Irans hat jedenfalls eindeutig auf hohe Konzentrationen von atmosphärischem Staub und eine erhöhte Staubablagerung für die Zeit um 510 N.CHR. — mit einer Fehlermarge auf 2σ-Niveau von ± 78 Jahren, d.h. dass 95 % der Daten innerhalb von zwei Standardabweichungen vom Mittelwert liegen — hingewiesen, s. SHARIFI *et al.* 2015, S. 221, Tafel 1. Untersucht wurden dabei insbesondere Variationen der relativen Häufigkeiten feuerfester (Al, Zr, Ti und Si), redoxsensibler (Fe) und mobiler (K und Rb) Elemente, des gesamten organischen Kohlenstoffs (TOC), des d13CTOC, der verbindungsspezifischen Wasserstoffisotope des Blattwachses (dD), der Kohlenstoffakkumulationsraten und der Staubflüsse, deren Gesamtbild eine große Lücke in den vorhandenen terrestrischen Paläoklima-Daten aus dem Inneren Westasiens zu schließen vermag (zu beachten ist vor allem der deutlich wahrnehmbare Ausschlag im Abschnitt F *ibid.*, S. 227, Fig. 9).

37 S. NEWFIELD 2018b, S. 463–467 für weitere Überlegungen zum möglichen Ursprung beider Ausbrüche; die erste Eruption von 535/6 verortet er an einem mittleren Breitengrad auf der Nordhalbkugel (vielleicht in Nordamerika), die zweite um 539/540 situiert er näher zum Äquator (entweder am El Chichón in Südosten von Mexiko oder am Ilopango in El Salvador). Die Sonnenverschleierung im Mittelmeerbecken im Jahr 536 wurde aber möglicherweise durch einen kleineren, lokalen Ausbruch verursacht, während der Temperaturrückgang den größeren Ausbrüchen zuzuschreiben wäre

langfristigen Auswirkungen dieser Vulkanausbrüche. Während manche Forscher darin die Ursache für eine über ein Jahrhundert währende kleine Eiszeit mit schwerwiegenden Folgen sehen,[38] sind andere weitaus zurückhaltender. Ohne die klimatische Anomalie kleinreden zu wollen und die Auswirkungen auf die mentale und körperliche Gesundheit der Menschen (etwa eine durch Mangelernährung verursachte Zunahme von Immunschwächen[39] oder einen Vitamin D-Mangel aufgrund fehlender Sonneneinstrahlung[40]) zu verneinen, schätzen sie die sozialen, demographischen, wirtschaftlichen und politischen Folgen viel geringer und vor allem zeitlich begrenzter (bis 545–550) ein.[41] Ein unmittelbarer, kausaler Zusammenhang zwischen den klimatischen Ereignissen und dem Ausbruch der spätantiken Pest steht daher nicht unumstößlich fest und bedarf wohl noch der weiteren Überprüfung;[42] es ist nicht auszuschließen, dass der Temperaturrückgang und seine Folgen in Wirklichkeit nur eine bereits eingesetzte Entwicklung beschleunigt haben, ohne sie verursacht zu haben.[43]

Die literarischen Zeugnisse für die Anwesenheit der spätantiken Pest im sasanidischen Perserreich sind rasch aufgelistet und beschränken sich im Wesentlichen auf die Jahre 542 und 628. Nachdem die Pest nach dem ersten Ausbruch der Krankheit Mitte Juli 541 in der ägyptischen Hafenstadt Pelousion nacheinander Mitte August in östlicher Richtung Gaza und im Laufe des Septembers in die andere Richtung Alexandria erreicht hatte, verbreitete sie sich immer weiter.[44] Ende März oder Anfang April 542 war sie in der oströmischen Hauptstadt Konstantinopel angekommen, wo sie bis August wütete.[45] In den

(*ibid.*, S. 465–466). Der Niederschlag der Aschewolken ist jedenfalls bis heute in den in Grönland und der Antarktis entnommenen Eisbohrkernen nachweisbar (s. Larsen *et al.* 2008, sowie Ferris *et al.* 2011; vgl. Newfield 2018b, S. 462–463). Die Folgen der Katastrophe waren deshalb nicht nur in Asien bis nach China und Korea (s. Newfield 2018b, S. 451), sondern auch in Europa von den britischen Inseln bis nach Skandinavien spürbar (s. Gräslund/Price 2012).

38 So sahen etwa Büntgen/Myglan/Ljungqvist *et al.* (2016) und Büntgen *et al.* (2020) darin die Ursache für eine etwa bis 660 andauernde, LALIA (‚Late Antique Little Ice Age') genannte spätantike Eiszeit, die letztendlich in ihren Augen ein Mitauslöser für die spätantike Pest gewesen ist, für politische Unruhe bis nach China gesorgt hat, s. auch Schamiloglu 2016, S. 309–310, Migrationen der Turkvölker in der asiatischen Steppe heraufbeschworen hat und sogar das Ende des Sasanidenreiches eingeläutet haben soll, vgl. auch Dols 1974, S. 372 Anm. 6 und Conrad 1985, S. 304–311, der die spätantike Pest für einen der Gründe der ‚abbasidischen Revolution' um 750 hält, s. dazu die Beurteilung von Eisenberg/Mordechai 2020, S. 1664 Anm. 159.

39 S. Newfield 2018a, S. 106.

40 S. Helama/Jones/Briffa 2017, sowie Helama *et al.* 2018.

41 S. Newfield 2018a/b, vgl. auch Haldon *et al.* 2018a, S. 4.

42 S. Newfield 2018a, S. 97–101, sowie Newfield 2018b, S. 467–475.

43 S. Newfield 2018b, S. 473: „Rather than a watershed, it (*i.e.*, the climate anomaly [*meine Anmerkung*]) was an accelerator of change already underway".

44 S. Kislinger/Stathakopoulos 1999, S. 85–89.

45 S. Stathakopoulos 2004, S. 113–114. Wie Kislinger/Stathakopoulos 1999, S. 90–93 erläutern, ist das relativ späte Eintreffen der Pest in Konstantinopel, etwa neun Monate

ersten Monaten des Jahres 542 gelangte sie nach Jerusalem und wohl bis zum Frühsommer 542 traf sie auch in Antiochien, der größten und bedeutendsten Stadt des östlichen Mittelmeerraums, ein. Weitere syrische Städte landeinwärts (Emesa, Epiphaneia, Apameia) erlitten bald dasselbe Schicksal und auch in mehreren kleinasiatischen Regionen (Kilikien, Kappadokien, Galatien, Bithynien) griff die Krankheit um sich.[46] Zehn Jahre zuvor hatten Xusrō I. (r. 531–579) und Justinian (r. 527–565) noch einen ‚Ewigen Frieden' zwischen Persern und Oströmern abgeschlossen, aber im Frühling 540 beging der persische König als Erster Vertragsbruch[47] und eroberte im Juni 540 Antiochien, das er verwüstete und dessen Einwohner er in großer Zahl als Arbeitskräfte nach Mesopotamien übersiedelte.[48] Zwar wurden nach einem Waffenstillstand neuerliche Friedensgespräche initiiert, aber als Xusrō zu weiteren Kriegshandlungen überging, fühlte sich Justinian auch nicht länger an irgendwelchen Auflagen gebunden.[49] Nach dem Winter gingen die kriegerischen Auseinandersetzungen zwischen den Großmächten bis August 541 weiter, als beide Parteien wegen der hochsommerlichen Hitze heimkehrten.[50]

Im dritten Kriegsjahr stießen die Perser zunächst nach Sergiopolis (ar-Ruṣāfa) im Nordosten Syriens vor, das Xusrō vergeblich einzunehmen versuchte, wonach er weiter gen Norden nach Kallinikon (ar-Raqqa) zog, das er hingegen erobern konnte. Dort muss er wohl auch von der schlimmen Erkrankung Justinians an der Pest erfahren haben.[51] Die Nachricht veranlasste ihn dazu, im Herbst 542 selber den Rückzug in die Heimat nach ‚Adarbigana' (dem früheren Media Atropatene) anzutreten.[52] Obwohl der persische Vorstoß abrupt abgebrochen wurde,

nach dem Erstausbruch in Pelousion, wohl damit zu erklären, dass die letzten Schiffe mit Getreidelieferungen aus Ägypten nach Konstantinopel vermutlich gegen Ende August den Hafen von Alexandria bereits verlassen hatten, d.h. wenige Wochen bevor der Erreger — unter Berücksichtigung der Inkubationszeit — die dort ansässigen Schiffsbesatzungen hätte befallen können.

46 S. STATHAKOPOULOS 2004, S. 114–115, 282–283.

47 Proc., *Pers.* 2.5.1 (ed./tr. DEWING 1916, S. 294–295), s. BÖRM 2016, S. 635.

48 Ausführlich beschrieben von Proc., *Pers.* 2.8.1–2.9.18 (ed./tr. DEWING 1916, S. 324–343); zur Eroberung und Übersiedlung s. JACKSON BONNER 2011, S. 55–57. Über die Folgen der Eroberung (540) und der Pest (542) gehen die Meinungen auseinander: abgesehen von den Deportationen, s. HUYSE 2022, S. 22 Anm. 53 und 28 mit Anm. 122, sah KENNEDY 2007, S. 92–95 in mehreren syrischen Städten Anzeichen dafür, dass die Bautätigkeit nach 540–542 stark zurückgefahren wurde; bereits errichtete Bauwerke wurden zwar noch instandgesetzt oder ausgebessert, aber Neubauten kaum noch in Angriff genommen. Dagegen führen andere an, dass nur eine einzige Inschrift ausdrücklich auf die Pest Bezug nimmt und es vielerorts Hinweise auf wirtschaftlichen Wohlstand und Bevölkerungswachstum gibt (s. HALDON *et al.* 2018c, S. 3; MORDECHAI 2018, S. 39 [Resilienz von Antiochien im 6. Jh.]; EISENBERG/MORDECHAI 2019, S. 168–169; MORDECHAI/EISENBERG 2019, S. 27).

49 S. KISLINGER/STATHAKOPOULOS 1999, S. 80.

50 S. KISLINGER/STATHAKOPOULOS 1999, S. 81.

51 Proc., *Anecd.* 4.1 (ed./tr. DEWING 1935, S. 42–43) und *Pers.* 2.23.20 (ed./tr. DEWING 1916, S. 472–473), s. KISLINGER/STATHAKOPOULOS 1999, S. 82–84.

52 S. STATHAKOPOULOS 2004, S. 115 und 147; JACKSON BONNER 2020, S. 191.

hatte die Krankheit das Heer und den König jedoch bereits mit voller Wucht getroffen,[53] auch wenn sich sowohl Xusrō als auch Justinian persönlich davon wieder vollständig erholten.[54] Dennoch blieb die ganze Angelegenheit nicht folgenlos für den sasanidischen Herrscher, da sein ältester Sohn Anōš(ag)zād gegen ihn in Aufstand kam, indem er sich auf die voreilige Nachricht der angeblich tödlichen Erkrankung seines Vaters hin zum König ausrufen ließ.[55] Die Revolte wurde jedoch niedergeschlagen und Anōš(ag)zāds Gesicht entstellt und die Augenlider verstümmelt, so dass er niemals mehr die Thronfolge antreten konnte, da bei den Sasaniden die körperliche Unversehrtheit eine Bedingung dafür war.[56]

Nach Auskunft der nicht-zeitgenössischen Chronik von Seʿert aus dem 11. Jh. wurde das Reich eines ungenannten Königs in seinem zehnten Regierungsjahr von der Pest (syr. *wabā'*) getroffen,[57] die sich daraufhin über ganz „Persien, Indien und Abyssinien (syr. *al-Habāsha*)" verbreitete.[58] Land und Herrscher sind

53 Proc., *Pers.* 2.24.5/8 (ed./tr. Dewing 1916, S. 474–475), s. Kislinger/Stathakopoulos 1999, S. 94. Obwohl Prokop Xusrō und seine Armee zunächst in Ādurbādagān (Āzerbāyjān) ankommen lässt (2.24.1), wo der persische König von der Erkrankung Justinians erfährt (2.24.5) und die Pest erst danach die Perser befällt (2.24.5), dürfte wenig Zweifel darüber bestehen, dass die Krankheit nicht bereits in Ādurbādagān anwesend gewesen war, sondern König und Heer sich bereits in Syrien angesteckt hatten und von dort die Infektion auf dem Heimweg mit eingeschleppt hatten, wo sie erst nach Ablauf der Inkubationszeit ausgebrochen war. Ähnlich sehen es auch Kisslinger/Stathakopoulos 1999, S. 94 mit Anm. 114 und Jackson Bonner 2012, S. 50 mit Anm. 54. Jedenfalls hat Xusrō laut Prokop (2.24.12) Ādurbādagān aus Angst vor der Krankheit (δέει τῷ ἐκ τῆς νόσου) bereits kurze Zeit danach verlassen und sich auf dem Weg nach Assyrien begeben, das noch nicht verseucht war (ἔνθα δὴ οὔπω ἐνδεδημήκει τὸ τοῦ λοιμοῦ πάθος).

54 S. Jackson Bonner 2020, S. 194 mit Anm. 123 zur Gesundung des sasanidischen Königs. Seine Armee scheint es allerdings schlimmer erwischt zu haben: jedenfalls lässt Proc., *Pers.* 2.24.8 erahnen, dass Xusrō selbst mitsamt dem *ganzen* Heer von der Krankheit ergriffen worden war (αὐτὸν ὁμοῦ ξὺν παντὶ τῷ Περσῶν στρατῷ τῇ νόσῳ ἁλῶναι). Jackson Bonner (2011, S. 85–87) führt Argumente dafür an, dass die Heereskraft infolgedessen zahlenmäßig stark dezimiert gewesen sein könnte und mit frischen Mannschaften wieder aufgestockt werden musste. Dafür spräche auch, dass Johannes von Ephesos erwähnt (über den Umweg von Pseudo-Dionysios von Tell-Maḥrē [tr. Witakowski 1996, S. 77; tr. Harrak 1999, S. 97], der dessen Schriften als Quelle verwendet hat), dass ganz Palästina von der Seuche dermaßen heimgesucht worden war, dass zahlreiche Dörfer und Städte völlig verwaist zurückgeblieben waren. Mordechai/Eisenberg/Newfield/Izdebski/Kay/Poinar (2019, S. 25550), anders Meier (2020, S. 184–185), weisen jedoch darauf hin, dass palynologische Daten, die für das 1. nachchristliche Millennium im östlichen Mittelmeerbecken in Überfluss vorhanden sind, die Aussage des Kirchenhistorikers so nicht bestätigen: weder geht die Zahl der Getreidepollen — die auf landwirtschaftlichen Getreideanbau hindeuten — im 6. Jh. signifikant zurück, noch steigen umgekehrt Kiefernpollen in erheblichem Maße an (Kiefern gedeihen als eine der ersten Pflanzenarten auf verlassenen landwirtschaftlichen Flächen und Weiden).

55 S. Proc., *Goth.* 8.10.8–22 (ed./tr. Dewing 1928, S. 144–149).

56 Zur Geschichte der Rebellion s. Jackson Bonner 2011, S. 59–70, sowie Jackson Bonner 2020, S. 195–199.

57 S. *Histoire nestorienne* (ed. Scher), 182 [90]. Vgl. auch Morony 2007, S. 62.

58 S. *Histoire nestorienne* (ed. Scher), 183 [91]. Vgl. Morony 2007, S. 63.

nicht namentlich genannt, aber der vorangehende Kontext — in der von der Verwüstung Antiochiens durch Xusrō und der Deportierung dessen Einwohner nach Mesopotamien die Rede ist, die Justinian großes Leid bereiteten — legt nahe, dass der sasanidische König, eher als der oströmische Kaiser gemeint sein dürfte. Städte und Dörfer wurden verlassen; Lebensmittel und bewegliche Güter wurden aufgegeben, da niemand sie anzurühren traute. Alles deutet somit darauf hin, dass hier ebenfalls auf den Erstausbruch der Pest im Jahre 541/2 angespielt wird, da Xusrō I. unmittelbar nach dem Tod seines Vaters Kawād I. am 13. September 531 den Thron übernommen hatte. Laut des syrischen Continuators von Zacharias von Mytilene[59] verbreitete sich die Pest „bis nach Galatien, Kappadokien, Armenien, Antiochien, der Osrhoene, Mesopotamien, nach und nach zu den Persern, bis zu den Völkern des Nordostens".[60] Mehrere syrische Quellen berichten des Weiteren über eine Hungersnot in Mesopotamien, die womöglich einer (Pest?-)Epidemie verschuldet wurde; allerdings unterscheiden sich die spätantiken Schriftsteller in Einzelheiten und auch der Zeitpunkt (zwischen 545 und 547?) wird nicht einheitlich angegeben.[61] Die bereits erwähnte Chronik von Seʿert weiß noch über eine weitere Episode in Mesopotamien zu berichten, als Joseph, Katholikos der ‚Kirche des Ostens' in Seleukeia-Ktesiphon, Leichen beerdigen ließ, die auf die Straße geworfen waren und dort liegengelassen.[62] Nun war Joseph in der Zeit von 552 bis zu seiner Absetzung im Jahr 567 der 28. Katholikos gewesen. Seine Dienstzeit fällt somit mit dem zweiten großen Ausbruch der Pest zusammen, die von Amida (Diyarbakır) ausgegangen war[63] und dem eine längere Hungersnot (546–547 bis 554–555) vorangegangen war.[64] Womöglich hatte dieser Ausbruch nach einigen Monaten auch Mesopotamien erreicht.[65]

Mehrere arabische Historiker bringen außerdem den sasanidischen König Kawād II. (r. 628) mit einem Ausbruch der Pest in der Reichshauptstadt Ktesiphon (al-Madāʾin) im Jahr 6 H./627–628 in Verbindung.[66] Dieser Ausbruch ist auch bekannt als die ‚Pest von Shīrawayh'; der Name geht auf den Geburtsnamen Šīrōy

59 Die in griechischer Sprache verfasste Kirchengeschichte des Bischofs Zacharias von Mytilene (um 465 – nach 536) hat sich nicht erhalten, aber eine kurze syrische Zusammenfassung wurde von einem miaphysitischen Mönch (Pseudo-Zacharias) aus Amida um 569 in dessen eigene zwölfbändige Kirchengeschichte eingearbeitet.

60 Ps.-Zach. Rhet. 9.9a (tr. PHENIX/HORN 2011, S. 414–415). Auch Proc., *Pers.* 2.23.21 schreibt, dass die Pest bis nach Persien (ἐς τὴν Περσῶν γῆν) vorgedrungen war, sowie „zu allen übrigen Barbaren" (ἐς βαρβάρους τοὺς ἄλλους ἅπαντας). Vgl. noch MORONY 2007, S. 64.

61 S. STATHAKOPOULOS 2004, S. 298–299 (Nr. 125); vgl. GREATREX/PHENIX/HORN 2011, S. 417 Anm. 142.

62 S. *Histoire nestorienne* (ed. SCHER), S. 185–186 [93–94], vgl. MORONY 2007, S. 76; JACKSON BONNER 2020, S. 194.

63 S. STATHAKOPOULOS 2004, S. 115, 306–307 (Nr. 135), s. auch *ibid.*, S. 304 (Nr. 133).

64 S. STATHAKOPOULOS 2004, S. 299 (Nr. 126).

65 S. STATHAKOPOULOS 2004, S. 307–309 (Nr. 136)? Vgl. SARRIS 2022, S. 319.

66 DOLS 1974, S. 376; DOLS 1977, S. 20; CONRAD 1981, S. 64; CONRAD 1985, S. 160–162; STATHAKOPOULOS 2004, S. 120, 348 (Nr. 178); MATLOUBKARI/SHAIKH BAIKLOO ISLAM 2022, S. 72.

(gr. Σ(ε)ιρόης, Σηρόης) des ältesten (?) Sohnes Xusrō's II. aus dessen erster Ehe mit einer Frau aus Konstantinopel zurück, bevor er den Thronnamen Kawād übernahm. Wie viele andere Perser mit ihm soll er noch im selben Jahr nach einer nur acht Monate währende Regierungszeit von der Pest dahingerafft worden sein, aber die Quellen sind sich diesbezüglich nicht einig.[67] Daneben gibt es noch eine ‚Pest des Yazdgerd', nach einem Enkel desselben Königs Xusrō II. genannte Epidemie. Hierbei dürfte es sich um einen erneuten Ausbruch der Pest in der Regierungszeit des letzten sasanidischen Königs Yazdgerd III. (r. 632–651) gehandelt haben.[68] Vermutet wurde, dass sie mit dem Pestausbruch von ʿAmwās (17–18 H./638–639) in Palästina, unweit westlich von Jerusalem, identisch sein könnte, und die dort stationierten muslimisch-arabischen Truppen getroffen hatte.[69] Eine weitere Verbindung mit dem sasanidischen Perserreich scheint jedoch nicht gegeben zu sein.

Was diese wenigen literarischen Berichte über die Pest bei den Persern in spätsasanidischer Zeit gemein haben, ist dass sie fast ausschließlich die jeweiligen Herrscher (Xusrō I. bzw. Kawād II.) betreffen und sich nur auf die Grenzgebiete (Ādurbādagān, Mesopotamien) zum oströmischen Reich beziehen. Über die breite persische Bevölkerung außerhalb der Armee und des Hofes erfahren wir nur in sehr knappen, so allgemein gehaltenen Worten, dass sie kaum etwas darüber aussagen, ob die Pest auch in die weiter östlich gelegenen Gebiete des Perserreiches vordringen konnte. Allerdings erwähnen einige chinesische Quellen etwa zeitgleich mit der Pest von Shīrawayh kurz die Anwesenheit der Krankheit in Nordwest-China, in der wichtigen Ortschaft Hami (Qumul, das *Camul* von Marco Polo), einer auf der Seidenstraße gelegenen Stadt im östlichen Xinjiang nahe zur Grenze der heutigen Mongolei.[70] Auch Ratten — die Wirtsträger für die Flöhe, die das infektiöse Pestbakterium übertragen — sind für die Zeit Yazdgerds III. in chinesischen Chroniken erwähnt.[71] Theophylact Simocatta erzählt außerdem, dass Sogdoane (gr. Σουγδαηνή, d.h. Baktrien und

67 S. etwa Ṭabarī (tr. Nöldeke 1879), S. 385 (mit Anm. 4): „Die Pest soll sich in seinen Tagen ausgebreitet und die Perser bis auf wenige hingerafft haben. Seine Regierung währte 8 Monate". Vgl. dazu die Angaben des Geographen und Historikers Masʿūdī (896–956): „Pendant son règne, la peste se déclara dans l'Irak et d'autres provinces de la Babylonie et enleva plusieurs centaines de milliers d'habitants : les calculs les plus élevés disent la moitié de la population, et les plus modérés, le tiers" (tr. Barbier de Meynard/Pavet de Courteille 1863, S. 232), sowie des Geographen Maqdisī (945 – nach 1000): „Après lui, régna son fils Chiroûyé, dont la mère, Marie, était la fille de l'empereur grec Maurice. La peste éclata dans le pays et enleva les neuf dixièmes des hommes ; Chiroûyé en fut victime, après huit mois de règne" (tr. Huart 1903, S. 175).

68 S. Dols 1977, S. 20–21; Matloubkari/Shaikh Baikloo Islam 2022, S. 72.

69 Für weitere Einzelheiten zur möglichen Identifizierung s. Dols 1974, S. 376; Dols 1977, S. 21, vgl. Stathakopoulos 2004, S. 349–350 (Nr. 180); zum Ausbruch selbst s. Morony 2007, S. 65 und vor allem Conrad 1985, S. 167–246.

70 S. Dols 1974, S. 376 Anm. 51; Dols 1977, 20 Anm. 23, vgl. Stathakopoulos 2004, S. 121 und 348. Zu chinesischen Quellen aus der Zeit der Sui-Dynastie (581–618), die möglicherweise über die Beulenpest in China berichten, s. Buell 2012, S. 133–135.

71 S. Dols 1974, S. 376 (und Anm. 53).

Sogdien) einst — gegen Ende des 6. Jh.s? — von Seuchen und Erdbeben (λοιῶν καὶ σεισμῶν) heimgesucht wurde.[72]

Angesichts der dargelegten Dürftigkeit der literarischen Quellen bleibt dem Historiker daher nichts Anderes übrig, als nach möglichen archäologischen Indizien oder indirekten Anhaltspunkten für die Pest im sasanidischen Persien zu suchen, falls vorhanden. Der Idealfall ergäbe sich natürlich, wenn irgendwo auf dem Territorium des sasanidischen Reiches ein Massengrab mit gut erhaltenen menschlichen Skeletten entdeckt würde, die noch Spuren des Pestbakteriums enthielten, aber das ist bisher nicht geschehen. Zwei der bedeutendsten Ausgrabungen der letzten Jahrzehnte an der Nordgrenze des sasanidischen Reiches haben zwar menschliche Überreste zutage gefördert, aber insofern sie näher untersucht werden konnten, scheint nichts auf die Anwesenheit der Pest hinzudeuten. In beiden Fällen handelt es sich um den Bau von Verteidigungssystemen gegen die aus dem Norden anstürmenden Feinde (Chioniten und Kidariten nach 350, Hephthaliten nach 450).

Die erste der beiden Schutzanlagen, die sogenannte ‚Mauer von Gorgān‘ im Nordosten des Reiches stellt die längste Verteidigungslinie der Spätantike dar und übertrifft in ihrer Länge sogar den römischen Limes zu einem vergleichbaren Zeitpunkt. Über einer Länge von etwa 200 km zwischen dem Kaspischen Meer und dem Kopet-Dag-Gebirge verband eine 2 bis 5 m hohe und 10 m breite Befestigungsanlage 33 militärische Bastionen miteinander, die zusätzlich durch einen 3 m tiefen und bis zu 30 m breiten Graben davor geschützt wurden. Bei einer 2007 durchgeführten Magnetometer-Untersuchung im Laufe der von 2005 bis 2009 währenden Grabungskampagne wurden in einer der zusätzlichen Festungen im Hinterland (Qal‘a Kharāba in der heutigen Provinz Golestān, im westlichen Teil des Schutzwalls[73]), etwa eine Meile südlich des riesigen Verteidigungswalls auf der Höhe der Festung Nr. 29[74] menschliche Gebeine gefunden. Die südliche Festung wurde möglicherweise von Zivilisten genutzt;[75] wahrscheinlicher erscheint allerdings, dass sie als Garnisonslager für die Soldaten gedient hat, die die Mauer verteidigten. Der genaue, rechteckige Grundplan der Anlage, mit einer kleinen Zitadelle in der sudöstlichen Ecke, in deren Nähe die Gebeine gefunden wurden, legt jedenfalls die Vermutung eines militärischen Zwecks nahe.[76] Da die Bestattungen allem Anschein nach aus der islamischen Zeit nach der Aufgabe der Garnisonsanlage stammen und somit mit ziemlicher Sicherheit nicht mit dem

72 Theoph. Simoc., *Hist.* 7.8.13 (tr. WHITBY/WHITBY 1986, S. 191). Vgl. auch SCHAMILOGLU 2016, S. 309.

73 S. die Karte des Verteidigungswalls in REKAVANDI/SAUER *et al.* 2008, S. 152, Fig. 1.

74 S. das Satellitenfoto in REKAVANDI/SAUER *et al.* 2008, S. 159, Fig. 8.

75 Darauf könnte die Anwesenheit von Kinderknochen hindeuten, s. SAUER/REKAVANDI/WILKINSON/NOKANDEH *et al.* 2013, S. 326.

76 Womöglich weisen insbesondere die fein säuberlich, geradlinig an Erschließungskorridoren entlang und in nordwestlicher Richtung ausgerichteten doppelten Parallelreihen im Ostteil der Anlage auf den Aufbau von Zelten in einem temporären Militärlager hin, s. REKAVANDI/SAUER *et al.* 2008, S. 162.

sasanidischen Verteidigungswall in Verbindung gebracht werden können, wurde jedoch keine der dort bestatteten Knochen exhumiert.[77]

Die zweite der beiden Schutzanlagen liegt an der Nordwestgrenze des sasanidischen Reiches, in der Darialschlucht (MP. **Alānān dar* ‚Alanentor' [vgl. ŠKZ-mp 2]) im zentralen Kaukasus, die auch heute noch Georgien von Russland trennt. An einer Stelle am östlichen Fuß des Berges Kasbek verengt sich die Kluft zu einem schmalen Nadelöhr, mit 600 Meter hohen Steilwänden auf beiden Seiten, die nur weniger als 8 m voneinander entfernt sind. Durch seine Lage eignet sich der Ort somit hervorragend für den Bau eines militärischen Stützpunkts gegen die feindlichen Angriffe der Steppenkrieger aus dem Norden. Eine erste Bauphase der Festung wurde zwischen dem Ende des 4. Jh.s und der Mitte des 7. Jh.s durchgeführt.[78] Diese erfüllte offenbar eine rein (?) militärische Aufgabe: es wurden dort zwar keine Münzen vorgefunden, aber es kann natürlich nicht ausgeschlossen werden, dass der Ort dennoch eine wirtschaftliche Rolle im Handelsverkehr mit den nördlichen Nachbarn gespielt hat, falls die Erhebung etwaiger Zollgebühren *in natura* erfolgt wäre.[79] Etwa 2,5 km südlich der Festung befindet sich auch ein Friedhof, dessen älteste Gräber aus der Zeit vom 7./8. bis zum 8./10. Jh. datieren und daher außerhalb der Sasanidenzeit fallen.[80] Die Reste menschlicher Skelette, die dort im Laufe der Grabungskampagne 2013–2016 entdeckt wurden, waren in einem schlecht erhaltenen Zustand, und wurden einer paläopathologischen Untersuchung unterworfen.[81] Bei den 36 Individuen im Alter von 6–9 Monaten bis 35–45 Jahren[82] zeigten nur sechs Anzeichen erheblicher pathologischer Skelettläsionen.[83] Krankheit und Mangelernährung konnten zwar in mehreren Fällen festgestellt werden,[84] aber Spuren einer Pestinfektion waren offensichtlich nicht dabei.

Wenn weder literarische Quellen noch archäologische Funde (mittels *aDNA*) mit Spuren einer möglichen Pestepidemie im Herzen des sasanidischen Reiches — und nicht nur in den westlichen Randgebieten — dienen können, so gibt es noch eine letzte Möglichkeit fündig zu werden, indem dokumentarische

77 Zu den menschlichen Bestattungen an dieser Stelle, s. Sauer/Rekavandi/Wilkinson/Nokandeh *et al.* 2013, S. 325–327, insbes. S. 326–327.

78 S. Sauer/Chologauri *et al.* 2020, S. 19–51, 108–123. Im Jahr 395 hatten die Kidariten den Kaukasus überquert und waren sowohl ins oströmische Reich (bis Antiochien) als ins Sasanidenreich (bis Ktesiphon) vorgedrungen, bevor sie von den Persern zurückgedrängt wurden. Ob der Bau der Festung bereits vor diesem Angriff angefangen wurde oder erst infolgedessen, kann nicht mit Sicherheit ermittelt werden (dazu s. *ibid.*, S. 36–37). Die spätantike Burg scheint jedenfalls noch über das Ende der Sasanidendynastie hinaus benutzt gewesen zu sein, bis ein Dachbrand zwischen der Mitte des 7. Jh.s und dem frühen 8. Jh. für ein zeitweiliges Vakuum im Gebrauch sorgte. Wohl um 727 n.Chr. dürfte dann die Besatzung einer arabischen Garnison einen neuen Zeitabschnitt eingeläutet haben (dazu s. *ibid.*, S. 58).

79 S. Sauer/Chologauri *et al.* 2020, S. 58.

80 Zum Friedhof s. Sauer/Chologauri *et al.* 2020, S. 185–229.

81 S. Sauer/Chologauri *et al.* 2020, S. 707–722.

82 S. Sauer/Chologauri *et al.* 2020, S. 709.

83 S. Sauer/Chologauri *et al.* 2020, S. 715.

84 S. Sauer/Chologauri *et al.* 2020, S. 720.

Quellen (Inschriften, Papyri, Münzen, Gesetzestexte) auf Hinweise untersucht werden, die einen plötzlich erfolgten Bruch oder Wandel herrschender Normen und Bräuche im (politisch/militärisch/fiskalisch/juristisch-)administrativen, kulturell-religiösen oder sozialen Bereich suggerieren. Inschriften und Papyri sind ohnehin eher relativ selten im sasanidischen Iran und bleiben diesbezüglich leider stumm. Dagegen wurde die Vermutung geäußert, dass die eine oder andere Maßnahme im sasanidischen Gesetzbuch *Mādayān ī hazār dādestān (MHD)* ‚Buch der tausend Rechtsurteile' vor dem Hintergrund eines demographischen Schwunds zu erklären sein mag.[85] Das Werk ist das einzige seiner Art in mittelpersischer Sprache und weder im Umfang noch in der Gestaltung mit den oströmischen Codices vergleichbar. Anders als sein Name vorgibt, beabsichtigt es nicht eine umfassende Gesetzessammlung darzubieten, sondern ist es eine von einem gewissen Farroxmard ī Wahrāmān nach 617 verfasste kasuistische Kompilation von 840 reellen und hypothetischen Fällen im Bereich des zivilen Privatrechts und des Verwaltungsrechts (ohne religiösen Bezug auf zoroastrische Angelegenheiten, wie dies in späteren Werken aus dem 9.–10. Jh. der Fall ist).

Im Bereich des Eigentumsrechts lässt sich für das 5. und 6. Jh. eine eindeutige Tendenz in eine Richtung beobachten, die wegführt vom individuellen Privateigentum eines Grundstücks, hin zu einem gemeinschaftlich verwalteten, manchmal mehrere Dörfer — mitsamt umliegenden Feldern und dazugehörigen Pächtern — umfassenden Landgut (*dastgerd*) in der Hand mehrerer Mitglieder einer dem höheren Adel angehörigen Familie, in Anlehnung an das Vorbild der Krongüter im Besitz spätsasanidischer Herrscher.[86] Diese Landgüter möglichst unverteilt zusammenzuhalten war das Hauptziel der adligen Familien.[87] Die Tatsache, dass einerseits Grundbesitz immer öfter von Einzelpersonen auf Familien übertragen wurde, und dass andererseits Frauen größere Freiheiten im zivilrechtlichen Bereich (etwa im Ehe- und Erbrecht) zugestanden wurden, wird als Zeichen dafür verstanden, dass es einen Mangel an erwachsenen Männern gab, um die Landgüter verwaltungsmäßig zu beaufsichtigen[88] und es auch nicht genug gebärfähige Frauen aus dem Adelsstand im heiratsfähigen Alter gab.[89] Der Rückgang an (insbesondere adligen) Männern kann natürlich auch eine Folge der zahllosen Kriege gegen die hunnischen Völker (Kidariten und Hephthaliten) oder gegen Ostrom im 5./6. Jh., des mazdakitischen Aufstands (496)[90] — dem der Hochadel anfangs mit Wohlwollen gegenüberstand — oder noch der inneren Unruhen im 6. Jh. gewesen

85 Parallel dazu hat MEIER (2020, S. 179–180) gemeint, mehrere Anspielungen auf die Pest in oströmischen Gesetzestexten aus der Zeit Justinians (inbesondere in den Jahren 542–545) feststellen zu können, vgl. auch SARRIS 2022, S. 331.

86 S. MORONY 1981, S. 139, 147; CAMPOPIANO 2018, S. 467–468.

87 S. MORONY 1981, S. 143–147; CAMPOPIANO 2018, S. 471; ELMAN 2013, S. 103.

88 S. ELMAN 2013, S. 103.

89 S. ELMAN 2013, S. 104.

90 S. CAMPOPIANO 2018, S. 469–479.

sein, und muss gewiss nicht zwangsläufig auf einen möglichen Pestausbruch zurückzuführen sein.[91] Gegen einen demographischen Rücklauf im 5./6. Jh. spricht aber die Entwicklung der bereits angesprochenen ‚Mauer von Gorgān': während die ersten vorbereitenden Arbeiten dort bereits im 4. Jh. stattfanden, folgte die expansivste Bauphase zwischen 430 und 540, und kannte die Verteidigungslinie ihre größte Bevölkerungsdichte ausgerechnet im 6. Jh., bevor sie schließlich im Laufe der ersten Hälfte des 7. Jh.s nach und nach aufgegeben wurde.[92] Das Fehlen junger adligen Frauen, falls dieses denn der Realität entsprach und es dafür keine andere logische Erklärung gibt, mag hingegen der Pest zuzuschreiben sein.[93]

Die schrumpfende Zahl an männlichen Adligen hatte noch eine weitere — fiskalische — Konsequenz für die staatliche Schatztruhe, da es nunmehr an genügend kapitalkräftigen Steuerzahlern (und pachtzahlenden Feldarbeitern) mangelte.[94] Dadurch fehlte es zusehends auch an Einnahmen, um die kostspieligen Truppen zu bezahlen, und es konnten keine neuen Rekruten mehr einberufen werden. Um nicht völlig auf dringend notwendige Einkünfte in Zeiten einer Liquiditätskrise zu verzichten, wurde von Staats wegen die Möglichkeit von Darlehen auf unbestimmte Zeit[95] zur Abbezahlung der Schulden eingeräumt.[96] Die Idee dahinter war natürlich, eher die rechtzeitige Zahlung von Steuern als die Rückzahlung von Schulden zu bevorzugen. Die Staatsverschuldung (in der Form von Steuern) hatte somit die Priorität über private Schulden. Ein Kreditsystem, das jedoch nicht nur einzelnen Schuldnern, sondern auch deren Erben die Aufschiebung der Rückzahlungen ‚für immer' erlaubt, ist selbstverständlich auf Dauer zum Scheitern verurteilt.[97]

Angesichts eines stetig schwindenden, verarmten Hochadels und immer leerer werdender Kriegskassen sah sich Xusrō deshalb gezwungen, eine Reihe von

91 S. Elman 2013, S. 105–107. Auch das oströmische Reich hatte mit einem drastischen Rückgang an Humanressourcen zu kämpfen, für den es neben der Pest noch weitere Ursachen wie Erdbeben oder Hungersnöte gab, vgl. Stathakopoulos 2004, S. 163–165.

92 S. Sauer/Rekavandi/Wilkinson/Nokandeh *et al.* 2013, S. 596–608. Allerdings könnte man dieses Argument auch umkehren und anführen, dass solche gigantischen Baumaßnahmen zur Verteidigung der Reichsgrenzen im Nordwesten und -osten notwendig geworden waren, weil eben der Nachschub an jungen wehrhaften Männern fehlte, s. Matloubkari/Shaikh Baikloo Islam 2022, S. 70.

93 S. Elman 2013, S. 108.

94 Nach Meier 2016, S. 279–281 sah sich auch das oströmische Reich mit demselben Problem konfrontiert, vgl. auch Sarris 2022, S. 332, der auf das Fehlen von Arbeitern in jeglichen arbeitsintensiven Wirtschaftszweigen wie Kupferbergbau oder Weinanbau hinweist.

95 Zu dieser Art von Darlehen im spätsasanidischen Iran s. Macuch 2009, S. 189–190.

96 Auch in aus Ägypten stammenden Papyri meinte Meier (2016, S. 279 und 2020, S. 181–182) etwa zur Mitte des 6. Jh.s eine steigende Tendenz zu solchen langfristigen Verträgen erkennen zu können, vgl. auch Sarris 2022, S. 329, 332–333, 336; dagegen führen Mordechai/Eisenberg/Newfield/Izdebski/Kay 2020, S. 290–291 an, dass diese Tendenz schon gegen Ende des 4. Jh.s eingesetzt hatte und gegen Ende des 5. Jh.s verstärkt Fahrt aufnahm.

97 S. Elman 2013, S. 109–113.

sozialen, wirtschaftlichen und militärischen Maßnahmen durchzuführen.[98] Die grundlegenden Reformen beinhalteten unter anderem die Schaffung einer neuen Klasse des niedrigen Landadels (*dehgān*) und die Erfassung des Grundbesitzes in einem Katasterplan, sowie die Einführung einer Grundsteuer mit der Regelung einer — nach Vermögen gestaffelten — festen Kopfpauschale anstelle der vorherigen variablen Ertragssteuer. Diese Verfügung erlaubte dem König dadurch eine genauere Schätzung der zu erwartenden jährlichen Steuereinnahmen in die Staatskasse und eine bessere Planung der Kriegsausgaben. Erstaunlicherweise scheinen die eingreifenden Veränderungen keinerlei Einfluss auf das Münzwesen gehabt zu haben.[99] Anzeichen dafür, dass daneben ein möglicher Pestausbruch in Persien in irgendeiner Art und Weise Folgen für die Münzprägung gehabt haben könnte, gibt es ebenfalls nicht. Hätte die Pest dramatische Einwirkungen auf die iranische Bevölkerung gehabt, so hätte man demzufolge auch schwere wirtschaftliche Erschütterungen erwarten können. Während etwa die Stückzahlen der in Konstantinopel geprägten Münzen für das Jahr 542/3 erheblich zurückgegangen sind, lässt sich Ähnliches in der Münzprägung Xusrōs für die Jahre 542/3 oder 543/4 nicht beobachten.[100] Auch eine Gewichtsreduzierung der Goldmünzen (*solidi*)[101] oder der im täglichen Leben vielverwendeten Kupfermünzen, die in Konstantinopel im selben Zeitraum auf eine Finanzkrise hinzudeuten scheint,[102] gab es im Perserreich nicht. Zwar wurde auch hier das Gewicht der Drachme — des wichtigsten Münzwertes des Sasanidenreiches — reduziert, doch wurde dies bereits mehr als ein halbes Jahrhundert zuvor unter Pērōz I. (r. 459–484) durchgeführt und wurde der neue Gewichtsstandard danach bis zum Ende der arabo-sasanidischen Münzprägung unverändert beibehalten.[103]

Ein weiterer und letzter möglicher Effekt der spätantiken Pest, der jedoch schwerlich unwiderlegbar als kausal zu beweisen ist,[104] wird manchmal hinter dem raschen kulturellen Wandel vermutet, der sich im 6. Jh. vollzogen hat. Im religiösen Bereich konnte sich die Tendenz entweder durch eine kollektive Repaganisierung äußern, indem eine zutiefst verunsicherte Bevölkerung in Scharen vom Glauben abfiel,[105] oder im Gegenteil dadurch, dass sie massiv ihre Zuflucht zu einer verstärkten Religiosität suchte.[106] Allerdings dürften auch andere

98 S. dazu ausführlich RUBIN 1995, vgl. auch zusammenfassend HUYSE 2022, S. 26 Anm. 84.
99 S. SCHINDEL 2013, S. 817–818.
100 S. SCHINDEL 2022. Dennoch ist auch in Konstantinopel der Rückgang der Münzprägung nicht zwingend mit den Folgen der Pest zu erklären, da durch Justinians Reform des Münzwesens schon 538 ein neuer Typ von Kupfermünzen eingeführt worden war.
101 S. SARRIS 2022, S. 329, 333–334, vgl. SCHAMILOGLU 2016, S. 305.
102 S. MEIER 2016, S. 280.
103 S. SCHINDEL 2013, S. 825.
104 S. hierzu die von MORDECHAI/EISENBERG/NEWFIELD/IZDEBSKI/KAY 2020, S. 291–292 vorgebrachten Einwände.
105 S. MEIER 2016, S. 283.
106 Belege dafür findet MEIER 2016, S. 284–291 und 2020, S. 187–192 etwa im Aufstieg des Marienkults, der Entstehung der Ikonolatrie (so wurde einer Christusikone 544

Katastrophen (Erdbeben, Hungersnöte, Sonnen- und Mondfinsternisse, Invasionen und Verwüstungen, usw.) diese Neigungen verstärkt haben. Eine vielleicht ungewöhnliche Auswirkung der sukzessiven Pestausbrüche (und anderen Kalamitäten) ist wohl auch hinter dem Anstieg und der Entfaltung mehrerer Vernakularsprachen, Volksliteraturen sowie Lokalalphabete zu vermuten, da die Reihen der gut ausgebildeten Berufsschreiber in den dichtbevölkerten Stadtzentren und Klöstern stark ausgedünnt worden waren und es nun zusehends an fähigen Leuten fehlte, die die standardisierten Verkehrssprachen noch beherrschten.[107]

Obwohl die schriftliche und materielle Quellenlage in Persien zugegebenermaßen weitaus dürftiger ist als für das oströmische Reich, so scheint die Pest nach unserem derzeitigen Kenntnisstand also insgesamt keine tiefgreifende und langwierige Bedrohung für das Sasanidenreich dargestellt zu haben, falls es ihr denn überhaupt gelungen sein sollte, tief ins Landesinnere vorzudringen.[108] Da der Pesterreger jedoch — wie bereits angesprochen[109] — seinen Ursprung in Zentralasien oder Nordwest-China zu haben scheint, bleibt noch eine letzte Frage zu klären, auf welchem Weg er denn nach Westen gekommen ist wenn er kaum Spuren im Iran hinterlassen hat.[110] Grundsätzlich kann man sich dabei zwei Möglichkeiten vorstellen, entweder über dem Landweg entlang der Seidenstraße oder auf dem Seeweg über den Indischen Ozean zu den Häfen am Roten Meer. Welche der beiden Varianten den Vorzug verdient, bedarf nun im Nachfolgenden einer näheren Betrachtung.

---

nachgesagt, die Stadt Edessa vor den Persern gerettet zu haben, s. MEIER 2016, S. 286), der Sakralisierung des Kaisers, oder in der ‚Liturgifizierung' des religiösen Lebens (Steigerung von Andachtsübungen). Vergleichbares ließe sich auch für Mesopotamien in sasanidischer Zeit anführen, als der Katholikos Ezekiel (576–585) die Einhaltung einer dreitägigen ‚Fastenzeit von Nineve' als Reaktion auf das Eintreffen der Pest einführte, s. SARRIS 2022, S. 345. Zu ähnlichen Zuständen in Zentralasien s. SCHAMILOGLU 2016, S. 307–308.

107 S. SCHAMILOGLU 2016, S. 305–307.

108 S. auch HALDON *et al.* 2018c, S. 5. Der Vergleich mit anderen Pestepidemien aus jüngerer Zeit, wie die in Indien im 19. und 20. Jh., lehrt, dass sogar in aufs Schlimmste betroffenen Gegenden die Sterblichkeit zu keinem Zeitpunkt solch exzessive Höhen erreicht hat, dass sie die Bevölkerung flächendeckend hätte auslöschen können oder Institutionen dermaßen aus den Angeln hätte heben können, dass der Folgezustand ein fundamentaler Umbruch in Verwaltung, Kultur- oder Sozialleben bedeutet hätte, s. MORDECHAI/EISENBERG 2019, S. 40–44. Sogar für den Pestausbruch in Konstantinopel zur Zeit Justinians im Frühjahr 542 ergeben auf den Prinzipien der Stochastik fußenden Modellrechnungen, dass dieser unmöglich die eingangs erwähnten extremen demographischen Auswirkungen gehabt haben kann, wie sie von den ‚Maximalisten' auf der Grundlage von Augenzeugenberichten (allen voran Prokop, Euagrios und Johannes von Ephesos) vermutet wurde (s. oben S. 206 und Anm. 17). Zwischen objektiver Wirklichkeit und subjektivem Empfinden klafft unwiderlegbar eine Lücke, s. WHITE/MORDECHAI 2020, S. 3–11.

109 Vgl. die bereits oben in Anm. 24 erwähnte Literatur.

110 Vgl. auch SARRIS 2022, S. 343: „trying to reconstruct the movement of plague from Central Asia, via the Red Sea or through other routes prior to and during the Age of Justinian is a major desideratum".

Bereits in arsakidischer Zeit hatte es unter Mithridates II. (124/3–91 v.Chr.) erste Kontakte mit dem chinesischen Han-Kaiser Wudi (*Wǔdì*, r. 140–87 v.Chr.) gegeben.[111] Daneben entwickelte sich in den ersten beiden nachchristlichen Jahrhunderten auch der Seehandel mit Indien über den indischen Ozean. Da die Parther das lukrative Feld des Seehandels nicht ausschließlich den Römern überlassen wollten, gewannen neben den bekannten Häfen am Roten Meer (Myos Hormos, Berenike) auch bereits einige am Šaṭṭ al-ʿArab gelegene Handelsstädte im Königreich Charakene (Mesene/*Tiáozhī*), einem parthischen Vasallenstaat, an Bedeutung; der genannte Fluss verband den Persischen Golf mit Mesopotamien südlich des Zusammenflusses von Euphrat und Tigris.[112] Seit dem 1. Jh. n.Chr. holten palmyrenische Händler die angelieferten Waren mit ihren Karawanen auf dem Landweg aus diesen Handelsstädten (Spasinou Charax, Forat, Teredon, Apologos, usw.) ab.[113] Der größte Teil des Handels mit dem noch jungen Kušānreich und weiter östlich situierten Gebieten wurde jedoch über Land abgewickelt; der Seeweg über den Persischen Golf nahm unter den Arsakiden noch eine sehr untergeordnete Rolle ein. Er wird hauptsächlich in chinesischen Quellen erwähnt und nun offensichtlich auch durch vereinzelte archäologische Funde gestützt.[114] Unter den Sasaniden wurde die angefangene Entwicklung aber fortgesetzt: gegen Ende des 4. Jh.s oder Anfang des 5. Jh.s wurden die ersten Häfen am Persischen Golf entlang der persischen Küste errichtet.[115] Der kürzere Anfahrtsweg aus Indien, sowie günstige Strömungen ließen einen vielen schnelleren Transport der Schiffsladungen zu als über das Rote Meer. Als der alte persische König Xusrō I. 571 auch noch Yemen und Oman in sein Reich einverleiben konnte, überwachten die Sasaniden nunmehr den Schiffsverkehr auf beiden Seiten des Persischen Golfes und brachten somit wichtige Handelswege nach Indien und Süd-China unter ihre Kontrolle.[116] Im 6. Jh. hatte der Handel unter den Sasaniden seinen Höhepunkt erreicht. Die überschüssige Außenhandelsbilanz mit einer großen Gewinnspanne ermutigte die Sasaniden nun dazu, auf die sogdischen und baktrischen Zwischenhändler zu verzichten, die bis dahin als Mittelsmänner (und Bankkaufleute) für den Handel mit China aufgetreten waren.[117] Dieselben Zwischenhändler hatten auch — mit dem Einverständnis der Kušānherrscher, deren Territorium auf beiden Seiten des Hindukusch durchquert werden musste — die Verbindung zwischen Nordwest-China und den Häfen am Indischen Ozean gesichert, indem sie den steten Warenfluss hochwertiger Luxusgüter (Seide, Silber, Glasperlen, Lapislazuli, Gewürze, aro-

111 S. Wang Tao 2007, S. 87, 99–101; Gregoratti 2019, S. 57–58.
112 S. Gregoratti 2011 und 2019.
113 S. Gregoratti 2019, S. 59, 62–64, vgl. Payne 2018, S. 232, 234–235.
114 S. Gregoratti 2019, S. 60.
115 S. Huyse 2022, S. 25 mit den Literaturhinweisen in Anm. 78.
116 S. Huyse 2022, S. 26; Howard-Johnston 2017, S. 288–289, 295.
117 S. Payne 2018, S. 233–234, 237–238, 242, s. zusammenfassend Huyse 2022, S. 26 Anm. 83.

matische Gummiharze, usw.) in beide Richtungen mit ihren Karawanen auf sich genommen hatten.[118]

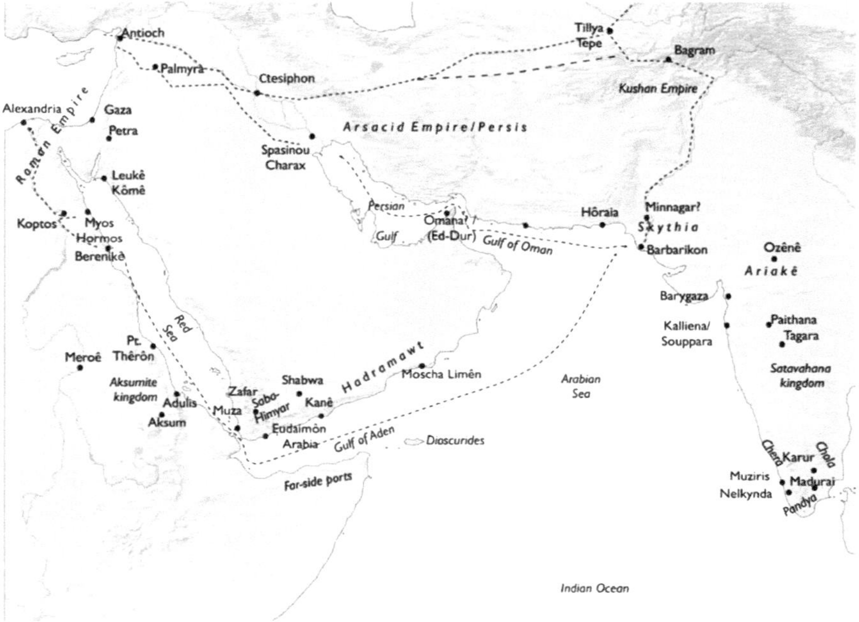

Fig. 1. Karte der Handelswege über Land und Meer von Afghanistan und Zentralasien nach Westen (Seland 2013, S. 67, Fig. 1)

Seit den 1960er Jahren hat sich weitestgehend die Ansicht durchgesetzt, dass die Beulenpest eine Nagetierkrankheit ist, die von Ratten über Flohbisse übertragen wird; Menschen sind dabei eigentlich überwiegend nur zufällige Nebenopfer.[119] Bereits in der Spätantike hatte Johannes von Ephesos (6. Jh.) beobachtet, dass die Krankheit nicht nur Menschen, sondern auch Haustiere und wilde Tiere, darunter Ratten, traf.[120] Gemeinhin wird angenommen, dass die infizierte

118 S. Payne 2018, S. 229. Bereits vor der Sasanidenzeit und der Einnahme des nordwestlichen Teils ihres Reiches — mit Baktrien und Gandhāra — durch Šābuhr I. (239/40–270) waren die Kušān als Händler zu Land auf der Seidenstraße und zur See im Indischen Ozean tätig, s. Seland 2013.

119 Die Geschichte dieser Entdeckung seit dem 19. Jh. und die bis heute anhaltenden Zweifel über die Ratte-Flöhe-Hypothese werden von Eisenberg/Mordechai (2020, S. 1655–1657) ausführlich geschildert. Die Lungenpest ist hingegen eine Tröpfcheninfektion, die von Mensch zu Mensch übertragen wird, s. oben Anm. 12; allerdings ist die Übertragung nicht so einfach wie allgemein angenommen wird, s. McCormick 2003, S. 1.

120 S. Joh. Ephes. *apud* Ps.-Dion. von Tell-Maḥrē = *Chronik von Zuqnīn* III (tr. Witakowski 1996, S. 87: „Also we saw that this great plague showed its effects on animals as well,

schwarze Hausratte (*Rattus rattus*) als Wirtstier und der in seinem Fell nistende, mit dem Bakterium *Y. pestis* infizierte Rattenfloh (*Xenopsylla cheopis*) die beiden Hauptverdächtigen für die Übertragung der Krankheit sind.[121] Angesichts dessen macht es stutzig, wie wenig Rattenknochen in den dennoch überaus zahlreichen Ausgrabungen im Mittelmeergebiet außerhalb Europas gefunden wurden.[122] Andererseits hatten spätrömische Augenzeugen sich schon über die hohe Sterblichkeit unter Ratten als Begleiterscheinung der spätantiken Pest gewundert.[123] Obwohl Rattenkolonien im römerzeitlichen Europa durchaus archäologisch gesichert sind,[124] ist der Grund für ihre Abwesenheit in der Levante nicht ganz klar.[125] Weil die Bevölkerungsdichte von Ratten[126] und Menschen parallel verläuft,[127] müsste ein Bevölkerungsanstieg oder -rückgang bei den Menschen sich logischerweise auch bei den Ratten demographisch bemerkbar machen. Tatsächlich hat eine rezente Untersuchung[128] ergeben, dass die hohe Zahl der schwarzen Ratten im Imperium Romanum der ersten nachchristlichen Jahrhunderte mit dem im 5. Jh. einsetzenden wirtschaftlichen Abschwung erheblich zurückgegangen war. Die geringere Menge an Getreidelieferungen für eine schwindende menschliche Bevölkerung war offensichtlich auch für die kommensalen Ratten nicht ohne Folgen geblieben. Nach dem Abklingen der spätantiken Pest im 6. Jh. haben sich die im klimatisch gemäßigten Europa ansässigen Rattenpopulationen in den folgenden Jahrhunderten (8.–10. Jh.) nach und nach erholt als die Städte wieder dichter bevölkert wurden und der Fernhandel wieder auflebte.[129]

---

not only on the domesticated but also on the wild, and even on the reptiles of the earth. One could see cattle, dogs and other animals, even rats, with swollen tumours, struck down and dying. Likewise wild animals could be found smitten by the same sentence, struck down and dying"); MORONY (2007, p. 71) und HARRAK (1999, S. 105) übersetzen syr. *'ūqbrē* mit ‚mice'.

121 S. oben Anm. 12.

122 Wiederholt haben MORDECHAI/EISENBERG 2019, S. 32–33 (s. die dort angegebenen Zahlen in Anm. 113) und EISENBERG/MORDECHAI 2019, S. 164 (s. auch hier oben Anm. 119 sowie WHITE/MORDECHAI 2020, S. 14) auf diesen Widerspruch aufmerksam gemacht und alternativ an die Lungenpest (wegen der höheren Sterblichkeitsrate) oder an Ektoparasiten wie menschliche Flöhe und Läuse gedacht. Dieselbe Beobachtung zur geringen Zahl der Rattenknochenfunde gilt im Übrigen auch für die Ausgrabungen an der Darialschlucht (zu den dort gefundenen Rattenknochen [1] s. SAUER/CHOLOGAURI *et al.* 2020, S. 780–787; und an der Mauer von Gorgān s. SAUER/REKAVANDI/WILKINSON/NOKANDEH *et al.* 2013, S. 575 [0]; an einigen Stellen war der Boden der Vorratsstellen außerdem so beschaffen, dass Nagetiere keinen Zugang zu den Getreidevorräten haben konnten, s. *ibid.*, S. 212).

123 S. MCCORMICK 2003, S. 4.

124 S. MCCORMICK 2003, S. 9.

125 S. MCCORMICK 2003, S. 15: „Whether this lack of hard data is due to insufficient investigation, to greater deterioration of fine rat bones after an additional millennium in the soil, or to lesser expansion of rat populations is unclear".

126 Dazu s. MCCORMICK 2003, S. 14 und WHITE/MORDECHAI 2020, S. 11.

127 S. MCCORMICK 2003, S. 16.

128 S. HE YU *et al.* 2022.

129 S. auch MCCORMICK 2003, S. 23.

Weiterhin gilt es zu beachten, dass die schwarze Ratte eher sedentär veranlagt ist. Unter der Annahme eines maximalen Bewegungsradius von etwa 200 m bei einer geschätzten Lebensspanne von ungefähr zwei Jahren würde dies bedeuten, dass eine Rattenkolonie im Durchschnitt rund fünf Jahre bräuchte um nur einen einzigen Kilometer zurückzulegen, oder anders gesagt, dass sie im Laufe eines ganzen Jahrhunderts höchstens 20 km vorankäme.[130] Damit können wir getrost davon ausgehen, dass die schwarze Ratte es niemals aus eigener Kraft, ohne menschliches Zutun, geschafft hätte, die Strecke von etwa 4 000 km zu überbrücken, die — sagen wir — Kokand an den westlichen Ausläufern des Tian-Shan-Gebirges vom syrischen Antiochien trennen. Genauso schwer vorstellbar erscheint es, dass die Ratten als blinde Passagiere im Gepäck versteckt auf dem Rücken von Kamelen, Pferden oder Mauleseln gereist wären.[131] Von den vor zwanzig Jahren bekannten Kolonien schwarzer Ratten in römischer Zeit ließ sich beziffern, dass sich knapp Dreiviertel in einer Entfernung von weniger als 10 km zu Meeresküsten oder Flussufern aufgehalten hatten und gar fast die Hälfte in Ufernähe von Binnengewässern gefunden wurde.[132] In den allermeisten Fällen dürften sie ihre Endbestimmung nur durch eine Mitfahrt auf See- oder Binnenschiffen erreicht haben. Genau wegen dieser Vorliebe für Bootsfahrten wird die schwarze Ratte manchmal auch als Schiffsratte bezeichnet.

Hausratten folgen Menschen, weil sie in deren Nähe Nahrung in Überfluss finden. Deshalb verwundert es nicht, dass man sie vor allem in den urbanen Zentren antrifft, wo ihnen mangelhafte Hygienezustände mit unzulänglichen Abwassersystemen und riesigen Müllhalden, sowie das enge Zusammenleben von Menschen und Haustieren in dichtgedrängten Wohneinheiten ein ideales Umfeld zum Vermehren bieten.[133] Die Ausdehnung der Rattenpopulationen und der Pest von einer Großstadt zur nächsten erfolgte immer nach demselben Muster, entlang der Hauptverkehrsadern von den Küsten ins Landesinnere.[134] Auch Dörfer wurden so erreicht, wo die Pest ihre Wirkung allerdings weniger

130 S. McCormick 2003, S. 10 mit Anm. 13.

131 S. McCormick 2003, S. 130, vgl. Buell 2012, S. 142 im Zusammenhang mit der Pestepidemie im 14. Jh.

132 S. McCormick 2003, S. 11.

133 S. Conrad 1996, S. 85–93; Sarris 2022, S. 324–325. Es sollte allerdings nicht vergessen werden, dass die Umstände, die eine Vermehrung der Rattenpopulationen begünstigen, hier nur allgemein formuliert sind. Wo sie im konkreten Fall zu einer höheren Sterblichkeit unter den Menschen im Zusammenhang mit der Pest führen, kann allerdings nur durch archäologische Funde genauer bestimmt werden, da spätantike Texte darüber nichts aussagen, vgl. auch White/Mordechai 2020, S. 15.

134 S. Conrad 1996, S. 94–96; McCormick 2003, S. 12; Schamiloglu 2016, S. 295. Auch der mittelalterliche ‚schwarze Tod‘ hatte sich auf diese Art und Weise zwischen 1346 und 1353 über ganz Europa ausgebreitet. Über Schiffe mit infizierter Besatzung war der Krankheitserreger von Genua nach Marseille gelangt, von wo aus die Pandemie ihren Aufmarsch der Rhone entlang unaufhaltsam nach Norden fortsetzen konnte. Auch Landwege, die über wichtige Verkehrsadern bevölkerungsreiche Städte miteinander verbanden, trugen zur Ausdehnung bei.

unmittelbar durch ihre inhärente letale Kraft entfaltete, sondern sekundär durch die Fluchtbewegungen die sie auslöste, wodurch die umliegenden Felder mangels Arbeiter oft brach liegen blieben oder Ernten auf den Feldern verrotteten.[135] Dagegen gedeihen Ratten in der Umgebung von Nomaden nicht so gut, weil diese sich selten lange an einem Ort aufhalten und meistens in kleinen Sozialverbänden leben; dadurch blieben durch eine nomadische Bevölkerung geprägte Regionen fast vollständig von der Pest verschont.[136]

Letztendlich kristallisiert sich ein glaubhaftes Szenario immer mehr heraus, das jedoch jederzeit durch Neufunde in Frage gestellt werden kann: Wenn der Pesterreger wirklich von Zentralasien oder Nordwest-China nach Europa gekommen ist,[137] dann kann das nach dem Überqueren des Hindukusch am Khaiberpass oder des Karakorumgebirges von Kaschgar aus eigentlich nur auf großen, mit Karren befahrbaren Verbindungs- und Handelswegen der südlichen Abzweigung der Seidenstraße durch das Industal geschehen sein, oder mit Binnenschiffen auf dem Wasserweg.[138] Im ausgehenden Gupta-Reich, das um 550

135 S. CONRAD 1996, S. 97–98, 111, vgl. SCHAMILOGlu 2016, S. 305. Aus diesem Grund hat sich Justinian laut Prokop (Proc., *Anecd.* 23.20–22 [ed./tr. DEWING 1935, S. 274–277]) auch dazu entschieden, verlassenes Ackerland neuen Eigentümern zuzuweisen, damit diese die Felder bearbeiten konnten und die jährlichen Steuern und Abgaben der vormaligen verstorbenen oder geflohenen Besitzer an deren Statt anteilig übernehmen konnten, s. CONRAD 1996, S. 108; MEIER 2016, S. 281 mit Anm. 81. Eine ähnliche Geschichte mit anderem Lösungsansatz erzählt Bīrūnī über den sasanidischen König Pērōz I. (459–484): als eine große Dürre das Reich getroffen hatte, erließ der König die Steuern, öffnete die Speicher und lieh Geld von den zoroastrischen Tempeln um es unter die Bevölkerung zu verteilen und ihre Not zu lindern, so dass niemand Hunger leiden musste (tr. SACHAU 1879, S. 215). Selbstverständlich kam die Situation ihm auch gelegen, um die Macht der Priester und Tempel zu beschränken, s. MATLOUBKARI/SHAIKH BAIKLOO ISLAM 2022, S. 70.

136 S. CONRAD 1996, S. 99–102; SCHAMILOGLU 2016, S. 303. Neuerdings wurde eine archeogenomische Untersuchung am Skelett zweier Individuen aus der Umayyadenzeit (661–750) durchgeführt, die in Tell Qarasa (Süd-Syrien) oben auf einer neolithischen Site begraben waren. Die Analyse ergab jedoch, dass sie nicht von örtlichen Beduinen abstammten, sondern genetisch mit einer Untergruppe aus der Wüste Negev in Israel für den einen, aus Saudi-Arabien für den anderen nah verwandt waren. Beide waren noch jung; da ihre Knochen keine Verletzungen aufwiesen und ihre in die Richtung von Mekka ausgelegte Körper außerhalb eines Friedhofskontexts gefunden wurden, wird vermutet, dass es sich um zwei muslimische Pilger auf der Durchreise gehandelt haben könnte, die vielleicht einem Pestausbruch erliegen waren und deshalb in größter Eile an Ort und Stelle bestattet wurden, s. SRIGYAN *et al.* 2022.

137 S. oben Anm. 24.

138 Zum dichten Netzwerk von fein verästelten Überlandverbindungen, die über die hohen Gipfel des Hindukusch (gr. Παροπάμισος) und des Karakorumgebirges durch die Täler des Hunza, des Gilgit und des Oberen Indus führten und dadurch den Osten Zentralasiens und den Westen des Tarimbeckens an die ‚nördliche Route' (skt. *uttarāpatha*) von Taxila bis Mathurā — und darüber hinaus — in Nordwestindien anknüpften, s. NEELIS (2002) mit weiteren Einzelheiten zur historischen Bedeutung des Wegennetzes für den Fernreiseverkehr, den Handel und die Übertragung von Religionen (Zoroastrismus, Manichäismus, Buddhismus). Der Indus war nicht über seinen gesamten Lauf von der Quelle

teilweise von den iranischen Alkhon-Hunnen (Αλχοννο, *Hūṇā*) übernommen wurde, verbanden der Indus und seine Zuflüsse die Städte in der Region Gandhāra (Peschawar, Taxila/Sirsukh) mit der von den Römern ehemals genutzten, knapp 1 500 km entfernten Hafenstadt Barbarikon (nahe Karachi).[139] Genauere Untersuchungen wären hier gewiss sehr willkommen. Die von den Karawanen benutzten Trampelpfade der weiter nördlich verlaufenden westlichen Route der Seidenstraße eigneten sich dafür hingegen wohl eher nicht. Ein *argumentum e silentio* ist selbstverständlich immer mit äußerster Vorsicht zu betrachten, aber wenn sich der Pesterreger tatsächlich auf dem Landweg nach Westen ausgebreitet hätte, erstaunt es schon, dass sich darüber sowohl die (späteren) schriftlichen wie auch die archäologischen Quellen — bisher? — vollkommen ausschweigen. Inwiefern China selbst vor dem 7. Jh. von der Pest betroffen war, ist ebenfalls schwer zu beurteilen, denn auch die zahlreicherer verfügbaren chinesischen Schriftquellen sind diesbezüglich nicht viel ergiebiger.[140]

im westlichen Tibet bis zur Mündung in das Arabische Meer zu befahren, sondern wird erst im Norden Pakistans schiffbar, wo der Kābul (ved./avest. Kubhā, gr. Κωφήν) auf der Höhe von Attock (etwa 85 km westlich von Islamabad) in den Indus mündet. Genau diesen Weg scheint auch Skylax von Karyanda bei seiner — meistens in der Zeit zwischen 519 und 516 v.Chr. angesetzten — Erkundungsfahrt auf dem Indus im Auftrag des achaimenidischen Königs Dareios' I. (522–486) genommen zu haben. Die Annahme einer Reise über den Kābul (und erst anschließend über den Indus) würde zumindest eine Erklärung dafür bieten, dass Skylax nach Herodots Angaben (Hdt. 4.44) von Kaspatyros (d.h. wohl Peschawar) in der Region Paktyika aus in *östliche* Richtung stromabwärts bis zum Meer gefahren sei (für weitere Einzelheiten s. vor allem Karttunen 1989, S. 40–48 sowie Parker 2008, S. 15, 22 Anm. 46). Knapp zwei Jahrhunderte später erkundete Nearchos als Oberbefehlshaber der neugegründeten Flotte Alexanders des Großen 326 v.Chr. zunächst den Hydaspes (h. Jhelam) stromabwärts bis zur Mündung in den Akesines (h. Chenāb) — am Zusammenfluss von Akesines und Indus hat Alexander daraufhin eine Stadt gegründet, die er Ἀλεξάνδρεια ἐπὶ Ἰνδῷ nannte und mit thrakischen Veteranen und Einheimischen besiedeln ließ —, bevor er in Alexanders Auftrag im darauffolgenden Jahr eine beschwerliche Seereise von Patala im Indusdelta nach Mesopotamien bis zur Mündung von Tigris und Euphrat in den Persischen Golf unternahm, s. etwa Karttunen 1989, S. 58–59, 90 und Parker 2008, S. 38–39. Die Physiognomie des heutigen Indusdeltas ist im Übrigen nicht ganz mit seiner Ausdehnung in der Antike deckungsgleich, da sich die Deltafront seit dem Alexanderzug um etwa 60–100 km vorgeschoben hat. Der Versuch einer Rekonstruktion des Wachstums und sonstiger Veränderungen im Indusdelta seit der Zeit Alexanders des Großen wurde von Wilhelmy (1968) auf der Grundlage von Berichten in schriftlichen Quellen, von der Beobachtung morphologischer Entwicklungen und vom Studium antiker Karten vorgenommen.

139 Zu dieser Hafenstadt und den dort von den Römern im 1. Jh. verhandelten Waren, s. *Periplus Maris Erythraei* 38–39 (tr. Schoff 1912, S. 37; ed./tr. Casson 1989, S. 72–75). Noch weiter südlich befinden sich in Gujarat Barygaza und weitere Hafenstädte, s. Casson 1989, S. 21–26.

140 Vor der Tang-Zeit (618–907) sind die Informationen recht spärlich, s. oben Anm. 70. Der früheste Ausbruch der Beulenpest mag im Jahr 610 stattgefunden haben, s. Schamiloglu 2016, S. 298, aber erst unter der Tang-Dynastie gibt es Berichte über Ausbrüche in den Jahren 636–655, 682 und 707, s. Schamiloglu 2016, S. 297, 310.

Dass es sich bei der ‚justinianischen Pest' (*ca.* 541–544) um die Beulenpest gehandelt hat,[141] dürfte mittlerweile über jeden Zweifel erhaben sein. Das muss nicht zwingend bei jedem späteren, schriftlich überlieferten Pestausbruch der Fall gewesen sein, aber mit Bezug auf den ersten Ausbruch sprechen dafür nicht nur die übereinstimmenden Beschreibungen der Symptome durch die spätantiken Autoren und die Verbreitung der Krankheit über schwarze Ratten (*Rattus rattus*), sondern auch der Anteil, der dabei speziell von den Rattenflöhen (*Xenopsylla cheopis*) eingenommen wird. Wenn die infizierten Ratten an der Pest sterben, müssen sich die Flöhe neue Wirte (Menschen) suchen, denen sie das mit Pestbakterien belastete Blut übertragen können. Von der Evolution wurden Rattenflöhe dank der Physiologie ihres Verdauungstraktes geradezu perfekt dafür ausgestattet, um in einem komplexen Übertragungszyklus das Bakterium *Y. pestis* genetisch zu einem der virulentesten Pathogene der Menschheitsgeschichte werden zu lassen.[142] Seit einem Jahrhundert wissen wir, dass Außentemperatur und relativer Sättigungsgrad der Luft (Luftfeuchtigkeit) dabei ebenfalls eine Rolle spielen, wobei letzterer Faktor der wichtigere ist.[143]

Heutzutage findet man die Pest noch in Asien, Gesamtamerika und vor allem in Afrika auf der Insel Madagaskar. Im Hochland der Insel wird der Krankheitserreger hauptsächlich durch zwei nebeneinander lebende Floharten übertragen, die bereits angesprochene Art *Xenopsylla cheopis*, die vor allem auf drinnen in Wohnungen lebenden Hausratten anzutreffen ist, und die endemische Art *Synopsyllus fonquerniei*, die eher bei draußen in der Natur verbleibenden Ratten vorkommt. Eine neuere Untersuchung[144] hat ans Licht gebracht, dass die Flöhe insgesamt häufiger in warmer und feuchter Umgebung vorkommen, wobei höhere Temperaturen unter Laborbedingungen eine schnellere Entwicklung der Larven und Puppen zu begünstigen scheinen (aber keinen Einfluss auf die bereits erwachsenen Insekten haben), während eine höhere Luftfeuchtigkeit zu einer längeren Lebensdauer führt. Die endemische Flohart kommt außerdem besser mit den kühleren Bedingungen in den Höhenlagen über 800 m zurecht,

141 Nach einer offenen Diskussion aller Argumente für und wider kommen auch WHITE/MORDECHAI (2020, S. 13–15) zu der Schlussfolgerung, dass es sich bei der ersten Pestepidemie um Beulenpest gehandelt hat.

142 S. HINNEBUSCH 2005. Zu den entscheidenden genetischen Veränderungen des Bakteriums gehören seine Fähigkeit, sich an die Umgebungstemperatur des Flohs anzupassen; die Ausstattung mit den Genen *hms* und *ymt*, die erforderlich sind, um eine übertragbare Infektion beim Floh hervorzurufen; und die Fähigkeit, eine Art verklumpten Biofilm zu entwickeln, um den Vordermagen des Flohs zu blockieren.

143 S. BACOT/MARTIN 1924. Die beiden Forscher fanden heraus, dass die Überlebenschancen der Rattenflöhe bei hoher Luftfeuchtigkeit, aber konstanter Temperatur und stillstehender Luft, am besten waren; je trockener die Umgebungsluft, desto schneller trockneten die Flöhe auch aus und starben. Umgekehrt verkürzte sich ihre Lebensspanne um die Hälfte bis zu zwei Dritteln bei konstanter Luftfeuchtigkeit aber ansteigender Temperatur. Bei gleichzeitiger Erhöhung von Luftfeuchtigkeit und Temperatur verkürzte sich ebenfalls die Lebensdauer, allerdings weniger stark (um ein Drittel) als im vorherigen Fall.

144 S. KREPPEL *et al.* 2016.

so dass beide Arten mit ihren unterschiedlichen saisonalen Zyklen eigentlich komplementär sind. Anders gesagt ist die endemische Art gerade dann[145] am stärksten vertreten, wenn die exotische Art zahlenmäßig zurückgeht.[146] Dass die heutige madagassische *Xenopsylla cheopis* die wärmere Regensaison mit einer Durchschnittstemperatur von 23 °C bis 28 °C und einer relativen Luftfeuchtigkeit von 84% bis 94% vorzieht, könnte *mutatis mutandis* auch ein weiteres Argument dafür sein, dass der Pesterreger per Schiff nach Westen gekommen ist. In der warmen und feuchten Umgebung unter Deck hätten sich Flöhe auf Schiffen bestimmt sehr wohl gefühlt.[147]

Da die Pest Mesopotamien erst Ende 542 erreicht hat,[148] knapp zweieinhalb Jahre nach dem Erstausbruch in Pelousion, nachdem vorher auch noch Konstantinopel und das östliche Mittelmeergebiet befallen worden waren, spricht alles dafür, dass es nicht persische Händler gewesen sind, die die Krankheit über eine der an den Ufern des Persischen Golfes gelegenen Hafenstädte eingeschleppt haben, sondern in der Tat — wie oft angenommen — oströmische oder syrische Händler, die sie in den auf der ägyptischen Seite gelegenen Hafenstädten am Roten Meer oder am Suezkanal (Clysma) an Land gebracht haben.[149] Da außerdem sowohl der ‚justinianischen Pest' als auch dem ‚schwarzen Tod' jeweils ein bis zwei Jahrhunderte zuvor wiederholte Invasionen nomadischer Völker vorangegangen sind (iranischer Hunnen im 4. und 5. Jh. [zunächst der Kidariten und Chioniten, gefolgt von den Hephthaliten], sowie der Mongolen im 13. Jh.), ist die Frage nach einer möglichen Verkettung der

145 In den ländlichen Gegenden auf Madagaskar beginnt die trockene und kalte Saison im Juli und erreicht ihren Höhepunkt zwischen September und Januar.

146 Auch Konrad (1996, S. 104) hatte darauf hingewiesen, dass die Pest im Grunde eine saisonale Krankheit war, die in den Monaten Oktober bis Januar weniger Probleme machte, was auch mit einer wetterbedingt ruhigeren Periode für die Seefahrt zusammenhängen konnte, vgl. auch oben Anm. 45.

147 Allerdings geht die Lebensdauer beider Floharten unter Laborbedingungen jedoch ab einer Temperatur von 32 °C und einer relativen Luftfeuchtigkeit von 90 % eindeutig zurück, s. Kreppel *et al.* 2016, S. 4. Bei Schifffahrten auf dem Nil und dem Roten Meer wäre diese Temperatur sicherlich noch um einiges überschritten worden und hätte im Sommer — freilich bei geringerer relativer Luftfeuchtigkeit um die 30 % — bis zu 40 °C erreichen können, s. Matloubkari/Shaikh Baikloo Islam 2022, S. 72. Andererseits hätte die in den Jahren 536–550 weitverbreitete Abkühlung um bis zu 3–4 °C dem entgegenwirken können, vgl. oben Anm. 32. Die hohen Temperaturen und die hohe Luftfeuchtigkeit könnten vielleicht auch eine Erklärung dafür bieten, warum die Pest im 14. Jh. weniger Tote in Indien gefordert hat.

148 Wie heftig und wie lang die Beulenpest in Mesopotamien wüten konnte, ist nicht sicher zu ermitteln, aber man kann sich des Eindrucks nicht erwehren, dass es dabei nur um vereinzelte, lokal begrenzte Ausbruchsherde gegangen ist, die insgesamt nur für wenige Monate auflodern konnten.

149 S. etwa McCormick 2003, S. 7–8; Harper 2017, S. 215–219; Newfield 2018a, S. 98; Keller *et al.* 2019a, S. 12368; Eisenberg/Mordechai 2019, S. 166 mit weiteren Literaturhinweisen in Anm. 48; Jackson Bonner 2020, S. 191.

Ereignisse aufzuwerfen.[150] Sie erscheint durchaus berechtigt, lässt sich jedoch derzeit wie so viele andere im Zusammenhang mit der Pest noch nicht endgültig beantworten.[151]

Bibliographie

Primärquellen (Textausgaben und Übersetzungen)

BARBIER DE MEYNARD, C./[A.] PAVET DE COURTEILLE 1863: *Maçoudi. Les Prairies d'Or. Texte et Traduction.* Tome deuxième. Paris.

CASSON, L. 1989: *The Periplus Maris Erythraei. Text with Introduction, Translation, and Commentary.* Princeton.

CROKE, B. 1995: *The Chronicle of Marcellinus. Translation and Commentary.* Sydney (Byzantina Australiensia 7).

DEWING, H.B. 1914: *Procopius. With an English Translation.* Vol. 1: *History of the Wars, Books I and II.* London/New York.

— 1916: *Procopius. With an English Translation.* Vol. 2: *History of the Wars, Books III and IV.* London/New York.

— 1928: *Procopius. With an English Translation.* Vol. 5: *History of the Wars, Books VII (continued) and VIII.* London/New York.

— 1935: *Procopius. With an English Translation.* Vol. 6: *The Anecdota or Secret History.* London/New York.

GREATREX, G. (ed.)/R.R. PHENIX/C.B. HORN (tr. from Syriac and Arabic sources) 2011: *The Chronicle of Pseudo-Zachariah Rhetor. Church and War in Late Antiquity.* Liverpool (Translated Texts for Historians 55).

HAMILTON, F.J./E.W. BROOKS 1899: *The Syriac Chronicle Known as that of Zachariah of Mitylene. Translated into English.* London.

HARRAK, A. 1999: *The Chronicle of Zuqnīn. Parts III and IV. A.D. 488–775. Translated from Syriac with Notes and Introduction.* Toronto (Mediaeval Sources in Translation 36).

HODGKIN, TH. 1886: *The Letters of Cassiodorus Being a Condensed Translation of the Variae Epistulae of Magnus Aurelius Cassiodorus Senator. With an Introduction.* London.

150 Wie zuletzt etwa von SARRIS (2022, S. 344) geschehen. Anzumerken wäre noch, dass die hunnischen Einfälle ins sasanidische Reich im 4. und 5. Jh. mit einer Periode großer andauernder Dürre (ca. 340–380) einhergehen. Hungersnot und ein Rückgang des Viehbestandes könnten daher die Hunnen zu ihren Übergriffen bei den südlichen Nachbarn angestiftet haben, s. MATLOUBKARI/SHAIKH BAIKLOO ISLAM 2022, S. 66–70.

151 Aufgrund der ursprünglichen Fehldatierung des Genoms eines in Nord-Ossetien ausgegrabenen Mannes, der nach molekularer Datierungsanalyse seiner Knochen um einige Jahrhunderte (von 6.–9. Jh. auf ca. 1030 N.CHR. [732–1274]) hochdatiert werden muss, haben Keller *et al.* 2019a/b die Hypothese eines Zusammenhangs mit den hunnischen Invasionen verworfen. Dabei handelt es sich jedoch um den isolierten Fall eines einzigen Individuums, der auf jeden Fall noch Bekräftigung oder Widerlegung durch weitere archäologische Funde bräuchte.

Huart, C. 1903: *Le Livre de la Création et de l'Histoire de Motahhar ben Ṭahîr el-Maqdisî, attribué à Abou-Zéïd Aḥmed ben Sahl el-Balkhî, publié et traduit d'après le Manuscrit de Constantinople.* Tome troisième. Paris.

Mommsen, Th. 1894: *Chronica minora saec. IV. V. VI.* Band 2. Berlin (Monumenta Germaniae Historica. Auctores Antiquissimi 11).

Nöldeke, Th. 1879: *Geschichte der Perser und Araber zur Zeit der Sasaniden. Geschichte aus der arabischen Chronik des Tabari übersetzt und mit ausführlichen Erläuterungen versehen.* Leiden.

Sachau, E. 1879: *The Chronology of Ancient Nations. An English Version of the Arabic Text of the Athâr-ul-Bâkiya of al-Bîrûnî, or "Vestiges of the Past," Collected and Reduced to Writing by the Author in A.H. 390–1, A.D. 1000. Translated and Edited, with Notes and Index.* London.

Scher, A. 1911: *Histoire nestorienne (Chronique de Séert), seconde partie, fasc. 1.* Paris (Patrologia Orientalis VII.2).

Schoff, W.H. 1912: *The Periplus of the Erythraean Sea. Travel and Trade in the Indian Ocean by a Merchant of the First Century. Translated from the Greek and Annotated.* New York/London/Bombay/Calcutta.

Wachsmuth, C. 1897: *Ioannis Laurentii Lydi Liber de Ostentis et Calendaria Graeca Omnia.* Leipzig.

Whitby, M. 2000: *The Ecclesiastical History of Evagrius Scholasticus. Translated with an Introduction.* Liverpool (Translated Texts for Historians 33).

Whitby, M./M. Whitby 1986: *The History of Theophylact Simocatta. An English Translation with Introduction and Notes.* Oxford.

Witakowski, W. 1996: *Pseudo-Dionysius of Tel-Mahre. Chronicle (Known also as the Chronicle of Zuqnin).* Part III: *Translated with Notes and Introduction.* Liverpool (Translated Texts for Historians 22).

Sekundärquellen

Arjava, A. 2005: "The Mystery Cloud of 536 CE in the Mediterranean Sources." In: *Dumbarton Oaks Papers* 59, S. 73–94.

Bacot, A.W./C.J. Martin 1924: "The Respective Influences of Temperature and Moisture upon the Survival of the Rat Flea (*Xenopsylla Cheopis*) Away from its Host." In: *The Journal of Hygiene* 23, S. 98–105.

Biraben, J.N./J.Le Goff 1969: "La peste dans le Haut Moyen Age." In: *Annales* 24, S. 1484–1510 [= "The Plague in the Early Middle Ages." In: R. Forster/O. Ranum (eds.): *Biology of Man in History.* Baltimore/London. 1975, S. 48–80].

Börm, H. 2007: *Prokop und die Perser. Untersuchungen zu den römisch-sasanidischen Beziehungen in der Spätantike.* Stuttgart (Oriens et Occidens 16).

Buell, P.D. 2012: "Qubilai and the Rats." In: *Sudhoff's Archiv* 96, S. 127–144.

Büntgen, U./V. Myglan/F. Ljungqvist *et al.* 2016: "Cooling and Societal Change during the Late Antique Little Ice Age from 536 to around 660 AD." In: *Nature Geoscience* 9, S. 231–236. Available online: doi:10.1038/ngeo2652.

Büntgen, U. *et al.* 2020: "Prominent Role of Volcanism in Common Era Climate Variability and Human History." In: *Dendrochronologia* 64: 125757. Available online: doi:10.1016/dendro.2020.125757.

CAMPOPIANO, M. 2018: "Land Tenure, Land Tax and Social Conflictuality in Iraq from the Late Sasanian to the Early Islamic Period (Fifth to Ninth Centuries CE)." In: A. DELATTRE/M. LEGENDRE/P. SIJPESTEIJN (eds.): *Authority and Control in the Countryside. From Antiquity to Islam in the Mediterranean and Near East (6th–10th century)*. Leiden (Leiden Studies in Islam and Society 9), S. 464–499.

CONRAD, L.I. 1981: "Arabic Plague Chronologies and Treatises: Social and Historical Factors in the Formation of a Literary Genre." In: *Studia Islamica* 54, S. 51–93.

— 1985: *The Plague in the Early Medieval Near East*. Ann Arbor.

— 1996: "Die Pest und ihr soziales Umfeld im Nahen Osten des frühen Mittelalters." In: *Der Islam* 73, S. 81–112.

DOLS, M.W. 1974: "Plague in Early Islamic History." In: *JAOS* 94, S. 371–383.

— 1977: *The Black Death in the Middle East*. Princeton.

EISENBERG, M./L. MORDECHAI 2019: "The Justinianic Plague: An Interdisciplinary Review." In: *Byzantine and Modern Greek Studies* 43, S. 156–180.

EISENBERG, M./L. MORDECHAI 2020: "The Justinianic Plague and Global Pandemics: The Making of the Plague Concept." In: *The American Historical Review* 125, S. 1632–1667. Available online: doi:10.1093/ahr/rhaa510.

ELMAN, Y. 2013: "Law in the Crisis of Empire: A Sasanian Example." In: *Journal of Persianate Studies* 6, S. 101–114.

FERRIS, D.G. *et al.* 2011: "South Pole Ice Core Record of Explosive Volcanic Eruptions in the First and Second Millennia A.D. and Evidence of a Large Eruption in the Tropics around 535 A.D." In: *Journal of Geophysical Research* 116, D17308. Available online: doi:10.1029/2011JD015916.

GRÄSLUND, B./N. PRICE 2012: "Twilight of the Gods? The 'Dust Veil Event' of AD 536 in Critical Perspective." In: *Antiquity* 86, S. 428–443.

GREGORATTI, L. 2011: "A Parthian Port on the Persian Gulf: Characene and its Trade." In: *Anabasis. Studia Classica et Orientalia* 2, S. 209–229.

— 2019: "Indian Ocean Trade: The Role of Parthia." In: M.A. COBB (ed.): *The Indian Ocean Trade in Antiquity. Political, Cultural and Economic Impacts*. London/New York, S. 52–72.

HALDON, J. *et al.* 2018a: "Plagues, Climate Change, and the End of an Empire: A Response to Kyle Harper's The Fate of Rome (1): Climate." In: *History Compass* 2018:e12508. Available online: doi.org/10.1111/hic3.12508.

— 2018b: "Plagues, Climate Change, and the End of an Empire: A Response to Kyle Harper's The Fate of Rome (2): Plagues and a Crisis of Empire." In: *History Compass* 2018:e12506. Available online: doi.org/10.1111/hic3.12506.

— 2018c: "Plagues, Climate Change, and the End of an Empire: A Response to Kyle Harper's The Fate of Rome (3): Disease, Agency, and Collapse." In: *History Compass* 2018:e12507. Available online: doi.org/10.1111/hic3.12507.

HARPER, K. 2017: *The Fate of Rome. Climate, Disease, and the End of an Empire*. Princeton/Oxford.

HELAMA, S./PH.D. JONES/K.R. BRIFFA 2017: "Dark Ages Cold Period: A Literature Review and Directions for Future Research." In: *The Holocene* 27, 10, S. 1–7.

HELAMA, S. *et al.* 2018: "Volcanic Dust Veils from Sixth-Century Tree-Ring Isotopes Linked to Reduced Irradiance, Primary Production and Human Health." In: *Scientific Reports* 8:1339. Available online: doi:10.1038/s41598-018-19760-w.

HE YU *et al.* 2022: "Palaeogenomic Analysis of Black Rat (*Rattus rattus*) Reveals Multiple European Introductions Associated with Human Economic History." In: *Nature Communications* 13:2399. Available online: doi:10.1038/s41467-022-30009-z.

HINNEBUSCH, B.J. 2005: "The Evolution of Flea-Borne Transmission in *Yersinia pestis*." In: *Current Issues in Molecular Biology* 7, S. 197–212.

HOWARD-JOHNSTON, J. 2017: "The India Trade in Late Antiquity." In: E. SAUER (ed.): *Sasanian Persia between Rome and the Steppes of Eurasia*. Edinburgh, S. 284–304.

HUYSE, PH. 2022: "Introduction générale – L'empire sassanide dans le monde interconnecté de l'Antiquité tardive." In: *Antiquité Tardive* 30, S. 15–39.

JACKSON BONNER, M.R. 2011: *Three Neglected Sources of Sasanian History in the Reign of Khusraw Anushirvan*. Paris (Studia Iranica, Cahier 46).

— 2012: "Eastern Sources on the Roman and Persian War in the Near East 540–545." In: T. BERNHEIMER/A. SILVERSTEIN (eds.): *Late Antiquity: Eastern Perspectives*. Oxford, S. 42–56.

— 2020: *The Last Empire of Iran*. Piscataway (N.J.) [Gorgias Handbook Series].

KARTTUNEN, K. 1989: *India in Early Greek Literature*. Helsinki (Studia Orientalia 65).

KELLER, M. *et al.* 2019a: "Ancient *Yersinia pestis* Genomes from Across Western Europe Reveal Early Diversification During the First Pandemic (541–750)." In: *PNAS* 116, S. 12363–12372.

— 2019b: "Ancient *Yersinia pestis* Genomes Provide No Evidence for the Origins or Spread of the Justinianic Plague." In: *bioRxiv preprint*. Available online: doi:10.1101/819698.

KENNEDY, H.N. 2007: "Justinianic Plague in Syria and the Archaeological Evidence." In: L.K. LITTLE (ed.): *Plague and the End of Antiquity. The Pandemic of 541–750*. Cambridge, S. 87–95.

KISLINGER, E./D. STATHAKOPOULOS 1999: "Pest und Perserkriege. Chronologische Überlegungen zum Geschehen 540–545." In: *Byzantion* 69, S. 76–98.

KREPPEL, K.S. *et al.* 2016: "Effect of Temperature and Relative Humidity on the Development Times and Survival of *Synopsyllus fonquerniei* and *Xenopsylla cheopis*, the Flea Vectors of Plague in Madagascar." In: *Parasites & Vectors* 9:82. Available online: doi:10.1186/s13071-016-1366-z.

LARSEN, L.B. *et al.* 2008: "New Ice Core Evidence for a Volcanic Cause of the A.D. 536 Dust Veil." In: *Geophysical Research Letters* 35, L04708. Available online: doi:10.1029/2007GL032450.

MACUCH, M. 2009: "Judicial and Legal Systems. iii. Sasanian Legal System." In: E. YARSHATER (ed.): *Encyclopædia Iranica* XV, S. 181–196.

MATLOUBKARI, E./B. SHAIKH BAIKLOO ISLAM 2022: "Climate Change and Challenges of the Last Ancient Dynasty of Iran: The Decline and Fall of the Sassanid Empire." In: *Persica Antiqua* 2, S. 61–75.

MCCORMICK, M. 2003: "Rats, Communications, and Plague: Toward an Ecological History." In: *The Journal of Interdisciplinary History* 34, S. 1–25.

MEIER, M. 2016: "The 'Justinianic Plague': The Economic Consequences of the Pandemic in the Eastern Roman Empire and its Cultural and Religious Effects." In: *Early Medieval Europe* 24, S. 267–292.

— 2020: "The 'Justinianic Plague': 'An Inconsequential Pandemic'? A Reply." In: *Medizinhistorisches Journal* 55, S. 172–199.

MORDECHAI, L. 2018: "Antioch in the Sixth Century: Resilience or Vulnerability?" In: A. IZDEBSKI/M. MULRYAN (eds.): *Environment and Society in the Long Late Antiquity.* Leiden (Late Antique Archaeology 12), S. 25–41.

MORDECHAI, L./M. EISENBERG 2019: "Rejecting Catastrophe: The Case of the Justinianic Plague." In: *Past and Present* 244, S. 3–50. Available online: doi:10.1093/pastj/gtz009.

MORDECHAI, L./M. EISENBERG/T.P. NEWFIELD/A. IZDEBSKI/J. KAY/H. POINAR 2019: "The Justinianic Plague: An Inconsequential Pandemic?" In: *PNAS* 116/51, 25546-25554 (and supplementary information). Available online: doi:10.1073/pnas.1903797116.

MORDECHAI, L./M. EISENBERG/T.P. NEWFIELD/A. IZDEBSKI/J. KAY 2020: "Quantitative Analysis and Plagued Assumptions: A Response to Mischa Meier." In: *Medizinhistorisches Journal* 55, S. 290–293.

MORONY, M. 1981: "Landholding in Seventh-Century Iraq: Late Sasanian and Early Islamic Patterns." In: A.L. UDOVITCH (ed.): *The Islamic Middle East, 700–1900: Studies in Economic and Social History.* Princeton (N.J.), S. 135–175.

— 2007: "For Whom Does the Writer Write? The First Bubonic Plague Pandemic According to Syriac Sources." In: L.K. LITTLE (ed.): *Plague and the End of Antiquity. The Pandemic of 541–750.* Cambridge, S. 59–86.

NEELIS, J. 2002: "La Vieille Route Reconsidered: Alternative Paths for Early Transmission of Buddhism Beyond the Borderlands of South Asia." In: *Bulletin of the Asia Institute* 16, S. 143–164.

NEWFIELD, T.P. 2018a: "Mysterious and Mortiferous Clouds: The Climate Cooling and Disease Burden of Late Antiquity." In: A. IZDEBSKI/M. MULRYAN (eds.): *Environment and Society in the Long Late Antiquity.* Leiden (Late Antique Archaeology 12), S. 89–115.

— 2018b: "The Climate Downturn of 536–50." In: S. WHITE/CH. PFISTER/F. MAUELSHAGEN (eds.): *The Palgrave Handbook of Climate History.* London, S. 447–493.

PARKER, G. 2008: *The Making of Roman India.* Cambridge.

PAYNE, R.E. 2018: "The Silk Road and the Iranian Political Economy in Late Antiquity." In : *Bulletin of the School of Oriental and African Studies* 81, S. 227–250.

REKAVANDI H.O./E.W. SAUER *et al.* 2008: "Sasanian Walls, Hinterland Fortresses and Abandoned Ancient Irrigated Landscapes." In: *Iran* 46, S. 151–178.

RUBIN, Z. 1995: "The Reforms of Khusro Anūshirwān." In: A. CAMERON (ed.): *The Byzantine and Early Islamic Near East.* III. *States, Resources and Armies.* Princeton (N.J.) (Studies in Late Antiquity and Early Islam 1), S. 227–296.

SARRIS, P. 2022: "New Approaches to the 'Plague of Justinian'." In: *Past and Present* 254, S. 315–346.

SAUER, E.W./H.O. REKAVANDI/ T.J. WILKINSON/J. NOKANDEH *et al.* 2013: *Persia's Imperial Power in Late Antiquity. The Great Wall of Gorgān and Frontier Landscapes of Sasanian Iran.* Oxford and Oakville (The British Institute of Persian Studies. Archaeological Monographs Series II).

SAUER, E.W./L. CHOLOGAURI *et al.* 2020: *Dariali: The 'Caspian Gates' in the Caucasus from Antiquity to the Age of the Huns and the Middle Ages.* 2 Bde. Oxford/Philadelphia (The British Institute of Persian Studies. Archaeological Monographs Series VI).

SCHAMILOGLU, U. 2016: "The Plague in the Time of Justinian and Central Eurasian History." In: I. ZIMONYI/O. KARATAY (eds.): *Central Eurasia in the Middle Ages. Studies in Honour of Peter B. Golden*. Wiesbaden, S. 293–311.

SCHINDEL, N. 2013: "Sasanian Coinage." In: D.T. POTTS (ed.): *The Oxford Handbook of Ancient Iran*. Oxford, S. 814–839.

— 2022: "The Justinianic Plague and Sasanian Iran: The Numismatic Evidence." In: *Sasanian Studies: Late Antique Iranian World/Sasanidische Studien: Spätantike iranische Welt* 1, S. 259–276.

SELAND, E.H. 2013: "Ancient Afghanistan and the Indian Ocean: Maritime Links of the Kushan Empire ca. 50–200 CE." In: *Journal of Indian Ocean Archaeology* 9, S. 66–74.

SHARIFI, A. *et al.* 2015: "Abrupt Climate Variability since the Last Deglaciation Based on a High-Resolution, Multi-Proxy Peat Record from NW Iran: The Hand that Rocked the Cradle of Civilization?" In: *Quaternary Science Reviews* 123, S. 215–230. Available online: doi:10.1016/j.quascirev.2015.07.006.

SPYROU, M.A. *et al.* 2018: "Analysis of 3800-year-old *Yersinia pestis* Genomes Suggests Bronze Age Origin for Bubonic Plague." In: *Nature Communications* 9:2234. Available online: doi:10.1038/s41467-018-04550-9.

SRIGYAN, M. *et al.* 2022: "Bioarchaeological Evidence of One of the Earliest Islamic Burials in the Levant." In: *Communications Biology* 5:554. Available online: doi:10.1038/s42003-022-03508-4.

STATHAKOPOULOS, D.CH. 2004: *Famine and Pestilence in the Late Roman and Early Byzantine Empire. A Systematic Survey of Subsistence Crises and Epidemics.* Farnham/Aldershot (Birmingham Byzantine and Ottoman Monographs 9) [= London/New York, 2016].

— 2012: "Death in the Countryside. Some Thoughts on the Effects of Famine and Epidemics." In: *Antiquité Tardive* 20, S. 105–114.

WANG TAO 2007: "Parthia in China. A Re-Examination of the Historical Records." In: V. S. CURTIS/S. STEWART (eds.): *The Age of the Parthians*. London (The Idea of Iran 2), S. 87–104.

WHITE, L.A./L. MORDECHAI 2020: "Modeling the Justinianic Plague: Comparing Hypothesized Transmission Routes." In: *PLoS ONE* 15:e0231256. Available online: doi:10.1371/journal.pone.0231256.

WILHELMY, H. 1968: "Indusdelta und Rann of Kutch." In: *Erdkunde* 22, S. 177–191.

Notizen zur Überlieferung und zum Gebrauch der *Yašt*s

GÖTZ KÖNIG, Berlin

Die in der Regel sehr unterschiedlichen Zugänge von Gläubigen und Wissenschaftlern zu den Texten einer Religion zeugen unterschiedliche Bilder vom religiösen Text einer Glaubensgemeinschaft. Neben den durch Produktion und Transmission bewirkten Differenzen im religiösen Text treten solche, die auf Rezeption sich gründen. Unter den Texten des Avesta ist solche Rezeptionsasymmetrie von Gläubigen und Forschern vor allem zwischen den liturgischen Feldern *Drōn/Āfrīngān* bzw. *Yasna*, sowie innerhalb der Gruppe der *Yašt*s zu konstatieren. Wurden die von den Gläubigen im Gebet bevorzugten *Yašt*s von den Gelehrten nicht selten abschätzig behandelt („ärmlicher Formelkram" [LOMMEL]), so scheint, was den Iranisten wertvoll, die sog. ‚Großen *Yašts*', den Gläubigen – und nicht erst deren jüngsten Generationen – nach Ausweis der Handschriften und Praxis kaum von Bedeutung: trotz ihrer liturgischen Rahmen und *Karde*-Formeln scheinen die *Großen Yašt*s, auch wenn sekundäre Nachrichten diesbezüglich widersprüchlich sind, liturgisch obdachlos zu sein. Zwar gibt ANQUETIL im *Zend-Avesta* Hinweise zur Zelebration aller *Yašt*s, und noch CHOKSY/KOTWAL 2005 und KOTWAL/HINTZE 2008 behaupten deren allgemeine Rezitationspraxis (allerdings mit Abweichungen zu ANQUETILS Angaben); doch unterstützen die Handschriften des eigentlichen *Xorde Avesta* (XA), d.h. die strukturierten Handschriften jenseits der Sammelmanuskripte ab F1 (1591) bzw. E1 (1601), diese Behauptungen keineswegs. Betrachten wir die 22 im *Tamām Xorde Avesta* (TXA) überlieferten *Yašt*s – d.h. Texte, die den spezifischen finalen liturgischen *Yašt*-Rahmen besitzen –, so ist im Falle von sechs Texten (Yt 5, 8, 10, 15, 17, 19) und in gewisser Weise auch im Falle von Yt 13 (welcher *Yašt* in Iran nur in der *Faroxšī*-Form transmittiert wird) zu konstatieren, daß diese lediglich im TXA und in (den späten) *Xorde Avesta*-Ergänzungshandschriften, nicht aber im „eigentlichen *Xorde Avesta*" (GELDNER) geführt werden (und also keine iranische Transmission kennen):

Yt	1	2	3	4	5	6	7	8	9	10	11	11a	12	13	14	15	16	17	18	19	20	21
< Nask Bayān[1]	o (Teil I?)				o*			o*	o	o*		o	o	o	●	●*	●	●*	●	●*		
< Nask Hādōxt											●											
< unbekannter Quelle	● (Teil II?)	●	●	●																	●	●
Yašts Faržiyat	●		●								●	●									?	?
IrXA Sāde	●	●	●	●		(●)[2]			●		●	●		*Faroxšī*	●							
IndXA Sāde	●	●	●	●		●	●		●		●	●	●		●		●		●		●	●
PÜ ir.	●					●[3]	●[4]				●	●										
PÜ ind.	●	●[5]	●	●[6]		●[7]	●[8]				●	●			●[9]						●	●
NpÜ ir.[10]	●	●[11]	●				●[12]		●		●	●			●							
NpÜ[13] ind.	●		●	●							●	●			●						●	●
SÜ	●										●										●[14]	
GujÜ bis ca. 1750	●																				●	
GujÜ ab ca. 1750[15]	●	●[16]	●								●	●			●						●	●

1 Die mit * gekennzeichneten *Yašts* sind nur im TXA (und den *Xorde Avesta*-Ergänzungshandschriften des 19. Jh.) bezeugt.
2 Die Yt 5, 6, 7 und 8 treten nur in Geldners ML2 und in der Handschrift 6306(DorostXANew) (19. Jh.) auf, in einer Folge Yt 1 bis 8. Ich halte es für wahrscheinlich, daß hier eine Übernahme aus der indischen TXA-Tradition statthatte, wie man sie auch an der Handschrift Ml2 oder im Druck-*Xorde Avesta* R. Xorsand & Širmard-e Nōzar von 1272 Y feststellen kann.
3 Als PÜ von Ny 1.
4 Als PÜ von Ny 3.
5 Siehe Katrak418d. Nicht zu überprüfen.
6 Siehe Katrak418d. Nicht zu überprüfen.
7 Als PÜ von Ny 1.
8 Als PÜ von Ny 3.
9 Aus NpÜ übersetzt.
10 Wichtigstes Ms. scheint MF28 zu sein. Allerdings bleibt in Dhabhars Beschreibung der Handschrift (1923c, S. 24f.) unklar, ob alle Stücke mit NpÜ versehen sind; möglicherweise ist MF28 eher als Sāde-Handschrift einzustufen. Siehe daneben besonders MF25, MF42.
11 Nur MF28.
12 Als PÜ von Ny 3.
13 Katrak279 führt am Ende der Hs. Yt 9+10 (sec.man.), unklar ist aus der Notiz, ob auch diese mit NpÜ versehen sind.
14 Mb2.
15 In MF72 von 1816: Yt 1, 2, 3, 11, 11a, 20, 21, 4, 9, 14, 18.
16 Nur R29, am Ms.-Ende.

Die Auswertung der (teilweise nur durch Katalogbeschreibungen oder Editionen bekannten) Handschriften zeigt also, daß aus dem *Bayān*, abgesehen vom (bis ins 18. Jh. nur in Iran auftretenden) *Faroxšī*, nur Yt 1, 9, 11a, 12, 14, 16, 18 in *Xorde Avesta*-Handschriften begegnen, jedoch alle Nicht-*Bayān*-*Yašt*s (Yt 2, 3, 4, 11, 20, 21). Schlüsseln wir dieses Ergebnis nach drei weiteren Kriterien auf — nach Klasse (ohne/mit Übersetzung), Ort (Iran/Indien) und Zeit (vor/seit dem 18. Jh.) —, so treten zum einen sehr ungleiche Verteilungen der *Yašt*s hervor, zum anderen lassen sich Angleichungsbewegungen zwischen den unterschiedlichen Teilmengen erkennen:

Yt	1	2	3	4	5	6	7	8	9	10	11	11a	12	13	14	15	16	17	18	19	20	21
I) XA Sāde ir.+ind.	•	•	•	•		ind	ind		•		•	•	ind		•		ind		ind		ind	ind
II) XA Ü älter (14./15. Jh.)	•										•											
IIIa) XA Ü jünger (ab 16. Jh.)	•	•	•	•					•		•	•			•						•	•
IIIb) davon ir. Hss.	•	?	• (np.)	?							•	•										

Die Tabelle zeigt, daß das X(orde) A(vest) mit Ü(bersetzung) des 14./15. Jh. (II) — die Hs. H2 (und damit möglicherweise auch K1=J9[17]) stammt, so Bharucha 1906–1933 I, S. vii, von P. Rām Kāmdīn — und das ältere XASāde (I) in der Anzahl der *Yašt*s zunächst weit auseinanderliegen, daß aber in den Folgejahrhunderten eine Angleichung einsetzt. Während die Menge der im XASāde bezeugten *Yašt*s im IndXA — am umfangreichsten ist das ältere IndXASāde, s. Jm4 (1352): Yt 1, 2, 3, 6, 9, 11, 14, 16; O3[18] (1646): Yt 1, 2, 3, 4, 9, 11, 12, 14, 16, 18, 20, 21 — die des IrXA zunächst übersteigt, sich dieser aber historisch angleicht, ist darüberhinaus eine Angleichung der Menge des XASāde an das Übersetzungs-*Xorde Avesta* insgesamt festzustellen.

17 K1=J9 zeigt einen H2 sehr ähnlichen Duktus. Das in K1=J9 geführte Āśīrvād-Datum gibt das Jahr 1343/44, was für P. Rām Kāmdīn zu früh liegt, doch kann das Āśīrvād-Datum kopiert sein.

18 Die Hs. O3 ist nicht nur eine derjenigen Handschriften, die als erste nach Europa gelangten, sondern hatte für die Gestaltung der Geldner-Edition hervorragenden Wert, s. Geldner 1896–1904 II, S. 16: „Als Muster <der „Khorda-Awesta-Codices" [GK]> mag der Oxforder Codex (O3) angeführt werden, dessen Inhalt als Durchschnittsinhalt dieser Mss. gelten darf. Er enthält der Reihe nach: das Awesta-Alphabet, die 5 Nyāishs, die 3 Āfrīngāns, die 5 Gāhs, die Yashts 1. 2. 3. 4. 9. 11. 12. 14. 16. 18. 20. 21, zahlreiche Nīrangs."

Die alten Gravitationszentren des Übersetzungs-*Xorde Avesta* scheinen die Yt 1[19] und Yt 11 zu sein; es sind die einzigen *Yašts*, die das ältere SkrXA (14./15. Jh.) kennt, Yt 11 (K1=J9) (noch?) ohne Übersetzung. Mehrere Prozesse gehen von diesen Zentren aus: a) die Anlagerung anderer *Yašts* in den Folgejahrhunderten; b) die Anähnelung des XASāde an das jüngere Übersetzungs-*Xorde Avesta*; c) das Abdrängen einiger *Yašts* aus dem Kreis des *Xorde Avesta Sāde*, die diesem in älterer Zeit noch zugehörten.[20]

Diese handschriftlichen Entwicklungen sind vor allem für die indische Gemeinde nachzuvollziehen, aus welcher *Xorde Avesta*-Handschriften aus einem Zeitraum zwischen dem 14. und 19. Jh. überliefert sind (während iranische *Xorde Avesta*-Handschriften nur aus dem frühen 18. Jh. aus der Hand des Rostam Goštāsp Erdašīr und sodann aus dem späten 18. und dem 19. Jh. bekannt sind). Die Entwicklungen sind jedoch nicht sämtlich als indische Besonderheiten zu werten, bewegen sie sich doch auf einen Zustand hin, der auch aus Iran bekannt ist. Eine entscheidende Rolle für die Veränderungsprozesse in Indien fällt vermutlich dem IrXASāde zu, über das wir durch die Handschriften des Rostam Goštāsp Erdašīr zumindest für das frühe 18. Jh. (ältestes Stratum) gut informiert sind:

F2 (7075)	MF29 (6110)	MF28 (7305)	Katrak90 < Ms. des Frēdōn Marzbān	K36 (6115)	MF3 (6095)	YL17-02233 (6135)	ML15286 (3060)
1726 (WEST: 1706)	1704	1706	1718	1724	1700	1723	1697/1716 (?)
PahlXA im *Faržiyat*-Umfang	XA im *Faržiyat*-Umfang	extensives XA (mit NpÜ) mit *Drōns*	XA mit *Drōns*	extensives XA mit *Drōns*	XA + *Drōn*/*Farοxšī*	XA + *Drōn*/*Faroxšī*	*Faroxšī*[21]
Yt 1.1–22	Yt 1, 3, 11, 11a	Yt 1, 2, 3, 11, 14	keine detaillierten Informationen	Yt 1, 3, 11, 11a; Yt 14 (sec.man.); ANogNavar	Yt 1; Yt 13	Yt 1, 3, 11, 11a; Yt 13	Yt 13

19 Yt 1 liegt in einer kürzeren und längeren Rezension vor. Während die Sāde-Hss. i.d.R. die Langversion führen, tritt in den Übersetzungshandschriften zunächst nur Yt 1.1–22/23 auf. Auffällig ist im alten Sanskrit-XA H2 von 1415, daß zunächst Yt 1.1–23 mit SÜ, dann Yt 1.24–29 + 31–33 ohne SÜ notiert ist.

20 Es fällt im übrigen auf, daß im ältesten IndXASāde wie im ältesten SkrXA Yt 11a (= Y 57) nicht vertreten ist, dessen älteste Übersetzungstradition (Pahl.) das vermutlich auf iranisches Vorbild zurückgehende T12 (1552) des Āsadīn Kākā bezeugt (darin: Yt 1, 11a; im besonderen Schlußteil des Ms. Yt 11). Wenn Yt 11a nicht im älteren IndXA vertreten, wohl aber: a) im vielleicht auf iranischem Import beruhenden PahlXA T12, b) im IrXA (Pahl. und Sāde) und c) im *Bayān*, die Fäden von b) und c) aber bei Āsadīn Kākā zusammenlaufen (F1 von 1591), dann könnte das zu einer Folgerung berechtigen: daß es im 16. Jh. zu einem Hss.-Export nach Indien kam, der dort die *Xorde Avesta*-Tradition in verschiedener Weise nachhaltig beeinflußte, so in der Einführung von Yt 11a in das eigentliche *Xorde Avesta*, vor allem aber durch Einbau des *Bayān* (bzw. von dessen Fragment) in die indische *Yašt*-Überlieferung und der Kreation des TXA.

21 Für ein nur noch fragmentarisch enthaltenen Yt 13 (Faroxšī) von Rostam Goštāsp s. Katrak742c.

Diese Auswahl von *Yašts* — Yt 1, 3, 11, 11a, teilweise Yt 14 (in K36 *sec.man.* eingefügt) — wird schließlich seit dem späteren 18. Jh. alle Handschriften-Klassen dominieren, neben dem iranischen dann auch das indische XASāde, das PahlXA wie das GujXA; die indischen Handschriften fügen lediglich Yt 20 + Yt 21 hinzu. Ein Spiegel ältester Verhältnisse scheint diese Auswahl jedoch nicht zu sein. Ohne das Problem der Pahlavi-Übersetzung des *Xorde Avesta* hier noch einmal darstellen zu wollen, möchte ich nur darauf hinweisen, daß die Übersetzungen von Yt 1 Teil II, von Yt 20 + Yt 21 wie von Yt 3 + Yt 14 möglicherweise Re-Pahlavisierungen einer NpÜ (unter Zuzug älterer PÜs für einzelne Textteile) sind.[22] Offenbar standen die genannten *Yašts* den Gläubigen im frühen 2. Jt. noch nicht zur Rezitation zur Verfügung (es sei denn, sie beherrschten deren avestischen Text, was etwa für Yt 21 anzunehmen ist).

*

Der Grund für die *Yašt*-Auswahl des iranischen und sodann indischen *Xorde Avesta* ist keineswegs unbekannt: Yt 1, 3, 11, 11a sind diejenigen *Yašts*, welche die Iraner den Indern als die der verpflichtenden Tagesgebete, des *Farżiyat*, mitteilten (Kama Bohra 1527[23]; T29 von 1642[24]; akzeptiert dann im *Farżiyat Nāme* [spätes 17. Jh.])[25], welches Pensum die Inder wohl um die Fabrikate Yt 20+21 erweiterten (wie sie schon Āsadīn Kākā dem TXA angefügt hatte). Doch wie wir im Fall der handschriftlichen Überlieferung erst nach der Mitte des 2. Jt. ein Einschwingen aller Handschriftenklassen auf die genannten *Yašts* beobachten können, so scheint auch der obligate Gebrauch von Yt 1, 3, 11, 11a im *Farżiyat* bereits eine Erweiterungsform darzustellen. Betrachten wir den Gebrauch jener vier *Yašts* im Tageszyklus, so läßt sich erkennen, daß Yt 11a und Yt 3 nie unabhängig von Yt 1 und Yt 11, oder vielmehr: nie unabhängig von Yt 11, rezitiert werden. Autonomen Gebrauch zeigen nur Yt 1+11:

22 Kein Ms. belegt die Existenz einer PÜ von Yt 14 vor dem 19. Jh. Eine NpÜ wurde im 18. Jh. von Dārāb Rustām Sanjāna angefertigt, s. R22 (nach 1867) (Dhabhar 1923a, S. 140), R116 (1800) (Dhabhar 1923a, S. 161f.), KJJA (Dhabhar 1927, S. 34f., mit der Vermutung „As stated above, the often ungrammatical and modern Pahlavi versions, e.g., of some of the longer pieces of prayers such as Patit Aderbad (longer Pahlavi version), Ardibehesht Yasht, the Behram Yasht, etc., seem to have been done into that language from Persian version, such as the one found in this MS"). Auch die PÜ von Yt 3 ist nicht im IrXA und vermutlich auch nicht vor dem 19. Jh. bezeugt; NpÜs enthalten die ir. Hss. MF25 und MF42 (spätes 18. Jh.), die ältesten GujÜ finden sich in R114 (1761) und E50 (1779). PÜs von Yt 20 + Yt 21 finden sich im undatierten T52, U1, U3, Katrak601, daneben in D (1810), T11 und F6 von 1851; F6 zeigt zuerst den Pāzand-Text, dann eine Pahlavi-Übersetzung, das Pahlavi ist also sekundär.

23 Siehe Dhabhar 1932, S. 299.

24 Choksy/Kotwal 2005, S. 247.

25 Choksy/Kotwal 2005, S. 247, nach Modi 1924, S. 4–9.

Nacht-Tag	Tag (Preis des Lichts)		Nacht (Abwehr der Finsternis)	
Yt 11, YtArW	-	Yt 11	YtArW	
Ny 1 + Ny 2 / Nām Stāyišn			**Yt 11+Yt 11a**	**Yt 11(+Yt 11a?)**
SrB, NerKB	**(SrB, NerKB)**	**(SrB, NerKB)**	**(SrB, NerKB)**	**SrB, NerKB**
Yt 1		-	Yt 1	
Ny 5 (an das Feuer) zu allen fünf Gāhs				

Diese Überlegungen führen zu dem Ergebnis, daß der Kern der täglichen Gebetspflichten zum einen in den auf den Leib sich beziehenden Gebeten besteht (NerKB; SrB; Pādyāb), zum anderen in jenen Gebeten, die sich auf *Yazata*s hin ausrichten, welche in besonderer Weise mit der ‚Theologie' von Licht/Dunkelheit sowie der des Feuers verbunden sind:

Sonne (+ Mihr) (Ohrmazd)	Srōš (Ardwahišt)
Feuer	

Der Befund einer Redundanz im Gebrauch von *Yašt*s im Rahmen des *Farżiyat* korrespondiert mit dem Befund, daß das älteste SkrXA (in dem Yt 11 allerdings ohne SÜ erscheint) diese Redundanz (offenbar noch) nicht kennt, sondern allein die Spannung der Yt 1 + Yt 11. Die strukturelle Spannung zwischen Yt 1 + Yt 11, d.h. zwischen Ohrmazd und Srōš, ist vermutlich auf den Wandel der Tageszeiten zu beziehen: die einzige Zeit ohne Anrufung des Srōš ist der Mittag, die einzige Zeit ohne Anrufung des Ohrmazd die darauffolgende des frühen Abends, des Sonnenuntergangs[26]; in der mitternächtlichen Zeit tritt der Wirkung von Yt 11 verstärkend die Rezitation von Yt 11a hinzu. Im Bedeutungshintergrund dieser Zeitorganisation stehen der Dualismus von Tag / Nacht, Licht / Finsternis bzw. dessen Übergangsformen. Ein nah verwandter Dualismus dirigiert das Erscheinen von Yt 3 + Ny 1/2. Yt 3 (Ardwahišt / Feuer) tritt niemals ohne die Rezitation von Yt 11 auf, d.h. nur in den dunklen bzw. Übergangsperioden des Tages; der Mittag/Nachmittag ist indes von Ny 1(+2) bestimmt. Der hier zugrundeliegende Dualismus ist der von Feuer (= Licht in der Nacht) und Sonne (Licht am Tag).[27]

Häufig begegnet Yt 14 in den Handschriften, und dem Text ist auch — vermutlich spät — eine Pahlavi-Übersetzung zuteil geworden (s. Fn. 22) Gleichwohl ist Yt 14 nicht fester Bestandteil der Tagesgebetspflichten. Ich vermute,

26 Zu Sraōšas Wirken bei *frāšmō.dāti-* s. Y 57.10, 16, s.a. Yt 4.8.

27 Das ältere Stratum der Hss. des PahlXA und das SkrXA führen nur Ny 1, 3, 5; im IrXASāde ist Ny 1 und Ny 2 erweitert, Ny 4 ist in Iran wohl kein *Niyāyišn* (sondern begegnet als *Mayā Yašt* [siehe KÖNIG 2022]). Die *Niyāyišn* dienten also der Verehrung von Sonne, Mond und Feuer — man vgl. dazu die Nachrichten MX 53.4–5, PRDd 40.1–5, *Xwad Patit* 7; zu den iranischen Sāde-Hss. vgl. die Information *Patit Irani* 19 —, eine bildliche Darstellung dessen liegt m.E. im Grabrelief der Achämeniden vor.

daß die Beliebtheit des Textes nicht allein von Wahrāms/Bahrāms Identifizierung mit dem Panth-Yazad, dem Reisegott, herrührt, sondern mit der Tatsache zusammenhängt, daß wohl der Gott es ist, der den höchsten Feuern den Namen gab (der Grund hierfür ist bis heute allerdings unklar). Die Tagesgebetspflichten fokussieren somit stark die *Hamkārān* des Feuers: Ardwahišt, Srōš, Wahrām.

*

Obgleich die meisten *Yašts* niemals dem *Faržiyat* als jener Textzusammenstellung zuzählten, welche, einem *Stundenbuch* ähnlich, das rituelle Pensum aller Gläubigen vor allem des Tages umfaßt, und obgleich das Fehlen von Übersetzungen darauf hindeutet, daß diese *Non-Faržiyat-Yašts* auch sonst unter den Laien nicht in Gebrauch standen, ist deren Überlieferung dennoch, und zwar vor allem in der älteren indischen Tradition, relativ umfangreich. Handelt es sich bei der Überlieferung der *Non-Faržiyat-Yašts* also nur um einen glücklichen Zufall, oder folgt diese bestimmten Intentionen oder Traditionen?

An den Handschriften des *Xorde Avesta* läßt sich jedoch noch eine weitere Entwicklungsreihe ablesen, die offenbar nicht vom Tag-Nacht- bzw. Sonne-Feuer-Dualismus bestimmt ist, sondern vom Konzept der Amahraspanden. Es fällt ja bereits bei der Verwendung von Yt 1, 3 wie auch von Yt 11/11a und Yt 14 auf, daß die mit diesen Texten Verehrten dem Kreis eben dieser besonderen Gottheiten zugehören.[28] Yt 2 + Yt 4, Verehrungstexte für die gesamte Gruppe der Amahraspanden bzw. für die fünfte Amahraspand, Hordad, zählen nicht nur zu den weit verbreiteten *Xorde Avesta-Yašts*, sondern zeigen auch Ansätze einer Übersetzungstradition. Darin mag das Bestreben kenntlich werden, die Tagesgebete nicht allein nach jenem polaren Tag-Nacht-Konzept auszurichten,

28 Zu Vərəϑraγnas Erhebung zum siebten Amahraspand und der Parallele zum armenischen Vahagn-Mythos s. de Menasce 1947–48, zu seinem Aufstieg s.a. den aus M55 ausgezogenen Text in Bartholomae 1915, S. 183; der liturgische Text K36 fol. 50+24 v 1-7 Pā<d>šāh Warharām Īzad feiert „den König der Könige“ Bahrām als *Amešāsfand*. Zu(r ausgezeichneten Position des) Bahrām im Gebet *Nām Stāyišn* s. Russell 1991, S. 129 (allerdings muß einschränkend gesagt werden, daß allein die indische Textversion die Erhöhung des Bahrām zur vermutlich achten Amahraspand kennt (*vīspa. sətāišne. dādār. hōrməzda. harvispa. āgāh. tuānā. tuągar. hafta. aməṣ̌āspəṇt̰. bahirąm. yazd. pərōz. gar. dušman. zaδār. amahe. hutāst.* [Dhabhars §8]), während die iranischen Textzeugen Bahrām nicht erwähnen. In der Tir Andaz-Übersetzung von Yt 14 werden die Amahraspand wie Bahrām als *ferešte* „Engel“ bezeichnet (NpÜ Yt 14.45). Sollte in KSM 48–49 (*ud dūr ul … ud gāh 1 zarrēn … xwadāy … … abar … zan [šud ?] … [andar] rōzan ī wahrām nišast* „Und fern hoch ... und ein goldener Thron* ... Herr ... ... auf ... Frau ist gegangen (?). [Und] … hat sich in das Licht des Wahrām gesetzt.“) vom Gott Wahrām (und nicht vom Wahrām-Feuer, das zwar im Himmel, jedoch eigentlich nicht vor Ohrmazd brennt [s. Bd 18, WZ 3, PY 17.11]) die Rede sein, so würde das seine Funktion als Amahraspand wohl bestätigen und schon auf die frühe Sasanidenzeit zurückdatieren lassen. *Vgl. AWN 11.1, da sich Wahman Amahraspand *az gāh ī zarrēnkard* „vom aus Gold gefertigten Thron“ erhebt.

sondern sie in Hinsicht auf eine Amahraspanden-Verehrung auszuweiten.[29] Auffällig schließlich ist, daß eine bedeutende Anzahl der Handschriften des *Xorde Avesta* und seiner Ergänzungen Yt 9 führt (s.u.). Der Text ist der eher unbedeutenden Gottheit Druwāsp gewidmet. Unter den Parsen wird der Text jedoch häufiger als das *Yašt* für Gōš betrachtet, denn an das Rind ist das entsprechende Tages-*Xšnūman* gerichtet (Genitiv: *gə̄uš. tašne. / gə̄uš. urune.*; Akk. aber: *gə̄uš. huδåŋhō. uruuānəm. yazamaide.*). Möglicherweise ist die Rezitation von Yt 9 als der Ersatz einer ausgefallenen Wahman-Verehrung zu verstehen.

Aus den beiden nachstehenden Tabellen läßt sich die *Yašt*-Überlieferung Irans ablesen. Aus ihnen geht hervor, daß die iranische Handschriftentradition der *Yašt*s mit den Notwendigkeiten des *Faržiyat* (Yt 1, 3, 11, 11a) enggeführt ist. Seit ca. 1800 treten weitere *Yašt*s im iranischen *Xorde Avesta* auf, insbesondere die oben genannten Amahraspanden-*Yašt*s Yt 2+4, Yt 9+14:

			Yašt:	1	2	3	4	5	6	7	8	9	11	11a	Yt14
6095	MF3(Geldner) (= MF45 [Dhabhar])	XA mit Faroxši	1700	●											
6110	MF29		1704	●		●							●	●	
6115	K36 (= M1 in Westergaard) (cf. MF3, W1)		1724	●		●							●	●	● (sec.m.)
6135	YL17–02233	XA mit Faroxši	1723	●		●							●	●	
6185	MF31	XA mit Faroxši	späteres 18. Jh.	●	●	●						●	●	●	●
6195	W1 (= old W6)		frühes 19. Jh.	●		●							●	●	
6220	Lb16 (Sgn.: Or[ient] 1588)	unvollständig	vor 1835	●											
6291	Ethé1943 (= Ouseley120)	unvollständig am Ende	frühes 19. Jh.												
6297	W3 (= old No. 5)	XA mit Faroxši	?												

29 Soweit die Tatsache, daß ein *Yašt* für Hordad existiert, nicht aber für Šahrewar, Spandarmad und Amurdad, und wohl auch nicht für Wahman – die Behauptung der einheimischen Tradition, Yt 1.II sei ein solcher Text, ist kaum glaubhaft, zumal in diesem Ārmaiti stärker hervortritt – nicht bloßer Transmissionszufall sein sollte, könnte deren Grund darin zu suchen sein, daß der Tag Hordad im ersten Jahresmonat besonders gefeiert wird („Nawrōz Xordādī" = „Barād") (s. Pahlavi Text 25 *Māh ī Frawardīn Rōz ī Hordad*), wie ebenso im letzten (Spandarmad) (Nourūz–e Dariaē = Hordad–Sāl–Gāh = Nawrōz–i Zāwuli; s. dazu KARANJIA 2010, S. 69f.).

			Yašt:	1	2	3	4	5	6	7	8	9	11	11a	Yt14
6187	MZK6_ XwAIsf1	unvollständig am Beginn; XA mit Faroxši	1803	●		●	●					●	●	●	●
6190	RR3 (RostamiXA)	XA mit Faroxši		●		●	●					●	●	●	●
6298	NiknamXA	unvollständig am Beginn	?	●		●							●	●	
6306	DorostXA-New	unvollständiges TXA		●	●	●	●	●	●	●	●				
8102	MZK8														●
8101	KM8			●		●	●					●	●	●	●
3100	K38 (= M3 in Westergaard)	Faroxši + XA Texte; unvollständig am Beginn; engst verwandt mit Suppl. persan1191	1814 (1183 Y)				●					●			●
3095	Suppl. persan1191 (= Blochet XXVI)	Faroxši + XA Texte; engst verwandt mit K38	„commencement du XIXesiècle“ (Blochet)										●		●

Die Transmission von Yt 13, ein *Yašt*, der vor allem an den Jahresendtagen gefeiert wird, erfolgt in iranischen Handschriften fast immer in der *Faroxšī*-Form, d.h. mit vorgeschaltetem *Drōn*-Text und Anweisungen zur Performanz.[30] Selten sind Notate ohne *Drōn*. Entweder wird das *Faroxšī* im Rahmen von eigentlichen *Xorde Avesta*-Handschriften geführt, oder in Handschriften, die neben dem *Faroxšī* auch einige *Xorde Avesta*-Texte aufweisen, schließlich aber in speziellen *Faroxšī*-Handschriften, die entweder nur das *Faroxšī* beinhalten oder dieses mit einigen kleineren Texten verbinden. Neben den schon genannten Handschriften K38 und Suppl.persan1191 handelt es sich in Iran um folgende Handschriften:

30 Siehe zur Überlieferung Andrés–Toledo 2015.

3050	Minocher Jamaspji11		ca. 1550 (?) (Angabe nicht vertrauenswürdig)
3055	Yazd3973		1607, 1717
3057	VL1		1617/1717
3060	ML15286	zur Sequenz Yt 13 + StS s.a. YL17, MF3	1697 (?); 1716/17
3065	K13	> M50	1721
3070	M50 (= Haug5)	< K13	1723 (Karanjia: 1721)
3080	MF16 (= MF1 Geldner [part 1])	> F3	1721, 1816, 1826
3085	X892.5 Av3 U		1755
Katrak756b	Katrak756b		1767
3087	R18	vgl. K13, M50	1800
Katrak139	Katrak139	eng verwandt mit R18	?
6215	ĀBYazd	unvollständig am Beginn und Ende	1834 (?); 1892
3130	F3	< MF16; vgl. YL YL17–02233	1865–1883
Katrak257	Katrak257		„old“ (Katrak)
Katrak792b	Katrak792b		„old“ (Katrak)
Katrak115	Katrak115		„old“ (Katrak)
Katrak116	Katrak116		„old“ (Katrak)
Katrak445	Katrak445		„seems old“ (Katrak)
3164	Hoshangji25		?
3165	Hoshangji26		?
Katrak156	Katrak156		?
Katrak742c	Katrak742c part III	Sammelhandschrift, 3 Teile	?
s.a.	Suppl.persan47.15d (= Blochet LXVII; Anquetil XV)		?
3140	Lb5 (= Sachau No. 5)		„modern“ (Geldner)

Das Folgende bietet eine auch die indischen Handschriften (ohne TXA) einbeziehende Zusammenstellung der Überlieferung jener *Yašts*, die a) neben den *Farżiyat-Yašts* im iranischen wie indischen *Xorde Avesta* erscheinen, und die b), wenn auch unvollständig, über Übersetzungen verfügen (die iranischen Handschriften sind grau markiert). Am häufigsten ist von diesen *Yašts* (Yt 2, 4, 9, 14) in *Xorde Avesta*-Handschriften und deren Ergänzungen Yt 14 vertreten. Um ca. ein Drittel weniger als Yt 14 finden sich Notationen von Yt 2, 4 und 9. Allerdings führt deren Bezeugung bis ins 14. Jh. zurück, ins älteste IndXASāde Jm4(6050) von 1352 sowie bis zur Handschrift M51(9775) des P. Rām Kāmdīn von 1397. Die Überlieferung von Yt 2+4 in M51 ist in mehrfacher Hinsicht eigentümlich: a) in der Tatsache der Aufnahme in einem Kodex, der vor allem (anonyme) Pahlavi-Literatur transmittiert; b) im Fehlen beider Texte in K20, ein Manuskript, das zumindest in den mit M51 gemeinsamen Textsequenzen mit diesem auf eine gemeinsame (iranische) Vorlage (die Handschrift des Rostam Mihrābān) zurückgeht; c) im Fehlen einer (gemäß den anderen Avesta-Texten in M51 erwartbaren) Pahlavi-Übersetzung; in der orthographischen Übereinstimmung mit der Transmission in F1. Letzteres weist darauf hin, daß Ende des 14. Jh. bzw. in der Zeit vor dem Handschriften-Export nach Indien eine Pahlavi- oder neupersische Übersetzung von Yt 2+4 nicht mehr oder noch nicht vorhanden war. Allerdings ist es bemerkenswert, daß in beiden *Yašts* der liturgische Rahmen extrem abbreviert ist, so daß Yt 2 scheinbar auf den Zaubertext Yt 2.11–14 zusammenschrumpft.[31] Diese Art der Textwiedergabe ist i.d.R. aus dem PahlXA bekannt, während Sāde-Handschriften den Rahmen vollständig oder doch abbreviert notieren.

Betrachten wir die Liste der Textzeugen von Yt 2+4, 9+14, so fällt auf:[32]

1. Yt 2, 4, 9, 14 sind für Jahrhunderte nur Teil der Sāde-Transmission (und damit vielleicht den Laien unzugänglich);
2. eine Pahlavi-Überlieferung fehlt, bei Yt 14 dürfte sie sekundär auf np. Übersetzung aufruhen;
3. Übersetzungen in indische Sprachen sind späte Produkte:

31 Ein verwandter (von GELDNER aber als Yt 2 bestimmter) Text iranischer Handschriften ist der als „Drōn Haft Amšāsfand" (K36, MF28) bzw. „Doʿā Haft Amšāsfand" (K38 und Schwestermanuskript Suppl.persan1191 [= Blochet XXVI]) bezeichnete *Drōn*-Text (in Gen./Akk.), vermutlich identisch mit dem *Xšnūman Drōn-e Haft Amešasfand* (T31, MF16 [ir. Hss.]), *Xšnūman Haft Amešasfand* (EMU12), der nur die gesammelten *Xšnūmans* aus Yt 2, nicht aber den Zaubertext — den eigentlichen *Yašt*-Text — führt.

32 er Prozeß der Autopsie neu aufgefundener Xorde Avesta-Handschriften aus Iran hat in einigen weiteren Handschriften (18., vor allem 19. Jh.) Textzeugen der vier Yašts bekannt werden lassen, so: DorostXANew(6306): Yt 2, Yt 4; KM8(8101), MZK9(6180): Yt 4, Yt 9, Yt 14. Nachzutragen ist das (in Indien gefertigte) iranische Xorde Avesta MF75(6860), das Yt 4 enthält.

			Yt 2	Yt 4	Yt 9	Yt 14
XA Sāde	Jm4(6050)	1352	●	●	●	●
	O3(6060)	1646	●	●	●	●
	MF90(6070), mit Mayā Yt	1664		●	●	
	L18(6085)	1672	●	●	●	●
	Mb1(6090)	1689				
	L11(6130)	1723				●
	K36(6115)	1724				● sec.man.
	U8(6155)	1773	●			●
	B5 (= B.U.L. X.7)	1789				●
	MF31(6185), mit Faroxšī	spätes 18. Jh.	●		●	●
	MZK6_XwAIsf1(6187), mit Faroxšī	1803	Yt 2.11–12, vgl. M66(9070), RR3(6190)	●	●	●
	RR3(6190)		Yt 2.11–12, vgl. M66(9070), MZK6_XwAIsf1(6187)			●
	Katrak131	„old“ (Katrak)			●	
	J17(6265)	„old“ (Geldner)	●	●	●	●
	J16(6275)	„modern“(Geldner)	●			●
TXA 1591 –späteres 19. Jh., ca. 35 Hss. (indisch)			●	●	●	●
XA Sāde np. Schrift	MF43(6855)	1797				●
	K37(6870)	„modern“(Geldner)		●	●	●
	R25(6875)	?		●	●	●
	MF76(6880)	?		●	●	●

			Yt 2	Yt 4	Yt 9	Yt 14
	G100(7946)[33]				●	●
NpXA	MF28(7305)	1706		●		●
	KJJA(7330)	1800				●
	Katrak279	(frühes 19. Jh.)			●	
	R22(7355)	>1867		●		●
SkrXA	EMU7(7590)	„modern“(Geldner)	●	●	●	●
	RBR1 (= R)(7600)	1865 und später				● (Yt 14 mit PÜ dem Kol. [1865] angehängt[34])
	EMU2(7605)	?				
GujXA	MF74(7890)	1812				●
	R29(7895)	1815	● (am Ms.-Ende)			
	MF72(7900)	1816	●	●	●	●
	U9(7943)	zw. 1830 & 1870				●
XA ähnliche Mss.	Suppl.persan50(8030)	2. Hälfte 17. Jh.		●		
	M65(8047)	Mitte 18. Jh.				●
	M70(8050)	1792	● (führt Yt 2 mit YH zusammen)	●		●
	Ethé1941(8060) ir.?	<1811		●		●
	MF62(8072) XA?	1822(?)		●		
	R20(8090)	nach 1859				● (Yt 14 mit PÜ + Pahlavi-Texte)
	Suppl.persan1216(8099)	2. Hälfte 19. Jh.				● (Yt 14 mit PÜ + Pahlavi-Texte)

33 Die Hs. G100(7946) ist gegenwärtig noch nicht autopsiert. Die kurze Beschreibung in Kotwal/Sheffield/Gandhi 2008 gibt nur wenige Verweise auf den Inhalt: „Khordeh Avesta in Avestan and Pazand with some translations in Old Gujarati. ... Begins with a description of the 21 Nasks of the Avesta, ends in the 2nd Kardag of the Gosht Yasht.“

34 Bharucha 1906, S. xxi f.; Dhabhar 1927, S. 33.

			Yt 2	Yt 4	Yt 9	Yt 14
	E3(8110)	?			●	
	K1(8125)	?				● (Yt 14 mit PÜ + Pahlavi-Texte)[35]
	F55(8130)	?				●
	T15 (7050)[36]	?				●
	Katrak19b	?	●			
Yt Mss.	MinocherJamas-pji208(8505)	(14. Jh.?)				●
	MinocherJamaspji10(8515), Kadmi-Ms.	(16. Jh.?)		●		●
	Katrak91	1772	●	●		
	G54(8565)	1798	●	●	●	●
	Katrak122	1809				●
	Hoshangji39(8595)	1818		●	●	
	G75(8605)	1821				●
	MF62(8072)	1822(?)	●	●	●	
	Katrak43	1831			●	
	T49(8625)	1835	●	●		●
	Katrak40	1842				●
	K40(8640)	1842				●
	F103(8645)	1866	●	●	●	
	K16(8670) < E1	19. Jh.		●		●
	Katrak243	„old“ (Katrak)				●
	Katrak239	„old“ (Katrak)			●	
	Katrak306	„old“ (Katrak)		●	●	

35 DHABHAR 1927, S. 34.
36 *Xorde Avesta-* + Pahlavi-Texte, Yt 14, 20, 21 mit PÜ.

			Yt 2	Yt 4	Yt 9	Yt 14
	MF41(8692), ir. Stil	?	●			
	G12(8694)	?			●	
	MF60(8696)	?		●	●	
	B.U.L. X.6(8698)	?			●	
	Katrak418d (+PÜ [so Katrak])	?	●	●		
	Katrak552	?		●		
	Katrak803e < ir.	?		●		
	Katrak753d	(undatiert)				●
	Katrak753f (mit PÜ)	(undatiert)				●
Mss. mit XA Texten	M66(9070)	17. Jh.?	● Yt 2.11–12 (zitiert im „Nērang against pestilence“, fol. 4 r 11 – 5 r 11), RR3(6190), MZK6_XwAIsf1(6187)			
	MinocherJamaspji62(9644)	?				●
	M51b(9775)	1397	● Yt 2.11–14	●		
	M49(9835)	1757	● Yt 2.8–9, 11–14 + NpÜ Do'ā Haft Amšasfand	● + NpÜ		●
	(Naples) Pers6(9505)[37]			●		
Faroxšī	Suppl.persan1191(3095)	frühes 19. Jh.			●	
	K38(3100)	1814			●	●
	27 Hss.+TXA			30 Hss.+ TXA	27 Hss.+ TXA	46 Hss. + TXA

37 Das Ms. NaplesPers.6 ist eine Sammelhandschrift. Das erste darin enthaltene, unvollständige Manuskript ist in Pāzand geschrieben und scheint, dem Papier nach zu urteilen, durchaus alt zu sein. CERETI 1998, S. 158, gibt leider keine vollständige Beschreibung der Handschrift. Seinen Angaben zufolge gründet auf einem älteren *Xorde Avesta*-Ms.: „This manuscript consists of miscellaneous texts taken from the Khorda Avesta“ (CERETI), darunter Stücke aus dem *Stayišn Sīrōze* (fol. 18r Dēn šnāsīδāre; fol. 20r Amešaspənd šnāsīδāre; fol. 25r Srōš šnāsīδāre), Texte aus dem Komplex der *Āfrīnagān*: fol. 28r Ciϑrəm buiiāṯ (= Do'ā-ye Bahrām-e Varjāvand); fol. 113v Afrīngạn i Gāhạnbār; fol. 120r Ruz Xordād māh Farwardīn; fol. 134r Ataš Niyayišn; fol. 146v Hurdād Yašt.

Der Fall des *Tamām Xorde Avesta*

Die Rekonstruktion der Transmissionsgeschichte der *Yašts* vor dem Einsetzen der Handschriften ist ein problematisches Unternehmen. Seit WESTERGAARD ist sie Gegenstand von einander widerstreitenden Hypothesen, die eigentümlicherweise jedoch in einem Punkt übereinkommen: in ihrer Fokussierung derjenigen *Yašts*, die für das *Xorde Avesta* nach Ausweis der Handschriften und des *Faržiyat*s keine oder kaum eine Bedeutung besitzen. Noch KELLENS, dessen *Considérations* von 1998 gerade zu erweisen trachteten, daß das überlieferte Avesta nicht fragmenthaft das *Große Avesta* der Sasanidenzeit fortsetzt, sondern vielmehr eine besondere liturgische Edition zweier voneinander getrennter Textensembles, geht nicht nur wie GELDNER im Bereich der sog. *Kurzen Liturgien*, also des *Xorde Avesta*, von der (nur in Indien existierenden) F1- bzw. *Tamām Xorde Avesta*-Tradition aus, sondern es sind von den *Kurzen Liturgien* lediglich die großen *Yašts*, auf die er — und zwar als Teile der Langzeremonie — einzig reflektiert. Diese im Grunde quer zu KELLENS' generellem Erkenntnisinteresse stehende Behandlung der *Yašts* kann wohl nur als ein Erbe von GELDNERS *Prolegomena* gewertet werden, in denen ebenfalls nur die sog. großen *Yašts*, die über keine „Vulgata", also über keine mündliche Tradition verfügen, behandelt wurden. Ein weiteres GELDNERsches Erbe bei KELLENS ist die Ausrichtung der Theorie von einer (sasanidenzeitlichen) liturgischen Edition von *Kurzen Liturgien* an den Kodizes des *Tamām Xorde Avesta* aus der ersten Hälfte des 17. Jh., deren Bedeutung für GELDNERS Edition das Bild einer definitiven Gruppe von 21 (bzw. 22) *Yašts* in der Forschung verfestigte (in ANQUETILS Handschrift P3 waren nur 18 *Yašts* enthalten). Doch gibt es überhaupt einen zwingenden Grund, das *Tamām Xorde Avesta* als Fortsetzer einer spätantiken liturgischen Kreation anzusehen (und damit die Prinzipien der postulierten spätantiken Edition wiederum vom *Tamām Xorde Avesta* abhängen zu lassen)?[38] Das *Tamām Xorde Avesta* begegnet als eine indische Besonderheit des 2. Jt. und ist ohne alte iranische Parallele (ML2 ist ein spätes Hybrid). Der Aufbau des *Tamām Xorde Avesta* folgt zwar der generellen Architektur des *Xorde Avesta*, ordnet aber i.d.R. die Texte nach vollständigen Textgruppen (z.B. Ny 1–5) und nicht nach liturgischen Erfordernissen wie im eigentlichen *Xorde Avesta*. An der Textgruppe, die in der Forschungsdiskussion zum *Tamām Xorde Avesta* die größte Aufmerksamkeit erfahren hat, den *Yašts*, fällt auf: a) sie ist aus mindestens zwei Quellen zusammengestellt, von denen eine einst vermutlich 16 Texte zählte (es

38 Nur zwei generelle Bemerkungen zu KELLENS' Theorie seien hier vorgebracht: 1. Es gibt im Bereich der sog. *Kurzen Liturgien* keinen zwingenden Grund gegen die ältere (und auch einheimische) Annahme, daß diese „Fragmente" des *Großen Avesta* sind; einzig eine rituelle Versorgung der 30 (27) verschiedenen Monatstage konnte nicht durch das *Bayān* geleistet werden, doch ist die Annahme solcher Versorgung lediglich ein Postulat. 2. KELLENS scheint davon auszugehen, daß das Große Avesta nicht zelebriert wurde; doch konnten noch im frühen 9. Jh. alle *Nask* liturgisch gefeiert werden (s. RĀF 144.2 [TD2 400.14–401.10]).

handelt sich vermutlich um das *Nask Bayān* [s. die Tabelle S. 200]); b) die Textgruppe umfaßt weniger Texte, als die allgemeine Annahme, daß jeder Monatstag (jeder *Yazata*) durch einen spezifischen *Yašt* gefeiert wurde, erwarten läßt; c) die Yt 20+21, die in Iran überhaupt unbekannt sind, sind mit keinem Monatstag verbunden.[39] Diese Beobachtungen legen den Schluß nahe, daß das *Tamām Xorde Avesta* eine sekundäre, auf dem eigentlichen *Xorde Avesta* aufbauende und dieses umgestaltende Kreation ist. Im Bereich der als Gruppe gefaßten *Yašts* wurden offenbar zusammengestellt: a) *Yašts*, die im eigentlichen *Xorde Avesta* enthalten waren; b) *Yašts*, die sich in einem nach „Fragards" geordneten Manuskript fanden.[40] Das eigentliche *Xorde Avesta* aber, dessen (einer) Strukturkern[41] das *Faržiyat* ist, scheint den von Kellens behaupteten Ādurbād-Eingriff nicht nur nicht zu fordern, sondern die Tatsache, daß zwar alle eigentlichen *Xorde Avesta*-Handschriften an einer generellen Architektur partizipieren, diese Architektur aber historisch und lokal besonders wie schließlich auch individuell ausformulieren, läßt an der Berechtigung solcher Forderung zweifeln. Einzig mag zu irgendeinem Zeitpunkt in der Antike oder Spätantike festgelegt worden sein, a) welche Texte zu welchen Zeiten obligat zu rezitieren waren (das *Faržiyat*), b) wie zu irgendeinem Zeitpunkt nach dem Übergang auf das Schriftmedium eine diesem angepaßte strukturelle Ordnung auszugestalten war.

*

An der *Yašt*-Überlieferung sind zwei Verluste besonders auffällig:

1. das weitgehende Fehlen von älteren Übersetzungen. Nur Übersetzungsreste des *Nasks Bayān-Yašt* sind erhalten.[42] Deren Charakter läßt vermuten, daß sie einer Art Übersetzung angehörten, die von derjenigen, wie sie die uns gekommenen Pahlavi-Übersetzungen erkennen lassen ist, abweicht. Ältere vollständige Pahlavi-Übersetzungen scheinen jenseits von Yt 1 Teil I (worin sich der einzige 'klassische' Kommentatorentext der *Yašt*-Übersetzungen findet) und

39 Es ist keineswegs unmöglich anzunehmen, daß es sich bei Yt 20+21 um indische Textfabrikate handelt. Auch in vielen anderen Fällen, daß Stücke des *Tamām Xorde Avesta* keine Parallele im iranischen *Xorde Avesta* haben, muß nicht immer von Verlust oder Transmissionzufall ausgegangen werden.

40 In F1 und E1 sind lediglich die *Yašts* 14–19 als solche *Fragards* ausgewiesen, obgleich ein Manuskript des *Nask Bayān* von den *Yašts* 1–13 (Yt 11 stammt aus dem *Nask Hādōxt*) weitere 10 Texte enthalten haben muß. Möglicherweise war von der Handschrift des *Bayān* — die auffälligerweise eine Sāde-Handschrift war — nur noch deren hinterer Teil übrig. Allerdings führt das auf die Frage, woher dann die Yt 5, 8 und 10 stammen, die doch wohl niemals Teil des eigentlichen *Xorde Avesta* waren.

41 Den zweiten Strukturkern bilden Texte höherer ritueller Performanz, die i.d.R. auch Priester erfordern, so das *Faroxšī* und die *Āfrīnagān*, zwei dem *Drōn* verbundene Rituale, oder die Feier der *Gāϑā*(s) als Totenzeremonie (das *Yašt Gāhān*).

42 König 2015. Man beachte ferner auch die mutmaßlichen Reste einer alten Pahlavi-Übersetzung von Yt 8 im *Bundahišn*.

vielleicht Yt 11 verloren zu sein (die Pahlavi-Übersetzungen von Yt 3 und Yt 14 sind sekundär). Der Grund für das Vorhandensein alter Pahlavi-Übersetzungen von Yt 1.I und Yt 11 dürfte darin liegen, daß eben diese *Yašts* bereits in der Zeit, als Laien die Tagesgebete in Pahlavi rezitierten, den Tagesgebeten zuzählten (die Scheidung zwischen alten und jungen Pahlavi-Übersetzungen von *Xorde Avesta*-Texten stellt eine wichtige Hilfe zur Rekonstruktion des *Xorde Avesta* bzw. des *Faržiyat* vor der Jahrtausendwende dar[43]).

2. die Einbuße verschiedener Performierungsweisen, bei den sog. großen *Yašts* sogar das Ausscheiden aus jeglicher mündlicher Tradition. Hinsichtlich der Rekonstruktion von Formen der Darbringung der *Yašts* ist es in den vergangenen Jahren gelungen, die *Drōn*-Formation, wie sie bis heute im *Faroxšī* überlebt hat, als allgemeine Darbringungsform wahrscheinlich zu machen, ebenfalls den Einbau von *Yašts* in die *Yasna*-Formation.[44] Unklar ist jedoch, wie und wie lange die *Yašts* als Libationsform zelebriert wurden. Diese Praxis reicht bis zum Zeitpunkt der 'Komposition' der sog. *Großen Yašts* zurück. So beschreibt Yt 10, wie die korrekte Begrüßung und Verehrung des Miϑra zu gestalten sei (Yt 10.6):

təm. pairi.jasāi. vaṇtaca. nəmaŋhaca.	ich will ihm mit Preis und Verneigung die
təm. yazāi. surunuuata. yasna. …	Referenz erweisen, mit einem hörbaren
zaōϑrābiiō.	*Yasna* … samt Libationen verehren

Die libierende Verehrungsform prägt sodann die finalen Rahmen der meisten *Yašts* (sie fehlt nur bei Yt 1, 13, 18, 20[?], 21, unter den *Niyāyišn* bei Ny 5 und beim *Mayā Yašt*) bzw. die *Karde*-Rahmen der *Großen Yašts*.[45] Dieser Rahmen nennt auch notwendige liquide Stoffe (Haōma-Milch) sowie das Hantieren mit dem *barəsman*:

ahe. raiia. x^v*arənaŋhaca.*	Ob seiner Pracht und <seines> x^v*arənahs*
təm. yazāi.	**will ich ihm opfern,**
surunuuata. yasna.	**mit einem hörbaren *yasna*,**
XY	XY
haōmaiiō. gauua.	**mit Haōma, welcher <ist> mit Milch <vermischt>,**
barəsmana.	**mit *barəsman*,**

43 Dhabhars Entscheidung, in seiner Edition (1927) weder zwischen alter und junger Übersetzung zu scheiden, noch auch den iranischen von indischen Übersetzungstext abzuheben, hat zu einem gänzlich verzerrten Bild vom ‚Pahlavi Xorde Avesta' geführt.

44 Kotwal/Kreyenbroek 2003; Kreyenbroek 2004, 2008; Cantera 2013.

45 Es handelt sich (gemäß der modularen Beschreibform der avestischen Liturgien) um dasjenige 'partikulare Modul', welches die Gruppen "Niyāyišn" und "Yašt" definiert. Der Autor ist mittlerweile der Ansicht, daß dieses Modul zunächst integraler Teil des Individualtextes von YtXwar bzw. YtMah war, von wo aus es sich ausgebreitet und im Rahmen der liturgischen Formular-Bildung als 'Modul' etabliert hat, wohl zunächst in den großen Yašts (die das Modul teilweise literarisch einbinden), schließlich in einigen Texten, die dem Faržiyat hinzugetreten sind.

hizuuō. daŋhaŋha. mąϑraca.	mit der Zunge Fertigkeit, mit *mąϑra* und Wort und
vacaca. š́iiaoϑnaca.	Tat,
zaoϑrābiiasca.	**und mit Opfergüssen** und mit richtig gesprochenen
aršuxδaēibiiasca. vāyžibiiō.	Worten.
yeŋ́he. hātąm. ...	*yeŋ́he. hātąm. ...*

Zu dieser Rahmenformel steht in performativem Widerspruch die rein rezitierende Ausführung der *Yašts* und *Niyāyišn*s, wie sie zumindest aus den vergangenen Jahrhunderten bekannt ist. Das deutet auf Veränderungen in der rituellen Praxis hin.

Hinsichtlich der Performation von *Yašts* bleibt das Folgende festzuhalten:

1a. *Yašts* (wie auch die *Niyāyišn*s an Sonne/Mihr und Mond) wurden standardmäßig zur Zeit der Rahmenkomposition mit Libationen dargebracht.

1b. *Yašts* konnten möglicherweise ‚für sich' rezitiert/performiert werden, sicher aber (man vergleiche die *Āfrīngān*s) im Zusammenhang mit dem *Drōn*, und vermutlich auch im Zusammenhang mit dem *Yasna* (*Visparad*). Der älteste Beleg für eine Zeremonie bestehend aus *Drōn*, *Yasna* und *Āfrīngān* dürfte sich in der sasanidischen Inschrift ŠPs-I finden.

2. Eine Performation von *Yašts*, insbesondere im Zusammenhang mit anderen Ritualformationen, weist auf die Notwendigkeit von Priestern hin. Möglicherweise besteht ein Zusammenhang zwischen der ehemaligen priesterlichen Performanz und a) dem weitgehenden Fehlen von Pahlavi-Übersetzungen (Priester rezitieren in avestischer Sprache), b) den Eigentümlichkeiten der Reste von Pahlavi-Übersetzungen der sog. *Großen Yašts*, welche vermutlich nicht wie die bekannten Pahlavi-Übersetzungen des *Xorde Avesta* zum rezitativen Gebrauch angefertigt wurden.

3. Die Tatsache, daß wohl nur im Fall der beiden zentralen *Faržiyat-Yašts* alte Übersetzungen vorhanden sind, zeigt die Altertümlichkeit des *Faržiyat*-Wesens unter den Laien an. Einen Kontrast hierzu bilden die älteren indischen Sāde-Handschriften (Jm4, O3), die zwar keine *Tamām Xorde Avesta* Handschriften sind, jedoch weit mehr *Yašts* aufnehmen, als *Yašts* im *Faržiyat* erforderlich sind. Möglicherweise sind diese ältesten Handschriften ein Zeugnis dafür, daß noch in den ersten Jahrhunderten des 2. Jt. neben den *Faržiyat-Yašts* einige andere *Yašts* — gemein ist diesen, mit Ausnahme von Yt 14, daß sie keine *Karde*-Teilung aufweisen, also relativ kurz sind — von den Priestern täglich rezitiert werden konnten, vielleicht bei besonderen Ereignissen, vielleicht im Zusammenhang mit anderen Texten.

*

Nur wenige Informationen zur rituellen Einbettung von *Yašt*s finden sich auch in der Pahlavi-Literatur. Av. *yasna-*[46] ist ins Pahlavi vereinzelt als *yasn* (bisweilen: *yast* geschrieben) entlehnt. Der allgemeine Sinn des Wortes ist „Zeremonie“ bzw. „zeremonieller Text“, das Wort kann folglich unterschiedliche Texte/Textgruppen bezeichnen. Als *yasn* wird z.B. in Šnš 13.15 das *Wisparad* bezeichnet (*yasn Wisparad*). Sodann wird der Ausdruck in Zusammenhang mit *Nask*-Bezeichnungen gebraucht: Dk 8.15.1, HKR 9, ZWY 7.22, ASS12 *Bagān yasn*; Šnš 13.1 *Stōtān yasn*; Šnš 12.17 *Bāy-yasn*. *Yasn* steht in Šnš 13.51 abbrevierend für das *Yasna Haptaŋhāiti* (*Ahuwayt gāh … Yasn … Uštwad gāh* etc.).[47] Im ZWY begegnet der *yasn*-Ausdruck allerdings in Zusammenhang mit Namen, die möglicherweise als *Yašt*s aufzufassen sind.[48] Bevorzugt weisen

46 Die jungavestische Wendung *aōxtō.nāmana yasna yaz-* „mit einem den Namen <einer Gottheit> nennenden *yasna* <diese> verehren“ (zu dieser Formel s. Panaino 1994, S. 172) zeigt an, daß der Ausdruck für die Verehrung/den Hymnus an die einzelne Gottheit derselbe ist wie für das Opfer schlechthin (*yasna*). Ein *Yašt* scheint im Avestischen also als ein *yasna aōxtō.nāman* bezeichnet worden zu sein. Eine PÜ dessen findet sich im Referat des *Bayān Nask* Dk 8.15.2 (MF 82.3–14) als *yast* [**yasn*?] *guft-nām* (Übersetzungen des Referatstextes finden sich jenseits von West (1892) in Darmesteter 1892–1893 II, S. XXVII; Geldner 1896–1904, S. 19; König 2012, S. 361f.). PRDd 40.1–5 scheint auf das Xorde Avesta/ Faržiyat des ausgehenden 1. Jt. hinzuweisen, neben Ny 1+3 und den *Āfrīnagān* ist die Rede von: *Ohrmazd-*ēsn ud abārīg *yašn ham-ēdōn bawēd* „Bei der Verehrung für Ohrmazd und anderer *yašn* verhält es sich ebenso.“

47 Desgleichen in Šnš 13.16 *yasn bun kardag 9 wizist u-š bun Humatanām u-š sar Humatanām*.

48 Die Passage WZ 3.15, die *yasn* mit zwei weiteren liturgischen Termini zusammenstellt, ist von Gignoux/Tafazzoli wie folgt übersetzt worden:

*u-š abar *paywahīd ō Ohrmazd pad yasn ud niyāyišn ud nām-barišnīh*	„et il (Tištar) supplia Ohrmazd qui lui apporta la force par le sacrifice, les litanies et la lounge“ (Gignoux/Tafazzoli 1993, S. 43)

Vielleicht liegt es näher, unter dem Ausdruck *pad yasn ud niyāyišn* einen Hinweis auf *Xorde Avesta*-Liturgien („Yašt und Niyāyišn”) zu sehen. Er entspräche den Eigenbezeichnungen *niiāiš u yast/yašt* einiger XA/TXA-Mss.: E1 (1601 n. Chr.) *kətāb. niiāiš. u. ẏašt. u. baēą̄n. ẏašt. u ńīraṇghā. u. cīzə. ki. hərbəδąn. u. bahidīnąnrā kār. āiiat̰.* (fol. 488r 2–6) „Buch <der> *Niyāyeš*<es> und *Yašt*<s> und des *Bayān Yašt* und der *Nīrang*s und der <anderen> Gegenstände, die die Priester und Laien verwenden“; vgl. O3 (1646 n. Chr.) „book of the Nēāsts (and) the Yasts“ (Kol.); P8 (1697 n. Chr. [Unvala 1940, S. 9]); Zend Add. 8996 (1854 n. Chr. [Unvala 1940, S. 108]); K12 (1801 n. Chr. [Unvala 1940, S. 136]). Die Darbringung eines *niyāyišn* „für Ohrmazd“ erklärt sich aus dem üblichen liturgischen Beginn dieser Texte, die immer eine Referenz an Ohrmazd einschließen, s. Ny 1: (ind.) *nəmasə.tē. ahura. mazda.* (3x); (ir.) *nəmō. huuarəxšaētāi. auruuat̰.aspāi.* (3x) *xšnaōϑra. ahurahe. mazdå. nəmasə.tē. ahura. mazda.* (3x). Auch der Text Dk 3.81 (DkM 81.7–17; B 59.3–10), unsere älteste datierbare Pahlavi-Quelle zu den Tagesgebeten, spricht vom *niyāyišn <ī> dādār ohrmazd*, welches „der Sonne gegenüber“ (*ō xwaršēd*) in Avestisch darzubringen sei, sowie von einer *yasn-*ōšmurišnīh* (Text: *ōšmurišnīg*), die im Text „weiter unten notiert“ sei, welcher tatsächlich das Substitutsgebet *Nām Stāyišn* (= *Doā–e Niyāyeš–e Īrān*) ist.

die Passagen auf *yasn* für Amahraspanden — ein Phänomen, das an die oben konstatierte bevorzugte Aufnahme von an Amahraspanden gerichtete *Yašts* im *Xorde Avesta* erinnert[49] —, insbesondere für Hordad:

ZWY 2.1

pad zand ī ***Wahman-Yasn Hordad-Yasn ud Aštād Yasn*** *paydāg …*	Im *Zand* des ***Wahman-Yasn Hordad-Yasn*** **und** ***Aštād Yasn*** heißt es …[50]

ZWY 7.24 gibt Notizen zu deren zeremonieller Ausführung, die auf eine *Lange Liturgie* weisen:

ZWY 7.24

*ud frāz rawēd Pišišōtan ī bāmīg abāg 100 ud 50 mard kē siyā samōr dārēnd ō ādur ī xwarrahōmand ī rōšn-kerb xwānēnd ī pad dādgāh nišast *ān*[51] *ī Ādur-farrōbāy ī pērōzgar*	Es ziehen der lichte Pišišōtan mit 150 Männern, die schwarze Säbel zum *xwarrah*versehenen Feuer,[52] das man „Licht-Körper" (*rōšn-kirb*[53]) nennt und das am *dādgāh* installiert ist, dem Sitz (?) des siegreichen Ādurfarrōbāy-Feuers.
u-š pad ham-zōdīh yazišn frāz sāzēnd barsom frāz wistarēnd ud yazēnd ***Hordad ud Amurdad yasn*** *pad nērang ī Nērangestān ī dēnīg*	Und sie feiern in Zōt-Gemeinschaft das Opfer (*yazišn*), spreitet das *Barsom*, feiert das ***Yašt (yasn)*** **für Hordad ud Amurdad** mit der Performanz (*nērang*) des *Nērangestān ī dēnīg*.

Der Ausdruck *nām-barišnīh* (vermutlich PÜ von [unbezeugtem] av. *nāman-* + *bərəti-*) ist von Gignoux/Tafazzoli 1993, S. 148, unspezifisch als „hommage" bestimmt worden. Die beiden weiteren Wortbelege (beide im *Dēnkard*) ergeben keine weitere Klärung. Dk 3.169 redet vom *ēzišnīg nām-barišnīh ī yazdān* „rituellen *nām-barišnīh* der Götter"; Dk 5.24.17 bezeichnet u.a. *Barsom* und *Drōn*: *nihang-ēw ī pad nām-barišnīh hangirdīg hēnd* „ein Partikulares, das mittels/in der *nām-barišnīh* aufgenommen ist".

49 Auffällig ist desweiteren, daß das *Nām Stāyišn*, das offenbar als Substitution der Tagesgebete dienen konnte (s. Fn. 48), neben Ohrmazd besonders die sechs (so die iranische Fassung) bzw. sieben oder acht (so die indische Fassung) Amahraspanden hervorhebt.

50 Die folgende Notiz bezieht sich auf Mazdak, der tatsächlich noch einmal in ZWY 3.28 genannt wird. Doch bleibt es auffällig, daß das *Wahman-Yasn* auf sich selbst als Quelle verweist.

51 In K20 139r 20 eine im Anfang unklare Schreibung (ys)yn'n; DH yd'n/h'n; K43 ø (s. Cereti 1991, S. 119).

52 Auch in der Moderne findet sich ein Zusammenhang zwischen Waffen und Feuer(gründung) — Tertium dessen dürfte die Wahrām-Gottheit sein — bzw. Waffen und Feuerkammern der Tempel, s. Darmesteter 1892–1893, I, S. LXII; Modi 1937, S. 213f.; Boyce 1968, S. 52f.; Gropp 1969, S. 152; Boyd/Kotwal 1983, S. 311; Boyce 1987, S. 2. Vgl. zu ai. Verhältnissen Haug 1907, S. 280.

53 *Rōšn-kirb* findet auch im Rahmen der Daēnā-Kosmographie (s. Y 9.26) Verwendung, s. Dd 36.100 *xwarrah ī dēn ī mēnōg pad ān ī rōšn-kirb asāmānīhā ham-pērāmōn ī āsmān parwandīhēd* „Das *xwarrah* der *dēn ī mēnōg* umrundet unendlich durch/in jenen/jenem ‘Lichtleib’ den Himmel".

Aus der Angabe ZWY 2.1, daß auch das *Hordad Yasn* und *Aštād Yasn* Notizen zu Mazdak enthielten, folgt, daß diese beiden *Yašt*s — ob ihr avestischer Text der bekannte von Yt 4+18 war, bleibt freilich ungewiß — eine Pahlavi-Übersetzung besaßen. Für die Identität mit Yt 4+18 mag sprechen, daß diese beiden Texte auch im frühen indischen XASāde vertreten sind.

Die Stelle ZWY 7.24 gibt in Hinsicht auf die Frage nach der Zelebration zu erkennen, daß diese a) durch Priester, b) im Zusammenhang mit dem *Yasna* mit *Barsom*, c) mit performativen Handlungen (*Barsom* spreiten), und zwar einer Performanz (*nērang*) erfolgte, wie sie im *Nērangestān ī dēnīg* notiert ist, d.h., soweit es sich hier um einen Verweis auf das *Nērangestān* handeln sollte, den dortigen Angaben zur Feier als *keh*- oder *meh*-Ritual entspricht.

Verwandt mit ZWY 7.24 könnte die komplexe rituelle Sequenz in AWN 3.11 sein, die die Himmelfahrt des Wirāz einleitet:

u-šān drōn yašt ud wirāz wāz grift ud xwarišn xward ud myazd rāyēnīd <ud> wāz be guft ud stāyišn ī ohrmazd ud amahrspandān ud ***spās ī Hordad ud Amurdad amahrspandān*** *hangārd ud āfrīnagān guft*	Sie feierten ein *Drōn:* Wirāz eröffnete die Zeremonie (*wāz grift*) und aß (vom *Drōn*) und führte das Myazd[54] durch und sprach das (schließende?) *wāz*; <dann> rezitierte er das *stāyišn* für Ohrmazd und die Amahraspanden und den **Dank**[55] **an die Amahraspanden Hordad und Amurdad** und sprach die *Āfrīnagān*-Texte.

Der gesamte Ausdruck *wirāz wāz grift ud xwarišn xward ud myazd rāyēnīd <ud> wāz be guft ud stāyišn ī ohrmazd ud amahrspandān ud spās ī Hordad ud Amurdad amahrspandān hangārd* entspricht weitgehend Wendungen, wie sie sich als rituelle Selbstbeschreibung im avestischen *Drōn*-Text finden.[56] Der Teilausdruck *spās ī Hordad ud Amurdad amahrspandān hangārd* scheint den „Dank“ an die Nahrungsgaben zu formulieren (schon im Avesta können

54 Die Verbindung *myazd rāyēn-* scheint singulär zu sein, meist geht *myazd* mit *kun-* oder *sāz-*.

55 Die Wendung *spās hangar-* wird einige Male in der Pahlavi-Literatur verwendet. Hauptfundstellen sind AWN und KN, undeutlich bleibt, ob der Ausdruck eine partikulare Bedeutung besitzt (AWN 15.7, vgl. damit: Dk 5.24.25; KN 4.8, KN 11.15, KN 14.18; vgl. a. NM 1.1.2, Dk 6 D5). Zu den Dankes-Texten im (iranischen) Xorde Avesta s. KÖNIG 2023.

56 Im avestischen Text des *Drōn* werden als *x^{v}arəϑəm. miiazdəm.* „Nahrung Miiazda“ stets genannt *hauruuata. amərətāta. gāuš. hudā̊.* (die beiden:) Wasser und Pflanze <sowie> das ‚gutgebende Rindervieh‘ (= Milch oder Fett), das Xšnūman geht an Ahura Mazdā, Aməṣ̌a Spəṇtas, Sraōša, s. Y 3.1 *barəsmana. paiti.bərəta. haδa.zaōϑre. hāuuanōiš. raϑβō.* ***x^{v}arəϑəm. miiazdəm.*** *āiiese. yešti.* ***hauruuata. amərətāta. gāuš. hudā̊.*** *xšnūmaine. ahurahe. mazdā̊. aməṣ̌anąm. spəṇtanąm. xšnūmaine. sraōšahe. aṣ̌ehe. aṣ̌iuuatō. vərəϑrājanō. frādat̰.gaēϑahe.*, vgl. Y 8.1 *aṣ̌aiia. daδą*mi. ***x^{v}arəϑəm. miiazdəm. hauruuata. amərətāta. gāuš. hudā̊.*** *haōməmca. para.haōməmca.* etc. Y 3.20 (= Y 7.20) ***x^{v}arəϑəm. miiazdəm.*** *āiiese. yešti.* ***hauruuata. amərətāta. gāuš. hudā̊.*** *xšnūmaine. sraōšahe. aṣ̌iiehe. taxmahe. tanumąϑrahe. darši.draōš. āhūiriiehe. aōxtō.nāmanō. yazatahe.*

Hauruuatāt und Amərətatāt für Wasser und Pflanzen metonymisch einstehen, eine Metonymie, die auch in der in AWN beschriebenen Zeremonie aus *Drōn* + *Myazd* und den *Āfrīnagān* sinnreich wäre). Ob der Teilausdruck indes eine Reformulierung von ZWY 7.24 *yazēnd Hordad ud Amurdad yasn* darstellt, ist unklar; auffällig an der Formulierung AWN 3.11 ist zumindest, daß das *spas* separat, nach dem *stāyišn ī ohrmazd ud amahrspandān* und vor der Rezitation der *Āfrīnagān* aufgeführt wird.

Die *Āfrīnagān*-Zeremonien gehören wie das auch mit ihnen verbundene *Drōn* zu den in der nicht-parsischen Forschung weitgehend vergessenen Zeremonien. Datiert das Vergessen des *Drōn* schon auf ANQUETIL zurück, so ist ANQUETIL neben DARMESTETER jedoch lange Zeit der wohl einzige ‚westliche' Forscher, der ein klares Bewußtsein von dem liturgischen Komplex *Āfrīnagān-Āfrīn* besaß (s. ANQUETIL 1771 II, S. 56–100) und diesen Komplex in seinem *Zend-Avesta* auch angemessen darstellt hat (während alle übrigen Textedioren in bezug auf die *Āfrīnagān* geradezu sinnzerstörend gearbeitet haben). Die Durchsicht der Pahlavi- und Pāzand-Literatur läßt indes erkennen, daß die *Āfrīnagān*-Zeremonien ein ganz zentraler Baustein im Ritualgefüge des Zoroastrismus seit alters her waren — sie sind notwendig vor allem für die Zelebration der sechs Jahresfeste und im Rahmen des Totengedenkens —, und daß sie diese Bedeutung (anders als etwa das *Yasna* in Iran) bis heute nicht eingebüßt haben. Vollständige *Āfrīnagān*-Zeremonien umfassen — unsere ältesten Quellen sind diesbezüglich ANQUETIL und *Rewāyat*-Texte des 16. + 17. Jh. — fast immer das (als *Āfrīnagān* Dahman bekannte) Y 60 (also der Text *Dahmā Āfrīti* [zu einem namensgleichen, interkalierten *Yašt* s. CANTERA 2013 nach KELLENS 1996]) und das *Āfrīnagān Srōš* (= Y 57.1–8 = Yt 11.0–7). Vielleicht mag nicht auszuschließen sein, daß in älterer Zeit auch andere *Yašt*-Texte mit den *Āfrīnagān*-Zeremonien zusammengestellt werden konnten. Gerade zum Hordad-Tag haben sich ja besondere *Āfrīnagān*s bis heute erhalten, so das *Āfrīnagān des Tages Hordad des Monats Frawardīgān* (= *Āfrīnagān* Valava), das *Āfrīnagān des Tages Hordad des Monats Spandarmad* (= *Hordad–Sāl–Gāh* = *Nawrōz–i Zāwuli*).

Abkürzungen

ANogNavar	Āfrīngān Nōg Nāwar
AWN	Ardā Wirāz Nāmag
Bd	Bundahišn
Dd	Dādestān ī dēnīg
Dk	Dēnkard
GujÜ	Gujarati-Übersetzung
ir.	iranisch
ind.	indisch
KN	Kārnāmag
KSM	Kirdīr Sar Mašhad

NerKB	Nērang Kustīg Bastan
MX	Mēnōg ī xrad
NM	Nāmagīhā Manuščihr
NpÜ	Neupersische Übersetzung
Ny	Niyāyišn
PahlXA	Pahlavi Xorde Avesta
PRDd	Pahlavī Rivāyat zum Dādestān ī dēnīg
PÜ	Pahlavi-Übersetzung
PY	Pahlavi-Yasna
RĀF	Rivāyat Ādurfarrbay und Farrbay-Srōš
SkrXA	Sanskrit-Xorde Avesta
SrB,	Srōš Bāj
SÜ	Sanskrit-Übersetzung
WZ	Wizīdagīhā ī Zādspram
TXA	Tamām Xorde Avesta
XA	Xorde Avesta
XASāde	Xorde Avesta Sāde
Y	Yasna
YH	Yasna Haptaŋhāiti
Yt	Yašt
ZWY	Zand ī Wahman Yasn

Bibliographie

ANDRÉS–TOLEDO, M. 2015: "Ceremonies in the Xorde Avesta Manscripts: the Drōn Frawardīn Yašt. In: *Estudios Iranios y Turanios* 2, S. 29–41.

ANQUETIL DUPERRON, A.H. 1771: *Zend-Avesta: Ouvrage de Zoroastre* I-II. Paris [Repr. New York/London 1984].

BARTHOLOMAE, CHR. 1915: *Die Zendhandschriften der K. Hof- und Staatsbibliothek in München*. München.

BHARUCHA, E.D. 1906–1933: *Collected Sanskrit Writings of the Parsis; Old translations of Avestâ and Pahlavi-Pâzend books as well as other original compositions; with various readings and notes*. Vols. I–VI. Collated, corrected, and ed. by ERVAD DADABHAI BHARUCHA. Bombay.

BLOCHET, E. 1900: *Catalogue des Manuscrits Mazdéens … de la Bibliothèque Nationale*. Besançon [2.ed. Paris 1905].

BOYCE, M. 1968: "On the Sacred Fires of the Zoroastrians." In: *BSOAS* 31, S. 52–68, 287–288.

— 1987: "Ātaš." In: *EIr* 3, S. 1–5.

BOYD, J./F.M. KOTWAL 1983: "Worship in a Zoroastrian Fire Temple." In: *IIJ* 26, S. 293–318.

CANTERA, A. 2013: "Talking with God: The Zoroastrian *ham.paršti* or Intercalation Ceremonies." In: *Journal Asiatique* 301, S. 85–138.

CERETI, C.G. 1998: "Zoroastrian Manuscripts in Italy: Past and Present." In: *Proceedings of the Third European Conference of Iranian Studies, held in Cambridge,*

11th to 15th September 1995. Part 1 Old and Middle Iranian Studies. Ed. by N. Sims-Williams. Wiesbaden, pp. 153–161.

Choksy, J.K./F.M. Kotwal 2005: "Praise and piety: Niyāyišn and yašts in the history of Zoroastrian praxis." In: *BSOAS* 68, S. 215–252.

Darmesteter, J. 1892–1893: *Le Zend-Avesta. Traduction nouvelle avec commentaire historique et philologique.* 3 Bde. Paris.

Geldner, K. Fr. 1896–1904: "Awestaliteratur." In: *GrIrPh* II.1, S. 1–53.

Dhabhar, E.B.N. 1923a: *The K.R.Cama Oriental Institute Catalogue. Classified Catalogue of Printed Books and Manuscripts, with Supplement and Indexes.* 2 vols. Bombay.

— 1923b: *Descriptive catalogue of all Manuscripts in the first Dastur Meherji Rana Library, Navsari.* Bombay.

— 1923c: *Descriptive catalogue of some Manuscripts bearing on Zoroastrianism and pertaining to the different collections in the Mulla Feroze Library.* Bombay.

— 1927: *Zand-i Khūrtak Avistāk.* Bombay.

— 1932: *The Persian Rivayats of Hormazyar Framarz and others. Their Version with Introduction and Notes.* Bombay.

Gignoux, Ph./A. Tafazzoli 1993: *Anthologie de Zādspram. Édition critique du texte pehlevi, traduit et commenté.* Paris (StIr, Cahier 13).

Haug, M. 1907 [4. ed.]: *Essays on the Sacred Language, Writings, and Religion of the Parsis.* London.

Karanjia, R.P. 2010: *The Bāj-Dharnā (Drōn Yasht): A Zoroastrian Ritual for Consecration and Commemoration, History, Performance, Text and Translation.* Mumbai.

Katrak, J.C. 1941: *Oriental treasures being a condensed tabular descriptive statement of over a thousand manuscripts and of their colophons written in Iranian and Indian languages and lying in private libraries of Parsis in different centres of Gujarat.* Bombay.

Kellens, J. 1996: "Commentaire sur les premiers chapitres du Yasna." In: *Journal Asiatique* 284, S. 37–108.

— 1998: "Considérations sur l'histoire de l'Avesta." In: *Journal Asiatique* 286, S. 451–519.

König, G. 2012: "Das Nask Bayān und das Xorde Avesta." In: Cantera, A. (Hrsg.): *The Transmission of the Avesta.* Wiesbaden, S. 355–394.

— 2015: "Zur Überlieferungsgeschichte der *Yašts*: Reste der exegetischen Tradition. Die Pahlavi-Übersetzungen von Yt 13 in Dk 7." In: Cantera, A. (ed.): *Estudios de Iran y Turan* 1, *Fs Pirart.* Girona, S. 131–149.

— 2017: "Bayān Yasn. State of the Art." In: *Iran and the Caucasus.* Leiden, S. 13–38.

— 2022: "Notizen zum Xorde Avesta III: Existierte ein Niyāyišn für Arəduuī/die Wasser in Iran?" In: *ZDMG* 172, pp. 373–406.

— 2023: "Nicht-avestische Texte im Xorde Avesta: die Texte des Danksagens." In: *Estudios Iranios y Turanios* 5, pp. 23–46.

Kotwal, F.M./A. Hintze 2008: *The Khorda Avesta and Yăst Codex E1.* Facsimile edition. Wiesbaden.

Kotwal, F.M./Ph. Kreyenbroek 2003: *The Hērbedestān and Nērangestān.* Vol. III: *Nērangestān, Fragard 2.* Paris (StIr, Cahier 30).

Kotwal, F. /D. Sheffield/Bh. Gandhi 2008: *Preliminary Descriptive List of Manuscripts Donated to the First Dastur Meherjirana Library since 1923.* Navsari.

KREYENBROEK, PH. G. 2004: "Ritual and Rituals in the Nērangestān." In: M. STAUSBERG (ed.): *Zoroastrian Ritual in Context. Studies in the History of Religions.* Leiden, S. 317–331.
KREYENBROEK, PH. G. 2008: "The Term Bâgân Yasn and the Function of the Yashts in the Zoroastrian Ritual." In: M. JAAFARI-DEHAGHI (ed.): *One for the Earth: Prof. Dr. Mahyar Nawabi, Memorial Volume.* Tehran, S. 81–94.
DE MENASCE, J. 1947–48: "La promotion de Vahrām." In: *RHR* 133, S. 5–18.
MODI, J.J. 1924: "A few Parsee Nîrangs (Incantations or Religious Formulæ)." In: *Anthropological Papers III. Papers Read before the Anthropological Society.* Bombay. S. 52–71.
— 1937: *The Religious Ceremonies and Customs of the Parsees.* Bombay [21937].
PANAINO, A. 1994: "Philologia avestica IV, Av. yaštay-/yešti; yašta; pahl. yašt. Quelques réflexions sur les titres des hymnes de l'Avesta." In: *StIr* 23, S. 163–185.
RUSSELL, J.R. 1991: "The Doʿā-ye Nām Stāyišn." In: *Corolla Iranica. Papers in honour of Prof. Dr. David Neil MacKenzie on the occasion of his 65th birthday on April 8th, 1991.* Ed. by R.E. EMMERICK and D. WEBER. Fr./M., S. 127–132.
UNVALA, J.M. 1940: *Collection of Colophons of Manuscripts bearing on Zoroastrianism in some Libraries of Europe.* Bombay.
WEST, E.W. 1892: *Pahlavi Texts.* Part IV: *Contents of the Nasks.* Oxford (SBE 37).

"Let Buyruq Sangun Live Long and be Divinely Blessed" Another Sogdian Dedicatory Inscription

PAVEL LURJE, St. Petersburg/BORIS ZHELEZNYAKOV, Almaty

1. Context of Find and Archaeological Significance[1]

The early Middle Age epigraphic monuments of Chu valley and neighboring Talas valley are written in two scripts: the Old Turkic runiform writing and in Sogdian. In some areas of Semirechie the Turko-Sogdian bilingualism continued throughout early Middle Ages. The dictionary of Maḥmūd of Kāshghar contains the information that allows for the exact understanding of this process.[2] In V.A. LIVSHITS' articles a history of research of Sogdian inscriptions in Semirechie has been outlined since their first discovery in 1941. The inscriptions are carved on the rims of *khums* (pythos, large pottery vessels) and often convey deep respect for the person to whom the *khum* was donated.[3]

The development of literacy and its usage are the main aspects of the cultural manifestations of Turko-Sogdian "symbiosis", which has been previously discussed. LIVSHITS divides Sogdian inscriptions of Chu-Talas into two groups: the rock inscriptions of Terek-say and Kulan-say and pottery inscriptions from the Chu valley.[4]

The town site of Burana is located in the eastern part of the Chu valley on the territory of Kyrgyzstan. It has been compared to the medieval town of Balāsāghūn, and its identification has been substantiated by translations of Moslem epitaphs dating to the 12th to 13th centuries found at the site published completely in 2019 by VLADIMIR N. NASTICH.[5] The main investigations in the research on Burana was made by archaeologist PETR N. KOZHEMJAKO. The central part of the site, *shahristān*, is delineated by the traces of the fortification wall, in some sections up to 4 m high and 20 m wide at the base. The walls are

1 Part 1 by BORIS ZHELEZNYAKOV, part 2, 3 and note 15 by PAVEL LURJE. The authors are grateful to Prof. YOSHIDA YUTAKA, Prof. JENS WILKENS, Dr. ASAN TORGOEV and VALERIJ KOL'CHENKO for their learned comments on the earlier draft of the paper, and CLAUDIA CHANG for correcting our English style.

2 LIVSHITS 2013, p. 62.

3 *Ibid.*, pp. 64–65.

4 LIVSHITS 2004a, pp. 55–57.

5 NASTICH 2019, pp. 281–289.

oriented in the cardinal directions, the area is 570 x 500 x 600 x 570 m. The outer rampart was discovered by KOZHEMJAKO and has a length of 15 km. Its remaining height reaches 1,7 m and its width is 3 m.[6]

The archaeological site of Burana dates back to the 9th–13th (14th) centuries. The well-known Medieval city of Balasagun with which the site of Burana is identified was the capital of the Eastern Karakhanid Kaganate. The heyday of this city was in the 11th–12th centuries[7]. The discovery of the storage vessel (*khum*) rim was made in the vicinity of the Nestorian cemetery, 20 m south of the wall of *shahristan*, not far from the foundation of the structure.

The Christian cemetery of the "Church of the East," in the location to the south of *shahristān*, has been well known since 1880s.[8]

A church and a monastery at the neighboring site Ak-Beshim have been previously studied[9], so one can safely assume that a church and a community of "Nestorian" Christians at Burana dates to the Qarluq-Karakhanide period (9th–11th century) and even later.

In early 2010, a local inhabitant accidentally discovered a rim of *khum* with inscription and depiction of a swastika at the site of Burana. An artefact hoard was discovered as well, most likely concealed inside the *khum*. The location of the find is indicated as 20–25 m to the north of the northern wall of *shahristān*, near the north-eastern corner (fig. 1). Further information on the hoard is being collected and will be published in the near future. The finds were examined by the renown numismatist PAVEL N. PETROV. He has reported his findings and shared a photo from his archive to one of the authors. The authors are grateful to PAVEL N. PETROV for this information.

The rim of the vessel is about 6,5 cm wide and comprises three fragments, the outer rim is *circa* 40 cm in diameter. A fragment of the inscription is on the top flat surface of the rim. In addition to the inscription, the rim also has a depiction of a swastika with hooks facing the right (right-hand double swastika), carved on surface of clay after the vessel's firing.

Such symbols are often found across the entire regions of the Middle East and Central Asia. DZHANGAR JA. IL'YASOV studied a large number of carved swastikas on *khums* from Kampyrtepa (middle Amu Darya) dating to the 2nd century CE layer; SERGEJ BOLELOV found similar images as well. Some swastikas are as large as 10 cm in diameter.[10] ILYASOV cites TIGRAN K. MKRTYCHEV's opinion that the "right-hand" swastika might be a combination of a Buddhist symbol and a clan tamga but are not dated earlier than mid-5th century.[11] However, there was a similar swastika on the golden scabbard from male burial 4 at Tillya-tepe in northern

6 KOZHEMJAKO 1959, pp. 12f.
7 AMANBAEVA *et al.* 2015, pp. 27, 35.
8 PANTUSOV 1888, pp. 98a–101a.
9 SEMENOV 2002.
10 ILYASOV 2010.
11 MKRTYCHEV 1996.

Afghanistan (excavation of Viktor I. Sarianidi); the monument now attributed to the second quarter of the 1st century CE.[12] Consequently the tradition of marking *khums* and other artefacts with right-hand swastika has been dated to the beginning of the Common era, often attributed specifically to the Kushans.

From these data we can also draw connections between finds at Torkultobe, where there are depictions of cross with sides of equal length and swastika on a stone vessel. The stone vessel was found by chance in 1930s and dated by comparative analogies with materials from the 10th–12th century,[13] i. e. the Qarakhanid Period. The symbols on the stone vessel intrigued many scholars beginning with Mikhail Je. Masson and Aleksandr N. Bernshtam. The attribution of this vessel with symbols of the cross and pigeon to local Christians is widely accepted. It also has signs and/or symbols that place it into earlier chronological periods and thus contradicts a Moslem affiliation. There are a significant number of relief depictions of the swastika on the bronzes from the "Nickson collection" found from the burials of the Onghuts, a group who accepted Christianity in the 12th century. These monuments are located close to the Chinese-Mongol border. Both right-hand and left-hand swastikas are found in large quantities there.[14] This well-known collection is kept in the museum of Hongkong, and its artefacts demonstrate once again the universal meaning of swastika, a popular symbol in many regions of Southern, Eastern and Central Asia in the Middle Ages.[15]

In our case, the symbol has additional hooks which separate at a 45 degree angle from the four terminal ends of the swastika. Perhaps one can interpret these elaborated symbols as a kind of clan tamga of the owner or person commemorated on the vessel. Perhaps the dedication symbol represented a person who had accepted Buddhism or Christianity by adopting the swastika as his tamga, then later his direct descendent added these finials to it. Whether this was deliberate or not, they are crudely carved without great accuracy. Perhaps this suggests that the dedicatee had a high status.

2. Edition and Commentary

The inscription is incised in the middle of the rim after firing in small but distinctive letters. A swastika-like sign marks the beginning of the phrase. A verb

12 Ilyasov 2010, p. 220.
13 Baypakov/Ternovaja 2018, pp. 26ff.
14 Drake 1962.
15 One can take into account a rim of *khum* from Kara-tobe-Sauran (Smagulov 2010, p. 32), where a symbol which can be understood as peculiar shape of swastika or cross overlaps with a Sogdian or Uighur inscription in a rather untrained hand *c(l)ʾ(y)p[ʾ]* = Syriac *clīpā* "cross" (see Lurje 2022, p. 226, fig. 5). Yoshida Yutaka (per litteras) kindly suggested another reading *cwlp(ʾn)* for Turkic *Čolpan* "Venus".

is needed to finalize the phrase after the lacuna. We do not know if there were other parts of the inscription on the missing half of the rim. (fig. 2–4)

Transliteration:

pwyrwγ snkwn βrzy zwʾt βγʾnyk šʾtwx [βwʾt?]

Translation:

"Let Buyruq Säŋün live long (and be) divinely blessed".

Commentary:

pwyrwγ snkwn a Turkish name or title *Buyruq Säŋün* "minister general". *Buyruq/buryuq/bïruq* is attested in Runic, Uighur, and Moslem texts; recently the oblique plural *pw(yrw)xty* was deciphered on the Sogdian version of the Karabalgasun inscription, 16(1)[16], the name *Buyruq Alp Sangun* appears on the Uighur stake inscription from Khocho,[17] *säŋün* (from Chinese *jiangjun* 將軍, Early Middle Chinese pronunciation *tsiaŋʰ-kun* "general") is widely known in Sogdian texts as well as *snkwn* or *sʾnkwn*, and in the compound Turkish names it usually is placed at the end.[18]

βrzy zwʾt optative 3 sg. "let him live long". Apparently, the same expression *βrz ʾzwʾt* appears on another dedicatory inscription from Ak-tobe (no. 5 below).[19] The final *y* in *βrzy* is a late spelling of *βrzʾk*. A less likely alternative would be *ryzy zwʾt* "live (according to his) will".

βγʾnyk šʾtwx "divine happy", both words *βγʾnyk* and *šʾtwx* are well known in Sogdian, and the similar expression *smʾncyk šʾtwxyʾ* "heavenly bliss" appears in Christian Sogdian C2 57 R 7–8.[20] On the original photo of the inscription one can recognize a hook above the last line of *x*, thus inclining one to read *šʾtwxy*.

16 YOSHIDA 2020, pp. 56ff, 131.

17 Analyzed in RYBATZKI 2006, p. 220a. I am grateful to JENS WILKENS for this reference.

18 The wide range of Sogdian attestations of the title can be supplemented now by an ink inscription *sʾnkw(n)* on a potsherd from Panjakent in a layer pre-dating the fire of 722 (RASPOPOVA 2017, no. 5; LURJE, *forthcoming* a, where the frontal vocalization *säŋün* is advocated on Sogdian material, if it was indeed borrowed through Turkic and not directly from Chinese). The compound *tʾy sʾnkwn* "big general" (Chinese *Da jiangjun*) appears on a well-wishing fragment SI 4905 V 16 (CHUNAKOVA 2019, p. 23).
It should be also noted that this term, in another phonetic shape of the borrowing, namely *sayun* (NADELYAEV *et al.* 1969, p. 481; LURJE 2010, p. 340) surely appears in the place-name *Balāsāγūn*, which is identified with the Burana site. Cf. its Chinese name *Péiluójiāngjūn* 裴羅將軍 with the same *jiāngjūn* = *säŋün* in Xin Tangshu 43b, 38, 3b ("ville de général *pʾei-lo*" according to CHAVANNES 1903, p. 10, updated translation in DICKENS 2023, p. 59.

19 LIVSHITS 2008, pp. 365f; 2015, pp. 279–282; YOSHIDA 2022, p. 604. A good photo of the inscription can be consulted in AKIMBEK/BAIBUGUNOV 2013, p. 80.

20 SIMS-WILLIAMS 1985, p. 113.

However, the resolution of this photo is very low, and this part of the inscription is absent from the most recent photo of better quality, so this hook appears to be an accidental artefact. A verb in optative would be expected at the end, one like *βw'ʾt*, *x'ʾt*, *y'ʾt*, *β'ʾt*, *'skw'ʾt* or alike. If the oblique case *š'ʾtwxy* is incised indeed, then some other wording of the final part of the inscription might be considered.

3. Dedicatory Inscriptions from Chu Valley: a Preliminary General Overview

This inscription belongs to a group of late Sogdian dedicatory texts incised on the rims of *khums* (large pottery vessels) found on different sites of Chu valley (mainly found in its eastern part, see the map 8) in present-day Kyrgyzstan and Kazakhstan. Eight of them have been published by V.A. LIVSHITS,[21] another one by G. BABAYAROV, K. TABALDIEV, A. KUBATIN and B. GHOIBOV, and corrected by N. SIMS-WILLIAMS and YOSHIDA Y. (fig. 6);[22] another fragment from

21 Five of them can be consulted in LIVSHITS 2008, pp. 353–368; 2015, pp. 271–282, basing on earlier articles. One fragmented inscription from Krasnaya Rechka is reproduced on fig. 106, p. 277 without reading (no. 6 here). The reading is provided in LIVSHITS 2002, p. 131: *'yny ty'r' prβytk(w)[ ](.)šy x'r* "this vessel is presented…" (somewhat different in LIVSHITS 1981, p. 80). The fragment no. 7 from Yakaligh (Kysmychi site) is published in LIVSHITS 2008, p. 332 (= 2015, p. 253). Transliteration and translation of another fragmented inscriptions is found in LIVSHITS 1981, p. 80., its image is found in the LIVSHITS' archive, folder Sogd 82: Semirechie.

22 BOBOYOROV/G'OYIBOV/KUBATIN 2020, pp. 59–63; the English preprint was distributed in 2011 by BABAYAROV and TABALDIEV in the Sogdian-L mailing list and at https://www.academia.edu/8343984/Gaybulla_Babayarov_Kubatbek_Tabaldiev_New_Sogdian_inscriptions_ from_Kyrgyzstan (last accessed 25.10.23). The rim from Sadovoe site is preserved now in the museum of Kyrgyz-Turkish Manas University in Bishkek.
The corrected reading by N. SIMS-WILLIAMS appeared also in the mailing list and was included in the article YOSHIDA 2018, p. 172, where reading *myδkry* "every day" instead of *myδk'y* "of Mēthak" was proposed.
When I saw a good photo of the inscription (taken by KUBAT TABALDIEV) in Manas Ordo museum in Talas in July 2022 and drafted a reading immediately, I regrettably forgot the studies made above, and noticed YOSHIDA's article too late to use it in the brief reedition of the inscription (LURJE 2022).
The reading of BABAYAROV *at al.* is *xwt'wy MYLK'Y βδnkt pry tkyn* "From / To the Lord, the ruler of Badankat / Bulankat (to) the Fri-tegin", the one of SIMS-WILLIAMS is *xwt'wy myδk'y kδ'rt wrytkyn* "[So-and-so] made [this *khum*(?)] for(?) Lord Methak, Uri-tegin …", and that of YOSHIDA is *xwt'wy myδkry kδ'rt wřytkyn* «…王の時代に Uri-tegin が作った» ("created by Uri-tegin in the King›s time").
I think now that Yoshida's reading is closest to a correct rendering, although I cannot exclude that the second word, *M'LK'y, MYLK'y* is an abnormal spelling of the ideogram *MLK'* "king" in the oblique case (cf. variation *MR'Y/MRY'*, the form *MLKY* [not oblique!] in the Manichaean "Murder of the Magi" fragment, 30, HENNING 1944, p. 138). On the usage of the word *xwt'w* in the Semirechie coinage see LURJE 2013a.

an unspecified site by LURJE[23], and the beginning of an inscription from Novopokrovka 2 by CHR. RECK,[24] the one above is the twelfth.

Examining the corpus of the dedicatory rim inscriptions, first we see that there was no obligatory formulary for these texts. The inscriptions usually start with *ʾyny* "this" the recipient and the donor(s) are mentioned, but the other parts are quite varied, and I provide here translations:

(No. 1, from Krasnaya Rechka [medieval Nawēkath?]) "This vessel (was made) for Yaruq-tegin, the teacher. The master craftsman (?) is Pashtwan. May he (the teacher?) be diligent. Amen, Amen";

(No. 2, from Novopokrovka [medieval Pākāb?]) "This vessel is a gift of the people (or 'community') of Pākāp. May this wine be drunk (at) a happy moment, insightful (?) Sovereign. For the Sovereign Alp-bilgä, who has received charisma from the gods, (as) his own (?). (May he be) happy and prosperous";

(No. 3, from Krasnaya Rechka) "He who has counted no loss will also not see his wealth, so, O Man, drink (wine)!";[25]

(No. 4 from Ak-Beshim [Suyab]) "This vessel along with crockery (?) ..., a gift for His Majesty Alan the Prosperous";

(No. 5 from Ak-tobe-Stepninskoe) "[This wine (?)] along with this large vessel was made in a blessed year, on a joyful day, in the Year of the Hare, in the month of Shnākhandā, on Thursday, on the day Rāmrōch. [Wr]itten: 'Alīmkhān 'Abbās, may he live 160 long years, may (he) remain rich (and) powerful!"'.[26]

(No. 6, from Krasnaya Rechka) "this vessel is presented...".

---

kδʾrt is the well attested abbreviated III Sg. preterite from *ʾkrtw δʾrt* "(he) did". Babayarov *et al.* read *βδnkt* and consider it to be a toponym.
wry tk-yn is a name of a manufacturer, it is Turkic *Urï Tegin* "child – prince". The names with *tk(ʾ)yn* in Sogdian records are quite numerous, cf. the names *ʾwry* from Turfan and *wry trxʾn* from Ladakh (LURJE 2010, no. 198, 1343). BABAYAROV *et al.* read *pry tkyn*, a Sogdo-Turkic compound "dear prince".

23 LURJE 2018, pp. 110–111.

24 RECK *apud* KOLCHENKO, ROTT 2019 pp. 371–372. Incidentally, I see the word *ʾʾγʾr* "splendour" instead of RECK's *ʾnxʾr* "star" or *ʾzγʾr* "humidity". The next incomplete word could be *pc[ʾrt* "for". The term *yʾm*, apart from Middle and New Persian *jām* "bowl" has a parallel in Sogdian *yʾmk* (LIVSHITS/LUKONIN 1964, pp. 168, 173). I agree with CHRISTIANE RECK that the second inscription from Novopokrovka does not contain Sogdian words, perhaps it begins with Uighur *PW* – *bu* "this" and contains *XWT* – *qut* "glory".

25 I would prefer now a somewhat different translation: "Don't count each person's whatever damage, so (you) do not diminish (your) own treasure and drink, o man!", note alliteration *šmār / xwār* in what can be understood as two hemistichs in the inscription: *āδḗ xō ēčē γíšip nē šmār ||xēp γaznú wān nē kišī ərt martí xwār.*

26 LIVSHITS 2015, pp. 271–282; our numbering.

(No. 7, from Kysmychi [which was tentatively identified with Yakalygh by A.N. BERNSHTAM]) "... bishop Shirfan (or Säŋün)[27]..."

(No. 8, from Krasnaja Rechka) "this vessel (belongs to) master Pashtawan..."[28]

(No. 9, from Sadovoe) "Urï tegin has done in the days (?) of king...".

(No. 10, from unspecified site) "... Shakh (?) Farukh..."

(No. 11, from Novopokrovka 2) "this bowl for splendour (?)..."

(No. 12, from Burana [Balāsaghūn]) "let Buyruq Säŋün live long (and be) divinely blessed".[29]

These inscriptions can be included in the series of so-called "Turko-Sogdian" texts: the ones written in Sogdian in the 9th–early 11th century show the very profound Turkic influence on many aspects of the language.[30] The Turkic features of these inscriptions include numerous Turkic names and titles; presence of Uighur letters *l* and *q*;[31] calqued expressions: *ʾlʾn prn pyδʾr* = **Alan qutï üčün* "for the sake of the majesty Alan", *MN βγyš[t]y prnβyrty* = *täŋridä(n) qut bolmïš* "he having received glory from god(s)", perhaps *šyr wyn-* = *jaqšï kör-*

27 So LURJE 2013b, p. 248, note 64.

28 LIVSHITS 1981, read *ʾyny γwyck γwštʾry pstwn*, I would modify into *ʾyny xwyck (xw)štry (pš)twn xw*, cf. DZHUMAGULOV, p. 37, fig. 20 for a legible photo.

29 I know two unpublished (and unclear in reading) rim inscriptions kept in the Institute of History and Archaeology of Kyrgyz Academy of Sciences in Bishkek.
The complete small *khum* (no. 13) contains two short phrases between stamps, I cannot explain it (on one side I see something like *γ/x/š-r/ʾ-p* (hardly *xyp* "own") *βl*. However, the stamps, decoration of the rim and handwriting are quite similar to our no. 11. Asan TORGOEV kindly informed me that this vessel was discovered at Krasnaya Rechka and the shape of the rim indicates 11th century.
An almost complete rim (no. 14) with very low relief inscription made before baking. Of four or five words I can recognize only *xypδ* "own". According to TORGOEV, it was also found in one of the Chu valley sites and should be dated to the 10th–11th century.
Photos of two more small fragments are found in V.A. LIVSHITS' archive (folder Sogd-82). One of them (no. 15) seems to contain the word *]γwδ(y)* "vessel";
Another one (no. 16), found in the suburb of Krasnaya Rechka in 1984, starts with *ʾyny* "this", the next word is difficult (*sʾrth* "caravan"?, *snkwn*?).
It is more than likely that I missed some more unpublished fragments.
After this paper was submitted, VALERY KOLʼCHENKO reported on yet another rim, discovered in August 2023 at Ken-Bulun in the eastern part of the valley by the expedition organized by the A.Kh. Khalikov Institute of Archeology of Academy of Sciences of Tatarstan and Institute of History, Archaeology and Ethnography of Academy of Sciences of Kyrgyzstan. The publication of this inscription is under preparation.

30 The principal studies on Turko-Sogdian are SIMS-WILLIAMS 2008, YOSHIDA 2009. The rock inscriptions from upper Talas valley in Semirechie and coin legends can be considered Turko-Sogdian monuments as well.

31 I. e., *γ* with two dots above in the name *yrwγ̈tkyn* in no. 1, as seen on the photo sent to me by VALERIJ KOLCHENKO. Two dots above *β* in *βrγwncy* (or *βrγwʾcy* for *βrγʾwcy*?) on the same inscription perhaps indicate reading *f*.

"to love, be dear",[32] literally "to see good" ("insightful" in LIVSHITS' translation; cf. Tajiki *naγz didan*). Other late Sogdian features (which are also present in Turko-Sogdian) show the predominance of the preterite and the absence of the imperfect past tenses, reduction of *xypδ* "own" into *xyp* (as Yaghnobi *xep*), loss of final vowels of the light stem (*zmn* < *zmnw* "time").

As for the religious affiliation of the inscriptions, the names represent the standard Turkic world-view. The inscription 1 from Kransaya Rechka addressing *mlpʾny* = Syriac *malpānā* "teacher" and ending in *amen amen* is Christian. no. 8 with the same name Pashtwan found in the same year by the same archaeological expedition might be also Christian.[33] The inscription 4 (dedication to Alan) was found *in situ* in the storage room ("*khum-khāna*") of the Christian monastery at Ak-Beshim and thus is Christian due to its archaeological context. The partially preserved rim from Krasnaya Rechka (no. 6) mentioning *taghara* vessel has the same stamp as the one from Ak-Beshim, as well as similar wording, so it is also most likely related to Christian producers. The relation of a swastika-like sign on the inscription published above (no. 12) to Christianity, and the Christian population of Burana has already been discussed by BORIS ZHELEZNYAKOV; crosses have been reportedly found in the same hoard.[34]

As for no. 9, one can notice that the word *myδkry* "in the days", if indeed used here, is a feature of Christian Sogdian, and there are no unambiguous attestations of it in secular, Buddhist or Manichaean texts.[35] The first part of the name *Ürï-tegin* "young prince" has two parallels in Sogdian onomastics (from Turfan and Ladakh), both pertaining to the Christians.[36] Moreover, the abbreviated preterite *kδʾrt* "(he) did" is a feature of Christian (*qϑʾrt*) and Manichaean scribal tradition and is exceptional in Buddhist texts, where one wrote plene *ʾkrtw δʾrt*, and seems to be absent elsewhere in epigraphy. Yutaka YOSHIDA noticed the peculiar dots above the letter *r* in the name *wr̈ytkyn*, which has been found in Christian Uighur and Uighur texts of the Qarakhanid Period.[37] Considering all these features together (none of them being decisive *per se*) one has strong circumstantial evidence that the inscription was produced by Christians as well.

32 So far I know, for the first time recorded in Qutadghu Bilig (K 21_{11}) of Yusuf of Balasaghun, the 11th century author from the Chu valley (NADELJAEV *at al.* 1969, p. 238b).

33 GORJACHEVA (1988, pp. 69f) writes that the name Pastun(= Pashtwan) appeared three times in the pottery inscriptions from Krasnaja rechka, predominantly on khums (that would mean that this third attestation was *not* a *khum*! Cf. LIVSHITS 2004b, p. 138 with n. 132).

34 The inscription *ʾyl tʾγ msyδr* "El tagh the presbiter" (LIVSHITS 2008, pp. 355f = 2015, p. 273) with the title *msyδ/dr* known both from Manichaean and Christian Sogdian texts is excluded from the present discussion because it is not a dedicatory inscription on the rim but likely a property mark on the shoulder of a *khum*.

35 SIMS-WILLIAMS/DURKIN-MEISTERERNST 2012, p. 118. On the possible Manichaean attestation see also LURJE 2010, no. 726.

36 LURJE 2010, no. 198, 1343.

37 YOSHIDA 2022, p. 610, n. 59.

Inscription from Kaindy – Yakaligh (no. 7) perhaps contains the Manichaean term *spsy* "bishop" and no. 10 has the name-part *βrwγ* "Farrukh", which was typical for Manichaean elects. One can cautiously consider them Manichaean. Novopokrovka 2 is famous for the hoard of Buddhist bronzes and stone objects, but the inscribed rim no. 9 was found in a context of a baker's shop of Qarakhanid period, not a Buddhist sanctuary; and no. 2 was found in 1940 during excavations of the Big Chu canal by A.N. BERNSHTAM, while the Buddhist hoard was discovered in 1960th at a distance no less than 400 meters from the nearest point on the canal.[38] So, there are no indications that these inscriptions were related to Buddhism in any way.

The *khum* from Ak-tobe Stepninskoe (inscription 5) is devoted to *ʾlymxn ʾpʾs*, *ʿAlīm-xān ʿAbbās*, the bearer of a Moslem name.[39] Incidentally, at the same site a short inscription of ownership on the body of a basin can be read as *ʾxmʾt* = Arabic *Aḥmad* in Sogdian script (fig. 7), and an Arabic ostracon was found there too.[40] V.A. LIVSHITS noticed the similarity of style of the inscription no. 3 to the Persian poetry of ʿUmar Khayyām and his predecessors, so the author could also be considered a somewhat libertine Moslem.

These dedicatory inscriptions on *khums* haven't been attested so far among the epigraphy of Sogdiana proper or from Sogdian colonies further to the east or to the west. Thus, one can consider them as only characteristic of the Chu valley towns of the 9th–early 11th century. What was the driver for producing these rather complex and variable dedications? I propose that the answers to this question require a closer examination of the contemporary art in the south-west: in already Islamic Khorasan and Mawarannahr (at that time Sogdian fell from literary usage there). The inscriptions on glazed pottery are quite uniform and, although they contain dedication words or aphorisms, the inscriptions lack names of the customers and producers. On the silver and bronze ware, however, we see the names of customers or owners, as well as various dedications in Arabic and sometimes Persian, from some period on the names of artisans appear as well.[41] The inscriptions in elaborate Kufi script are a part of decorative program of the vessels.

38 GORJACHEVA 1988, p. 57; KOLCHENKO/ROTT 2019 pp. 366ff.

39 The name element *ʿAbbās* and the epithet *ʿĀlim* are both attested in the numismatics of Qarakhanides, the first Moslem dynasty in Semirechie, let alone the commonest title *khān*, see KOCHNEV 2006, pp. 25, 148. YUTAKA YOSHIDA doubts that the name is Moslem and thinks that the inscription was executed in the year 160 of post-Yazdgerd era, that is September 25, 811 (YOSHIDA 2022, pp. 604f). Incidentally, according to ASAN TORGOEV, the shape of the rim can be dated to the 9th century or later, but there are no documented layers of pre-Samanid period on the site.

40 Images reproduced in AKYMBET/BAIBUGUNOV 2014, p. 80, fig. 2.2, 2.3.

41 As a couple of examples, on the bowl a personal inscription "to/property of Khumar Tegin the treasurer" is accompanied by semi-poetic Persian piece "for the sake of this pleasant (but) prohibited job which is permitted to you, keep your heart joyful"; another pitcher has a shorter formula "bless of the Allah and prosperity and happiness to al-Husayn ibn al-ʿAli", see MARSHAK 2017, pp. 131–136.

The principal difference between the eastern Islamic silver and bronze ware from these almost contemporary *khums* of the Chu valley lies in the status difference between the objects themselves. The former are individual works of art of high quality and status and the latter are examples of serial production of cheap pottery found in great quantities during the excavations. The *khums* per se could not be high status gifts (perhaps only for Eeyore the Donkey). On some inscriptions it is clear, and on others it may be assumed that it was not the vessel, but rather its contents — wine — that was the subject of the gift. The inscribed *khum* from Ak-beshim (no. 4) was found in a storage room close to the basin of wine-press. This *khum*, judging from its section, could contain a solid amount of 75–80 liters of liquid.[42]

Not being able to present DIETER WEBER, the pillar of Middle Iranian epigraphy, a *khum* full of Sogdian wine on his anniversary, we can just wish him to "live long and be divinely blessed"!

Figures

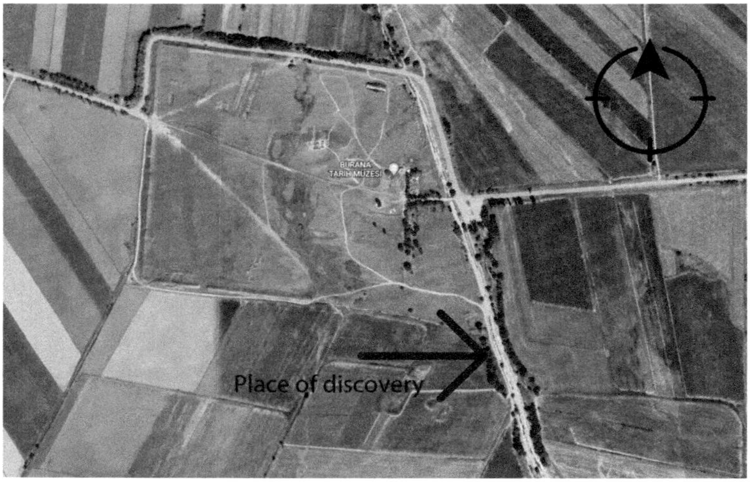

Fig. 1. Plan of Burana with indication of reported place of find.

42 Calculated from the scaled profile published by SEMENOV (2002, pp. 47, 57–68). GORJACHEVA (1988, p. 56) claims that the *khum* from Novopokrovka (our no. 2) could contain some 300 liters.
Having submitted the present paper, we had the pleasure to read the forthcoming artilce by S.R. IL'JASOVA and B.M. BABADZHANOV "Vinnye stikhi na khumakh XII veka s gorodishha Sodmalik-ata", due to be published in Arkheologija Kazakhstana, No. 1 (23), 2024. The authors publish three *khums* with New Persian (Arabic script) Bacchic quatrains discovered in the vicinity of Tashkent. So far, they are the closest analogy to Sogdian dedications on khum rims from Semirechie discussed above.

Fig. 2. Montage of the initial photographs of the rim.

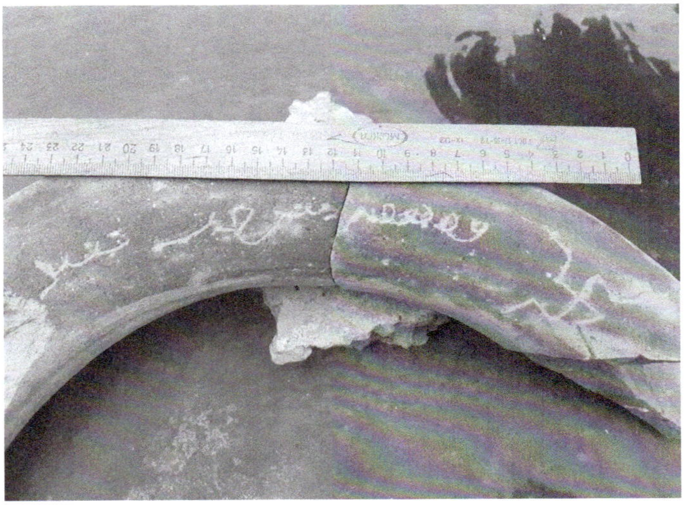

Fig. 3. Photo of surviving part of the rim.

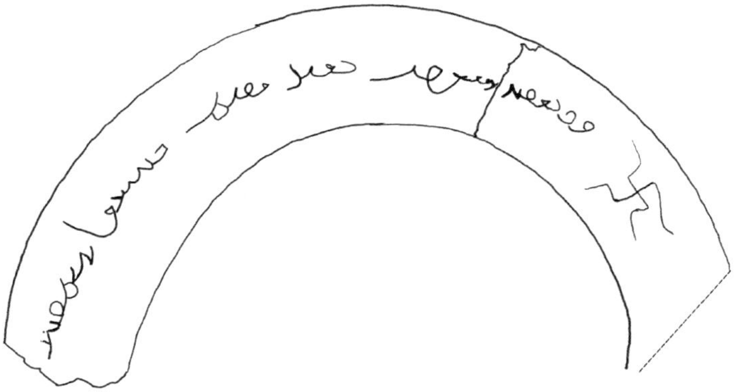

Fig. 4. Tracing of the rim.

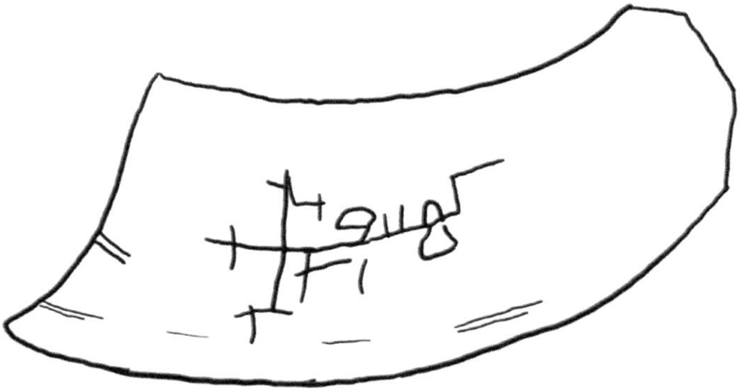

Fig. 5. Rim with the cross from Sauran.

Fig. 6. Photo of inscription from Sadovoe (by KUVAT TABALDIEV).

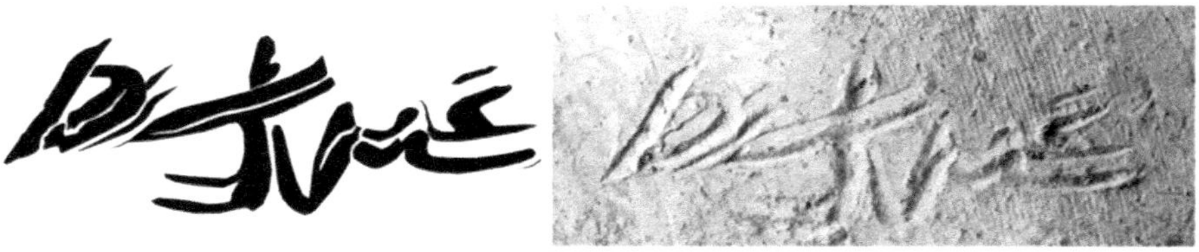

Fig. 7. Inscription Ahmad from Ak-tobe (after AKYMBEK/BAYBUGUNOV 2014).

Fig. 8. Map of Chu valley with indication of location of finds of inscribed rims.

Bibliography

AKYMBEK, Y./B. BAIBUGUNOV 2014: "Inscriptions on ceramics of medieval city Aktobe." In: *Procedia - Social and Behavioral Sciences* 122 (*2nd World Conference on Design, Arts and Education DAE-2013*), pp. 77–81.

AMANBAYEVA, B.E./V.A. KOL'CHENKO/A.T. SULAIMANOVA 2015: *Archeologicheskie pamyatniki na kyrgyzstanskom uchastke Velikogo Shelkovogo puti*. Bishkek.

BAYPAKOV, K.M./G.A. TERNOVAJA 2018: "Khristianstvo v Juzhnom Kazakhstane I Semirech'e (VI–XIV vv.)." In: *Religii Central'noj Azii i Azerbajdzhana*. Tom IV. *Khristianstvo*. Samarkand, pp. 8–47.

BOBOYOROV, G./B. G'OYIBOV/A. KUBATIN 2020: *O'rta Osiyo bitiklari*. I. *Sug'diy yozma yodgorliklar*. Toshkent.

CHAVANNES, E. 1903: *Documents sur les Tou-Kiue (turks) occidentaux*. (Сборник трудов Орхонской Экспедиции, VI). St.-Pétersbourg.

CHUNAKOVA O.M. 2019:*Rukopisi iz Vostochnogo Turkestana. Srednepersidskie, parfjanskie i sogdijskie fragment v sobranii Instituta vostochnykh rukopisej*. Sankt-Peterburg.

DICKENS, M. 2023: Where was the Christian Metropolitan Bishop of Nawakath located?" In: *Bulletin of the International Institute for Central Asian Studies* 35, pp. 50–65. Available online: https://www.unesco-iicas.org/library/0/%D0%92%D0%B5%D1%81%D1%82%D0%BD%D0%B8%D0%BA+%D0%9C%D0%98%D0%A6%D0%90%D0%98 (last accessed 19.12.2023).

DRAKE F.S. 1962: "Nestorian Crosses and Nestorian Christians in China under the Mongols." In: *Journal of the Hong Kong Branch of the Royal Asiatic Society* 2, pp. 11–25, pl. I–IV.

DZHUMAGULOV CH. 1963: *Épigrafika Kirgizii*. Vypusk I. Frunze.

GORJACHEVA, V.D. 1988: *Gorod zolotogo verbljuda*. Bishkek.

HENNING, W.B. 1944: "The murder of the Magi." In: *Journal of the Royal Asiatic Society* 76, pp. 133–144.

ILYASOV, J. 2010: "Nomad Heritage. Kushan Tamga- Signs from Southern Uzbekistan." In: *Traditional Marking Systems. A Preliminary Survey*. London/Dover, pp. 213–225.

KOCHNEV, B.D. 2006: *Numizmaticheskaja istorija karakhanidskogo kaganata (991 – 1209). Chast' I*. Moskva.

KOZHEMJAKO P.N. 1959: *Rannesrednevekovye goroda i poselenija Chujskoj doliny*. Frunze.

LIVSHITS [LIVSHIC], V.A. 1981: "Sogdijcy v Semirech'je: lingvisticheskie i épigraficheskie svidetel'stva." In: *Pis'mennye pamjatniki i problemy istorii kul'tury narodov Vostoka* XV, pp. 76–85 [reprinted in *Krasnaja rechka i Burana. Materialy i issledovanija Kirgizskij arkheologicheskoj ékrpedicii*. Frunze, 1989, pp. 78–85).

— 2002: "Sogdijskaja nadpis' na venchike khuma iz Ak-Beshima." In: G.L. SEMENOV (ed.): *Sujab Ak-Beshim*. Sankt-Peterburg, pp. 128–133.

— 2004a "Predshestvenniki Khayyama v Semirech'e v VIII–IX vekakh." In: *Dialog civilizacij. Vzaimodejstvie kul'tur, narodov i gosudarstv v zone Velikogo Shelkovogo puti* 1 (4), pp. 55–57.

— 2004b "Sogdijskie teksty, dokumenty i épigrafika." In: V.M. PLOSKIKH (ed.): *Istochnikovedenie Kyrgyzstana (s drevnosti do konca XIX veka)*. Bishkek, pp. 117–148.

— 2008: *Sogdijskaja épigrafika Srednej Azii i Semirech'ja*. Sankt-Peterburg.

— 2013: "Sogdijsko-tjurkskie lingvisticheskie kontakty." In: *Lavrovskij sbornik. Materialy XXXVI i XXXVII Sredneaziatsko-kavkazskikh chtenij 2012 – 2013 gg. Étnologija, istorija, erkheologija, kul'turologija*. Sankt-Peterburg, pp. 62–68.

— 2015: *Sogdian epigraphy of Central Asia and Semirech'e*. Tr. by T. STABLEFORD, ed. by N. SIMS-WILLIAMS. London (*Corpus inscriptionum iranicarum* Pt. II Vol. III) [English translation of LIVSHITS, 2008].

LIVSHITS, VA./V.G. LUKONIN 1964: "Srednepersidskie i sogdijskie nadpisi na serebrjanykh sosudakh." In: *Vestnik drevnej istorii* 3 (89), pp. 155–176.

LURJE, P.B 2010: *Personal names in Sogdian texts* (*Iranisches Personennamenbuch* II/8). Vienna.

— 2013a: "Karluki i jaglakary v sogdijskoj numizmatike Semirech'ja." In: *Tjurkologicheskij sbornik 2011 – 2012*. Moskva, pp. 220–230.

— 2013b: "O sledakh manikheizma v Srednej Azii." In: P. LURJE/A. TORGOEV (eds.): *Sogdijcy, ikh predshestvenniki, sovremenniki i nasledniki (Trudy Gosudarstvennogo Érmitazha,* LXII). Sankt-Peterburg, pp. 219–251.

— 2018: "Novye dannye o sledakh manikhejstva v Semirech'e." In: K. BAYPAKOV *et al.* (eds.): *Central'naya Azija na Velikom shëlkovom puti: dialog kul'tur i konfessij ot drevnosti do sovremennosti*, Almaty, pp. 109–116.

— forthcoming: "Two Sino-Turkic Titles in Sogdian Texts." In: M. ÖLMEZ (ed.): *Soğud Toplantisi…* Istanbul.

— 2022: "K sogdijskoj épigrafike Srednej Syrdar'i i Semirech'ja." In: *V mezhdunarodnyj kongress arkheologii jevrazijskikh stepej*. Turkestan, pp. 225–228.

MARSHAK, B.I. 2017: *Istorija vostochnoj torevtiki III–XIII vv. i problemy kul'turnoj preemstvennosti*. Sankt-Peterburg.

MKRTYCHEV, T.K. 1996: "Purna-ghata na Kara-tepe." In: B.J. STAVISKIJ (ed.): *Buddijskie kompleksy Kara-tepe v Starom Termeze: osnovnye itogi rabot 1978–89 gg.* Moskva, pp. 220–223.

NADELJAEV, V.M./D.M. NASILOV/ É.R. TENISHEV/A.M. SHHERBAK (eds) 1969: *Drevnetjurkskij slovar'*. Leningrad.

NASTICH, V.N. 2019: *Musul'namskaja épigrafika Fergany i Semrech'ja: pamjatniki arabskogo pis'ma XI–XVII vv. na territorii Kyrgyzstana*. Saint Petersburg.

PANTUSOV, N.N. 1888: *Plan rabot po raskopkam v 1886 drevnego nestorianskogo kladbischa bliz goroda Tokmak na urochosche Burana. Ob issledovanii nadv. sov. Pantusovym nestorianskikh kladbisch bliz gor. Pishpeka i Tokmokskoj oblasti*. Kept in the archive of IIMK RAN, 40-b.

RASPOPOVA, V.I. 2017: *Épigrafika Pendzhikenta (Iz raskopok 1947–2006 gg.)*. Sankt-Peterburg.

RYBATZKI, V. 2006: *Die Personennamen und Titel der mittelmongolischen Dokumente. Eine lexikalische Untersuchung*. Helsinki. Available online: https://core.ac.uk/download/pdf/14914743.pdf (last accessed 02.10.2022).

SEMENOV, G.L. 2002: "Raskopki 1996–1998 gg." In: G.L. SEMENOV (ed.): *Sujab Ak-Beshim*. Sankt-Peterburg, pp. 11–114.

Sims-Williams, N. 1985: *The Christian Sogdian Manuscript C2 (Berliner Turfantexte* XII*)*. Berlin.
— 2008: "Sogdian-Turkish bilingualism and linguistic interference in 9th – 10th century Dunhuang." In: Z. Zarshenas (ed.): *Ǧašn-nāme-ye doktor Badr-al-zamān Qarīb (Papers in Honour of Professor B. Gharib).* Tehran, pp. 41–51.
Sims-Williams, N./D. Durkin-Meisterernst 2012: *Dictionary of Manichaean Sogdian and Bactrian (Dictionary of Manichaean Texts,* vol. III, pt. 2). Turnhout.
Yoshida, Y. 2009: "Turko-Sogdian features." In: W. Sundermann *et al.* (eds.): *Exegisti monumenta! Festschrift in Honour of Nicholas Sims-Williams.* Wiesbaden, pp. 571–85.
— 2018: "貨幣の銘文に反映されたチュルク族によるソグド支配 (Turkic rule of Sogdiana reflected in coinage and inscriptions, Kahei no meibun ni han'ei sa reta churuku-zoku ni yoru sogudo shihai." In: 京都大學文學部研究紀要 = *Memoirs of the Faculty of Letters, Kyoto University* (Kyōtodai gakumon gaku-bu kenkyū kiyō) 57, pp. 155–182.
— 2020: "Studies of the Karabalgasun Inscription: Edition of the Sogdian Version." In: *Modern Asian Studies Review* 11, pp. 1–139. Available online: https://toyo-bunko.repo.nii.ac.jp/index.php?action= pages_view_main&active_action=repository_action_common_download&item_id=7313&item_no=1&attribute_id=22&file_no=1&page_id=25&block_id=47 (last accessed 04.04.2022).
— 2022: "Sogdian Christians in China, Turfan and Sogdiana." In: K. Perry/G. Mikkelsen (eds.): *Byzantium to China: Religion, History and Culture on the Silk Roads. Studies in Honour of Samuel N.C. Lieu*. Leiden/Boston, pp. 596–617.

Trading with Infidels: A Balancing Act in Zoroastrian Legal Reasoning

MARIA MACUCH, Berlin

Many of the Pahlavi original documents, which have been made accessible by the dedicatee deal with economic and legal affairs in the Zoroastrian communities of the early Islamic period reflecting various aspects of daily life in a changing environment. In his invaluable studies DIETER WEBER has called our attention to some of the presumably earliest attestations of terms and titles in these documents indicating en passant the changes brought about by the Arab conquest of Iran and the advent of Islam, such as the adapted *bismillah*-formula *(pad nām ī yazd* 'in the name of God'*;* instead of pl. *yazdān,* 'gods'), the title *amīr* and the term *mazgit* 'mosque'.[1] Dealings with Arabs *(tāzīgān)*[2] and members of other religious communities, such as the Eastern or Nestorian Christians (*dēn asūrīg)*[3], are also touched upon in these documents. Although these are only short allusions with no further context due to the concise nature of these records, we can reasonably infer that interaction between Mazdeans and adherents of other religions, specifically Muslims and converted Zoroastrians, increased on various levels in the first centuries of Islam, and that a range of questions, both of a practical and theoretical nature, arose in the Zoroastrian communities regarding how to treat specific transactions with non-Mazdeans and whether these were legal or illegal from the viewpoint of Zoroastrian law. In this short contribution dedicated to my esteemed colleague and dear friend, DIETER WEBER, I propose to scrutinize two sections of the *Dādestān ī dēnīg, pursišn* 49 and 52, in which problems regarding trading activities between members of the Zoroastrian community and non-Mazdeans are discussed from a legal, economic and social perspective.

It is well known that the *Dādestān ī dēnīg* ("Religious Decisions"; Dd), comprising altogether 92 questions and answers, is the work of a single author, Manuščihr, son of Juwānǰam,[4] the supreme spiritual authority of the Zoroastrians and "Leader of the Religion" *(pēšōbāy ī dēn),*[5] in the second half of the

1 See specifically WEBER 2020, pp. 143–147 and 151–158, with further references.
2 WEBER 2020, pp. 151–153.
3 WEBER 2020, pp. 162–163.
4 GIGNOUX/TAFAZZOLI 1993 read the patronymic as Gušnǰam.
5 This is the title used in the introduction to the Dd, § 25 (KREYENBROEK 1995, pp. 174, 176; JAAFARI-DEHAGHI 1998, pp. 38–39); other titles of Manuščihr are: *hērbed* (headings of Epistles I and II), *hērbed xwadāy* 'Lord of the *hērbeds*' (Epistle III), *rad* of Pārs and

ninth century in post-Sasanian Iran. In his treatise on diverse ritual, eschatological and apocalyptic matters Manuščihr also includes several questions on legal issues (*pursišn* 49–62) pertaining to family law, inheritance and succession and discusses in the style of "responsa" literature problems arising in the Zoroastrian community from legal transactions between co-religionists as well as between Mazdeans and adherents of other religions. These legal passages are unique from several points of view. They show not only the surprising tenacity of specific Zoroastrian legal institutions long after the downfall of the Sasanians, but also reveal the manner in which the highest Zoroastrian authority reached his judgement: by balancing a basic rule or decision on principle against the concrete circumstances of a case, weighing up contradictory aspects of the problem, and reflecting on the impact of the legal transaction on the involved parties as well as on the Zoroastrian community as a whole.[6] In this respect the sections on trade in this treatise differ fundamentally from the rather simple answers to legal questions transmitted in other post-Sasanian Pahlavi texts of the *riwāyat* type, in which usually straightforward answers are presented to questions of a juristic nature with no discussion of the specific circumstances of the case or the practical consequences for the future of the Zoroastrian community.[7]

All the legal sections, encompassing *pursišn* 49 to 62, are in the part of the text which has not yet been edited and translated adequately. The fairly recent edition of the *Dādestān ī dēnīg* by JAAFARI-DEHAGHI 1998 is based on the edition of the Pahlavi text by T.D. ANKLESARIA 1911, encompassing the first forty questions, hence contains only the so-called first part of the text, *pursišn* 1–40, excluding the legal sections.[8] The rest, or so-called second part, of the Pahlavi text, *pursišn* 41 to 92 containing the legal passages, has been edited by a descendant of the latter, P.K. ANKLESARIA, based on a collation of the most important manuscripts of the Dd in a thesis presented to the University of London in 1958. The thesis contains a valuable description of the most important surviving manuscripts of the Dd and the reconstruction of a stemma in the introduction, but the edition of the Pahlavi text is unfortunately both unreliable and unusable. It consists of a reconstructed hand-written text in Pahlavi script, has no transliteration, transcription or translation and has never been published. Moreover, the editor has chosen to include only a choice of manuscript variants in his apparatus. In his own words, he discards the "individual mistakes of a manuscript", reducing his apparatus to a few "variants (properly understood)".[9] Given the

Kirmān and *framādār* 'Commander, Chief' (colophons to Dd and Epistle II; see WEST 1882, p. xiii; JAAFARI-DEHAGHI 1998, p. 24).

6 This approach is also demonstrated in *pursišn* 51, which I have discussed in MACUCH 2022.

7 For a general comparison of *responsa* literature in Zoroastrian, Jewish and Islamic law see JANY 2017, who, however, does not include the legal passages of the Dd in his discussion.

8 JAAFARI-DEHAGHI 1998, p. 28.

9 P.K. ANKLESARIA 1958, "Abstract", p. V.

well-known ambiguities and stumbling blocks of the Pahlavi script, this approach is hardly convincing and leaves us with the choices and amendments of the editor, which in several cases show that he has misunderstood crucial parts of the text. The following transcription of *pursišn* 49 and 52 therefore does *not* follow P.K. ANKLESARIA's reconstruction of the Pahlavi text, but is based on the oldest available manuscripts of the Iranian tradition, K35[10] (941 A.Y. = 1572 C.E.) and TD4a[11] (961 A.Y. = 1592 C.E.). Apart from the outdated (and partly incomprehensible) translation of WEST (1882) over a century ago, there is no recent transliteration, transcription or translation of these passages.

I. Text and Translation of *Pursišn* 49 (K35, fol. 170r, l. 4–170v., l. 5; TD4a, pp. 318.7–319.11)[12]

1. *čehel-nohom pursišn pāsox*[13] *ān (ī) pursēd kū kē*[14] *may* (⟨HS⟩) *frōšēd*[15] *be ō an-ērān ag-dēnān frōšēd*[16] *ēg-iš dādestān čē.*
2. *pāsox ēd kū abēr saxt garān wināh bīm ud wad pēšagīhā.*
3. *bē agar kardan*[17] *ī-š ān may-frōšīh rāy may az awēšān kē may a-paymān xwarēnd*[18] *may xward*[19] *rāy wattar bawēnd*[20] *wēš abāz dārīhēd ō awēšān kē may pad paymān*[21] *xwarēnd may xwardan rāy weh bawānd*[22] *wēš rasēd kū ān ī ka ōy*[23] *ān may-frōšīh nē kard ēg-iš ān may*[24]*-frōšīh rāy tuwān ī pad xwāstag*[25] *kē-šān abāz dāštan mardōm pad wehdēnīh* ⁺*pattāyēnēd*[26] *ud*[27] *az*

10 *Codices Avestici et Pahlavici Universitatis Hafniensis* 1934 (vol. III); (abbr. K in P.K. ANKLESARIA 1958, pp. 38–39).
11 *Pahlavi Codices and Iranian Researches* 1978 (vol. 52); (abbr. T in P.K. ANKLESARIA 1958, pp. 38–39). The surviving manuscripts of the Dd have been described by WEST 1882, pp. xv-xix, P.K. ANKLESARIA 1958, pp. 7–37 (reconstruction of the stemma p. 48) and JAAFARI-DEHAGHI 1998, pp. 26–28 (reconstruction of the stemma p. 28).
12 ANKLESARIA 1958, p. 106; WEST 1882, pp. 176–177.
13 K35: om.; TD4a: ⟨p'shw Y⟩.
14 K35: om.; TD4a: ⟨MNW⟩.
15 K35: om.; TD4a: ⟨MZḆNW-x_2⟩;
16 K35: ⟨MZḆNW-x_2⟩ super-lin. ⟨-yym⟩; TD4a: ⟨MZḆNW-x_1⟩.
17 K35: ⟨krtn' ⟩; TD4a: ⟨krt'⟩.
18 K35: om.; TD4a: ⟨'ŠTH̱nd⟩.
19 K35: only ⟨ŠTH̱t' ⟩;TD4a: ⟨HS 'ŠT' 'ŠTH̱' t'⟩.
20 K35: ins. ⟨W⟩; TD4a: om.
21 K35: ⟨ptm'n' ⟩; TD4a: ⟨ptm'n' Y⟩.
22 K35: ⟨YHWWNynnd⟩; TD4a: ⟨YHWWN'nd⟩.
23 K35: ⟨'LH̱'⟩; TD4a: ⟨'L⟩.
24 K35: om.; TD4a: ⟨HS⟩.
25 K35: ⟨hw'stk' Y⟩; TD4a: om. ⟨Y⟩.
26 Both K35 and TD4a: ⟨ptyynyd'⟩.
27 K35: ⟨W⟩; TD4a: om.

šudan[28] *ī ō agdēnīh*[29] *wardēnēd rawāgīh ī*[30] *wināh bast*[31] *kirbag rawāgēnēd*[32] *ān*[33] *bawēd wehān ayārīh ud dēn-pānagīh winēh hamēmālīh ud*[34] *kirbag ayārīh ī ka nē kunēd ān may-frōšīh nē bawēd ī wēš frāy az winēh*[35] *winēh ud* +*wadīh*[36] *ī a-dādīhā xwarišnīh ī may rawāgīhēd ayāb-iš any meh-dādestānīh ud meh kirbag ī*[37] *ēwarīg.*

4. *andar ēdōn ōy kē may*[38] *ō*[39] *an-ērān ud ag-dēnān abarīg-iz kē*[40] *mastīh*[41] *rāy a-dādīh az-iš bawēd frōšēd*[42] *was winēhīhā nē dastwarīhā.*

1. Forty-ninth question (and) answer. That (which) you ask: One who sells wine *(may),* (if) he sells it to non-Iranians *(an-ērān),* infidels *(ag-dēnān),* then what is the judgment *(dādestān)*?
2. The answer (is) this: (There is) concern *(bīm)* that it (is) a very grievous sin *(saxt garān winēh)* and an evil profession *(wad pēšagīhā).*
3. But if by practicing wine-selling (to non-Iranians; infidels) the wine is kept away more *(wēš abāz dārīhēd)* from those who drink wine immoderately *(a-paymān* 'without measure') and become worse due to drinking wine and (if) more accrues *(wēš rasēd)* to those who may become better by drinking wine moderately *(pad paymān)* than if he (=the seller) had not sold the wine (to non-Iranians; infidels), then because of that sale they (=the Zoroastrians) (stay) solvent *(tuwān)* with regard to property *(xwāstag),* due to his restraining them, (and) the people are induced to remain in the Good Religion and to refrain from converting to the evil religion (and) the dissemination *(rawāgīh)* of sin is impeded (and) virtuous deeds are disseminated: this means aiding the righteous and guarding the Religion (and) opposing sin (and) promoting virtuous deeds. If he (=the seller) does not do (this), (if) no wine-selling (to infidels) takes place, (then there is) a large increase in sin (and) sin and evil are disseminated because of the unlawful *(a-dādīhā)* drinking of wine. Or he (acts) otherwise (*ayāb-iš any):* (this is) *meh-dādestānīh* ('greater justice') and a great(er) virtuous deed (*meh kirbag),* which is binding *(ēwarīg).*

28 K35: ⟨'ZLWNt'⟩; TD4a: ⟨'ZLWNytn'⟩.
29 K35: ⟨'kdyn' yh⟩; TD4a: ⟨'k 'dyn' yh⟩.
30 K35: ⟨Y⟩; TD4a: om.
31 K35: ⟨bst'⟩; TD4a: ⟨bstk'⟩.
32 K35: ⟨rwb'kynyt⟩; TD4a: ⟨rwb'ynytn'⟩.
33 K35: om.; TD4a: ins. ⟨Y⟩.
34 K35: ins. ⟨W⟩; TD4a: om.
35 K35: ⟨wn's⟩; TD4a: ⟨wn's⟩, super. lin. ⟨HS⟩.
36 K35: ⟨wt' Y⟩; TD4a: ⟨wyn'⟩.
37 K35: ⟨krpk' yh⟩, super lin.: ⟨Y⟩ (above ⟨–yh⟩); TD4a: ⟨krpk' Y⟩.
38 K35: ⟨wn's⟩; TD4a: ⟨HS⟩.
39 K35: ⟨'L⟩; TD4a: ⟨'LH̱⟩.
40 K35: ⟨MNW⟩; TD4a: ⟨Y⟩.
41 K35: ⟨mst' yh⟩; TD4a: ⟨mst' Y⟩.
42 K35: om.; TD4a: ins. ⟨W⟩.

4. This (answer) implies (lit.: 'in this thus'): He who sells to non-Iranians and infidels and others, to whom (sale of wine) is unlawful due to drunkenness *(mastīh)*, (is) very sinful *(was winābīhā)*; (it is) not authorized *(nē dastwarīhā)*.

II. Background, Terminology and Content of *Pursišn* 49

This remarkable *pursišn* sheds light not only on the legal problem of commercial interaction between a Zoroastrian and a non-Mazdean, but also on the manner of reasoning employed by the Leader of the Mazdeans in his discussion of the problem by taking recourse to one of the methods used in Zoroastrian law to circumvent a strict rule or decision on principle, called *meh-dādestānīh*. The economic background of the general question put to Manuščihr on the sale of wine *(may)* to infidels is not elucidated, but we have good reason to assume that wine-growing and viticulture played an important role in the socioeconomic fabric of certain regions of Iran within the framework of an economy that relied essentially on agricultural resources. Wine products and wine growing are alluded to in several Pahlavi original documents. Berk. 93.6 refers to the "(trading) value of the wine/must" *(wahāg ī bādag)* and mentions in line 4 a *maydārīg*, "wine-grower; vintner (?)"; a *maydār* is mentioned Berk. 34.2.[43] Another more elaborate original document from Tabarestān (Tab. 13) records a dispute regarding the amount of rent *(tāg)* to be paid in kind for the lease of a vineyard *(razestān)* yielding grapes, which are processed into wine by the harvesters. The dispute is settled by an agreement determining that the exact amount of rent should be calculated on the basis of the amount of produce as follows: for each yield of grapes weighing 6 *kabīz* (one-tenth of a *grīw*, the measure for solid matters) one-third of a *dēg* ('cauldron', the measure for liquids) of wine is to be delivered as rent.[44]

These documents (besides other sources)[45] indicate that there was a long tradition in viticulture and viniculture in Iran, which continued to be a source of income in the Islamic period. Our *pursišn* furthermore suggests that the

43 On these terms and the documents see Weber 2014, pp. 186–187, and (with a revised reading of Berk. 93) Weber 2020, pp. 149–150.

44 Weber 2017, pp. 133–135; Macuch 2017a, pp. 167–172.

45 Wine *(may)* is mentioned as a liquid offering in ritual texts (see e.g. attestations in the *Nērangestān*, Kotwal/Kreyenbroek 2003, glossary, p. 308), but the expression does not always necessarily refer to wine made of grapes (as, for instance, in *may ī han-iz asp pēm*, "koumiss, the wine of the mare's milk"; Kotwal/Kreyenbroek 1995, *Nēr.* 12.2, pp. 82–83). Wine also played a prominent part in the New Year's celebrations according to an age-old Iranian custom. The eleventh century *Nowrūz-nāme*, "Book of the New Year", describes how on the first day of the *nowrūz* celebrations the Chief Mobed *(mowbedān mowbed)* presents the king with a golden goblet filled with wine, among other gifts. In his New-Year's wishes he asks the king to "drink (the elixir) of immortality from Jamšid's cup" *(anōšag xwar pad jām-e Jam)*. This New Year's custom might have been the origin of the connotation of a famous metaphor in Sufi literature with wine drinking: the *jām-e Jam*

commercial activities of the Mazdean wine-growers, vintners and merchants included the sale of wine and wine products to the adherents of other faiths, but that trading with wine in this manner was basically prohibited in Zoroastrian law.

The simple question put to the high-priest in this context is: what is his judgment *(dādestān)* regarding the sale of wine *(may)* by a Zoroastrian to non-Mazdeans? Two terms designate the groups to which wine is sold: *an-ērān*, lit. 'non-Iranians', and *ag-dēnān*, lit. 'adherents of the/an evil religion'. Were these just two general expressions for 'foreigners' and 'unbelievers, infidels' (i.e. generally all non-Mazdeans) or do they designate two distinctive groups?[46] It is well known that the word *ēr* 'Iranian' is not only an ethnic designation, but is also used in the broader sense of 'Mazdean', whereas *an-ēr* 'non-Iranian' specifically denotes the 'non-Mazdean'. The term seems to have been tied, at least in the Sasanian era, to the two criteria of "citizenship" (the status of a *mard ī šahr)* and of religious affiliation: if a person converted from Zoroastrianism to another faith he became not only an 'infidel' *(ag-dēn)*, but also an *an-ēr*, a 'non-Iranian'.[47] Hence the *an-ēr* is not always a foreigner in the ethnic sense of the word, but could also be a convert, who was regarded prior to his conversion as an 'Iranian' *(ēr)*. On the other hand, *ēr* is in several attestations clearly an ethnic term, as in *Dēnkard* III (140) describing the division of humankind into individual groups in accordance with the specific traits that unite and separate them.[48] According to this text, 'people' *(mardomān)* are generally divided into two separate categories: Iranians *(ērān)*, who build a union *(hamīh)* due to their 'Iranian character' *(ērīg xēm)* and are distinguished *(ǰudāgīh)* from non-Iranians *(an-ērān)* because of their 'un-Iranian character' *(an-ērīg xēm)*. The Iranians *(ērān)* in turn are also split into two groups: Zoroastrians *(hu-dēnān)*, who build a union *(hamīh)* due to following the law of the Good Religion *(hu-dēnīg dād)* and are distinguished *(ǰudāgīh)* from the adherents of evil religions *(ag-dēnān)*, who follow the 'law(s) of evil religion(s)' *(ag-dēnīg dād)*. In this text *ēr* is obviously an ethnic term that includes both Zoroastrians *(hu-dēnān)* and infidels *(ag-dēnān)*, the latter being defined as Iranians who do not abide by

---

'cup of Jamšīd', a vessel which imparts (spiritual/mystical) knowledge of the whole world. See REMPIS 1951, pp. 235–238, and MACUCH 2009, pp. 194–195.

46 *Pursišn* 52 (to be discussed below) has the general *ǰud-dēnān*, "believers of another faith".

47 On these categories see MACUCH 2010, pp. 199–201.

48 DkD 109.7–10 (DkM 143.20–144.2): *hād hamīh ud ǰudāgīh ēwēnagān was u-š ēk andar mardomān hamīh ī abāg ērān pad ērīg xēm ǰudāgīh az an-ērān pad an-ērīg xēm. ud ēk andar ērān hamīh ī abāg hu-dēnān pad hu-dēnīg dād ǰudāgīh az ag-dēnān pad ag-denīg dād.* "That is, there are many kinds of unions and separations: One is among people *(mardomān)* the union *(hamīh)* of the Iranians *(ērān)* because of (their) Iranian character, the separation *(ǰudāgīh)* from the non-Iranians *(an-ērān)* because of (their) non-Iranian character. And one is among the Iranians *(ērān)* the union of the adherents of the Good Religion *(hudēnān)* because of the law of the Good Religion, the separation from the adherents of the evil religion(s) *(agdēnān)* because of the law of the evil religion(s)." Compare DE MENASCE 1973, nr. 140, p. 145.

Zoroastrian law. Although *ag-dēn* can refer generally to any other religion apart from Zoroastrianism, the term denotes in late Pahlavi texts specifically the convert from Mazdaism to Islam, as in REA 4.1–3.[49] The reference to Islam is unequivocal in this passage, since it explicitly mentions circumcision: the convert from Zoroastrianism, called *ag-dēn*, is a man whose organ *(handām)* has been mutilated *(drōš)* according to the practice *(kardag)* of the *ag-dēnān*, i.e. Muslims (it is rather unlikely that Jews should be meant in the context of conversion, particularly in this text of the Islamic period). Given the various connotations of *an-ēr* and *ag-dēn* and the broad use of these terms, we have good reason to assume that these expressions denote generally foreigners and non-Mazdeans respectively, but can also designate converts from Zoroastrianism to Islam.

One of the noteworthy features of this *pursišn* (and many of the following legal sections of the Dd) is the flexibility with which Manuščihr handles the concrete problem by combining a rule of canonical law (called *čāštag* 'doctrine' in Pahlavi legal texts) with a divergent or even completely contrary judgment based on the discussion of the exceptional circumstances of the case in the interest of greater justice *(meh-dādestānīh)*.[50] It will be useful to consider the four elements of his answer in detail:

1. According to the decision on principle in canonical law, selling wine to non-Mazdeans is prohibited to Mazdeans (it is a "very grievous sin", *saxt garān wināh*, and an "evil profession", *wad pēšagīhā)*.
2. On the other hand, the immediate consequences of wine-selling to non-Mazdeans (foreigners, infidels, converts) have to be taken into consideration. These may be positive for the Zoroastrian community as a whole and contribute to its wellbeing due to several reasons: (a) members of the community who drink wine immoderately *(a-paymān)* would have less access to the intoxicating beverage with the result that they would improve by drinking

49 REA 4.1–3 (B.T. Anklesaria 1962, pp. 9–10): (1) *pursišn. pus ag-dēn har ān ī-š az pidar ud mādar pad weh-dēnīh rasēd ēg-iš pad ag-dēnīh bawēd ayāb nē* (2) *pāsox. mard kē az weh-dēnīh ō ag-dēnīh šawēd ud pad ag-dēnīh be rasēd pad gyāg tanāpuhr-ē(w) wināh ka andar sāl drahnāy pad rāh ī wehdēnīh hilēd margarzān.* (3) *agar-aš pad handām drōš ī čiyōn ag-dēnān pad kardag darēnd ud ān ī-š az handām burēnd ō āb ud ātaxš andar zamīg nihānīh rasēd ēg kamist margarzān wināh bawēd.* "(1) Question. A son (is) an adherent of the evil religion *(ag-dēn)*. Does every thing (=property) that he receives *(rasēd)* from (his) father and mother as a Zoroastrian remain in effect during (his) adherence to the evil religion *(pad ag-dēnīh)* or not? (2) Answer. A man who converts from the Good Religion to the evil religion and as a member of the evil religion receives (property of the parents): this is immediately (considered as) a *tanāpuhr* sin. If he leaves the path of the Good Religion in the course of a year, he (is) *margarzān*. (3) If an organ *(handām)* (of his body has received) a mutilation *(drōš)*, as is the practice *(kardag)* among the adherents of the evil religion, and that which they cut from the organ, reaches water or fire (or is) concealed in the earth, then it is at the very least a *margarzān* sin." See also de Menasce 1962, p. 77; Safa-Isfahani's 1980 edition (here: pp. 20–22) is on the whole unreliable.

50 On this technical term see Macuch 2017b, pp. 367–368, and 2019.

wine moderately *(pad paymān)*;[51] (b) Mazdeans would be restrained *(abāz dāštan)* from spending their money (or other means) on wine with the result that they would remain solvent *(tuwān)* and their property *(xwāstag)* intact; (c) this in turn would encourage them to remain in the Good Religion instead of converting to Islam *(ag-dēn)* because of economic reasons. Hence, in this context selling wine to infidels has beneficent results: it leads to aiding the righteous *(wehān ayārīh)*, guarding the Religion *(dēn-pānagīh)*, opposing sin *(wināh hamēmālīh)* and promoting virtuous deeds *(kirbag ayārīh)*.

3. Manuščihr's conclusion is somewhat twisted, but nevertheless clear: if selling wine to infidels has this positive effect on the Zoroastrian community and prohibiting it would lead to an increase in sin *(wēš frāy az wināh)*, to sin and evil *(wināh ud +wadīh)* due to the "unlawful drinking of wine" *(a-dādīhā xwarišnīh ī may)*, then the case must be judged otherwise than by retaining the basic rule. Under these circumstances and in accordance with the notion of *meh-dādestānīh*, 'extension of justice; greater justice', his divergent ruling explicitly supports the sale of wine to infidels, assessing the transaction even as a "binding virtuous deed" *(meh kirbag ī ēwarīg)*. The last expression *ēwarīg* '(legally) binding, reliable, valid' is a technical term (besides *ēwar/ēwarīh*) denoting a procedure or judgement (or a document or seal) that is unconditionally valid, cannot be contested and is hence legally binding (its opposite is *warōmand/warōmandīh* 'disputable, suspect; uncertainty, doubtfulness', referring to a provisional procedure or judgement that can be revised and does not have a legally binding character).[52] By using the term *ēwarīg* Manuščihr underlines the compulsory character of his assessment of this type of trade as a "virtuous deed" *(meh kirbag)* under the described circumstances and with the elucidated consequences.
4. This exceptional ruling (based on *meh-dādestānīh)* does not eliminate the decision on principle: the sale of wine to infidels and drunkards remains basically prohibited *(nē dastwarīhā* "it is not authorized").

Although Manuščihr's judgment of the case deviates considerably from the canonical ruling, this approach to a concrete legal dilemma is by no means exceptional.[53] The problem of discrepancy between legal theory and practice

51 On the idea of *paymān* see SHAKED 1987.

52 On *ēwar/ēwarīh* see MACUCH 2017a, p. 181, with further references. The contrast between the two types of judgement is summarized DkM 723.19: *abar dādestān pad ēwarīh ān ī pad warōmandīh* "on legally binding judgements and doubtful ones".

53 According to Manuščihr's own words in the introduction to the Dd, his approach to the questions posed in this work derives from "two sources" *(az dō bun)*: (1) from the "interpretation of essentials by the innate wisdom of the Leader of the Religion" *(mādayān nimūdārīh ī +āsn-xrad ī dēn-pēšōbāy)* (that is, in this case, his own assessment) and (2), "more importantly" *(mādayān-tar)*, from the "foundation (laid) by the blessed earlier leaders, the great *pōryōtkēšān* (ancient masters of Mazdaism)" *(nihādag ī hufraward pēšēnīgān ī meh-pōryōtkēšān)* (Dd, introduction, § 23; compare KREYENBROEK 1995, pp. 173 and 176;

was well known in Zoroastrian (specifically Sasanian) law and tackled by various means. One of these was to distinguish between legal proceedings, which strictly followed the 'doctrine' (*čāštag*) of canonical law, and those that were adjudicated on the basis of other criteria, called *kardag* or legal 'practice'.[54] Another method of circumventing canonical law was to apply the two devices called *passand* (lit. 'pleasure, liking'), a technical term denoting 'leniency (in justice); reduction of justice to the minimum required by law' (Syriac *ḥasīrūt dīnā* 'decrease of justice' in Jesubōxt's *Corpus Iuris*) and its opposite, *weh-dādestānīh* (lit. 'better justice') or, in later Pahlavi texts, *meh-dādestanīh* (lit. 'greater/higher justice'), meaning 'extension of justice; doing more than the minimum required by law' (Syriac *yaṯīrūt dīnā* 'extension of justice').[55] By applying the concept of *weh-dādestānīh/meh-dādestanīh* to a specific case a legal right could be extended beyond the boundaries set by canonical law, and, as in our *pursišn,* even a principal decision could be overruled in the interest of 'better/greater justice'. In the late Pahlavi texts the term *meh-dādestānīh* (and its adverbial form *meh-dādestānīhā* with the comparative ending, *meh-dādestānīhātar,* 'greater justice') seems to have replaced the Sasanian *weh-dādestānīh* (and *weh-dādestāntar),* but was employed — at least in a legal context — with the same technical meaning.[56]

Manuščihr explicitly makes use of this device to present a surprisingly pragmatic solution in his discussion of the effects of wine trading with infidels by balancing the arguments in favour of an extensive legal approach against the evils that might ensue by a restrictive handling of the problem. Besides religious considerations, he takes both the economic situation and the social dimension of the transaction into account in his discussion. Selling wine to infidels reduces the amount of wine that can be sold to members of the Zoroastrian community *without* leading to a significant reduction of income for the Mazdean trader. From a social point of view, the consequences are positive if selling wine outside the Zoroastrian community impedes immoderate drinking within the community. Likewise, the economic effect can be favourable if it restrains Mazdeans from wasting their property on wine, losing their solvency and having to leave the Zoroastrian community. He basically argues that protecting the community from the evils of immoderate drinking, insolvency and conversion to Islam is definitely 'better/greater justice' than attempting to implement a judgment based

Jaafari-Dehaghi 1998, pp. 36–37). He "essentially (follows) the truth of the statements of the former authorities" *(mādayān rāstīh ī pēšēnīgān dastwarān gōwišn),* but adheres to the "authorities of his time and family" *(dastwarān ī zamānag ud dūdag),* if the ancient authorities represent "divergent opinions" *(ǰud-dādestānīh būd)* (Dd, introduction, § 20; Kreyenbroek 1995, pp. 173 and 176; Jaafari-Dehaghi 1998, pp. 36–37).

54 On these two terms with examples see Macuch 1981, pp. 146–162; Colditz 2015, pp. 230–237.

55 Sachau 1914, pp. 13f., 289f.

56 On these two concepts see Macuch 2019.

on legal doctrine, which might thwart the positive effects described above. This pragmatic approach to the problem in legal practice, however, does not affect the validity of the basic doctrine prohibiting the sale of wine to non-Mazdeans.

III. Text and Translation of *Pursišn* 52 (K35, fol. 171v.,16–172r.,15; TD4a, pp. 323.13–324.15)[57]

1. *panǰāh-dōwom pursišn pāsox*[58] *ān ī*[59] *pursēd kū andar šahr bē šahr mardōm ī*[60] *wehdēn xrīd frōxt ī pad gōspand*[61] *abāg ǰud-dēnān windakkarān*[62] *kunēnd ud ō awēšān frōxšēnd*[63] *ēg-iš dādestān čē ud*[64]
2. *ka wehdēn ka nē mad ēstēnd pad*[65] *arz nē xrīnēnd*[66] *bē ō windakkarān*[67] *ǰud-dēnān frōxšēnd*[68] *ēg-iš*[69] *dādestān čē*
3. *ān kē-š*[70] *zīwišn*[71] *čiš ēg-iš dādestān čē*
4. *pāsox ēd kū ōwōn kār kardan*[72] *abēr garān wināhīhā ud*[73] *wad* ⁺*pēšagīhā*[74] *pad wizār ud tuwān*[75] *an-hangār kardan pad ōwōn sūd xwāstan nē dastwarīhā*
5. *bē*[76] *agar ān wehdēn kē nibišt kū*[77] *ziwīšn čiš*[78] *ud pad any-iz ēč kār ī frārōn pēšag ī čiš kam wināhtar ziwīšn xwāstan*[79] *nē tuwān purr xrīdār*

57 ANKLESARIA 1958, p. 110; WEST 1882, pp. 182–183.
58 K35: ⟨p'shw⟩; TD4a: om.
59 K35: ⟨Y⟩; TD4a: om.
60 K35: ⟨Y⟩; TD4a: om.
61 K35: ⟨gwspnd⟩; TD4a: ⟨gwspnd'n⟩.
62 K35: ⟨wndk gl'n'⟩; TD4a: ⟨wndgl'n⟩.
63 K35: ⟨MZḆN⟩; super lin. ⟨MZḆNNnd⟩; TD4a: ⟨ MZḆNNx_2⟩.
64 K35: om.; TD4a: ⟨W⟩.
65 K35: om.; TD4a: ⟨pṯ'⟩.
66 Both mss.: ⟨ZḆNNx_2⟩.
67 K35: ⟨wndk gl'n'⟩; TD4a: ⟨wndgl'n⟩.
68 K35: ⟨MZḆNNx_2⟩; TD4a: ⟨ MZḆNNx_1⟩.
69 K35: ⟨'DN'-š⟩; TD4a: om.
70 K35: written twice: ⟨ZK MNW-š ZK MNW-š⟩; TD4a: ⟨ZK MNW-š⟩.
71 K35: ⟨zywšn'⟩; TD4a: ⟨ZḆNNx_1 zywšn'⟩.
72 K35: ⟨'wgwn' k'l krtn'⟩; TD4a: om. the whole passage beginning with ⟨'wgwn'⟩.
73 K35: ⟨W⟩; TD4a: om.
74 Both mss.: ⟨pyšyh'⟩. The correct form ⟨pyškyh'⟩ (in *wad pēšagīha*) is attested in a parallel context Dd. *pursišn* 49 (see above).
75 K35: ⟨tb'n⟩; TD4a: ⟨twb'n⟩.
76 K35: ⟨BR'⟩; TD4a: ⟨BR' W⟩.
77 K35: om.; TD4a: ⟨'YK⟩.
78 TD4a: ins. ⟨k'l⟩; K35: om.
79 K35: ⟨BʻYHWNst'⟩; TD4a: ⟨BʻYHWNstn'.

ī[80] *wehdēn ayāft be ō wehdēnān*[81] *frōxšēd*[82] *čiyōn-iš kam winābtar tuwān kē*[83] *hamkār ziwišn xwāstan pādixšāy čē ēk-iz mard ī ahlaw abāg ahlawān ī-š andar sālārīh ziwīstan ēdōn*[84] *tuwān ka gōspandān be ō ōzanišn an-ērān*[85] *xwarišnīh frōxšēd was gōspand be-iz ō* +*kāhēnišn*[86] *ērān dārišn mad xwārtar kū mard ī ahlaw pad an-ayābišnīh ī ziwišn marg bīm ōzad.*[87]

1. Fifty-second question (and) answer. That which you ask: (When) adherents of the Good Religion practice buying (and) selling small livestock (=sheep; *gōspand)* in the country (and) outside the country with traders of another religion *(ǰud-dēnān windakkarān)* and sell to them, what is the decision?
2. If adherents of the Good Religion *(wehdēn)* are not present *(nē mad ēstēnd*, lit. "have not come") (or) do not buy (according to) value (and) they (=the Zoroastrian vendors) sell (the sheep) to traders of another religion *(windakkarān ǰud-dēnān)*, what is the decision?
3. Regarding the (person), whose living *(zīwišn čiš)* is made (by trade), what is the decision?
4. The answer (is): practising this (is) a very severe sin *(abēr garān winābīhā)* and it is an evil profession *(wad* +*pēšagīhā);* it is not authorized *(nē dastwarīhā)* to do this inconsiderately *(an-hangār)* for payment *(pad wizār)* and being solvent *(tuwān),* in order to seek profit *(sūd).*
5. But if that adherent of the Good Religion *(wehdēn)*, who (you) have written about, makes a living *(zīwišn čiš)* (by trade) and he cannot seek a living by any other righteous profession *(kār ī frārōn pēšag)*, which is less sinful, by obtaining fully (solvent) buyers of the Good Religion, and selling to the adherents of the Good Religion, as this is less sinful, he is authorized *(pādixšāy)* to seek an associate *(hamkār)* in making a living, since this one righteous man *(mard ī ahlaw)* together with the righteous, who are under his guardianship *(sālārīh)*, can live thus, when he sells sheep for slaughtering to be eaten by non-Iranians *(an-ērān).* Even (if) the number of sheep for maintaining Iranians is decreased *(be-iz ō* +*kāhēnišn … mad)*, this is a smaller (sin) than (when) a righteous man (has) fear of death (and) is killed due to not being able to obtain a living.

80 K35: ⟨Y⟩; TD4a: om.
81 K35: ⟨wyhdyn' 'n⟩; TD4a: ⟨ŠPYLdyn' 'n⟩.
82 K35: ⟨MZB̲NNx$_2$⟩; TD4a: ⟨ MZB̲NNx$_1$⟩.
83 K35: ⟨MNW⟩; TD4a: ⟨MN⟩.
84 TD4a: ins. ⟨Y⟩; K35: om.
85 TD4a: ins. ⟨Y⟩; K35: om.
86 K35: ⟨ksyn' šn⟩; TD4a: ⟨ks'nšn'⟩.
87 K35: ⟨YKTLWYN' t'⟩; TD4a: ⟨YKTLWNt'⟩.

IV. Background, Terminology and Content of *Pursišn* 52

The same method of combining a decision on principle with a judgment contrary to legal doctrine based on a discussion of the concrete circumstances of a case can be observed in the second *pursišn* dealing with the sale of small livestock or sheep *(gōspand)*[88] to non-Mazdeans. The transfer of livestock to an unbeliever was obviously perceived as a grave offence from the viewpoint of religious law due to a commonly known central doctrine, which did not have to be explicitly elucidated: the special status of beneficent *(spəṇta)* animals of the good creation in Zoroastrianism. Cattle belonged generally to the group of beneficent animals, which were protected by the rules governing the *ruwānīg* ('pertaining to the soul') category of law. According to the *stōrestān* ('chapter on large livestock, cattle') in *Dēnkard* 8 it was considered as a 'sin against the soul' *(ruwānīg wināh)* to "unlawfully beat and wound" *(adādīhā zanišn ud rēš)* large and small cattle *(stōrān gōspandān)*. Harming animals in this manner was liable to a financial penalty *(tōzišn)* and a fine *(tāwān)* to be paid to the owner of the cattle *(gōspand-xwēš)*. Judgement in these cases also had to take into consideration *(āmār)*, whether the offence against the animal was committed wilfully and intentionally *(andar nigerišnīg)* or by negligence *(sūdagīhā)*.[89] It was forbidden to kill a domestic or tame animal 'unlawfully' *(adādīhā)*, that is, without observing specific rules and prescribed rites. One of these rules prohibited the slaughter of an animal that had not yet reached maturity (usually less than a year old);[90] another one prescribed that the sacrificial animal had to be first stunned with a log *(čōb)* before being killed with the knife *(gōspand čōb pēš az kārd frāz burdan* "striking the *gōspand* with a log before applying the knife"). Two reasons are given for the latter rule: (1) compassion with the animal *(abaxšišn ī abar gōspand)*: by stunning the animal first it would "fear less and sense less pain" *(kam bīmīh ud kam dardīh)*; (2) it prevents the killing of an animal on impulse (*nē halagīhā zūd zūd pad har zamān ārzōg tēzīhā ōzadan ī gōspand* "[so that] the *gōspand* is not slayed rashly, quickly on impulse any time one wishes to").[91]

88 Av. *gaospəṇta-* 'beneficent bull/cow/animal' was used as a generic term for all beneficent animals, due to their descent from the seed of the sole-created bull/cow/animal *(gauu-aēuuō.dāta-*; MP *gāw ī ēw-dād)* according to the ancient creation myth; see Boyce 1975, pp. 138–140. On *gauu-* 'cow, animal' as the chief representative of the animal world (*gauu-paṇcō.hiiā-* "animal of five kinds", designating the five classes of animal) and the expression *māh- gaočiϑra-* "the moon that holds the seed of the animal" see Hintze 2009 [2005], pp. 61–62. The expression *gōspand* continued to be employed as a general term for 'cattle, livestock', but by Sasanian times (and later) it designated mainly small livestock, sheep and goats, and finally sheep alone, *stōr* being used for large cattle.

89 DkD 553.20–554.12 (DkM 728.5–23). On the treatment of animals in Zoroastrian law see Macuch 2003 with a transcription and translation of the whole passage on p. 179.

90 Boyce 1975, p. 297–298; Macuch 2003, p. 171.

91 DkD 364.16–21 (DkM 466.12–18); transcription and translation of the passage in Macuch 2003, p. 171.

As ALBERTO CANTERA has shown, the Zoroastrian ritual knew two distinct types of animal sacrifice. The *gōspand* was either slaughtered during the actual performance of the Long Liturgy which included the killing of the animal *(ka gōspand pad yašt)* or the animal was slayed before the liturgy and its meat was prepared and cooked beforehand to be presented as an offering (specifically in the *yazišn ī yazdān,* liturgies to deities other than Ahura Mazdā).[92]

None of the above mentioned rules and restrictions, which were incumbent on Zoroastrians, would be in effect if livestock bred within the Zoroastrian community were sold to infidel traders outside the community. According to the passage cited above, restricting the slaughter of cattle as beings of the beneficent creation to the context of sacrifice (in either of the two above mentioned forms) would lead to "less slaying of cattle" *(kam kušišn-iz ī gōspand)* and would prevent the animals from being killed "unlawfully and rashly" *(adādīhā ud halakīhā).*[93] Moreover, by observing the prescribed rituals the animal would only lose its physical life whereas its spirit would be released to depart to the other world.[94]

Apart from these beliefs, the food derived from cattle was obviously regarded as superior. In another passage of the Dd (30.13) Manuščihr describes the products of the *gōspand* as the "best material/earthly food" *(andar gētīgīg xwarišn ān ī az gōspandān bar pāšom guft ēstēd* "among the material food the products of cattle are regarded as the best"); among these the most excellent are milk *(šīr),* butter *(rōyn)* and spring butter.[95] Another text (RivDd 23.17) reflects this high assessment of the food derived from animal products in the nourishment given to the souls of the righteous in the hereafter, consisting of "mare's milk, and cream (or: marrow) and butter and sweet wine, or butter which is made in spring" *(pēm ī asp ud mazg ud rōyn ud may ī šīrēn ayāb rōyn ī mēdyozarm).*[96] Besides its products the meat of the animal was valued, both in the context of sacrifice and from a nutritional and economic point of view, as we may deduce from an ancient phrase attested in the context of remunerating persons engaged as guardian *(sālār)* of the family or as 'proxy' *(stūr).* The technical term *srēnag/sēnag masāy ud bāzā masāy*, lit. 'the size of a buttock/breast and size of a forefoot', derived from Av. *sraoni.masah-* 'the size of a buttock' and **bāzu.masah-* 'the size of a forefoot', designates in legal texts the 'daily ration' of a mature man.[97] The phrase illustrates well the original custom of paying in kind by allocating meat rations from the front and hind part of a slaughtered animal ('the

92 See the extensive and detailed description of animal sacrifice in CANTERA 2022, specifically p. 90, with an overview of the main types of ceremonies on p. 91.

93 DkD 364.18–19 (DkM 466.15).

94 BOYCE 1975, p. 149.

95 Compare JAAFARI-DEHAGHI 1998, pp. 94–95.

96 WILLIAMS 1990, I, pp. 120–121; II, p. 49.

97 The alternative *sēnag* 'breast' is attested in several manuscripts and is a late variant of the original *srēnag* 'forefoot'. For attestations of the Avestan terms see BARTHOLOMAE 1904, col. 1633 and 956, respectively. On this technical phrase in a legal context see MACUCH 1990 with further references.

size of a buttock and size of a forefoot') as remuneration for the fulfilment of a duty. Persons engaged as guardian and proxy were entitled to a portion of the family income corresponding to the daily ration they would receive in terms of pieces of meat. By the Sasanian period the phrase had become a technical term, not to be taken literally, but rather as the basis for calculating the share of income due to these persons for performing important tasks in the family.

In the light of the rules regarding beneficent animals of the good creation according to the *ruwānīg* category of law and the ritual significance of killing cattle according to prescribed rites, besides the relevance of their meat and their products from an nutritional and economic viewpoint, it is hardly surprising that our *pursišn* targets the difficult dilemma of selling livestock bred by Zoroastrians to unbelievers. The high-priest is asked to give judgement *(dādestān)* on three interconnected questions:

1. Are Zoroastrians (*wehdēn)* who practice trade (*xrīd frōxt* 'buying, selling') inside and outside the country (*andar šahr bē šahr)* allowed to sell small cattle/sheep *(gōspand)* to traders of another religion *(ǰud-dēnān windakkarān)?*
2. Is it allowed if there are no Zoroastrian (*wehdēn)* buyers or none who can buy according to the value of the animal (*pad arz nē xrīnēnd)?*
3. Is it allowed if the trader's livelihood *(zīwišn čiš)* depends on trade?

Whereas the previous *pursišn* uses the expressions *an-ēr* and *ag-dēn* to denote generally foreigners, infidels and converts, our passage employs the term *ǰud-dēnān,* lit. 'adherents of another religion', in combination with a word written  ⟨wndk gl'n'⟩ in K35 (fol. 172r., 3) and  ⟨wndgl'n⟩ in TD4a (p. 323, 15,17), which I have read *windakkarān*. Although one could suggest an alternative reading, following the spelling in TD4a, as ⟨wnyk gl'n'/wnygl'n⟩ *wanīgarān,* I prefer the proposed one due to several reasons. First of all, of the two manuscripts used to reconstruct the text K35 is definitely more reliable than TD4a in the legal passages, as it retains rare expressions and technical terms, which have been altered beyond recognition or even completely removed in the latter manuscript.[98] Moreover, the established meaning of *wanīgar* 'squanderer, prodigal, spendthrift; person, who spends wastefully' simply does not make sense in the context of our *pursišn.*[99] Even in combination with

98 See for example the discussion of technical terms in *pursišn* 51 (Macuch 2022), which are preserved (at least rudimentarily) in K35, whereas they have been completely eliminated in TD4a.

99 On *wanīgar(īh)* see Tafazzoli 1971, pp. 195–197, and Shaked 1979, glossary, pp. 363–364, with further references. The pejorative meaning of *wanīgar(īh)* is elucidated in several passages of *Dēnkard* 6, as in B14.1: *čē rādīh wehīh u-š wanīgarīh petyārag* "For generosity (is) goodness and squandering (is) its adversary" (compare Shaked, *ibid.*, p. 136–137); or B15.1: *wanīgarīh az gehān be barišn bē ēdōn barišn kū rādīh be nē kāhēd* "Squandering should be driven away from the world, but in a manner that generosity should not diminish" (Shaked, *ibid.*, pp. 140–141); the person designated as *wanīgar* is described in E24: *wanīgar ān bawēd kē ō wattarān čiš dahēd* "The squanderer is the one who gives things to

ǰud-dēn and with a pejorative meaning it is too far-fetched to be acceptable, whereas *windakkar* with the literal meaning of 'person, who acquires, obtains something, who makes a gain', in the sense of 'trader' or 'merchant', fits in perfectly with the context of our passage discussing the problem of trade with non-Mazdeans. If the reading is correct (as the spelling in K35 suggests), the noun is easily derived from *wind- (windādan, wind-* 'to find, obtain, acquire, get, gain, win') + suffixes *-ag* + *-gar/-kar*.[100] As far as I can see, there is no further attestation of this expression in a Pahlavi text, but other derivations from the same stem are attested, compare the very frequent *windišn* 'gain, income, earnings'[101] and *windagīh* 'gain, profit'.[102] Is *windakkar* simply a synonym for the common *wāzāragān* 'merchant' or does it have a specific meaning? The choice of this word might have a concrete reason: any person, who actively makes a gain by selling and buying goods, regardless of his profession, may have been called *windakkar*, lit. 'profit-maker', whereas *wāzāragān* would have expressly denoted the *professional* trader or merchant. We may further surmise that the use of this word together with *ǰud-dēnān* created a pejorative connotation. In a list of offences in *Dēnkard* 8 *windagīh* is in fact employed in a negative context as the sin of taking advantage of destitute people (*niyāzagān* 'needy, poor') in order to make a profit: *abar niyāzagān-windagīh ud zūr-afrāhīh ud druxt-padīrišnīh wināh* "On the sin of making profit of the needy (*niyāzagān-windagīh*) and false teaching and accepting deceit" (DkD 562.14–15 = DkM 738.20–21). Another question that cannot be answered definitely, is, whether *ǰud-dēnān windakkarān* (or: in reversed sequence, *windakkarān ǰud-dēnān* in the second attestation) designates two groups of people, i.e. lit. "adherents of another religion *and* traders" or only one group, "traders of another religion". I have chosen the second variant, but the problem of selling cattle to non-Mazdeans might not have been relevant only in dealings with persons who practiced trade on a regular professional basis.

Manuščihr's answer again consists of several parts in a sequence similar to the previous *pursišn*, but without the repetition of the principle decision at the end:

1. According to the decision on principle based on canonical law the sale of *gōspand* to non-Mazdean traders is prohibited (it is a "very severe sin", *abēr garān winābīhā* and an "evil profession", *wad* ⁺*pēšagīhā*). It is not authorized (*nē dastwarīhā*) to practice this profession with the intention of seeking gain in an inconsiderate manner, that is, "for payment" (*pad wizār*), for "[being] solvent" (*tuwān*) and for "profit" (*sūd*).

evil people" (Shaked, *ibid.*, pp. 194–195.). West 1882, p. 182, reads this expression in our passage as *vanîkgarān*, but translates "trader" with no further explanation.

100 MacKenzie 1971, p. 91; Nyberg 1974, p. 213; Ir. $\sqrt{}$*u̯aid*² 'to find', Cheung 2007, pp. 409–410; Av.$\sqrt{}$²*vaēd* 'to find', Bartholomae 1904, col. 1318; on the suffix *-gar/-kar* see Durkin-Meisterernst 2014, p. 167–169, §§ 326, 333.

101 For attestations see Macuch 1993, word index, p. 738.

102 DkD 562.14 (DkM 738. 21; see below).

2. On the other hand, the concrete circumstances of a case have to be taken into consideration before reaching a final decision. An exception to the general rule is admissible under the following conditions: (a) the livelihood *(zīwišn čiš)* of the Zoroastrian depends on selling cattle and he cannot make a living by any other means; (b) the Zoroastrian trader is not able to sell his livestock to fully solvent co-religionists who would buy his goods at market price.
3. Under the said conditions the Mazdean *(wehdēn)* trader is authorized *(pādixšāy)* to seek a "collaborator, fellow-worker, associate" *(hamkār)* in order to make a living. Manuščihr justifies this decision contrary to legal doctrine by arguing that the Zoroastrian trader is a "righteous man" *(mard ī ahlaw)*, who, together with all the righteous *(ahlawān)* under his guardianship *(sālārīh)*, can only make a living by selling cattle/sheep to be slaughtered and eaten by non-Iranians *(an-ērān)*. Then he states a counter-argument, which he immediately refutes: the result of trading with non-Mazdeans would be a decrease in the number of cattle available for maintaining *(dārišn)* Iranians *(ērān)*, i.e. Mazdeans.[103] He argues: it would be less sinful *(xwārtar)* to accept a diminution of the obtainable amount of livestock in the Zoroastrian community than to risk the death of a righteous man *(mard ī ahlaw)*, who is not able to make a living, as well as persons dependent on him. That is, Manuščihr permits under these specific circumstances trade of livestock with unbelievers, although it is explicitly prohibited in legal doctrine.

The last part of the answer employs two well-known, but ambiguous terms, *hamkār* 'collaborator, partner, fellow-worker, associate, assistant' and *mard ī ahlaw* 'righteous, pious man' which are not further elucidated. Does *hamkār* in this context have a specific meaning? Generally the expression could designate an associate of any individual, the partner of a person belonging to any profession. In our context *hamkār* could refer to a fellow-trader or business partner of the Zoroastrian trader, but, if Manuščihr had his own profession in mind, the term could refer to a member of the priestly class, who would control and sanction the deal between the Zoroastrian vendor and the infidel purchaser. Given the abovementioned rules regarding the obligation of Zoroastrians to protect beneficent animals of the good creation, this use of the word would make far more sense in our context. According to MODI (1937, p. 455) and BOYCE (1968, p. 285) the expression *hamkār* assumed a technical meaning among the Parsis of Navsari as the designation for a qualified priest. The members of the priestly profession were all denoted as *hamkār*s and, in an extension of this use of the word, dinners given to the qualified priests of the town also came to be known by the name of *hamkār* or *hamkār-sāth*.

103 See commentary on *pursišn* 49.

The technical meaning of 'qualified priest' might in fact have evolved at a far earlier period than assumed by these two authors. In the long *pursišn* 47 of the Dd dealing with specifics of the *yazišn* ceremony Manuščihr employs *hamkār* in this specific sense of a person, who assists or works together with the chief officiating priest *(zōt)*: Dd 47.13: *yaštārān gāh (čiyōn ast) xwad gāh* *+ī zōt (ud) hamkārān gyāg urwīs* "The place of the celebrators of the liturgy (*yaštārān*) (is) itself the place of the chief officiating priest *(zōt)* and his fellow-helpers/associates *(hamkārān)*, the place of the ritual table (*gyāg urwīs)*".[104] The *gyāg urwīs* (or *urwīsgāh*, Nēr. 40.11) 'place of the ritual table' is the name of the consecrated space within which the ritual is performed, or, in the words of KOTWAL/KREYENBROEK, "the ritual precinct enclosed by furrows *(pāvī)*, in which the ritual table *(urwīs)* stands, and in which the high ritual are [sic] performed".[105] Another passage of the same *pursišn* is more elaborate, listing the individual tasks of the performers of the *yazišn*, consisting of the *zōt* and his fellow-helpers, *hamkār*:

> Dd 47.23 (K35.166v.8–13; TD4a, p. 310, 9–14): *ōy*[106] *ī*[107] *zōt ī*[108] *weh-pēšōbāyīh*[109] *abārīg hamkārīhā*[110] *ast kē pad abestāg*[111] *ast kē*[112] *pad ātaxš ān ēw-jadārīh ast kē frāz*[113] *burdārīhā ast kē pad bē burdārīhā ast kē +āsnadārīhā*[114] *ast kē gumēzakkarīhā ast kē kār-framūdārīhā ud xwēš niyābag dēnīhā*[115] *andar +rāyēnišn*[116] *andar yazišn rāyēnēd.*
>
> "The *zōt* (chief officiating priest) of good leadership (and) the other associates *(hamkārīhā):* there is one who (is) for (reciting) the Avesta (*pad abestāg*), one who maintains *(ēw-jadārīh)* the fire *(ātaxš)*, one who brings forward (*frāz burdārīhā*) (the firewood), one who carries it away (*bē burdārīhā*); one who washes it (*+āsnadārīhā*), one who makes mixtures (*gumēzakkarīhā*), one who

104 K35, fol. 165v, 4–5; TD4a, p. 307, 13–14 (inserts *čiyōn ast* after *yaštārān gāh)*; compare WEST 1882, p. 163.

105 KOTWAL/KREYENBROEK 2003, p. 173, fn. 684; WEST 1882, p. 163, fn. 4. On the *urwīsgāh* see also MODI 1937, pp. 248–249.

106 K35 ⟨'LH⟩; TD4a ⟨'L⟩.

107 TD4a: om.

108 K35 ⟨zwt Y⟩; TD4a ⟨zwtyh⟩.

109 TD4a inserts ⟨Y⟩; K35: om.

110 Both mss. ⟨hmk'lyhs⟩.

111 K35 ⟨'pst'k⟩; TD4a ⟨'psyt wyh⟩.

112 TD4a inserts ⟨MNW⟩; K35 om.

113 K35 inserts ⟨'p'⟩; TD4a om. (although *kē frāz āb burdārīhā* 'who brings forward the water' makes sense, it does not fit in with the tasks of the associate priests mentioned in the parallel passages referred to below; *āb* is probably an addition of the copyist trying to make sense of the text, but the act of 'bringing forward' most likely refers in this context to firewood, compare Dk §9.12.7 cited below).

114 Both mss. ⟨'ynt'lyh'⟩.

115 K35 ⟨-yh'⟩ *super lin.;* TD4a ⟨gh'n⟩; ⟨BYN⟩ *super lin.*

116 K35 ⟨l'dynsn⟩; TD4a ⟨l'dynyt⟩.

give orders (*kār-framūdārīhā*) and performs according to (his) own (individual) religious suitability (*xwēš niyābag dēnīhā*) within the arrangement the *yazišn*." [117]

This enumeration of associates or qualified priests (*hamkārān, hamkārīhā*) in Dd 47.13 and 23 corresponds roughly to a passage of the *Sūdgar Nask* (*Dēnkard*, Book 9, §9.12.7), listing in a similar manner the priests involved in the performance of the Long Liturgy,[118] whose names and functions are explicated in *Nērangestān* 54–59[119] and mentioned in *Widēwdād* 5.57–58.[120] YUHAN VEVAINA excerpts the following names and functions of the seven (associate) priests (to which our text refers indirectly without giving their precise designations): "*hāuuanān (=hāwan)* 'the Pressing priest'; *ātrauuaxša (=ātarwaxš)* 'the Fire-lighting priest'; *frabərətar (=frabardār)* 'the Presenting priest'; *ābərət (=ābard)* 'the Tending priest'; *āsnatar- (=āsnadār)* 'the Washing priest'; *raēϑβiškara- (=rehbiškar)* 'the Mingling priest'; *sraošāuuarəza- (=srōšāwarz)* 'the Auditing priest'."[121] In a recent article on the historical evolution of ritual performance and the functions of the auxiliary priests ALBERTO CANTERA elucidates that a priestly college consisting of eight priests performed the greater Long Liturgy (*yašt ī meh):* one main priest (*zaōtar-*) and the seven auxiliary priests listed above, whereas only two priests, the *zaōtar- (=zōt)* and an auxiliary priest, performed the lesser Long Liturgy (*yašt ī keh*). In the further development of the performance the auxiliary priests gradually lost their importance due to two concurrent changes: (a) the functions of the seven auxiliary priests were gradually assumed by the *zaōtar;* (b) the auxiliary priests could exchange functions, gradually reducing the number of priests to only one auxiliary priest, the *rāspīg*.[122]

The list of *hamkārs* in Dd. 47.23 might represent an intermediate stage in this evolution from the ancient ritual to modern practice as performed at the time of Manuščihr in the ninth century. In any case, there can be no doubt that the term refers in this context to a person with specific duties within the performance of the ritual, who works in alliance with the *zōt* and is a member of the priestly class. The use of *hamkār* in this sense in both this long *pursišn* and in our text makes it rather likely that Manuščihr had some kind of priestly function

117 WEST 1882, p. 167, has a completely different translation.

118 According to the recent edition of VEVAINA 2023, p. 154, (commentary in VEVAINA 2024, p. 206): "§9.12.7 *abar čihrīh-mizdīh ī āsnūdār ud pāk- ud pādyāb-kardār ī ān ī ātaxš sraxt ud ēsm abar-burdār ud frāz-āsnādār ud frāz-kardār ī ātaxš ud bē-burdār ī ēsm ī garān framūd dādīg-kār dēg ud kudāmag aziš wināh ī ōy [ī] ǰumbēnīdār.* 'About the reward in kind of the one who purifies the corner/side [= Av. *ϑraxti-*] of the fire (altar) and the one who makes (it) clean and pure; and (about) the one who brings the firewood; the one who washes (it); the one who makes the Fire; and the one who removes the firewood, for which a cauldron, made in accordance with the Law, is ordered; (and about) the sin of the one who moves the leftovers from him.'"

119 KOTWAL/KREYENBROEK 2003, pp. 262–267.

120 MOAZAMI 2014, pp. 160–161. For further attestations see VEVAINA 2024, p. 206.

121 VEVAINA 2024, p. 206.

122 CANTERA 2021, pp. 2–4.

in mind in authorizing the Zoroastrian *(wehdēn)* trader to choose a *hamkār* for his dealings with non-Mazdeans. If this interpretation is correct, *hamkār* would designate as a technical term one of the fellow-helpers or associate priests, whose task would be to control and sanction the (otherwise prohibited) deal between the Zoroastrian trader and his non-Mazdean business partner. Interestingly, in the immediately following passage Manuščihr no longer designates the Mazdean trader just as a *wehdēn*, but calls him a *mard ī ahlaw,* 'righteous, pious man', an expression reserved for the most zealous Zoroastrians.[123] Although this term is not less ambiguous than *hamkār*, its sudden use under the described circumstances does not seem to be arbitrary. The choice of this wording seems to suggest that by involving a fellow-helper/associate priest in his dealings the Mazdean trader has reached a very high degree of religiosity, which makes him a *mard ī ahlaw*. Hence, we may surmise that Manuščihr not only exceptionally permits the sale of cattle/sheep to infidel traders under the said circumstances, but explicitly sanctions the act, if the deal is confirmed by a member of the priestly class.

Conclusions

The two passages of the Dd dealing with the legal problem of trade with non-Mazdeans demonstrate how crucial it had become by the 9th century for the dwindling Zoroastrian communities to overcome legal barriers preventing commercial and economic interaction with adherents of other religions, be it foreigners, infidel traders or Zoroastrian converts to Islam. The inconsistencies and contradictions to Zoroastrian canonical law might have been particularly apparent in the two discussed cases involving the sale of wine *(may)*, due to its intoxicating effect, and of cattle/sheep *(gōspand)*, due to the special status of beneficent animals in Zoroastrianism. In both cases transactions with non-Mazdeans are explicitly prohibited in canonical law. But in his response the high-priest Manuščihr reveals how the restrictive doctrines of legal theory could be circumvented in practice by applying the well-tested method called *meh-dādestānīh* 'extension of justice; greater justice'. He replies to the questions put to him by conveying two contradictory judgements, one based on canonical law, the other on an analysis of the concrete circumstances of the issue in question in the spirit of 'greater justice'. His answer consists of three distinct parts:

1. A *basic rule* or principle decision following the precepts of canonical law (*pursišn* 49 repeats this basic rule at the end of the response).
2. A *discussion* of the concrete consequences of the transaction, which takes the living conditions of Zoroastrians into account and the possible economic and social impact of the deal on the Zoroastrian community as a whole.

123 On the various connotations of *mard ī ahlaw* see König 2005 and recently Shaked 2022.

3. A *divergent ruling* contrary to the principle decision based on the arguments in the discussion using the legal device of 'greater justice'.

Although the sale of wine (*pursišn* 49) to unbelievers is prohibited in canonical law, the high-priest explicitly permits it under the condition that the deal is in the interest of the Zoroastrian community as a whole, that it keeps society intact by preventing excessive drinking within the community, and by averting the loss of solvency and property, which would cause Zoroastrians to leave the community and convert to Islam *(ag-dēn)*. Likewise, the sale of cattle to infidel traders (*pursišn* 52) is basically prohibited, but permitted by the high-priest, if the Zoroastrian trader has no other means of making a living and cannot sell to his co-religionists. Although there would be a decrease of livestock available to the Zoroastrian community, it is a 'lesser (sin)' *(xwārtar)* to seek a bargain with non-Mazdeans than to risk the life of a righteous man and all the persons in his guardianship. The trader is explicitly authorized *(pādixšāy)* to seek the help of an associate priest *(hamkār)* whose task would be, as we may infer, to sanction the deal. These passages shed light not only on the economic difficulties Zoroastrian communities were confronted with in the early Islamic period, but show how the ensuing legal dilemma was dealt with in a pragmatic manner without giving up fundamental precepts. As the highest legal authority of this period, Manuščihr explicitly upholds the basic principles of legal doctrine, but skilfully uses the device of extending justice to find a solution compatible with the concrete interests of individual Mazdeans and the Zoroastrian community as a whole.

Bibliography

ANKLESARIA, B.T. 1962 (ed.): *Rivâyat-î Hêmît-î Ašavahištân.* Vol. I. Bombay.

ANKLESARIA, T.D. 1911: *The Datistan-i-Dinik.* Part I: *Pursishn I-XL.* Bombay.

ANKLESARIA, P.K. 1958: *A Critical Edition of the Unedited Portion of the Dādestān i Dīnīk.* (Unpublished thesis submitted to the University of London).

BARTHOLOMAE, CH. 1904: *Altiranisches Wörterbuch.* Straßburg [reprint: Berlin 1962].

BOYCE, M. 1968: "The Pious Foundations of the Zoroastrians." In: *Bulletin of the Society of Oriental and African Studies* 31, pp. 270–289.

— 1975: *A History of Zoroastrianism.* Vol. I: *The Early Period.* Leiden/Köln.

CANTERA, A. 2021: "The *sraōšāuuarəza*-priest and the usage of the *srōš-barišnīh* in the greater Long Liturgy". In: *Journal of the Royal Asiatic Society* 3rd Series 31/3, pp. 479–514.

— 2022: "The Offering to Satisfy the ratu *(miiazda ratufrī)*: the Dual System of the Animal Sacrifice in Zoroastrian Rituals." In: A. CANTERA/M. MACUCH/N. SIMS-WILLIAMS (eds.): *The Reward of the Righteous. Festschrift in Honour of Almut Hintze.* Wiesbaden (Iranica 30), pp. 39–96.

CHEUNG, J. 2007: *Etymological Dictionary of the Iranian Verb.* Leiden/Boston.

Codices Avestici et Pahlavici Universitatis Hafniensis 1934. *Vol. III: The Pahlavi Codex K35. First part containing the Pahlavi Rivāyat I, Dādhastān ē Dēnīgh and the Pahlavi Rivāyat II.* With an introduction by A. CHRISTENSEN. Copenhagen.

COLDITZ, I 2015: "Iteration im zoroastrischen Recht. Rechtsfindung zwischen kanonischer Norm und Rechtspraxis". In: E. CANCIK-KIRSCHBAUM/A. TRANINGER (eds.): *Wissen in Bewegung. Institution – Iteration – Transfer.* Wiesbaden (Episteme in Bewegung. Beiträge zu einer transdisziplinären Wissensgeschichte 1), pp. 223–239.

GIGNOUX, PH./A. TAFAZZOLI 1993: *Anthologie de Zādspram.* Paris (Studia Iranica Cahier 13).

HINTZE, A. 2009 [2005]: "The Cow that Came from the Moon. The Avestan expression *māh- gaociϑra-*." In: C. ALTMAN BROMBERG/N. SIMS-WILLIAMS/U. SIMS-WILLIAMS (eds.): *Iranian and Zoroastrian Studies in Honor of Prods Oktor Skjærvø. Bulletin of the Asia Institute* 19, pp. 59–68.

JAAFARI-DEHAGHI, M. 1998: *Dādestān ī Dēnīg.* Part I: *Transcription, Translation and Commentary.* Paris (Studia Iranica Cahier 20).

JANY, J. 2017: "Übermittler von Rechtswissen in der zoroastrischen, jüdischen und islamischen Rechtskultur: *Dādestān, Responsa, Fatwā.*" In: I. COLDITZ/B. JOKISCH/M. MACUCH (eds.): *Transferprozesse in spätantiken Rechtssystemen. Rezeption, Transformation und Rekontextualisierung von Rechtsbegriffen.* Wiesbaden (Episteme in Bewegung 10), pp. 31–42.

KÖNIG, G. 2005: "Zur Figur des "Wahrhaftigen Menschen" *(mard ī ahlaw)* in der zoroastrischen Literatur." In: *Zeitschrift der Deutschen Morgenländischen Gesellschaft* 155, pp. 161–188.

KOTWAL, F.M. and KREYENBROEK, PH.G. 1995: *The Hērbedestān and Nērangestān.* Vol. II: *Nērangestān, Fragard 1.* Paris (Studia Iranica Cahier 16).

— 2003: *The Hērbedestān and Nērangestān.* Vol. III: *Nērangestān, Fragard 2.* Paris (Studia Iranica Cahier 30).

KREYENBROEK, PH. 1995: "The Introduction to the *Dādestān ī Dēnīg.*" In: R. GYSELEN (ed.): *Au Carrefour des Religions. Mélanges offerts à Philippe Gignoux.* Bures-sur-Yvette (Res Orientales VII), pp. 171–176.

MACKENZIE, D.N. 1971: *A Concise Pahlavi Dictionary.* London.

MACUCH, M. 1981: *Das sasanidische Rechtsbuch Mātakdān i hazār Dātistān (Teil II).* (Abhandlungen für die Kunde des Morgenlandes XLV, 1). Wiesbaden.

— 1990: "Eine alte Bemessungsgrundlage für die 'Tagesration' in den Pahlavi-Schriften." In: R. GYSELEN (ed.): *Salaires, prix, poids et mesures.* Paris (Res Orientales II), pp. 139–142.

— 1993: *Rechtskasuistik und Gerichtspraxis zu Beginn des siebenten Jahrhunderts in Iran: Die Rechtssammlung des Farroḫmard i Wahrāmān.* Wiesbaden (Iranica 1).

— 2003: "On the Treatment of Animals in Zoroastrian Law." In: A. VAN TONGERLOO (ed.): *Iranica Selecta: Studies in honour of Professor Wojciech Skalmowski on the occasion of his seventieth birthday.* Turnhout (Silk Road Studies 8), pp. 167–190.

— 2009: "Pahlavi Literature." In: R.E. EMMERICK/M. MACUCH (eds.): *The Literature of Pre-Islamic Iran. Companion Volume I to A History of Persian Literature.* (History of Persian Literature XVII) London, pp. 116–190.

— 2010: "Legal Constructions of Identity in the Sasanian Period." In: C.G. CERETI (ed.): *Iranian Identity in the Course of History. Proceedings of the Conference Held in Rome, 21–24 September 2005.* Roma (Orientalia Romana 9), pp. 193–212.
— 2017a: "Pahlavi Legal Documents from Tabarestān on Lease, Loan and Compensation: The Juristic Context (Tab. 13,14, 15, 17, 18, 23)". In: R. GYSELEN (ed.): *Sasanian Coins, Middle-Persian Etymology and the Tabarestān Archive.* Bures-sur-Yvette (Res Orientales XXVI), pp. 165–195.
— 2017b: "A Case of Loan and Mortgage in a Late Pahlavi Text". In: Team "Turfanforschung" (ed.): *Zur Lichten Heimat. Studien zu Manichäismus, Iranistik und Zentralasienkunde im Gedenken an Werner Sundermann.* Wiesbaden (Iranica 25), pp. 355–370.
— 2019: "A Pahlavi Legal Term in Jesubōxt's Corpus Iuris." In: J. RUBANOVICH/G. HERMAN (eds.): *Irano-Judaica VII: Studies Relating to Jewish Contacts with Persian Culture Throughout the Ages.* Jerusalem, pp. 73–102.
— 2022: "A Legal Transaction in the Zoroastrian Community and its Social Consequences." In: A. CANTERA/M. MACUCH/N. SIMS-WILLIAMS (eds.): *The Reward of the Righteous. Festschrift in Honour of Almut Hintze.* Wiesbaden (Iranica 30), pp. 307–320.
DE MENASCE, J. 1962: "La 'Rivāyat d'Ēmēt i Ašavahištān". In: *Revue de l'Histoire des Religions* 162, pp. 69–88.
— 1973: *Le troisième livre du Dēnkart.* Paris (Bibliothèque des Oeuvres Classiques Persanes 4).
MOAZAMI, M. 2014: *Wrestling with the Demons of the Pahlavi Widēwdēd. Transcription, Translation and Commentary.* Leiden/Boston (Iran Studies 9).
MODI, J.J. 1937: *The Religious Ceremonies and Customs of the Parsees.* Bombay.
NYBERG, H.S. 1974: *A Manual of Pahlavi.* Part II: *Glossary.* Wiesbaden.
Pahlavi Codices and Iranian Researches 1978. Vol. 52, *Manuscript TD4a. The Pahlavi Rivāyat, Dātistān-i Dīnīk, Nāmakīhā-i Manushchihr and Vichītakīhā-i Zātasparam etc.* K.M. JAMASPASA, M. NAWABI, M. TAVOUSI (eds.). Shiraz.
REMPIS, CH. 1951: "Die ältesten Dichtungen in Neupersisch." In: *Zeitschrift der Deutschen Morgenländischen Gesellschaft* 101, pp. 220–240.
SACHAU, E. 1914: *Syrische Rechtsbücher, 3. Band: Corpus juris des persischen Erzbischofs Jesubocht. Erbrecht oder Canones des persischen Erzbischofs Simeon. Eherecht des Patriarchen Mâr Abhâ.* Berlin.
SAFA-ISFEHANI, N. 1980: *Rivāyat-ī Hēmīt-ī Ašawahištān. A Study in Zoroastrian Law.* Cambridge, Mass. (Harvard Iranian Series 2).
SHAKED, SH. 1979: *The Wisdom of the Sasanian Sages (Dēnkard VI).* Boulder, Colorado (Persian Heritage Series 34).
— 1987: "Paymān: An Iranian Idea in Contact with Greek Thought and Islam." In: *Transition Periods in Iranian History.* Leuven (Studia Iranica. Cahier 5), pp. 217–240.
— 2022: "Piety in Pahlavi Literature. Notes on *mard ī ahlaw* and Other Themes." In: A. CANTERA/M. MACUCH/N. SIMS-WILLIAMS (eds.): *The Reward of the Righteous. Festschrift in Honour of Almut Hintze.* Wiesbaden (Iranica 30), pp. 467–480.
TAFAZZOLI, A. 1971: "Pahlavica." In: *Acta Orientalia* XXXIII, pp. 193–204.
VEVAINA, Y.S.-D. 2023: *The Sūdgar Nask of Dēnkard Book 9. Text, Translation and Critical Apparatus.* Wiesbaden (Iranica 31).

— 2024: *Zoroastrian Hermeneutics in Late Antiquity. Commentary on the Sūdgar Nask, Dēnkard Book 9.* Wiesbaden (Iranica 32).

Weber, D. 2014: "Arabic Activities Reflected in the Documents of the 'Pahlavi Archive' (late 7th and early 8th centuries)." In: R. Gyselen (ed.): *Documents, argenteries et monnaies de tradition sassanide.* Bures-sur-Yvette (Res Orientales XXII) pp. 179–188.

— 2017: "Pahlavi Legal Documents from Tabarestān on Lease, Loan and Compensation: A Philological Study (Tab. 13, 14, 15, 17, 18, 23)." In: R. Gyselen (ed.): *Sasanian Coins, Middle-Persian Etymology and the Tabarestān Archive.* Bures-sur-Yvette (Res Orientales XXVI), pp. 131–163.

— 2020: "Living together in Changing Iran. Pahlavi Documents on Arabs and Christians in Early Islamic Times." In: *Annales islamologiques* 54, pp. 139–164.

West, E.W. 1882: *The Dādistān-ī Dīnīk and the Epistles of Mānuškīhar.* Oxford (Sacred Books of the East, 18) [reprint 1965].

Williams, A.V. 1990: *The Pahlavi Rivāyat Accompanying the Dādestān ī Dēnīg,* Part I: *Transliteration, Transcription and Glossary;* Part II: *Translation, Commentary and Pahlavi Text.* Copenhagen.

Blowing out *saṃsāra* in Khotan

MAURO MAGGI, Rome

By spotting ghost words in the secondary literature on Khotanese, I have taken part on several occasions in what HAROLD W. BAILEY styled 'an easy old game, hunting the hapax' and what he described as '[t]hat kind of scholarship [which] removes all the interesting words from the dictionaries', as RONALD E. EMMERICK reported.[1] It is scarcely with any hesitation, however, that I now suggest recognising a previously unidentified word, virtually a hapax, in the tenth-century Late Khotanese *Book of Vimalakīrti* (Vim for short), where *kṣąca* occurs twice in a single passage in the Paris manuscript (verses 242c and 244d, see below). This lexical study is offered as a tribute to a devoted scholar and fine philologist who has made significant contributions to our knowledge of Iranian languages, including Khotanese.[2]

BAILEY read the word in question as *kṣāṃca* in both editions of the third volume of his *Khotanese texts*, but did not include it in his *Dictionary of Khotan Saka*. Since '[t]he Buddhist Sanskrit vocabulary, and particularly the varieties of Prakrit, ... with few exceptions are excluded' from the *Dictionary*,[3] BAILEY must have regarded the word as of Indian origin, maybe as an oblique case or a derivative of *kṣāṃtti-* 'patience, acceptance', a loanword from the still imperfectly understood Buddhist Sanskrit technical term *kṣānti-* 'intellectual receptivity; the being ready in advance to accept knowledge' (from *kṣam-* 'to be patient, endure; to forgive; to allow; etc').[4] Whether this was BAILEY's idea or not, *kṣāṃtti-*, which is also contained in the compound *anąpattya-kṣātta* 'acceptance that phenomena have no origination' immediately after the first occurrence of *kṣāṃca*, does not fit the context and occurs only in Late Khotanese where it is extremely rare.[5]

1 See EMMERICK 2002, p. 11.

2 I am grateful to ALESSANDRO DEL TOMBA, BHIKKHUNĪ DHAMMADINNĀ, and DOUG HITCH for the useful suggestions they made after reading a draft of this article.

3 Dict. vii.

4 See BHSD 199 and cf. MW 326.

5 E.g. Vim 215 (IOL Khot S 10 375 Catalogue 498) *kṣ⟨ā⟩\tta/* = (P 2026 10 KT 3.48) *kṣāṃttä* (I number verses according to my unpublished edition of the text). More frequent is Old Khotanese *kṣāndi-*, borrowed through Prakrit as voicing of *-nt-* to *-nd-* indicates, which is the only form to be found in the fifth-century *Book of Zambasta* (see LEUMANN 1933–1936, p. 414).

I think that *kṣāṃca* is spelled with unetymological *anusvāra* and should be transcribed as *kṣąca*, that it means 'blowing out (a flame), extinguishing' as we shall see presently, and that the passage where it occurs (Vim 242–244 [P 2026 55–59 KT 3.50]) should be read and translated thus:[6]

242 *parąmārtha bāvaña ṣṭāna*
ku ṣṭa na rū aśta na saña
na vā sa[ṃ](56)*tsārä*[7] *na kṣąca*
ṣāʾ anąpattya-kṣātta agunai tsāṣṭä naṣāʾda \40 2/[8]

243 *ṣaʾ bvau*(57)*ma cu paysaida*
ṣaʾ rä jsāna bvāma pā rusta[9]
varä drąma na bīde
(58) *sa khu dai āca pasūśte*[10] *\40 3/*[11]

244 *sa* ra *va*[12] *beʾysūśtä harśtä*
ttaña beḍa vasva akhauṣṭa
kū (59)*ṣṭa na rū aśtä*[13] *na saña*
na vā satsārä na kṣąca

'(242) When one is staying in meditation on the ultimate reality (*paramārtha*), where there is neither form (*rūpa*) nor notion (*saṃjñā*), neither cycle of birth (*saṃsāra*) nor 'blowing out' (Kh. *kṣąca*), (then) this acceptance that phenomena have no origination (*anutpattika-(dharma)-kṣānti*) is markless, calm, tranquil. (243) The (analytical) knowledge, when one recognises (by it the ultimate reality), also this knowledge is indeed then lost. No such thing is found there (any more) just as a flame of fire burns (and leaves no trace of the fire-drill used to kindle it). (244) And only awakening remains there at that time, pure, unmoved, where there is neither form (*rūpa*) nor notion (*saṃjñā*), neither cycle of birth (*saṃsāra*) nor 'blowing out' (Kh. *kṣąca*).'

My translation of v. 243 basically follows the one offered by EMMERICK in *Studies in the vocabulary of Khotanese*, who removed the ⟨*na*⟩ unnecessarily supple-

6 The passage is not preserved in the London manuscript (IOL Khot S 10 = Ch. 00266 224–386 Catalogue 489–499). The following conventions are used: *italics* (or roman in quotations in italics) = letters not entirely visible (manuscript partially broken or erased); [abc] = restoration of a lacuna (manuscript broken or erased); [[abc]] = deletion by the copyist; \abc/ = interlinear addition in connection with an insertion mark (absence of the mark is pointed out in a note); <abc> = editorial supplement where the manuscript has no lacuna. Manuscript line numbers are raised and enclosed in parentheses. In the translation, the Sanskrit original forms of the technical Buddhist loanwords occurring in the text are included in parentheses.

7 Restoration by BAILEY.

8 *40 2* under *da* without insertion mark.

9 BAILEY *pārusta*.

10 BAILEY supplements ⟨*na*⟩ before *pasūśte*.

11 *40 3* under *dai* without insertion mark.

12 BAILEY *sarava*.

13 BAILEY *aśtą*.

mented by BAILEY before *pasūśte*: 'This bodhi, when one recognises (by it the ultimate reality, *paramārtha*)—this bodhi is indeed then lost. No such (thing) is found there just as a flame of fire burns'.[14] The verse is in all likelihood an abridged quotation from *Ratnakūṭa* (*Kāśyapaparivarta*) 69: *tad yathā kāśyapa kāṣṭhadvayaṃ pratītyāgnir jāyate iti jātaś ca samānas tad eva kāṣṭhadvayaṃ dahati | evam eva kāśyapa bhūtapratyavekṣāṃ pratītyāryaṃ prajñendriyaṃ jāyate jātaṃ ca tām eva bhūtapratyavekṣāṃ dahatīti*[15] 'Just as, O Kāśyapa, from a couple of pieces of wood fire is born and, as soon as fire is born, it burns up that very couple of pieces of wood, exactly so, O Kāśyapa, from the analytical knowledge of reality the noble faculty of wisdom is born and, once it is born, it burns up exactly that analytical knowledge of reality (from which it was born)'.

It is worth noting in passing that the third singular present indicative active *pasūśte* 'burns' (< Old Khotanese **pasuśtä* with short *u*) is the only occurrence of the 'inchoative' **pasus-* 'to burn' (formally active but with intransitive meaning), which is formed and inflected like *vasus-* 'to become pure, be purified' (third singular *vasuśtä*) from the Iranian root **sau̯č-* 'to burn'. This **pasus-* can thus be added to the fifty-eight Khotanese *s*-verbs without Old Iranian antecedents and largely constituting a Middle Iranian innovation, as was shown by DIETER WEBER, and brings the total of such verbs to fifty-nine and from 87% to no less than 92% of all Khotanese *s*-verbs.[16]

Coming back to *kṣa̧ca*, it should first be made clear that the passage under consideration refers to the Mahāyānist and more specifically Mādhyamika conception that, through analytical knowledge of the everyday world and then through meditative absorption beyond discursive thought, one attains the superior knowledge of the ultimate truth, according to which all things have no independent origination and are empty of intrinsic existence: even the cycle of births (*saṃsāra*) and its extinction (*nirvāṇa*) are identical in that they both are intrinsically non-existent, so that '*nirvāṇa* is attainable here and now through the correct understanding of the empty nature of the here and now [*saṃsāra*] and then through letting it all go'.[17]

14 See Studies 1.70–71 and cf. 20–21 on BAILEY's ⟨*na*⟩.

15 The text is taken from the quotation in Sthiramati's *Madhyāntavibhāgaṭīkā* (ed. PANDEYA 1971, p. 184), as the paragraph is not entirely preserved in the Sanskrit original due to a lacuna of three folios in the manuscript. See MAGGI 2005 for a discussion of the quotations of *Ratnakūṭa* 69 in *Book of Zambasta* 4.95, 8.44, 9.16, and the Late Khotanese *Mañjuśrīnarātmyāvatārasūtra* P 4099 392–393 KBT 133.

16 See SGS 79 s.v. *pasūjs-* and cf. WEBER 1970, pp. 275–276 s.v. *vasus-* and 306–307. EMMERICK's wording in Studies 1.20 may give the erroneous impression that *pasūśte* is from *pasūjs-*, which is not the case since its third singular pasūste is well attested in both Old and Late Khotanese. BAILEY's **pa(ti)-saučati* as the antecedent of *pasūśte* in Dict. 225 is possible but not very likely because in this case *pasūśte* (< OKh. **pasūśtä* with long *ū* and the palatalising ending *-ʲtä*, cf. *sūśtä* from the simplex *sūjs-*, SGS 193 no. 1) would be third singular active of *pasūjs-*, which, however, is regularly conjugated in the middle.

17 See WILLIAMS 2009, pp. 74–79 (quotation from p. 76, italics added) for a general summary exposition of these concepts with reference to the sources.

It is apparent that *kṣą̄ca* is an occasional translation for *nirvāṇa*. Exegetical translations of this kind are also to be found, in the *Book of Vimalakīrti*, with the names of the ten stages of the bodhisattva path (*bhūmi*), whose Sanskrit names are either mentioned or simply implied and then provided with explanations that include their Khotanese renderings. For an example, the explanation of the fourth stage omits its Sanskrit name *arciṣmatī* and runs thus: Vim 100 (IOL Khot S 10 = Ch. 00266 224) Catalogue 489 *ācausta tcūra*[[+]]*ma*[18] *y⟨ā⟩va padaśta aharīne kīḍaiśa'* 'The fourth (stage) is "flaming" (Kh. *ācausta* = Skt. *arciṣmatī*) until it burns his (i.e. the bodhisattva's) afflictions (*kleśa*) entirely'.[19]

Formally, the form *kṣāṃca* in the manuscript looks like a derivative containing the suffix *-kyā-/-cā-*, which forms nouns from nouns, adjectives, past participles, and present stems. Derivatives from verb stems (past or present) are usually abstract nouns.[20] Derivation from **kṣaunda-*, past participle to *kṣam-* 'to endure; to please; to forgive', is not only semantically unfitting, but is also phonologically impossible because of the lack of voicing of the suffix to *-gyā-/-jā-*, which is expected with past participles ending in *-da-*[21] and which would have given **kṣauṃjā-*. Skt. *nirvāṇa* 'extinction' is from the root ²*vā-* 'to pass by; to exhaust, extinguish' (< Indo-European **h₁u̯eh₂-*)[22] and, actually, 'the extinguishing of fire ... is the prevailing Buddhist conception of the term'. However, 'in the older texts do we find references to a simile of the wind and the flame',[23] that is, to extinction of fire by blowing, which points to a folk-etymological connection with the root ¹*vā-* 'to blow' (< Indo-European **h₂u̯eh₁-*).[24] In light of the old simile of *nirvāṇa* as the extinction of a fire by wind, it is possible to suggest an interpretation and an etymology of *kṣāṃca*.

The blowing of wind is expressed in the *Book of Zambasta* by the verb ¹*kṣäv-*, which EMMERICK translated 'to throw' in his *Saka grammatical studies* and 'to toss (about)' in the *Book of Zambasta*. EMMERICK was probably right in assigning ¹*kṣäv-* 'to throw' (< **kṣuv-*, cf. *nikṣuv-* 'to urge') and its passive *kṣiy-* 'to be thrown' to the Ir. root **xšaub-* (cf. Avestan *xšuf-sa-* 'to become agitated', Skt. *kṣubh-* 'to shake, tremble, be agitated') and in suggesting that '[a] suppletive system < O.Ir. **xšvaip-* and **xšaub-* is ... possible' and that '[p]ossibly *kṣäv-* and [*]*kṣuv-* have been conflated'. Such a conflation is very likely because of the semantic and phonetic proximity of the two Ir. roots **xšu̯aib-* 'to vibrate, tremble, shake' and **xšaub-* 'to rustle, tremble':[25] the transitive ¹*kṣäv-* is from

18 In the 2nd ed. of KBT, Bailey reads *tcūra buma* straightaway, but the third *akṣara* was deleted by the copyist.

19 My translation. See MAGGI 2004, esp. pp. 132 and 134–135.

20 See DEGENER 1989, pp. 199-200 §§ 38.1, 38.3.1–4, and 38.4.3.

21 DEGENER 1989, pp. 199–200 §§ 38.3.1.

22 EWAia 2.538 s.v. *vā²* and LIV 254.

23 PTSD 362 s.v. *nibbāna*.

24 EWAia 2.537 s.v. *vā¹* and LIV 287.

25 EDIV 459 s.v. **xšu̯aip/b*, 454 s.v. **xšaub*. See PANAINO 1990, p. 96 on Avestan *xšuuaēβa-* 'vibrant, sparkling' with further references. The stem of the Khotanese passive can be

*xšub-ai̯a-/xšu̯ib-ai̯a-; the intransitive (= passive) *kṣi-* is from *xšub-i̯a-/xšu̯ib-i̯a-; and the past participle *kṣautta-* is from *xšaufta- (to *xšaub-).[26] His translation of these verbs, however, apparently still depended on their superseded etymological interpretation by ERNST LEUMANN as cognates of Skt. *kṣip-* 'to throw' (Ir. *xšaip-).[27] The meanings of ^{1}*kṣäv-* and *kṣi-* need, therefore, to be clarified by reviewing their occurrences in the *Book of Zambasta* (Z for short) — where they are only to be found, including the occurrence in Z 4.63 that EMMERICK ascribed to ^{2}*kṣäv-* 'to cry (of birds)'[28] — and by verifying whether the basic meaning 'to make tremble, shake' of the root (in transitive forms) suits the contexts. In particular, since all passages involve wind as the subject or the agent (*padama-* and *bāta-* 'wind', *branthi-* 'whirlwind'), a first possible semantic specialisation is from a general '*to make tremble, shake' — established by comparison but not actually attested in Khotanese — to a more specific 'to blow about (of wind)':[29]

Z 2.43 *ku vā dumä sarbätä mästä grraśdīndi gguvaṭhuta dāña haṃdāri ṣṭāna kṣiyāre huṣka āhūḍe padamna* '... *elsewhere* [EMMERICK: Where][30] much smoke rises [in the cemetery], there are stewing (things) half-burnt in the fire. Other, dry bones are being *blown about* [EMMERICK: thrown about] by the wind';

Z 2.44 *ggūne pharu śśāre tcabrīye diśe vīri brīnthe jsa kṣautte* 'Many hairs lie scattered [in the cemetery], *blown about* [EMMERICK: tossed] in (all) directions by a whirlwind';

Z 4.62-63 *bāta varata nuṣṭhura tsīndä ... dī kuṃbiye dau ni buysairu diśe vīri ṣṣundä kṣävīru* '(62) The winds there [i.e. in hell] become fierce ... (63) Would they not extinguish the fire under the pot (and) *blow about* [^{1}*kṣäv-*] the ravens in (all) directions [if these things would indeed exist]?[31] [EMMERICK: The ravens would caw in (all) directions (^{2}*kṣäv-*; without question mark)]';

---

conveniently described as *kṣi-* according to HITCH (2016, pp. 285, 288).

26 SGS 24–25 (cf. KT 6.55 s.v. *kṣäv-*); DEGENER 1989, p. 225 § 42.6.16 f–g.

27 See LEUMANN 1933–1936, p. 414. Derivation from *xšaip- (still in EDIV 452–453) is unsatisfactory, as it does not explain the past participle *kṣautta-*. HITCH (2016, p. 285 n. 36), who basically keeps EMMERICK's meanings and LEUMANN's etymology, renounces distinguishing between ^{1}*kṣäv-* and ^{2}*kṣäv-* ['to cry'] and suggests 'that *xšaip- ['to throw' after EDIV] and *xšai- ['be anxious, worried, lament, weep' after EDIV] have merged in Khotanese, with the former as the active *kṣäv-* and the latter as the passive *kṣi-* ['to be disturbed'] counterpart, but both carrying the blended semantics'.

28 SGS 25: '< *xšiu̯-, u̯-extension to *xšai- "lament"' (cf. KT 6.55–56 s.v. *kṣävīru*, Dict. 68, and EDIV 452 s.v. *xšai). The only two remaining attested forms of ^{2}*kṣäv-* are the third singular present indicative LKh. P 2936 6 KT 3.108 *kṣavū* (< *kṣavä < OKh. *kṣävätä + *u* 'and') and the third plural present optative LKh. P 2891 39 KT 3.81 *kṣvīrä*.

29 I take Z quotations and translations from EMMERICK 1968 unless otherwise indicated; in translations, my alternative renderings are in *italics* and my amplifications and additions in square brackets.

30 This verse follows a lacuna of one folio and the collocation *ku vā* is in all likelihood part of a sequence *ku vā ... ku vā ...* 'somewhere ..., elsewhere ...' (cf. MAGGI 2017, p. 155 n. 21).

31 So already LEUMANN 1933–1936, p. 60: 'würden sie die Raben treiben [oder: aussenden]?'.

Z 20.40 *ggūne padamna kṣautte vūmūva jāte* 'Their hair is *blown about* [EMMERICK: tossed about] by the wind [in the cemetery], scattered, destroyed';

Z 20.48-49 *ṣṣamana dätāndi kädä nu udvīyu hämäte trām[u] nä aursi brrītye jsa īṣṭä puṣṣo 8 kho ju dai mästä . kvī padamä kṣävätä puṣṣo o* ... '(48) The monks saw [the cemetery and the rotting corpses exposed there]. Very great disgust arose in them. So did their desire turn back completely from passion, (49) as a great fire when the wind utterly *blows* it *out* [← 'to blow about (of wind)', see below] or ... (EMMERICK: So did their desire turn back completely from passion. As a great fire when the wind utterly tosses it or ...)'.

Z 21.23 *nauni bajāṣṣä . karä ni paphanīndi gguvaʾ padamäna kṣyār[e] ttā ttin[* 'No soft sounds [from the lips of the now dead women] gladden the ears. They are *blown about* [EMMERICK: tossed about] by the wind [in the cemetery] ...' (the subject is unfortunately lost in the gap).

Though the blowing of wind rather encourages a large fire, the use of the verb *buysai-* 'to extinguish' in Z 4.63[32] proves that extinction of fire by wind was actually contemplated and lends support to my translation 'the wind utterly blows it out' in Z 20.49. A semantic development [1] '*to make tremble, shake' → [2] 'to blow about (of wind)' (Z 2.44, 4.63, 20.40) → [3] 'to blow out, extinguish (fire by wind)' (Z 20.49) is well conceivable.

The shift [1] '*to make tremble, shake' → [2] 'to blow about (of wind)' may have been favoured by the Indo-Iranian initial consonant cluster **kš(u̯)-* that is found with an onomatopoeic effect in roots that involve moving air and producing fizzling and acute sounds (cf. Ir. **xšnauš-* 'to sneeze' and **xšu̯aid-* 'to whistle'; Skt. *kṣav-* 'to sneeze' and *kṣved-/kṣveḍ-* 'to squeak (of wheels)'), as DOUG HITCH suggests to me.[33]

The further shift [2] 'to blow about (of wind)' → [3] 'to blow out, extinguish (fire by wind)' is natural and finds confirmation precisely in our *kṣāṃca*.

In fact, if read as *kṣą̄ca* with unetymological anusvāra, the word can be safely regarded as a variant spelling for **kṣauca* on account of the common Late Khotanese alternation *au/ą̄*. Morphologically, this **kṣaucā-* is easily explained as a *-kyā-/-cā-* derivative from *kṣautta-*, the past participle of ¹*kṣäv-* (and *kṣi-*). As for semantics, **kṣaucā-* is employed in the *Book of Vimalakīrti* passage in the sense of 'blowing out' and provides a literal translation of Skt. *nirvāṇa* according to the early Buddhist exegetical tradition.

32 Cf. SGS 101. The stem is better described as *buysa-* (see HITCH 2017, esp. p. 518).

33 Letter of 13 August 2020. See EDIV 458 and EWAia 1.429–430, 441 for the roots and their probable onomatopoeic character.

Bibliography

BHSD = F. Edgerton 1953: *Buddhist Hybrid Sanskrit grammar and dictionary. 2: Dictionary.* New Haven.

Catalogue = P.O. Skjærvø 2002: *Khotanese manuscripts from Chinese Turkestan in the British Library: a complete catalogue with texts and translations*, with contributions by U. Sims-Williams. London.

Degener, A. 1989: *Khotanische Suffixe.* Stuttgart.

Dict. = H.W. Bailey 1979: *Dictionary of Khotan Saka.* Cambridge.

EDIV = J. Cheung 2007: *Etymological dictionary of the Iranian verb.* Leiden.

Emmerick, R.E. 1968: *The Book of Zambasta, a Khotanese poem on Buddhism.* London.

— 2002: "Hunting the hapax: Sir Harold W. Bailey (1899-1996)". In: N. Sims-Williams (ed.): *Indo-Iranian languages and peoples.* London, pp. 1–17.

EWAia = M. Mayrhofer 1992–2001: *Etymologisches Wörterbuch des Altindoarischen.* Heidelberg: 1: 1992; 2: 1996; 3: 2001.

Hitch, D. 2016: "Contracted semivowels in Old Khotanese". In: *Indo-Iranian journal* 59, pp. 259–294.

— 2017: "Old Khotanese type A stems in *-a-* and *-e-*". In: *Bulletin of the School of Oriental and African Studies* 80, pp. 491–523.

KBT = H.W. Bailey 1951: *Khotanese Buddhist texts.* London [2nd ed. Cambridge 1981).

KT 1–7 = H.W. Bailey 1945–1985: *Khotanese texts.* Cambridge: 1: 1945; 2: 1954; 3: 1956 [1–3, 2nd ed. in one vol., 1969; repr. 1980]; 4: *Saka texts from Khotan in the Hedin collection.* 1961 [repr. 1979]; 5: 1963 [repr. with corrections 1980]; 6: *Prolexis to the Book of Zambasta.* 1967; 7: 1985.

Leumann, E. 1933–1936: *Das nordarische (sakische) Lehrgedicht des Buddhismus: Text und Übersetzung*, aus dem Nachlaß hrsg. von M. Leumann. Brockhaus.

LIV = Rix, H. 2001: *Lexikon der indogermanischen Verben: die Wurzeln und ihre Primärstammbildungen*, bearb. von M. Kümmel *et al.*, 2., erw. und verb. Aufl., bearb. von M. Kümmel und H. Rix. Reichert.

Maggi, M. 2004: 'Le bhūmi nel *Libro di Vimalakīrti* cotanese.' In: C.G. Cereti /B. Melasecchi/F. Vajifdar (eds.): *Orientalia Romana. 7: Varia Iranica*, Roma, pp. 131–136.

Maggi, M. 2005: "Annotations on the *Book of Zambasta*, II: Khotanese *maṃkyā-*". In: *Bulletin of the Asia Institute*, n.s. 19 (*Iranian and Zoroastrian studies in honor of Prods Oktor Skjærvø*), pp. 103–109.

— 2017: "Khotanese *baṣṣä* and *bihaḍe*". In: A. Crisanti *et al.* (eds.): *Anantaratnaprabhava: studi in onore di Giuliano Boccali.* Milano, pp. 153–162.

MW = M. Monier-Williams 1899: *A Sanskrit-English dictionary.* Oxford.

Panaino, A. 1990: *Tištriya.* 1: *The Avestan hymn to Sirius.* Roma.

Pandeya, R.: 1971: *Madhyānta-vibhāga-śāstra, containing the Kārikā-s of Maitreya, Bhāṣya of Vasubhandhu and Ṭīkā by Sthiramati.* Delhi.

PTSD = T.W. Rhys Davids/W. Stede 1921–1925: *The Pali Text Society's Pali-English dictionary.* Oxford.

SGS = R.E. Emmerick 1968: *Saka grammatical studies.* London.

Studies 1 = R.E. Emmerick/P.O. Skjærvø 1982–1997: *Studies in the vocabulary of Khotanese.* Wien: 1: 1982; 2: 1987; 3: ed. by R.E. Emmerick, contributed by G. Canevascini *et al*, 1997.

WEBER, D. 1970: *Die Stellung der sog[enannten] Inchoativa im Mitteliranischen.* Göttingen.
WILLIAMS, P. 2009: *Mahāyāna Buddhism: the doctrinal foundations.* 2nd ed. Abingdon.

A Brief Note on an Avestan Quotation in the *Wizīrgerd ī Dēnīg*[1]

Jaime Martínez Porro, Berlin

The meta-ritual texts of Pahlavi and Persian literature (i.e. especially the *Nērangestān* and the Persian *Revāyāts*) are fundamental tools for reconstructing the texts of the Zoroastrian rituals in the Avestan language. They also play an important role for the analysis of the ritual instructions in Pahlavi, Persian and Gujarati accompanying the Avestan texts. Besides these sources other literary works in Pahlavi, such as the *Šāyešt nē Šāyešt* or the *Wizīrgerd ī Dēnīg*, also convey important information on the rituals in the Avestan language.

Thanks to the analysis of the entire aforementioned material progress has been made in research in recent years regarding the performative dimension of Avestan rituals, which is essential for a deeper comprehension of the texts and the connection between text, recitation and ritual performance. This new approach has been mostly developed within the projects Avestan Digital Archive (ADA) and Corpus Avesticum Berolinense (CAB).[2]

The present brief note deals with the following text in the *Wizīrgerd ī Dēnīg* (Sanjana 1848, pp. 184–185):

> ʾywk Z̲NE AYK̲ BYN pnck OD whyštwyšt AYK̲ hmsptmmydym [Y] BYRH Y sp̄ndrmt BYN ycšnʾ W nydʾdšnʾ W dlwn yštnʾ LA šʾyt KLYTWNtnʾ ME Z̲NE 5 YWM MN BYRH ywdtʾk YHS̲NNt YKOYMWNyt cygwn MN ʾp̄stʾk Y nygʾtwm pytʾk
> *āaṯ aētahē paṇca aiiara hamaspϑmaiδəm paiti ratūm spəṇtaiiā̊ ārmitōiš mā̊ŋhō nōiṯ frasrāuuaiiōiṯ*

1 This article originated within the project “Corpus Avesticum: eine text-kritische Edition der zoroastrischen Rituale in awestischer Sprache” (CA 955/2-2), funded by the Deutsche Forschungsgemeinschaft. The numbering follows the one of the ceremonies as they are displayed at the CAB-website (https://cab.geschkult.fu-berlin.de/). There, an explanation to the numbering is provided (https://cab.geschkult.fu-berlin.de/exist/apps/cab/files/The_Numbering_in_CAB.pdf).

2 Several contributions have been dedicated to this specific subject within this framework, such as the reconstruction of the ceremony of Visperad-e Dō-Hōmāst (Cantera 2020; Cantera/Martínez Porro 2022), the performative variation in the rituals of the last ten days of the year (Cantera 2018) and the variation in the *šnūman* in the ceremonies of intercalation depending on the occasions when they were performed (Martínez Porro 2022). Furthermore, an edition of the ritual instructions in Pahlavi is under preparation (Cantera *forthcoming*). An edition of ritual instructions in Gujarati for the Paragnā, Yasna and Visperad (Redard/Daruwalla 2021) has already been prepared in the context of the MUYA project.

ʾytwn' Z̲K 5 YWM hmsptmydym Q̲DM ltyh sp̄ndrmt bwndk mynšn' mʾh AYK̲ sp̄ndrmt BYRH LA prʾc slʾyt AYK̲ LA KLYTWNyt ME HT MN plymwšyh Q̲DM KLYTWNyt ʾp̄stʾk ptylptk LA YHWWNyt.

ēk ēn kū andar panjag tā wahištōišt kū hamaspadmēdyam [ī] māh ī spandarmad andar yazišn ud neyāyešn ud drōn yaštan nē šāyed xwāndan čē ēn panj rōz az māh judāg dāšt estēd ciyōn az abastāg ī nigādom paydāg
āat̰ aētahē paṇca aiiara hamaspəϑmaiδəm paiti ratūm spəṇtaiiå ārmitōiš måŋhō nōit̰ frasrāuuaiiōit̰
ēdōn ēn panj rōz hamaspadmēdyam abar radīh spandarmad bowandag mēnišn māh kū spandarmad māh nē frāz srāyēd kū nē xwānēd čē az ⁺frāmōšīh abar xwānēd ābastag padīriftag nē bawēd.

"It is not admissible for the one who performs the Yasna, the Neyāyešn and the Drōn during the pentad until the (day) Wahištōišt — i.e. during the Hamaspadmēdyam — to recite the month of Spandarmad, since these five days are kept separated from the month. This way is revealed in the Avesta (in the text) of the Nigādom:
āat̰ aētahē paṇca aiiara hamaspəϑmaiδəm paiti ratūm spəṇtaiiå ārmitōiš måŋhō nōit̰ frasrāuuaiiōit̰
Thus, (in) these five days at the time of the Hamaspadmēdyam, he should not recite, he should not read the month of the right minded Spandarmad that is the month Spandarmad. If, by oversight, he reads it, the Avestan becomes inadmissible."

The most important part of this text is the Avestan ritual instruction. This falls within the same tradition of the well-known ritual quotations in the Avestan *Nērangestān*, which are very likely from an old period (Sasanian or Pre-Sasanian) when Avestan was still a living language, at least for the members of the clergy (CANTERA 2014, pp. 210ff.). The text shows, once again, a continuity in the performance of Avestan rituals despite some changes that occured between the last canonization of the rituals and the period of our first manuscripts (CANTERA 2014, pp. 187ff.). Specifically, we can compare the Avestan quotation in the *Wizīrgerd ī Dēnīg* with the information conveyed in Persian meta-ritual literature in one of the *Revāyāts*.

In the Persian *Revāyāt* of Kama Bohra, on the consecration of the *dar panǧi-ye veh*[3] *yazešn*[4], the question is as follows (UNVALA 1922, p. 453):[5]

3 A description of this pentad (*panǧi-ye veh*) is found in the Greater or Iranian *Bundahišn* 1A.22 (ANKLESARIA 1956, pp. 28–29): *nām ī ān 5 rōz truftag ast kē 5 gāh ī gāhānīg ast kē panjag ī weh gōwed. pad dēn ēn ast Ahunwayd gāh Uštawayd gāh Spandōmēn gāh Wohušahr gāh Wahištōišt gāh* "On the names of these five intercalary days, there is one who says 'the five periods of Gāhānīg', there is one who says 'the good pentad'. In the Dēn these are the period (day) Ahunwayd, the period (day) Uštawayd, the period (day) Spandōmēn, the period (day) Wohušahr and the period (day) Wahištōišt". In the *Revāyāt* they are called also the *panǧ ruz-e gāṣābiyo* "the five days of the *gāϑābiiō*" (the Av. word introducing both the date and the dedication during the Gāϑā-days) or *panǧi(-ye) veh* "the good pentad".

4 In this case Per. *yazešn* refers to the *Yasna* in the case of the *yazešn-e gāṣābiyo*, but to the *Visperad* in the *yazešn dar gāhānbār*, as the *karde* of the *Visperad* are quoted in the description of the ceremony.

5 I would like to thank BEHNAM ATAEI, graduate student at the Corpus Avesticum Berolinense, for the transliterations of the Persian texts. Translations were carried out by JAIME MARTINEZ PORRO.

> *yazešn dar panǧi-ye veh yazešn dar gāhānbār yazešn-e gāṣābiyo cun mibāyad kardan*
> "How should the Yasna be performed on the *panǧi-ye veh* (days), the Yasna with (the dedication of) Gāhānbār (or) the Yasna (with the dedication) of *gāṣābiyo* (Av. *gāϑābiiō*)?"

Afterwards, Kama Bohra gives both variants of the Yasna with the dedication of Gāhānbār and with the dedication of the *Gāϑās*. In both cases, the day and the month are recited the same way and the main difference is the dedication.[6]

In the case of the *yazešn dar gāhānbār*, the date is given just in dative (Unvala 1922, p. 454):

> (Av.) (Y1.12a) niuuaē. *negāh ruz māh* (Av.) gāϑābiiō spəṇtābiiō ratuxšaϑrābiiō aṣ̌ōnebiiō (Y1.12b) niuuaē. ahunuuiϑiiå. gāϑiiå.
> "(Av.) (Y1.12a) *niuuaē.* (and) he should observe the day and the month (Av.) *gāϑābiiō spəṇtābiiō ratuxšaϑrābiiō aṣ̌ōnebiiō* (Y1.12b) *niuuaē. ahunuuiϑiiå. gāϑiiå.*"

For the *yazešn-e gāṣābiyo*, the text is more complete, giving the date both in dative and accusative (Unvala 1922, pp. 455, 457)

> (Av.) (Y1.1a) niuuaēδiiemi haṇkāraiieme *tā sar* (Av.) (Y1.11a) miϑrahe daxiiunąm daŋhōpatōiš (Y1.12a) *negāh ruz māh* (Av.) gāϑābiiō spəṇtābiiō ratuxšaϑrābiiō aṣ̌aonebiiō (Y1.12b) niuuaē. ahunuuatiiå gāϑaiiå (Y1.13a) niuuaē. tauua āϑrō.
> "(Av.) (Y1.1a) *niuuaēδiiemi haṇkāraiieme* to the end (and recite) (Av.) (Y1.11a) *miϑrahe daxiiunąm daŋhōpatōiš* (Y1.12a). (He should) consider the day and the month (and recite) (Av.) *gāϑābiiō spəṇtābiiō ratuxšaϑrābiiō aṣ̌aonebiiō* (Y1.12b) *niuuaē. ahunuuatiiå gāϑaiiå* (Y1.13a) *niuuaē. tauua āϑrō.*"
> [...]
> (Av.) (Y6.1a) daδuuåŋhəm ahurəm mazdąm yaz. *tā* (Y6.10b) miϑrəm vīspanąm daxiiunąm daŋhupaitīm yaz. *negāh ruz māh* (Y6.11a) gāϑå spəṇtå ratuxšaϑrå aṣ̌aonīš yaz. (Y6.12a) ahunuuaitīm gāϑąm aṣ̌auuanəm aṣ̌ahe ratūm yaz. (Y6.13a) ϑβąm ātarəm
> "(Av.) (Y6.1a) *daδuuåŋhəm ahurəm mazdąm yaz.* until (Y6.10b) *miϑrəm vīspanąm daxiiunąm daŋhupaitīm yaz.* (He should) consider the day and the month (and recite) (Y6.11a) *gāϑå spəṇtå ratuxšaϑrå aṣ̌aonīš yaz.* (Y6.12a) *ahunuuaitīm gāϑąm aṣ̌auuanəm aṣ̌ahe ratūm yaz.* (Y6.13a) *ϑβąm ātarəm*".

The same applies for the Drōn, as it is again recorded in the *Revāyāt* of Kama Bohra (Unvala 1922, pp. 509–511). Moreover, in the *Revāyāt* of Kāmdin Šāpur we are informed how each single day of the pentad must be recited (Unvala 1922, pp. 573–574).[7]

6 See reconstruction of the ceremony of the last ten days of the year in Cantera (2018).

7 *dar panǧ ruz-e gāṣābiyo negāh pa ruz māh pa* (Av.) āiiese ẏešti *andar ruz-e pardom ahnavad geh* (Av.) gāϑābiiō spəṇtābiiō ratuxšaϑrābiiō aṣ̌aonibiiō āiie. ahunauuaitiiå gāϑaiiå āiie. *ruz-e dovvom pa oštavad geh* (Av.) gāϑābiiō spəṇtābiiō ratuxšaϑrābiiō aṣ̌aonibiiō āiie. uštauuaitiiå gāϑaiiå āiie. *ruz-e sevvom pa esfantmad geh* (Av.) gāϑābiiō spəṇtābiiō ratuxšaϑrābiiō aṣ̌aōnibiiō āiie. spəṇtā mainiiəuš gāϑaiiå āiie. *ruz-e cahārom pa vohuḫešatr gāh* (Av.) gāϑābiiō spəṇtābiiō ratuxšaϑrābiiō aṣ̌aonibiiō āiie. vōhuxšaϑraiiå gāϑaiiå āiie.

There is, however, one missing ceremony among those mentioned in the *Wizīrgerd ī Dēnīg*: the *Neyayešn*. According to GÖTZ KÖNIG,[8] the recitation of the date (the day and the month) is an innovation of the Indian priests as it only appears in the Indian manuscripts containing the *Neyayešn*. The date is absent in the Iranian manuscripts and there is no single trace suggesting that this text was lost in Iran at any point of the transmission.[9] Moreover, the mention of the date appears in the Indian manuscripts after the formulas that close the Avestan rituals,[10] which is an unexpected position for it.

If KÖNIG's suggestion is correct, this change in the text of the ritual should have occured before the 14th century. Among the manuscripts used by GELDNER for the edition of the *Neyayešn* — in which the recitation of the day and month is given —, ms. 6050 [Jm4], the oldest one, was written in 721 YE (1352 CE) (GELDNER 1896, p. v).

If we take this hypothesis into consideration together with the text of our quotation, we will have to deal with the date of the *Wizīrgerd ī Dēnīg*, which is problematic. We can accept that the compilation of the texts contained in the

---

ruz-e pangom vahištuyašt gāh (Av.) gāθābiiō spəṇtābiiō ratuxšaθrābiiō ašaonibiiō āiie. vahištōištōiš gāθaiiā̊ āiie. *dar pang ruz-e gāsābiyo fa yazamaydi cenin āvāyad ḫvāndan. ruz-e pardom beahnavad geh* (Av.) gāθā̊ spəṇtā̊ ratuxšaθrā̊ ašaonīš ẏaz. ahunauuaitīm gāθąm ašaonīm ašahe ratūm ẏaz. *ruz-e dovvom pa oštavad geh* (Av.) gāθā̊ spəṇtā̊ ratu. xšaθrā̊ ašaonīš ẏaz. uštauuaitīm gāθąm ašaonīm ašahe ratūm ẏaz. *sevvom ruz pa esfantmad geh* (Av.) gāθā̊ spəṇtā̊ ratu.xšaθrā̊ ašaonīš ẏaz. spəṇtā.mainniiūm gāθąm ašaonīm ašahe ratūm. ẏaz. *cahārom ruz vohuḫešatr geh* (Av.) gāθā̊ spəṇtā̊ ratu.xšaθrā̊ ašaonīš ẏaz. vōhuxšaθrąm gāθąm ašaonīm ašahe ratūm ẏaz. *ruz-e pangom vahištuyašt geh* (Av.) gāθā̊ spəṇtā̊ ratu.xšaθrā̊ ašaonīš ẏaz. vahištōištəm gāθąm ašaonīm ašahe ratūm ẏaz.

"On the five days of the *gāsābiyo* (he should) consider the day and the month (and recite) with (Av.) *āiiese ẏešti* during the first day, i.e. the Ahunwad Gāh, (Av.) *gāθābiiō spəṇtābiiō ratuxšaθrābiiō ašaonibiiō āiie. ahunauuaitiiā̊ gāθaiiā̊ āiie.* (During) the second day the Uštavad Gāh (Av.) *gāθābiiō spəṇtābiiō ratuxšaθrābiiō ašaonibiiō āiie. uštauuaitiiā̊ gāθaiiā̊ āiie.* (During) the third day at the Spandamad Gāh (Av.) *gāθābiiō spəṇtābiiō ratuxšaθrābiiō ašaōnibiiō āiie. spəṇtā mainiiəuš gāθaiiā̊ āiie.* (During) the fourth day at the Vohuxšatr Gāh (Av.) *gāθābiiō spəṇtābiiō ratuxšaθrābiiō ašaonibiiō āiie. vōhuxšaθraiiā̊ gāθaiiā̊ āiie.* (During) the fifth day at the Vahištoišt Gāh (Av.) *gāθābiiō spəṇtābiiō ratuxšaθrābiiō ašaonibiiō āiie. vahištōištōiš gāθaiiā̊ āiie.* On the five days of the *gāsābiyo* with (Av.) *yazamaide* as well must be recited, (during) the first day at the Ahunwad Gāh (Av.) *gāθā̊ spəṇtā̊ ratuxšaθrā̊ ašaonīš ẏaz. ahunauuaitīm gāθąm ašaonīm ašahe ratūm ẏaz.* (During) the second day at the Uštavad Gāh (Av.) *gāθā̊ spəṇtā̊ ratu. xšaθrā̊ ašaonīš ẏaz. uštauuaitīm gāθąm ašaonīm ašahe ratūm ẏaz.* (During) the third day, at the Spandamad Gāh (Av.) *gāθā̊ spəṇtā̊ ratu.xšaθrā̊* ašaonīš ẏaz. *spəṇtā.mainniiūm gāθąm ašaonīm ašahe ratūm. ẏaz.* (During) the fourth day, at the Vohuxšatr Gāh (Av.) *gāθā̊ spəṇtā̊ ratu.xšaθrā̊ ašaonīš ẏaz. vōhuxšaθrąm gāθąm ašaonīm ašahe ratūm ẏaz.* (During) the fifth day at the Vahištoišt Gāh (Av.) *gāθā̊ spəṇtā̊ ratu.xšaθrā̊ ašaonīš ẏaz. vahištōištəm gāθąm ašaonīm ašahe ratūm ẏaz.*

8 By personal communication.

9 The edition of the *Neyāyešn* according to the Iranian manuscripts is available at https://cab.geschkult.fu-berlin.de at the Ceremony Generator CAB 3.0.

10 Edited by GELDNER in Y72.9-10 (CAB Y72.14-20): *aŋ́āi raēsca… ašəm vohū… hazaŋhrəm baēšazanąm… ašəm vohū… jasa.mē… amahe hutāštahe… ašəm vohū…*

Wizīrgerd ī Dēnīg took place between the 10th and the 13th centuries, following Sheffield's hypothesis (SHEFFIELD 2005). The colophon recorded in the edition by SANJANA (1848) goes back to 609 YE (1239 CE). If we compare it with the date of the oldest dated Indian manuscript containing the *Neyāyešn*, i.e. 6050 [Jm4], written in 721 YE (1352 CE), two hypotheses are possible: either this change in the Indian tradition occurred before the 14th century and it had already been recorded in the *Wizīrgerd ī Dēnīg*, or the *Wizīrgerd ī Dēnīg* has undergone several changes during its transmission in India, between the 13th and the 19th centuries, and SANJANA's copy attests an altered version of the older text. According to CANTERA's analysis of ritual information,[11] the latter is most likely the correct one.

In this sense, this text represents a perfect example of "antiquité et dynamisme" (CANTERA 2014, pp. 187ff.). On the one hand, the Avestan ritual instruction evidently goes back to Sasanian or pre-Sasanian times, when the priests were still able to compose ritual instructions in Avestan (CANTERA 2014, pp. 210ff.). This instruction finds a continuity in Pahlavi and Persian meta-ritual literature (the *Wizīrgerd ī Dēnīg* and the *Revāyāts*) up to the most recent notices, as we have seen. On the other hand, it is very likely that the Indian clergy, according to their local practice which differs from the Iranian one, introduced the mention of the *Neyāyešn* into the Pahlavi text of the *Wizīrgerd ī Dēnīg*.

Bibliography

ANKLESARIA, B.T. 1956: *Zand-Ākāsīh, Iranian or Greater Bundahišn. Transliteration and Translation in English*. Bombay.

CANTERA, A. 2014: *Vers une édition de la liturgie longue zoroastrienne: pensées et travaux préliminaires*. Paris.

— 2018: Textual performative variation in the Long Liturgy: the ceremonies of the last ten days of the years. *Dabir* 6, pp. 16–49.

— 2020: "A brief note on the possibilities and limitations involved in reconstructing the historical performances of the Avestan liturgies: The case of the Dō-Hōmāst." In: *Estudios Iranios y Turanios* 4, pp. 7–28.

CANTERA, A./J. MARTÍNEZ PORRO 2022: "Sasanian rituals and their continuity in the Avestan liturgical manuscripts: the double Āb-zōhr of the Dō-Hōmāst." In: *Sasanian Studie: Late Antique Iranian World* 1, pp. 29–40.

GELDNER, K.F. 1896: Prolegomena. In K.F. GELDNER (ed.): *Avesta. The Sacred Books of the Parsis.* Stuttgart, pp. i–liv.

MARTÍNEZ-PORRO, J. 2022: The timing of the Vidēvdād and Vištāsp Yašt ceremonies. In: A. CANTERA/M. MACUCH/N. SIMS-WILLIAMS (eds.): *The Reward of the Righteous. Festschrift in Honour of Almut Hintze.* Wiesbaden (Iranica 30), pp. 335–359.

11 By personal communication. Cantera stated during preparation of the edition of the Nērangs, that some ritual information recorded in the *Wizīrgerd ī Dēnīg* concerning the Long Liturgy only represents the Indian tradition after 1600 CE. This speaks for a modification of the text between the 13th century and the time of Sanjana's copy.

REDARD, C./K.D. DARUWALLA 2021: *The Gujarati Ritual Directions of the Paragnā, Yasna and Visperad Ceremonies*. Leiden.
SANJANA, P.B. (ed.) 1848: *Vajarkard Dini*. Bombay.
SHEFFIELD, D. 2005: "The Wizirgerd i Denig and the Evil Spirit:Questions of Authenticity in Post-Classical Zoroastrianism." In: *Bulletin of the Asia Institute* 19, pp. 181–189.
UNVALA, M.R. 1922: *Dârâb Hormazyâr's Rivâyat*. Bombay.

Fragments from a Sogdian Cosmogonical Manuscript in Manichaean Script

Enrico Morano, Turin/Berlin

This paper offers a complete edition of all the fragments from a lost Sogdian Manichaean book in Manichaean script on cosmogony of the Berlin Turfan Collection. Most of the fragments are here edited, and commented upon, for the first time, and shed new light on some parts of the Manichaean cosmogony. Two appendices are dedicated to the edition of unpublished Sogdian texts which contain related subjects.

Amongst the Berlin Turfan collection there are at least four sets of manuscripts written in Sogdian in Manichaean Script which are from books on cosmogony[1]. The most extensive of these, Ms4 in my article, consists of 15 fragments, written in a clear, particular, cursive bold Manichaean script[2]. Although no entire page has been preserved, yet joining some fragments together, three sheets can be reconstructed in their larger part. Here is a description of the manuscripts as given in Morano 2019, pp. 197–198:[3]

> "Each page had at least 17 lines, but possibly more: the most complete fragment, M5701+, has 17 incomplete lines, vertical red lines ruling both margins, which appear to have been probably cut off with a sharp tool, and regular, linear tear marks above and below, while M264a preserves the upper part of the sheet, with the first 8 lines and both ruled margins, again cut off regularly. A third almost complete page of the manuscript, M141+, has 17 incomplete lines, but no margins and the upper cut seems to be linear and regular like in the other two sheets. We know the original width of the inner margin from M6291, an internal fragment of a double sheet, and from M5991: it was 1.75 cm. The outer margin is known from M485b: 2.5 cm. From the same manuscript there are in the Berlin collection several smaller fragments, which I was not able to join, or to assign, to any other fragment."

There follows the list of all the fragments from the same codex I found in the Berlin Turfan collection, which will be edited entirely and commented upon here:

1 A description of all these fragments is given in Morano 2019, pp. 196–198 (= Morano 2022, pp. 205–213) as Ms1–4.

2 See Morano 2018, p. 31.

3 In that article I published the three most complete fragments, M 264a, pp. 198–199; M5701+, pp. 200–201; M141+, pp. 201–203. (= Morano 2022, pp. 213–222). For the sake of completeness, I republish these three texts here, with some changes and additions.

M141+M6795, M264a, M485b, M5701+6796+2308, M5991, M6067, M6099, M6099a (not described in Boyce 1960[4]), M6100, M6291, M6790, M6800.[5]

1. The Father of Greatness

M264a (Fig. 1–2)

Upper part of the sheet, with the first 9 lines fairly complete. Parts of both margins preserved, cut regularly through the red ruling lines. The lower part of the page is partly torn off, only the initial/final characters of the lines are preserved. At least one line at the end is missing. 12.4 x 12.2 cm.

In this page the Father of Greatness, called *rwxšnʾγrδmncyk ʾxšywnyy βγyy* "the Lord God of the Paradise of Light", is exalted above the other gods, and said to be different from the other gods in seven things. Of these, only the first (he is, and has always been, immortal and permanent, while the other gods were created and blessed by him), the fourth (he is the father of all the gods, and they are all his sons) and the fifth (he is brighter than all the gods) are complete; the second (he is more exalted than all gods ...) the third (... he knows past, present and future), the sixth and the seventh being only partly preserved.

/R/1/ [....ʿ](y)nyy (III) (ʾ..)[......] (.yk/x..ʾ..) /2/ s(fry)tyt ○○ ʾʾfrytyt ○○ ʾt[y](y) nyjtyṭ /3/ xnd(t) (○)○ {blank} ○○ ʾrtyy (x)w(n)[yy](ẖ) /4/ rwxšnʾγrδmncyk ʾxšywnyy βγyy pr /5/ VII zngʾn ʾʾc ○○ cn sʾt βγyyštyẖ /6/ nyʾzngstr wmʾt ○○ I pr nwšʾkyʾ ʾtyẖ /7/ ʾʾs[tn](k)yʾ [○](○) (w)ʾnw ʾtyy rʾmndt n(w)[šy](yẖ) /8/ (wmʾ)[t ʾtyy ʾ]ʾstnyy ○○ cn ʾʾδʾẖ /9/ sfrytyy ʾtyẖ [ʾ](ʾ)frytyy nyy xcyẖ (○○) /10/ pʾrwtyy pʾ(r)[ykt βγyyš](t) cn wny(ẖ) /11/ βyksʾr s(f)[rytyt ʾtyy ʾʾfry](tyt)[wmʾtnd] /12/ ○○ ○○ δβ[tyk 18–20] /13/ cn sʾt β(γ)[yšty 18–20] /14/ ptrštr x(c)[yẖ 18–20] /15/ xyδ [20–22] /16/ pt(r)[štr 20–22] . . .
one line missing
/V/1/ cyndr βyk c(w) ʾ(st)yy ○○ c(w) βw(t)kʾ[m pr] /2/ bywn[6] γrβt(y) ʾtyẖ (p)tz(ʾ)nd ○○ ○○ /3/ IIIImyk (x)[y](δ) ʾxšywnyy βγyy wnyy sʾt /4/ βγyyštyy ptryy xcyy ○○ ʾtyy xww wyšʾnd /5/ sʾt wnyy ʾʾjwnd xndt ○○ sʾt xyδ /6/ ʾxšywnyy βγyy sʾr nmʾc

4 The fragment was earlier stuck to M6099, and after the restoration it was given the number M6099a.

5 I am very grateful to the Berlin-Brandenburgische Akademie der Wissenschaften and to the Staatsbibliothek zu Berlin — Preußischer Kulturbesitz for allowing me to study and publish these texts and to Abdurishid Jakup, Christiane Reck and to all the staff of the Akademienvorhaben "Turfanforschung" for the kind hospitality they always offer me. Thanks are also due to Nicholas Sims-Williams and Federico Dragoni for reading a draft of this article and for giving me suggestions and critical remarks.

6 Written ⟨bywn⟩ without dots. GMS §434 quotes it as ⟨βywn⟩.

βrynyt γwβnyt /7/ (ʾ)t[y](ẖ) ʾʾfrynyt[7] xndt ○○ ○○ (p)ncmyk /8/ xyδ ʾxšywnyy βγyy rwxš[nyʾ]k (cn) sʾt /9/ βγyštyy wʾf[yy](δ rw)xšndry(y) xcyy ○○ cʾnw /10/ [my](š)yy βγ(y)[y rwxšndryy](c)[n] sʾt ʾstʾrytyy /11/ [xcy ○○] ○○ [VImyk .... β](γy)štyy wʾfryδ /12/ [22–23](m) rwγ(n)[y]xsʾ /13/ [22–23](.) ○○ VIImyk /14/ [22–23]pʾrγztr ʾtyy /15/ [23–25](p)tkʾrʾẖ /16/ [26–28](y) cn . . .
one line missing

Translation

/R/1/ [...]these 3 [...] /2/ are created, blessed and emanated. /3/ {blank} And he, /4/ the Lord God of the Paradise of Light, in /5/ 7 sorts of things was /6/ different from all the Gods. Firstly in immortality and /7/ permanence. For he has always been immortal /8/ [and] permanent. By anyone /9/ he is not created and blessed, /10/ but the oth[er gods] out of him /11/ [were] creat[ed and bless]ed. /12/ Se[condly: ...] /13/ than all the God[s ...] /14/ is more exalted [...] /15/ this/these [...] /16/ [more] exalted . . .
one line missing

/V/1/ inside (and) outside what it is, what it will be, /2/ by foresight he knows and understands. /3/ Fourthly. The Lord God is the father /4/ of all the Gods. And they /5/ are all his sons. To that same /6/ Lord God they are all bringing honour, praise /7/ and blessing. Fifthly. /8/ The brightness of the Lord God is as much brigh[ter] than all /9/ the Gods, as /10/ the [S]un God[is brighter]than all the stars. /11/ [Sixthly ... than all the]gods, so much /12/ [...]oil, musk /13/ [...] Seventhly /14/ [...]more excellent and /15/ [...] appearance /16/ [...] than . . .
one line missing

Commentary

/R/4/ rwxšnʾγrδmncyk ʾxšywnyy βγyy — the same expression is found in L73+L77/R/3–4: cn rwxšnʾγrδmncyk ʾxšywnʾ βγʾ ○○, "from the ruler king of the paradise", Yoshida 2001, pp. 111–112.

/V/2/ bywn (sic), used adverbially, "foreseeingly", according to GMS §434, but see DMT III.2^2, p. 72a; γrβt(y) ʾtyẖ (p)tz(ʾ)nd — hendiadys: "he knows", see GMS §1637.

7 Haplology for ⟨ʾʾfrynynyt⟩, see DMT III.2^2, p. 5a.

2. How the Living Spirit Divided the World

M5701 [T II 116[8]]+**M6796** [T II K[9]]+**M2308**[10] (Fig. 3–4)

The three pieces, joined together, form an almost entire page containing 17 lines of which the last 3 are almost complete. Margins appear to be cut regularly with a sharp tool at the top, bottom and through the internal margin, where the red ruling lines are still preserved. 12.5 x 9.8 cm.

The text in this page describes how the Living Spirit created the walls and ditches and divided the world into four parts with Mount Sumeru in the middle, and four mountains as frontier guards of the world. He then separated, accordingly, the sky upwards and day and night.

/R/1/ xndt ○○ ○○ [....] xww tβ[tyy 8–10] /2/ δʾt pr pδkwyy [XX] XX XX (β)[rywr fsʾx] /3/ ○○ ○○ ʾtyy xww jʾr ʾʾ[pny? 9–11] /4/ XX XX XX βrywr fsʾ(x)[12–13] /5/ cywyδyy βystr [15–17] /6/ [f]s[ʾx] (p)r pδkwyy [15–17] /7/ [pr](kn)yy pδkwyy C[βrywr fsʾx βwt] /8/ ○○ ○○ ʾtyy štyk[15–17] /9/ XX XX [XX] βrywr fnsʾ(x) [12–14] /10/ ʾ(..y[11] ...) prkn pr pδk[wyy 14–16] /11/ βrywr fsʾx xcyy ○○ [14–16] /12/ mzyx δ[ʾ](t) kyy wyspw(w)[14–16] /13/ δʾrt skwn ○○ ○○ ʾtyy (..)[13–14] /14/ XX XX XX XX βrywr fnsʾx xcyy [○○ ○○] /15/ ʾrtyy ptsʾr wʾδ jywndy(y) (IIII) [yxwʾk] /16/ mnβxš ○○ cn smwt(r)ʾ cyndr(p)ʾr ○○ [....] /17/ xwrsncyk ʾfcmbδ (ʾtyh̠ x)wrtxyz[cyk]

/V/1/ [cn pʾškyrʾnc](y)k ʾtyy (n)[ymy](δ)cyk fcmbδ /2/ [13–14 ○○] ○○ ʾt[yy] pr myδʾn smyr /3/ [γryy 9–10](c)y IIII ʾfcmbδyy yxwʾk /4/ [15–16](sm)yr γryy pδyʾh̠ cn /5/ [16–18](.) ptysʾc ○○ ○○ /6/ [18–20]kyrʾn ○○ ʾwnw cw /7/ [18–20](.) ○○ ○○ ʾrty(h̠)[...] /8/ [18–20]βrzkwyy ʾtyy pδkwyy /9/ [15–16 f](s)ʾxyt xnd ○○ ○○ ʾrty /10/ [15–16]ʾ ○○ cn xwrsnyy kww /11/ [xwrtxyz sʾr](cn) smyr γrʾ xww ʾwrδpʾr /12/ [14–15] IIII γryy cn s(m)yr γrʾ /13/ [8– 10](cy ʾ)fcmbδyy wmʾndyy pʾšʾy /14/ [6–7](.)ʾtyy ○○ cʾnw ʾskyy smʾnyy /15/ [4–5 ʾn](βy)ndʾnd ○○ ʾrtyy cʾδr xʾ γrtʾ /16/ [....](s)yʾk δʾrʾnd ○○ ʾtyy xww ○○ myδ ʾtyh̠ /17/ [xʾ xš](p)ʾ yxwnng β[w](t) ○○ ○○ ʾrtyy xʾ myδ

Translation

/R/1/ are. [...] he se[aled(?) ...] /2/ a wall with the width of 60 [myriad parasang]. /3/ And the poison(ous)[12] w[atery ditch? ...] /4/ 60 myriad parasang [...] /5/ outside that [...] /6/ parasang in width [...] /7/ the width of the ditch 100 [myriad parasang(?)]. /8/ And the third[ditch(?)... is] /9/ 60 myriad parasang [...] /10/ and ... ditch with the wid[th ...of ...] /11/ is [...] myriad parasang. [...] /12/ great wall

8 T II (violet ink stamp) 116 (pencil) recto l. 3.

9 Written with pencil between the second and third line of the verso.

10 No site-signature.

11 The reading ⟨ʾ(ʾp)y⟩ is very doubtful.

12 On the three poisons see MORANO *forthcoming*.

that all [...] /13/ holds. And [...] /14/ is 80 myriad parasang [...] /15/ and moreover the Living Spirit divided 4[parts.] /16/ Inside the Ocean [...] /17/ the eastern world and the west[ern]

/V/1/ [from the north]ern and the southern world. /2/ A[nd] in the middle [...] (Mount) Sumeru /3/ [...] 4 parts of the world /4/ [...] at the foot of Mount Sumeru from /5/ [...]he fixed. /6/ [...] regions. This [is] what /7/ [...]. And [...] /8/ [...]length and width /9/ [...]are [... para]sangs(obl. pl.?). And /10/ [...]. From East to /11/ [West] from Mount Sumeru /12/ those on the farther side [...] the 4 mountains from mount Sumeru /13/ [...] he threw [... on] the boundary of the world. /14/ [...] While above in the sky /15/ they[13] follow (one another) and below the mountains /16/ hold [them in] shadow. Thus the day and /17/ [the] night are separated. And the day...

Commentary

/R/1, ff./ cf. M99/I/R/10/17:[14] ʾwd zmyg ʿyw wzrg ʾwd ʿstbr pd dwʾzdẖ dr ○ ʿy hmbdyc ʾsmʾnʾn dr ○○ ○○ʾwd ʾbr hm zmyq pyrʾmwn chʾr prysp ʾwd sẖ pʾrgyn kyrd ○ ʾwd pd hʾn ʿy ʾndrwn pʾrgyn dywʾn ʾndr przyd “And he made one great and strong earth with twelve Gates which correspond to the gates of heaven. And above this same earth he built in circuit four walls and three moats, and in that (which is) the inner moat he imprisoned the demons”. Šābuhragān, 272 (M535+/V/8/):[15] [hʾ]n sẖ pʾ(r)gyn ʿy [zh]ryn ṭʾryn “those three poisonous dark ditches”. Cf. also M498c/II/R/[16]: /1/ ʾṭ(y .. C)[... pr] /2/ pδkwy XX XX XX βrywr (fs)[ʾx ...] /3/ βwṭ ○○ ○○ ʾr(ṭ)[y ...] “/1/ and 100+[... in] /2/ width 60 myriad parasang [...] /3/ is. And [...]” [...] /V/1/ [...](..)ẖ /2/ [18–20](.)nyʾ prm ʾfcmβδ /3/ [20–22](ʾ)xšywn(y)[..](...) ◦◦ “/1/ [...] /2/ [...] in this world /3/ [...] the Lord”. See also the appendix below (M128).

/R/3/ ʾtyy xww jʾr ʾʾ[pny(?): on this poison, left by the dark powers in the waters, see also M873a/B/ii/3–8: jhr ʾwṯ qrmbg cy ʾmyxt pṯ hw hwyn tʾr zʾwrʾn ky ʾc bwn wy[ʾg •••] [h](ʾ)mʾxw[nd ••• •••] [ʾw](ṯ p)[d ••• •••] “The poison and refuse which those dark powers who ... from the base place ... companion ... . and in ...”[17] One can also compare M128/V/8–9/: ○○ ʾṭy cywyδδyy βyk(s)[ʾ](r) / jʾr ʾʾpnyy (prkn)[13–14] “Outside it a watery poisonous ditch ...” see Appendix below. The contexts of these two passages, although incomplete, look very similar. Cf. also *Šābuhragān* 272 (M535+/V/8/)[18]: [hʾ]n sẖ pʾ(r)gyn ʿy [zh]ryn ṭʾryn “those 3 poisonous dark ditches”.

13 I.e. the sun and the moon?
14 Cf. JACKSON 1932, pp. 34 ff. = HUTTER 1992, pp. 15–17.
15 MACKENZIE 1979, p. 515.
16 Publ. MORANO 2009, pp. 196–197.
17 DURKIN-MEISTERERNST 2014, p. 223.
18 MACKENZIE 1979, p. 515.

/R/10/ ʾ(ʾ.. ...) prkn pr pδk[wyy ...]: unfortunately the first 5–6 characters of the line are badly damaged, and only the first alef can be read clearly. The words could perhaps be restored to ʾ(ʾpny jʾr) "watery poison"; see commentary on /R/3/ above.

/V/3/ On the four quarters of the world see SUNDERMANN 2001a, p. 183.

/V/4/](sm)yr γryy pδyʾẖ "at the foot of Mount Sumeru" cf. HENNING 1937, p. 54 on 489 who translates "am Fusse des Sumeru-Berges" and cf. The Book of Giants G 20–23 (= M7800/I/V/1–4)[19]: ʾty nymyy cn xwrtxyz / **kyrʾn pr 4 mzyx γrtyʾ pδʾmn / kw smyrγryy pδww kww 32 / knδ sʾr ʾškrtδʾrnd** kyy wʾδjyw[nd] (yẖ) cn ʾʾγʾzyẖ / wyšndyẖ pyδʾr pršṭʾṭyẖ / wmʾṭ ○○ ʾṭyy ʾryʾnwyjn nʾm / jγyrʾnd ○ "... And they led one half of them eastwards, and the other half westwards, on the skirts of four huge mountains, **towards the foot of the Sumeru mountain**, into thirty-two towns which the Living Spirit had prepared for them in the beginning. And one calls (that place) Aryān-waižan".

3. Adam

M141 [T II K][20]+**6795** (Fig. 5–6)

The fragment contains 17 lines, none of them complete and, like M5701+, is cut regularly with a sharp tool above, below and through one margin. The margins are not preserved, but there are faint traces of the ruling red vertical line of one margin. The two fragments are joined and glassed together. 11.9 x 9.8 cm.

The text consists of a description of the birth of Adam, born to the two archdemons Šaklūn and Pēsūs, after they had devoured 80 thousand abortions and copulated,[21] followed by an explanation (xwyckʾwyy)[22] on the body of Adam. Although the context looks rather clear, the interpretation of some details is difficult and this description, as far as I know, has no parallels in known Manichaean literature.[23]

/R/1/ mzy(x) γrkw(s)[y 16–18] /2/ (.)ywʾncyy c(x)[r? 16–18] /3/ (p)syy tʾwʾn(d)[yy ...](δ)ʾn (β)[12–14] /4/ (w)ytwr ʾtyšyy xʾ tmb(ʾ)[r 11–13] /5/ [○]○ ○○ ʾtyẖ pr [XX XX] XX XX [zʾr pjwkty] /6/ mʾ(j)yy xww ʾʾδʾm ○○ (ʾty)šyy (xw)[4–5] /7/ tmbʾr

19 HENNING 1943, pp. 68–69.
20 T II (violet ink stamp) K (pencil) on recto between ll. 5 and 8.
21 On the Manichaean myth of the birth of Adam see SUNDERMANN 1994, pp. 45–46.
22 This word appears two more times in these fragments. In this book each section was evidently followed by an explanation.
23 For a list of Iranian Manichaean Turfan fragments in which Adam is quoted see COLDITZ 2018, pp. 184–185, with further literature.

cn pš’kt δy[w](z)’ktyy ○○ ’(t)[yšyy] /8/ xww rw’n cn pnc mrδ(’)spndyy (z)[’wryy] /9/ ’ktwδ’rt ○○ jw’n ○○ z’wr ○○ rwxšny(’)[k ○○] /10/ kršn’wty’ ○○ ’tyh̲ βwδ [○○ 5–6] /11/ ’stkyy ○○ pδδ(y)’ ○○ r’k ○○ y’t[yh̲ ○○] /12/ crm ○○ xwrnyy ○○ mγzyy ○○ ’[6–7] /13/ γwn’yy cyndr βstwδ’rt (○)[○ .... kyn ○○] /14/ yp’k ○○ ’’βrxsyy ○○ t[’](f)[[24]...] (pr)[6– 8] /15/ mndγrβ’ky’ δwn γ(wr)s [12–14] /16/ cw pr s’r[25] p’šyt w’[st 14–16] /17/ (x)’ ’’(z) ’βrxs(y)y ’tyh̲ [12–14]
/V/1/ [20]h̲ w(β’t) /2/ [20]n’m ○○ p(r) /3/ [11–12](’’δ’m m’)nwk βwt ○○ (○) [○] /4/ [8–10 xwyc]k’wyy w’nw βwt ○○ kt mn’nd(y) /5/ [6–7](k)[.](.)’(ry.)[26][...]r myšyy βγyy kršn ○○ (○)[○] /6/ [’ty]yh̲ (wn)[y] wyδ’syγwny ’’δc p(r) /7/ [6–7] ’fcmb[δ](y) ○○ cn m’tyy ’tyh̲ /8/ [6–7]ptr’ s(y)γtr ○○ ○○ ’tyy ’δ’myy /9/ [tmb’]ryy ptr’z ○○ z’r II C wβ’z wm’t ○(○) /10/ [6–7 ’t]y ryn(c)k ’nkwšṭ nw’ fns’x /11/ [wm’t ○○ ’](r)tyšyy cn tmb’r βyks’r IIII /12/ [8–10]’y rwxšny’k ’rδyf’skwn ○○ /13/ [12–14 ’](r)tyh̲ tym w’nw /14/ [10–12](t) (c’nw) šklwn ’ty pysws /15/ [7–8 pjwqt] xwrtδ’r’nd ○○ ’tyh̲ II /16/ [12–14 γnd’]kty(y) pckwyryy prštyt /17/ [10–12 ’’yw]štyt (wm’t’nd) ○○ ’tyh̲

Translation

/R/1/ the big mountainside[...] /2/ demonish(?) whe[el? ...] /3/ the strong enquiry(?)[27] [...] /4/ until his body [...] /5/ And from the 80 [thousand abortions (?)] /6/ Adam was born. His [...] /7/ body from the abortions of the children of demons, [and his] /8/ soul from the elements’ p[ower (?)] /9/ (she=Āz) has made: life, strength, brightness, /10/ beauty and perfume [...] /11/ [as] bones, nerves, veins, flesh, [...] /12/ skin, blood, marrow [and] /13/ hair she bound above[28] [... hatred,] /14/ anger, lust, [... vehemence] /15/ ignorance with around(?) [...] /16/ on top guardians she pl[aced(?)...] /17/ Āz dissoluteness and [...]

/V/1/ [...] may be /2/ [...]. In/to /3/ [...] Adam is similar. /4/ [... explan]ation is thus: similar(?) /5/ [...] [...] the beauty of the Sun God. /6/ [An]d he [had] something wonderful in /7/ [...]world. From the mother and /8/ [...]father more beautiful. Adam’s /9/ body’s dimension was one thousand 200 fathoms /10/ [...] and his little finger nine parasang /11/ [...] and from his body outwards 4 /12/ [...] brightness shone. /13/ [...] and thus again /14/ [...]when Šaklūn and Pēsūs /15/

24 Cf. ⟨t’β-n’k⟩ (in Sogdian script) ‘angry’, see DMT III.2[2], p. 224a. Here perhaps a substantive formed on the root *t’p-* meaning something like ‘act of being inflamed with anger, vehemence, irascibility’? In Sundermann 1992, p. 69, 42b there is a lacuna between ⟨ryzh⟩ and ⟨mntγrβ’kyh⟩. The corresponding list in the Chinese *Traité* (214) is 怨憎 “Hatred”, 嗔恚 “Irascibility”, 婬慾 “Lewdness”, 忿怒 “Anger” and 愚癡 “Foolishness”, see Lieu/Mikkelsen 2017, p. 55.

25 Written ⟨cw pr s’r for cwprs’r⟩.

26 Read perhaps ⟨’s](k)[ys]’r y(.)[⟩ ‘upwards’?

27 Federico Dragoni suggests to me that here psyy might be the “question” referring to the Call, which is strong, loud and violent in a context similar to a text published in Dragoni/Morano 2022, pp. 79ff.

28 I.e. “over the body”.

[...] ate [the abortions]. And in fear of the 2 /16/ [... e]vil ones having run away 14 /17/ [... were exci]ted(?). And

Commentary

/R/1/ On γrkwsy "mountainside", see RECK 2009, p. 388 and DRAGONI/ MORANO 2022, p. 81.

/R/2/ The word (.)yw'ncyy, clearly legible except the first character, is difficult to interpret. If the first missing letter is δ, then δyw'ncyy could be the feminine adjective or noun derived from δyw, "demon"; c(x)[emend cx[r "wheel" or cx[ty "to fight, contend"? Perhaps "the wheel of the demoness (= Āz)"? Or "fight with the demoness"?

/R/6 ff./ SUNDERMANN 1973, p. 27 n. 52 "Üblicher ist die Deutung des menschlichen Körpers als einer dämonischen Pentade. Daneben finden sich Heptaden verschiedener Zusammensetzung, so in M9 (Mir. Man. II, 300 Zeilen 18—20): "Knochen, Fleisch, Haut, Blut, Atem, . . . und Kot", in M5750/V/II/12—14/: 'stg mgj py rg xwn crm 'wd mwy Knochen, Gehirn (oder: Mark), Sehnen (oder: Nerven), Adern, Blut, Haut und Haare" (allerdings als die „acht vermischten Wege" bezeichnet!), Kephalaia I S. 107, 28—32: „Mark, Knochen, [Sehne,] Fleisch, Adern, Blut [, Haut"]." A partial list of these parts of the body is found, with additional information, in a small Leningrad fragment, L33: [cnn] w'tny tm' nw-100 **r('k)** cnn ['']trn'y (t)m' [p]nc-100 nnpy **y'ty** cnn ''pny tm' **βykcrm** cnn myγny tm' 'krt(y)[ ] 'yny[ ] mwr[ ] pw(.)[ ] "[... nerves from] the hell of wind. 900 veins from the hell of fire. 500 moist(?) flesh from the hell of water. Outer skins were made from the hell of fog. This .... "[29]. See also LIEU & MIKKELSEN 2017, pp. 68–69 §42b [rty] 'δw 'xšp' (m)[wn'w xnt ° ZK] (')prtmcykw ['](x)šp' (x)[wty xcy](Z)K t'r'kw δyw''šty-ch [tn](p')r ○○ rty šy ZKh XII ['z-] (m)[n]th xwty xnt ZK [pnc]w ''st'nkw tnp'rmy-šth ['nδ](my't) **'stky pδy-' r'kh [y't'](k)** ZY **crm** °° ZY xw pncw [t'r'k](w w't)y-n'kt cyt'kt [ZK]**(k)y-n yp'k ryz-h** [Z](Y) [...]γ/x(...)kw **(mntγ)rβ'k(yh)**[° ''z](?) (ZY wyt'wn)y(h xw) [']('t)[r] "[And] the Two Nights [are these: the] First Night [is] the dark, demonic [b] ody. And its Twelve [Hou]rs are the [fiv]e original(?) [pa]rts of the body: Bones, Sinews, Veins, [Fle]sh and Skin. And the five [da]rk spiritual demons: Hatred, Anger, Desire, [Vehemence(?)] and Foolishness, the [devouring] Fi[re] of [Gree] d and *Covetousness ... "; M1004+/R/ii/11–16/ (Middle Persian)[30]: [···](.)[··· 'st] (w)ynd / [b](x)šyhy(d) 'y xwd / (h)ynd hpt'n drwxš'n / ○ nxwyn **crm** ○ dwdyg / **pyt** ○ sdyg **rg** ○ tswm / **xwn** ○ pnzwm **py** ○ š(šwm) "[...mat]ter is distributed which (in) itself is seven she-demons: The first one is the skin, the second one the flesh, the third one the vein(s), the fourth one the blood, the fifth one the sinews,

29 YOSHIDA 2000, p. 77, with the interesting note: "it seems certain that the text is concerned with the creation of a microcosm or a human being".

30 SUNDERMANN 1973, p. 27, ll. 363–368.

the sixth …"; §10 (Parthian = Tr. 039–043) [cw'gwn 'rd'w fr](w)rdyn ° w'(d) rwšn (')b [ẅ 'dwr zynd'n] (')hynd ° pd pnj q'rw'n ['hrmyng'n ° 'w'gwn] **xyn dybhr 'wrjwg** ° '(s)[**tftyft wdyšn'sgyft**] bndb'n'n 'hynd ° pd pnj [w'd jywndg pwhr nyš'n ° 'wd](')'z 'wd 'wrjwg (p)[d mdy'n nš'st pd xrwštg ẅ](p)dw'xtg (n)[yš'n] "[She made Bones, Sinews, Veins, Flesh and Skin to be a prison for the Five Lights,] just as the righteous *Fr]awardīn*, Wind, Light, Water [and Fire] are [prisons] for the five [diabolical] armies. [In this way] (also) Hatred, Anger, Covetousness, Ty[ranny and Foolishness] are prison warders, in [the manner of] the five [Sons of the Living Spirit. And] Greed and Covetousness [were set] in [the middle, in the] m[anner of Calling and] Answer".[31]

/R/9 ff./ According to the Sogdian text M14/V/17–23/ (Waldschmidt/Lentz 1933, p. 548) 'The twelve limbs of the sojourning soul are: life, power, light, beauty and perfume; in the same text the Five Commandments, 'truth, non-injury, chastity, purity of mouth (and) blessed poverty; vigilance and zeal' are described by the phrase *rw'nyy m'šq γryw*, 'the substance (and) essence of the soul'[32]: M14/17/ δβtyk myn'ndyy rw'n δw'ṭs /18/ 'nδmyyṭ mwnw xnd ○ **jw'n** ○ **z'wr** /19/ **(r)wxšny'q** ○ **qršn'wṭy'** ○ 'ṭy /20/ **βwwδ** ○ ○ pnc cxš'pδδ ○ /21/ ršṭy'k ○ pw'zrmy' ○ δyncyhryft /22/ [○] qwcyzprṭy' ○ frnxwndc δšt'wc /23/ [○](w) yγr'ṭky' 'nspsṭqy' ○ "Secondly of the sojourning soul twelve members are the following: life, power, light, beauty and sweet smell: the five commandments: truth, not hurting, religious appearance (i.e. chastity), purity of the mouth, blessed poverty, watchfulness, eagerness to serve". M14/R/24–25/ ○ rw'nyy m'šq / γryw **jw'n z'wr rwxšny''q qršn'wṭy' βwwδ** "the being of the substance of the soul (are): (25) life, power, light, beauty, fragrance". Cf. also Sundermann 1981, p. 37, ll. 374–378: ZY ms 'nγ-wn m'yδ xcy 'prtmyk 'nδm'k ZKn rw'n \ ZK **'zw'nh** ptšmyrty δβtyk 'nδm'k **z'wr** \ ptšmyrty °'štyk 'nδm'k **rxwšny'kh** ptšmyrty \ ctβ'rmyk 'nδm'k **kršn'wty'kh** ptšmyrty pncmyk \ 'nδm'k **βwδh** ptšmyrty "The soul too [is] just like that: as the [first] limb of the soul (375) is to be considered [life], power [is to be considered] as the second limb, [as the third] (limb) light, the (fourth) [limb], is to be considered as [beauty], the fifth [limb] as fragrance". For all these lists see also additional unpublished texts edited below in Appendix 2.

/V/5/ myšyy βγyy kršn, cf. M7800/II/R/5ff: 'ṭyy myδ[ry β](γyy) qšn /6/ wšy' 'kṭwδ'(r)n(d) (m)'γ'z(nd ṭkwš'ṭ) "and they remembered the beauty of the Sun God; they began to look out for him".[33]

/V/9–12/ "Adam's /9/ body's dimension was one thousand 200 fathoms[34] /10/ and his little finger nine parasang /11/ […] and from his body outwards 4 /12/ […]

31 Lieu/Mikkelsen 2017, p. 10.
32 See Sims-Williams 1985, p. 574.
33 Sundermann 1994, pp. 45f.
34 For ⟨wβ'z⟩ = Av. *vibāzu* "fathom" see Henning 1942, p. 236 n.4.

brightness shone". The measurements of Adam's body given here are certainly just hyperbolic, but indeed somewhat strange: his little finger is nine parasang long and it appears to be longer than his body (1200 fathom). A fathom (i.e. the span of two outstretched arms) is about six feet or two metres, so 1200 fathoms is about 2 km. In the gospel fsx translates "mile", but even 9 miles is much more than 2 km! The restoration tmb'ryy seems pretty certain, so Adam is 2 km tall, but it's not so obvious that the 9 miles must be the length of his little finger. Maybe the line could be interpreted "[from his] little finger [something shone/streamed?] for 9 miles"? I thank NICHOLAS SIMS-WILLIAMS for the latter interpretation. Ultimately, as FEDERICO DRAGONI points out to me, the infinite variations in the measurements of the Buddha's or Maitreya's body in Buddhist literature may have had symbolic references, which we are not able to recover any more.

/V/14–15/ (cw) šklwn 'ty pysws [...]xwrtδ'r'nd: cf. M7800/II/V/12–19/: 'rtyy IIII βrywr pjwwk ww šklwn xwrtδ'rt 'tyy IIII βrywr x' pysws 'rty I δβty' 'pryw pcywznd 'rty w'nw w'βnd kt m'ncyk šm'r' kw myšyyβγw s'r δ'ryym w'nw kt xwny ky cn m'x ''jy't kww βγyštt "And Šaklūn devoured forty thousand abortions, and Pēsūs forty thousand. And they copulated with each other, and thus they said: "The intentional thought, we have it towards the Sun God, so that what will be born from us [will resemble] the gods".[35]

4. Small Fragments Without or with Unclear Context

M6099 - M6099a [*T II D 163] (Fig. 7–8 and 9–10)

Two small fragments that were glued on top of each other, separated after restoration. M6099 4.1 x 5.1 cm; M6099a 3.4 x 3.3 cm.

The contexts of these fragments are too poor to understand where to place them in the cosmogonical narration. Perhaps this section deals with the fallen Light particles desiring to return to their own Paradise.

M6099

{lines missing}		*{lines missing}*	
/A/1/	[17–18](')[8–10]	/A/1/	[...]
/A/2/	[15–16]('β)y'p[....]	/A/2/	[...] attainment[36][...]
/A/3/	[15–16](k) pr n'(ywk)[....]	/A/3/	[...] in deep[...]

35 SUNDERMANN 1994, pp. 45f.

36 See DMT III.2[2], p. 2b.

/A/4/ [15–16](.) frʾšk[yrʾn]
/A/5/ [18–20 w](š)tmʾk xypδ
/A/6/ [22–24 ʾ](kδʾr)ʾ[nd(?)](sʾr?)
{*lines missing*}
{*lines missing*}
/B/1/ [7–8](..y)[17–18]
/B/2/ [4–5](ʾβrxsyy?)[16–17]
/B/3/ [...](mʾ....)[16–17]
/B/4/ [...]yny(y) (II ʾxš)[ʾwnt(?) 12–13]
/B/5/ (r)ʾ(m)ʾ(ndy ..)[16–17]
/B/6/ [....](.)wky(y)[*18–20]*
{*lines missing*}

/A/4/ [...] south
/A/5/ [...] own Paradise
/A/6/ [...] they made(?) [...]
{*lines missing*}
{*lines missing*}
/B/1/ [...]
/B/2/ [...] desire(?)[...]
/B/3/ [...]
/B/4/ [...] 2 realms(?)
/B/5/ always [...]
/B/6/ [...*]*
{*lines missing*}

M6099a

{*lines missing*}
/A/1/ [.?.](.)ẖ
/A/2/ [.?.](j)wʾndyẖ
/A/3/ [.?.](δ) pww wyʾky
/A/4/ [.?.]cʾnw xw(w)
/A/5/ [.?.](tyy .β)[..]
{*lines missing*}
{*lines missing*}
/B/1/ traces
/B/2/ [.?. jw](ʾ)nd(yy s)[...](.)[.?.]
/B/3/ [.?.](xyδ)[.?.]
/B/4/ [.?. w](δyδδ)[.?.]
/B/5/ traces
{*lines missing*}

{*lines missing*}
/A/1/ [...]
/A/2/ [...]living [...]
/A/3/ [...]without place[...]
/A/4/ [...]when he[...]
/A/5/ [...]
{*lines missing*}
{*lines missing*}
/B/1/ traces
/B/2/ [... L]iving[Spirit(?)...]
/B/3/ [...]that [...]
/B/4/ [...]there[...]
/B/5/ traces
{*lines missing*}

M6100 [(T II) D 163[37]] (Fig. 11–12)

End of page (the bottom part of the sheet appears to be cut horizontally with a sharp tool) with a bit of ruled outer or inner margin. 2.9 x 4.3 cm.

Although the context is not quite clear, the fragment is interesting for the quotation of the Living Spirit and of the 3 ptyc[yẖ (see commentary below).

{*12 lines missing*}
/A/1/ [...](k/x)[22–24]
/A/2/ (ʾ)tyy III ptyc[yẖ 18–20]
/A/3/ wʾδ jywndyy [18–20]
/A/4/ ʾtyy cn twʾ n(.)[16–18]

{*12 lines missing*}
/A/1/ [...]
/A/2/ and [...] the 3 Aməša Spəntas[...]
/A/3/ the Living Spirit [...]
/A/4/ and from thy/thee [...]

37 Written in pencil above the first line of side /B/.

/A/5/ δyw nyy ''jy't (○)[16–18]	/A/5/ demon will not be born. [...]
{end of page}	*{end of page}*
{13 lines missing}	*{13 lines missing}*
/B/1/ [18–20]ky ○○ 'rty cywy[δ]	/B/1/ [...] and then
/B/2/ [20–22](..w)' pnc	/B/2/ [...] five
/B/3/ [16–18 mrδ's]p[n]dt [x]' γrt'ẖ ○○	/B/3/ [... Amə]ša Spəntas the mountains.
/B/4/ [16–18](.)s(try)c 'tyẖ	/B/4/ [...] woman and
{end of page}	*{end of page}*

Commentary

/A/2/ The '3 ptycyẖ', who are mentioned in M583/ii/V/16/, probably also in M583/ii/R/13/ (Waldschmidt/Lentz 1933, pp. 68–70 [545–47]) and here, may be identified with the 'three Aməša Spəntas' quoted in M6132/B/2 (Reck 2003, pp. 330–331), the 'three gods' of the parallel Arabic and Turkish accounts (see DMT III.2[2], p. 189a).

M6067 [T II D163[38]] (Fig. 13–14)

Small fragment with 4 lines with incomplete words. Part of inner(?) margin, 1.3 cm, preserved; ruled with red lines. Context undefined, with an explanation (xwyck'wyy) of the preceding missing text

{lines missing}	*{lines missing}*
/R/1/ p'[26–27]	/R/1/ [...]
/R/2/ 'ty(ẖ) [25–26]	/R/2/ and[...]
/R/3/ ʿ/V[26–27]	/R/3/ 5(?)[...]
/R/4/ (.)[28–29]	/R/4/ [...]
{lines missing}	*{lines missing}*
{lines missing}	*{lines missing}*
/V/1/ [26–27]'t ○○	/V/1/ [...]
/V/2/ [26–27 xwyc](k)'wyy ○○	/V/2/ [... expla]nation.
/V/3/ [22–24 p'š](k)[y]r'n ○○	/V/3/ [... nor]thern
/V/4/ [26–27](.δ)	/V/4/ [...](..)
{lines missing}	*{lines missing}*

M5991 [T II D 163[39]] (Fig. 15–16)

Small fragment with beginning/ends of 4 lines. Inner margin, 1.8 cm, preserved. Context undefined, but the recto seems to suggest a battle against dragons.

38 D 163 written reversed in pencil on the verso inner margin.

39 D 163 written in pencil on the recto inner margin.

{*lines missing?*}	{*lines missing?*}
/R/1/ xns βys[tr?[40] 20–22]	/R/1/ strong outside(?)[...]
/R/2/ c’nw kyrmyy [20–22]	/R/2/ when a snake’s[...]
/R/3/ xnγr wy’ n’(q)[20–22]	/R/3/ sword in a dragon(?) [...]
/R/4/ ’spnyn(y)[22–24]	/R/4/ of iron [...]
{*lines missing*}	{*lines missing*}
{*lines missing?*}	{*lines missing?*}
/V/1/ [20–22](y)t myn’ndk’m ○○	/V/1/ [...] they will stay.
/V/2/ [20–22 c’]nw cywyδ	/V/2/ [...]then
/V/3/ [20–22](n)yjt’h̲ wβ’t	/V/3/ [...] may die
/V/4/ [22–24](βγ)yy ○○ ’tyy	/V/4/ [...] god. And
{*lines missing*}	{*lines missing*}

/R/3/ xnγr wy’ n’(q)[thus I. Gershevitch’s reading n’(q) “dragon”, in his Notebook kept in the Ancient India and Iran Trust in Cambridge.

M6291[T II D 185[41]] (Fig. 17–18)

Central part of a double sheet. Beginnings/ends of lines only. /I/: 3 x 3.3 cm; /II/: 2.9 x 3 cm.

Text without context followed by an explanation.

{*lines missing*}	{*lines missing*}
/I/R/1/ ’tyy (γ)[24-25]	/I/R/1/ and [...]
/I/R/2/ ’skw[24-25]	/I/R/2/ was/were[...]
/I/R/3/ p’δy[24-25]	/I/R/3/ foot/feet[...]
/I/R/4/ mrδ[’spndt 20-21]	/I/R/4/ ele[ments ...]
{*lines missing*}	{*lines missing*}
{*lines missing*}	{*lines missing*}
/I/V/1/ [24-25 pr](x)st	/I/V/1/ [re]mains
/I/V/2/ [24-25]qršn	/I/V/2/ [...]beauty
/I/V/3/ [24-25]r’z	/I/V/3/ [...]mystery
/I/V/4/ [26-27 xwyc](k’)wyy	/I/V/4/ [...] explanation
{*lines missing*}	{*lines missing*}
{*lines missing*}	{*lines missing*}
/II/R/1/ p(.)[26-27]	/II/R/1/ [...]
/II/R/2/ ○○ [26-27]	/II/R/2/ . [...]
/II/R/3/ cw[26-27]	/II/R/3/ which [...]
/II/R/4/ (’t)[y? 26-27]	/II/R/4/ and(?)[...]
{*lines missing*}	{*lines missing*}

40 Or ⟨βys[tyt⟩ ‘bound (pl.)’? So ‘[beats] strongly thhose who are bound’?

41 Written in pencil on the inner margin of /I/V/.

{*lines missing*}		{*lines missing*}	
/II/V/1/	[27-28](.)	/II/V/1/	[...]
/II/V/2/	[26-27 z]'wr	/II/V/2/	[p]ower
/II/V/3/	[26-27 ']tyẖ	/II/V/3/	[... a]nd
/II/V/4/	[27-28](yy)	/II/V/4/	[...]
{*lines missing*}		{*lines missing*}	

M485b (Fig. 19–20)

Small squarish fragment with beginning/ends of lines. Some complete words. Not joining, but perhaps belonging to, the same page as M141+, see above. 4.1 x 4.9 cm. Ruled outer margin 2.5 cm.[42]

Context unknown, perhaps from the narration of the creation of the protoplasts (recto) and a battle against bird-shaped demons? (verso).

{*lines missing?*}[43]		{*lines missing?*}	
/R/1/	[25–26] pš'k[t]	/R/1/	[25–26] abortions
/R/2/	[25–26](β)[y](k)s'r xr(t)	/R/2/	[25–26] went outside
/R/3/	[25–26](s)kwn ○○ kt	/R/3/	[...]. When
/R/4/	[25–26]sk ○○ kt	/R/4/	[...]. When
/R/5/	[25–26](sk) ○○ kt	/R/5/	[...]. When
{*lines missing*}		{*lines missing*}	
{*lines missing*}		{*lines missing*}	
/V/1/	[w](rz) pty(s)['c 25–26]	/V/1/	he/she prepared a wonder[...]
/V/2/	ʿst[25–26]	/V/2/	[...]
/V/3/	kt C z'r[25–26]	/V/3/	when 100 thousand [...]
/V/4/	sy'k k(w)[25–26]	/V/4/	shadow[...]
/V/5/	w'(z)t[25–26]	/V/5/	wings[...][44]
{*lines missing*}		{*lines missing*}	

M6800 [T II K[45]] (Fig. 21–22)

Small damaged fragment with beginning/ends of lines, worm-eaten. Cut through one of the ruled margins delimited with a red line. 6.1 x 4.2 cm.

Context unclear, perhaps about the creation by the Living Spirit of the shadow

42 On the outer margin of the verso there are faint imprints in red ink from another manuscript with different handwriting.

43 The small portion above the first line looks as if it were cut regularly with a sharp tool, like in M5701+, see above. If this is correct, the first line was the first of the page.

44 Cf. M5563/V/3–5/ (unpubl., cosmogonic context): 'rṭpṭs'r m(r)xšy(p)[.](ṭ) / qršnyṭ δywṭ prw xy[pδ ...] prndṭ 'ṭy w'zṭ wnyẖ[...] 'Afterwards the bird-shaped(?) demons, with their feathers and wings' ... On m(r)xšyp[.](ṭ) / qršnyṭ see DMT III.2[2], p. 137a.

45 T II (violet ink stamp) k (pencil) between ll. 1 and 2 of side /A/.

/A/		/A/	
{*lines missing*}		{*lines missing*}	
/A/1/	*[...](t) (k/x)[...](..)[10-12]*	/A/1/	[...]
/A/2/	*[wʾs](t)ynd* ○○[46] *wyδ[14-16 wʾδ]*	/A/2/	they placed. that [...]
/A/3/	*[j](w)ʾndyy wβytyy[15-17]*	/A/3/	the living [Spirit] may be [...]
/A/4/	*(x)[w]ʾcnʾk w(β)[y](t)[y 10-12]*	/A/4/	may be ill/suffering [...]
/A/5/	*mwrtyy wβyty(y)[16-18]*	/A/5/	may be dead [...]
/A/6/	*V(I)myk (X)*[47] *[16-18]*	/A/6/	sixthly: 10[...]
/A/7/	*ʾwtʾ(k)[22-24]*	/A/7/	place[...]
/A/8/	*(w.)[26-28]*	/A/8/	[...]
{*lines missing*}		{*lines missing*}	
/B/		/B/	
{*lines missing*}		{*lines missing*}	
/B/1/	*[16-18](mrc)[..]w(m)[ʾt?]*	/B/1/	[...] death [...]was
/B/2/	*[12-13](t)[...](ʾ)nwzytynd (.)[4-5]*	/B/2/	[...] may they assemble [...]
/B/3/	*[16-18] nyy ʿysytyn[d]*	/B/3/	[...] may they not come
/B/4/	*[16-18](s)yʾk kwnʾ(s)[kwn]*	/B/4/	[...] he made the shadow
/B/5/	*[15-17](.)ʾt kδʾm ʾʾδyy*	/B/5/	[...] whoever
/B/6/	*[16-18](y)nd wδ[y]ẖ*	/B/6/	[...]they [...] there
/B/7/	*[20-22](δ)yẖ*	/B/7/	[...]
/B/8/	*[26-28]sk*	/B/8/	[...]
{*lines missing*}		{*lines missing*}	

M6790 [T II K[48]] (Fig. 23–24)

Long narrow fragment, tattered and with holes. Only a few entire words are preserved. The bottom part of one side is almost completely faded. Horizontal gridlines visible on one side. 8.8 x 5 cm.

The fragment is possibly similar in contents to M6100 (see above) for the quotation of the 3 ptycyẖ and of the third son of the Living Spirit. The context is unfortunately to poor to place the fragment in the narration.

/A/		/A/	
{*lines missing*}		{*lines missing*}	
/A/1/	[.?.](.)[.?.]	/A/1/	[...]
/A/2/	[.?.](y.)nd ○○[.?.]	/A/2/	[...]
/A/3/	[.?.](..ʾy)n w(y)[.?.]	/A/3/	[...]
/A/4/	[.?.]y (○○)[.?.]	/A/4/	[...]
/A/5/	[.?.](kδ)ryy[49] pš(pʾ)[ry .?.]	/A/5/	[...]then the progress[...]
/A/6/	[.?. w]ndn ○○ kt III (p)[tycyẖ .?.]	/A/6/	[...]so many. When the 3 ptycyẖ
/A/7/	[.?.(k/x)..](s) ptsʾr [.?.]	/A/7/	[...] but [...]

46 Red only, one above the other.

47 Probably other numbers followed in the lost part.

48 T II (violet ink stamp) k (pencil) between ll. 8–9 of side /A/.

49 Or ⟨rw](x)[š]ndryy⟩?

/A/8/ [.?. p](n)cmyk (z)’ty(ẖ)[.?.]
/A/9/ [.?. (k/x..y)[.?.](.) wšγny(y) (β)[γyy .?.]
/A/10/ [.?.] ○○ w’(nw)[.?.]
/A/11/ [.?.](c)yy nyy (.)[.?.]
/A/12/ [.?.]δyy [.?.]
/A/13/ [.?.](pr m)[.?.]
{*lines missing*}

/B/
{*lines missing*}
/B/1/ [.?.](k/x)[.?.]
/B/2/ [.?.](.wn) ○○ [.?.]
/B/3/ [.?.](.ẖ) wy(.)[.?.]
/B/4/ [.?.](..)[...] wδyy (’)[.?.]
/B/5/ [.?.](ẖ) pr xy(δ)
/B/6/ [.?.] ○○ ’rty(ẖ)[.?.]
/B/7/ [.?.](k/x)[.]y smwtry’[.?.]
/B/8/ [.?.](’rtyẖ)[...] xypδδ)[.?.]
/B/9/ [.?.](mzyx? ○○ (δsmyk?) [.?.]
/B/10/ [.?.](.. ’)kr(t)yẖ
/B/11/ [.?.](ẖ f)[.?.]
/B/12/ traces
{*lines missing*}

/A/8/ [...]fifthly: the son [...]
/A/9/ [...] God Adamas [...]
/A/10/ [...]
/A/11/ [...] not [...]
/A/12/ [...]
/A/13/ [...]in [...]
{*lines missing*}

/B/
{*lines missing*}
/B/1/ [...]
/B/2/ [...]
/B/3/ [...]
/B/4/ [...] there [...]
/B/5/ [...] in that [...]
/B/6/ [...] and [...]
/B/7/ [...] in the ocean[...]
/B/7/ [...]and [...]
/B/9/ [... g]reat. Tenth(?)[...]
/B/10/ [...] done/made [...]
/B/11/ [...]
/B/12/ [...]
{*lines missing*}

Commentary

/A/6/ ○○ kt III (p)[tycyẖ .?.], see above commentary on M6100.

/A/8/ [.?. p](n)cmyk (z)’ty(ẖ)[.?.]: these two words, taken together, should mean ‘fifth son’, but, since wšγnyy βγyy, the third son, is quoted in the following line, it makes it preferable to interpret the two words as separated: ‘Fiftly: the son ...’

/A/9/ wšγny(y) (β)[γyy is the third son of the Living Spirit, Adamas of Light, see VAN LINDT, pp. 100–103. The Sogdian name appears also in M583/I/R/8/, see WALDSCHMIDT/LENTZ 1933, p. 68.

Appendix 1

The following fragment, unpublished so far, is not from the same manuscript of the preceding collection, but it contains a text that resembles the contents of the other fragments.

M128 (Fig. 25–26)

Irregular, triangular fragment, parts of both side margins, only one line almost complete. 9.7 x 11.4 cm. Unpublished.

This fragment contains a narration, followed by an explanation, of the way the Living Spirit prepared the 4 walls and the two ditches. From recto 10 onwards there followed an explanation (xwyck'wyy), unfortunately not preserved.

/R/
{*lines missing*}
/R/1/ [...]'s(k)[wn 15–16]
/R/2/ 'ṭy II δ'ṭy[y 14–15]
/R/3/ pṭšprṭy(y k/x)[14–15]
/R/4/ kww c'δrcyq (.)[10–12]
/R/5/ ○○ 'ṭy δβṭyk (δ')[ṭ 10–12]
/R/6/ kww 'nxrwzn prys(ṭ)[○○ ○○]
/R/7/ {red}pṭymṭy IIII δ'ṭ III pr(kn ..) [...]
/R/8/ {blank}
/R/9/ {blank}
/R/10/ {red} [''γšt ......](xw)yck'w(y)y
/R/11/ [16–18](..δ)'wy
{*lines missing*}

/V/
{*lines missing*}
/V/1/ [17–18](.)'(β)[...]
/V/2/ [11–12](...) XX XX XX
/V/3/ [14–15 nyy](')s(?)
/V/4/ [5–6 sm'nx]šyδδ(?) ○○ 'rṭyšyy
/V/5/ [6–7](š)yy 'ṭyh̠ IIII
/V/6/ [....](k/x)yy ○ wδδyy 'skw'nd
/V/7/ [...](○○)[50] (m)s XIIII ṭmṭ' wδyδδ
/V/8/ (psγṭ)y xnd ○○ 'ṭy cywyδδyy βyk(s)['](r)
/V/9/ j'r ''pnyy (prkn)[13–14]
/V/10/ βwṭ pr yγ[r](ṭ)[y'k 10–12]
/V/11/ XX XX (XX)[15–16]
{*lines missing*}

Translation

/R/1/ [...] /2/ and 2 walls [...] /3/ are arranged [...] /4/ to the lower [...] /5/ The second wall [...] /6/ reaches the zodiac circle. [...] /7/ The 4 walls and 3 ditches' (discourse) is finished. /8/ *blank* /9/ *blank* /10/ [here begins the] explanation [...]

/V/1/ [...] / 2/ [...] 60 /3/ [...] to[ok(?) ...] /4/ [...]the King [of Heaven(?)]. And his /5/ [...] and 4 [...] /6/ [...]. There are /7/ [...]. 14 Hells /8/ are also fashioned there. Outside it [he settled] /9/ a watery poisonous ditch [...] /10/ it is in extension [...] /11/ 60 [...]

Commentary

/V/4/ [10–11 sm'nx]šyδδ. The restoration is doubtful. If so, the King of Heaven, the second son of the Living Spirit, could be brought into play. In M178/V/9–14/ sm'nxšyδδ, 'the King of Heaven' is called by Wišparkar (the Living Spirit) and is seated on a throne in the seventh heaven and made the Lord over all the ten Firmaments: 'rṭy pts'r xw wyšprkr 'yy (107)/ 10/ sm'nxšyδ jyγyr o 'rṭyšw (108)/ 11/ wy' 'βṭmyk sm'nyyh̠ pr (109)/ 12/ γ'δwk nyšyδ'nd 'ty pr mγwn (110) / 13/ δs' sm'n 'xšyδ 'ty xwt'w (111)/ 14/ qwn'nd.[51]

/V/7/ XIIII ṭmṭ' "14 hells": in M99/I/V/16–19/ there are 12 hells: 'wd 'bgwhg 'y (92)17/ ch'r qyšwr t'r 'wyš wrwpṭn (93)18/ r'y ° dw'zdh̠ dwšwx ° sh̠ (94)19/ sh̠ 'ndr 'yw p'ygws ps'xt̠ "And for sweeping thereto the dirt of the darkness of the four climes, he prepared twelve hells, three to each region".[52]

50 Reversed from the other side.
51 Henning 1948, pp. 312f.
52 Hutter 1992, pp. 16ff.

/V/8–9/ “Outside it [he settled] a watery poisonous ditch”, see above M5701/V/10/ and commentary thereof. Literally the espression j’r ’’pnyy (prkn) means “poison watery ditch”, i.e. “a ditch with poisoned water”.

Appendix 2

The following unpublished fragments contain lists of the cardinal sins, Light elements, limbs of the soul and of the dharma body.

M123 (Fig. 27–28)

Small fragment from a bottom corner. Three incomplete lines. Ruled margin. 4 x 10.2 cm.

/A/
{*lines missing*}
/1/ [13–14](y) ○ kyn yp’q
/2/ [ryj zwstmbky](’) ’ṭyy mndγ(r)β’ky’
/3/ [......](f)r βγnyy z’wr ○ ’wzmṭyẖ
{*end of page*}

/B/
{*lines missing*}
/1/ p’zy(y) z(yn) ’[13–14]
/2/ ny(z)β’nyṭ ○ βyk(s)[’r](.γ)[......]
/3/ II (m)yδδ’ny ○ ’mr’cy’ (m)[.....]
{*end of page*}

Translation

/A/1/ ... Hatred, anger, /2/ [greed, tyranny] and ignorance /3/ [...] naked(?) power[53]. Condemned

/B/1/ the weapon of the face(?) [...] /2/ passions. Outside [...] /3/ between 2. Confidency(?)[54] [...]

So10260(1) (Fig. 29–30)

On the Light elements, the limbs of the soul and the dharma body.[55]

/A/
/1/ [7–8 c](yw)yšn [....]
/2/ [....](.) xypδ CWRH w’n’kw ’’š’(r.)[....]

/B/
/1/ [12–13](C)WRH [5–6]
/2/ [...... Z](Kh) kršn’wty’kh ZKh ’’(.)[

53 Or ‘the power of the temple’?

54 ⟨’mr’cy’⟩ is an unknown hapax in an unknown context. FEDERICO DRAGONI (p.c.) tentatively considers the word as an abstract of a substantive ’mr’c “confidant”, formed by the preverb ’m- < **ham*- (with -m- instead of expected -n-!) + r’c “secret”. The same formation is found in NP *hamrāz* “confidant”. The abstract might have had the meaning “trustworthiness” or the like.

55 See full description of the fragment in RECK 2006, p. 51 nr. 43.

/3/ ’YKZ-Y ZK c(rm) ky ZY prw w’tδ’rty C[WRH]
/4/ ZKw ctβ’r pyš’k šrt(?) δ’rt o(o)[rty]
/5/ c’n’kw ZK ’stky pδyh r’kh (y)[’](t)[’k]
/6/ [Z](K) crm xwty xcy[....](δ)[6–7]

/3/ [.....](w) ’šm’r’kh ZY ZKn šm’r’kh ZK(n)
/4/ [......] CWRH wyt’w p’z-nyh βwt
/5/ [..........](kr)šn z-rγwn’k xcy oo Z-Kwyh
/6/ [7–8](h) CWRH β(w)δh xc[y]

Translation

/A/1/ ... from them ... /2/ one’s own body thus ... /3/ if the skin, which is in the living beings’ b[ody], /4/ the four limbs[56] he has shaped(?)[57]. And ... /5/ like the bones, tendons, veins, flesh /6/ the skin is ...

/B/1/ ... the body ... /2/ ... the beauty of (someone) [and] /3/ ... thinking and meditation[58] /4/ ... the body is endurance /5/ ... the shape is green. In the /6/ ... the body is fragrance

So18500 (Fig. 31–32)

From the same manuscript as So10260(1)[59].

/A/
{*lines missing*}
/1/ [...](.) pδy(h)[...]
/2/ [...](k)t’yk(w) (Z)K rxwšny ’r(.)[...]
/3/ [...]t ZY pr ’(rt)’w βrw[rtyy]
/4/ [...](.) ’skwty ’YKZ-Y ZK (y’t)[’k]
/5/ [...C](W)RH pδyh ZY ’stkt’[60] ○[...]
/6/ [...](.) p’r’γz kršn ’’p(h) ’xšy(w)[...]
/7/ [...](..)[...]’nγwncyδ ptryδty šwt[...]
/8/ [prw w’t]δ’rt(y) CWR(H) ZKh (y)[...]
{*lines missing*}

/B/
{*lines missing*}
/1/ [...](..’y) ZY [
/2/ [...](C)WRH ’šyh (γ)[...](...)[...]
/3/ [...δ]rm’ykw CWRH pyrp’z[-n ...]
/4/ [...](.) kršn kp’(w)t’k xcy ○[...]
/5/ [...](’r)txwšt ZKh m’škh CW[RH...]
/6/ [...](w)y ZY ZKn rxwšny’kh ZK(n)[...]
/7/ [... C]WRH m’nprm’t’k ZY [...](.)[...]
/8/ [...](.) δrm’ykw (C)WRH (p.)[...]
/9/ {*traces*}
{*lines missing*}

56 See Sundermann 1992, pp. 68f., 42b and Lieu/Mikkelsen 2017, p. 54.

57 As Christiane Reck informs me, Sundermann tentatively connected this unknown word with Av. *tβarəs-* “schneidend gestalten, schaffen, hervorbringen”, see Bartholomae 1904, col. 795. Federico Dragoni (p.c.) rather thinks a suitable derivation might be from PIr. **fšar-*[2] “to squeeze, press out”, see Cheung 2007, p. 93, cf. MP *’pš’l-* “to press (out)”, if we assume loss of -f- in an expected **(’)šfr-* > *(’)šr*. The idea of “squeezing” or “pressing” the skin etc. on a body seems quite suitable semantically. It might also be connected to Khot. *ṣṣarr-* “to incite”, for which see Dragoni 2023, pp. 186f. (to press >> to incite?).

58 Federico Dragoni suggests “continuous meditation”.

59 See full description of the fragment in Reck 2006, p. 228, nr. 292.

60 See Sundermann 1992, pp. 68f., 42b.

Translation

/A/1/ ... tendon ... /2/ ... the light ... /3/ ... and in the Artāw Frawarti[61] ... /4/ ... is like flesh ... /5/ ... body, tendons and bones ... /6/ ... excellent shape the Water Lord(?) ... /7/ ... so like mixed goes ... /8/ in the living beings' body the ...

/B/1/ ... and ... /2/ ... body memory ... /3/ ... dharma body of believing mind ... /4/ ... Shape is blue. ... /5/ ... Artaxušt the substance of the body /6/ ... and the light the ... /7/ ... body mind and ... /8/ ... dharma body ... /9/ ...

Commentary

CHRISTIANE RECK kindly informs me about a free interpretation of part of this text by SUNDERMANN as follows: "[Und des Windes] [Substanz]-Leib ist Gedächtnis, der Dharma-Leib ist Glaubenssinn, die Gestalt ist blau. Und von Artaxušt ist der Substanzleib [...], und vom Licht ist [der Substanzleib] Gedachter Sinn und [u.] der Dharma-Leib [ist ... und die Gestalt ist ...]"

61 Name of the first light element, Ether, cf. SUNDERMANN 1992, p. 132 and SUNDERMANN 1979b, p. 101, nr. 3/4.2.1.

Plates

Fig. 1. M264a recto
All images: Depositum der Berlin-Brandenburgischen Akademie der Wissenschaften in der Staatsbibliothek zu Berlin–Preussischer Kulturbesitz.

Fig. 2. M264a verso

Fig. 3. M5701+M6796+M2308 recto [montage]

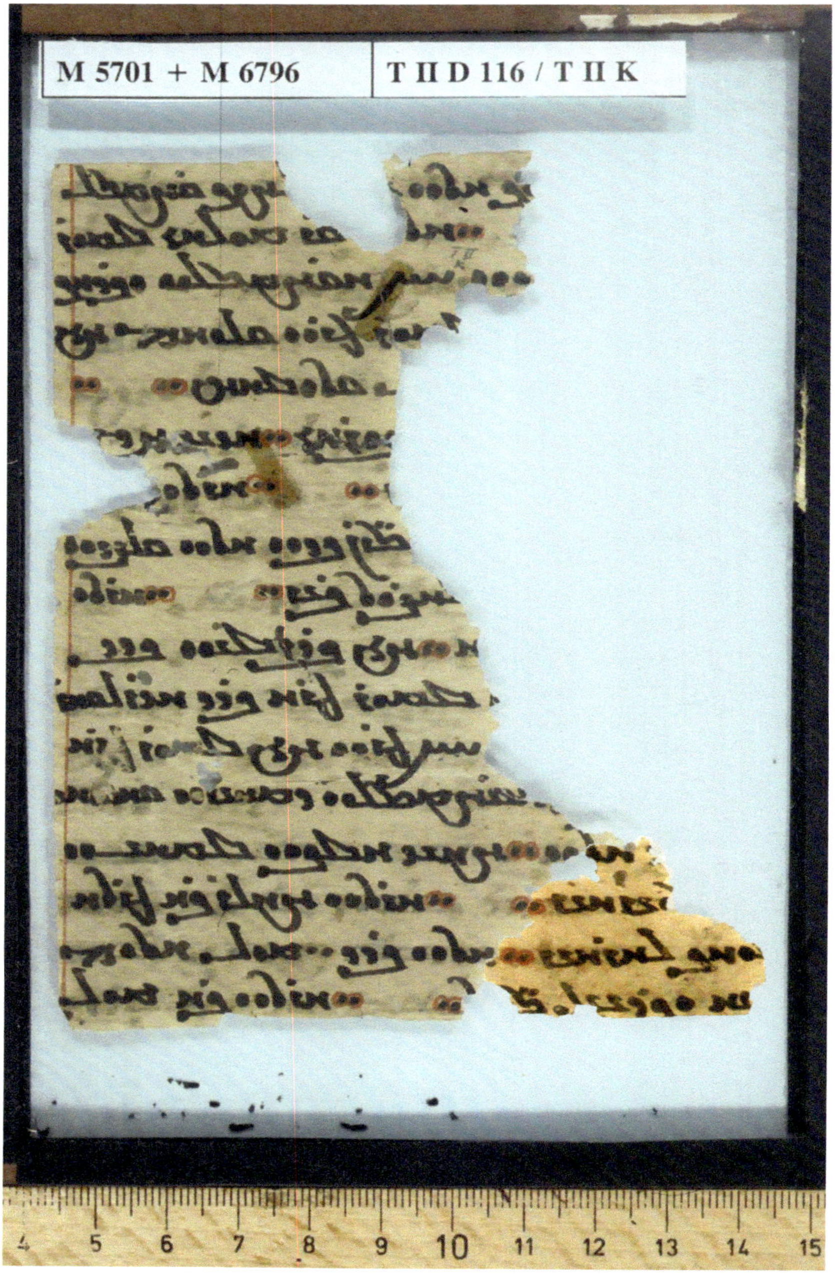

Fig. 4. M5701+M6796+M2308 verso [montage]

Fig. 5. M141+M6795 recto

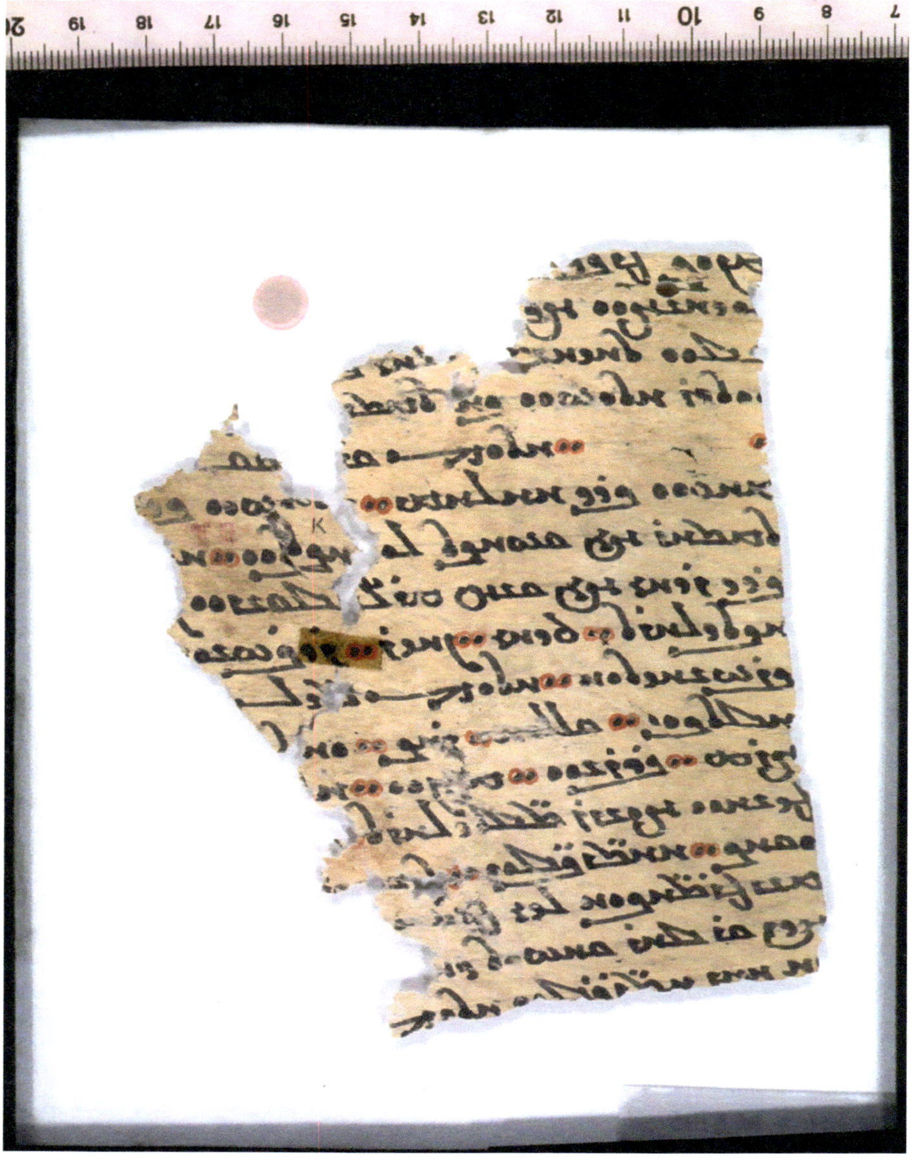

Fig. 6. M141+M6795 verso

Fig. 7. M6099/A/

Fig. 8. M6099/B/

Fig. 9. M6099a/A/

Fig. 10. M6099a/B/

Fig. 11. M6100/A/

Fig. 12. M6100/B/

Fig. 13. M6067/A/

Fig. 14. M6067/B/

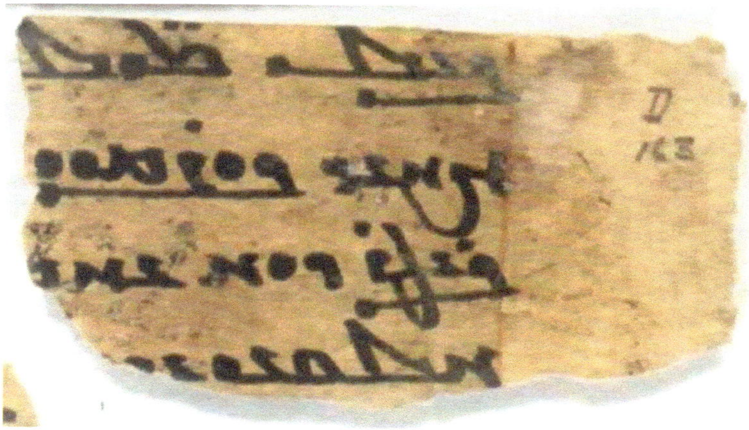

Fig. 15. M5991 recto

Fig. 16. M5991 verso

Fig. 17. M6291 side 1

Fig. 18. M6291 side 2

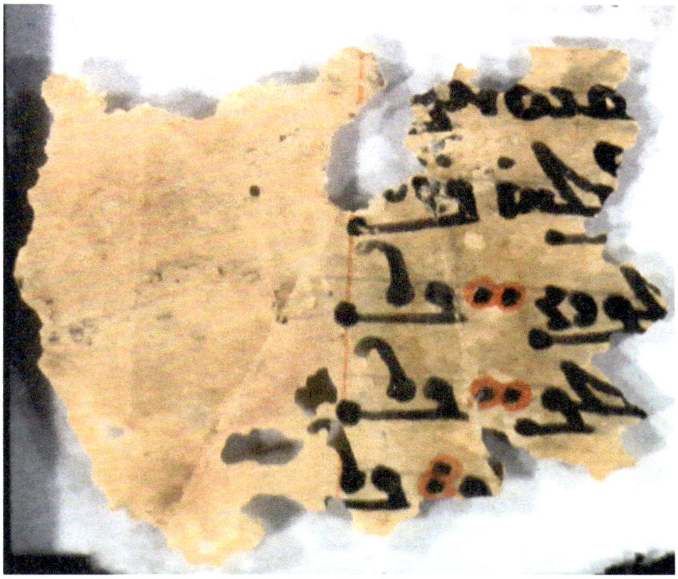

Fig. 19. M485b recto

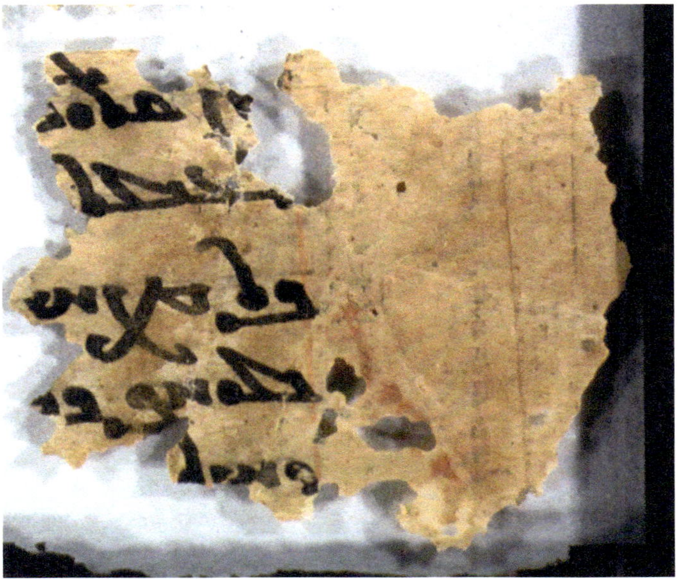

Fig. 20. M485b verso

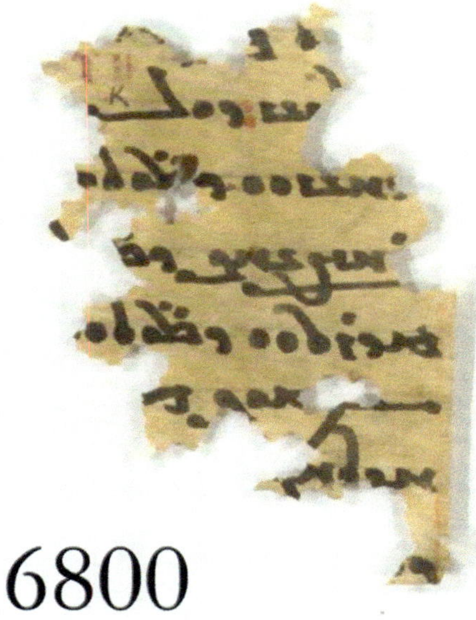

Fig. 21. M6800 recto

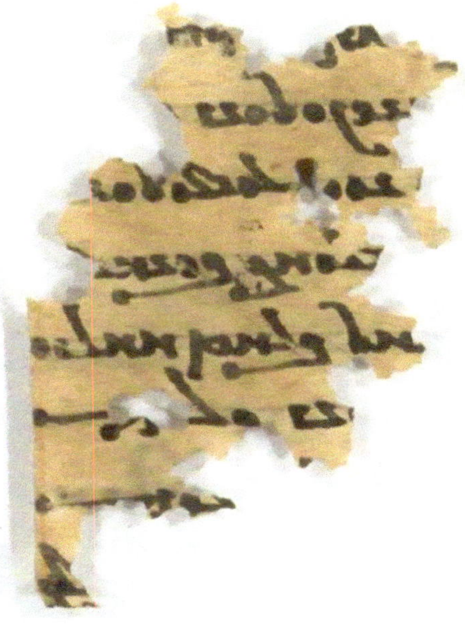

Fig. 22. M6800 verso

Fig. 23–24. M6790 /A/ and /B/

Fig. 25. M128 recto

Fig. 26. M128 verso

Fig. 27. M123/A/

Fig. 28. M123/B/

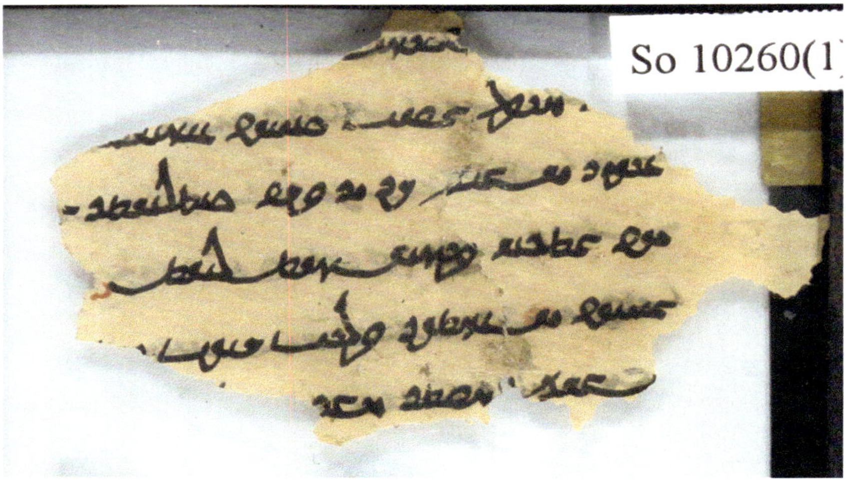

Fig. 29. So10260(1)/A/

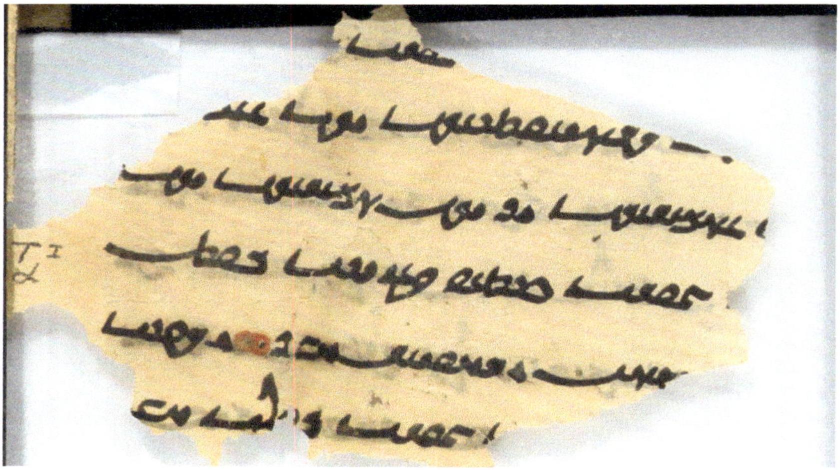

Fig. 30. So10260(1)/B/

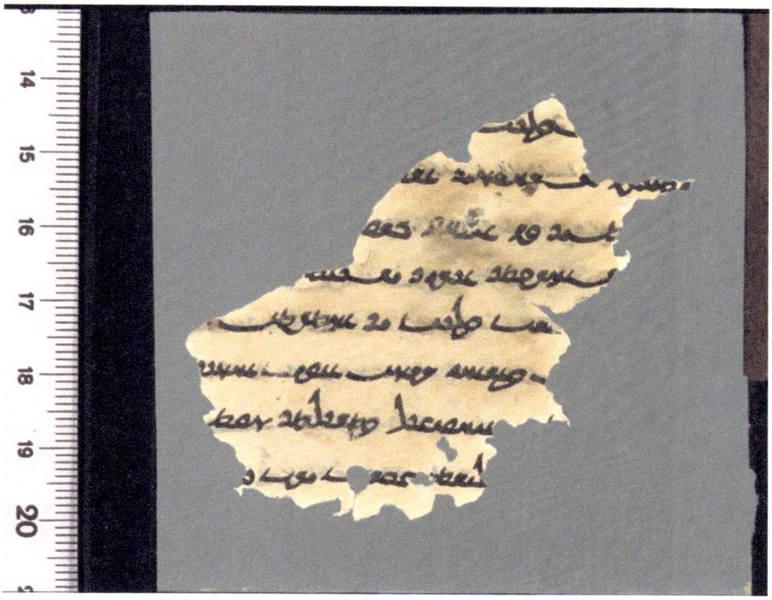

Fig. 31. So18500/A/

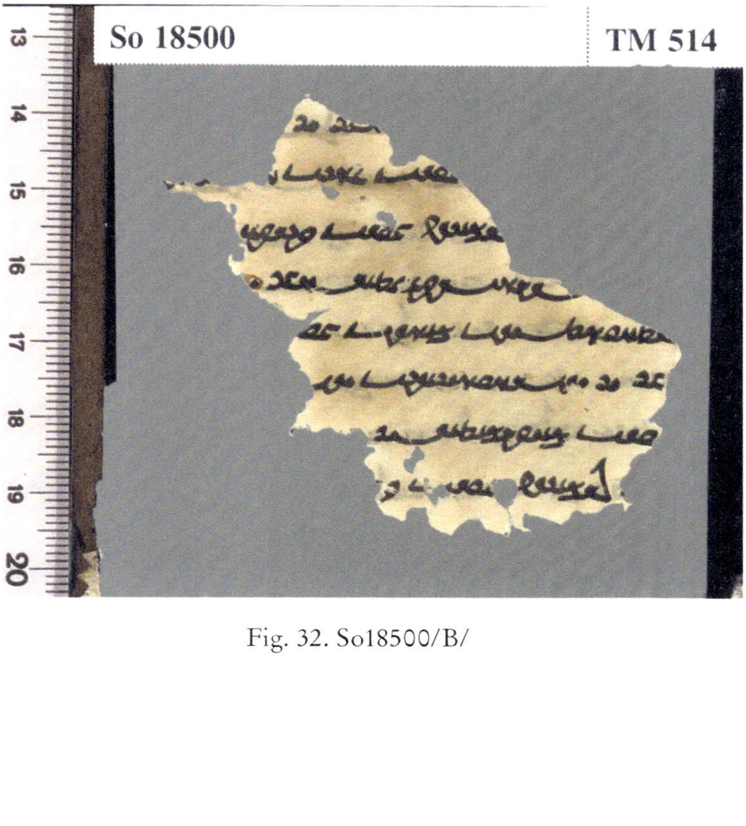

Fig. 32. So18500/B/

Bibiography

BARTHOLOMAE, CH. 1904: *Altiranisches Wörterbuch*. Straßburg.

BOYCE, M. 1960: *A Catalogue of the Iranian Manuscripts in Manichean Script in the German Turfan Collection*. Berlin.

CHEUNG, J. 2007: *Etymological Dictionary of the Iranian Verb*. Leiden/Boston.

COLDITZ, I. 2018: *Iranische Personennamen in manichäischer Überlieferung*. Vienna (SÖAW 889. Iranische Onomastik 16. IPNB 2,1).

DMT III.2[2] = SIMS-WILLIAMS, N./D. DURKIN-MEISTERERNST 2022: *Dictionary of Manichaean Sogdian and Bactrian*. Second edition revised and enlarged by N. SIMS-WILLIAMS. Turnhout.

DRAGONI, F. 2023: *Watañi lāntaṃ. Khotanese and Tumshuqese Loanwords in Tocharian*. Wiesbaden.

DRAGONI, F./E. MORANO 2022: "A Sogdian manuscript in Manichaean Script on Cosmogony and Rules for the Elect and Hearers in Mānistāns". In: *Manichaica Taurinensia*. Turnhout (Analecta Manichaica II), pp. 75–94.

DURKIN-MEISTERERNST, D. 2014: *Miscellaneous Hymns*. Turhnout (Berliner Turfantexte XXXI).

GMS = GERSHEVITCH, I. 1961: *A Grammar of Manichean Sogdian*. Oxford, Turnhout.

HENNING, W.B. 1936: "Ein manichäisches Bet- und Beichtbuch". In: *APAW* 10, Berlin [reprinted Henning 1977, I, pp. 417–557].

— 1942: "An Astronomical Chapter of the Bundahishn". In: *JRAS*, pp. 133–144. [repr. HENNING 1977, II, pp. 95–114].

— 1943: "The Book of Giants". In: *BSOAS* 11/1, pp. 52–74 [repr. HENNING 1977, II, pp. 115–137].

— 1948: "A Sogdian Fragment of the Manichaean Cosmogony". In: *Bulletin of the School of Oriental and African Studies* 12, pp. 306–318 [repr. HENNING 1977, II, pp. 301–313].

HENNING 1977 = W.B. HENNING 1977: *Selected Papers* I-II. Téhéran/Liège (Acta Iranica 14–15 2ème série, Hommages et Opera Minora).

HUTTER, M. 1992: *Manis kosmogonische Šabuhragan-Texte. Edition, Kommentar und literatur-geschichtliche Einordnung der manichäisch-mittelpersischen Handschriften M 98/99 I und M 7980–7984*. Wiesbaden (Studies in Oriental Religions 21).

JACKSON, A.V.W. 1932: *Researches in Manichaeism, with special reference to the Turfan fragments*. New York (Columbia University Indo-Iranian Series).

LIEU, S.N.C./G. MIKKELSEN 2017: *Tractatus Manichaicus Sinicus*. Turnhout (Corpus Fontium Manichaeorum, Series Sinica I., 1).

MACKENZIE, D.N. 1979: "Mani's Šābuhragān". In: *Bulletin of the School of Oriental and African Studies* 42, pp. 500–534.

MORANO, E. 2007: "A working catalogue of the Berlin Sogdian fragments in Manichaean script". In: M. MACUCH/M. MAGGI/W. SUNDERMANN (eds.): *Iranian Languages and Texts from Iran and Turan: Ronald E. Emmerick Memorial Volume*.Wiesbaden, pp. 239–271.

— 2009: "Sogdian Tales in Manichaean Script". In: D. DURKIN-MEISTERERNST/CH. RECK/D. WEBER (eds): *Literarische Stoffe und ihre Gestaltung in mitteliranischer*

Zeit. Kolloquium anlässlich des 70. Geburtstages von Werner Sundermann. Wiesbaden (Beiträge zur Iranistik 31), pp. 173–200 + Taf. II–VI.
— 2018: "Some codicological remarks on the corpus of the Berlin Manichaean Sogdian texts in Manichaean script: among books, glossaries, letters, booklets, bilingual and trilingual texts, normal, bold and cursive script". In: CH. BARBATI/O. CHUNAKOVA (eds.): *Studies in Early Medieval Iranian Manuscript Traditions other than Islamic. Written Monuments of the Orient* 2018 (2), pp. 11–38.
— 2019: "Manichaean Sogdian Cosmogonical Texts in Manichaean Script". In: *Competing Narratives between Nomadic People and their Sedentary Neighbours. Proceedings of the 7th International Conference on the Medieval History of the Eurasian Steppe, Nov. 9–12, 2018, Shanghai University, China* (Studia Uralo-altaica, University of Szeged), pp. 195–215.
— 2022: 恩里克 · 莫朗诺 (Enrico Morano, 《摩尼教粟特语创世文书》, 陈浩主编《欧亚草原历史研究》, 北京: 商务印书馆, 2022年, 第205–225页 [MORANO, E. "Monijiao Suteyu chuangshi wenshu". In: CHEN HAO (ed.): *Ouya caoyuan lishi yanjiu*, Beijing, pp. 205–225.]
— *forthcoming:* "The Sermon on the Three Poisons. An unpublished Manichaean Sogdian page in Sogdian script".
RECK, CH. 2003: "Die Beschreibung der Daēnā in einem soghdischen manichäischen Text". In: C.G. CERETI *et al.* (eds.): *Religious themes and texts of pre-Islamic Iran and Central Asia. Studies in honour of Professor Gherardo Gnoli.* Wiesbaden, pp. 323–38.
— 2006: *Mitteliranische Handschriften.* Teil 1: *Berliner Turfanfragmente manichäischen Inhalts in soghdischer Schrift.* Stuttgart (VOHD 18, 1)
— 2009: "The Ascension of the Light Elements and the Imprisonment of Ahriman. The cosmogonical and eschatological part of a Sogdian 'Sammelhandschrift'". In: W. SUNDERMANN *et al.* (eds.): *Exegisti monumenta. Festschrift in honour of Nicholas Sims-Williams.* Wiesbaden, pp. 369–398.
SIMS-WILLIAMS, N. 1985: "The Manichaean commandments: A survey of the sources". In: *Papers in honour of Professor Mary Boyce* II. Leiden (Acta Iranica 25), pp. 573–82.
SUNDERMANN, W. 1973: *Mittelpersische und parthische kosmogonische und Parabeltexte der Manichäer.* Berlin (Berliner Turfantexte IV).
— 1979a: "The Five Sons Of The Manichaean God Mithra" In: U. BIANCHI (ed.): *Mysteria Mithrae. Atti Del Seminario Internazionale Su 'La specificità storico-religiosa dei misteri di Mithra, con particolare riferimento alle fonti documentarie di Roma e Ostia'*, Roma e Ostia 28–31 Marzo 1978. Leiden/Roma (Études Préliminaires Aux Religions Orientales dans l'Empire Romain 80), pp. 777–787 [= SUNDERMANN 2001b, II, pp. 799–801].
— 1979b: "Namen von Göttern, Dämonen und Menschen in iranischen Versionen des manichäischen Mythos". In: *AOF* 6, pp. 95–133 [= SUNDERMANN 2001b, I, pp. 121–163].
— 1981: *Mitteliranische manichäische Texte kirchengeschichtlichen Inhalts.* Berlin, (Berliner Turfantexte XI).
— 1992: *Der Sermon vom Licht Nous.* Berlin (Berliner Turfantexte XXVII).
— 1994: "Mani's 'Book of the Giants' and the Jewish books of Enoch: a case of terminological difference and what it implies". In: *Irano-Judaica* III, pp. 40–48. [= SUNDERMANN 2001b, II, pp. 697–706].

— 2001a: "On human races, semi-human beings and monsters". In: P. MIRECKI/J. BEDUHN (eds.): *The Light and the Darkness. Studies in Manichaeism and its World*. Leiden/Boston/Cologne,pp. 181–99.

— 2001b: *Manichaica Iranica. Ausgewählte Schriften von Werner Sundermann*. 2 vols. Ed. by CH. RECK/D. WEBER/C. LEURINI/A. PANAINO. Roma (SOR 89).

VAN LINDT, P. 1992: *The Names of Manichaean Mythological Figures. A Comparative Study on Terminology in the Coptic Sources*. Wiebaden (Studies in Oriental Religions 26).

WALDSCHMIDT, E./W. LENTZ 1933: "Manichäische Dogmatik aus chinesischen und iranischen Texten". In: *SPAW* 13, Berlin.

YOSHIDA, Y. 2000: "First Fruits of Ryūkoku-Berlin Joint Project on the Turfan Iranian Manuscripts". In: *Acta Asiatica* 78, pp. 71–85.

— 2001: "On the Sogdian fragments of the St. Petersburg collection". In: *Contributions to the Studies of Eurasian Languages*, Series 3, *Issues in Eurasian Languages* 1, pp. 105–117.

The 'Starred' Frawahr and the 'Katasterization' of Humanity

ANTONIO PANAINO, Bologna

A very striking statement contained in chapter 49, 22–23[1] of the *Dādestān ī Mēnōg ī Xrad* has usually passed unnoticed despite its cosmological relevance. I take the present occasion to dedicate the discussion of this remarkable passage to DIETER WEBER, a dear friend and a colleague to whom our scholarly community owes the decipherment and interpretation of so many difficult Middle Persian texts.

The passage under discussion runs as follows:

> (22) *ud abārīg a-mar ud an-ōšmār axtarān ī paydāg hēnd frawahr ī gētīgān guft estēd* (23) *čē hāmōyēn dām ud dahišn ī dādār ohrmazd ō gētīg dād kē zāyišnīg ud kē-iz ārōyišnīg hēnd, harw tan-ēw rāy hamgōhr frawahr ēd ī xwēš paydāg.*
> "(22) And other countless and innumerable stars that are visible are called the *frawahr* of the material (creatures), (23) because of all the creation that the creator Ohrmazd fashioned within the material world — which are animal or even vegetable — it is evident that for everyone possessing a body, there is its own (corresponding) *frawahr* of the same nature (in the heavens)".

This statement can be partly explained thanks to the previous passage contained in the same chapter:[2]

> (15) *ud stārag ī haftōring abāg nō ud nawad ud nō sad ud nō hazār ud nō bēwar frawahr ī ahlawān pad dar ud widard ī dōšox gumārd estēd* (16) *pad abāz dāštan ī ān-ag nō ud nawad ud nō sad ud nō hazār ud nō bēwar dēwān ud druzān ud parīgān ud jādūgān ī pad hamēstārīh ī spihr ud axtarān hēnd.* (17) *u-š rawišn pērāmōn ī dušox* (18) *u-š mādagwar kār ēn čiyōn dwāzdah kadag ī axtarān pad dast dārēd pad drust šudan ud āmadan.* (19) *ud awēšān-iz dwāzdah axtarān hamgōnag pad nērōg ud ayārīh ī haftōring rawēnd.* (20) *ud harw axtar-ēw ka pad harborz andar rasēd pušt ō haftōring kunēd* (21) *ud panāh az haftōring xwāhēd.*
> "(15) And the star Haftōring was appointed with 99,999 *frawahr* of the righteous ones at the doors and the gates of hell (16) in order to withhold the 99,999 demons and *druz*, witches and wizards who are in opposition to the sphere and (its) stars. (17) And its motion is around the hell (18) and its essential job is that of keeping within its hands the twelve Houses of the constellations so that they (can) move

1 ANKLESARIA 1913, p. 137; BAUSANI 1963, p. 156.
2 ANKLESARIA 1913, pp. 137–138; BAUSANI 1963, p. 156–157.

on and come back orderly. (19) And even those twelve constellations so proceed thanks to the strength and the support of Haftōring. (20) And every constellation, when it descends on the Harborz, brings support to Haftōring (21) and seeks protection from Haftōring".

The presence of 99,999 *frawahr* together with Haftōring, Ursa Major, in the northern heaven, is justified because this celestial position is the one through which Ahreman pierced the celestial sphere and entered the creation. In another study, I have already shown that despite our perception, the northern direction was imagined as inferior, i.e. as placed below, because Ahreman and his demons were rising from the kingdom of the darkness toward the light, which was higher with respect to them.[3] Although they entered and invaded the earth and the atmosphere (as already stated in Yt 13,13),[4] they were unable to ascend higher than the heaven of the stars. Actually, they were blocked by the barrier formed by the stars (*stārag*) of "the unmixable sphere" (*spihr ī a-gumēzišnīh*).[5] Thus, all the demons with the leader were imprisoned between the lower heaven and the earth, including its subterranean spaces.

For this reason, the specific location of 99,999 *frawahr* around the seven stars of the Big Dipper is not surprising, and it forms a pendant with the 99,999 *frawahr*, which protect the semen deposited by Zardošt in the bottom of the lake *Kayānseh*.[6] This doctrine is already present in the Younger *Avesta*, and precisely in Yt 13,59–60.[7] These two stanzas state firstly that 99,999 *Frauuaṣ̌is* protect the *Vourukaṣ̌a* Sea, and then that the same number of *Frauuaṣ̌is* is involved in the protection of the seven *Haptō.iriṇga* stars. Thus, we find a perfect symmetry between the 99,999 *Frauuaṣ̌is* watching over the hole through which the demonic army entered the creation (and then was entrapped within), and the other group of 99,999 *Frauuaṣ̌is* guarding Zoroaster's semen. This is one of the few interesting examples of direct correspondence between heaven and earth within the Mazdean tradition.

If the symbolic value of the figure, 99,999 insists on a multiplication of the power attributed to number "three", more relevant is the explicit statement assigning to the countless stars of the heaven the privilege to be considered as (literally "called") *frawahr*. The patent idea here presented simply shows that every living being, animal or vegetable, has an astral correspondence in the sky. This form of astralization is more or less comparable with the processes of

3 See PANAINO 2019, pp. 134–141.
4 MALANDRA 1971, pp. 69, 113–114; KELLENS 1975, p. 13; LECOQ 2016, p. 480.
5 For a more detailed discussion of the cosmologic role of this layer of the heaven within Mazdean uranography and in particular its relation with the astral level of the *stārō spəṇtō.mainiauua-* (i.e. the "stars belonging to Spəṇta Mainiiu)", see PANAINO 2019, pp. 77–88, *passim*.
6 Cf. Yt 13,62; KELLENS 1975, p. 20. See PANAINO *forthcoming*.
7 MALANDRA 1971, pp. 80, 124, 198–199; KELLENS 1975, p. 20; LECOQ 2016, p. 496.

katasterization,[8] i.e. the phenomenon of the transfer of individual souls as stars to heaven. This practice became current in the Hellenistic and Late Antique astrology[9], but it was usually restricted to few privileged persons or heroes, while the doctrine attested in the *Mēnōg ī Xrad* implies a universalistic cosmological idea, and seems to derive directly and independently from a coherent development of a genuine Mazdean tradition. In fact, according to the *Frawardīn Yašt*, the *frauuaṣ̌is* reacted to the invasion of Aŋra Mainiiu, directing the motion of the heaven, whose turning rotation eventually blocked the demonic army within the celestial trap arranged by Ahura Mazdā (Yt 13, 57–58).[10] The importance of this cosmological tradition has been focused on by KELLENS,[11] and for other reasons, by the present author,[12] but the fact that the foundational role played by the *frauuaṣ̌is* had inspired a further development in the Zoroastrian astral mythology had escaped our full consideration.

Within the framework of the Avestan literature, the *frauuaṣ̌is* and the stars have been clearly distinguished (as in Yt 13,16),[13] but it is evident that the *frauuaṣ̌is* contribute to maintaining the upraised sky (Yt 13,29),[14] supporting the work of the star *Satauuaēsa-* (Yt 13,43–44)[15] and the cosmic order. It is in this context that a phenomenon such as a progressive association between the myriads of stars, in particular those of the Via Lactea (or Milky Way, which with its large spiral and its opposed arms was associated not only with Anāhitā,[16] but also with the *Xwarrah ī weh-dēn*),[17] took place. The divinity of the Glory of the Good Religion was a divinity whose legacy was preserved also in the Manichaean tradition and probably extended its prestige to Central Asia.[18] The difference in the visible brightness of the stars (their *magnitudo*, a concept certainly known in Sasanian

8 The καταστερισμός was a process through which a prestigious human being, a king, a princess, a hero, etc. was transformed after death into a star or a constellation (from καταστερίζω, i.e. "to place (someone/something) among the stars"): from κατά "down" + ἀστήρ "star"; on this process, see DOMENICUCCI 1996.

9 See already the presentation of the astral mysticism offered by CUMONT 1912, pp. 139–166, *passim*.

10 MALANDRA 1971, pp. 79, 123, 198–199; KELLENS 1975, pp. 19–20; LECOQ 2016, pp. 495.

11 KELLENS 2001.

12 For the origin of the spinning impulse impressed onto the celestial sphere after Ahreman's attack, see PANAINO 2019, pp. 78–79, 156–158. There are in fact two different traditions: one, earlier and Avestan, which attributed the *Frauuaṣ̌is* with a central role in this action, while some Pahlavi texts explain this motion as due to the impact given by Ahreman himself.

13 MALANDRA 1971, pp. 70, 114; LECOQ 2016, p. 481.

14 MALANDRA 1971, pp. 73, 117, 179; KELLENS 1975, pp. 15–16; LECOQ 2016, pp. 485–486.

15 MALANDRA 1971, pp. 76-77, 120–121, 189; KELLENS 1975, p. 18; LECOQ 2016, p. 491.

16 See WITZEL 1984.

17 HENNING 1942, pp. 233 (= 1977, 2: 99). For the occurrence in the *Bundahišn*, see now PAKZAD (2005, p. 39), who edited this passage as ch. 2,11.

18 SUNDERMANN 1979: 97, 102, 132, n. 239 (= 2001, I: 123, 128, 132, n. 239). Note that in the Manichaean sources, the name of this divine being concerns also the "Nous" or "Licht-Nous"; cf. also SUNDERMANN 1992.

times)[19] were thus associated with the quality of the living beings on the earth. In this way, we can infer the implicit existence of a sort of "moral" catalogue of the stars, in which the most brilliant ones were, as traditionally, associated with prestigious divinities, such as *Tištriia-*,[20] *Vanaṇt-*,[21] *Satauuaēsa-*,[22] *Haptō. iriṇga-*,[23] etc., while those of minor magnitude, including the ones practically invisible with a naked eye were associated (according to a comparative graduation) with the *frawahr* of the human beings. The idea of an astral component of the soul, associated with the individual *frawahr* — I insist —, is not *per se* an Avestan doctrine, but its emergence in a Late Antique or early Medieval context should not impress modern scholars, although I do not insist on the exclusive impact of a strong astrological external influence, because the overlapping between the celestial role played by the *frauuašis* and their interpretation as minor stars was not so peculiar and improbable. I think that it would be unnecessary to find here a direct echo of a Platonic doctrine, such as the one attested in the *Timaeus* 40b, where it is stated that after death the soul of a right man would reach again "his native star" (οἴκησιν ἄστρου), or with Gnostic traditions concerning the ascent of the souls (like the Manichean Column of Glory).[24]

This example in my opinion just shows the diffusion, since earliest times, of a tradition, which linked human individual destiny to the heavenly stars, although in the Mazdean framework these *frawahr* cannot be exclusively ascribed to dead persons, but with past, present and future generations, as if it were possible to see in the nocturnal sky not only the stars of our ancestors, but even ours and those of our last great-grandsons. We must also observe that this association did not find a special development and that it did not underpin further mythological cycles. It was just like a fascinating simile, a nice mythical-poetic intuition, without any further special theological or narrative implications.

The only echo of this doctrine seems to be found in the Renaissance, when Marsilius Ficinus[25] (in his *De vita coelitus comparanda*, "On obtaining life from the heavens", ch. 1) stated that:[26]

> *Neque in mundo vivente toto quicquam reperitur tam deforme, cui non adsit anima, cui non insit et animae munus. Congruitates igitur eiusmodi formarum ad rationes animae mundi Zoroaster divinas illices appellavit, quas et Synesisus magicas esse illecebras confirmavit.*

19 See PANAINO 2004.
20 See PANAINO 1990; 1995.
21 See PANAINO 1987.
22 About the identification of *Satauuaēsa-*, Pahlavi *Sadwēs*, see PANAINO 2008.
23 Cf. PANAINO 1996; for the classification of these stars, see PANAINO 2015.
24 See already PANAINO 2000.
25 About the importance of the Zoroastrian and pseudo-Zoroastrian traditions in the works of Marsilius Ficinus, see STAUSBERG, 1998, I, pp. 93–228.
26 See FICINO in the edition by KASKE/CLARK (1989, p. 244). Cf. also CILIBERTO 2005, p. 173. Cf. CATÀ 2010, p. 635.

"There is nothing to be found in this whole living world so deformed that Soul does not attend it, that a gift of the Soul is not in it. Therefore Zoroaster called such correspondences of forms to the reasons existing in the World-soul divine lures (*divinas illices*) and Synesius corroborated that they are magical baits".

The complexity of the idea of the *illices*,[27] the divine "lures", "baits", or "fascinations", which connect the divine world and the terrestrial one, cannot be treated here, because this subject concerns one central motif within the *Theologia Platonica* of Ficino, involving also Iamblichus, Synesius, and the *Chaldaean Oracles*.[28] Furthermore, the ways through which the esoteric concept of a stellar soul was developed are so many that a direct derivation or, alternatively, just a later survival of an Iranian tradition seems to me highly improbable, and in any case too difficult to be proved. Certainly, the presence of a reference to the fact that Zoroaster would have attributed divine roots to all the living beings in the astral dimension deserves to be considered in further researches, and certainly this particular reference contained in the *Dādestān ī Mēnōg ī Xrad* strikes us as an interesting witness, whose relevance and influence cannot be at the moment under-evaluated or forgotten.

Bibliography

ANKLESARIA, T.D. 1913: *Dânâk-u Mainyô-i Khrad. Pahlavi Pazand and Sanskrit Texts*. Bombay.

BAUSANI, A. 1963: *Testi religiosi zoroastriani tradotti dall'originale pahlavi con introduzione e note*. Catania (settima edizione).

CAFÀ, C. 2010: "L'idea di 'anima stellata' nel Quattrocento fiorentino. Andrea da Barberino e la Teoria psico-astrologica di Marsilio Ficino." In: *Bruniana & Campanelliana* 16/2, pp. 627–637.

CILIBERTO, M. 2005: *Pensare per Contrari. Disincanto e Utopia nel Rinascimento*. Roma (Storia e Letteratura. raccolta di Studi e Testi 226).

CUMONT, F. 1912: *Astrology and Religion Among the Greeks and Romans*. New York/London (American Lectures on the History of Religions, Series of 1911–1912).

DOMENICUCCI, P. 1996: *Astra Caesarum. Astronomia, astrologia e catasterismo da Cesare a Domiziano*. Pisa (Testi e studi di cultura classica 16).

FICINO, M. 1989: *Thee Books on Life*. A. Critical Edition and Translation with Introduction and Notes by C. V. KASKE and J. R. CLARK. Binghamton/New York (Medieval & Renaissance Texts & Studies Series 57. Renaissance Text Series 11).

KELLENS, J. 1975: *Fravardin Yašt* (1–70). *Introduction, édition et glossaire*. Wiesbaden (Iranische Texte, Heft 8).

— 2001: "Les saisons des rivières". In: M. STAUSBERG in Verbindung mit O. SUNDQVIST und A. VAN NAHL (eds): *Kontinuität und Bruche in der Religionsgeschichte. Festschrift für Anders Hultgård zu seinem 65. Geburtstag am 23. 12. 2001*. Berlin/

27 On this term and its complexity, see again STAUSBERG 1998, I, p. 157, and n. 391.

28 See CILIBERTO 2005, pp. 173–174.

New York (Ergänzungsbände zum Reallexikon der Germanischen Altertumskunde 31), pp. 471–480.

LECOQ, P. 2016: *Les livres de l'Avesta. Textes sacrés des Zoroastriens.* Paris.

MALANDRA, W.W. 1971: *The Fravaši Yašt. Introduction, Text, Translation and Commentary.* University of Pennsylvania, Ph.D. Ann Arbor, Michigan. (University Microfilms).

PAKZAD, F. 2005: *Bundahišn. Zoroastrische Kosmogonie und Kosmologie.* Band I. *Kritische Edition.* Tehran (Ancient Iranian Studies Series, 2).

PANAINO, A. 1987: "L'inno avestico a Vanant." In: *Atti del Sodalizio Glottologico Milanese* [1989], pp. 21–30.

— 1990: *Tištrya.* Part I: *The Avestan Hymn to Sirius.* Roma (Serie Orientale Roma, LXVIII, 1).

— 1995: *Tištrya.* Part II: *The Iranian Myth of the Star Sirius.* Roma (Serie Orientale Roma, LXVIII, 2).

— 1996: "Uranographia Iranica II. Avestan *hapta.srū-* and *mərəzu-*: Ursa Minor and the North Pole?" In: *Archiv für Orienforschung*, 42–43 [1995/1996 [1996], pp. 190–207.

— 2000: "Manichaean Concepts in the Pahlavi Commentary of *Māh Nyāyišn*, par. 4 ?" In: R.E. EMMERICK/W. SUNDERMANN/P. ZIEME (eds): *Studia Manichaica. IV. Internationaler Kongreß zum Manichäismus. Berlin, 14.–18. Juli 1997.* Berlin (Berichte und Abhandlungen/Berlin-Brandenburgische Akademie der Wissenschaften), pp. 464–480.

— 2004: "On the Dimension of the Astral Bodies in Zoroastrian Literature: between tradition and scientific astronomy." In CH. BURNETT/J.P. HOGENDIJK/K. PLOFKER/M. YANO (eds): *Studies in the History of the Exact Sciences in Honour of David Pingree.* Leiden/Boston (Islamic Philosophy, Theology and Science: Texts and Studies 54), pp. 267–286.

— 2008: "Again about α Cygni in the Sasanian Astronomical Tradition." In: Z. ZARSHENAS (ed.): *Papers in Honour of Professor B. Gharib.* Tehran, pp. 33–39.

— 2015: "*The Classification of Astral Bodies in the framework of an Historical Survey of Iranian traditions.*" In: U. BLÄSING/V. ARAKELOVA/M. WEINREICH (eds): *Studies on Iran and The Caucasus in Honour of Garnik Asatrian.* Leiden (Middle East and Islamic Studies), pp. 229–244.

— 2019a: *A Walk through the Iranian Heavens. Spherical and Non-Spherical Models in the Imagination of Ancient Iran and Its Neighbors.* (Ancient Iran Series 9).

— forthcoming: "Lake *Kąsaoiia-*: from the Mythical Geography of Later Avestan to its Ideological and Political Adaptation." With two Appendices by M. SCHWARTZ. In B. GENITO (ed.): *The Joint Iranian-Italian Archaeological Excavations at Dāhāne-ye Ghōlaman (Sistan, Iran). (Reports 1959, 1962, 1964, 1965, 1975–1976).* Napoli/Roma.

STAUSBERG, M. 1998: *Faszination Zarathushtra. Zoroaster und die Europäische Religionsgeschichte der Frühen Neuzeit.* 2 Bände. Mit einem Geleitwort von C. COLPE. Berlin/New York (Religionsgeschichtliche Versuche und Verarbeite, 42, 1–2).

SUNDERMANN, W. 1979: "Name von Götter, Dämonen und Menschen in iranische Versionen des manichäischen Mythos." In: *Altorientalische Forschung* 6, pp. 95–133.

— 1992: *Der Sermon der Licht-Nous: eine Lehrschrift des östlichen Manichäismus. Edition der parthischen und soghdischen Version.* (Berliner Turfantexte 17). Berlin.

— 2001: *Manichaica Iranica. Ausgewählte Schriften von Werner Sundermann.* 2 Bände. Herausgegeben von C. Reck/D. Weber/Cl. Leurini/A. Panaino. Roma (Serie Orientale Roma 89,1/2).

Witzel, M. 1984) "Sur le chemin du ciel." In: *Bulletin des Études Indiennes* 2, pp. 213–279.

Studies of 'Watermarks of Technology' from the Turfan Collection in Berlin

ANNA-GRETHE RISCHEL, Copenhagen

1. Introduction

Since my retirement in 2005 I have continued my studies of the technological development of the art of papermaking as paper conservator emerita in the department of Environmental Archaeology and Materials Science, the National Museum of Denmark. In connection with the International Dunhuang Project digitization of the Turfan collection in Berlin 2009–2010 in cooperation with Dr. Simone-Christiane Raschmann at the Berlin-Brandenburgische Akademie der Wissenschaften, I had access to study a random collection of more than 300 Turfan manuscripts and fragments, framed between sealed glass plates. The macroscopic observation of each document was registered chronologically on working tables, where my suggestion for collection of a tiny sample of paper for the microscopic analysis was marked on a photo or on a tracing of the document and agreed upon by Dr. Raschmann. The microscopic paper analysis of the tiny samples, collected simultaneously in connection with the studies of the selected Turfan manuscripts in Berlin, took place in Denmark at the National Museum of Denmark and at the School of Conservation, the Royal Academy of Fine Arts in Copenhagen. The combination of macroscopic and microscopic analysis served originally as a tool in paper conservation for describing the condition of an object before treatment. Much information is to be found macroscopically by just looking at a sheet of paper. Mechanical damages and damages from water, insects, and micro-organisms, illustrating the visible condition and strength of the paper, are easily observed with the naked eye in direct light, raking light, and light held against the paper. The internal condition and strength of the paper, must however, be examined through microscopic observation. Just a tiny piece of paper is needed for an optical estimate of the condition of the separated material of individual fibres and that is essential in studies of manuscripts, prints and drawings.

2. Scientific Analysis of Paper

JULIUS VON WIESNER, professor in plant anatomy and physiology in Vienna, Austria founded at the end of the 19th-century the scientific analysis of paper, built on optical microscopic observation, chemical spot tests and identification of the fibre materials through comparative analysis with a reference material of plants of known origin. His analysis in 1886–1887 of Arab paper manuscripts and of European rag paper through microscopic observation of the fibre materials completely changed European history that hitherto had built entirely on palaeographic interpretation of written sources. VON WIESNER proved with microscopic analysis that rag paper was not a 13th-century European invention but adopted by the Arabs in Samarkand in the 8th-century[1]. Arab papermakers had brought the knowledge of the production of rag paper to the Mediterranean region and to the Iberian Peninsula, from where it spread via Italy to the rest of Europe and further westwards.[2]

3. Archaeological Discoveries of Ancient Paper

Simultaneously with VON WIESNER's microscopic documentation in Vienna of the 8th-century origin of rag paper European archaeological excavations in East Turkestan discovered the existence of much older texts, written on birch bark, wood and paper. New studies of these manuscripts not only included palaeographic studies of texts of hitherto unknown languages and scripts and information preserved on paper about civilizations and cultures along the ancient Silk Roads in East Turkestan and Central Asia, but also microscopic analysis of these ancient paper materials, discovered by the archaeologists. Samples of paper without texts from the archaeological excavations along the Silk Roads were sent from Britain to VON WIESNER who expected to find paper qualities of recycled textile fibres similar to the Arab rag paper examined in 1886–1887. Use of local plants for the paper production were also a possibility, and VON WIESNER therefore collected local East Turkestan plants, fit for

1 WIESNER 1911, p. 26: "Schon in der ersten Periode ihrer Papiererzeugung aus Pflanzenfasern haben die Chinesen, wie später die Araber, es verstanden, Papier ganz und gar aus Hadern herzustellen. Die chinesische Hadern-Papier Erzeugung ist also etwa sechshundert Jahre älter als die arabische."

2 ENAMI 2010, p. 12: "The story is widely accepted among historians of the transferring of paper craft from China to the West at the battle between Chinese army and Arab army in 751 at Talas. However, the real reason why Arabs and later Europeans had continued the primitive papermaking craft using cloth rag until the 19th-century is yet unclear in spite of the fact that sophisticated papermaking technology using tree bark, shrub or other plant fibre had been widely spread in China, Central Asian oases kingdoms and Asian countries already in the 8th-century."

papermaking, and used his microscopic observation and description of these plants as reference material together with the description of the rag fibres in his comparative analysis of the East Turkestan paper samples.[3]

4. A Reference Material and Key for Identifying the Paper Technology and Fibre Material

JULIUS VON WIESNER's reference material of plants as a key for botanical fibre identification of the ancient archaeological Central-Asian paper qualities inspired me in 1987 to a pilot project, where a selection of new Oriental paper of known origin and technology, collected in Nepal, Thailand and Japan functioned as my reference material and key for identifying the paper technology and fibre materials of 19th-century anonymous Japanese papers. Since 1991 have I adapted this comparative method of paper analysis to study and shed light on the origin of fibre materials and technology of early European paper as well as ancient Arab and Central Asian paper from Lou-lan and the Turfan Region.

Common check lists served as schemes for a systematic macroscopic and microscopic description of the paper. Collection of optical data of each item together with photographic documentation, numbering, drawings, tracings, and notes were of importance for the analysis of the papers. This combination of macroscopic and microscopic analyses of paper proved to be a useful method for a possible identification of the origin of the fibre materials and paper technologies used. In a comparative analysis, it was possible with a reference material of paper of known origin and technology to encircle the provenance and date of these anonymous manuscripts through traces of the technology and leading elements of the fibre materials.[4]

3 WIESNER 1902, p. 47: "Zwischen der chinesischen und arabischen Hadernpapierbereitung besteht somit ein großer Unterschild. Die Chinesen erfanden die Fabrication des Rohfaserpapieres. Die aus den Rinden durch chemische Mittel isolierte Pflanzenfaser repräsentiert ein edleres Papiermaterial als jene Masse, welche die Chinesen durch starke Zerstampfung aus Hadern bereiteten. Nach meinem Dafürhalten benützten die Chinesen die Hadernmasse nur als billiges Surrogat, welches der wertvollen Rohfaser zugesetzt wurde, um die Papiermasse zu vermehren. Als die Hadern von den Chinesen zur Papierbereitung herangezogen wurden, waren dieselben Abfälle ohne sonstige Verwendbarkeit, also ein so gut wie wertloser Gegenstand. In fein Zerstampften Zustande der Rohfasermasse zugesetzt, bildet sie ein bloßes Surrogat."

4 RISCHEL 2019, p. 14: "Identification of the Lou-lan fibre material through microscopic analysis of tiny specimens of individual fibers testifies that mixtures of hemp, ramie, flax and mulberry fibers from recycled textile material as described in Ts'ai Lun's report from 105 AD still dominate the 3rd-century Lou-lan writing material. In order to obtain a paper surface, fit for writing with ink, a coating combined with a sizing and/or glazing of the new writing has taken place."

5. The Turfan Collection in Berlin-Brandenburgische Akademie der Wissenschaften

The systematic macroscopic registration of observations, tracing of the documents and suggestion for collection of samples of paper without inscriptions from already damaged edges for the microscopic analysis took place in 2009–2010 at Berlin-Brandenburgische Akademie der Wissenschaften in Berlin, where the collection is kept. Here the macroscopic part of the analysis dealt with systematic observation, documentation, and registration of the whole piece of paper, including its morphology, surface structure, transparency, stiffness, quality, shade of colour, fibre distribution, impressions from the mould sieve, and the drying process.

6. Examples of the Turfan Collection Project Notes in February 2009

Agr 001-Turfan **U5** TM 342 Language: Old Turkish, script: Runic

Macroscopic observation
Photocopy with measures and sketch
Paper length: 20. 5cm; paper width/height: 15. 0cm
Laid lines: 13/ 3cm, impression of irregular distributed laid lines from a screen of reed/straw.

2 lines with text, written with black ink and with addition of red circles on both sides of the paper; the text is slightly visible through the paper, and the characters are written on the same lines on both sides. Irregular lustreless surface, traces of brush strokes on verso, soft and plain paper quality, opaque and of a sand grey shade. The fibre distribution is slightly patchy with a few coarse fibres. The condition of the brittle paper with mechanical damages is good. Sample collected 17/02 2009. (Fig. 1)

Agr 002-Turfan **Ps 6** 124-126 Language: Middle Persian, script: Pahlavi

Carbon 14 analysis, date 870
Macroscopic observation
Photocopy with measure and sketch
Paper length: 10. 2cm; paper width/height: 9. 5cm (cut edges)
Laid lines: 11/ 3cm, impression of irregular distributed laid lines from a screen of reed/straw.

Fig. 1. Probenentnahme Turfan Sammlung 17.02.09. Agr 001 Turfan

18 lines with text, three lines are written with red ink. The paper has a lustreless surface of a thin and transparent quality with a clay brownish shade. Uniform and even fibre distribution of the fragmented and brittle paper. Sample collected 17/02 2009.

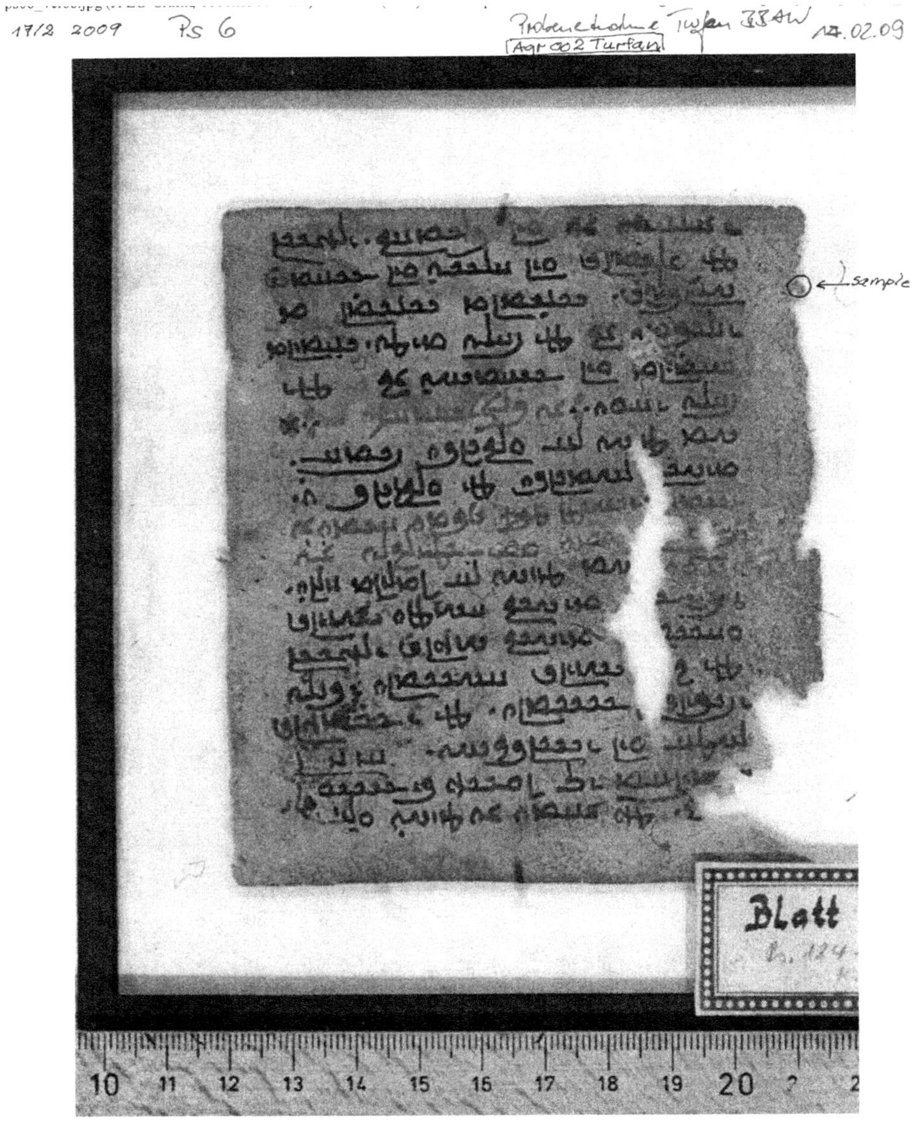

Fig. 2. Probenentnahme Turfan 17.02.09. Agr 002 Turfan

Agr 016-Turfan **Ps 7** Language: Middle Persian, script: Pahlavi

Carbon 14 analysis

Probenentnahme Carbon 14 Analysis: Restaurierungsprotokol 17.10.08. Probenentnahme für C 14 Test. Probe größer als 0, 5cm2, da Papier sehr geringes Gewicht. Masse: 11. 3 x 8. 6cm. Risse, Fehlstellen Klebestreifen Seide. Oberfläche verschmutzt. Papierstruktur teilweise sehr unstabil.

Macroscopic observation:

Photocopy and tracing with notes

Paper length: 9. 3cm; paper width/height: 11. 2cm

Laid lines: 21/ 3cm, impression of regular distributed laid lines from a screen of bamboo splints.

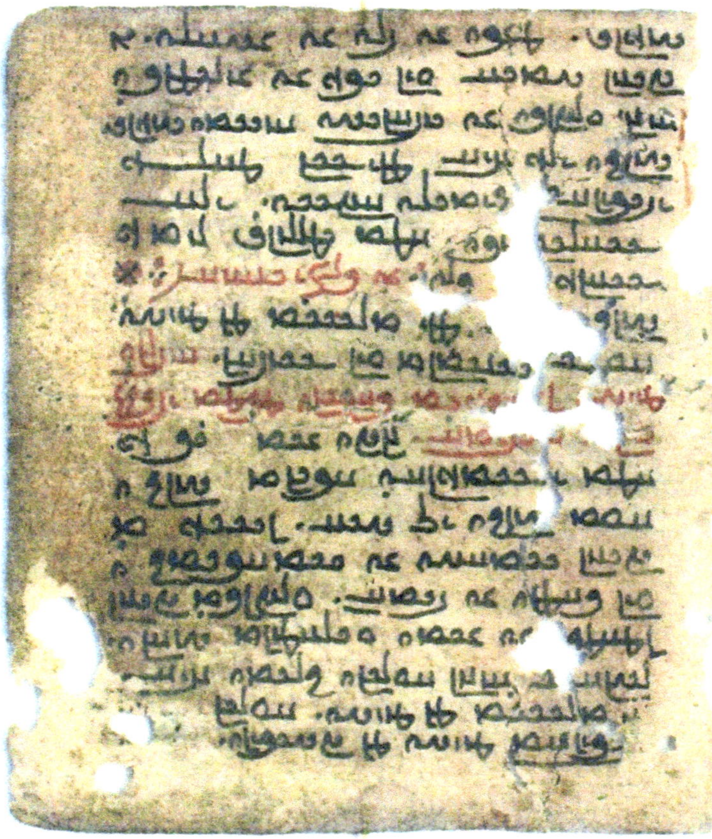

Fig. 3. Bl 7

19 lines of texts with black and red ink are written on both sides. The opaque and fragile paper has a lustreless, sized surface, the shade is clay brown, and the fibre distribution is uniform and even. The condition of the fragmented paper with mechanical damages is brittle. Sample collected 18/02 2009.

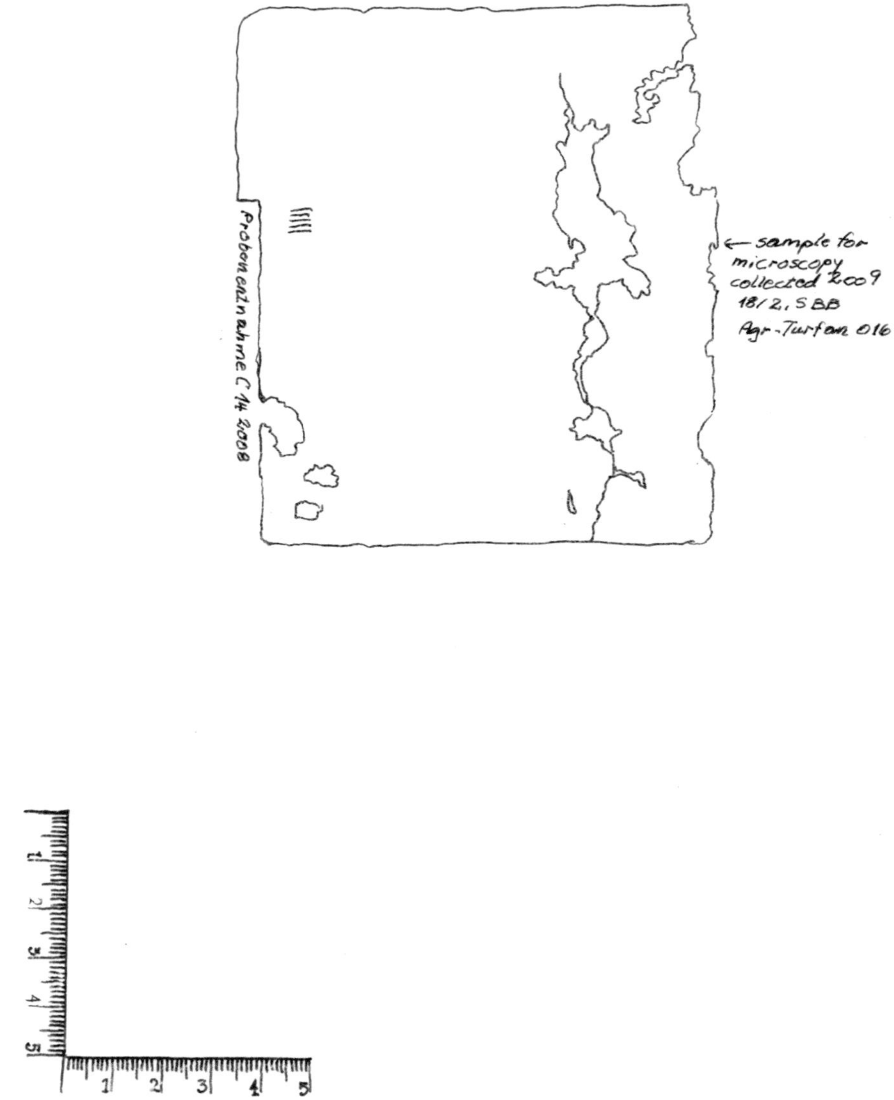

Fig. 4. Tracing of Ps 7 Turfan 18.02.09. Agr 016 Turfan

7. Connection Between Languages, Scripts, Tools and Fibre Materials

Turfan Analysis 002 **Ps 6** 124,126, C 14 analysis
Language/script: Middle Persian/Pahlavi

Macroscopic observation of the impression of a regular distribution of **11** laid lines/ 3cm from a sieve of reeds/straw. Microscopic observation of recycled hemp- & flax (?) fibres.

Turfan Analysis 016 **Ps 7** C14 analysis
Language/script: Middle Persian/Pahlavi

Macroscopic observation of the impression of a regular distribution of **21** laid lines/3 cm from a sieve of bamboo splints. Microscopic observation of recycled hemp & flax fibres.

Turfan Analysis 003 **M 7984** T III 260 e
Language/script: Middle Persian/Manichaean

Macroscopic observation of the impression of a regular distribution of **21** laid lines/ 3cm from a sieve of bamboo splints. Microscopic observation of recycled ramie/hemp & flax fibres.

Turfan Analysis 089 **M 765 c**
Language script: Sogdian/Manichaean

Macroscopic observation of the impression of a regular distribution of **32** laid lines/ 3cm from a screen of bamboo splints. Microscopic observation of recycled ramie/hemp & flax fibres.

Turfan Analysis 108 **M 1923 T III M 148**
Language/script: Parthian/Manichaean

Macroscopic observation of the impression of a regular distribution of **21-23** laid lines / 3cm from a sieve of bamboo splints. Microscopic observation of recycled ramie/hemp & flax fibres.

Turfan Analysis 307 **THT 4122 B**/ T III MQR 63/ Toch
Language/script: Tocharian B/Brahmi

Macroscopic observation of the impression of a regular distribution of **20-21** laid lines/ 3cm from a sieve of bamboo splints. Microscopic observation of recycled hemp & flax fibres.

Turfan Analysis 288 **SHT 2330**
Language/script: Sanskrit/Brahmi

Macroscopic observation of the impression of a regular distribution of **20** laid lines/ 3cm from a sieve of reeds or of bamboo splints. Microscopic observation of recycled hemp/flax/mulberry & cotton fibres.

Turfan Analysis 245 **SHT III 842**/ K 14207 Gö 763/ R
Language/script: Sanskrit/Brahmi IV

Macroscopic observation of the impression of a regular distribution of **20** laid lines/ 3cm from a sieve of reeds or of bamboo splints. Microscopic observation of recycled hemp/flax/mulberry & cotton fibres.

Turfan Analysis 259 **SHT VI 1217, i-p**/ X 433/ Gö 260
Language/script: Sanskrit/Brahmi IV

Macroscopic observation of the impression of a regular distribution of **20** laid lines/ 3cm from a sieve of reeds or of bamboo splints. Microscopic observation of recycled hemp & flax fibres.

Turfan Analysis 013 **SHT I 191**/ K 1233
Language/script: Sanskrit/Brahmi (V)

Macroscopic observation of the impression of a regular distribution of **26** laid lines/ 3cm from a sieve of bamboo splints. Microscopic observation of recycled hemp & flax fibres.

Turfan Analysis 015 **SHT I 134**/ K 237/ Gö 58, Bl. 60
Language/script: Sanskrit/Brahmi (V)

Macroscopic observation of the impression of a regular distribution of **22** laid lines/ 3cm from a sieve of bamboo splints. Microscopic observation of recycled hemp -6 flax fibres.

Turfan Analysis 067 **SHT I 400** Gö 154, S. 362 Bl.172 R
Language/script: Sanskrit/Brahmi V

Macroscopic observation of the impression of a regular distribution of 20 laid lines/ 3cm from a sieve of reeds or bamboo splints. Microscopic observation of mulberry fibres.

Turfan Analysis 258 **SHT 219**/ K 1373/VIII 6-27
Language/script: Sanskrit/Brahmi V

Macroscopic observation of the impression of a regular distribution of **20** laid lines/ 3cm from a sieve of reeds or bamboo splints. Microscopic observation of recycled ramie/hemp & flax fibres.

Turfan Analysis 073 SHT I 498 Gö 163, S. 364 R. Sang 74
Language/script: Sanskrit/Brahmi VI

Macroscopic observation of the impression of a regular distribution of **22** laid lines/ 3cm from a sieve of bamboo splints. Microscopic observation of mulberry fibres.

Turfan Analysis 029 **U 6067**
Language/script: Old Turkish/Uighur

Macroscopic observation of the impression of a regular distribution of **21** laid lines/ 3cm from a sieve of bamboo splints. Microscopic observation of mulberry fibre material (?).

Turfan Analysis 057 **U 5453** T I D 575
Language/script: Old Turkish/Uighur

Macroscopic observation of the impression of a regular distribution of **21** laid lines/ 3cm from a sieve of bamboo splints. Microscopic observation of recycled ramie/hemp & mulberry fibres.

Turfan Analysis 097 **U 5578** T II D 104
Language/script: Old Turkish/Uighur

Macroscopic observation of the impression of a regular distribution of **20** laid lines/ 3cm from a sieve of reeds or bamboo splints. Microscopic observation of mulberry fibres.

Turfan Analysis 107 **U 5965**
Language/script: Old Turkish/Uighur

Macroscopic observation of the impression of a regular distribution of **23** laid lines/ 3cm from a sieve of bamboo splints. Microscopic observation of mulberry fibres.

Turfan Analysis 110 **U 6067 a**
Language/script: Old Turkish/Uighur

Macroscopic observation of the impression of a regular distribution of **26** laid lines/ 3cm from a sieve of bamboo splints. Microscopic observation of mulberry fibres.

Turfan Analysis 111 **U 6067 b**
Language/script: Old Turkish/Uighur

Macroscopic observation of the impression of a regular distribution of **26** laid lines/ 3cm from a sieve of bamboo splints. Microscopic observation of mulberry fibres.

Turfan Analysis 112 **U 6067 c**
Language/script: Old Turkish/Uighur

Macroscopic observation of the impression of a regular distribution of **26** laid lines/ 3cm from a sieve of bamboo splints. Microscopic observation of mulberry fibres.

Turfan Analysis 113 **U 6067 d**
Language/script: Old Turkish/Uighur

Macroscopic observation of the impression of a regular distribution of **26** laid lines/ 3cm from a sieve of bamboo splints. Microscopic observation of mulberry fibres.

Turfan Analysis 114 **U 6067 e**
Language/script: Old Turkish/Uighur

Macroscopic observation of the impression of a regular distribution of **26** laid lines/ 3cm from a sieve of bamboo splints. Microscopic observation of mulberry fibres.

Turfan Analysis 177 B5/ **U 7005**
Language/script: Old Turkish/Uighur

Macroscopic observation of the impression of a regular distribution of **23** laid lines/ 3cm from a sieve of bamboo splints. Microscopic observation of mulberry fibres.

Turfan Analysis 203 **B 10/ U 7031**/ T II S. 2
Language/script: Old Turkish/Uighur

Macroscopic observation of the impression of a regular distribution of **20** laid lines/ 3cm from a sieve of reeds or bamboo splints. Microscopic observation of mulberry fibres.

Turfan Analysis 212 **B 15 b/ U 7044**/ T III TV 49
Language/script: Old Turkish/Uighur

Macroscopic observation of the impression of a regular distribution of **20** laid lines/ 3cm from a sieve of reeds of bamboo splints. Microscopic observation of recycled ramie/hemp & flax fibres.

Turfan Analysis 308 **B 21/ U 7054**
Language/script: Old Turkish/Uighur

Macroscopic observation of the impression of a regular distribution of **20** laid lines/ 3cm from a sieve of reeds or of bamboo splints. Microscopic observation of bamboo fibres.

Turfan Analysis 080 **U 6873 (a)**
Language/script: Old Turkish/Brahmi

Macroscopic observation of the impression of a regular distribution of **21** laid lines / 3cm from a sieve of bamboo splints. Microscopic observation of recycled rami/hemp & flax fibres.

Turfan Analysis 081 **U 6873 (b)**
Language/script: Old Turkish/Brahmi

Macroscopic observation of the impression of a regular distribution of **21** laid lines/ 3cm from a sieve of bamboo splints. Microscopic observation of recycled hemp & flax fibres.

Turfan Analysis 082 **U 3395** TM 472 500
Language/script: Old Turkish/Brahmi

Macroscopic observation of the impression of a regular distribution of **22** laid lines/ 3cm from a sieve of bamboo splints. Microscopic observation of recycled ramie/hemp & flax fibres.

Turfan Analysis 085 **U 2293** T I α-b
Language/script: Old Turkish/Brahmi

Macroscopic observation of the impression of a regular distribution of **20** laid lines/ 3cm from a sieve of reeds or of bamboo splints. Microscopic observation of mulberry fibres.

8. Watermarks of Technology

The technological watermark of chain lines and laid lines is created during the sheet formation as an embossment in the new sheet of paper during the drainage of the water. In the flexible and loose lying Oriental sieve, the numbers of laid lines/ 3 cm indicate, if the sieve is constructed of slightly irregular reeds or grasses available everywhere, or if the sieve is constructed of regular thin and close-lying bamboo splints of Chinese origin. The fibre distribution in the sheet of paper also leaves 'watermarks' of the movements during the sheet formation of the mould, and traces of brush strokes tell about the flattening of the still humid sheet on drying boards.

9. Conclusion

I have experienced in my studies of Oriental and Occidental papers without watermarks that information about the technology and fibre materials and eventual provenance can be observed through macroscopic and microscopic analysis. In my search for information about a possible provenance of the Turfan manuscripts examined, I have found a useful method in combining the manuscript languages and scripts with the 'technical watermarks', preserved as embossment in the paper during the sheet formation on the flexible sieve, where the number of laid lines indicate either a local production or a Chinese production of the paper. Usually only one sheet of paper of the random collection of manuscripts was available for me of the Turfan material that I studied in 2009–2010, except for the Turfan Analysis 002 and 016. Here, in 2009, I was given paper samples of two folios, folio 6, 17/02 and folio 7 18/02 of the Pahlavi psalter. The result of the microscopic analysis of these two folios is that the paper material was made of recycled fibre material. Interestingly, however the macroscopic analysis of these two folios yielded different results. While both folios are made from recycled fibre material, the number of laid lines of Ps6 (Pahlavi psalter folio 6) points to: locally produced paper of recycled fibre material, while the number of laid lines of Ps7 (Pahlavi psalter folio 7) indicates imported Chinese paper of recycled fibre material. Thus, locally produced Central Asian paper and imported Chinese paper were here combined as two sheets of the manuscript.

Appendix

Macroscopic-Microscopic observation of Asian paper

Sample no.	Catalogue no. & language/script	Fibre materials and laid lines 1
001-Turfan	U 5 (TM 342)	Recycled ramie/hemp/flax fibres
	Old Turkish/ Runic	13/ 3cm
006-Turfan	U 5519 (T II 954)	Recyced hemp/flax fibres
	Old Turkish/Uighur	13/ 3cm
029-Turfan	U 6067	Mulberry fibres (?)
	Old Turkish/Uighur	21/ 3cm
031-Turfan	U 5589 (T II D 150.501)	Mulberry fibres
	Old Turkish/Uighur	10/ 3cm
035-Turfan	U 6055	Mulberry fibres
	Old Turkish/Uighur	11/ 3cm
036-Turfan	U 6076	Recycled ramie/hemp/flax fibres
	Old Turkish/Uighur	13/ 3cm
037-Turfan	U 639 (T III 5625)	Recycled ramie/hemp/flax fibres
	Old Turkish/Uighur	08/ 3cm
038-Turfan	U 3144 (T III 84.48)	Recycled hemp/flax fibres
	Old Turkish/Uighur	09/ 3cm

039-Turfan	U 2405 (T II 509)	Recycled ramie/hemp/flax fibres
	Old Turkish/Uighur	09/ 3cm
040-Turfan	U 5538	Recycled ramie/hemp/flax fibres
	Old Turkish/Uighur	10/ 3cm
041-Turfan	U 5720 (T II)	Mulberry fibres
	Old Turkish/Uighur	08/ 3cm
042-Turfan	U 5290	Mulberry fibres
	Old Turkish/Uighur	
043-Turfan	U 835 (T II M 12-2)	Mulberry fibres
	Old Turkish/Uighur	
051-Turfan	U 5856	Mulberry fibres
	Old Turkish/Uighur	11/ 3cm
052-Turfan	U 6281	Mulberry fibres
	Old Turkish/Uighur	11/ 3cm (?)
053-Turfan	U 6256	Mulberry fibres
	Old Turkish/Uighur	11/ 3cm
054-Turfan	U 6287	Mulberry fibres
	Old Turkish/Uighur	9-11/ 3cm
055-Turfan	U 6266	Recycled ramie/hemp/mulberry fibres
	Old Turkish/Uighur	11/ 3cm
056-Turfan	U 5841 (T III D)	Mulberry fibres
	Old Turkish/Uighur	14/ 3cm
057-Turfan	U 5453 (T I D 575)	Recycled ramie/hemp/mulberry fibres
	Old Turkish/Uighur	21/ 3cm
093-Turfan	U 5833 (T III 99 b)	Recycled ramie/hemp/flax fibres
	Old Turkish/Uighur	11/ 3cm
096-Turfan	U 1923 (T III M 148	Mulberry fibres
	Old Turkish/Uighur	13/ 3cm
097-Turfan	U 5578 (T II D 104)	Mulberry fibres
	Old Turkish/Uighur	20/ 3cm

Sample no	Catalogue no. & language/script	Fibre materials & laid lines 2
102-Turfan	U 6317	Recycled ramie/hemp/mulberry fibres
	Old Turkish/Uighur	20/ 3cm
103-Turfan	U 6198	Recycled hemp/flax/mulberry fibres
	Old Turkish/Uighur	13/ 3cm

104-Turfan	U 3189 (T III BT.V. 51-11)	Recycled ramie/hemp/flax fibres
	Old Turkish/Uighur	
106-Turfan	U 6157	Mulberry fibres
	Old Turkish/Uighur	11/ 3cm
107-Turfan	U 5965	Mulberry fibres
	Old Turkish/Uighur	23/ 3cm
110-Turfan	U 6067 a	Mulberry fibres
	Old Turkish/Uighur	26/ 3cm
111-Turfan	U 6067 b	Mulberry fibres
	Old Turkish/Uighur	26/ 3cm
112-Turfan	U 6067 c	Mulberry fibres
	Old Turkish/Uighur	26/ 3 cm
113-Turfan	U 6067 d	Mulberry fibres
	Old Turkish/Uighur	26/ 3cm
114-Turfan	U 6067 e	Mulberry fibres
	Old Turkish/Uighur	26/ 3cm
142-Turfan	Mainz 870	Recycled hemp/flax/cotton fibres
	Old Turkish/Uighur	10/ 3cm
143-Turfan	Mainz 870	Recycled ramie/hemp/flax fibres
	Old Turkish/Uighur	13/ 3cm
144-Turfan	Mainz 871 (T II S.2 B)	Recycled ramie/hemp/flax fibres
	Old Turkish/Uighur	10/ 3cm
145-Turfan	Mainz 872	Recycled ramie/hemp/flax fibres
	Old Turkish/Uighur	11/ 3cm
146-Turfan	Mainz 873	Recycled ramie/hemp/flax fibres
	Old Turkish/Uighur	11/ 3cm
147-Turfan	Mainz 874 (T II S.2 B)	Recycled hemp/flax/mulberry fibres
	Old Turkish/Uighur	10/ 3cm
148-Turfan	Mainz 875	Recycled ramie/hemp/flax/ cotton fibr.
	Old Turkish/Uighur	11/ 3cm
149-Turfan	Mainz 876	Recl.ramie/hemp/flax/cotton/ mulber.f
	Old Turkish/Uighur	15/ 3cm
150-Turfan	Mainz 877	Recl.ramie/hemp/flax/cotton/ mulber.f
	Old Turkish/Uighur	13/ 3cm
151-Turfan	Mainz 878	Recycled ramie/hemp/flax fibres
	Old Turkish/Uighur	11/ 3cm

152-Turfan	Mainz 879/(T II S 2 B No. 383)	Recycled hemp/flax/cotton fibres
	Old Turkish/Uighur	09/ 3cm
153-Turfan	Mainz 880	Recycled ramie/hemp/mulberry fibres
	Old Turkish/Uighur	09/ 3cm
154-Turfan	Mainz 881	Recycled ramie/hemp fibres
	Old Turkish/Uighur	10/ 3cm
155-Turfan	Mainz 882	Recycled hemp/flax fibres
	Old Turkish/Uighur	10/ 3cm

Sample no.	Catalogue no. & language/script	Fibre materials and laid lines 3
156-Turfan	Mainz 883	Recycled ramie/hemp/flax fibres
	Old Turkish/Uighur	
157-Turfan	Mainz 884	Recycled ramie/hemp/cotton fibres
	Old Turkish/Uighur	09/ 3cm
158-Turfan	Mainz 885	Recycled ramie/hemp/flax fibres
	Old Turkish/Uighur	9-10/ 3cm
159-Turfan	Mainz 886	Recycled ramie/hemp/flax fibres
	Old Turkish/Uighur	10/ 3cm
160-Turfan	Mainz 887 (T II S. 2 B No 352)	Recycled hemp/flax/cotton fibres
	Old Turkish/Uighur	9-10/ 3cm
161-Turfan	Mainz 888 (T II S. 2 B)	Recycled ramie/hemp/flax fibres
	Old Turkish/Uighur	10/ 3cm
162-Turfan	Mainz 889	Recycled ramie/hemp/flax fibres
	Old Turkish/Uighur	13/ 3cm
163-Turfan	Mainz 890	Recycled ramie/hemp fibres
	Old Turkish/Uighur	10/ 3cm (?)
164-Turfan	Mainz 891	Recycled ramie/hemp/flax fibres
	Old Turkish/Uighur	9-10/ 3cm (?)
165-Turfan	Mainz 892	Recycled ramie/hemp/flax fibres
	Old Turkish/Uighur	10/ 3cm
166-Turfan	Mainz 892	Recycled ramie/hemp/flax fibres
	Old Turkish/Uighur	10/ 3cm
167-Turfan	Mainz 1012	Recycled hemp/flax fibres
	Old Turkish/Uighur	15/ 3cm (?)
168-Turfan	Mainz 1013	Recycled ramie/hemp/flax fibres
	Old Turkish/Uighur	10/ 3cm
169-Turfan	Mainz 1014 (T II S 2 B No. 357)	Recycled ramie/hemp fibres
	Old Turkish/Uighur	09/ 3cm

170-Turfan	Mainz 1015	Recycled ramie/hemp/flax fibres
	Old Turkish/Uighur	10/ 3cm
171-Turfan	Mainz 1016	Recycled ramie/hemp/flax fibres
	Old Turkish/Uighur	10/ 3cm
172-Turfan	U 7000	Recycled ramie/hemp/flax fibres
	Old Turkish/Uighur	
174-Turfan	U 7002	Recycled ramie/hemp/flax fibres
	Old Turkish/Uighur	16/ 3cm
175-Turfan	U 7003 (T III T.V.)	Mulberry fibres
	Old Turkish/Uighur	11/ 3cm
176-Turfan	U 7004	Mulberry fibres
	Old Turkish/Uighur	9-11/ 3cm
177-Turfan	U 7005	Mulberry fibres
	Old Turkish/Uighur	23/ 3cm
178-Turfan	U 7006 (T II Y 49)	Recycled ramie/hemp/flax/ mulberry f.
	Old Turkish/Uighur	13/ 3cm
179-Turfan	U 7007 (T II Y 40.6)	Recycled hemp/flax/cotton fibres
	Old Turkish/Uighur	11/ 3cm
180-Turfan	U 7008	Mulberry fibres
	Old Turkish/Uighur	17/ 3cm

Sample no.	Catalogue no. & language/script	Fibre materials and laid lines 4
181-Turfan	U 7009	Mulberry fibres
	Old Turkish/Uighur	17/ 3cm
182-Turfan	U 7010	Mulberry fibres
	Old Turkish/Uighur	17/ 3cm
183-Turfan	U 7011 (TM 32)	Mulberry fibres
	Old Turkish/Uighur	16/ 3cm
184-Turfan	U 7012 (T II D 228)	Mulberry fibres
	Old Turkish/Uighur	17/ 3cm
185-Turfan	U 7013	Mulberry fibres
	Old Turkish/Uighur	16/ 3cm
186-Turfan	U 7014	Mulberry fibres
	Old Turkish/Uighur	16/ 3cm (?)
187-Turfan	U 7015 (T I ų)	Mulberry fibres
	Old Turkish/Uighur	16-17/ 3cm
188-Turfan	U 7016	Mulberry fibres
	Old Turkish/Uighur	16/ 3cm

189-Turfan	U 7017	Mulberry fibres
	Old Turkish/Uighur	16/ 3cm (?)
190-Turfan	U 7018 ([I] D 377)	Mulberry fibres
	Old Turkish/Uighur	16/ 3cm (?)
191-Turfan	U 7019 (T I α)	Mulberry fibres
	Old Turkish/Uighur	16/ 3cm
192-Turfan	U 7020	Mulberry fibres
	Old Turkish/Uighur	16/ 3cm
193-Turfan	U 7021	Mulberry fibres
	Old Turkish/Uighur	16/ 3cm
194-Turfan	U 7022 (T I)	Mulberry fibres
	Old Turkish/Uighur	19/ 3cm
195-Turfan	U 7023 (T.M. 40)	Mulberry fibres
	Old Turkish/Uighur	19/ 3cm
196-Turfan	U 7024 (T I ụ)	Mulberry fibres
	Old Turkish/Uighur	17/ 3cm
197-Turfan	U 7025	Mulberry fibres
	Old Turkish/Uighur	17/ 3cm
198-Turfan	U 7026 (T II)	Mulberry fibres
	Old Turkish/Uighur	17/ 3cm
199-Turfan	U 7027 (T i ụ) (2 sheets w. attach. sh)	Mulberry fibres
	Old Turkish/Uighur	17/ 3cm
200-Turfan	U 7028 (T III M 178)	Mulberry fibres
	Old Turkish/Uighur	17/ 3cm
201-Turfan	U 7029	Recycled ramie/flax/silk fibres
	Old Turkish/Uighur	
202-Turfan	U 7030 (T I D)	Recycled ramie/hemp/flax fibres
	Old Turkish/Uighur	16/ 3cm
203-Turfan	U 7031 (T II S. 2)	Mulberry fibres
	Old Turkish/Uighur	20/ 3cm
204-Turfan	U 7032 (T II S)	Recycled ramie/hemp/flax fibres
	Old Turkish/Uighur	10 & 15/ 3cm

Sample no.	Catalogue no. & language/script	Fibre materials & laid lines 5
205-Turfan	U 7033 (T I α)	Recycled ramie/hemp/flax fibres
	Old Turkish/Uighur	15/ 3cm
206-Turfan	U 7034 (T I D)	Recycl. ramie/hemp/flax/cotton fibres
	Old Turkish/Uighur	15/ 3cm

207-Turfan	U 7035 (T II Y 18)	Recycl. ramie/hemp/flax/cotton fibres
	Old Turkish/Uighur	11/ 3cm
208-Turfan	U 7036 (T II Y 5)	Rec.ramie/hemp/flax/cotton/ mulberry
	Old Turkish/Uighur	11/ 3cm
209-Turfan	U 7037 (T II Y 14)	Recycl. ramie/hemp/flax/cotton fibres
	Old Turkish/Uighur	13/ 3cm
210-Turfan	U 7038 (T II D 85)	Recycled ramie/hemp/flax fibres
	Old Turkish/Uighur	14/ 3cm
211-Turfan	U 7039 (T III 234)	Recycled ramie/hemp/flax fibres
	Old Turkish/Uighur	15/ 3cm
212-Turfan	U 7044 (T III TV 49)	Recycled ramie/hemp/flax fibres
	Old Turkish/Uighur	20/ 3cm
213-Turfan	U 7045 (T I D)	Recycled ramie/hemp/flax fibres
	Old Turkish/Uighur	15/ 3cm
214-Turfan	U 7046	Recycled ramie/hemp/flax fibres
	Old Turkish/Uighur	15/ 3cm
301-Turfan	U 5065 (T III M 120)	Mulberry fibres
	Old Turkish/Uighur	16/ 3cm
302-Turfan	U 7047	Recycled ramie/hemp/flax fibres
	Old Turkish/Uighur	09/ 3cm
303-Turfan	U 7048	Recycled ramie/hemp/flax fibres
	Old Turkish/Uighur	
304-Turfan	U 7049 (T II Toyoq)	Mulberry fibres
	Old Turkish/Uighur	10/ 3cm
305-Turfan	U 7051	Recycled ramie/hemp/flax fibres
	Old Turkish/Uighur	15/ 3cm
306-Turfan	U 7052	Recycled ramie/hemp/flax fibres
	Old Turkish/Uighur	
308-Turfan	U 7054	Bamboo fibres
	Old Turkish/Uighur	20/ 3cm
309-Turfan	U 7058 (T II Y 21)	Recycl. ramie/hemp/flax/cotton fibres
	Old Turkish/Uighur	11/ 3cm
310-Turfan	U 7059 (T III TV. 57)	Recycled ramie/hemp/flax fibres
	Old Turkish/Uighur	17-18/ 3cm
311-Turfan	U 7061 (T III M 127)	Recycled ramie/hemp/flax fibres
	Old Turkish/Uighur	14/ 3cm

312-Turfan	U 7068 (T II Y 63)	Recycled ramie/hemp/flax fibres
	Old Turkish/Uighur	09/ 3cm
313-Turfan	U 7069 (T II T)	Recycled ramie/hemp/flax fibres
	Old Turkish/Uighur	13/ 3cm
314-Turfan	U 7070 (T III T)	Recycled ramie/flax fibres
	Old Turkish/Uighur	
032-Turfan	U 331 (T II D 121)	Mulberry fibres
	Old Turkish/Syriac/Uighur	14/ 3cm

Sample no.	Catalogue no. & language/script	Fibre materials & laid lines 6
044-Turfan	U 6869	Recycled hemp/flax fibres
	Old Turkish/Brahmi	11/ 3cm
045-Turfan	U 6866	Recycled ramie/hemp/flax fibres
	Old Turkish/Brahmi	10/ 3cm
046-Turfan	U 6865	Recycled ramie/hemp/flax fibres
	Old Turkish/Brahmi	10/ 3cm
047-Turfan	U 6868	Recyc. ramie/hemp/flax/mul-berry fibr.
	Old Turkish/Brahmi	9-10/ 3cm
048-Turfan	U 6861	Recycled ramie/hemp/flax fibres
	Old Turkish/Brahmi	10-11/ 3cm
049-Turfan	U 6860	Recycled ramie/hemp/flax fibres
	Old Turkish/Brahmi	11/ 3cm
050-Turfan	U 6867	Recycled ramie/hemp/flax fibres
	Old Turkish/Brahmi	10/ 3cm
080-Turfan	U 6873a	Recycled ramie/hemp/flax fibres
	Old Turkish/Brahmi	21/ 3cm
081-Turfan	U 6873b	Recycled hemp/flax fibres
	Old Turkish/Brahmi	21/ 3cm
082-Turfan	U 3395 (T I/ T M 472.500)	Recycled ramie/hemp/flax fibres
	Old Turkish/Brahmi	22/ 3cm
084-Turfan	U 5555 (T II D 68.501)	Recycled hemp/flax fibres
	Old Turkish/Brahmi	15/ 3cm
085-Turfan	U 2293 (T I α)	Mulberry fibres
	Old Turkish/Brahmi	20/ 3cm
115-Turfan	U 6903 (T I α)	Recycled ramie/hemp/flax fibres
	Old Turkish/Brahmi	13/ 3cm
116-Turfan	U 6904	Recycled ramie/hemp/flax fibres
	Old Turkish/Brahmi	11/ 3cm

117-Turfan	U 6902 (T III M 140)	Recycled ramie/hemp/flax fibres
	Old Turkish/Brahmi	
118-Turfan	U 6898	Recycl. ramie/hemp/flax/ mulberry fibr.
	Old Turkish/Brahmi	11/ 3cm
119-Turfan	U 6891	Recycled hemp/flax fibres
	Old Turkish/Brahmi	11/ 3cm (?)
120-Turfan	U 6893	Recycled ramie/flax/cotton fibres
	Old Turkish/Brahmi	11/ 3cm
121-Turfan	U 6890 (T III M 145)	Recycled ramie/hemp/flax fibres
	Old Turkish/Brahmi	11/ 3cm
122-Turfan	U 6895 (T II S 51)	Recycled ramie/hemp/flax fibres
	Old Turkish/Brahmi	13/ 3cm
123-Turfan	U 6894	Recycled ramie/hemp/flax fibres
	Old Turkish/Brahmi	15/ 3cm
124-Turfan	U 6899	Recycl. ramie/hemp/flax/ mulberry fibr.
	Old Turkish/Brahmi	15/ 3cm
125-Turfan	U 6852	Recycled ramie/hemp/flax fibres
	Old Turkish/Brahmi	11/ 3cm
126-Turfan	U 6859	Recycl. ramie/hemp/flax/ mulberry fibr.
	Old Turkish/Brahmi	11/ 3cm

Sample no.	Catalogue no. & language/script	Fibre materials & laid lines 7
127-Turfan	U 6855	Recycled ramie/hemp/flax fibres
	Old Turkish/Brahmi	09/ 3cm
128-Turfan	U 6857 (T III S 51)	Recycled ramie/hemp/fibres
	Old Turkish/Brahmi	
129-Turfan	U 6892 ([ ] M 262)	Recycled hemp/flax fibres
	Old Turkish/Brahmi	10/ 3cm
130-Turfan	U 6854	Recycled hemp/flax fibres
	Old Turkish/Brahmi	11/ 3cm
131-Turfan	U 6851	Recycl. ramie/hemp/flax/ mulberry fibr.
	Old Turkish/Brahmi	10/ 3cm
132-Turfan	U 6858	Recycled ramie/hemp/flax fibres
	Old Turkish/Brahmi	10/ 3cm
133-Turfan	U 6853	Recycled hemp/flax fibres
	Old Turkish/Brahmi	11/ 3cm

134-Turfan	U 6840 (T III S 51)	Recycled ramie/hemp/flax fibres
	Old Turkish/Brahmi	16/ 3cm
135-Turfan	U 6841	Recycled ramie/hemp/flax fibres
	Old Turkish/Brahmi	15/ 3cm
136-Turfan	U 6847	Recycled hemp/flax fibres
	Old Turkish/Brahmi	11/ 3cm
137-Turfan	U 6842	Recycled ramie/hemp/flax/ cotton fibr.
	Old Turkish/Brahmi	10/ 3cm
138-Turfan	U 6843	Recycled ramie/hemp/cotton fibres
	Old Turkish/Brahmi	
139-Turfan	U 6844	Recycled ramie/hemp/flax/ cotton fibr.
	Old Turkish/Brahmi	11/ 3cm
140-Turfan	U 6845	Recycled ramie/hemp/flax fibres
	Old Turkish/Brahmi	11/ 3cm
141-Turfan	U 6846	Recycled ramie/hemp/flax/ cotton fibr.
	Old Turkish/Brahmi	11/ 3cm
233-Turfan	SHT 2471	Mulberry fibres
	Sanskrit/Brahmi	17/ 3cm
256-Turfan	SHT 4511	Recycledhemp/flax fibres
	Sanskrit/Brahmi	
261-Turfan	SHT 4450	Sample 1&2 Recycl. hemp/flax/ cotton fibr.
	Sanskrit/Brahmi	11-15/ 3cm
269-Turfan	SHT 4466	Recycled hemp/flax fibres
	Sanskrit/Brahmi	13/ 3cm
270-Turfan	SHT 4467	Recycled hemp/flax/cotton fibres
	Sanskrit/Brahmi	11/ 3cm
271-Turfan	SHT 4468	Recycl. ramie/hemp/flax/cotton fibres
	Sanskrit/Brahmi	14/ 3cm
272-Turfan	SHT 4469	Recycled ramie/hemp/flax fibres
	Sanskrit/Brahmi	15/ 3cm
273-Turfan	SHT 4303	Recycled hemp/flax/mulberry fibres
	Sanskrit/Brahmi	15/ 3cm
274-Turfan	SHT 4303	Recycled hemp/flax/mulberry fibres
	Sanskrit/Brahmi	15/ 3cm

Sample no.	Catalogue no. & language/script	Fibre materials & laid lines 8
275-Turfan	SHT 4303	Mulberry fibres
	Sanskrit/Brahmi	15/ 3cm
276-Turfan	SHT 4303	Recycled hemp/mulberry fibres
	Sanskrit/Brahmi	15/ 3cm
277-Turfan	SHT 4303	Recycled hemp/mulberry fibres
	Sanskrit/Brahmi	15/ 3cm
278 b-Turf.	SHT 2641, 11 fragments	Recycled hemp/mulberry fibres
	Sanskrit/Brahmi	
278 e-Turf.	SHT 2641, 11 fragments	Recycled hemp/flax/mulberry fibres
	Sanskrit/Brahmi	19/ 3cm
278 h-Turf.	SHT 2641, 11 fragments	Recycled hemp/mulberry fibres
	Sanskrit/Brahmi	
278 i-Turf.	SHT 2641, 11 fragments	Mulberry fibres
	Sanskrit/Brahmi	15/ 3cm
281-Turfan	SHT 2329	Recycled ramie/hemp/flax fibres
	Sanskrit/Brahmi	11/ 3cm
283-Turfan	SHT 3363	Recycled hemp/flax fibres
	Sanskrit/Brahmi	19/ 3cm
284-Turfan	SHT 3361	Recycled ramie/hemp/flax fibres
	Sanskrit/Brahmi	11/ 3cm
285-Turfan	SHT 3364	Recycled ramie/hemp/flax/silk fibres
	Sanskrit/Brahmi	19/ 3cm
286-Turfan	SHT 3362	Recycled ramie/hemp/flax fibres
	Sanskrit/Brahmi	15/ 3cm
287-Turfan	SHT 3365	Recycled ramie/hemp/flax fibres
	Sanskrit/Brahmi	11/ 3cm
288-Turfan	SHT 2330	Recycled ramie/hemp/flax fibres
	Sanskrit/Brahmi	20/ 3cm
291-Turfan	SHT 3368	Recycl. ramie/hemp/flax/cotton fibres
	Sanskrit/Brahmi	11/ 3cm
297-Turfan	SHT 4432	Recycled ramie/hemp/flax fibres
	Sanskrit/Brahmi	
298-Turfan	SHT 4433	Recycled ramie/hemp/flax fibres
	Sanskrit/Brahmi	11/ 3cm
020-Turfan	SHT 381/6 (T III Šo 13, 19)	Recycled hemp/flax fibres
	Sanskrit/Brahmi III	

070-Turfan	SHT 381/2 (T III Šo 26)	Recycled ramie/hemp/flax fibres
	Sanskrit/Brahmi III	
215-Turfan	SHT 645/9.3 (D 754)	Recycled ramie/hemp/ flax fibres
	Sanskrit/Brahmi S III	19/ 3cm
215-Turfan	SHT 645 /9.4 (D 754)	Mulberry fibres
	Sanskrit/Brahmi S III	19/ 3cm
216-Turfan	SHT 645/9.5 (D 754)	Mulberry fibres
	Sanskrit/Brahmi S III	19/ 3cm
217-Turfan	SHT 645/7.4-7.5 (D 754)	Recycled hemp/cotton fibres
	Sanskrit/Brahmi S III	
238-Turfan	SHT 1211	Recycled hemp/cotton fibres
	Sanskrit/Brahmi S III	

Sample no.	Catalogue no. & language/script	Fibre materials & laid lines [9]
245-Turfan	SHT 842 (T III MQR B 10)	Recycled hem/flax/mulberry/ cotton fi.
	Sanskrit/Brahmi IV	20/ 3cm
257-Turfan	SHT 1763b1	Recycled hemp/flax fibres
	Sanskrit/Brahmi IV	15/ 3cm
259-Turfan	SHT 1217i-p	Recycled hemp/flax fibres
	Sanskrit/Brahmi IV	20/ 3cm
011-Turfan	SHT 159b	Mulberry fibres
	Sanskrit/Brahmi (V)	
012-Turfan	SHT 147 (T III MQR)	Mulberry fibres
	Sanskrit/Brahmi (V)	
013-Turfan	SHT 191g-o	Recycled hemp/flax fibres
	Sanskrit/Brahmi (V)	26/ 3cm
014-Turfan	SHT 106y-aa	Mulberry fibres
	Sanskrit/Brahmi (V)	
015-Turfan	SHT 134 (T III MQ 17)	Recycled hemp/flax fibres
	Sanskrit/Brahmi (V)	22/ 3cm
017-Turfan	SHT 269/10 (T III MQR)	Recycled hemp/flax fibres
	Sanskrit/Brahmi (V)	
018-Turfan	SHT 197/15	Recycled hemp/mulberry fibres
	Sanskrit/Brahmi (V)	
019-Turfan	SHT 197/21	Mulberry fibres
	Sanskrit/Brahmi (V)	
021-Turfan	SHT 192h	Recycled hemp/flax fibres
	Sanskrit/Brahmi V	

022-Turfan	SHT 109b (T III MQR)	Mulberry fibres
	Sanskrit/Brahmi V	
065-Turfan	SHT 400 S. 362 a-f,c	Mulberry fibres
	Sanskrit/Brahmi V	
066-Turfan	SHT 400 S. 362 a-f,f	Mulberry fibres
	Sanskrit/Brahmi V	
067-Turfan	SHT 400/31 (T III Šo 97, 99)	Mulberry fibres
	Sanskrit/Brahmi V	20/ 3cm
068-Turfan	SHT 400 /4 (T III Šo 65)	Mulberry fibres
	Sanskrit/Brahmi V	
069-Turfan	SHT 400/4 (T III Šo 79)	Mulberry fibres
	Sanskrit/Brahmi V	
071-Turfan	SHT 308	Mulberry fibres
	Sanskrit/Brahmi V	
072-Turfan	SHT 450/6 (T III Šo 5, 8, 22)	Mulberry fibres
	Sanskrit/Brahmi V	15/ 3cm
075-Turfan	SHT 412/6 (T III Šo 34)	Mulberry fibres
	Sanskrit/Brahmi V	
076-Turfan	SHT 412/12 (T III Šo 33, 34)	Mulberry fibres
	Sanskrit/Brahmi V	15/ 3cm
077-Turfan	SHT 308c (T III MQR)	Mulberry fibres
	Sanskrit/Brahmi V	
220-Turfan	SHT 447/21 (T III Šo 63, 78, 91)	Recycled hemp/flax fibres
	Sanskrit/Brahmi V	11/ 3cm

Sample no.	Catalogue no. & language/script	Fibre materials & laid lines 10
221-Turfan	SHT 428b (T III Šo 33)	Mulberry fibres
	Sanskrit/Brahmi V	
223-Turfan	SHT 1623/6 (T III MQ)	Recycled ramie/hemp/flax fibres
	Sanskrit/Brahmi V	
226-Turfan	SHT 856 (T III MQR)	Recycled ramie/hemp/flax/ cotton fib.
	Sanskrit/Brahmi V	11/ 3cm
227-Turfan	SHT 160a	Recycled hemp/flax/cotton fibres
	Sanskrit/Brahmi V	16/ 3cm
228-Turfan	SHT 160b	Mulberry fibres
	Sanskrit/Brahmi V	16/ 3cm
229-Turfan	SHT 242 (T III MQR) fragment 1	Mulberry fibres
	Sanskrit/Brahmi V	

230-Turfan	SHT 242 (T III MQR) fragment 2	Mulberry fibres
	Sanskrit/Brahmi V	
231-Turfan	SHT 154e	Recycled hemp/flax/cotton fibres
	Sanskrit/Brahmi V	19/ 3cm
232-Turfan	SHT 1780	Mulberry fibres
	Sanskrit/Brahmi V	17/ 3cm
234-Turfan	SHT 316 (T III MQR)	Mulberry fibres
	Sanskrit/Brahmi V	17/ 3cm
235-Turfan	SHT 891 (T III MQ 43)	Mulberry fibres
	Sanskrit/Brahmi V	16-17/ 3cm
236-Turfan	SHT 1248	Recycled hemp/flax/cotton fibres
	Sanskrit/Brahmi V	
237-Turfan	SHT 1260b	Recycled hemp/flax/cotton fibres
	Sanskrit/Brahmi V	15/ 3cm (?)
239-Turfan	SHT 336 (T III MQR)	Mulberry fibres
	Sanskrit/Brahmi V	16/ 3cm (?)
240-Turfan	SHT 961c (T III Šo 33, 34)	Recycled ramie/hemp/flax/ mulberry fi.
	Sanskrit/Brahmi V	15/ 3cm
242-Turfan	SHT 972 (T III Šo 25)	Recycled hemp/flax fibres
	Sanskrit/Brahmi V	19/ 3cm
243-Turfan	SHT 706/3	Mulberry fibres
	Sanskrit/Brahmi V	
244-Turfan	SHT 937 (T III Šo 24)	Recycled ramie/hemp/flax fibres
	Sanskrit/Brahmi V	19/ 3cm
248-Turfan	SHT 412/54 Šo 34)	Mulberry fibres
	Sanskrit/Brahmi V	
249-Turfan	SHT 866a (T III MQR)	Recycled ramie/hemp/flax fibres
	Sanskrit/Brahmi V	
249-Turfan	SHT 866b (T III MQR)	Recycled ramie/hemp/flax fibres
	Sanskrit/Brahmi V	16/ 3cm
249-Turfan	SHT 866c (T III MQR)	Recycled ramie/hemp/flax/ cotton fib.
	Sanskrit/Brahmi V	
250-Turfan	SHT 907 (T III MQR)	Recycled hemp/flax/cotton fibres
	Sanskrit/Brahmi V	14/ 3cm
255-Turfan	SHT 412/33.2 (T III Šo 34)	Mulberry fibres
	Sanskrit/Brahmi V	17/ 3cm

Sample no.	Catalogue no. & language/script	Fibre materials & laid lines 11
258-Turfan	SHT 219 (T III MQ 190, 308 gr. H.)	Recycled ramie/hemp/flax fibres
	Sanskrit/Brahmi V	20/ 3cm
260-Turfan	SHT 1779a1-2,b,c	Mulberry fibres
	Sanskrit/Brahmi V	15/ 3cm
290-Turfan	SHT 335a (T III MQR)	Recycled ramie/hemp/flax/ cotton fib.
	Sanskrit/Brahmi V	15/ 3cm
073-Turfan	SHT 498/4 (T III Šo 33)	Mulberry fibres
	Sanskrit/Brahmi VI	22/ 3cm
074-Turfan	SHT 498/3 (T III Šo 34)	Mulberry fibres
	Sanskrit/Brahmi VI	
224-Turfan	SHT 1111 (T II S 10)	Recycled hemp/flax/cotton fibres
	Sanskrit/Brahmi VI	14/ 3cm
225-Turfan	SHT 1109 (T III M 137)	Recycled hemp/flax/cotton fibres
	Sanskrit/Brahmi VI	11/ 3cm
241-Turfan	SHT 360b	Recycled ramie/hemp fibres
	Sanskrit/Brahmi VI	14/ 3cm
247-Turfan	SHT 1098a,d (T III M 145)	Recycled ramie/hemp/flax fibres
	Sanskrit/Brahmi VI	
251-Turfan	SHT 1093 ([T] M 135)	Recycled hemp/flax/cotton fibres
	Sanskrit/Brahmi VI	10/ 3cm
252-Turfan	SHT 1091 (T III MQR)	Recycled hemp/flax fibres
	Sanskrit/Brahmi VI	
253-Turfan	SHT 514 (T III Šo 90, 97)	Recycled hemp/flax fibres
	Sanskrit/Brahmi VI	
254-Turfan	SHT 626 (T II Y 7)	Recycled hemp/flax fibres
	Sanskrit/Brahmi VI	
279 a-Turf.	SHT 1762a (T III D 318)	Mulberry fibres
	Sanskrit/Brahmi VI	
279 b-Turf.	SHT 1762b (T III D 318)	Mulberry fibres
	Sanskrit/Brahmi VI	
279 c-Turf.	SHT 1762c	Mulberry fibres
	Sanskrit/Brahmi VI	
279 d-Turf.	SHT 1762d (T III D 318)	Mulberry fibres
	Sanskrit/Brahmi VI	
279 e-Turfan	SHT 1762e	Mulberry fibres
	Sanskrit/Brahmi VI	

279 f-Turfan	SHT 1762f (T III D 318)	Mulberry fibres
	Sanskrit/Brahmi VI	
279 g-Turfan	SHT 1762g (T III D 318)	Mulberry fibres
	Sanskrit/Brahmi VI	
279 h-Turfan	SHT 1762h (T III D 318)	Mulberry fibres
	Sanskrit/Brahmi VI	
279 i-Turfan	SHT 1762i (T III D 318)	Mulberry fibres
	Sanskrit/Brahmi VI	
282-Turfan	SHT 1456	Recycled ramie/hemp/flax fibres
	Sanskrit/Brahmi VI	
247-Turfan	SHT 1098a,d (T III M 145)	Recycled ramie/hemp/flax fibres
	Sanskrit/Brahmi VI	11/ 3cm

Sample no.	Catalogue no. & language/script	Fibre materials & laid lines 12
246-Turfan	SHT 1098a,d/THT 4083	Recycled ramie/hemp/flax fibres
	Sanscrit/Brahmi VI/Tocharian A/Brahmi	11/ 3cm
222-Turfan	SHT 1621/THT 4090	Mulberry fibres
	Sanskrit/Brahmi V/ Tocharian B/ Brahmi	15/ 3cm
060-Turfan	M 8635-M8635(a)	Recycled ramie/hemp/flax fibres
	Manichaean/Manichaean	
061-Turfan	M 8635-M 8635(b)	Recycled ramie/hemp/flax fibres
	Manichaean/Manichaean	
062-Turfan	M 5860 (T II D 138)	Mulberry fibres
	Manichaean/Manichaean	
003-Turfan	M 7984 (T III 260 e)	Recycled ramie/hemp/flax fibres
	Middle Persian/Manichaean	21/ 3cm
004-Turfan	M 470a,b,c, M 497b	Mulberry fibres
	Middle Persian/Manichaean	
078-Turfan	M 1364 - M 1367 (T I)	Mulberry fibres
	Middle Persian/Manichaean	16/ 3cm
299-Turfan	M 482 + M 477b	Mulberry fibres
	Middle Persian/Manichaean	16/ 3cm
002-Turfan	Ps 6 C14 analysis	Recycled hemp/flax fibres
	Middle Persian/Pahlavi	11/ 3cm
016-Turfan	Ps 7 C14 analysis	Recycled hemp/flax fibres
	Middle Persian/Pahlavi	21/ 3cm

058-Turfan	M 7100	Recycled ramie/hemp/flax fibres
	Middle Persian/Parthian/ Manichaean	
059-Turfan	M 7106	Recycled hemp/flax fibres
	Middle Persian/Parthian/ Manichaean	11/ 3cm
079-Turfan	So 18.212 (TM 388)	Mulberry fibres
	Middle Persian/Parthian/ Sogdian	
064-Turfan	M 104 + M 459 e	Recycled ramie/hemp/flax fibres
	Parthian/Manichaean	11/ 3cm
108-Turfan	M 1923 (T III M 148)	Mulberry fibres
	Parthian/Manichaean	21/ 3cm
005-Turfan	M 112, M 146a, M 336c	Recycled ramie/hemp/flax fibres
	Sogdian/Manichaean	11/ 3cm
088-Turfan	M 765b	Mulberry fibres
	Sogdian/Manichaean	
089-Turfan	M 765c	Recycled ramie/hemp/flax fibres
	Sogdian/Manichaean	32/ 3cm
090-Turfan	M 765d	Recycled hemp/flax fibres
	Sogdian/Manichaean	
091-Turfan	M 765g	Recycled ramie/hemp/flax fibres
	Sogdian/Manichaean	
092-Turfan	M 765k	Recycled ramie/hemp/flax fibres
	Sogdian/Manichaean	

Sample no.	Catalogue no. & language/script	Fibre materials & laid lines 13
083-Turfan	n 386 (T II B 25)	Recycled hemp/flax fibres
	Sogdian/Nestorian	8-9/ 3cm
086-Turfan	Mainz 404a	Recycled ramie/hemp fibres
	Sogdian/Sogdian	9/ 3cm
087-Turfan	Mainz 404b	Recycled hemp/flax fibres
	Sogdian/Sogdian	9/ 3cm
100-Turfan	So 18432 (T III S (462?)	Recycled ramie/hemp/flax fibres
	Sogdian/Sogdian	15/ 3cm
101-Turfan	So 18220 (TM 389)	Recycled hemp/flax/mulberry fibres
	Sogdian/Sogdian	14/ 3cm

007-Turfan	SyrHT 221 (T II B 66) 1.& last page	Recycled ramie/hemp/flax/ mulberry f.
	Syriac/Syriac	11/ 3cm
008-Turfan	SyrHT 221 (T II B 66) 2.& next last page	Recycled hemp/flax/mulberry fibres
	Syriac/Syriac	11/ 3cm
009-Turfan	SyrHT 72 (T II B 24) p. 1	Recycled ramie/hemp/flax/ mulberry f.
	Syriac/Syriac	13/ 3cm
010-Turfan	SyrHT 72 (T II B 24) p. 2	Recycled ramie/hemp/flax/ mulberry f.
	Syriac/Syriac	11/ 3cm
023-Turfan	SyrHT 72 (T II B 24) p. 6/5	Recycled hemp/flax/mulberry fibres
	Syriac/Syriac	13/ 3cm
024-Turfan	SyrHT 72 (T II B 24) p. 8/9	Recycled hemp/flax fibres
	Syriac/Syriac	13/ 3cm
025-Turfan	SyrHT 71 (T II B 23) p. 1	Recycled hemp/flax fibres
	Syriac/Syriac	9-11/ 3cm
026-Turfan	SyrHT 71 (II B 23) p. 2	Recycled ramie/hemp/flax fibres
	Syriac/Syriac	9-11/ 3cm
027-Turfan	SyrHT 71 (T II B 23) p. 3	Recycled hemp/flax/mulberry fibres
	Syriac/Syriac	9/ 3cm
028-Turfan	SyrHT 71 (T II B 23) p. 4	Recycled hemp/flax fibres
	Syriac/Syriac	9/ 3cm
094-Turfan	U 328 (T III Kurutka)	Mulberry fibres
	Syriac/Nestorian	15/ 3 cm
218-Turfan	THT 137 (T III MQR 43)	Recycled hemp/flax fibres
	Tocharian B/Brahmi	13/ 3 cm
219-Turfan	THT 138 (T III MQR 42)	Recycled hemp/flax fibres
	Tocharian B/Brahmi	14/ 3cm
267-Turfan	THT 251 (T III Š 29.3)	Recycled hemp/flax fibres
	Tocharian B/Brahmi	16/ 3cm
268-Turfan	THT 451 (T III MQ 17.41)	Recycled ramie/hemp/flax fibres
	Tocharian B/Brahmi	16/ 3cm
280-Turfan	THT 4101	Recycled hemp/flax fibres
	Tocharian/Brahmi	11/ 3cm

293-Turfan	THT 4100	Recycled ramie/hemp/flax fibres
	Tocharian/Brahmi	14/ 3 cm
307-Turfan	THT 4122 (T III MQ 63)	Recycled hemp/ flax fibres
	Tocharian B/Brahmi	20-23/ 3cm
030-Turfan	Ch/U 6949 (T II M)	Recycled ramie/hemp/cotton fibres
	Chinese/Old Turkish/Chinese/ Uighur	

Sample no.	Catalogue no. & language/script	Fibre materials & laid lines 14
033-Turfan	Ch/U 7491	Mulberry fibres
	Chinese/Old Turkish/Uighur	
034-Turfan	Ch/U 6106 (T II Y 59.16)	Recycled ramie/hemp/flax fibres
	Chinese/Old Turkish/Uighur	13/ 3cm
063-Turfan	Ch/U 6958	Recycled hemp/flax/mulberry fibres
	Chinese/Old Turkish/Uighur	10/ 3cm
095-Turfan	Ch/U 6754 (T II 1210)	Recycled ramie/hamp/flax/ mulberry f.
	Chinese(Chinese/Old Turkish/ Uighur	11/ 3cm
098-Turfan	Bs 2 (T II Y 3)	Recycled ramie/hemp fibres
	Chinese/Chinese/Sogdian/ Brahmi	15/ 3cm
105-Turfan	M 7391 (T II Toyoq 15a)	Recycled hemp/flax fibres
	Chinese/Chinese/Sogdian/ Manichaean	15/ 3cm
109-Turfan	Ch/U 6949 (T II M)	Recycled ramie/hemp/flax/ cotton fibr.
	Chinese/Chinese/Old Turkish/ Uighur	
173-Turfan	U 7001 (T I D)	Bamboo/Rice straw fibres
	Chinese/Chinese/Old Turkish/ Uighur	
099-Turfan	Ch/U 6512 (T III 66)	Recycled ramie/hemp/flax fibres
	Chinese/Chinese/Old Turkish/ Uighur	15/ 3cm

Bibliography

ENAMI, K. *et al.* 2010: "Origin of the difference in papermaking technologies between those transferred to the East and the West from the motherland China". In: *Paper History. Journal of the International Association of Paper Historians* 14, 2, pp. 12–22.

RISCHEL, A.-G. 2014: "Julius von Wiesner and his importance for scientific research and analysis of paper". In: *Paper History. Journal of the International Association of Paper Historians* 18, 1, pp. 31–38.

— 2019a: "The provenance of paper analysis of a Syriac Service Book and other Syriac manuscripts in the Turfan Collection". In: *Paper History. Journal of the International Association of Paper Historians* 23, 1, pp. 8–13.

— 2019b: "Lou-lan documents – a stepping stone on the true Paper Road". In: *Paper History. Journal of the International Association of Paper Historians* 23, 1, pp. 9–18.

VON WIESNER, J. 1902: *Mikroskopische Untersuchung alter ostturkestanischer und anderer asiatischer Papiere nebst histologischen Beiträgen zur mikroskopischen Papieruntersuchung.* Wien.

— 1911: *Über die ältesten bis jetzt aufgefundenen Hadernpapiere, ein neuer Beitrag zur Geschichte des Papiers.* Wien (Sitzungsberichte der Kais. Akademie der Wissenschaften in Wien. Philosophisch-Historische Klasse. 168. Band 6).

Minima Iranica for Dieter

ADRIANO V. ROSSI, Naples

My scientific familiarity with DIETER WEBER goes back to my post-graduate period, when under the guidance of ALESSANDRO BAUSANI, GIORGIO R. CARDONA and GHERARDO GNOLI I was particularly interested both in the Indo-Iranian frontier areas and Book Pahlavi, which was for many years the subject of my courses at L'Orientale in Naples.

Since those years, in the framework of a multi-year project originally funded by Orientale, CNR and IsMEO (now ISMEO), I began to put together a dialectological database that in the course of time, with the collaboration of many of my former pupils and more than any other, of ELA FILIPPONE, has reached considerable dimensions.

The following notes were written down while reading DIETER's papers (as well as other scholars' with whom I was in contact at the time), with the intention to enrich the etymological section of the cited database. Since there has never been any opportunity to make public many of these reflections of mine, I have chosen to publish some of them now – even if in skeletal form – in honour of DIETER, an outstanding scholar both of Pahlavi studies and of general Iranian philology, with many sincere and affectionate wishes for a long and productive work.[*]

1. In a list of possible matches OIr. **au* ~ Gk. -ω/ο-, WEBER (1986, p. 174 and fn. 29) mentions the anthroponyms *Βωροβαρακος/Βορασπος*,[1] which compares with Oss. *bur/bor* 'gelb', Prs. *bōr*[2] 'rotbraun; Fuchs (Pferd)', all derived by

* This research is carried out within the frame of the Ethnolinguistics of the Iranian area Project (no. 9710425417 and ff.), also drawing on lexical material from the Archives of the Comparative Etymological Balochi Dictionary Project (no. MM10422399), both directed by myself and funded by the Italian Ministry of Education/University at L'Orientale University, Naples, and ISMEO, Rome. Those works containg an alphabetic list are referred to by the name of the author and date of publication, without indication of page.

1 The Sogdian anthroponym βwr'kk/βwrk /Vōrak/ is now compared with anthroponyms *Βωρακος*, Elam. *Baurakka* by LURJE (2010, p. 150 no. 327), all according to the scholar < Sogd. **bwr* 'brown' in the sense of "Brown" (personal name). There (no. 326) also βwr /Vōr/ "Brown" is attested, but the nominal type, despite what is asserted by LURJE (ibidem), is not widespread enough to make the interpretation safe.

2 Sic WEBER 1986, p. 174, but the form should be considered as Early New Persian; today Eastern Persian has *bōr*, Tajik *būr*, standard Persian (of Iran) *bur*.

WEBER from a common Iranian protoform **baura-*. If we look at the members of the etymological family of Prs. *bur*, a word specific to the chromatic lexicon generally translated with "blond" in modern Prs. bilingual dictionaries,[3] we will see that their meanings vary from 'grey' (said of coats of animals) in Luri, Madaglashti[4] and many Kurdish dialects[5], to 'yellow' or 'blond' in Ossetic,[6] 'gold-yellow' in Āmorei, Mazandarani and at Jiroft (here particularly said of hair colour),[7] it designates *gusfand-e sefid māyel be zard* (a 'white-yellow sheep') in Davani,[8] while 'to become *bur* of shame' means 'to become *red* of shame' in Fārsi, Zarandi, Qamšei, Baxtiāri, Gilaki[9] and many other languages.

Modern discussions of the name of the beaver in connection with our color label date back to the following remark in BARTHOLOMAE's article on LAv. *baβra-*: "ai. vgl. *babhrắv-* Adj. 'rotbraun', auch Tiername."[10] From there, the connection was accepted by POKORNY,[11] and BARTHOLOMAE himself, going back twenty years later to the same word, connected to it Prs. *bur*, Bal. *bor*, Oss. *bur/bor*, Baxt. *būr*, Zaza *bur*,[12] and derived the whole set from Ir. **barṷa-*, obviously an *ad hoc* reconstruction.[13] MAYRHOFER (1996, p. 210), of whom WEBER quotes an early opinion (MAYRHOFER 1960, p. 146 fn. 74), more or less coinciding with his more recent position, maintains that "das 'Biber'-Wort[14] ist von den Farb-Adj. [...] nicht zu trennen," a position also accepted by RASTORGUEVA-EDEL'MAN (2003, p. 153) and BORBOR (2015, p. 556: "Whereas the etymology of the colour brown connected to beaver appears convincing [POKORNY, pp. 136–37], its application to *bōr* is hypothetical"); HASANDUST (2016, no. 913: "ešteqāq-e movāfeq nist") suspends his judgment.

3 But e.g. also 'roux; fauve; marron clair, noisette (yeux)' in LAZARD 1990 s. v.

4 UNVALA 1958, p. 14 *būr* 'grey'.

5 Cf. CHYET 2020 s. v. *bor*[1]: 'gray/grey; color between brown and white'.

6 ABAEV 1958 s. v. *būr/bor* 'želtyj', but *būr k̑yzg* 'rusaja (zlatokudraja) devuška'.

7 ᶜĀDELXĀNI 2000 s. v. *bur*; SOTUDE 1962 s. v. *bur*; NAFS DEHQĀNI 1998 s. v. *bur*.

8 SALĀMI 2002 s. v. *bu:r*.

9 BABAK 1996 s. v. *bur*; TĀHER 1965 s. v. *bur*; SARLAK 2002 s. v. *bur*; FARZPUR MĀČIĀNI 1964 s. v..

10 BARTHOLOMAE 1904, p. 925. On the symbolic implications of the name of the beaver in the Iranian culture cf. also OMIDSALAR 1984, p. 136ff.; in what follows the main stress is not, anyhow, on the etymological proposals **bawra-* and **barwa-*, on which some material is found in MAYRHOFER 1996, p. 210, and RASTORGUEVA-ÈDEL'MAN 2003, pp. 151–154.

11 POKORNY 1959, p. 136: 5. *bher-* 'glänzend, hellbraun'.

12 The connection of Prs. *bur* with Ossetic, Pashto and Balochi analogous colour words was already in HORN 1893, p. 53 no. 234.

13 BARTHOLOMAE 1924/1925, p. 5: "[...] das ich aus iran. **barṷa-* (, idg. **belṷo-* = lat. *fulvo-s*) herleite, mit dem bei farbenbezeichnenden Adjektiven häufig auftretenden *ṷo*-Suffix"). Due to the unsatisfactory documentation of the time, NIr. cognates in BARTHOLOMAE are mostly quoted in inaccurate transcription or with inexact meanings.

14 Cf. LAv. *baβra-* 'beaver.'

Discussing a passage of the *Bundahišn* (TD_2 20.2–3) where scholars usually agree in seeing an occurrence of 'borax',[15] NYBERG included in the first (German) edition of his *Handbook* an article **bōrak* "unsicherer Bed.",[16] accepting **baru̯a-* as reconstructed by Bartholomae, and originating the series Avestan – Middle Iranian – New Iranian still current in the literature. In fact, as remarked by DARIUSH BORBOR,[17] there is no certainty at all that in Pahlavi *bōr* was ever used to denote any shade of 'reddish-brown, bay (horse)',[18] 'red', or 'rose',[19] nor is it — as far as I know — ever used to indicate any horse coat, barring, perhaps, the passage contained in the Indian *Bundahišn* (13.30: *panǰom asp hašt sardag: spēd syā zard bōr komayt tāzīg pārsīg astar xar ī gōr asp ī ābīg abārīg asp sardagān*) where anyhow some adjectives point to colour labels, other refer to horse coats or types.[20]

The coat of a blue roan horse[21] is anyhow perfectly perceptible, especially by non-experts, in association with more than one colour. In this particular coat pattern, horses will have a mixture of black and white hairs all over their body, making them appear greyish blue. Blue roans can often be mistaken for grey horses. The best representation of this kind of perceptive mixing – even if not in connection with horse coats - is the dictionary gloss by AFGHANINEVIS (1956 s.v. *bor*): 'rangi ast maxlut syā o sefid [is a colour mixed between black and white]':

15 So e.g. CHOKSY 1986, p. 212 s. v. *bōrag*. On the origin of the borax name in Middle Persian cf. the following remark appearing at the end of NYBERG's short treatment in his *Glossary*: "*bōrak*, NP *bōrah*, Syr. Lw. *bōrqā*, Arab *baurāq* 'borax, nitre', whose colour is silver-grey. The Arab translation of this name is *al-šabhā'*, from *'ašhab-* 'grey, grizzled'" (NYBERG 1974, p. 48 s. v. *bor-*gil*). Contra, BORBOR 2015, p. 559.

16 NYBERG 1931, p. 37.

17 BORBOR 2015, p. 556 fn. 10; cf. also BORBOR 2002, pp. 191–192.

18 As e.g. MACKENZIE (1986 s. v.) translates, referring to a Prs. unquoted word (in the form: " | N ~ ") which is assumed by default (according to MACKENZIE's symbolics) to have "the same" meaning as the Phl. term; cf. MACKENZIE (1986, p. xvii): "After the vertical stroke the corresponding forms from Manichaean Middle-Persian (M) and/or Parthian (P) are given wherever possible [...] Later forms of the word are quoted from [...] the earliest New Persian".

19 As is commonly assumed on the basis of *Borhān-e Qāteᶜ*, *Dehxodā* etc.

20 In any case, the text is not in order, most manuscripts do not bear the detailed list of types of horses (cf. BEHZADI 1368/1989, p. 151), so we don't know what the scribe who added (among other labels) *bōr* meant. The only other passage mentioning *bōr* is Gr. Bd. 17.9 *xargōš ī bōr*, where BAILEY (n.d., p. 61 Text, p. 53 Translation) recognizes "the yellow hare", AGOSTINI-THROPE 2020, p. 93: "the brown rabbit".

21 On the perception of horse coat colours see the remarks by PORTER (1992, p. 76): "il n'est pas rare de voir dans les miniatures persanes des chevaux oranges, rouges, violets ou bleus, ce qui montre que leur couleur naturelle est moins importante que l'impressione general qui doit être transmise, par le jeu des couleurs et de la composition") and BORBOR (2015, p. 554): "A blue roan horse, according to our researches of hundreds of Iranian miniature paintings was one of the most, if not the most desired colour of a horse by the heroes and the royalty".

at least in Dari Persian, this meaning is preserved; see also Hazaragi *pešak-e bor* 'grey cat' (but *duxtar-e bormuy* 'girl with red-brown (*auburn*) eyes').[22]

Moving from this perspective, one could even suggest a possible link of the etymological family of *bor/būr* with *al-burāq*, 'the Prophet's horse'. I would recall the interesting remarks advanced fifty years ago by ANGELO PIEMONTESE (1974) in a noteworthy paper on this horse: its colour *bur-āq* (most probably an Iranian *–āk* derivative from **bur*) could be hinted at not because of its 'whiteness' (in our terms) but because of its shining appearance.[23]

DARIUSH BORBOR's argument that the main works of classical Persian literature give unambiguous evidence showing that *bor/būr* cannot point to a dark hue such as 'brown' or 'red-brown' while instead points to a light shade of 'grey', 'light blue', 'blue roan',[24] must therefore be accepted in its general outline, and prevail over the attempt to establish an (uncertain) etymological history of what may or may not be a larger lexical family. However, it should not be ignored that today's dialectal distribution of items connectable to *bor/būr* shows some important invariables:

(1) the label practically never represents an autonomous and general cromonym: instead, it always refers to parts of living beings (hair, hair, eyes, etc.);[25]
(2) in general, in the Iranian West it indicates lighter nuances, darker as you go eastwards;
(3) radically different perceptions can occur depending on the brightness and nature of the colored surface, e.g. Maz. *bur* 'yellow' HASANDUST (2011, p. 742), 'date colour (hair)' SOTUDE (1962 s.v.); cf. ZOLFAGHARI (2017, p. 321): "the concepts of colors in a Bakhtiari nomad's world is not necessarily compatible with the standard urban or scientific descriptions. For example, the very frequent word *keu* may cover a range of colors we normally call blue, dark blue, marine, gray, amethystine, dark turquoise and many other varieties of blue, purple and red black combinations. In the same way, *ga zærd-mure*, to my eyes was a light brown or an ochre cow and not a yellow one.")

22 BAU 2003 s.v. *bor*.
23 This association is rejected by BORBOR (2015, p. 559), even if I had occasions to discuss with him how different component of brightness can change the perception of hues, before and after his communication subsequently printed as BORBOR 2015.
24 According to BORBOR (2015, p. 557) the formulation was put forward by him in 2010, but the notion — together with general considerations on the change in the perception of hue according to changing lighting conditions — is already widely present in ROSSI (2006 *passim*).
25 A circumstance that is not evident — understandably, given the nature of synthetic comparison underlying the work — in the meritorious work by HASANDUST, which includes Sanglechi *bōr* and Wakhi *būr* in the section 'Grey' (HASANDUST 2011, p. 741), Oss. *būr/bor* in 'Yellow' (pp. 742–743), Prs. *bōr* and Munji *vūr* in 'Red' (pp. 746–747), while an entire section is devoted to 'Brown' (according to HASANDUST < MPrs. *bōr* 'reddish brown') with Bal. *bor* ('light brown'), Bartangi *vūr*, Prs. *bōr*, Roshani, Shughni *vůr*, Yaghnobi *vur*, Yazgholami *bər*.

2. Accepting the suggestion of SCHWENTNER according to which Lat. *zanc(h)a/ zanga* (also *tzan°*) 'shoe' would be a loan from Middle Iranian ("das latinisierte parthisch-persische Wort *zanga*", SCHWENTNER [1955, p. 242]) indicating the lower parts of the leg, WEBER (1989a) comments on Persian, Ossetian, and Pashto terms that sound assonant with the Latin term, and indicate terminal parts of the body of animals and humans. WEBER (1989a, p. 128), using existing documentation, rightly establishes a primary meaning 'krumm' ~ 'Haken' which he attributes to the protoform Ir. **čanga-*[26] taken from ABAEV (1958, p. 313f.) and BIELMEIER (1977, p. 273f.). Subsequently, and particularly starting from MAYRHOFER (1992 s.v. *jaṅghā-*), the idea of the nominal group linking to the verbal base IE **ĝʰengʰ-* 'schreiten' (RIX 2001, pp. 175–176) has gained ground. CHEUNG (2007), in my opinion rightly, does not accept the verbal basis among those that are certainly Iranian, contrary to MAYRHOFER (1992 s.v. *jaṅghā-*) who considers it a verbal basis surely Indo-Iranian; SADOVSKI (2017, p. 579) mentions the neo-Iranian continuations of the nominal base Ir. **ʧanga-*, without adding any comment. The Neo-Iranian cognates of the whole lexical family are now analysed in detail in RASTORGUEVA-ÈDEL'MAN (2003, pp. 219–221) and FILIPPONE (2010, pp. 80–83 = § 4.2), this last comments over 100 linked entries.

3. WEBER (1989b) notes that in correspondence to Phl. *dahān/dahan* (/dahan/?) and MMP *dhyn* (/dahen/?), Manichaean Parthian has for 'mouth' the isolated rwmb, which also (sometimes) means 'word' or 'speech'.[27] The same meanings, real and translated, are found in Sogd. rwβ.[28] The etymology of Sogd. rwβ has been considered, starting from BENVENISTE (1940, p. 203 ad 44), connected not only to Parth. rwmb but also to Prs. *ram/rum(m)* 'flesh about the mouth' (obsolete).[29] As WEBER (1989a, p. 96) rightly noted, BAILEY's attempt to bring the Sogdian word back to a root **rauf-*, **raup-* 'tear out'[30] is not likely, because "Sogd. *rwβ* is so spelt also in Man. script [...] and therefore demands an etymon with **b*".[31] However, it could also be that the (apparently) isolated Parth. rwmb, instead of being compared to Sogd. rwβ, is to be connected with different WIr. forms. indicating parts of the face in the mouth area, available only now, by virtue of the increasing dialectological documentation, and not at the time when WEBER published his paper. Note the alternance of the vocalization *a/u* in the

26 Which the scholar cites (probably by oversight) as **čanka-*.
27 Some of the available Parthian contexts are illustrated by WEBER (1989b, pp. 94–95).
28 SIMS-WILLIAMS 2012 s.v. Some of the available Sogdian contexts are illustrated by WEBER (1989b, p. 95).
29 STEINGASS 1892 s.v.
30 On whose (possible but questionable) Iranian documentation see now CHEUNG 2007, pp. 195–196 s.v. *Hraup.
31 SIMS-WILLIAMS 1983, p. 46.

following documentation, which anyhow is not a problem being this alternance widely witnessed throughout the history of Iranian.[32]

The available forms are:

> Khwarezmian RNB-RˀW 'with running nose' (MacKenzie 1970, p. 550) ("*-rˀw* appears to be the pause form of *rw-* /raw/ 'be runny (nose)'"[33])
> Sangesari *ruf* 'face' (Azami/Windfuhr 1972), if with Sang. *p* ~ *f* as in *sapāl* ~ *safāl* 'skin of wheat kernel', etc.
> Shirazi *rip* 'mouth, snout' (Xazduz 2002, p. 119), if with Shir. *i* < *u* as in *kin* < *kun* 'bottom', etc.

Moreover, assuming the phonetic action of the initial alternation *r* ~ *l*, widespread in many areas of West Iranian:[34]

Qāini *lam* 'cheek' (Zomorrodiān 1989)

> Birǰandi *lam* 'inner mouth' (Rezāi 1994)
> Gilaki *lamče* (Rams) 'area around the mouth' (Šokri 2006), *-če* is a Gil. rimorphematizing suffix
> Šuštari *lamač* 'the corner of the mouth' (MacKinnon 1974, p. 226), *-ač* as in Šušt. *loviča* 'lip' vs *low* 'lip'.

In the phonosymbolic perspective envisaged by Filippone (2020, pp. 136–138), one could also reconnect here a whole set of *lombus*-words for 'cheek':

> Prs. *lombus* (note "*lumbōs*" Steingass 1892) 'inner mouth, inside surface of the cheek',
> Afgh. Prs. *lumbus* 'all round the cheek' (Afghāninevis 1956)
> (Herati) *lombus* 'lower part of the cheeks, mouth, lips' (Ioannesyan 2009),
> (Xor.) Qāini *læmbus* 'cheek, face' (Zomorrodiān 1989)

32 Weber (1989b, p. 96) mentions without particular comments the alternation Prs. *ram/rum* from Steingass (1892). The existence of this phenomenon in Parthian is testified by cases such as rwbyšn 'movement' (Durkin-Meisternernst [2004 s.v.] transcribes /rōbišn/ but it should probably more exactly be understood as *ravišn* [with <b> = [β]] as in Ghilain 1939, p. 67).

33 MacKenzie 1970, p. 550.

34 Especially Fārs and Lārestān. Examples from the body part terminology: Aheli *li* 'face' (Prs. *ru*), *lom* 'pubic hair' (Prs. *roma* id., Steingass) (Salāmi 2007), Āškenani *leš* 'beard' (Prs. *riš*), *li* 'face', *lom* 'pubic hair' (Salāmi 2009), Banāruyei *leš* 'beard', *lom* 'pubic hair', *lon* 'face', *lu* 'face' (Salāmi 2009), Bastaki *leš* 'beard', *li* 'face', *lodi* 'guts' (Prs. *rude*), *lom* 'pubic hair', but *ridāh* 'guts', *ron* 'thigh' (*rān*) (Bastaki 1980), Evazi *lān* 'thigh', *leš* 'beard', *lom* 'pubic hair', *lu* 'face' (Salāmi 2009), Farāmarzāni *leš* 'beard', *li* 'face', *lodi* 'guts', *lom* 'pubic hair' (Farāmarzi 1984), Fedaghi *leš* 'beard', *li* 'face', *lom* 'pubic hair', *loŋ* 'thigh' (Salāmi 2009), Firuzabadi *leš* 'beard', *lom* 'pubic hair', *løn* 'thigh', *lu* 'face' (Estaxri 2016), Gerači *leš* 'beard', *li/le:* 'face', *lom* 'pubic hair' (Salāmi 2007), Kāriani *leš* 'beard', *lom* 'pubic hair', *lon* 'thigh', *lu* 'face' (Salāmi 2007), Kurdei *leš* 'beard', *li* 'face', *lom* 'pubic hair' (Salāmi 2009), Lārestāni *leš* 'beard', *lo/lû/ru* 'face', *lom* 'pubic hair', *lon/run* 'thigh' (Salāmi 2009), Kalāti *leš* 'beard', *løm* 'pubic hair', *løn* 'thigh', *lu* 'face' (Salāmi 2007), Xonji *leš* 'beard', *lom* 'pubic hair', *lon* 'thigh', *lu* 'face' (Salāmi 2007).

Birǰandi *lambus* 'cheek' (REZĀI 1994)
Gilaki (Rahimābād) *leumpus* 'cheek' (PĀYANDE 1987)
Tāleqāni *lambūz* 'cheek' (FALLĀHI/SĀDEQIĀN 2011)

identifying in them one of the sound-symbolic building blocks for 'cheek' active in Iranian, i.e. the LVP[35] building block (with or without nasal insertions, with or without an *-r* or other extensions). This set of words may convey not only the usual notion of 'roundness' or 'swelling' but also those of 'fleshiness' and 'fatness'.

Further forms such as

Jiroft *lapûz* (also reduplicative *laklapûz*) 'mouth and surrounding areas' (NAFS DEHQĀNI 1998)
Lori *lāvus* 'inner mouth' (HASANDUST 2016 s.v. *lunbōs*), also *lawsa* 'area around the mouth' (derivative in *-a*)
Kurd. *lavus* 'inner mouth' (MONCHI-ZADEH 1990, no. 345)
Sistāni *lāmos, lāmosk* 'all around the mouth', MOHAMMADI XOMAK 2000 (*-osk* is a Sist. ri-morphemizing suffix; note that Sist. *ā* does not represent historically long **ā*),

all characterized by a final syllable *°us/ûs/os* preceded by labial, could suggest the composition of an initial element of the group *lam* with an element of the group of Prs. *puze*, Classical Prs. *pōz* 'snout',[36] with assimilation at morpheme boundary, perhaps acting in parallel with the sound-symbolic processes described by FILIPPONE (2020).

Bibliography

ABAEV, V.I. 1958: *Istoriko-ètimologičeskij slovar' osetinskogo jazyka*. Tom I: *A–K'*. Moskva/Leningrad.
ʿĀDELXĀNI, H. 2000 (1379): *Farhang-e Āmorei*. Arak.
AFGHĀNINEVIS, ʿA. 1956 (1335): *Loγāt-e ʿāmiāne-ye fārsi-ye Afγānistān*. Kabul.
AGOSTINI, D./S. THROPE 2020: *The Bundahišn: The Zoroastrian Book of Creation*. Oxford.
AZAMI, C.A./G.L. WINDFUHR 1972: *A Dictionary of Sangesari*. Tehran.
BĀBAK, A. 1996 (1375): *Barresi-ye zabānšenāxti. Guyeš-e Zarand*. Kermān.
BAILEY, H.W. n.d.: *Bundahishn* (Linguistic commentary supplemented by transliteration, translation and word-index). Vols. I-II. Unpublished manuscript [revised version of the unpublished D. Phil. thesis, Oxford 1933].
BARTHOLOMAE, CH. 1904: *Altiranisches Wörterbuch*. Strassburg.

35 I.e. any liquid + any vowel + any labial stop, as e.g. Prs. *lop(p)* 'cheek', which, according to MONCHI-ZADEH (1990, p. 119 no. 345) "ist sicher aus *lunb* entstanden"; anyhow etymologically unclear.
36 On the Pashto cognates cf. lastly MORGENSTIERNE 2003 s.v. *poza*.

— 1925: "Zur Kenntnis der mitteliranischen Mundarten, VI". In: *SHAW* phil.-hist. Kl., pp. 1–92.

BASTAKI, ʿA.A. 1980 (1359): *Farhang-e bastaki.* Tehrān.

BAU, P. 2003: *Dictionnaire persan-français et français-persan.* Paris.

BEHZADI, R. 1989 (1368): *Bondaheš-e hendi. Matni be zabān-e pārsi-ye miāne.* Tehrān.

BENVENISTE, E. 1940: *Textes sogdiens édités traduits et commentés.* Paris.

BIELMEIER, R. 1977: *Historische Untersuchungen zur Erb- und Lehnwortschatzanteil im ossetischen Grundwortschatz.* Frankfurt a.M.

BORBOR, D. 2002: "Notes on the New Iranian toponomastics (The element *-būr*)". In: *Iran and the Caucasus* 6, pp. 189–192.

— 2015 (1394): "A Revision of the Diachrony, Synchrony, Etymology and Gloss of the New Persian *bōr* (بور)". In: *Proceedings of the Second International Conference on Iranian Languages and Dialects (past and present).* Tehran, pp. 558–559.

CHEUNG, J. 2007: *Etymological Dictionary of the Iranian Verb.* Leiden/Boston.

CHYET, M.L. 2020: *Ferhenga birûskî. Kurmancî – Înglîzî. Kurmanji – English Dictionary.* Vols. 1–2. London.

CHOKSY, J.K. 1986: "An annotated index of the Greater or Iranian Bundahišn (TD 2)". In: *Studia Iranica* 15, pp. 203–242.

DURKIN-MEISTERERNST, D. 2004: *Dictionary of Manichaean Middle Persian and Parthian.* Turnhout.

ESTAXRI, ʿA. 2016 (1395): *Šahr-e Gur (Firuzābād) dar āine-ye tārix.* Širāz. [Word-list at pp. 128ff.]

FALLĀHI, K./F. SĀDEQIĀN 2011 (1390): *Darāmadi bar guyeš va farhang-e Tāleqān.* Tehrān.

FARĀMARZI, H. 1984 (1363): *Farhang-e Farāmarzān.* Tehrān.

FARZPUR MĀČIĀNI, M. 1964 (1343): "Zabān va farhang-e Māčiān". In: *Našrie-ye dāneškade-ye adabiāt-e Tabriz* 16/3, pp. 177–296.

FILIPPONE, E. 2010: *The Fingers and their Names in the Iranian Languages.* Wien.

— 2020: "The Sound-Symbolic Component in the Iranian Lexicon of the Body Parts: Some Case Studies ('Pupil', 'Cheek', 'Buttock')". In: *Word formation, grammar and lexicology Contrastive, multilingual and comparative-historical perspectives.* Hamburg, pp. 121–147.

GHILAIN, A. 1939: *Essai sur la langue parthe.* Louvain/Leuven.

HASANDUST, M. 2011: *Comparative-Thematic Dictionary of the New Iranian Languages and Dialects.* 2 vol. Tehran.

— ²2016 (1395): *Farhang-e rišešenāsi-ye zabān-e fārsi.* 5 vol. Tehrān.

HORN, P. 1893: *Grundriss der neupersichen Etymologie.* Strassburg.

IOANNESYAN, Y. 2009: *Afghan Folktales from Herat. Persian Texts in Transcription and Translation.* Amherts, NY.

LAZARD, G. 1990: *Dictionnaire persan-français.* Leiden/Téhéran.

LURJE, P.B. 2010: *Personal names in Sogdian texts.* Wien (IPNB, II, 8).

MACKENZIE, D. N. 1970: "The Kwarezmian Glossary–I". In: *BSOAS* 33, pp. 540–559.

— ²1986: *A concise Pahlavi dictionary.* London.

MAYRHOFER, M. 1992: *Etymologisches Wörterbuch des Altindoarischen* I. Heidelberg.

— 1996: *Etymologisches Wörterbuch des Altindoarischen* II. Heidelberg.

MacKinnon, C.R. 1974: *The Phonology and Morphology of Dezfuli-Shushtari: a Study in West-Persian dialectology*. Doct. thesis, University of California, Los Angeles.
Mohammadi Xomak, J. 2000 (1379): *Vāženāme-ye sakzi (farhang-e loγāt-e sistāni)*.
Monchi-Zadeh, D. 1990: *Wörter aus Xurāsān und ihre Herkunft*. Leiden.
Morgenstierne, G. 2003: *A New Etymological Vocabulary of Pashto*. Compiled and edited by J. Elfenbein/D.N. MacKenzie/N. Sims-Williams. Wiesbaden.
Nafs Dehqāni, E. 1998 (1377): *Barrasi-ye guyeš-e Jiroft va Kahnuj*. Kermān.
Nyberg, H.S. 1931: *Hilfsbuch des Pehlevi*. Vol. II: *Glossar*. Uppsala.
— 1974: *A manual of Pahlavi*. Vol. II: *Glossary*. Wiesbaden.
Omidsalar, M. 1984: "The beast *babr-e bayān*: contributions to Iranian folklore and etymology". In: *Studia Iranica* 13, pp. 129–142.
Pāyande, M. 1987 (1366): *Farhang-e Gil o Dilam — Fārsi be Gilaki*. Tehrān.
Piemontese, A. 1974: "Note morfologiche ed etimologiche su al-Burāq". In: *Annali di Ca' Foscari* 13/3 (Serie orientale 5), pp. 109–133.
Pokorny, J. 1959: *Indogermanisches etymologisches Wörterbuch*. Bern/Munich.
Porter, Y. 1992: *Peinture et arts du livre. Essai sur la littérature technique indo-persane*. Paris/Téhéran.
Rastorgueva, V.S./D.I. Edel'man 2003: *Ètimologičeskij slovar' iranskix jazykov*. Vol. 2: *b-d*. Moskva.
Rezāi, J. 1994: *Vāženāme-ye guyeš-e Birjand*. Tehrān.
Rix, H. [2]2001 : *Lexikon der indogermanischen Verben*. Wiesbaden.
Rossi, A.V. 2006: "Colours and lexical taxonomies: Linguistic and cultural categories in Iranian". In: A. Panaino/R. Zipoli (eds.): *Proceedings of the 5th Conference of the Societas Iranologica Europæa*, II: *Classical and Contemporary Iranian Studies*. Milano, pp. 459–480.
Sadovski, V. 2017: "The lexicon of Iranian". In: *Handbook of Comparative and Historical Indo-European Linguistics*. Berlin/Boston, pp. 566–599.
Salāmi, ʿA. 2002 (1381): *Farhang-e guyeš-e Davāni*. Tehrān.
— 2007 (1386): *Ganǰine-ye guyeššenāsi-ye Fārs*. Vol. 4. Tehrān.
— 2009 (1388): *Ganǰine-ye guyeššenāsi-ye Fārs*. Vol. 5. Tehrān.
Sarlak, R. 2002 (1381): *Guyeš-e Baxtiāri-ye Čahārlang*. Tehrān 2002.
Schwentner, E. 1955: "Lat. *zanca* 'Schuh'". In: *Zeitschrift für vergleichende Sprachforschung auf dem Gebiete der Indogermanischen Sprachen* 72, pp. 241–243.
Sims-Williams, N. 1983: "Chotano-Sogdica". In: *Bulletin of the School of Oriental and African Studies* 46, pp. 40–51.
Sims-Williams, N./D. Durkin-Meisterernst 2012: *Dictionary of Manichaean Sogdian and Bactrian*. Turnhout.
Sotude, M. 1962 (1342): *Farhang-e semnāni, sorxei, lāsgerdi, sangesari, šāmirzādi*. Tehrān.
Steingass, F. 1892: *A Comprehensive Persian-English Dictionary*. London.
Šokri, G. 2006 (1385): *Guyeš-e rāmsari*. Tehrān.
Tāher, Gh. 1965 (1344): "Loγatnāme-ye lahjehā-ye Qamšei". In: *Farhang-e Irānzamin* 13, pp. 279–297.
Unvala, J.M. 1958: "Contributions to modern Persian dialectology: The Lurī and Dizfūlī dialects". In: *Indo-Iranica* 1, 1/3, pp. 1–16.

WEBER, D. 1986: "ΑΣΦΩΡΟΥΓΟΣ und Verwandtes". In: *Archäologische Mitteilungen aus Iran* 19 (Festschrift Prof. Dr. W. Hinz), pp. 171–175.
— 1989a: "Eine iranistische Kleinigkeit (zu lat. *zanca* 'Schuh')". In: *Historische Sprachwissenschaft (Historical Linguistics)* 102, pp. 127–128.
— 1989b: "Eine iranisch-baltische Parallele (parth. *rwmb* 'Mund')". In: *Indogermanische Forschungen* 94, pp. 94–100.
XAZDUZ, M. 2002: *Kākuye širāzi*. Širāz.
ZOLFAGHARI, S. 2017: *The Bakhtiaris. An anthropological-linguistic lexical study of Haft Lang nomads of southwestern Iran*. Leiden.
ZOMORRODIĀN, R. 1989 (1368): *Barresi-ye guyeš-e Qāin*. Mašhad.

Zur Bronzeprägung des Ohrmazd IV.

Nikolaus Schindel, Wien

Die Münzprägung des sasanidischen Großkönigs Ohrmazd IV. (579–590) mag im Vergleich zu der seines Vaters Khusro I. (531–579) oder seines Sohnes Khusro II. (590–628) eintönig wirken. Auf jeden Fall hat sie bisher wenig Aufmerksamkeit in der numismatischen Forschung auf sich gezogen: In den meisten Handbüchern wird sie nur knapp erwähnt;[1] allein Malek Iradj Mochiri hat die tatsächlich oder vorgeblich östlichen Prägungen, die er in einen Zusammenhang mit den von Wahram Cobin geleiteten Türkenkriegen sah, in einiger Ausführlichkeit besprochen,[2] wobei etliche seiner Resultate in SNS 5 (Ohrmazd IV.) kritisch hinterfragt werden müssen. Im Gegensatz zu seinen meisten Vorgängern verwendete Ohrmazd IV. nur einen einzigen Avers- und einen Reverstyp für seine gesamte Prägung.[3] Bis vor kurzem waren zudem nur silberne Drachmen bekannt.[4] Goldmünzen fehlen weiterhin; sollten zweifelsfrei authentische Belege noch auftauchen, so würde man sich aufgrund der Usancen in der spätsasanidischen Münzprägung erwarten, dass sie beidseitig von den Drachmen deutlich abgesetzte Sondertypen zeigen.[5] Dass von einem König, der immerhin knappe zwölf Jahre lang regierte,[6] bisher keine goldenen Dinare bekanntgeworden sind, ist übrigens nicht so überraschend, wie man auf den ersten Blick glauben könnte. Denn von Kawad I., der auf 43 Regierungsjahre (abgekürzt RJ) kam, ist bisher nur ein einziger Dinar aufgetaucht,[7] und die 48

1 Vgl. etwa Göbl 1954, pp. 119 f.; Göbl 1971, p. 52, Prägetabelle 11, Taf. 12, Abb. 200–202; unter den 315 Münzen, die Gyselen 2004 vorstellt, findet sich gerade eine Drachme des Ohrmazd IV. (p. 124, Nr. 268). Malek (1993, p. 237) listet keine einzige Einzelstudie zu Ohrmazd IV. auf. Heute kann man Amini 2005 nennen, immerhin eine recht reichhaltige Materialzusammenstellung, wenn auch ohne Quellenangaben. Für einen historischen Überblick zu Ohrmazd IV. etwa Shahbazi 2004.

2 Mochiri 1977, pp. 37–127.

3 Göbl 1971, Prägetabelle 11. Nach den Kriterien für die Typendefinition, wie sie in der Reihe „Sylloge Nummorum Sasanidarum“ gelten, sehe ich auch heute noch keine typologischen Varianten unter Ohrmazd IV.; freilich ist meine Materialsammlung für SNS 5 noch nicht abgeschlossen.

4 Vgl. etwa Göbl 1971, Prägetabelle 11 oder Malek 1993, p. 237.

5 Vgl. Schindel 2006b.

6 Dass Münzen aus RJ 13 existieren, obwohl Ohrmazd IV. noch vor Ablauf seines RJ 12 abgesetzt wurde, ist am ehesten damit zu erklären, dass die Münzprägung im Vorhinein erfolgen konnte, vgl. Szaivert 1975, Bd. 1, p. 20.

7 Schindel 2004, Bd. 2, pp. 467f.; Bd. 2, Taf. 137, Abb. 300.

Jahre des Khusro I. sind durch bislang lediglich vier zweifelsfrei authentische Goldmünzen aus drei verschiedenen Jahrgängen belegt.[8] Ich habe mehrfach die Meinung vertreten, dass die sasanidische Goldprägung in erster Linie zeremoniellen Zwecken diente, wobei Gold natürlich auch Geldwert besaß.[9]

Wie aber sieht es mit der Kupferprägung aus, die zweifellos für niedrigwertige finanzielle Transaktionen des alltäglichen Lebens diente? Die längste Zeit waren von Ohrmazd IV. nur Drachmen bekannt.[10] Erst 2010 sind die ersten gesicherten Belege für AE-Münzen des Ohrmazd IV. aufgetaucht.[11] Sie stammen offenkundig aus einem kleinen Börsenfund und werden im Nationalmuseum Teheran verwahrt.[12] Es ist festzuhalten, dass in den letzten Jahren die Zahl der sasanidischen Bronzemünzen im Münzhandel (zumal in Auktionen) deutlich angestiegen ist. Neben Ausgaben des immer schon recht gut vertretenen 3. Jhdts. sind heutzutage auch AE-Münzen der spätsasanidischen Zeit deutlich häufiger als vor 20 Jahren. Da anzunehmen ist, dass dieser Trend anhalten wird, dürfte sich das Gesamtbild in Zukunft noch weiter verändern; daher ist dieser Beitrag durchaus als vorläufig anzusehen. Ein paar gesicherte Erkenntnisse lassen sich aber dennoch bereits jetzt erarbeiten.

Zunächst einmal: Auch wenn AE-Münzen des Ohrmazd IV. existieren, so sind sie doch alles andere als häufig. Das mag daran liegen, dass spätsasanidische Bronzeausgaben oft schlecht ausgeprägt sind, sodass nicht alle für eine vollständige Bestimmung relevanten Details — Averslegende, Astralsymbole außerhalb des Bildrandes, Münzstättenangabe und Jahreszahl — sicher bestimmt werden können; oftmals bleiben sämtliche genannten Parameter unklar. Selbst wenn der Schrötling all diese Angaben sauber aufnahm, so erschwert oft die Korrosion (die durch den geringen Durchmesser erleichtert wird) die Lesbarkeit. Hier kann in Zukunft nur die Zunahme des der Forschung zur Verfügung stehenden Materials die Lage verbessern, hoffentlich auch aus regulären archäologischen Grabungen. Angemerkt sei, dass vom Usurpator Wistahm, der einige Jahre lang

8 SCHINDEL 2022, Bd. 1, pp. 93–96; die bisher belegten Jahrgänge sind RJ 13, RJ 21 und RJ 44 (zwei beidseitig stempelidente Münzen).

9 SCHINDEL 2004, Bd. 1, pp. 99–103; SCHINDEL 2005b; SCHINDEL 2006a; eine andere Meinung etwa bei GARIBOLDI 2006, meines Erachtens freilich ohne überzeugende Argumente, zumal in Anbetracht der immer noch großen Seltenheit sasanidischer Goldmünzen des 5. und 6. Jhdts.

10 Subärate Fälschungen, also Kupfermünzen mit Bronzekern, die in betrügerischer Absicht hergestellt wurden, bleiben hier klarerweise unberücksichtigt; vgl. dazu GÖBL 1959; SCHINDEL 2004, Bd. 1, pp. 194 f.; SCHINDEL 2014, pp. 30 f. Derartige Stücke sind im sasanidischen Rom — im Vergleich etwa zum kaiserlichen Rom des 2. und 3. Jhdts. — sehr selten. In einer Partie von über 100 sasanidischen AE-Münzen, die ich momentan bearbeite, fanden sich keine Exemplare des Ohrmazd IV.

11 CURTIS *et al* 2010, Taf. 100 f., Nr. 1457–1472; einige Anmerkungen zu diesem Band bei MALEK 2011, konkret zu den AE-Münzen des Ohrmazd IV. pp. 478f. Frühere Zusammenfassungen zur sasanidischen AE-Prägung, die heute aufgrund der verbesserten Materiallage als überholt zu haben gelten, etwa bei GÖBL 1971, p. 29 mit den Materialnachweisen in Prägetabelle 1–13 oder HERRLI 1983.

12 Ich habe VESTA CURTIS herzlich zu danken.

Rayy beherrschte, bislang vier AE-Münzen bekanntgeworden sind,[13] die somit relativ gesehen als häufiger zu gelten haben als die Buntmetallprägungen des Ohrmazd IV., wenn man den genannten Börsenfund abrechnet.

Betrachten wir zunächst einmal die bisher aufgetauchten AE-Münzen dieses Königs. Insgesamt 20 Exemplare stammen aus dem oben angesprochenen Börsenfund im Iranischen Nationalmuseum (Nr. 2–8, 10–22). Eine Münze befindet sich in der neuen Sammlung Schaaf (Nr. 9);[14] ein weiteres Stück ist 2020 im Münzhandel aufgetaucht (Nr. 1). Einige andere AE-Münzen lassen keine sichere Entscheidung zwischen dem typologisch und in seinen späteren Jahren stilistisch sehr ähnlichen Khusro I. zu.[15] Die Verteilung nach Münzstätten[16] sieht bei den mit der erforderlichen Sicherheit Ohrmazd IV. zuweisbaren Münzen folgendermaßen aus (Tab. 1; die Reihung erfolgt nach dem lateinischen Alphabet):

Tab. 1. AE-Münzen des Ohrmazd IV. nach Münzstätten

Münzstätte	Stückzahl	Katalognummer
ART	4	2–5
DA	8	6–13
ST	1	14
WYHC	1	1
Unbestimmbar	8	15–22

Gleich vier Münzen (Nr. 2–5) zeigen eindeutig die Signatur ART (Ardashir-khwarrah in Fars).[17] Das gut belegte DA (Darabgerd in Fars)[18] bietet gleichfalls keine Probleme – beide Buchstaben der Sigle sind sicher lesbar, zumal auf den Münzen des Ohrmazd IV. das Pehlevi-` noch gut vom *h* unterschieden werden kann (man betrachte etwa den Königsnamen auf der Vorderseite). Nicht so eindeutig ist

13 Schindel 2015; es steht zu hoffen, dass in Zukunft mehr derartige Münzen auftauchen werden.

14 Ich habe Robert Schaaf herzlich für die Bereitstellung des Bildes zu danken; als Schindel 2014 erschien, befand sich diese Münze klarerweise noch nicht in der Slg. Schaaf.

15 Diese werden in SNS 5 katalogisiert werden, vergleichbar den nicht genauer bestimmbaren Münzen in Schindel 2004, Bd. 2, Taf. 141.

16 Die Lokalisierung der verschiedenen sasanidischen Münzstättensignaturen stellt eines der wichtigsten, aber auch umstrittensten Forschungsfelder in der sasanidischen Numismatik dar. Methodisch von grundlegender Bedeutung ist Herzfeld 1938; vgl. weiters Walker 1941, pp. XCIX–CXLIII; Bivar 1963; Gaube 1973; Szaivert 1975 (unpubliziert, aber methodisch wichtig); Gyselen 1983; Album/Goodwin 2002; Schindel 2004, Bd. 1, pp. 128–178; Schindel 2005a; Schindel (online); Schindel 2018; Schindel 2022, Bd. 1, pp. 113–202.

17 Schindel 2004, Bd. 1, p. 130, 150 mit Literatur.

18 Schindel 2004, Bd. 1, pp. 134, 156f. mit Literatur.

hingegen der Beleg aus ST (Nr. 14):[19] Ich glaube, am Ende den senkrechten Strich eines *t* ausmachen zu können, davor die beiden gerundeten Elemente des *s*; auf jeden Fall sieht die Sigle anders als ART aus. In Anbetracht des Umstandes, dass zwölf von 14 bestimmbaren AE-Münzen des Ohrmazd IV. beim momentanen Materialstand aus Fars stammen, ist eine Deutung auf eine weitere Prägestätte in dieser Region naheliegend (wenngleich natürlich nicht zwingend). Nr. 1 zeigt am Ende den Halbkreis, der typisch für das *c* ist. Mir sind unter Ohrmazd IV. nur zwei reguläre Siglen bekannt,[20] die dieses Zeichen enthalten, nämlich das sehr seltene WLC (Georgien)[21] sowie WYHC, die häufigste Drachmenmünzstätte des Königs (vgl. Tab. 3), die die Reichshauptstadt Ctesiphon unter dem Namen Weh-az-Andiyok-Khusro meint.[22] Die übrigen Reste der Sigle passen weit besser zur zweiten Variante, da einerseits vor dem *c* ein *h* zu stehen scheint und andererseits das unverkennbare *l* fehlt. Drei der Münzen mit RJ 6 (Nr. 17, 19, 21) scheinen einen kurzen Münzstättennamen zu tragen, der mit einem *r* oder *w* endet; man würde an AW (Ohrmazd-Ardashir in Khuzistan)[23] denken, doch sieht es für mich so aus, als ob das letzte Zeichen nach rechts unverbunden wäre, was nicht zu dieser Lesung passt. Auch ist die Jahreszahl auf allen drei Münzen recht verderbt ausgeführt, sodass man auch beim Namen des Prägeorts mit einer ungenauen Schreibung zu rechnen hat, die in Anbetracht der unvollständigen Ausprägung eine zuverlässige Deutung verunmöglicht. Ich habe übrigens nach Stempelverbindungen gesucht in der Hoffnung, unbestimmbare Stücke auf diese Weise einem Prägeort oder -jahr zuweisen zu können, fand aber keine sichere Koppelung im Revers; freilich sind aufgrund der schlechten Erhaltung und Ausprägung belastbare Beobachtungen von gleichen Stempeln grundsätzlich schwierig.

Wenn wir uns auf die Regierungsjahre konzentrieren, so sehen die Zahlen wie folgt aus (Tab. 2):

Tab. 2. AE-Münzen des Ohrmazd IV. nach Prägejahren

Regierungsjahr	Stückzahl	Katalognummer
1		
2	7	2, 3, 6–10

19 Schindel 2004, Bd. 1, pp. 143, 167 f. mit Literatur.

20 WLCAN (bei Mochiri 1977, pp. 102f. „Gorzevān“) ist keine offizielle sasanidischen Reichsmünzstätte, sondern dürfte eine tatsächlich deutlich nach 590 zu datierende Prägecharge im Kaukasus bezeichnen.

21 Schindel 2019, pp. 111–116 mit Literatur.

22 Schindel 2004, Bd. 1, pp. 145, 170f. mit Literatur. Übrigens spricht das Fehlen von AE-Münzen aus WYHC im Börsenfund in Teheran, in dem sonst nur Münzstätten in Fars sicher nachweisbar sind, gegen die alternative Gleichsetzung von WYHC mit Weh-az-Amid-Kawad in ebendieser Region.

23 Schindel 2004, Bd. 1, pp. 131, 151 mit Literatur.

Regierungsjahr	Stückzahl	Katalognummer
3	1	4
4		
5	1	15
6	6	16–21
7		
8		
9		
10		
11		
12		
13		
Unbestimmbar	7	1, 5, 11–14, 22

Ich habe absichtlich alle 13 auf Drachmen belegte Regierungsjahre des Ohrmazd IV. in Tab. 2 berücksichtigt, um dadurch die noch bestehenden Lücken in der AE-Prägung aufzuzeigen — denn bislang sind lediglich sind erst vier verschiedene Jahrgänge mit Sicherheit nachweisbar. RJ 2 ist auf mehreren Stücken klar und deutlich lesbar (vgl. Nr. 9), auch RJ 3 ist recht sicher bestimmbar, mag auch das zweite *t* auf dem bisher einzigen Beleg undeutlich sein (Nr. 4). Die Lesung der Zahl 5 auf Nr. 15 ist vergleichsweise unsicher; das runde Zeichen in der Mitte, gefolgt von einem längeren waagrechten Strichten, lässt aber an *HWMŠA* denken, mag auch das waagrechte Element über dem Kreis angebracht sein. Die Zahl 6 (*ŠTA*) wird im Gegensatz zu *TLYN* deutlich ungenauer und verderbter ausgeführt (vgl. Nr. 16), wenngleich einige Belege sie mit Sicherheit überliefern — Nr. 20 etwa zeigt das *t* in der Mitte in aller gewünschten Klarheit, und da Ohrmazd IV. ja nur auf 13 Jahre kam, besteht an der Lesung dieser Jahreszahl (zumindest meiner Meinung nach) kein ernsthafter Zweifel. Auf Nr. 17 ist die Zahl zur Kombination eines waagrechten, eines senkrechten und eines weiteren waagrechten Strichs verkommen; aufgrund der Parallelen liegt auch hier eine Lesung als *ŠTA* (6) nahe. Wenn man die Lesung von Nr. 15 auf RJ 5 akzeptiert, dann sind bislang (wie gesagt) vier der 13 auf Münzen bezeugten Jahrgänge des Ohrmazd IV. in der AE-Prägung belegt. Zwar stammen bis auf Nr. 9 (Slg. Schaaf) alle Exemplare mit lesbarer Jahresangabe aus dem genannten Fund, doch bezeugt dieser immerhin drei verschiedene Jahre sicher (RJ 2, 3, 6), ein weiteres vielleicht (RJ 5). Auch unter Wistahm sind bisher lediglich zwei Jahrgänge in der AE-Prägung belegt (RJ 2 und 5).[24] Übrigens prägte dieser

24 Schindel 2015.

Usurpator in sechs verschiedenen Jahren Drachmen, was bedeutet, dass es auch hier Lücken in der AE-Prägung gibt.[25] Für einen Vergleich der AE-Prägungen dieser beiden Könige muss man bedenken, dass man, wenn man lediglich die Münzstätten berücksichtigt, die durch zwei Dutzend Drachmen oder mehr belegt sind, auf immerhin 24 verschiedene Siglen kommt (Tab. 3).[26] Potenziell also ist also Zahl für die Prägestätten und -jahre, aus denen AE-Ausgaben des Ohrmazd IV. stammen könnten, im Vergleich zu Wistahm um etwa den Faktor 50 größer. Beim momentanen Materialstand, der keineswegs als vollständig, aber doch als repräsentativ gelten darf, stammen etwa 1800 Drachmen des Ohrmazd IV. aus diesen über 20 verschiedenen Siglen, denen 100 Silbermünzen des Wistahm in TYLER-SMITHs Stempelcorpus gegenüberstehen. Daraus könnte man folgern, dass die AE-Prägung des letztgenannten Königs stärker war als die des Ohrmazd IV., da das Verhältnis bei den Drachmen etwa 18:1 ist, beim Kupfer unter Einrechnung des Börsenfundes in Teheran hingegen momentan nur 5:1. Wenn man aber diesen geschlossenen Fundkomplex — zu dem es beim AE des Wistahm bislang keine Parallelen gibt — beiseitelässt und nur die aus Einzelfunden stammenden Bronzemünzen berücksichtigt, so ist das Verhältnis 2:1 zugunsten des Wistahm, was bedeutet, das bislang die Bronzemünzen des Ohrmazd IV. massiv unterrepräsentiert sind.

Die folgenden Tab. 3 dokumentiert zur Untermauerung des bisher Gesagten die mir momentan bekannten Stückzahlen von Drachmen des Ohrmazd IV., geordnet absteigend nach Belegzahlen pro Münzstätte. Hier zeigt sich, dass die Prägeorte in Fars — die aufgrund des genannten Schatzfundes bei den AE-Ausgaben dominieren — im Silber zwar auch gut belegt sind, aber bei weitem nicht so prominent figurieren. Freilich ist im Silber die Materialbasis wesentlich breiter, weshalb ein einziger Fund die Verhältnisse nicht derartig massiv wie im Kupfer verzerren kann.

Tab. 3. Drachmen des Ohrmazd IV. nach Münzstätten (in absteigender numerischer Reihenfolge)

Münzstätte	Stückzahl
WYHC	197
YZ	171
GD	156
BYŠ	130
AY	124
NAL/WAL	103

25 TYLER-SMITH 2017, pp. 97–110, 257–279.
26 Bei einigen der schwach belegten Siglen am Ende von Tab. 3 können sich im Rahmen der Kontrollarbeiten an SNS 5 noch Änderungen ergeben.

Münzstätte	Stückzahl
MY	101
AW	86
LD	82
WH	81
ST	76
APL	73
WYH	70
LAM	59
GW	47
DA	42
ART	42
AYLAN	34
BN	33
ML	31
SK	27
ŠY	26
PL	26
LYW	24
BHL	21
AHM	17
KL	15
NY	13
MLWYNALTY	12
HL	10
AM	9
SML	7
LWH	6
AT	3
AL	3
AYL	2
ALM	2
LHW	2
WLC	1

Kommen wir aber nochmals zu den Münzstätten, konkret zu WYHC. Diese Signatur ist gerade in der spätsasanidischen Zeit von herausragender Bedeutung,[27] weshalb ihre korrekte Lesung und Identifizierung von besonderer Wichtigkeit ist. Interessant ist nun, dass WYHC trotz seiner Häufigkeit in der Drachmenprägung (vgl. Tab. 3) in der AE-Prägung selten ist, und zwar nicht nur unter Ohrmazd IV. (Tab. 1), sondern auch unter seinem Vorgänger Khusro I. (Tab. 4): Unter diesem König ist WYHC in der AE-Prägung noch gar nicht belegt.

Tab. 4.[28] AE-Münzen des Khusro I. nach Münzstätten (in alphabetischer Reihenfolge)

Münzstätte	Stückzahl
ALM	1
ART	3
AS	3
AY	2
BYŠ	4
DA	2
GW	1
LAM	1
LYW	2
ML	7
MLL?	2
NY	1
ST	2
ŠY	1

Auch unter Khusro I. ist Fars in der Bronzeprägung am stärksten vertreten, wobei in der untenstehenden Tab. 5 die Fundmünzen aus Marw,[29] die das Gesamtbild verzerren würden, nicht berücksichtigt sind.

27 Vgl. die knappen, aber wichtigen Bemerkungen von BELLINGER 1946.
28 Das Folgende nach SCHINDEL 2022, Bd. 1, pp. 100f., Tab. 39f.
29 LOGINOV/NIKITIN 1993.

Tab. 5. AE-Münzen des Khusro I. nach Regionen und in Prozent (in alphabetischer Reihenfolge)[30]

Münzstätte	Stückzahl	Prozent
Armenien	1	3%
Asuristan	3	9%
Fars	14	44%
Gurgan	1	3%
Khorassan	9	28%
Khuzistan	3	9%
Medien	1	3%

Die Bedeutung von Asuristan lässt sich in der Drachmenprägung eindeutig nachweisen, wie ja die besonders hohe Produktivität von WYHC beweist. In der AE-Prägung hingegen ist weder diese Münzstätte noch die Region, in der sie liegt, besonders materialstark, wie sich sowohl für Ohrmazd IV. (Tab. 1) als auch für Khusro I. (Tab. 4, 5) beweisen lässt. Zwar ist die Materiallage noch schlecht, doch können wir dies im Moment nicht grundlegend ändern.

Wenngleich wir nun wissen, dass auch Ohrmazd IV. Bronzemünzen prägte, so zeigt sich jenseits aller Zufälle der Materialüberlieferung doch, dass die AE-Prägung im Vergleich zum Silber nebensächlich war: Vergleicht man die Gesamtsumme in Tab. 1 und Tab. 3, so kommt momentan auf 22 AE-Münzen und 1984 Drachmen, was einem Verhältnis von 1 zu 90 entspricht. Zwar wurden sasanidische AE-Münzen seltener und in geringeren Zahlen thesauriert,[31] aber dennoch ändert das nichts daran, dass die Silberdrachme bei weitem die wichtigste Nominalienstufe im sasanidischen Iran war.

30 Für die administrative Geographie des Sasanidenreichs neuerdings Gyselen 2019.

31 Der größte sasanidische AE-Schatzfund befindet sich in Tel Aviv und enthält etwa 1800 Münzen, zum überwiegenden Teil Beischläge zu Khusro II., vgl. Schindel 2009, pp. 32–43, 116–155, Taf. 21–26. Für einen Überblick zu den spätsasanidischen Drachmenhorten etwa Akbarzadeh/Schindel 2017, pp. 19–55.

Katalog

Asuristan

WYHC (Weh-az-Amid-Khusro/Ctesiphon)

1. 0,74 g. 14 mm. 2 h. RJ unbestimmbar. Privat.

Fars

ART (Ardashir-khwarrah)

2. 0,61 g. 19 mm. 3 h. RJ 2. CURTIS *et al.* 2010, Nr. 1457.
3. 0,60 g. 16 mm. 3 h. RJ 2. CURTIS *et al.* 2010, Nr. 1458.
4. 0,79 g. 18 mm. 3 h. Lesung der Sigle unsicher; RJ 3. CURTIS *et al.* 2010, Nr. 1467.
5. 0,61 g. 16 mm. 6 h. RJ unbestimmbar. CURTIS *et al.* 2010, Nr. 1459.

DA (Darabgerd)

6. 0,84 g. 17 mm. 9 h. RJ 2. CURTIS *et al.* 2010, Nr. 1460.
7. 0,68 g. 19 mm. 1 h. RJ 2. CURTIS *et al.* 2010, Nr. 1461.
8. 0,65 g. 16 mm. 2 h. Überprägt. RJ 2. CURTIS *et al.* 2010, Nr. 1462.
9. 0,43 g. 20 mm. 8 h. RJ 2. Slg. Schaaf.
10. 0,82 g. 17 mm. 5 h. RJ 2 (?). CURTIS *et al.* 2010, Nr. 1463.
11. 0,67 g. 18 mm. 5 h. RJ unbestimmbar. CURTIS *et al.* 2010, Nr. 1464.
12. 0,58 g. 17 mm. 3 h. RJ unbestimmbar. CURTIS *et al.* 2010, Nr. 1465.
13. 17 mm. 3 h. RJ unbestimmbar. CURTIS *et al.* 2010, Nr. 1466.

ST (Stakhr)

14. 0,59 g. 15 mm. 5 h. Lesung der Sigle unsicher; RJ unbestimmbar. CURTIS *et al.* 2010, Nr. 1474.

Unbestimmbar

15. 0,82 g. 17 mm. 9 h. RJ 5 (?). CURTIS *et al.* 2010, Nr. 1470.
16. 0,78 g. 17 mm. 1 h. RJ 6. CURTIS *et al.* 2010, Nr. 1471.
17. 0,65 g. 19 mm. 9 h. RJ 6. CURTIS *et al.* 2010, Nr. 1473.
18. 0,58 g. 17 mm. 9 h. RJ 6. CURTIS *et al.* 2010, Nr. 1475.
19. 17 mm. 12 h. RJ 6. CURTIS *et al.* 2010, Nr. 1476.
20. 16 mm. 6 h. RJ 6. CURTIS *et al.* 2010, Nr. 1468.
21. 0,77 g. 17 mm. 7 h. RJ 6 (?). CURTIS *et al.* 2010, Nr. 1472.
22. 0,87 g. 17 mm. 9 h. RJ unbestimmbar. CURTIS *et al.* 2010, Nr. 1469.

Abb. 1. Nr. 1.

Abb. 2. Nr. 9.

Abb. 3. Drachme des Ohrmazd IV, WYHC/RJ 10. Vormals Slg. Eichler.

Abb. 4. Drachme des Ohrmazd IV, BYŠ/RJ 7. Privat.

Bibliographie

AKBARZADEH, D./N. SCHINDEL 2017: *Sylloge Nummorum Sasanidarum Iran. A late Sasanian coin hoard from Orumiyeh*. Wien.

ALBUM, S./T. GOODWIN 2002: *Sylloge of the Islamic Coins in the Ashmolean*. Volume 1: *The Pre-Reform Coinage of the Early Islamic Period*. Oxford.

AMINI, A. 2005: *Hormozd IV: 12 years reign, 13 years Coins*. Teheran.

BELLINGER, A.R. 1946: "A note on the Sassanian mint monograms". In: *Numismatic Review* 3/2, p. 48.

BIVAR, A.D.H. 1963: "A Sassanian Hoard from Hilla". In: *Numismatic Chronicle*, pp. 157–178.

CURTIS, V. S./E.M. ASKARI/E. PENDLETON 2010: *Sasanian Coins. A Sylloge of the Sasanian Coins in the National Museum of Iran*. Vol. 1: *Ardashir I – Hormizd IV*. London.

GARIBOLDI, A. 2006: "The Role of Gold and Silver in the Sasanian Economy". In: A. PANAINO/A. PIRAS (Hrsg.): *Proceedings of the 5th Conference of the Societas Iranologica Europaea*. Volume I. *Ancient & Middle Iranian Studies*. Mailand, pp. 415–435.

GAUBE, H. 1973: *Arabosasanidische Numismatik*. Braunschweig.

GÖBL, R. 1954: "Aufbau der Münzprägung". In: F. ALTHEIM/R. STIEHL, *Ein asiatischer Staat. Feudalismus unter den Sasaniden und ihren Nachbarn*. Wiesbaden, pp. 51–128.

— 1959: "Zu einigen Fälschungen vorislamischer orientalischer Münzen". In: *Mitteilungen der Österreichischen Numismatischen Gesellschaft* 11/1, pp. 1–4.

— 1971: *Sasanian Numismatics*. Braunschweig.

GYSELEN, R. 1983: "Sigles d'ateliers monétaires sasanides: interpretation et identification". In: R. GYSELEN/L. KALUS (eds.): *Deux trésors monétaires des premiers temps de l'Islam*. Paris, pp. 141–158.

— 2004: "New Evidence for Sasanian Numismatics: The Collection of Ahmad Saeedi". In: *Res Orientales* 16, pp. 49–140.

— 2019: *La Geographie Administrative de l'Empire Sassanide: Les Temoignages Epigraphiques En Moyen-Perse*. Paris.
Herrli, H. 1983: "Die Kupfer-Nominale des sasanidischen Münzsystems". *Münzen Revue* 15/1, pp. 15–19, 15/2, pp. 103–105; 15/3, pp. 188–190; 15/4, pp. 26f.
Herzfeld, E. 1938: "Notes on the Achaemenid Coinage and some Sasanian Mint-names". In: J. Allan/H. Mattingly/E.G. Robinson (Hrsg.): *Transactions of the International Numismatic Congress organized and held in London by the Royal Numismatic Society, June 30 - July 3, 1936 on the occasion of its centenary*. London, pp. 413–426.
Loginov, S.D./Nikitin, A.B. 1993: "Sasanian Coins of the Late 4th-7th Centuries from Merv". In: *Mesopotamia* 28, pp. 271–296
Malek, H.M. 1993: "A Survey of Research on Sasanian Numismatics". In: *Numismatic Chronicle*, pp. 227–269.
— 2011: "Sasanian Numismatic Research in the Context of the Muzeh Melli Iran". In: *Numismatic Chronicle*, pp. 469–486.
Mochiri, M.I. 1977: Étude de numismatique iranienne sous les Sassanides et Arabe-Sassanides. *Tome II*. Teheran.
Schindel, N. 2004: *Sylloge Nummorum Sasanidarum Paris – Berlin – Wien.* Band III: *Shapur II.–Kawad I. / 2. Regierung*. 2 Bde. Wien.
— 2005a: "Sasanian Mint Abbreviations: The Evidence of Style". In: *Numismatic Chronicle* 165, pp. 287–299.
— 2005b: "Besprechung zu Andrea Gariboldi, La monetazione Sasanide nelle civiche raccolte numismatiche di Milano". *Studia Iranica* 34/2, pp. 302–306.
— 2005c: "Sasanian Coinage". In: *Encyclopædia Iranica* (Online unter: http://www.iranicaonline.org/articles/sasanian-coinage).
— 2006a: "Sasanian Gold Coinage: An Overview". In: *Dal denarius al dinar. L`oriente e la moneta Romana*. Rom, pp. 105–129.
— 2006b: "Khusro I. oder Khusro II.?". In: *Mitteilungen der Österreichischen Numismatischen Gesellschaft* 46/1, pp. 16–29.
— 2009: *Sylloge Nummorum Sasanidarum Israel*. Wien.
— 2014: Sylloge *Nummorum Sasanidarum. The Schaaf Collection*. Wien.
— 2015: "The Copper Coins of Wistahm", *Journal of the Oriental Numismatic Society* 223, pp. 9–10.
— 2018: "Sasanian mints – where and why?". In: B. Woytek (Hrsg.): *Infrastructure and Distribution in Ancient Economies. Proceedings of a conference held at the Austrian Academy of Sciences, Vienna, 28–31 October 2014*. Wien, pp. 497–517.
— 2019: "Sasanidische Münzen im Kaukasusgebiet". In: N. Asutay-Effenberger/F. Daim (Hrsg.): *Sasanidische Spuren in der byzantinischen, kaukasischen und islamischen Kunst und Kultur/Sasanian Elements in Byzantine, Caucasian and Islamic Art and Culture*. Mainz, pp. 107–126.
— 2022: *Sylloge Nummorum Sasanidarum Paris – Berlin – Wien.* Band IV: *Khusro I.* 2 Bde. Wien.
Shahbazi, A.S. 2004: "Hormozd IV". In: *Encyclopædia Iranica* XII/5, pp. 466–467 (Online unter: https://iranicaonline.org/articles/hormozd-iv).

SZAIVERT, W. 1975: *Die Tätigkeit der sāsānidischen Münzstätten ab der generellen Einführung der Signaturen und Datenangaben (Organisation, Technisches und historische Bezüge)*, ungedruckte Dissertation. 3 Bde. Wien.

TYLER-SMITH, S. 2017: *The Coinage Reforms (600-603) of Khusru II and the Revolt of Vistahm*. London.

WALKER, J. 1941: *A Catalogue of the Arab-Sassanian Coins (Umaiyad Governors in the East, Arab-Hephthalites, ʿAbbasid Governors in Tabaristan and Bukhara)*. London.

Mnemonica Iranica

MARTIN SCHWARTZ, Berkeley

It is my pleasure to dedicate this article in celebration of DIETER WEBER, a meticulous and magnanimous scholar.

The semantic as well as formal history of words pertaining to mental operations is often elusive. An example, with a solution suggested, will be detailed in this article: the Iranian for 'memory', **abiyāta-* and its verbal cognate **abiyāsa-*. It may first be observed that Indo-Iranian *√*smar* 'to remember' had come to mean 'to reckon, to count' etc. in Iranian, and it is dubious that even in Avestan *√*hmar* still had the meaning 'to remember', except perhaps as a marginal retention.

We find that in Sogdian the verbal notion 'to remember' was expressed by *šyā* (**uši-* 'awareness, intelligence') with various auxiliary verbs. Similarly, in Khwarezmian, *ʾxwʾzy-* (*m/xwʾzy-*) 'to remember' (wrongly compared with Parthian *wxʾz-* etc. 'to desire') is an old compound of **ʾx* f. 'mind' (cf. *mβywxydʾh c.xy* 'he learned it by heart') and **āzaya-* (=Avestan *āzaiia*) 'to drive, conduct'. *ʾxw* from Old Iranian **ahwā* finds its equivalent in Sogdian *ʾxw* seen in Christian Sogdian *ʾxwsyd* 'to encourage', with *wsyd* 'to stir, stimulate', and *ʾxwdʾwny* 'diligent' < 'giving the mind (over to...)', where, as in the Khwarezmian verb, *ʾxw* functions as accusative.

Etymologically problematic is Sogdian /ptfrāu/, as verb, 'to remember, to remind', and as noun, 'the act of remembering, memory'. SIMS-WILLIAMS (1989, p. 262) cites as a possibility GERSHEVITCH's etymology **pati-mrāwaya-* for Khwarezmian *pcrʾwȳ-*, and comments that the Khwarezmian word "can hardly be separated from Sogd. *ptfrʾw* 'to remember.'" In fact GERSHEVITCH's etymology fails for either or both words, since the consonantal change is unparalleled, and the root, **mrauH*, would give causative **-mrawaya-*, cf. Y 32.14 *mraoī* and not **mrāuuī*, and the meaning of GERSHEVITCH's etymon would be 'to make answer' and not 'to recall', cf. Y 32.2 *paitī.mraoṯ*.

YAKUBOVICH (2011, pp. 174ff) proceeds from the aporia of an etymological way of reconciling the foregoing Sogdian and Khwarezmian words, and, abandoning further explanation of the Khwarezmian form, suggests an origin in *√*frau* 'to swim, float'. His alleged parallel, an English expression 'to float up in memory', is unknown to me and not corroborated by an internet search. YAKUBOVICH's "main piece of evidence" for his etymology is [Iron] Ossetic *fæjlawyn* 'to undulate, go in waves', which is, however, different from 'float up', and his citation of Y 9.32, about a whore-witch whose mind 'floats' (*frafrauuaiti*) like a wind-driven cloud, it is the mind itself which is floating, and not a datum floating up *in* the mind, and it refers to loss of awareness, rather than to the presence of awareness involved in memory.

To return to the synonymous Sogdian and Khwarezmian for 'to remember', upon whose etymological connectedness SIMS-WILLIAMS (1989, p. 262) rightly insists, I posit **pati-srāwaya-* *'to call back' = 'to recall' for both. SIMS-WILLIAMS (*loc. cit.*) had doubted this because of Sogdian *ptsr'w* 'to consecrate (with a mantra)'; cf. CHEUNG 2007, p. 91, "**pati-srāwaya-* would not explain the Sogd. forms, which are surely related to [Khwarezmian] *pcr'wy-*." CHEUNG's only recourse, however, is to set up a root **frauʔ* 'to remember'.

SIMS-WILLIAMS now (in an email of November, 2020) notes that Sogdian *ptsrwm* 'mantra, spell' (which occurs as with verb *ptsr'w* at P 14, L. 6 *ptsrwm'y ptsr'w't*) "doesn't look like a regular Sogdian form" (**sr* normally gives Sogdian *š*), and that these words may be "from an archaic language of magical practitioners". In such an event, one may propose that **pati-srāwaya-* may have undergone an early semantic splittage, 1) 'to incantate' (cf. Middle Persian *srāy-* 'to sing, recite'), whose status as a solemn technical term preserved its *sr*, and 2) 'to call back, recall, remember'.

The Sogdian noun *ptsrwm* from 1) yielded a denominative verb *ptsrwm* (P 7, L. 67), whence, probably as an early loanword, the Khwarezmian verb *pcfrwmȳ-* (cf. SIMS-WILLIAMS 1989, p. 267), whose *-f-*, due to *p-* (in a further labial environment) is relevant, but cannot straightforwardly be used to explain Sogdian /ptfrāu/ 'to remember' < **pati-srāwaya-*. The decisive factor for the /f/, I propose, was the antonymy of Sogdian /ptfrāu/ 'remembering, memory' vs. /frāuči/ 'forgetfulness, oblivion' (with /-či/ an old verbal noun suffix, see GERSHEVITCH 1961, p. 152 §1002 and 153 §2006) whereby /pt-/ < **pati-*, taken with its adversative function, would make /ptfrāu/ be felt as virtually *'counter-forgetfulness'. A reverse relationship is wrongly envisaged by YAKUBOVICH (2011, p. 176 fn. 24) citing P. LURJE, for whom the /āu/ of /frāuči/ is an irregularity based on /ptfrāu/, but the former word, < **frāmršti-*, is like Common Sogdian /āu-/ < **hāma-* 'homo-' and Christian Sogdian *mr'w* 'to weep' < **brāma-*, GERSHEVITCH 1961, p. 53, § 351. By the way, Yaghnobi *fĭrómịč*, *fĭrómịš* 'forgetfulness, forgetting' have *m* from Tajik *faromüš*).

Khwarezmian *pcrw'k* 'reputation' is probably based not on a verb from √*srau* with preverb **pati-*, but from a compound **pati-srawah-* *'characterized by fame/rumor' (Avestan *srauuah-*), cf. Khwarezmian *pcfrn* 'lucky' < **farnah-* 'fortune'.

The preceding etymological discussions will serve to exemplify how the histories of words can entail complexities, a subtheme for what is to follow here.

For our focal noun, Old Iranian **abiyāta-* 'memory', we may start with two old forms attested in non-Iranian texts. The early Byzantine dictionary of HESYCHIUS ALEXANDRINUS, continuing a lexicographical tradition going back to some citation of a Greek historical work which touched on the Achaemenids, transmits a form *ABIATAKA (mss. αβιλτακα), glossed as μνήμονα 'memorious', and referring to Artaxerxes (II) Mnemon; this represents an Old Persian adjective **abiyāta-ka-*

'memorious'. Far to the east, Tocharian B *epiyac* and Tocharian A *opyāc* 'memory' represent a borrowing from an East Iranian language early enough for the word apparently to have merged with Proto-Tocharian reflexes of Indo-European **-ti-* abstracts (cf. ADAMS 2013, p. 95); thus **abiyāta-* 'memory' entered Proto-Tocharian before the well-attested wave of Tocharian borrowings from Middle Iranian (i.e. Bactrian and then Sogdian and Khotanese).

With regard to the foregoing view that Proto-Tocharian integrated **abiyāta-* as an indigenous **-ti-* stem, MICHAEL WEISS (e-mail of 28 August, 2020) wrote me that XAVIER TREMBLAY and others have derived the Proto-Tocharian form directly from Old Iranian **abiyāti-*. Against such a derivation I would note: 1) **abiyāta-* 'that which is remembered' has clear formal reflection in the Hesychian **ABIATAKA*, and (see the forms listed in my next paragraph) in Sogdian and Khotanese; 2) Parthian uses the auxiliary phrases *ʾbyʾd dʾr-*, *ʾbyʾd kr-* for 'gedenken' and *ʾbyʾd bw-* for 'gedacht sein', a fact which we owe to WEBER (1970, pp. 88f, § 39), where Khotanese phrasal parallels are also indicated (P.O. SKJÆRVØ, e-mail of 30 August, 2020, stresses that Khotanese *byāta* by itself means only 'that which is remembered'); with such auxiliaries also Parachi *awḗ* (MORGENSTIERNE 1929, p. 237) all of which reflect **abiyātam* 'that which is remembered'; and 3) **abiyāta-* is reflected as an internal object in compounds with **kāra-* and/or **-kara-* in the sense of 'memorializing, remembrance' in Christian Sogdian, Khotanese, Parthian, and Middle Persian. Thus the analysis of the Proto-Tocharian, as per ADAMS, is justified, and only Old Iranian **abiyāta-* lies behind all the nominal forms.

For the nominal forms from **abiyāta-* attested in Iranian, the following list suffices: Early Sogdian (in Sogdian script) *ʾβyʾtw*, cf. Christian Sogdian *byʾtqʾryc*; Old Khotanese *byāta-*; Manichean Parthian *ʾbyʾd* /aβyād/; Manichean Middle Persian *ʾyʾd*, Pahlavi *ʾbydʾtʾ*; both /ay(y)ād/; Persian *yād*, and Parachi *awḗ*. Apart from the verbal notion 'to remember' formed by **abiyāta-* in phrases with auxiliary verbs, there is an actual verbal stem **abiyāsa-* reflected in Bactrian, Parthian, and Middle Persian, which will prove etymologically important. First, however, an examination of the currently most visible etymological proposition for **abiyās, abiyāta-* is in order.

CHEUNG (2007, pp. 175f) gives as etymon Proto-Iranian **HiaH* 'to remember', commenting, "This root with the meaning 'to remember' is solely attested with the preverb **abi-*. It is probably originally identical to **HiaH* 'to go, drive to' (Skt. *yā* etc.) that acquired a specialized meaning with *abi-*: *'to come to mind' > *'to remember'." (In what follows, for the notation of [Indo-]Iranian, *y* will be used in place of *i̯*, and *w* will be used in place of *u̯*.)

CHEUNG comments: "The peculiar form OAv. ⁽⁺⁾*yāmǝŋg* gen. sg. 'course' (Y 48.2) may actually contain **HiaH* 'to go, drive to', on which, for instance, INSLER, *Gathas*, 286." The fact is that **yāmǝ̄ŋg* (*ǝ̄ sic*) is the late INSLER's excellent emendation for the text's *yā mǝ̄ŋg*; it was not implemented in subsequent Gatha-editions (although HUMBACH 1991 II, p. 197 mentions it as a "possible" alternative to his edition's maintaining the received text; cf. MAYRHOFER 1996, p. 409

"überlegenswert"). Since Indo-Iranian √*yā* (*Hi̯aH*) deserves fuller discussion, I take this opportunity to set forth the further evidence.

There is nothing "peculiar" about the emended **yāmə̄ṇg*, neither as an inflected form, nor for its stem **yāman-*; note e.g. Y 50.6 *rāzə̄ṇg*, genitive of *rāzar/n-* 'direction', cf. Y 34.12 *rāzarə̄ ... rāšnąm*. What INSLER had written was: "The peculiar *yā mə̄ṇg* if for orig. *yāmə̄ṇg*, gen. of *yāman-* 'course' = Ved. *yā́man-*". There is another Iranian reflex of √*yā* in Old Avestan *yāh-* (**yaHah-*). In SCHWARTZ 2014 I defend, in very great detail, the meaning 'chariot race, contest'. For this I availed myself of the systematic ring-compositional concentrism, whereby Y 30.2, which demands declaration of choice between the two sides, correlates with Y 30.10, which states that there will occur breakage of the pole-and-yoke device (of the chariot) of Wrongness, while the swift team of Rightness will remain yoked, and win in good fame. I further compared with Y 30.2/10 two Gathic passages with locative *yāhī* juxtaposed with a vocative possessive name ending *-aspa-* '-horse': Y 49.6 (Də̄jāmāspa) and theme of being yoked with Rightness for the best prize, and Y 46.14 (Vīštāspa) and theme of the righteous ally becoming famed. I concluded with a demonstration of the thematic relationship between Y 30.2 *yā̊ŋhō* and Y 48.2 **yāmə̄ṇg*, for which I also showed their intertextual lexical relationship, via the analytic charting which I now call by the acronym SCRIM (Serially Corresponding Recursive Intertextual Matching), cf. SCHWARTZ 2018, p. 117 (seq.), with a list of articles in which I had illustrated the principle, to which add SCHWARTZ 2019, p. 265, and SCHWARTZ 2022. I take this occasion to revise the SCRIM chart which shows the correspondence of *yā̊ŋhō* and **yāmə̄ṇg*:

30.1a′ *vaxšiiā*		48.1b″ *fraoxtā*
	√'speak'	
30.2c′ *parā ... yā̊ŋhō*		48.2b *parā ... *yāmə̄ṇg*
	'before the race/course' √'to course'	
30.3c′ *hudā̊ŋhō*		48.3b′ *hudā̊*
	'beneficent one'	
30.4b″ *aŋhat̰ apə̄məm*		48.4d *apə̄məm ... aŋhat̰*
	'will be (at) the last (...)'	
30.5a″ *vərəziiō*		48.5d′ *vərəziiātąm*
	'(to) effect'	
30.6c″ *ahūm*		48.6d′ *aŋhə̄uš*
	'existence'	
30.7c″ *paoruiiō*		48.6d″ *paouruiiehiiā*
	'first'	
30.8b″ *vohū manaŋhā*		48.7b *vaŋhə̄uš manaŋhō*
	'Good Mind'	

30.8c″ _aṣ̌āi_	‘Rightness’	48.8c′ _aṣ̌ā_
30.9c″ _aŋhat̰_	‘will be’	48.9d″ _aŋhat̰_
30.10a′ _adā_	‘when/then’	48.10a′ _kadā_
30.10b″ _hušitōiš_	‘fine dwelling’	48.11b″ _hušəitiš_
30.11c′ _sauuā_	√‘bring weal’	48.12a″ _saošiiaṇtō_
30.11d″ _at̰ … aŋhaitī_	‘and … will be’	48.12a′ _at̰ … aŋhən_

There are several difficulties with CHEUNG’s derivation of _*abi-yāsa-_, _*abi-yāta-_ as related to the verb of motion seen in Old Indic _√yā_. The fact that there is no independent evidence for such a root ‘to remind, to remember’ necessitates for CHEUNG’s hypothesis that _*abi-yāsa-_, _*abi-yāta-_ be from a specialized meaning of the root of motion _√yā_ with preverb _*abi_. However, in Vedic _abhi+√yā_ means ‘to encounter inimically’. In Iranian, the root is attested only in nouns, which leaves unlikely any inner-Iranian verbal formation _*abhi+√yā_. In addition, Old Indic has no verbal stem _*yācha-_ in support of Iranian _*abi-yāsa-_ from this root. Finally, the historical semantics of CHEUNG’s proposal are somewhat _ad hoc_. As will now be shown, an alternative explanation of the Iranian words in question is at hand, one which entails an established Iranian verbal stem _yāsa-_ for which a preverb _*abi_ is demonstrable with apt semantics.

Let us return to _*abiyāsa-_ ‘to remember’. It is represented in Middle Iranian, by Bactrian αβοιασ- (SIMS-WILLIAMS 2007, p. 186) /ayās-/; Manichean Parthian _aby’s-_ /aβyās-/; Manichean Middle Persian _ʾbyʾs-_, and Pahlavi _ʾbydʾs-_, both /ay(y) ās-/. Given the widespread _*abiyāta-_ plus auxiliary verb for ‘remember’, the verb _*abiyāsa-_ in the contiguous Bactrian-Parthian-Middle Persian continuum for ‘remember’ suggests an areal innovation in early Middle Iranian. This development may be attributed to the influence of the verb _*(-)grāsa-_, past stem _*(-)grāta-_ ‘to become awake, aware’, belonging to the same semantic field; see Appendix.

The etymological solution for the formal origin of _*abiyāsa-_, _*abiyāta-_ from a root ‘to (seize) hold, grasp’ (albeit with no semantic expatiation) was seen _in nucleo_ by WEBER (1970, pp. 87ff, § 39), s.v. Parthian _ʾbyʾs-_ etc., and cf. pp. 171f, § 106 s.v. Sogdian _nyʾs-_ ‘nehmen, fangen’, with citation of HENNING _apud_ GERSHEVITCH, as in my next paragraph.

GERSHEVITCH (1954, pp. 83f, §539) lists, under Old Iranian Present classes in Sogdian, inchoative _ʾʾs-_ ‘to take’ < _*ā-yasa-_, past stem _ʾyt-_ from _*ā-yata-_; and _nyʾs-_ ‘to take’ < _*ni-yāsa-_, past stem _nyʾt-_, from _*ni-yāta-_. The matter is continued in the footnotes, beginning (§539[2]) with reference to an observation by HENNING: "Acc. to H. the root *yam* seems to appear in two forms, *yam-* and *yamə-*; thus we have *yasa-* (*y̥m̥sk̂o-*), and *yāsa-* (*y̥m̥̄sk̂o-*), *yata-* and *yāta-*." In §539[3], *inter alia* an analogical Christian Sogdian *nymt-* /nyamt-/ is cited for *ny'̓s* /nyās/: *qt ny'st' 'dyy yw'nt nymtyt bntq'* "if you retain anybody's sins, they will be retained" (it may be added that Sogdian examples of present stem /nyās/, past stem /nyāt/ 'take, seize' are very common).

The relevant Old, Middle, and New Iranian examples of the verb-complex in question, including stems in *yasa-*: *yata-* and *yāsa-*: *yāta-*, are given fairly adequately (but without much formal discrimination) in CHEUNG 2007, pp. 211f s.v. **i̯am* 'to hold [etc.]'. As for the Avestan, which likewise includes stems **yāsa-* and **yasa-*, note the stems in *yāsa-* with preverbs *ā*, *apa*, and *ni*; for the last, we have the semantic correspondence of *niiāsa-* (*Yasht* 19.48 and 50) to Sogd. *nyās* 'to seize' (for the relationship between Sogdian *'yt* and *ny't* etc., see SIMS-WILLIAMS 1989, pp. 257f). As for the verb with preverb **ham*, CHEUNG's 'attend to' involves wrong analysis of Yasna 51.3a *həmiiaṇtū*; the latter means 'let them come together', from √*ay* 'to come, to go'; the passage says, "Let those come together with You via (their) (h)ear(ing), who are united/connected with You via their actions', which the context shows to refer to comprehension of the inner revelatory meaning of the utterances. However, **ham* occurs with *yāsa-* in Yasna 33.1c *həmiiāsaitē* "are held up together (in comparison)'. The problem (unnoted by CHEUNG) of what (to reformulate HENNING's observation in terms of laryngeals) may be stated as roots *yam* vs. *yamH* (*yāsa-*: *yāta-* belonging to the latter) will be resumed later.

Enough has already been said here for a new historical semantic explanation of **abiyāta-* 'memory' and **abiyāsa-* 'to remember': from **yāsa-* 'to hold', **abiyāsa-* would be *'to retain or maintain something (in the mind) for a period of time', and **abiyāta-*, 'something retained (in the mind) for a period of time', i.e. '(a) memory'. As for the preverb **abi*, there is one example, reflected in Christian Sogdian. It occurs in the martyrology of Placidus/Eustathius, fragments of which I identified in my unpublished dissertation (SCHWARTZ 1967, pp. 1–9, 151); the relevant textual details are readily accessible in SIMS-WILLIAMS 1985, pp. 161 and 164, and cf. SIMS-WILLIAMS 2016, p. 57. Here **by'm* (= Syriac *rby*) 'rear/foster' in *b'y'mnt* 'they reared/fostered [the children]'. *Contra* CHEUNG 2007, p. 212, the *b-* of **by'm* is not from **upa-*, which would give **p-*, but Estrangela Syriac script *b*, representing the Sogdian continuant /β/, as e.g. *by'tq'rc*, cited above, would be from **abi-*. Thus **by'm* /βyām/ 'to rear, foster' is from **abi+√yam* *'to retain/maintain for a period of time', compatible in meaning with what was proposed above for the meaning underlying our **abiyāsa-* and **abiyāta-* from the same preverb and ultimate root. For our verb /βyām/ comparable Sogdian verbs are Sogdian /ptyām/ 'to finish' < **pati+√yam* *'to bring containment', and /pyām/ 'to cure' < **api+√yam* or **upa+√yam* 'to sustain into the future, bring sustainment'. The series probably continues **-yāmaya-*.

It remains to explain why we have Iranian reflexes of roots **yam* as well as **yamH*. I propose a merger of two Indo-Iranian verb roots, **yam* 'to hold fast' and *√(H)amH* ‘to grab, seize, lay hold of’ (> ‘attack’); for the latter, see MAYRHOFER 1992, pp. 96f. This would have taken place after a preverb, likely **ni* or **abhi*, with **-i-HamH-* merging with **-i-yam-*. The merger resulted in Iranian **√yamH* alongside the more conservative **√yam*. A trace of Iranian **√(H) amH* may remain as **anta- < *(H)amHta-* in **anta-ahwa-* ‘characterized by consciousness having gone under attack’ > Middle Persian and Persian *andōh*, Khwarezmian *ʾndx*, Sogdian *ʾntwxc* ‘sorrow’.

The proposal that Indo-Iranian **√yamH* is the result of interaction between roots (a) **yam* and (b) **(H)amH*, is paralleled by two other pairs of roots, each pair again showing partial similarity phonologically and semantically: Proto-Indo-European **√h*$_2$*i̯emh*$_2$ ‘to replicate, duplicate, be twinned’ (for which see the excellently detailed BLAŽEK 2016, esp. pp. 368–371), and Proto-Indo-European **√ĝem* ‘to match, to pair, to couple’, first proposed by SCHWARTZ (1975); and (the second pair) (a) **√HyamH*, i.e. the Proto-Indo-Iranian outcome of Proto-Indo-European **√h*$_2$*i̯emh*$_2$ ‘to duplicate, to pair, to replicate’ and (b) Proto-Indo-Iranian **√yam* ‘to hold, to grasp’, these again citable as factors which brought about **√yamH* as variant of the latter root.

From **√ĝem* I derived, *inter alia*, Latin *geminus* ‘twin’, RigVedic *vijā́man-* ‘paired, matching, twinned’ (both with *-n-* formation like that in Old Irish *emon* ‘pair of twins’); RigVedic *ájāmi-* (in the hymn about the twins Yama and Yamī), if ‘not paired’; Greek γαμέω ‘to mate, to wed’; and the many words in Indo-European languages for male relationships through marriage, which reflect **ĝVm-*.

With all the foregoing I posited a series of Iranian words pertaining to compensation and requital as semantic developments of ‘to match, bring parity’: Avestan *zəmanā* ‘reward, payment, wages’; Mugh Sogdian *zʾmnʾk* ‘payment’; Pashto *zəman*, *zamnə* ‘stipend, debt’; and Khotanese *ysaṃtha-* ‘payment’. To these I related Sogdian *ōzām* ‘to requite, repay, compensate, condemn’, passive *ōzams*, past stem *ōzat*, to which now add Bactrian ωζαμο ‘liability’ and ωζι- / ωζαδο ‘to be a liability’ (SIMS-WILLIAMS 2007, pp. 281f).

Of these Iranian forms, none provides clear evidence for an Iranian laryngeal root **zamH* (as against **zam*), but Khwarezmian *ʾwzʾcyk* /ūzācīk/ f. ‘culpability, crime, offense’ < **awa-zāti-* must go back to **√zamH* and supports SIMS-WILLIAMS’ derivation of Bactrian ωζαδο from **awa-zāta-*. The contrast of Sogdian *ōzams-* vs. Khwarezmian *ūzācīk* as to the root vowel points to the secondary formation of a laryngeal root *zamH* (alongside non-laryngeal *zam*) for *‘to give parity, match’, due to the eventual influence of the semantically similar Proto-Indo-European **√h*$_2$*i̯emh*$_2$ (whence Vedic *yamá-*, Gathic *yə̄ma-* ‘twin’ < **h*$_2$*i̯emh*$_2$*ó-*).

CHEUNG (2007, p. 464) gives **zamH* ‘to repay, reward, compensate’, and cites my 1975 article, *inter alia* ignoring my having adduced Latin *geminus* and Vedic *vijā́man-*. CHEUNG contests my attribution of an underlying definition for PIE **√ĝem* ‘to match, make parity, couple’, whence I derived γαμέω ‘to mate, to marry’ and related Indo-European words pertaining to relationship through marriage. CHEUNG instead sees here reference to the bridal payment, and reconstructs PIE

*√ĝemH 'to compensate' as lying behind the Greek, for which he cites POKORNY 1959, p. 369 *ĝem(e)- 'heiraten', where there is no mention of payment. HAMP (1988) proceeds from the evidence in my 1975 article and agrees with my attributing to *√ĝem the primary sense of 'pairing, coupling' and states that Greek γάμος and γαμέω "simply reflect a specialized sense of 'mating', derived from 'pairing'", in accord with my view, and he denies that there is in these words any reference to the payment given to the bride. HAMP also notes lack of evidence for a final laryngeal in γαμέω and its non-Iranian cognates. HAMP thereby supports PIE *√ĝem (for which he denies a laryngeal root) 'to match, to pair', etc.

It may be further proposed that *√HyamH 'to duplicate, to pair' interacted with *√yam as 'to hold two things together, to clasp' (cf. e.g. Vedic *yáma-* 'reins'). Such an association is in effect seen independently from the SCRIM charts in SCHWARTZ 2002 [2006], pp. 59ff, as analyzed on pp. 55f, where the Gathic correspondence of **Yama-* 'the *Twin' with */yama-/ 'twin(ned)' (both < **HyamHá-*) is shown as further correlating with verbal forms, with and without preverbs, from *√yam 'to hold'.

In sum, in the background of Iranian *√yam becoming *√yamH we may have four different, formally and semantically overlapping roots, complexly interacting. The chief roots whereby *√yam became *√yamH were *√(H)amH and, arguably, *√HyamH.

With the foregoing remarks ancillary to the formation of **yāsa-*/**yāta-* (*√yamH), our account of the history of **abiyāta-* '(a) memory' and **abiyāsa-* 'to remember', both from *abi+√yamH 'to retain (in the mind)', comes to an end.

Appendix

An extra impetus for the verb **abiyāsa-* 'to retain, maintain' (alongside **abiyāta-* 'that which has been retained/maintained as a memory') becoming the verb for 'to remember' areally in Bactrian, Parthian, and Middle Persian was probably **-grāsa-* 'to become awake, aware' in the same semantic field as 'to remember'. In what follows, my account differs from that given by YAKUBOVICH (2013), which argues for a stative origin of some Middle Iranian intransitive verbs in *-ās-*, for which he makes use of the material in WEBER 1970, whence he speaks of "Weber's Law"; YAKUBOVICH also touches on Parthian *ʾbyʾs-* (p. 68 fn. 10) as a starting point for the developments he proposes.

The attestations for Avestan *fra*+√*grā* are all worth brief discussion. V 18.16, 24 *fraγrāta-* stem correctly given by KELLENS (1984, p. 157); the texts' *fraγrātō* is nominative, not locative of an improbable stem **fraγrātu-*, as implied by CHEUNG (2007, p. 173) and YAKUBOVICH (2013, p. 69). For the construction, I adopt the English translation of DARMESTETER (1880, pp. 193ff): 'Bushya[n]sta ... who lulls to sleep the whole ... world, as soon as it has awoke', in which *ahūm* 'existence, world' accusative and, in its own clause, *fraγrātō* 'having awoke' = 'being awake' agree as masculine nouns in decent syntax for the late "Vendidadic" grammar.

The second example for *fra*+√*grā* is N 19, in which a priest, lest he sleep though morning prayers, tells his colleague, 'You should awaken me, man' (*frā mā gāraiiōiš narə*). Despite his colleague's promise to 'get him up' (text *fraγrāraiiō*), 'he does not get [him] up' (*nōit̰ fraγrāγrāiieiti*). (From here, the corrupt *fraγrāraiiō*, a cross of *frā* ... *gāraiiōit̰* and *fraγrāγrāiieiti*, further induced by dissimilation, yielded the form *fraγrārāiieiti* at V 18.23.) I take *fraγrāγrāiia-* as 'to get someone up (be sure to awaken someone) by a series of actions' (e.g. calling, touching, shaking), with the fully reduplicative stem being frequentative-iterative, as in Gathic *zaozaomī* 'I keep on invoking'.

The last example of *fra*+√*grā* is the most plausible interpretation for the problematic Hadōxt Nask I.13 *fraγrisəmnō*, KELLENS' (1984, pp. 159f) reconstruction **fraγrāsəmnō*, which furnishes us with **-grāsa-* alongside **-grāta-* (*fraγrāta-* above).

The pair seen in Avestan **fraγrāsa-*: *fraγrāta-* would have been a factor motivating **abiyāsa-*, originally 'to maintain, retain', areally to become, in Early Middle Iranian, 'to remember', alongside the long-established **abiyāta-* 'that which is memorized' < *'that which is maintained (in the mind)', these sharing with **fraγrāsa-*: *fraγrāta-* 'to become awake' the semantic field 'to be aware'. For this phenomenon note Old Iranian *gāraya-* 'to awaken' > Yazghulami *žir-* 'to think'. **-grāsa-* is an "inchoative" like the inherited **źnāsa-* 'to know', whose form and meaning may also may also be relevant for **abiyāsa-*.

However, it is with preverb **wi-*, not **fra*, that **-grāsa-*: **-grāta-* is attested in Middle Iranian: Middle Persian and Parthian /wiγrās-/: /wiγrād/; Sogdian / wiγrās/: /wiγrāt/; and Khwarezmian /uγrās-/: /uγrād/ (*ʾγrʾs-*: *ʾγrʾd*, also attested without *ʾ*-); for **wi-* > Khwarezmian /u-/, cf. *ʾzdx* < /wazdah-/. Cf. further with **wi-* Ossetic D *(i)qal* 'awake'. I propose that the marginal **wi* was promoted (to replace **fra-*) in Middle Iranian **wigrāsa-*: **wigrāta-* by the rhyming influence of **abiyāsa-*: **abiyāta-*.

An approach again taking into account semantic fields provides alternate explanations for other forms discussed in YAKOBOVICH 2013. First, the group consisting of Psalter Pahlavi *ʾwnʾd-* /ōnāy-/, Khwarezmian (*ʾ*)*γnʾs-*: (*ʾ*)*γnʾsʾd*, Persian *γunaw-*: *γunūd*, and Christian Sogdian *γnʾw* 'to slumber' (it is odd that, in connection with Christian Sogdian *γnʾw* adduced by SIMS-WILLIAMS 1989, p. 261 from an unpublished text, nobody has mentioned the precise Yaghnobi cognate, *γnóu̯-* 'to slumber' [ANDREEV and PEŠČEREVA 1957, p. 258 '*dremat*"']). For the entire series one should proceed from ***√*gnā* (cf. HENNING 1971, p. 20b; YAKUBOVICH 2013, p. 69, where, however, as also for ***√*grā*, YAKUBOVICH posits an underlying stative formation). The Middle Persian form */ōnāy-/ would be parallel to the many stems like /nimāy-/ 'to show' < ***√*mā*. For the remaining forms, ***√*gnā* should be upheld against CHEUNG (2007, p. 119) root **gnauH*. SIMS-WILLIAMS (1989, p. 261), on the Khwarezmian verb, remarks, "CSogd. *γnʾwt* ... 'slumbers' ...

indicates that the root is in fact **gnu-*, hence Chor. **gnāu-sa-* (or influenced by its antonym (ʾ)*γnʾs-?*).” However, the reasoning in SIMS-WILLIAMS’ parenthetic speculation works better as a factor for the existence of **√gnā* as a phonic counter to its antonym **√grā*, so Khwarezmian (ʾ)*γrʾs-* served as a model for (ʾ)*γnās-*. Furthermore, Avestan *γənąna-* ‘a blow’, *γnāna-* ‘abortifacient’ yielded the basis of a root **gnā*, whence ‘to (be) knock(ed) out’, and would give, as in English, ‘to slumber’.

Persian *γunaw-*: *γunūd* would be from an East Iranian, most probably a Bactrian, loanword /γnāu/. Persian *γunaw-*, with its rare *-aw-* present stem, shows a past stem *γunūd* parallel to the common *baw-*: *būd* ‘to become’. Similarly *šunaw-*: *šunūd* ‘to hear’, where no laryngeal is involved. I explain the latter Sogdian and Persian (< Bactrian?) forms for ‘to slumber’ from **√gnā* crossed with **√nau* *‘to nod’ (cf. English ‘to nod out’ = ‘fall asleep’), evidenced by Sogdian /nāu/ ‘to shake one’s head’ and /nau-/ ‘to go slowly’, both attested in Manichean spellings, and Old Khotanese *vanau-* ‘to become inactive’, with preverb **awa-* as also reflected by Middle Persian /ōnāy-/ ‘to slumber’; phonetically, the cross was made easier by the spirantization **g* > *γ*, cf. the Greek cognates νεύω ‘I nod’, νυστάζω ‘I am getting sleepy, delay, slumber’.

Finally, the development of **√hwah* ‘to beat, thrash, thresh’ is rightly connected by YAKUBOVICH (2013, p. 68) to Parthian /xwās-/: /xwāsād/ ‘to be weak, tired’, Khwarezmian */xwās/: /xwād/ ‘be weak, tired’, Sogdian /xwāt/ ‘weak, tired’, with */xwāhāta-/ > */xwāt-/. It may be added that */xwāt(a)-/: */xwās(a)-/ was influenced, in the same semantic field, by */gnāt(a)-: */gnās(a)-/ (*‘be beat, knocked out’ > ‘to slumber’), with consequent semantic distinction from */xwāh(a)-: */xwāst(a-) ‘to beat, thrash, thresh’.

I have tried throughout this paper, *inter alia*, to show how taking into account associative processes within and across the realms of form and meaning can yield solutions to etymological problems, where linear explanations fail.[1]

Bibliography

ADAMS, D.Q. 2013: *A Dictionary of Tocharian B: Revised and Greatly Enlarged.* Amsterdam/New York.

ANDREEV, M.S./E.M.PEŠČEREVA 1957: *Jagnobskie Teksty.* Moscow/Leningrad.

BLAŽEK, V. 2016: “Iamos — the Greek Counterpart of the Indo-Iranian Twin-God *Yama-?” In: *Journal of Indo-European Studies* 44, pp. 350–379.

CHEUNG, J. 2007: *Etymological Dictionary of the Iranian Verb.* Leiden/Boston (Leiden Indo-European Etymological Dictionary Series 2).

DARMESTETER, J. 1880: *The Zend-Avesta, Part I. The Vendidad* (= F. MAX MÜLLER (ed.): *Sacred Books of the East* IV). Oxford [Repr. 1965 Delhi].

GERSHEVITCH, I. 1961: *A Grammar of Manichean Sogdian.* Oxford.

1 I thank DAVID BUYANER, ALMUT HINTZE, AGNES KORN, NICHOLAS SIMS-WILLIAMS, P.O. SKJÆRVØ, and MICHAEL WEISS for their substantive help and suggestions, and NATHAN LEVINE for his careful word-processing.

HAMP, E.P. 1988: "The Indo-European terms for 'marriage'". In: M.A. JAZAYERY and W. WINTER (eds.): *Languages and Cultures: Studies in Honor of Edgar C. Polomé*. Berlin, pp. 179–182.

HUMBACH, H. 1991: *The Gāthās of Zarathushtra and the Other Old Avestan Texts, in collaboration with Josef Elfenbein and Prods O. Skjærvø*. Part II: *Commentary*. Heidelberg.

INSLER, S. 1975: *The Gathas of Zarathustra*. Leiden (Acta Iranica Textes et Mémoires Vol. I).

KELLENS, J. 1984: *Le verbe avestique*. Wiesbaden.

MAYRHOFER, M. 1992: *Etymologisches Wörterbuch des Altindoarischen*. Band I. Heidelberg.

— 1996: *Etymologisches Wörterbuch des Altindoarischen*. Band II. Heidelberg.

MORGENSTIERNE, G. 1929: *Indo-Iranian Frontier Languages* I: *Parachi and Ormuri*. Oslo.

SCHWARTZ, M. 1967: *Studies in the Texts of the Sogdian Christians*. Doctoral dissertation, University of California, Berkeley.

— 1975: "Proto-Indo-European √*ĝem*." In: *Monumentum H.S. Nyberg* II. Leiden (Acta Iranica, Hommages et opera minora, Deuxième Série), pp. 195–211.

— 2002 [2006]: "How Zarathushtra Generated the Gathic Corpus." In: *Bulletin of the Asia Institute*, Volume 16, pp. 53–64.

— 2014: "Gathic Lexicography and Composition." In: *Iran Nameh* 29, 2, pp. 22–28.

— 2018: "A Preliterate Acrostic in the Gathas: Crosstextual and Compositional Evidence." In: *Dabir* 6, pp. 116–124.

— 2019: "An Early Trait of Gathic Performance." In: A. PANAINO/A. PIRAS/P. OGNIBENE (eds.): *Studi iranici ravennati* III. Bologna (Indo-Iranica et Orientalia, Series Lazur 17), pp. 261–268.

— 2022: "Gathic †*mąnarōiš*: A Hapax Expatiated Compositionally." In: A. CANTERA/M. MACUCH/N. SIMS-WILLIAMS (eds.): *Reward of the Righteous, Festschrift in Honour of Almut Hintze*. Wiesbaden, pp. 469–485.

SIMS-WILLIAMS, N. 1985: *The Christian Sogdian Manuscript C 2*. Berlin (Schriften zur Geschichte und Kultur des alten Orients, Berliner Turfantexte XII).

— 1989: "New Studies in the Verbal System of Old and Middle Iranian". In: *Bulletin of the School of Oriental and African Studies* (University of London) 52, 2, pp. 257–264.

— 2007: *Bactrian Documents from Northern Afghanistan*, II: *Letters and Buddhist Texts*. London.

— 2016: *A Dictionary: Christian Sogdian, Syriac, and English*. Wiesbaden (Beiträge zur Iranistik 41).

WEBER, D. 1970: *Die Stellung der sog. Inchoativa in Mitteliranischen*. PhD. Dissertation, Universität zu Göttingen.

YAKUBOVICH, I. 2011: "Sogdian Etymological Notes". In: *Acta Orientalia Hungarica* 69, 2, pp. 161–181.

— 2013: "Middle Iranian Intransitives in *-ās-*". In: P.B. LURJE/S.R. TOKHTASEV (eds.): *Commentationes Iranicae: Vladimiro Livshits Nonagenario Donum Natalicum*. St. Petersburg, pp. 64–73.

Further Notes on Sogdians in Khotan

Nicholas Sims-Williams, Cambridge

As is well known, the Sogdians were amongst the most energetic merchants on the so-called "Silk Road", who traded along the various branches of the Silk Road throughout China and even as far as Mongolia. They founded trading colonies at many of the important markets along these routes, and some of them settled permanently in the "Western Regions" and in China proper. Since Khotan was an important station on the road which skirted the southern edge of the Taklamakan desert, it was of course visited by Sogdian traders, who are referred to in Khotanese documents as *sūlia-* (nom. sg. *sūlī*, nom. pl. *sūlya*, etc.).

After earlier hesitations, it is now generally accepted that the basic meaning of *sūlia-* is "Sogdian", from which it also developed a secondary meaning "merchant".[1] Forms of this ethnonym containing [l] are widely attested, e.g. *suliǵa* in a famous Kharoṣṭhi document from Endere;[2] Pahlavi *swlyk*;[3] Manichaean Middle Persian *swγlyy*;[4] Chinese *suli* 窣利 (EMC swət-lih);[5] Tocharian B *Suklyī[ka]*.[6] The relationship of such forms to those with [d] or [δ], e.g. Sogdian *swγδyk*, Persian *suγdī*, Tibetan *sog-dag*, Chinese *sute* 粟特 (EMC suawk-dək), requires more of an explanation than Bailey's bland statement that "the variation of *d*, *δ*, *l* is banal".[7] At the time when Bailey wrote these words, it was natural for him to rely on the widespread assumption that the Sogdian letter <δ> was pronounced as [l] in certain varieties of Sogdian,[8] but an important article by Pavel Lurje and Ilya Yakubovich has shown that this assumption, which they term "the myth of Sogdian lambdacism", is without foundation.[9] Consequently the *-l*-forms of the word for "Sogdian" cannot be regarded as deriving directly from Sogdian, but must have been mediated via some other

1 Kumamoto 1982, pp. 191–196; Bailey 1985, pp. 76–78; Emmerick in Emmerick/Skjærvø 1987, pp. 148–149.

2 See Burrow 1940, p. 137.

3 *Vendidad* 1.4 etc.

4 *BBB*, line 462: *ʿyn pd swγlyy zgr* "this (hymn) to a Sogdian tune" (Henning 1937, p. 32). The phrase is certainly Middle Persian, not Sogdian as stated in Bailey 1985, p. 77.

5 EMC/LMC = Early/Late Middle Chinese (following Pulleyblank 1991).

6 Ching 2013, p. 346 (referring also to a personal name attested in forms such as Suklyike, Suklike).

7 Bailey 1985, p. 78.

8 Henning 1939, p. 97.

9 Lurje/Yakubovich 2017. Cf. also Sims-Williams 2016.

language. For both linguistic and historical reasons, the language in question is almost certainly Bactrian, in which the development of an earlier *d or *δ to [l] is regular and which is known to have contributed a large number of loanwords to neighbouring languages from the Kushan period onwards.

The word for "Sogdian" is not certainly attested in Bactrian. However, a Bactrian contract from the end of the 7th century C.E. names two brothers, Potan (πωτανο) and Miyar (μιιαρο), the sons of Farn-agad (φαρνοαγαδο) from Bunsuglig (βονοσογολιγο). In view of the element *Farn-* rather than Bactrian *Farr-*, the father's name is probably Sogdian, and the same may be true of Miyar, for which the only likely cognate is the Sogdian personal name *myʾrxʾʾn*. This evidence that the family were Sogdians adds plausibility to a suggestion by PAVEL LURJE that the place-name Bunsuglig should be understood as "the Sogdian (σογολιγο) settlement (βονο)".[10] Another late but undated Bactrian document contains a family name Sugdukan (σογδοκανο), which may either represent a form closer to the Sogdian pronunciation of the ethnonym or result from a late Bactrian change of [γl] to [γd].[11] In any case, there can be little doubt that the Bactrian form of the word would have been [suγlīg], later [suγlī], providing a historically and linguistically plausible source for forms such as *suliǵa*, *swlyk*, *swγlyy* and *suli*.

The earliest evidence of Sogdians in Khotan is found in the Kharoṣṭhi document already mentioned, a contract for the sale of a camel to a certain Sogdian (*suliǵa*), which probably dates from the 3rd or 4th century C.E.[12] Although the document was found at Endere, a long way to the east of Khotan, it must have been written in the kingdom of Khotan, as it is dated according to the regnal years of a Khotanese king. The purchaser of the camel may have been a travelling merchant, but one of the witnesses is a Sogdian too. He was presumably a local resident, since a passer-by would hardly be qualified to act as a witness.

A larger body of evidence comes from the Tang period, when Sogdians in the Khotan region are mentioned in documents in several languages, including Chinese, Khotanese, Tibetan and Judaeo-Persian.[13] Several fragmentary Sogdian documents have also been found near Khotan, particularly in places on the northern and north-eastern borders of the ancient kingdom of Khotan, at the sites now known as Mazar Tagh and Dandan Uiliq. Their number has recently increased greatly as a result of the acquisition by the Library of Renmin University of China, Beijing, of a collection of manuscripts from the Khotan area which includes some thirteen Sogdian documents as well as religious texts

10 See SIMS-WILLIAMS 2010, p. 87 s.v. μιιαρο. By a regrettable oversight, the place-name is still transcribed "Bonchuqlïgh" (as if it were a Turkish word) in my edition of the text (Document S, in SIMS-WILLIAMS 2012, pp. 94–97).

11 See SIMS-WILLIAMS 2010, pp. 130–131 s.v. *σογδοκο; 2011, p. 245. The text in question is Doc. ag, lines 2–3, in SIMS-WILLIAMS 2012, pp. 156–157.

12 See BURROW 1940, p. 137.

13 References to much of the relevant material are collected in YOSHIDA 1997, pp. 568–569; RONG 2006, pp. 514–518; 2009, pp. 405–407; ZHANG 2018.

and secular documents in Chinese, Khotanese, Tibetan and Sanskrit. These new Sogdian documents have been published by Bi Bo and myself.[14]

Taken together, these sources show that Sogdians in the Khotan region were engaged in trading both on a local level and internationally. The resident Sogdians seem to have remained distinct from the local population, retaining their native language and perhaps, at least in somes cases, living in special "Sogdian villages",[15] where they paid their taxes and dealt in cloth and other commodities. To judge from certain Khotanese documents, some Sogdians seem to have been involved as moneylenders or tax-collectors.[16] Others were engaged in long distance trade, with their homeland to the west, with Turkic peoples to the north, with the Tibetans to the south, and even with the Chinese capital of Chang'an (modern Xi'an), far away to the east.[17] A collection of documents from the Khotan area recently acquired by the National Library of China includes a slip of paper (BH4-136), with a clay sealing and a Sogdian inscription naming a *srtp'w* "caravan-leader", which probably dates from the late 7th century: *(t)βty βγy'n [ZKn?] srtp'w 'kwt'kk* "Sealed by Vaghyan (son of) the caravan-leader Akutakk".[18] To judge from the Khotanese document to which it is attached (BH4-135), the Sogdian caravan obtained its supplies via a local Buddhist monastery. One Chinese document, a permit to pass the northern border of Khotan at Mazar Tagh, is issued to a Sogdian who is described as a "vice-ambassador",[19] but he was probably a merchant like most so-called "ambassadors" mentioned in Chinese documents and histories. This vice-ambassador can be identified as a Sogdian from his Chinese surname Kang 康, which indicates that his family came from Samarkand. Some other persons mentioned in the Chinese and Khotanese documents can be identified as Sogdians either from surnames of this type or from their characteristic personal names.[20]

Some of the Sogdians in Khotan seem to have obtained high status. A group of Chinese documents from Khotan refer to a gentleman who bears the surname Mi 米, indicating that his family came from Maymurgh near Samarkand, as well as several Chinese titles of high rank such as "general" and "commissioner in chief".[21]

14 Bi/Sims-Williams 2010; 2015; 2018.

15 Rong 2009, p. 407; Yoshida *apud* Bi/Sims-Williams 2015, p. 261 n. 2 (= 2018, p. 3 n. 2). On *bisā-* in the sense "village" see Duan 2008.

16 See Zhang 2018, esp. pp. 37–38.

17 See in particular Renmin document no. 5 in Bi/Sims-Williams 2015, pp. 262–270; 2018, pp. 61–72.

18 This is the most recent reading and interpretation of the Sogdian text (Yoshida 2017, p. 285). See also Bi/Sims-Williams 2018, p. 3 n. 1. For an edition of the Khotanese document see Duan 2016.

19 Rong 2009, p. 407.

20 See for example Yoshida 1997, p. 569.

21 Bi/Sims-Williams 2015, p. 270 (= 2018, p. 73).

The Sogdian witness in the Kharoṣṭhi document from Endere, *Nani-vadhaǵa*, i.e. Nanai-vandak "Slave of Nanai", bears a name which indicates his family background in Zoroastrianism, the traditional religion of the Sogdians.[22] Khotan was of course famous as a stronghold of Buddhism and by Tang times some of the Sogdians in Khotan had converted to this religion.[23] According to some scholars, pictures of deities and other works of art found at Dandan Uiliq show connections with the art of Panjikent in the Sogdian homeland and indicate Zoroastrian influence on the local form of Buddhism practised by the Sogdians in this region.[24] Some of the Sogdians in Khotan may of course have adhered to other religions. The writer of a Judaeo-Persian letter found near Khotan seems to be referred to in the text as a Sogdian (*sugdī*), and YOSHIDA has speculated that the writer of the Sogdian document Renmin no. 4 may also have been Jewish.[25] I must withdraw my own over-hasty suggestion that a Sogdian fragment from Mazar Tagh in the British Library belongs to a Manichaean text;[26] however, Renmin no. 3 refers to a presbyter or priest (*msyδr*), either a Manichaean or a Christian, though his name does not seem to be Sogdian.[27]

Two further Sogdian documents, one so far unpublished, the other so far misunderstood, add to our picture of the Sogdian community in the Khotan region.

The first is a fragment in the Francke–Körber collection of the Museum Fünf Kontinente, München (formerly the Museum für Volkerkunde), of whose existence I first learnt from Dr GERD GROPP in 1983. The fragment bears the signatures FK 859 and MTa 17, the latter of which should indicate that it was found at the site of Mazar Tagh. This provenance is perfectly plausible but should be treated with caution, since the manuscript was bought by FRANCKE from a dealer.[28] To judge from the contents, the fragment is the upper right-hand corner of a sheet of paper. The verso is blank, while the recto contains the beginning of the first four lines of a letter, written in a practised but not particularly elegant cursive (Fig. 1).

22 See LURJE 2011, p. 273, with references.

23 E.g. *Bodifen* 勃帝分 = *pwtyprn* "Glory of Buddha", *Budävaṃdai* = **pwtyβntk* "Slave of Buddha" (YOSHIDA 1997, p. 569). The phrase *[βγ'n-β]xtm pw(t)[y]* "the *devātideva* Buddha" in a fragment which seems to have been found at Dandan Uiliq suggests that this is a Buddhist text, but a Manichaean origin cannot be ruled out: see BI/SIMS-WILLIAMS 2010, p. 497 with nn. 4–6 (= 2018, p. 2 with nn. 3–5).

24 MODE 1992; see also RONG 2013. The most recent discussion is that of COMPARETI 2020.

25 YOSHIDA 2019, pp. 390–392.

26 "Fragment 12" in SIMS-WILLIAMS 1976, pp. 53–54. This opinion (unfortunately repeated in RONG 2006, p. 517) was based only on the spelling of *δβ'mpnwh* "wife" with *-mp-* rather than *-np-*, but this spelling is also attested in Renmin no. 8, a letter without any apparent religious content. It is now clear that such "non-standard" writings are not restricted to any single religious community.

27 BI/SIMS-WILLIAMS 2010, p. 502 (= 2018, p. 54).

28 GROPP 1984, p. 149 (where the signature is given as "Maz. T").

Fig. 1. FK 859 (MTa 17)
© Museum Fünf Kontinente, Munich, photo: NICOLAI KÄSTNER

1 pr RBkw (c)[yn'kh δykh ZY]
2 ptškw'nh['kw cnn]
3 wyspn'cw ''δ'(k)['yw γw'ncykstr
4 (βntk)šyr(?) [

"With great d[esire to see him, I send a letter and] respectful message [to the noble lord, the great hope, most necessary] of everyone, [the mighty support], Vande-shir(?) ...".

The choice of wording to fill the lacunae is of course only approximate, but there is not much doubt about the reading and restoration of most of the words which are at least partially preserved, since they all belong to standard formulae for beginning a polite letter. The opening words *pr RBkw cyn'kh* "with great desire" are found, variously spelt, as the first words of another letter from Khotan (Renmin no. 8) and of a small fragment in the Otani collection (O 2483).[29] The following phrase *δykh ZY ptškw'nh* "letter and respectful message", not fully preserved in Renmin no. 8, is attested in several other letters, sometimes as their opening words (Renmin no. 5 and no. 7), sometimes, as here, a little later in the opening formula.[30] The phrase *cnn wyspn'cw ''δ'k 'yw γw'ncykstr*

29 BENKATO 2018, p. 52.
30 L44, see BENKATO 2018, p. 14.

"most necessary of everyone" is again attested in Renmin no. 8, as well as in L44 (partly restored), L27 and Ch/So 10920.[31]

The first word of line 4 is partly illegible, being written with a flourish like a signature. Nevertheless, its position shows that it is not the name of the writer, but that of the addressee, placed at the beginning of a line and followed by a space as a sign of respect as in several other Sogdian letters such as Renmin nos. 5, 6 and 7. The most likely reading seems to be *βntkšyr*, a name also attested in Renmin no. 2 (where it may possibly refer to the same individual) and, in the variant spelling *βntyšyr*, in the Mug document Б9, line 1.[32] A Sogdian name consisting of the same two elements in the opposite order seems to be attested as Śirvaṃdai, i.e. **šyrβntk*, in the Chinese-Khotanese bilingual text X15.[33]

The second text to be edited here, the British Library fragment Or. 8212/74 = M. Tagh a.IV.00166, was first published by me more than forty years ago.[34] At that time few examples of late Sogdian documents were available for comparison, with the result that little sense could be made of this tattered fragment in cursive script (Fig. 2).

Fig. 2. Or. 8212/74 (M. Tagh a.IV.00166)
© British Library Board

31 BENKATO 2018, pp. 14, 34, 37. As noted in GERSHEVITCH 1954, p. 195 (§§1303, 1305), prefixing *ʾyw* "one" to a comparative gives it the force of a superlative. The translation "more necessary than everyone" (BENKATO 2018, p. 37) is not quite correct.

32 LURJE 2011, pp. 142–143.

33 YOSHIDA *apud* DUAN 2008, p. 67.

34 "Fragment 15" in SIMS-WILLIAMS 1976, p. 62. As noted there, the fragment is written on one side only and has no margins, although line 3 seems to be complete at the beginning. Photo in SIMS-WILLIAMS/HAMILTON 1990/2015, Pl. 28a.

1](ʾ)k ʾ(s)[
2]. mʾxw mδ(y)[
3 ʾskw(ym) (r)[tm]s[35] mʾt[36] γẓʾ [
4 [rtk]δ[] γẓʾ msʾ šwʾ ʾys(β)[
5].[ ].[ ]δδ[ ]δ[

"... [if you are well we are happy] ... we here are [well up to the present day. Moreov]er: there was(?) [in](?) Gazā ... [and wh]en he went from Gazā, he(?) came ...".

The phrase "we here are well up to the present day", partially preserved in lines 2–3, is common in the opening formulae of Sogdian letters, including those from Khotan. It almost always follows a parallel phrase enquiring about the health of the addressee, which suggests a restoration such as *[kδʾ ʾšmʾxw šyr](ʾ)k ʾ(s) [kwδʾ]* "if you are well (we are happy)" in lines 1–2.[37] What follows these formulae should be the body of the letter, which, as always, is less formulaic and therefore more difficult to interpret. The first problem here is *mʾt* or *mnt*, which is highly ambigous: *mʾt* "(there) was", "mother", "(so) that"; *mnt* "while", "without", "(to/for) us".[38] The second problem is *γẓʾ*, occurring in both line 3 and line 4. In the latter it it followed by *msʾ*, which is commonly used in late Sogdian texts as a postposition "from", with or without an accompanying preposition *cn/MN*.[39] This collocation suggests the possibility that the unknown *γẓʾ* may be a Sogdian spelling of Gaysāta [γazāʔa], the Khotanese name of Dandan Uiliq, Chinese *jiexie* 傑謝 (LMC kɦiat-sɦiaˋ),[40] one of the settlements in the north of the kingdom of Khotan where Sogdians are known to have been present. So far as I know, the place-name is never spelt without *-t-* in Khotanese, but an adjective *gaysāyia-* is attested in Or. 11252/33, line 6.[41] The same reduction of Khotanese *-āta* to *-ā* implied by the Sogdian spelling *γẓʾ* seems to be attested by *ʾspʾ* in Renmin no. 4, verso 6, which probably represents Khotanese *spāta* "general", later *spā*;[42] cf. also the transcription of this title as Tibetan *spa*, Chinese *sabo* 薩波 (LMC sat-pua). As recently noted, the same form may be attested as *sbʾ-* in a Judaeo-Persian letter, where *sbʾpwšy* can perhaps be understood as a combination of this Khotanese word with Chinese *fushi* 副使 "deputy, assistant", giving a meaning "vice commander".[43]

35 There is only an indeterminate trace of the supposed initial *r-*.
36 Or *mnt*.
37 See Benkato 2018, pp. 81–83, where these phrases in various letters including Renmin nos. 5 and 6 are tabulated and discussed.
38 1 pl. enclitic pronoun, of which this particular form is so far attested only in the spelling *mnd* in both Christian (Sims-Williams 2014, p. 71) and Manichaean Sogdian (*[ʾs](k)[w]ʾmn(t)ymnd* "our existence" M891a, R11, beside *[ʾskw](ʾ)mndyymn* "id.", M1697, A3, both unpublished).
39 See Sims-Williams/Hamilton 1990, p. 28 (= 2015, p. 34).
40 See Rong 2006, p. 516.
41 See Skjærvø 2002, pp. lxxvi, 101.
42 Bi/Sims-Williams 2010, p. 506 (= 2018, p. 60).
43 Bi/Sims-Williams 2018, p. 60.

If the identification of *γẓ'* as Gaysāta/Dandan Uiliq is correct, this is the second local place-name to be found in the Sogdian documents from Khotan. The British Library fragment H.143 MNS 18 = IOL Khot 158/5 contains two mentions of Khotan itself, as was discovered by YUTAKA YOSHIDA.[44]

The last text to be mentioned here seems to be a mirage. In 1976, D. N. MACKENZIE printed a list of British Library Sogdian fragments, many of them still unpublished at the time, in which he included Or. 8212/91 = M.T.75.D, describing it as a piece of wood with 2 lines of illegible Sogdian text.[45] RONG assumed that this fragment came from Mazar Tagh,[46] but YOSHIDA has pointed out that the signature indicates that it should rather have been found at Mazar Toghrak, noting further that he examined it in 1993 and thought that it was not Sogdian but rather one of the many Chinese-Khotanese bilinguals from this site.[47]

Finally, I would like to draw attention to the form *hvācai*, usually interpreted as an unknown Chinese title, which is attested in several Khotanese documents from the Khotan area.[48] It is worth considering whether this title may be equated with the Sogdian title *xw'c'k* [xwāčē] in a bilingual epitaph from Ye 鄴, the meaning of which must be close to that of *shangke* 商客 "travelling merchant" in the parallel Chinese text; see BI *et al.* 2017, pp. 313–314. In that article two possible etymologies for the Sogdian title are considered: it may be cognate with Sogdian *xw'kr* "merchant", where the element *xw'*- derives from **wahāka*- "trade", or it may be a slightly adapted loanword from Chinese *huozhu* 貨主 (EMC **xwa^h tɕuă'*) "seller", lit. "owner of goods", an expression attested in Chinese since Eastern Han times. In either case, following a suggestion by PAVEL LURJE, it is possible that Persian *x^{v}āǰa*, a title for rich merchants and other men of importance, may be a loanword from Sogdian *xw'c'k*.

The Khotanese documents in which this word has been noticed are the following:

(i) Hedin 26, ed. BAILEY 1961, pp. 38–39, 140–141. As BAILEY points out, *hvācai* here seems to be used as a plural: *gaysātaja auya auva haṃdastä daḍūsi āstaṃna hvācai ṣī śī'na ... mūri nāṃdä* "the village haṃdasta-official Daḍūsi and the other hvā cai ṣī śī'na men of the village Gaysāta received mūra-coins ..." (BAILEY's translation). The meaning of the syllables *ṣī śī' na* is unclear. The document ends with the finger-marks of Daḍūsi and eight other persons, presumably those referred to in the document as *hvācai*. Their names are a linguistic mixture, but include the likely Sogdian name Kānai (Sogdian *k'n'k*, *k'nk*, see LURJE 2011, pp. 201–202).

44 See YOSHIDA 2010, p. 6, where this text (shown in facsimile in SIMS-WILLIAMS/HAMILTON 1990/2015, Pl. 39a) was edited for the first time.

45 MACKENZIE 1976, p. ix.

46 RONG 2006, p. 517 n. 13.

47 YOSHIDA 2010, p. 7 (kindly interpreted for me by BILL MAK). On STEIN's signature "M.T." see KUMAMOTO 1996, p. 31.

48 These are conveniently listed in ZHANG 2018, p. 32.

(ii) SI P 103.7, ed. EMMERICK–VOROB'ËVA-DESJATOVSKAJA 1995, pp. 137–138. Here too, *hvācai* seems to be the subject of a plural verb, but the context provides no further information about the persons concerned.

(iii) SI P 103.12, ed. EMMERICK–VOROB'ËVA-DESJATOVSKAJA 1995, pp. 139–140. The *hvācai* is named as Puñūṃni.

(iv) IOL Khot 53/1 (M.T. c.0019), ed. BAILEY 1968, p. 83; SKJÆRVØ 2002, p. 289. The context is fragmentary, but the *hvācai* seems to be named as Vageyaṃni, i.e. Sogdian *βγy'n*, a name which we have already met as that of the son of the caravan-leader in the Sogdian text attached to the Khotanese document BH4-135.

(v) IOL Khot 48/8 (M.T. a.iv.00170), ed. BAILEY 1968, p. 96; SKJÆRVØ 2002, p. 283. No usable context.

(vi) Or. 6397/2, ed. BAILEY 1968, p. 55; SKJÆRVØ 2002, pp. 9–10; ZHANG 2018, pp. 32–33. In 1968 it seems that BAILEY took *sai*, the syllable following *hvācai*, as his name, but in BAILEY 1979, p. 478b s.v. *hāy-*, he writes "Hvā Cai-sai".

In some documents (Hedin 26, SI P 103.12) the *hvācai* are connected with the village Gaysāta (Dandan Uiliq), a place known to have been inhabited by Sogdians as mentioned above. Or. 6397/2 must also come from Gaysāta, as implied by the mention of Sīḍaka.[49] At least in SI P 103.12, the *hvācai* seem to play a role in the local administration, perhaps the collection of taxes.

To sum up, the evidence collected here suggests that *hvācai* may well derive from the Sogdian title *xw'c'k*, denoting a merchant or a particular type of merchant, which came to be used in Late Khotanese to refer both to certain Sogdian merchants and to those belonging to other ethnic groups.

The texts presented in this article are mere fragments, on which no more than a few words can be read, but I hope that they will nevertheless be of interest to my esteemed colleague DIETER WEBER, whose work on documents in cursive Pahlavi has often shown how much can be deduced from small and almost illegible fragments when they are considered in their historical context.

Bibliography

BAILEY, H.W. 1961: *Indo-Scythian Studies being Khotanese texts.* IV. Cambridge.
— 1968: *Saka Documents. Text volume.* London.
— 1985: *Indo-Scythian Studies being Khotanese texts.* VII. Cambridge.
BENKATO, A. 2018: *Studies on the Sogdian epistolary tradition.* Turnhout (Berliner Turfantexte 42).
BI, B./N. SIMS-WILLIAMS 2010: "Sogdian documents from Khotan. I: Four economic documents." In: *Journal of the American Oriental Society* 130/4, pp. 497–508.

49 Cf. YOSHIDA 2005, pp. 54–57.

— 2015: "Sogdian documents from Khotan. II: Letters and miscellaneous fragments." In: *Journal of the American Oriental Society* 135/2, pp. 261–282.

— 2018: *Sogdian Documents from Khotan in the Museum of Renmin University of China / Zhongguo renmin daxue bowuguan cang hetian chutu sute yu wenshu* 中国人民大学博物馆藏和田出土粟特语文书. Beijing.

BI, B./N. SIMS-WILLIAMS/YAN YAN 2017: "Another Sogdian-Chinese bilingual epitaph." In: *Bulletin of the School of Oriental and African Studies* 80/2, pp. 305–318.

BURROW, T. 1940: *A translation of the Kharoṣṭhi documents from Chinese Turkestan.* London.

CHING CH. 2013: "The activities of Sogdian Buddhists in Kucha as observed in the Tocharian B secular documents." In: M. DE CHIARA/M. MAGGI/G. MARTINI (eds.): *Buddhism among the Iranian peoples of Central Asia.* Vienna (Multilingualism and History of Knowledge. I), pp. 333–383.

COMPARETI, M. 2020: "The representation of non-Buddhist deities in Khotanese paintings and some related problems." In: X. LI (ed.): *Studies on the history and culture along the continental Silk Road.* Singapore (Silk Road Research Series), pp. 89–119.

DUAN Q. 2008: "*Bisā*- and *hālaa*- in a new Chinese-Khotanese bilingual document." In: *Journal of Inner Asian Art and Archaeology* 3, pp. 65–73.

— 2016: "Accounts in Khotanese with the signature of the leader of a Sogdian caravan." In: RONG XINJIANG/LUO FENG (eds.): *Sute ren zai zhongguo : kaogu faxian yu chutu wenxian de xin yinzheng* 粟特人在中国: 考古发现与出土文献的新印证 [Sogdians in China: New evidence in archaeological finds and excavated texts]. Beijing [in Chinese], pp. 96–115.

EMMERICK, R.E./P.O. SKJÆRVØ 1987: *Studies in the vocabulary of Khotanese.* II. Vienna.

EMMERICK, R.E./M.I. VOROB'ËVA-DESJATOVSKAJA 1995: *Saka Documents. Text volume.* III. London.

GERSHEVITCH 1954: *A grammar of Manichean Sogdian.* Oxford.

GROPP, G. 1984: "Eine neuentdeckte Sammlung khotanesischer Handschriftenfragmente in Deutschland." In: W. SKALMOWSKI/A. VAN TONGERLOO (eds.): *Middle Iranian Studies.* Leuven (Orientalia Lovaniensia Analecta 16), pp. 147–150.

HENNING, W.B. 1937: *Ein manichäisches Bet- und Beichtbuch.* Berlin (APAW 1936, No. 10).

— 1939: "Sogdian loan-words in New Persian." In: *Bulletin of the School of Oriental Studies* 10/1, pp. 93–106.

KUMAMOTO, H. 1982: *Khotanese official documents in the tenth century A.D.* PhD. dissertation, Philadelphia.

— 1996: "The Khotanese documents from the Khotan area." In: *Memoirs of the Research Department of the Toyo Bunko* 54, pp. 27–64.

LURJE, P.B. 2011: *Personal Names in Sogdian texts.* Vienna (Iranisches Personennamenbuch II/8).

LURJE, P.B./I. YAKUBOVICH 2017: "The myth of Sogdian lambdacism." In: *Zur lichten Heimat. Studien zu Manichäismus, Iranistik und Zentralasienkunde im Gedenken an Werner Sundermann.* Wiesbaden (Iranica 25), pp. 319–341.

MacKenzie, D.N. 1976: *The Buddhist Sogdian texts of the British Library*. Tehran/ Liège (Acta Iranica 10).

Mode, M. 1992: "Sogdian gods in exile – some iconographic evidence from Khotan in the light of recently excavated material from Sogdiana." In: *Silk Road Art and Archaeology* 2, pp. 179–214.

Pulleyblank, E.G. 1991: *Lexicon of reconstructed pronunciation in Early Middle Chinese, Late Middle Chinese, and Early Mandarin*. Vancouver.

Rong X. 2006: "Sogdians around the Ancient Tarim Basin." In: M. Compareti *et al.* (eds.): *Ērān ud Anērān. Studies presented to Boris Il'ič Maršak on the occasion of his 70th Birthday*. Venice, pp. 513–524.

— 2009: "Further Remarks on Sogdians in the Western Regions." In: W. Sundermann *et al.* (eds.): *Exegisti monumenta. Festschrift in Honour of Nicholas Sims-Williams*. Wiesbaden (Iranica 17), pp. 399–416.

— 2013: "Buddhist images or Zoroastrian deities? The mixture of religions on the Silk Road as seen in Khotan." In: S.R. Toxtasev/P.B. Lur'e (eds.): *Commentationes Iranicae. Sbornik statej k 90-letiju Vladimira Aronoviča Livšica*. St Petersburg, pp. 423–434.

Sims-Williams, N. 1976: "The Sogdian fragments of the British Library." In: *Indo-Iranian Journal* 18, pp. 43–82.

— 2010: *Bactrian Personal Names*. Vienna (Iranisches Personennamenbuch II/7).

— 2011: "Remarks on the phonology of the Manichaean Bactrian fragment." In: *Leksika, Ètimologija, Jazykovye Kontakty. K jubileju doktora filologičeskix nauk, professora Džoj Iosifovny Èdel'man. Moscow*, pp. 244–251.

— 2012: *Bactrian documents from Northern Afghanistan*. I: *Legal and economic documents*. Revised edition, London.

— 2014: *Biblical and other Christian Sogdian texts from the Turfan Collection*. Turnhout (Berliner Turfantexte 32).

— 2016: "From Aramaic to Manchu: Prehistory, life and after-life of the Sogdian script." In: Rong Xinjiang/Luo Feng (eds.): *Sute ren zai zhongguo : kaogu faxian yu chutu wenxian de xin yinzheng* 粟特人在中国: 考古发现与出土文献的新印证 [Sogdians in China: New evidence in archaeological finds and excavated texts]. Beijing, pp. 414–421.

Sims-Williams, N./J. Hamilton 1990: *Documents turco-sogdiens du IXe–Xe siècle de Touen-houang*. London (Corpus Inscriptionum Iranicarum, Part II, Vol. III/3).

— 2015: *Turco-Sogdian Documents from 9th–10th century Dunhuang*. London (Corpus Inscriptionum Iranicarum, Part II, Vol. III/3).

Skjærvø, P.O. 2002: *Khotanese manuscripts from Chinese Turkestan in the British Library*. London.

Yoshida, Y. 1997: [Review of R.E. Emmerick/M.I. Vorob'ëva-Desjatovskaja 1995]. In: *Bulletin of the School of Oriental and African Studies* 60/3, pp. 567–569.

— 2005: *Notes on the Khotanese documents of the 8th–9th centuries unearthed from Khotan*. Kobe [in Japanese].

— 2010: "On some recently discovered Sogdian materials – Edition of a draft letter written by an inexperienced scribe: a sample from the so far unnoticed Saigonji Tachibana texts." In: *Kyōto Daigaku Bungakubu kenkyū kiyō [Memoirs of the Faculty of Letters, Kyoto University]* 49, pp. 1–24 [in Japanese].

— 2017: "Kotan no yudaya-sogudo shonin? [Judaeo-Sogdian traders in Khotan?]" In: Y. DOHI/Y. KEGASAWA (eds.): *Tonko-Torufan monjo no sekai to sono jidai* [Documents from Dunhuang and Turfan: Their World and Time]. Tokyo, pp. 263–285.
— 2019: "Some new interpretations of the two Judeo-Persian letters from Khotan." In: A. HINTZE *et al.* (eds.): *A Thousand Judgements. Festschrift for Maria Macuch.* Wiesbaden, pp. 385–394.
ZHANG, Z. 2018: "Sogdians in Khotan." In: *The Silk Road* 16, pp. 30–43.

Training of Scribes along the Silk Road: A Case from Manichaean Sogdian[1]

YUTAKA YOSHIDA, Kyoto

0 Introduction: Khotanese Syllabaries Discovered in Dunhuang

In the preface to her edition of the Khotanese version of the *Aparimitāyuḥ sūtra* discovered in Dunhuang, DUAN QING shows that among the 20 folios in all, folios 7 and 8 are distinct from the others not only in their smaller size but also in their ductus (DUAN 1992, pp. 5f.).[2] Historical consideration of the relationship between the kingdom of Khotan and the local Dunhuang government enables one to date the manuscript to the 10th century (SKJÆRVØ 2002, pp. lxvi–lxix). DUAN QING argues that the two were copied in Dunhuang to replace two older and possibly damaged folios which had been prepared in Khotan. In other words, in those days, there existed Khotanese scribes in Dunhuang, who could copy these Buddhist manuscripts. This is far from astonishing, and one discovers several pieces of evidence to show that the training of scribes was conducted in Dunhuang. The most evident are numerous Chinese Buddhist texts reused for copying the syllabaries of the Khotanese Brahmi script on their backside.[3] In one case, in SKJÆRVØ's opinion, a teacher's model handwriting is also found in the same manuscript (SKJÆRVØ 2002, pp. 530–533: IOL Khot. S25). Sometimes one encounters an interesting sentence: *sāja thyau netcūka khu dāla na byehä: ca* "Learn quickly and thoroughly so that you may not receive the stick!" (SKJÆRVØ 2002, p. 533, line 108). Obviously a naughty or lazy novice got the whiplash. One may wonder what kind of teaching tools or textbooks were employed when the pupils were copying syllabaries. In this regard, we are lucky that one such teacher's copy of the syllabary has survived and been discovered in the Russian collection (EMMERICK/VOROV'ËVA-DESJATOVSKAJA 1993, plates 129–135; *idem* 1995, pp. 165–170: SI O 20). Although the editors of the text argued that this is also a

1 This article is a revised version of my paper read on the 2nd November 2019 at Beijing Forum 2019.

2 See also HOERNLE 1916, plate XV.

3 For the lists of manuscripts containing syllabaries see DRESDEN 1977, p. 82 and SKJÆRVØ 2002, p. 609 s.v. "syllabaries", in which reference to IOL Khot S. 1 and 15 should also be included.

pupil's writing practice (*ibid.* pp. 169–170), it differs from all the others in that it is not copied on the backside of a Chinese text but on nicely ruled poṭhi folios, and also in that characters are written with meticulous care. A phrase similar to the above-cited warning is also found in it: *sāja vaṭhāyā khu ma dạla na byeha*ʾ "Learn, pupil, so that you do not get my stick!" (EMMERICK/VOROV'ËVA-DESJATOVSKAJA 1995, p. 165, folio 1 verso line 5; translation, *ibid.* p. 169). Perhaps some pupils copied this warning as well, while others recognized that it was just a warning and was not meant for writing exercise.

1 Sogdian and Manichaean Alphabets

The Sogdian counterpart of the Khotanese syllabary would be an alphabet in Sogdian script. In fact, two Sogdian alphabets have been unearthed from Panjikant. The most well-preserved exemplar once studied by LIVSHITS contains 22 letters of the Aramaic alphabet plus extra *δ* (*lamed*)[4] (LIVSHITS 2015, pp. 227–232).[5] What comes after the last letter is hard to read but this part seems to end with words *šyr δpyryʾkh* "good writing" as so read by LIVSHITS. Thus, this alphabet does seem to have served as either a teaching or learning tool for Sogdian scribes. Among the Panjikant mural paintings one representation of a scribe has been discovered, who is depicted as holding a wood stick and a pen (Fig. 1).[6]

Fig. 1.

In the Mug documents of the early eighth century Panjikant kingdom, a word *δpʾyrpt* "chief scribe" is attested twice (B-1, col. 2, line 14 and B-17, 2, cf. LIVSHITS 2015, pp. 159f.), but in both cases the contexts do not enable us to understand the specific function of *δpʾyrpt* in the society. The word *δpʾyrpt* also appears in a contract of 639 CE unearthed in Turfan; there he authorizes the contract and his son is mentioned as drawing up the contract (YOSHIDA 2003,

4 This alphabet copied on an ostracon was first published by LIVSHITZ (1970). On the phonetic value of the extra letter *δ* see SIMS-WILLIAMS 1981, pp. 349f. In SIMS-WILLIAMS's opinion, it represents [l] and in this respect the Sogdian scribe followed the Uighur alphabet. Nevertheless, it is not known whether the Uighur alphabet ever existed already in the early eighth century, when the Sogdian ostracon was produced.

5 For the other alphabet see LIVSHITS 2015, p. 232, n. 37.

6 For the drawing of the painting see MARŠAK/RASPOPOVA 1987, p. 195 with drawings reproduced in plates VII–VIII.

pp. 159ff.). This fact suggests that scribe-ship is a family tradition that had been handed down from a father to his son. On the other hand, according to the *Xifanji* 西蕃記 "Records of western barbarians" of the early seventh century, in Sogdiana people began to teach boys when they became five years old so that they might be able to trade in foreign countries (CHAVANNES 1903, p. 133, n. 5). Thus, not only professional scribes but also ordinary traders could read and write Sogdian, which is betrayed by a number of commercial letters written in Sogdian.[7]

I once discovered a Sogdian alphabet among the Turfan manuscripts belonging to the Otani collection (Otani 2502). This alphabet differs from the Panjikant counterpart in the arrangement of 22 letters as well as in putting extra letters *p*, *δ*, and *t* at the end, of which the function is not clear to me. Whereas the cursive style of the letters is likely to go back to the 8th century, we cannot place this alphabet in the socio-cultural context of the Sogdian speaking people in the Turfan oasis. Since LIVSHITS totally misunderstands my explanation in Japanese of its somewhat complicated structure (YOSHIDA 1995, pp. 75–79; LIVSHITS 2015, p. 231), in what follows I reproduce the manuscript (Fig. 2) and give my transliteration of letters arranged in the way they are placed in the manuscript and provide each with a superscript number indicating the order in the alphabet, e.g. ^{17}p, which indicates that the letter *p* (*pe*) is the 17th in the Sogdian alphabet.

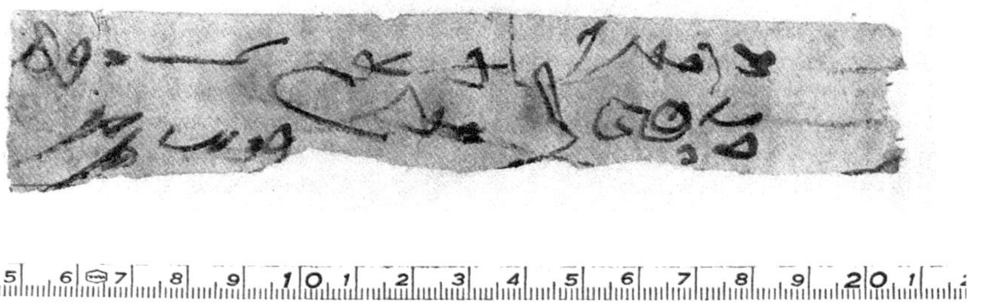

Fig. 2. Otani 2502[a]

^{1}(ʾ)	^{4}d	^{7}z	^{8}x	^{11}k	^{13}m		^{16}ʿ		^{18}c	^{20}r	pδt
^{2}(β)	^{5}h	^{9}ṭ		^{12}δ	^{14}n	^{15}s				^{21}š	
^{3}(γ)	^{6}w	^{10}y						^{17}p	^{19}q	^{22}t	

[a] A small stroke between the letters ^{4}d (*daleth*) and ^{7}z (*zain*) is just a slip of the pen.

7 One of the Ancient Letters of the early 4th century was dispatched by a woman to her husband, who had deserted his family in a Sogdian diaspora situated in Dunhuang (SIMS-WILLIAMS 2004, pp. 248f.); the letter is concluded with a postscript added by their daughter. This fact may indicate that Sogdian traders' female family were also literate, although the possibility must also be envisaged that the letter and its post script were drawn up by a public letter-writer.

It is to be noted that forms of the four letters not employed in writing Sogdian, *d* (*daleth*), *ṭ* (*teth*), ʿ (*ain*), and *q* (*koph*) are all basically identical with those found in the alphabet of Panjikant studied by LIVSHITS.[8]

As for the Manichaean script, two sets of the Manichaean alphabet have so far been discovered among the German Turfan collection: M409b, M 1571a (SUNDERMANN 1985, p. 95). Yet another very small fragment (Fig. 3; 4.0 cm x 6.5 cm) is found in the Russian Turfan collection: Dx. 8102.[9] It is written on the backside of a Chinese Buddhist text of the *Dazhidulun* 大智度論 (TT vol. 25, 65a16–17). What has remained on the fragment is only *](l)mn(s)[*, but in view of the sequence of these four letters there is practically no doubt about its being a part of the Manichaean alphabet.

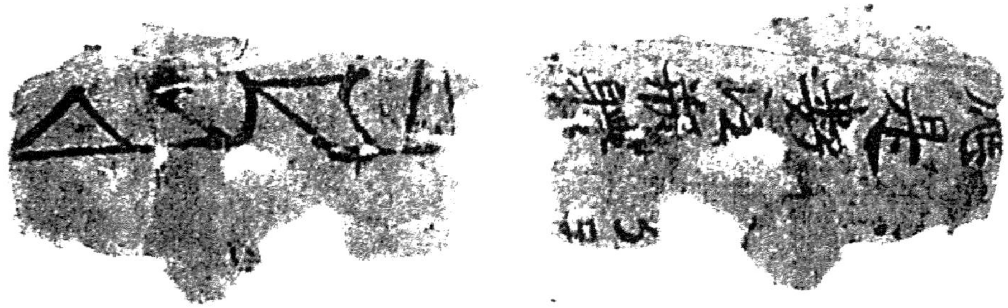

Fig. 3. Dx. 8102

Since Manichaean script was employed only by Manichaeans, it is clear that these alphabets served as teaching or learning tools for Manichaean scribes. Unlike the Brahmi script comprising so many characters and ligatures, the Manichaean and Sogdian scripts must have been easy to learn, because they ultimately go back to the Aramaic alphabet consisting of only 22 simple-formed letters. That seems to be the reason why we do not find scribal exercises of writing independent Sogdian or Manichaean characters.

8 However, their shapes do not represent what one would expect as the natural development of these letters. The two letters, *d* (*daleth*) and ʿ (*ain*), are known to be used in ideograms *ʿD, ʿL, ʿM,* and *ʿNYW* (SIMS-WILLIAMS 1981, pp. 348f.) and differ very much from those found in the alphabets. Incidentally, so far unnoticed attestation of *ʿNYW* is encountered in a document unearthed from Khara Khoja, Turfan (M96, p. 66, line 4): *[ ](x)wt'w KZNH ʿNY[W ...]* "The king ordered thus ..." (LI *et al.* 2012, p. 65).

9 It is reproduced in the *Dunhuang manuscripts collected in the St. Petersburg Institute of Oriental Studies of the Academy of Sciences of Russia* (俄藏敦煌文獻), vol. 14, Shanghai 2000, p. 23.

2 Copying Exercise of a Letter (Epistle) by a Manichaean Novice Scribe?

In the course of my studies of the three Manichaean letters discovered in Bäzäklik (*Three Manichaean Sogdian letters unearthed in Bäzäklik, Turfan,* Kyoto 2019), I surveyed letter fragments among the German, Otani and St. Petersburg collections exhaustively. In so doing I encountered a very unique case in which one letter seems to be copied twice or thrice. It is also interesting to note that a word *δpʾyrstn* "school", which has not hitherto been attested in Sogdian, occurs in this text. A group of four non-joining fragments Ch/So 14742, Otani 7281, Otani 10001, and ST 15[10] are written on the verso of a halved Chinese Buddhist scroll. The Chinese text[11] enables one to reconstruct their original order and the approximate size of gaps between them: (i) ST 15 (4 lines), <1-2 lines missing>, (ii) Otani 10001 (6 lines), <ca 6 lines missing>, (iii) Otani 7281 (3 lines), <1-2 lines missing>, (iv) Ch/So 14742 (25 lines). Although the text of Ch/So 14742 does not end with line 25, a space of a few lines is left blank after it. Obviously, the scribe stopped copying without completing the text. The text has been edited twice, first by me in 2010 and later by A. Benkato in 2018, who slightly modified my text (Yoshida 2010, pp. 7–24; Benkato 2018, pp. 16ff.).

From what has remained one can see that the letter is addressed to the writer's father: Otani 10001 /2/ *[ ]w xw nmʾc βrʾym*[12] /3/ *[ ](.) šw*[13] *(ʾ)xšnkw ʾptry* /4/ *[pr](y)ʾn pryt[m]* "I bring homage [...] you, the excellent father, [...] the most beloved [...]". *ʾptry* "father" is also encountered in line 15 of Ch/So 14742. The most interesting feature of this text is that a small fragment Ch/U 6886 shows a parallel text of lines 5–16 of Ch/So 14742. Let us see the two texts. For convenience' sake I only give first 16 lines of Ch/So 14742, which has counterpart in Ch/U 6886.[14]

10 ST stands for S[aigonji] T[achibana]; Mr. Zuicho Tachibana was a member of the Otani Expedition and kept a small number of manuscript remains at his temple called Saigonji. On the other fragments belonging to this collection see Yoshida 2010, pp. 7ff.

11 It is a part of the *Dabanniepanjing* 大般涅槃経 corresponding to TT. vol. 12, 431a8-b25.

12 *βrʾym* is the 1 pl. present indicative form, but here it is likely to be an error for the 1 sg. form *βrʾm*.

13 On this article/demonstrative of *iste*-deixis or *du*-deixis see Sims-Williams (1994), Yoshida (2009, pp. 291ff.), and *idem* (2019b, p. 270). Benkato mistakes it for the enclitic pronoun (2018, pp. 16, 100a).

14 For the remaining incomprehensible part (lines 16–25) I now correct two readings: *ʾʾnʾʾprs-ʾkyʾ* (lines 22–23) > *ʾnzʾnprs-ʾkyʾ* 'acknowledgement' (thus corrected in DMSB, 15a) and *mʾxxyδδwkcyk* (line 24) > *mʾx γyδδwkcyk* 'we (creatures) of the material world' (cf. Yoshida 2019a, p. 120).

Text

Ch/So 14742	Ch/U 6886[15]
1/ [ ]cnn	
2/ [ ](.) mrts’r	
3/ [ ](.) ZY ptm’k	
4/ s’r pwrny δ’rt’ ZY kδ’ry	
5/ ZKn βγy xwy-šty nβ’nt	[1][ ](x)wyšty nβ’nt
6/ pr ywk ZY pr ’βs’k	[2]pr ywkh ZY pr ’βs’kw
7/ wγtw δ’rt’ rty kδ’ry ZKn	wγtw δ’rt’ [3]rtkδry ZKn
8/ δp’yrstn šyr’kw ZY βγ	δp’y-rstny šyr’kk ZY βγ
9/ wrcy’ ’skwym xwyšty	[4]w’rcy’ ’skw’m xwy-šty
10/ pr mn’ nry ZY ywk m’n	pr mn’ [5]nry ZY ywkh m’n
11/ z’wr r’y’m skwn kštrw	z’wr zy’mtskwn [6]kštry
12/ βnty wnw (z)’wr ’sty myδ ZY	βnty cw t’w z’wr ’sty myδ
13/ ’xšp’ ’ntwxs’ skwn	[7]’xšph ’ntwxs’mskwn
14/ w’nw ZY ’sptrw-rw	w’nw ZY xwptrw
15/ β’w ZKn ’xšnkw ’ptry pr	[8]β’w ’xšnky ’ptry pr
16/ krm’yr ryt’ky’ …	krm’yr ryt’kyh

Translation

"[...] from [...] hither [... Since] you consider (*lit.* hold) [me] as full in respect to measure (i.e. as attained maturity), now you have sent me to the lord (and) teacher for teaching and training. Now I am staying in the school well and at peace, Sir. The teacher spends the energy (*lit.* power) of (his) mind[16] for my skill(?) and teaching. Whatever strength and power there is with (me, your) most humble servant, I am striving day and night so that I might become better. To the excellent father with honour [...]".[17]

When one compares the two texts, one soon notices that Ch/U 6886 is written more carefully. More important is the fact that while Ch/U 6886 is perfectly comprehensible, the corresponding text of Ch/So 14742 does not always make sense as it stands. Obviously, several words are miscopied. *kδ’ry* (line 7) "belly" is a simple error for *kδry* "now". *r’y’m skwn* (line 11) "I am weeping", which corresponds to *zy’mtskwn* "he is spending", makes no sense in the context.[18]

15 The superscript number preceding each word indicates the beginning of the corresponding line.

16 For my *m’n* BENKATO reads *mn’* 'my', which also suits the context.

17 BENKATO's translation differs considerably from mine. I cite the part corresponding to lines 1-16: "[...] from [...] hither [...] and to measure you have full (one). Now together with (you), Lord Master you said in teaching and instruction. Now about the scriptorium (it is?) well and, Sir, I am at peace. Master, in my skill and teaching I am spending my strength, I (your) humble servant. [What] strength (I have), I am striving day and night so that I become more perfect. About? the excellent father I venture (to write) in honour ...".

18 BENKATO reads it as *z’y’m skwn* and takes it for an error for *zy’mt skwn* or *zy’m’m skwn*. Judging from the initial letters of *z’wr* of line 11 and *ryt’ky’* of line 16, his reading seems

cw t'w z'wr 'sty "if there is strength (and) power" of Ch/U 6886 is paralleled by *wnw*[19] *(z)'wr 'sty*, whose *wnw* is likely to be an unsuccessful attempt to copy *cw t'w*. What I read *(z)'wr* is also ill-formed and the scribe may not have understood what he was copying. *'ntwxs'* (line 13) would be 2nd sg. subjunctive/imperative of *'ntwxs* "to strive", which can hardly be construed with the durative particle. Finally, an enigmatic *'sptrw-rw* (line 14) corresponds to *xwptrw* "better, more skilled". Considering his clumsy and awkward brushstrokes, I assume that the scribe of Ch/So 14742 was a novice who was not skillful enough to reproduce his teacher's exemplar in a comprehensible way.

One may also get a vague idea as to how the texts copied by a novice scribe look like, when one sees two practices of one passage from the *Manichaean Psalm* found in Pelliot sogdien 25 (Durkin-Meisterernst/Morano 2010, pp. 106f.). For example, in one case *''βrn* is written for a correct *''βryn'm* "I bless". Sometimes interlinear writing practices are also encountered, e.g. Helsinki C + Ch/U 6456 + L29,[20] and Ch/U 6434 (unpublished).[21]

In understanding the text, *ptm'k* (line 3) could serve as a keyword because its original meaning "measure" does not seem to make good sense in the context: *ptm'k s'r pwrny δ'rt'* "you (pl.) hold full toward the measure". In the context of a letter addressed to one's father, the 2 pl. form *δ'rt'* seems to be an honorific expression referring to the singular addressee (Yoshida 2006, pp. 88f.). The Middle Persian counterpart of Sogdian word *ptm'k* is *paymān* and it has a special meaning "full measure, maturity" in the combination *ō paymān āmadan* "to reach maturity" (MacKenzie 1971, p. 67). On this meaning of *ptm'k* see also the following sentence found in So 18140 I verso 6–7: ... *tnp'r δ'r'nt rty kw ptm'kh prys'nt k'm* "they have a body, and they will arrive at maturity" (Yoshida 2010, p. 18). Thus, in the writer's mind, his father considers him as *pwrny* "full" as regards maturity, and has sent him to a teacher for training in the school.[22] Accordingly, I venture to suppose that Ch/U 6886 was prepared by this particular teacher for training the pupil.

In this connection, I should like to draw attention to Ch/U 7058[23], which also seems to preserve a parallel sentence corresponding to Otani 7281, lines 2-3 and Ch/So 14742, lines 1–7 with a few variant readings. It is written on the backside of a Chinese Buddhist text (*Miaofalianhuajiang* 妙法蓮華経), of which the remaining part corresponds to TT, vol. 9, 55b1-9. This text was once

to be simply impossible. In any case one must emend it in one way or the other.

19 Benkato reads it as *t'w* and presumes that the preceding *cw* has been omitted.

20 Joining of the three fragments was discovered by me (cf. Reck 2006, p. 270, n. 2). For the edition of the joined text see Morano 2009.

21 See Sundermann's comments on this text: "Segenssprüche, eventuell als Briefformular, mit schülerhaften Nachschriften" (Reck 2006, pp. 268f. with n. 2).

22 Compare a similar case where a father urges his son to make exercise in writing encountered in a Manichaean community of Kellis, Egypt (Leurini 2017, p. 25).

23 See also Reck 2006, p. 284, for the general information and description of this fragment.

published by BENKATO (2018, p. 49), but his reading differs so much from the text read and restored by me that it is worth publishing my own text in this place.[24] Admittingly, the manuscript written in cursive script is badly damaged and in some places several other readings are possible.

Text

Ch/U 7058	Otani 7281
1 [kšt](r)y RYPW-myk[prm'n-]	2 [](k)štry prm'nptγw(š)[y]
2 [pt](γ)wšy βnty[rty βγ?]	3 [βnty rt](y) βγ[ ]
3 kδry pr mn' (β)[nty]	Ch/So 14742
4 w'nw βrtpδ p(r)['m'y 'krty?]	1 [ ]cnn
5 kt cnn r[ync'k t'yw'k 'skwny][25]	2 [ ](.) mrts'r
6 mrts'r p'rδ'r(t)[' ZY kw ptm'k]	3 [ ](.) ZY ptm'k
7 s'r pwrny[26] pr'(γ)[ty δ'rt' ZY]	4 s'r pwrny δ'rt' ZY kδ'ry
8 kδry ZKn βγ[y xwyšty nβ'nt]	5 ZKn βγy xwy-štr nβ'nt
9 pr ywk ZY p(r)['βs'kw wγtw]	6 pr ywk ZY pr ' βs'k
10 (δ)['rt']rty k[δry ZKn ?]	7 wγtw δ'rt' rty kδ'ry ZKn

Translation

> "… humble and 10,000th servant (and) slave. And, sir, now, to me (who am your) slave …, you de[igned to] inform (me) that since the [small childhood] thus far you brought (me) up, [and] you [consider that] (I have) fully reached [maturity]. Now you have sent me to the teacher for teaching and training. And now …"

In view of a few variant readings, even if my restoration is correct, it is not likely that Ch/U 7058 was copied directly from Ch/U 6886. But it is also unlikely that the two are totally independent from each other. Therefore, for the present I have no idea how to explain this situation. Possibly, all the three texts (a. Ch/So 14742, b. Ch/U 6886, and c. Ch/U 7058) may have gone back to one prototype, which was a teacher's copy for novice scribes to write to their fathers.

24 BENKATO's text and translation read as follows: /1/ *[..]'y RYPW-m(yk)[prm'n?]* /2/ *[pt](γ)wšy βnty [* /3/ *(kδ)ry pr mn' β[* /4/ *w'nw βrtpδ p(.)[* /5/ *kt cnn r(.)[* /6/ *mrts'r p'rδ(..)[* /7/ *s'r pk'ry p(k'ry)[* /8/ *kδry ZKn β(..)[* /9/ *pr ywk ZY p(r)['βs'k* /10/ *[ ] rty (β)[γ* "(1) … thousand-fold … (2) obedient(?) servant … (3) now to my … (4) thus informed … that from … (5) that from … (6) hither, guard … (7) to, individually … (8) now of the … (9) in teaching … (10) … And sir …".

25 Or just *r[ync'k 'skwny]*? For *ryncq skwn* 'childhood (Manichaean script)' see DMSB 176a s.v. *skwn*.

26 I admit that my reading of *pwrny* is not very satisfactory, whereas BENKATO's *pk'ry*, in particular the second letter *k*, also meets some difficulty, since it looks more like *r*.

3 Epistolary Formulae, Writing Practices, and Teacher's Copy

As a matter of fact, numerous scribal practices of the Sogdian epistolary formulae are found among the Turfan Manichaean Sogdian manuscripts. They are now collected by BENKATO in his book published in 2018. Apart from these Manichaean manuscripts, one ostracon unearthed from Old Merv and another from Penjikent also contain a short epistolary formula (BENKATO 2018, p. 73, n. 62). Drawing up letters must have been one of the most important functions of professional scribes and the training of novice scribes to copy epistolary formulae is most expected in the school education. One also finds practices of writing letters among the Dunhuang Khotanese manuscripts containing syllabaries. See for an example SKJÆRVØ (2002, pp. 527–528).

Among the texts collected by BENKATO, Ch/So 14730 (*ibid*., pp. 39f.) is most intriguing in that its clumsy and awkward handwriting certainly indicates that the manuscript was copied by a novice.[27] The text comprises two parts; the supposed addressee of the first part is one's mother (*m'th*) and that of the second is a king (*xwt'w*). The text is written on the verso of a halved Chinese scroll and on the Chinese side one finds the following sentence: *xwy-šty xypδ'w'nt xcy 'yšwy'n* "The teacher, (who is) master, is (named) Yišōyān"[28] written in a more careful handwriting different from that of the verso. This sentence seems to indicate that the novice's teacher was called Yišōyān. In a small fragment of another scribal practice of the epistolary formula, Ch/So 20102, one finds a correction by a scribe himself or by his teacher, who crossed the initial *p* of *pr'yštyty* and added *β* in its place (BENKATO 2018, p. 40).

Similar in its structure to Ch/So 14730 is a large manuscript Ch/So 10920 + Ch/So 19535, which is consisting of four parts, the fourth being broken in the middle. The first part again concerns one's mother who is also called *xwt'ynh* "queen", the second *'xšywn'k* "king, emperor, qaghan", and the third a religious leader(?).[29] Obviously, this text is a collection of several formulae addressed to various supposed recipients headed by a queen.

As far as the texts collected by BENKATO are concerned they are all written on the verso of in most cases halved Buddhist Chinese scrolls, in other words, copied on recycled paper. This situation may perhaps suggest that recycled paper was employed as a writing material for the scribal exercise of epistolary formulae. However, there is one exception, a small fragment So 18154 not edited by BENKATO, which again comprises a few epistolary formulae as those found in Ch/So 10920 +

27 Cf. BENKATO's remark: "Judging by the repetition of some words and phrases, the messy script, and the several insertions and cross-outs, the text was likely a kind of draft or scribal exercise." It is also to be noted that like Ch/So 14742 the manuscript ends with a large blank space, although the text itself does not come to the end.

28 BENKATO's *'yswy'n* is a misprint. His translation slightly differs from mine: "The master of teachers is Išō-yan[sic]".

29 For the edition see BENKATO 2018, pp. 37–38 and YOSHIDA 2019, pp. 56f.

Ch/So 19535, but is a fragment from a folio, which must have once constituted a booklet. Moreover, one also finds a rubric: *mwn'kw 'pcm(')[k]* "This (is for) a noble [recipient](?)" (YOSHIDA 2019, pp. 57–58). In view of the morphology of the manuscript and its semi-formal handwriting characteristic of Manichaean formal scriptures, it is fitting to regard So 18154 as a kind of textbook or teacher's copy, from which novice scribes copied epistolary formulae for practice.

Some Manichaean Sogdian letters are also written in Manichaean script and were published by BENKATO (2016). Among them, M7391 + M7392 and M7440 are scribal exercises of an opening phrase addressed to a recipient who is a religious leader. Thus, one may wonder if a similar teacher's copy written in Manichaean script also existed. As far as I can see from the published and unpublished fragments of the German Turfan collection, no such text has been discovered. But one folio fragment M1846 attests a text very much similar to an epistolary formula, and I wonder if this might also be a folio from a teacher's manual for training scribes to write letters in Manichaean script (YOSHIDA 2019, pp. 57, 174).[30]

Finally, it is also worth noting that Helsinki C + Ch/U 6456 + L29 mentioned above begins with a practice of the opening phrase of a letter but is followed by an attempt to copy a parable about a parrot, while another scribe(?) tried to copy several lines of the text between lines. Therefore, not only epistolary formulae but also parables seem to have been copied by way of scribal practice. In fact another copy of the same narrative about a parrot is encountered in L111, of which the other side contains a scribal exercise of an epistolary formula.

4 Miscellaneous Problems

Some of the above-mentioned manuscripts bear an old signature beginning with T representing Toyoq, in particular Ch/So 14742 (= T II T 1585), Ch/U 6886 (= T II T 1585), Ch/So 14730 (= T II Toyoq), M 7391 + M7392 (= T II T 15), and M7440 (= T II T 31), and were discovered in one of the Toyoq caves. Possibly the school (*δp'yrstn*) mentioned in Ch/So 14742 was situated there.[31] This institution must have been located within the church complex. According to the Chinese Manichaean text called *Compendium of the Doctrines and Styles of the Teaching of Mani, the Buddha of Light*, a Manichaean monastery comprises five buildings: (i) Jingtutang 経図堂 "hall of holy books and pictures", (ii) Zhaijiangtang 齋講堂

30 M1846 is announced to be published by MORANO and SIMS-WILLIAMS. I have come to know about their planned publication through the draft of the second edition of DMSB being revised by SIMS-WILLIAMS, who was kind enough to share it with me.

31 Basing on the analysis of all the Iranian fragments which are written in Manichaean script and were discovered in Toyoq, HU XIAODAN has come to the same conclusion (HU 2019, pp. 85–89). She supports her claim by referring to MIK III 34b (T II T 20), in which the Turkic Runic characters are transcribed in Manichaean script. It could have served as a tool for learning the phonetic values of the Runic characters.

"hall of fasting and explication", (iii) Lichantang 礼懺堂 "hall of adoration and confession", (iv) Jiaoshoutang 教授堂 "hall of instruction", (v) Bingsengtang 病僧堂 "hall for sick elects" (GULÁCSI 2016, p. 116). Scribes were most likely to have been trained in the Jiaoshuotang, or the hall of instruction.

We still do not know anything about the details of the scribal training and practices. The so-called word lists could have served as textbooks, and the exemplars which have been handed down to us may have been copied by novice scribes. In this regard, one may mention scribes' colophons or rather scribbles. One interesting case is a scribble entered on the Chinese side, i.e. the backside of the Sogdian text, which reads as follows: *ʾyny βγʾnykw kwy-šn pwsty wz-rkcwr ywγtym šyr xwpw δpʾyr wβʾm oo wʾxš δβryny wnxʾncwr* "I, Wuzurgčor, learned this book of 'Divine Sermon'. May I be a very good scribe! Word-giver (possibly dictator?) Wanxānčor" (Ch/So 13399a + 13401, cf. BENKATO 2017, pp. 108–109, where *wz-rkcwr* is read *(t)z-ʾkcwr*). A similar wish to become a good scribe is also found in a Christian Sogdian manuscript E45: *[pr] byγ (nʾ)m ywxn(w)n* šyr( )*dpyr b(ʾ)[n]* "[In] the name of God, [may I,] John, be a good scribe!" (SIMS-WILLIAMS 2012, p. 191). Indeed, to be a good scribe, one is expected to learn (*ywxs-/ywγt-*) much. When they learned texts, scribes sometimes wrote such scribbles/colophons saying: *ʾyny pwstk ʾzw ... ywγtym ky Lʾ pyrʾt ... sʾr psδʾ* "This text, I by the name of so-and-so learned. He who would not believe it, ask so-and-so" (YOSHIDA 2000, pp. 83–85; BENKATO 2017, pp. 102–111). It may not be a coincidence that these scribbles/colophons often accompany parable texts, since narratives were sometimes copied by novice scribes.

5 Concluding Remark

Young scribes must have been well aware that they were not skilled enough, and one actually finds such a phrase as *ayduq yangï bitkäči* "unskillful (and) young scribe" in a Manichaean Uighur manuscript (YOSHIDA 1993, pp. 132–133). Although the Sogdian counterpart has not so far been attested, the Middle Persian equivalent is found in M98: *mn yyšwʿprzy[nd] dby(r) ʿy nwg ʾwd ʾq(r)wg* "I, Yišōfrazend, young and unexperienced scribe" (YOSHIDA, *ibid.*). Since in those days bilingualism of Sogdian and Uighur prevailed among the Turfan Manichaeans, what has been known to Uighurists about Manichaean Uighur scribes is to be compared with what I have discussed in connection with Sogdian scribes, which is unfortunately far beyond my competence. In this respect, the Sogdian and Uighur alphabets are also to be compared in the hope that one may be able to trace the course or developments in which the Sogdian script was applied to the Uighur language most probably by those bilingual scribes.[32]

32 On the development of the Uighur script from the Sogdian see SIMS-WILLIAMS (1981), who sees "the Uyghur script as a natural development of the Sogdian, the unpremeditated outcome of the attempt to write Turkish by people familiar with the Sogdian alphabet"

Bibliography

BENKATO, A. 2016: "Sogdian letter fragments in Manichean script". In: *Studia Iranica* 45, pp. 197–220.

— 2017: *Āzandnāmē*. Wiesbaden.

— 2018: *Studies on the Sogdian epistolary tradition*. Turnhout (Berliner Turfantexte 41).

CHVANNES, E. 1903: *Documents sur les Tou-kiue occidentaux*. St. Petersburg.

DRESDEN, M.J. 1977: "Khotanese (Saka) manuscripts. A provisional handlist". In: *Varia 1976*. Leiden/Téhéran/Liège (Acta Iranica 16), pp. 27–85.

DSMB = N. SIMS-WILLIAMS/D. DURKIN-MEISTERERNST 2012: *Dictionary of Manichaean Sogdian and Bactrian*. Turnhout.

DUAN Q. 1992: *Das khotanische Aparimitāyuḥ sūtra*. Stuttgart.

DURKIN-MEISTERERNST, D. *et al.* (eds.) 2009: *Literarische Stoffe und ihre Gestaltung in mitteliranischer Zeit. Kolloquium anlässlich des 70. Geburtstags von Prof. Dr. W. Sundermann*. Wiesbaden (Beiträge zur Iranistik 31).

DURKIN-MEISTERERNST D./E. MORANO 2010: *Mani's Psalms. Middle Persian, Parthian and Sogdian texts in the Turfan Collection*. Turnhout (Berliner Turfantexte XXVII).

EMMERICK, R.E./M. VOROV'ËVA-DESJATOVSKAJA 1993: *Saka documents VII: The St. Petersburg collection*. London.

— 1995: *Saka documents. Text volume III: The St. Petersburg collections*. London.

GULÁCSI, Zs. 2015: *Mani's pictures*. Leiden/Boston.

HOERNLE, A.F.R. 1916: *Manuscripts remains of Buddhist literature found in Eastern Turkestan*. Oxford [reprint 1970].

HU XIAODAN 2019 "Interpretation of the Persian remnants of the ancient Mani in the Tuyugou of Turpan and discussion on the religious life of the Manichaeans (in Chinese)" [It is the English rendering of the Chinese original provided in the journal; it may rather be translated as 'Edition of Middle Persian fragments newly discovered in Toyoq, Turfan—with special discussion of the religious life of the Manichaean community in Toyoq as reflected in the Manichaean texts discovered there'], *The Western Regions Studies*, 2019/4, 83–89.

LEURINI, C. 2017: *Hymns in honour of the hierarchy and community, installation hymns and hymns in honour of church leaders and patrons. Middle Persian and Parthian hymns in the Berlin collection*. Turnhout (Berliner Turfantexte XL).

(SIMS-WILLIAMS 1981, p. 359). He also asserts that "the Uyghur script arose almost casually, from day-to-day contact between Turks and Sogdians, and not from the deliberations of a committee such as that which adapted the Roman script for the writing of Republican Turks" (SIMS-WILLIAMS, *ibid.*). Nevertheless, when one compares the Sogdian and Uighur alphabets, one sees two very great differences. One is that the four disused letters (*daleth, teth, ain, and koph*) and *h* (*he*) in Sogdian are no longer represented in the Uighur alphabet. The other is that four extra letters follow the main part consisting of 17 (= 22-5) letters; they are *l* (or hooked *resh*), *š*, *m*, and *q* (MORIYASU 1997). In the case of the Sogdian alphabet, the extra letters affixed at the end are different among those alphabets so far discovered. In Otani 2502 one finds enigmatic combination of *pδt* at the end, while in the Panjikant ostracon the letter *δ* (*lamed*) was added, of which the function is discussed by SIMS-WILLIAMS (1981, p. 350) and LIVSHITS (2015, pp. 229f.). In the Sogdian alphabet recorded in the Islamic sources one finds yet another three extra letters transcribed *θ*, *x*, and *δ* in Arabic script (YOSHIDA 1995, pp. 77ff.; LIVSHITS, *ibid.*).

LIVSHITZ, V.A. 1970: "A Sogdian alphabet from Panjikant". In: M. BOYCE/I. GERSHEVITCH (eds.): *W. B. Henning memorial volume.* London, pp. 256–263.

— 2015: *Sogdian epigraphy of Central Asia and Semirech'e.* London.

LI XIAOCHEN *et al.* 2012: "A study on ancient paper sheets from Astana—Khara Khoja graves in Turfa (in Chinese)". In: *Xiyuyanjiu* 2012/1, pp. 62–68.

MACKENZIE, D.N. 1971: *A concise Pahlavi dictionary.* Oxford.

MARŠAK B./V. RASPOPOVA 1987: "Une image sogdienne du dieu-patriarche de l'agriculture". In: *Studia Iranica* 16, pp. 193–199 with plates VII–VIII.

MORANO, E. 2009: "Sogdian tales in Manichaean script". In: D. DURKIN-MEISTERERNST *et al.* (eds.): *Literarische Stoffe und ihre Gestaltung in mitteliranischer Zeit. Kolloquium anlässlich des 70. Geburtstags von Prof. Dr. W. Sundermann.* Wiesbaden (Beiträge zur Iranistik 31), pp. 173–200.

MORIYASU, T. 1997: "A New Study of the Uighur Script: A foundation for solving the problem of the designation *Hui-hui*] (in Japanese)". In: *Tōhōgaku ronshū. Eastern Studies Fiftieth Anniversary Volume.* Tokyo, pp. 1238–1226 [reverse pagination; English summary, pp. 96–97].

RECK, CH. 2006: *Mitteliranische Handschriften.* Teil 1: *Berliner Turfanfragmente manichäischen Inhalts in soghdischer Schrift.* Stuttgart (Verzeichnis der Orientalischen Handschriften in Deutschland 18, 1).

SIMS-WILLIAMS, N. 1981: "The Sogdian sound-system and the origins of the Uyghur script". In: *Journal Asiatique* 269, pp. 347–360.

— 1994: "The triple system of deixis in Sogdian". In: *Transactions of the Philological Society* 92/1,pp. 41–53.

— 2004: "191 Sogdian letter no.3". In: S. WHITFIELD (ed.): *The Silk Road: Trade, travel, war and faith.* London, pp. 248–249.

— 2012: *Iranian manuscripts in Syriac script in the Berlin Turfan Collection.* Stuttgart.

SKJÆRVØ, O. with contributions by U. SIMS-WILLIAMS 2002: *Khotanese manuscripts from Chinese Turkestan in the British Library.* London.

SUNDERMANN, W. 1985: "Iran als Vermittler und Verbreiter fremder Schriftsysteme". In: *Das Altertum* 31/2, pp. 92–97.

YOSHIDA, Y. 1993: "Middle Iranian and Old Turkish—Notes on two sets of colophons or scribbles found in Manichaean texts— (in Japanese)". In: *Studies on the Inner Asian languages* 8, pp. 127–133.

— 1995: "Sogdian miscellany (in Japanese)". In: *Studies on the Inner Asian languages* 10, pp. 67–84.

— 2000: "First fruits of Ryūkoku-Berlin joint project on the Turfan Iranian manuscripts". In: *Acta Asiatica* 78, pp. 71–85.

— 2003: "Translation of the contract for the purchase of a slave girl found at Turfan and dated 639." Appendix to V. HANSEN's review article: "New work on the Sogdians, the most important traders on the Silk Road, A.D. 500–1000." In: *T'oung Pao* 89, pp. 159–161.

— 2006: "Honorific and polite expressions in Sogdian (in Japanese)". In: Department of Linguistics, Kyoto University (ed.): *Contribution to the Studies of Eurasian Languages* 10. Kyoto, pp. 81–94.

— 2009: "Sogdian". In: G. WINDFUHR (ed.): *The Iranian languages*, London/New York, pp. 279–335.

— 2010: "On some recently discovered Sogdian materials – Edition of a draft letter written by an inexperienced scribe: a sample from the so far unnoticed Saigonji Tachibana texts (in Japanese)". In: *Memoirs of the Faculty of Letters, Kyoto University* 49, pp. 1–24.
— 2019a:*Three Manichaean Sogdian letters unearthed in Bäzäklik, Turfan.* Kyoto.
— 2019b: "On the Sogdian articles". In: *Annual report of the International Research Institute for Advanced Buddhology at Soka University for the academic year 2018[2019]* XXII, pp. 261–285.

The Covenant that Binds: Ownership of Life in Late Antique Zoroastrianism

ARASH ZEINI, Oxford

It is a great privilege and a pleasant duty to present this paper to my teacher DIETER WEBER in honour of his significant and numerous contributions to the study of Pahlavi papyri and documents. In 2014, DIETER and I talked in Cambridge about the significance of Middle Persian *bun* as we encounter it in the Pahlavi documents and its relationship to *buneh* in New Persian.[1] I promised that I would work on this concept and hope to have fulfilled my promise, at least partially, by illuminating another aspect of *bun* that originates in the *Zand*.

*

In most cases, it is difficult to determine the extent to which religious treatises reflect social realities of their time. Even when they are prescriptive, their relationship with practical matters of life is more complex than immediately noticeable. A case at hand might be the treatment of animals. Zoroastrianism divides animals into the categories of beneficial, *ahuric* and demonic, *ahremanic* animals (Avestan *xrafstra-*, Middle Persian *xrafstar*).[2] For instance, according to *Bundahišn* 23.2, cats are a subspecies of wolves, which are a creation of *Ahreman*. Yet, I believe that contra to Zoroastrian prescriptions, Iranians must have kept cats for the simple and practical reason to hunt and control vermin.[3] OMIDSALAR (2020) discusses an episode in the *Šāhnāme* on the treatment of cats which might be a reflection of such practical concerns among Zoroastrians:

> Nevertheless, a story in the *Šāh-nāma* (Moscow ed., IX, p. 192 vv. 3082–87) suggests that cats were common both as pets and mousers at the time of Ḵosrow II Parvēz (r. 590, 591-628). According to this story Ḵosrow sent a wicked and ruthless man to Ray, the home town of Bahrām Čōbīn, as governor with the order to destroy it. The governor ordered all the house cats in the city killed, but this led to such an explosion in the mouse population that the inhabitants of the city were

1 DIETER WEBER has variously worked on *bun*. See, for instance, WEBER 2008a *apud* MACUCH, WEBER 2008b and WEBER 2019, p. 3.

2 On noxious animals, see MOAZAMI 2005 with references.

3 On cats in Zoroastrianism, see BOYCE 1975, p. 91; on cats among Zoroastrians of Iran, see the brief note in BOYCE 1977, p. 163, fn. 51; and on the history of cats in the region from a zooarchaeological perspective, see HARUDA *et al.* 2020.

forced to abandon their houses. The city was saved when the queen brought a kitten to entertain the king, persuading him to remove the wicked governor from his post (Moscow ed., IX, p. 193 vv. 3098–102).

Similar considerations apply to other religious domains that concern practical matters or aspects of daily life. BOYCE (1977, p. 139) describes Zoroastrian attitudes towards death as follows:[4]

> WHEN death comes, Zoroastrians have two pressing duties: to dispose of the polluting corpse with care and celerity, according to strict rules, and to do everything possible to help the disembodied soul to reach heaven and be blessed. The first duty should be fulfilled within a day, the second should last at least thirty years—a con- trast which marks the difference in value between dead body and living soul, the one belonging to Ahriman, the other to Ohrmazd. Both sets of rites, of the one day and the many years, include immensely ancient elements representing different historic layers of belief. Some of the beliefs themselves were discarded millennia ago, but the observances have long outlasted them.

Irrespective of whether we agree with the details of BOYCE's description, the danger posed by a polluting corpse cannot be underestimated in Zoroastrianism. The corpse of a righteous person poses an even bigger danger as it attracts more evil after death. Moreover, impurity caused by contact with dead matter is one of the oldest concerns in Zoroastrianism, having already been discussed in the *Wīdēwdād* (chapters 5–12). Thus, the question arises as to how Iranian kings, in particular, Zoroastrian kings could justify exposure to dead matter on a large scale as it would be the case on the battlefield.[5] How would a Zoroastrian king sanction and justify a war, if the act of killing is a major source of the highest degree of pollution and a great attraction to evil in this world? In which light shall we view the following declaration about the loyalty to a military commander:

> Dk 8.26.14[6]
> *abar mihr *ud dōšāram ī artēštārān āgenēn hamīh *ud ayārīh ī ēk abāg did framān-burdār ī-šān andar spāh-sālār ud menišnīg abespārdan ī tan ō ōš ud dōšīd ī mēnōy mizd abē-gumānīh pad tan ī pasēn*
> On the friendship and love of the warriors, together (in) the union of the assistance of one with the other. (And on) their obedience towards the commander of

4 For a general overview of funerary rites described in the Avestan (Av.) scripture, see BOYCE 1975, pp. 325–330.

5 On the religious identity of Sasanian kings, see their coinage and for an example the declaration of King Šābuhr in his inscription: [*an, maz*]*dēsn bay [šābuhr šāhān šāh ērān ud anērān kē čihr az yazdān pus mazdēsn bay ardaxšēr šāhān ērān kē čihr az yazdān nab bay pābag šāh ērānšahr xʷadāy hēm*] 'I, the Mazdean lord Šābuhr, the king of kings of the Iranians and non-Iranians, who is of divine seed, the son of the Mazdean lord Ardasxšēr, the king of kings of the Iranians, who is of divine seed, the grandson of lord Pābag, (I) am the king of the realm of the Iranians' (quoted after HUYSE 1999, p. 22, with my translation and normalisation of the transcription).

6 If not otherwise mentioned, I quote Pahlavi passages with modifications after transcriptions kindly provided by SKJÆRVØ.

the army, the thoughtful surrender of their body to death, and the love for the reward of the *mēnōy*, (and) the certainty of the future body.

In the following, I shall examine Zoroastrian terminology relating to the type of death which is known to other religions as martyrdom.[7]

*

Acts of religious devotion, be it more generally striving for a sacred cause, or more specifically martyrdom, are common concepts in religions such as Christianity and Islam, but rarely discussed in the case of Zoroastrianism. As religious ideals, they seem in part to be connected with the idea of proselytism, a dominant feature of both Christianity and Islam. In the case of Islam, a martyr is 'one who bears witness to God by dying in his cause'.[8] It remains a strong feature even today, particularly in Shīʿa Islam, and may be associated with *jihād* or '[m] ore fully, *jihād fī sabīl Allāh*, striving in the cause of God'.[9] Both devotion and martyrdom are understudied in Zoroastrianism, as the surviving rituals and the extant corpus of Zoroastrian texts do not seem amenable to these religious concepts. This is striking, particularly as during late antiquity, a formative era for Zoroastrianism, the Sasanians (224–651 CE) faced rivals and enemies to the west as well as the east of their territories. One can easily imagine the emergence of a literary or religious genre around emerging religious zeal and in the face of threats to identity be it religious or civil.

Martyrdom seems an alien concept in Zoroastrianism[10] through its association with death and blood, the former strongly linked with *ahremanic* forces and the latter with the highest orders of impurity. These notions resonate even with modern perceptions of Zoroastrianism. WALKER (2020), for instance, writes in *The Guardian*: 'Zoroastrianism does not prize concepts such as guilt, martyrdom or asceticism. There is, instead, an obligation to work hard, make money, enjoy the proceeds and give generously'. This in turn, seems to agree with a classification of Zoroastrianism as a non-proselytizing religion, which may accept converts but does not prioritise conversion.[11] This is while narratives

7 It is beyond the scope of this article to discuss the Zoroastrian concepts surrounding death, sacrifice, sacrificial death, pollution and impurity. CHOKSY (1989) has written on pollution and its connection with the evil forces, while HINTZE (2018) has more recently discussed the Zoroastrian afterlife and funerary practices. In a discussion of the *stūm* ritual, KOTWAL & CHOKSY (2004) highlight how the connection between human beings in this world and the souls of the deceased can be upheld.

8 BOWKER 1997, p. 882.

9 BOWKER 1997, p. 501. BOWKER clarifies that *Jihād* does not serve the purpose of conversion of others into Islam.

10 See also STAUSBERG 2015, p. 189, who states 'that the concept of a martyr had been absent in Zoroastrianism' before the 'martyr-discourse of the Islamic Republic'.

11 SHARMA (2014, pp. 429–430) mentions Zoroastrianism only briefly in his discussion of Hinduism as 'a non-proselytizing religion that accepts converts'.

of unjust dying for a cause greater than humans are not uncommon in Middle Persian (MP) texts. In the *Ardā Wīrāz nāmag* 1.1–7, for instance, we read:

AWN 1.1–11[12]
ēdōn gōwēnd kū ēw-bār ahlaw zarduxšt dēn ī padīrift andar gēhān rawāg bē kard tā bowandagīh 300 sāl dēn andar abēzagīh ud mardōm andar abē-gumānīh būd hēnd ud pas gizistag gannāg mēnōy druwand gumān kardan ī mardōmān pad ēn dēn rāy ān gizistag +aleksandar ī hrōmāyīg ī muzrāyīg-mānišn wiyābānēnīd ī pad garān sezd ud nibard ud yask ō ērān šahr āmad u-š ōy ērān dahībed ōzad ud dar ud xwadāyīh wišuft ud awērān kard ud ēn dēn čiyōn hamāg abestāg ud zand abar gāw pōstīhā ī wirāstag ud pad āb ī zarr nibištag andar staxr pābagān pad diz nibišt nihād estād ud ōy petyārag ī wad-baxt ī ahlomōγ ī druwand ī anāg-kardār +aleksandar hrōmāyīg [muzrāyīg-mānišn abar āwurd ud bē sōxt ud čand dastwarān ud dādwarān ud hērbedān ud mowbedān ud dēn-burdārān ud abzārōmandān ud dānāgān ī][13] *ērān šahr rāy bē kušt ud mehān kadag-xwadāyān ī ērān šahr ēk abāg did kēn ud an-āštīh +ō mayān abgand xwad škast ō dušox dwārist*
They say thus: Once the just Zarduxšt propagated in the world the religion which he had accepted, the religion remained for 300 years, until (the time of) completion, in (the state of) purity and the people in (the state of) certainty. And then, the hateful Gannāg Mēnōy, the sinful one, in order to make people doubt this religion, deceived that accursed Alexander, the Roman who was dwelling in Egypt, who came to Ērān Šahr with heavy might and fighting and illness. And he struck down the ruler of Ērān, and he destroyed and ruined court and kingship. And this *dēn*, that is, the entire *abestāg* and *Zand*, arranged on cow hide and written in gold, had been put in Pābag's Staxr at the fortress of writing. And that evil, unfortunate, heretic, liar, the evil-doer of Alexander, the Roman who was dwelling in Egypt, he brought and burnt it. And (he) killed many of the religious authorities and judges and teacher-priests and priests and believers, and skilled and knowledgeable ones of the land of the Iranians. And he incited hate and enmity in the midst of the great ones and the local rulers of the land of the Iranians. (Then) he destroyed himself and ran to hell.

The above passage begins with a reference to the acceptance and dissemination of the religion (*dēn ī padīrift andar gēhān rawāg bē kard*), perhaps pointing to a moment of religious zeal, perhaps even a reflection of the spread of Islam to the Sasanian domains.[14] However, in describing the destruction brought about by Alexander, the narrator adopts a matter-of-fact and unemotional tone. None of the kings, lords and religious dignitaries are described as martyrs, or as people

12 The first folio of K20 the missing (see NAWABI 1976), and VAHMAN (1986, p. 19–20) only reproduces folio 135r of H6, so that a sequence of text, noted below, is missing in his facsimile. I have thus supplemented my transcription with readings provided by VAHMAN (1986, p. 76). The numbering follows JAMASPJI ASA/HAUG (1872, pp. 3–4).
13 Sequence missing in H6 as reproduced by VAHMAN (1986, p. 19).
14 On disseminating the religion, see ZEINI 2020, pp. 100–103 & 112–114. I am currently working on another paper on religious identity and the dissemination of Zoroastrianism in late antiquity.

who died while upholding their beliefs or fighting for a sacred cause. In fact, they remain anonymous.

In another instance, highlighted by YARSHATER (1979, p. 90) and briefly discussed also by ROSE (2011, p. 172), the Middle Persian text *Ayādgār ī Zarerān* and the figure of Siyāwaxš have been suggested as forerunners of the Islamic rites of *ta'ziyeh*. The text, *Ayādgār ī Zarerān*, describes a religious battle at the time of king Wištāsp, the first king to accept the Zoroastrian religion (*ēn dēn ī abēzag ī mazdēsnān az ohrmazd padīrift* 'he accepted this pure religion of the Mazdeans from Ohrmazd'). Religious overtones are undoubtedly present and an uncontroversial feature of the text, but I fail to see that Zarēr's unjust death is 'bitterly lamented' as YARSHATER (1979, p. 90) suggests. The text celebrates the bravery of Zarēr and his son Bastwar, who is described as a child (MP *aburnāy*); Zarēr's courage as a military commander with an unwavering commitment to his king, and Bastwar as a child dedicated to his father. References to martyrdom or similar concepts are missing in the text, and the figure of Zarēr is not portrayed as martyr.[15]

The same applies to Siyāwaxš who is a rather marginalised figure in the Zoroastrian Middle Persian texts, and not connected with religious ideas. Both Zarēr and Siyāwaxš are killed unjustly by different types of enemies of the Iranians, both are victims of intrigues, and their death is revenged by their sons (*kēn ī pid*), Bastwar and Kay Husraw. In the Middle Persian text *Māh Frawardīn rōz ī Hordād* we read: *māh frawardīn rōz ī hordād Kay-Husraw Siyāwaxšān Frāsiyāg ī Tūr pad kēn ī pid ī xwēš bē ōzad* 'On the day Hordād of the month Frawardīn, Kay-Khosrow son of Siyāwaxš killed Frāsiyāg the Tūrānian to avenge his father'.[16] In the same text, we find another example of revenging an unjust death: *Māh [ī] Frawardīn rōz ī Hordād Manūščihr abar kēn ī Ērēč bērōn mad ud Salm ud Tōz rāy pad kēn ī *Ērēč bē ōzad* 'On the day Hordād of the month Frawardīn, Manuščihr came out to avenge Ērēč and killed Salm and Tōz to avenge Ērēč'.[17] While ancient Iranian epic traditions might have served as templates for Islamic rites, religious motifs and terminology akin to martyrdom are missing in both narratives discussed by YARSHATER (1979).

If martyrdom is not endorsed in Zoroastrianism on account of purity concerns, did the Mazdean religion discourage it, or did it frame striving for a sacred cause differently?

15 A detailed analysis of *Ayādgār ī Zarerān* is beyond the scope of this paper. I recognise the intensely dramatic and epic nature of the text, but maintain that the language is not dramatic and that Zarēr is not celebrated as a martyr of the religion. I share the view expressed by BOYCE (1987) that the text is rather epic in nature. Father and son encounters and conflicts are known from other Iranian material and this text is one such example. On the text, see MONCHI-ZADEH (1981) which should be consulted alongside a review by MACKENZIE (1984).

16 GRENET 2009, p. 163.

17 GRENET 2009, p. 163.

For this investigation, I borrow a simple working definition for martyr, and by extension martyrdom, from BOWKER (1997, p. 623): 'One who suffers death on behalf of his or her faith, often for refusing to renounce it'. Moreover, I expect that such instances are either celebrated, lamented, or portrayed in light of the struggle for a religious conviction. Similarly, in Islam already the 'Ḳurʾān refers to the reward for those slain in the way of God (*fī sabīl Allāh*)', presumably the martyr, whereby the wider Islamic jurisprudence maintains the purity of the martyr's lifeless body, going so far as to suggest that 'the martyr's bloodstained clothes will constitute proof of his status on the Day of Judgment' which is 'the main reason for holding that he should be buried in the garments in which he was killed'.[18] Although martyrdom is a far more complex concept both in Christianity and Islam, with possible cross-cultural influences between the two faiths, its association with death and blood are obvious in both religious traditions.[19] By contrast, Zoroastrianism shuns death as the work of evil. It views dead matter as the highest impurity, and likewise regards free flowing blood as impure. Martyrdom being intrinsically linked with death and bloodshed, both evil concepts in Zoroastrianism, the question naturally arises as to how such a religious mindset could approve dying or killing for a good cause, let alone celebrate it.[20] How then does Zoroastrianism solve this conundrum? What are the tools in the hands of the priests for spreading, protecting or defending the Mazdean religion?

On a purely lexical level, the concept of devotion is known in Middle Persian. MACKENZIE (1990, p. 39), for instance, lists *gyān-abespār* with the meanings, to my mind rather confusingly, 'reckless, desperate' and 'devoted'. The meaning 'devoted' is perhaps best illustrated in the following passages:[21]

Handarz ī anōšag-ruwan ādurbād ⁺ī mārspandān 10[22]

> *pad tis ⁺ī yazdān ud amahraspandān tuxšāg ud gyān-abespār bāš*
> In the affairs of the divine beings and the *Amahraspandān* be diligent and devoted.

Ayādgār ī wazurg-mihr 265[23]

> *anōšag-ruwān bawād wazurg-mihr ī bōxtagān ud awēšān kayān ud yalān ud wīrān kē gyān-abespārīh ī dēn ī māzdēsnān kerd hēnd*
> May the souls of Wazurg-mihr ī Bōxtagān and those kings, and heroes, and men who devoted[24] (themselves) to the religion of the Mazda-worshippers be immortal.

18 KOHLBERG 2012.
19 Literature on martyrdom abounds. For a multifaceted approach, see DIJKSTRA/KROESEN/KUIPER 2010.
20 For comparative perspectives in Jewish and Christian cultures, see HERMAN 2010 and FRANCISCO 2016.
21 *gyān-abespār* is not very widely attested in Zoroastrian Middle Persian texts. Most are within *Kārnāmag ī Ardaxšēr ī Pābagān*.
22 Text after JAMASP-ASANA 1913, p. 59.
23 Text after JAMASP-ASANA 1913, p. 101.
24 This is perhaps the only passage, where *gyān-abespārīh* can also be translated '… gave their lives for …'.

Mēnōy ī xrad 1.64[25]

> *pad spāsdārīh ī andar yazdān ud yašt ud niyāyišn ud yazišn ud azbāyišn ud hammōxtārīh ī frahang kardan tuxšāg ud gyān-abespār bāš*
> In gratitude towards the divine beings and sacrifice, and prayer, and worship, and invocation, and learning to practise *frahang*, be diligent and devoted.

As the semantics of the term seem in part to be informed by New Persian *ǰān-sipār*, literally 'entruster of life', it is unclear to me how MACKENZIE arrives at 'reckless, desperate'. NYBERG (1974, p. 106) offers a more nuanced list of collocations involving '*jān*' such as *jān apispārtan* 'to give one's life (*rād* for a p.)'. The association of *gyān-abespār* or *gyān abespurdan* with dying through commitment of life to a person or cause, seem to be clear. The compounded verb *gyān kandan* with the meaning 'give up the ghost; moment of death' seems to further underline this notion. With these terms and verbs in mind, the question arises as to whether *gyān-abespār* denotes devotion or whether the semantics also include a concept comparable to martyrdom. After all, the Persian, as opposed to Arabic, words for a martyr are جان‌باز *ǰānbāz* or جان‌باخته *ǰānbāxte*.

In the following, I will draw attention to a previously unrecognised use of Sasanian legal terminology in the Middle Persian translations of the *abestāg*. I hope to elucidate how Sasanian priests might have utilised the exegesis of the sacred word to extend their authority beyond matters of theology and scripture.

1. *bun ud bar*

In a number of *Zand* passages we encounter the expression ⟨bwn W bl⟩ *bun ud bar* 'capital and yield', which does not correspond to a phrase in the Avestan source text. So, for example, in the Middle Persian translation of Y 37.1c:

Y 37.1[26]
(a) *iϑā. āaṯ. yazamaide. ahurəm. mazdąm. yō. gąm.cā. aṣ̌əmcā. dāṯ*
(b) *apascā. dāṯ. uruuarā̊scā. vaŋᵛhīš*
(c) *raocā̊scā. dāṯ. būmīmcā. vīspācā. vohū*

(a) In this way, we then worship *Ahura Mazdā*, who created the cow and truth,
(b) he created the waters and the good plants,
(c) he created light and the earth, and all that is good.

PY 37.1
(a) *ēdar ēdōn yazom ohrmazd kē gōspand ud ahlāyīh-iz dād*
(b) *u-š āb-iz dād ud urwar-iz ī weh*
(c) *u-š rōšnīh dād ud būm-iz ud harwisp-iz ābādīh bun ud bar*

25 Text after ANKLESARIA 1913, p. 15.
26 Text after Pt4, the translation is mine. For a close reading of the Avestan and Middle Persian *Yasna Haptaŋhāiti*, see HINTZE 2007 and ZEINI 2020.

(a) Here, I thus worship *Ohrmazd*, who created cattle and righteousness too.
(b) And he also created water and the good plant(s) too.
(c) And he created light and also the earth and all prosperity too, (namely) capital and yield.

The Avestan passage assigns the creation of 'all that is good' (*vīspācā vohū*) to *Ahura Mazdā*. The *Zand* agrees, but adds the expression *bun ud bar* after *harwisp-iz ābādīh* 'also all prosperity', the latter translating Avestan *vīspācā vohū* 'all that is good'. In this passage, *vīspācā vohū* 'all that is good' and its Middle Persian translation *harwisp-iz ābādīh* 'also all prosperity' both signify the tangible creation, commonly known as *gētīy* in Zoroastrian Middle Persian texts. It is, however, unclear as to what *bun ud bar* signify after references to the *gētīy*. The meaning of the individual components, *bun* 'substance, capital, base, foundation, bottom' and *bar* 'fruit, yield, produce, profit', are sufficiently clear.[27] However, the priestly interpretation of the expression as a whole and its place and meaning in the *Yasna* have not been studied before.[28]

In the *Zand*, the expression *bun ud bar* regularly occurs after *harwisp huzāyišnīh*[29] 'all good birth'[30] and *harwisp ābādīh* 'all prosperity'.[31] We have already encountered *harwisp ābādīh* 'all prosperity', as referring to the tangible creation or *gētīy*. Although the attestation and spelling of *huzāyišnīh* are complicated in the manuscripts, this term too refers to the good creation of *Ohrmazd*, birth representing the act of creation.[32] The expression is also

27 See ZEINI 2020, p. 235, for other translations of *bun ud bar*.

28 I first discussed *bun ud bar* in ZEINI 2020. At the time, BUYANER (2014) had concurrently, but independently, carried out a study into the supposed Indo-European roots of Middle Persian metonymic figures including *bun ud bar*. I leave the evaluation of Buyaner's suggestion to the reader.

29 The manuscripts attest various spellings for *huzāyišnīh*. Pt4, for instance, reads ⟨hwz'šnyh⟩ in PY 3.8. The manuscripts F2 E7, M1 have ⟨hwz'yšnyh⟩ for *huzāyišnīh*, which informs my transcription, while J2 K5 have ⟨hwz'yšn'Y⟩ and ⟨hwz'y'šnyh⟩, respectively. In PY 1.6b, by contrast, all relevant manuscripts (Pt4 Mf4 F2 T6 E7 G14, J2 K5 M1) read ⟨hwz'šnyh⟩ *huzāyišnīh*.

30 See PY 1.6, 3.8, 4.11, 7.8, 13.4, 14.2, PWd 3.3, *Srōš Wāž* 1 and G 4.6 (*Ēbsrūsrim Gāh*). In PY 3.8, J2 and F2 replace *bun ud bar* with a comment from PY 2.6 (for J2, see DHABHAR 1949, p. 22). The MSS also alternate between *huzāyišnīh* and *huzīwišnīh* 'good life' for Avestan *hujiiātōe* 'good life' and *hujītaiiō* 'good life'. In PY 3.8, 4.11 and 7.8, Pt4 translates *hujiiātōe* as *huzāyišnīh*. F2 agrees with Pt4 with the exception of PY 7.8 where it has *huzīwišnīh*. Both MSS have *huzāyišnīh* for *hujītaiiō* in PY 13.4, but *huzīwišnīh* in PY 33.10. The expected translation is *huzīwišnīh* 'good life' rather than 'good birth'. See also BARTHOLOMAE 1904, pp. 609, 1821–1822, and DHABHAR 1949, pp. 86, 88.

31 See PY 5.1 (= 37.1), 8.5, 11.12, 12.9, Yt 1.7, *Zand ī Nān*, *Stāyišn Dēnīh* (= Y 12.8–9) and *Hōšbām*.

32 Not every occurrence of *harwisp*, *ābādīh*, *huzāyišnīh* or a combination thereof is glossed *bun ud bar*. For *harwisp huzāyišnīh* without the gloss, see PY 2.6, 3.8, 6.5 and 12.1. See PY 19.2 & 4, 22.3 & 22, 24.3 & 8, 25.3, 37.4, 42.3 and 70.1 for *harwisp ābādīh*. Also, in PY 31.10, the expression comes after *ēdōn ān ī harw 2*, while in *Petīt Pašēmānīg* 1.1.2 *bun ud bar* is not seemingly motivated by a word we can identify.

attested in PY 31.10 after *ēdōn ān harw 2*, and in *Patit ī Pašēmānīh* 1.1.2, where *bun ud bar* are not seemingly motivated by a word I can identify.[33]

On the one hand, the collocation *bun ud bar* seems to emphasise totality, which the exegetes could have associated with the preceding *harwisp* 'all, everything'.[34] On the other hand, the expression could have been motivated by the immediately preceding word, *huzāyišnīh* or *ābādīh*. The key to understanding the hermeneutics of *bun ud bar*, however, may lie in PY 31.10 where it occurs after *ēdōn ān harw 2* and in a further reflection:

> (P)Y 31.10a[35]
> *aṯ. hī. aiiā̊. frauuarətā. vāstrīm. ax́ iiāi. fšuiiaṇtəm.*
> Thus, of these two, she [i.e., the cow] chose the cattle keeper as her shepherd.
>
> *ēdōn ān harw 2* ^{tis} *bun ud bar ā-t* ^{tō}[36] *az* ^{ast}[37] *awēšān mardōmān ō ōy franāft ī warzīdār ī fšūnēnīdār kū-t gōspandān bun ud bar ō ōy dād ī tuxšāg paymānīg*
> Thus, you professed those 2 things, (namely) *bun ud bar*, of those people to that one, who is a farmer, a cattle keeper; that is, the cattle gave *bun ud bar* to that one, who is diligent (and) moderate.

In this passage, where the cow is offered a choice to follow a shepherd and guardian or a non-shepherd, the cow chooses the shepherd, and irrespective of the Avestan source text, the two options are contextualised as *bun ud bar*, which are offered to the dilligent farmer and shepherd. Here, we have a solid reference to the material creation, the *gētīy*, with the cow or cattle, but in the *Zand* also to the two important aspects of wealth and property, as the collocation *bun ud bar* is known from Sasanian legal texts as two aspects that apply to each legal object in Sasanian law.

2. Sasanian Law

In Sasanian property law a legal object is defined as *xwāstag* 'property, wealth; money'.[38] As Macuch (2015) convincingly points out, Sasanian jurists distinguished between two fundamental types of rights to legal objects: *xwēšīh* 'ownership' and *dārišn* 'possession'. *xwēšīh* entitles the owner to full control of

33 For a recent edition of the *patit* texts, see Buyaner 2016.
34 See also Dhabhar 1963, p. 101, fn. 3, who suggests 'everything from beginning to end' as one of the possible translations.
35 Text after Pt4, with modifications to the *Zand* text after comparison with other manuscripts. Translation is mine.
36 Superscript above *ā-t*.
37 Superscript above *az*.
38 Macuch has extensively discussed the terms *bun ud bar* in the context of the Sasanian judiciary system. See Macuch 1993, pp. 695,697; 2005, p. 381; 2007, p. 198; 2009a, pp. 262, 271; Macuch 2009b, pp. 96–97 and Macuch 2015. Macuch (2008) has also examined the term *bun* in the context of the Pahlavi documents. This section is largely based on Macuch 2015.

an object (e.g. the right to own, use or even dispose of an object), while *dārišn* denotes the possession of an object without full ownership (e.g. leasehold and tenancy). Moreover, Sasanian property law divided every legal object (*xwāstag*) into capital or substance (*bun*) and its fruit or yield (*bar*). This division allowed the legal system to differentiate between ownership or possession of an object's capital or yield. For instance, the title to a vineyard could be transferred to one person, while another held the estate in ownership. Ultimately, the distinction between *bun* 'substance' and *bar* 'yield' in relation to *xwēšīh* and *dārišn* was fundamental to the development of Sasanian institutions such as *stūrīh* 'substitute succession' and *ruwānagān* 'pious foundation'.

As MACUCH (2015, p. 5) fittingly observes, in legal texts the ownership is always expressed by the verbal compound *pad xwēšīh dāštan* 'to hold in ownership', while possession is expressed by the verb *dāštan* 'to hold'. As we shall see, the *Zand* retains the legal terminology and reinterprets the above terms in a theological context, placing the relationship between the deity, the *gētīy* as a legal object, and the rights of the humans to the tangible creation in the context of a legal contract.

3. The Covenant

A commentary in PY 12.9, the final stanza of the *Frawarāne*, elaborates on the concept of capital and yield and its relationship to *ābādīh* 'prosperity':

> (P)Y 12.9c[39]
> *ahurāi. mazdāi. vīspāi. vōhū. cinahmī. aēšā. astī. daēnaiiā̊. māzdaiiasnōiš. āstūitiš.*
> I assign all good things to *Ahura Mazdā*. This is the profession of the Mazda-worshipping religion/vision.
>
> *ō ohrmazd harwisp ābādīh čāšom kū bun ud bar hamāg pad xwēšīh ī ohrmazd dārom ēd-iš ast dēn ī mazdēsnān āstawānīh +bowandag*[40]
> I assign all prosperity to *Ohrmazd*; that is, I possess both capital and yield in *Ohrmazd*'s ownership. This is the complete confession of the religion of the Mazdeans.

In agreement with Y 37.1c, here too, all prosperity (*harwisp ābādīh*) is assigned (MP *čāšom*, Av. *cīšmahī*) to *Ohrmazd*. However, in the commentary that follows the exegetes construe this assignment as a covenant, employing what seems to be legal terminology: *Ohrmazd* alone has full ownership over the substance and yield of the *gētīy* (*pad xwēšīh ī ohrmazd*), the legal object (*xwāstag*), while the worshippers are entitled to its substance and yield as possessors (*dārom*). The twist, compared to purely legal language where *pad xwēšīh dāštan* expresses full ownership, lies in the addition of *Ohrmazd* into the phrase as the sole retainer of the ownership: *pad xwēšīh ī ohrmazd (dāštan)* 'to posses in the ownership of *Ohrmazd*'. Therefore, I would like to

39 Text after Pt4, translation is mine.
40 Pt4 reads ⟨bndk̂'⟩.

suggest that the expression *bun ud bar* 'capital and yield' refers to the tangible world, defining it as a legal object, of which the capital and yield are owned by the deity, while humans partake in the ownership as possessors, again of both the substance and its yield. Thus, two different groups seem to share in on the *gētīy* as the legal object.

Such notions of shared ownership also emerge from other passages where the terms and consequences of the covenant are further clarified :

> PY 0.5c[41]
> *frāz pad menišn ud frāz pad gōwišn ud frāz pad kunišn ud frāz pad axw menišnīg ud frāz pad tan ud ān-iz ī xwēš gyān kū tan pad xwēšīh ī ašmā dārom pad xwēšīh ī ašmā dāštan ēd kū agar-im tan ruwān rāy bē abāyēd dādan be dahom*
> (I offer) forth by thought, and (I offer) forth by speech, and (I offer) forth by deeds, and (I offer) forth by focusing on the existence, and (I offer) forth by (my) body and also that which is my life,[42] as I possess (my) body in your ownership; 'to possess in your ownership' means this: if I have to give my body on account of the soul, I will give (it) up.

Here, the human body, part of the tangible creation, is declared the property of the deities: *kū tan pad xwēšīh ī ašmā dārom*.[43] The next commentary immediately clarifies the ramification of this legal relationship: *pad xwēšīh ī ašmā dāštan ēd* '"to possess in your ownership" means this'. The logical conclusion for the exegetes is this: 'if I have to give (up) my body for the sake of the soul, I will give (it)'. As we can see, humans are not fully entitled to their own body, and it can be *sacrificed* for the soul should the need arise. This view has far reaching consequences in the late antique Zoroastrian literature.

A commentary on a paraphrase of PY 0.5 in another Middle Persian text (*Petīt Pašēmānīg*), elaborates on this concept:

> Pt 1.1.2[44]
> *tan gyān ud ham ruwān bun ud bar ī xwāstag ī-m ast pad xwēšīh ī yazadān dārom pad xwēšīh ī yazadān dāštan ēn bawēd kū agar tis-ēw az ān rasēd ka-m tan ī ruwān rāy be abāyēd dādan be dahom*
> The body and life together (make up) the soul.[45] I possess the substance and yield of my properties in the ownership of the *yazadān*; 'to possess in the ownership

41 Text after Pt4, translation is mine.

42 In translating *gyān* as 'life' I follow Modern Persian. Shaked (1994, p. 56) prefers 'vital soul' to distinguish *gyān* from *ruwān* 'soul'. But there is ample evidence that already in Middle Persian *gyān* meant 'life'.

43 *ašmā* could theoretically refer to *Ohrmazd*, the *Amahraspandān* or the *yazadān*, as is the case in Pt 1.1.2. However, as the *Amahraspandān* are addressed in (P)Y 0.5a it is likely that 0.5c refers to them.

44 Text after Dhabhar 1927, p. 55 with indicated modifications. Considering his notes on his translation (see Dhabhar 1963, pp. 100–101, 124–125), I have emended his readings, hoping to approximate the text of the manuscripts, as Dhabhar's text is not always reliable.

45 My interpretation of this clause is based on a sentence found in Pt 2.1.2: *tan ud gyān kē nām ī ōy ruwān ast* 'The body and life whose name is soul', found in Dhabhar 1927, p. 63.

of the *yazadān*' is this: if something happens, so that I have to give my body on account of the soul, I will give (it).

The substance and yield of the legal object (*xwāstag*) are once more described as possessions in the ownership of the deities. Although the passage avoids explicit language, I interpret it as follows: The human body and its life (*tan gyān*) are the substance and yield of the soul (*ruwān*) whose full ownership lies with the deities. Moreover, the explanation of the phrase *pad xwēšīh ī yazadān dāštan* 'to possess in the ownership of the deities', suggests, to my mind at least, that the body is not just dedicated to the soul, but must be given up on account of the soul, if the need arises. I will return to this passage.

This sense of belonging to *Ohrmazd* and other deities is reminiscent of a passage from the *čīdag handarz ī pōryōtkēšān*:

ČHP 1[46]
kē hēm ud kē xwēš hēm ... ohrmazd xwēš hēm ayāb ahreman yazadān xwēš hēm ayāb dēwān ... ohrmazd xwēš hēm nē ahreman yazadān xwēš hēm nē dēwān
Who am I and to whom do I belong? ... Do I belong to *Ohrmazd* or *Ahreman*? Do I belong to the deities or the demons? ... I belong to *Ohrmazd* and not *Ahreman*, I belong to the deities and not the demons.

Although the above passage's purpose is to highlight the ethical dualism of Zoroastrianism, broadly speaking, the expressed sense of belonging is not accidental and reminds the reader of the passages discussed before.

Let us now look at two Middle Persian passages that do not translate the sacred corpus. I believe we find an explicit reference to defending the religion with one's own life in a discussion of good rule in MX 14.16:

MX 14.16[47]
hupādixšāyīh ān bawēd kē ... (21) *ud dēn ī weh ī mazdēsnān rāy tan ud ān-iz ī xwēš gyān be abespārēd*
(16) Good rule is that one, which ... (21) and (the good ruler) will give up his body and his life for the good religion of the Mazdeans.

Defending the religion with one's own life seems to have been a privilege reserved for the king, but certainly not the only mode of commitment. An alternative type of giving is discussed in a summary of the *Yasna Haptaŋhāiti* in the Middle Persian compendium known as *Dēnkard* (*Bag Nask*):

Dk 9.57.28[48]
ud ēn-iz kū huframānīh ud abzōn ī ohrmazd kard bawēd kē tan ud gyān ō yazadān dahēd u-š tan gyān ō yazadān dād bawēd kē dōstīh ō dēn ī zardušt dahēd ud ēn-iz kū kē ō ohrmazd dōstīh dahēd ā-š az ohrmazd sālārīh rasēd

46 Text after JAMASP-ASANA 1897, p. 41.
47 Text after ANKLESARIA 1913, pp. 60–61.
48 Text after DRESDEN 1966, p. 212.

> And this too, that good command and increase of *Ohrmazd* are performed (by those) who give their body and life to the deities. And their body and life are given to the deities (when) they commit friendship to *Zardušt*'s religion. And this too: whoever gives friendship to *Ohrmazd*, will receive guardianship from *Ohrmazd*.

The intended meaning of this passage is not entirely clear. The dedication of body and life to the deities, which strengthens *Ohrmazd*, is defined as committing friendship to Zardušt's religion. However, the text is silent on the nature of this friendship. Do you commit friendship by giving your life for the religion? The *Dēnkard* passage does not answer the question.

Allow me to close this section with the following observation: The legal terminology employed in the *Zand* is absent from the passage on good rule and the *Dēnkard*'s summary of the *Yasna Haptaŋhāiti*. However, the sentiments expressed in both passages, can only be explained by way of the covenant discussed in the *Zand*. Thus, it seems that in the immediate exegesis of the *abestāg* greater attention was paid to an explicit and more precise interpretation of the sacred word, while the wider Pahlavi literature made use of the established wisdom.

4. Conclusions

I hope to have shown how the late antique exegesis of the *abestāg* defined the relationship between the divine and human spheres as a contract using legal terminology. Humans do not own their body and as possessors have an obligation towards the deity, which they fulfil by accepting to abandon body and life (*tan*, *gyān*) for the benefit of the soul (*ruwān*). Admittedly, the priestly perception of *bun* and *bar* remains elusive in the *Zand*. Thanks to the efforts of Maria Macuch we know the legal definition of capital and yield, but the finer details of the divine covenant are not entirely clear. We do not know, for instance, which parts of the tangible and intangible creation are understood to be capital and which parts yield. It is perceivable that the *gētīy*, the tangible part of the creation, is *bar*, and the *mēnōy*, the intangible creation, *bun*. Be that as it may, the dense and coded language of the *Zand* leaves many questions open and more research is needed before we can comprehend the Sasanian exegesis of the *abestāg*. However, the above observations allow a number of interpretations for our understanding of Sasanian Zoroastrianism. In the following, I draw attention to three possible conclusions.

4.1. First Conclusion

In a discussion of constituent parts of a human, SHAKED (1994, pp. 55–57) observes three schemes that emerge from Middle Persian texts.[49] I cannot discuss the passages in detail here, but it is worthwhile to revisit SHAKED's observations:

> Besides certain details where traces of Aristotelian thinking, and perhaps also of some other Greek writers, can be detected, there is a solid tradition which derives from the Avesta and which continues the vocabulary of the sacred scripture. In this tradition some elements were added to the accepted Avestan notions, while others were omitted.[50]

He identifies the following schemes. According to *Dēnkard* 3 humans consist of four spiritual entities: the soul (*ruwān*); the vital soul, or anima (*gyān*); the pre-existent soul (*frawahr*), and consciousness (*bōy*). In this scheme, the soul has the highest rank. In the *Bundahišn*, Shaked identifies five entities: body (*tan*); vital soul (=anima, *gyān*); soul (*ruwān*), associated with consciousness (*bōy*); form (*ēwēnag*); and pre-existent soul (*frawahr*). Finally, there is the view put forward by the ninth century Zoroastrian scholar-priest Zādspram. In agreement with the *Zand* and the *Bundahišn*, it seems to me, he divides the constituent parts of humans into the three categories of what belongs to the body (*tanīg*), life (*gyānīg*), and the soul (*ruwānīg*), each category holding another three constituent parts. Thus, although SHAKED's observations are accurate, his conclusion that 'there is a solid tradition which derives from the *abestāg* and which continues the vocabulary of the sacred scripture' may need a closer look and revision. As we can see, the scheme proposed by Zādspram, that is, his division into *tanīg* and *gyānīg* may agree with the *Zand* passages discussed in this paper where *tanīg* and *gyānīg* may be the categories of *bar* that can be given up for the *ruwānīg* category which might be the *bun*. The *Dēnkard* diverges from the *Zand*. Zādspram's deep knowledge of the *Zand* is well-known and has been pointed out.[51] The juxtaposition of *tan* and *gyān* in the discussion above corroborates the background to Zādspram's views. As I shall discuss in the following, Zādspram's tripartite division, reflects what the *Zand* and other Middle Persian texts tell us about *gyān*.

As I have already pointed out, the covenant requires of worshippers to give up their body and life if the need arises. We can infer from the other passages I have discussed above that the body will be sacrificed to guard the religion. The verbs used to express these notions are *gyān dādan* and *gyān abespurdan* or *abespārdan* 'commit, entrust, consign' life. The phrases are *tan ud gyān dādan* and *tan ud ān-iz ī xwēš gyān be abespārdan*, respectively. There is no doubt that New Persian *jān dādan*, meaning 'to die', continues the Middle Persian usage.

49 For another discussion of the composition of humans, see BAILEY 1943, also mentioned by SHAKED.

50 SHAKED 1994, p. 57.

51 See, for instance, GROPP 1991.

The case of *gyān abespurdan* is similar. MACKENZIE (1990, p. 39) gives the following relevant constructions for the noun *gyān*: *gyān kandan* meaning 'to give up the ghost; moment of death' and *gyān-abespār* 'reckless, desperate; devoted'. The first, *gyān kandan*, is also known in NP and confirms that a construction with the meaning 'to die' is possible for *gyān*. As a result, *gyān*, for which MACKENZIE (1990, p. 39) only gives the meaning 'soul, ghost' can be extended to denote 'life'. To distinguish *gyān* from *ruwān* 'soul', SHAKED (1994, p. 56) prefers 'vital soul' for *gyān*. I believe, however, that in much of the Middle Persian literature *gyān* refers to life. The second compound noted by MACKENZIE, *gyān-abespār*, is also known in NP. However, based on the previous observations, and NP *ǰān-sipār*, we can add a new nuance to the meaning of Middle Persian *gyān-abespār* and extend 'devoted' to mean 'someone who is willing to give up life'. As most will agree, the meaning of *ǰān sepurdan* is uncontroversial in New Persian. See for instance a verse by Adīb Pišāvari (ادیب پیشاوری):

سحر به بوی نسیمت به مژده جان سپرم   اگر امان دهد امشب فراق تا سحرم

> At dawn, I will give up life to the scent of your breeze, the joyful news, if the parting spares me tonight till dawn.

That *gyān* can and should be translated 'life' as opposed to 'soul' or 'vital soul' emerges from the following passage:[52]

> Bd 27.44[53]
> *astwihād wāy ī wattar kē gyān stānēd čiyōn gōwēd kū ka dast abar mardōm mālēd būšāsp ka-š sāyag abar abganēd tab ka-š pad čašm wēnēd gyān bē zanēd u-š marg xwānēnd*
> *Astwihād*, (that is) the evil *Wāy*, is the one who takes life. As it is said: When it touches a person with its hand, it is 'lethargy'; when it casts its shadow on one, it is 'fever'; and when it looks upon one with its eyes, it strikes life, and they call it 'death'.

The above passage is certainly an allusion to Bd 3.15:

> Bd 3.15[54]
> *u-š mardōm pad 5 bazišn frāz dād tan ud gyān ud ruwān ud ēwēnag ud frawahr čiyōn tan ān ī gētīy ud gyān ān ī abāg wād paywast estēd wēn āwarišn barišn ruwān ān ī abāg bōy andar tan āšnawēd wēnēd gōwēd dānēd ēwēnag ān ī pad xwaršēd-pāyag estēd frawahr ān ī pēš ī ohrmazd xwadāy pad ān čim ēdōn brēhēnīd kū*

52 While in many passages *ruwān* and *gyān* may seem to have been used interchangeably, I maintain that *ruwān* is the part that survives the death of a person, departing to the hereafter, while *gyān* is the part that ends, bringing about the death of a human.

53 I quote this passage from VEVAINA 2024, who kindly took the time to entertain my questions about *gyān* by going through the rich resource that is his forthcoming book. I have modified his translation to reflect my understanding of *gyān*.

54 Text after SKJÆRVØ's transcriptions, checked against PAKZAD 2005, pp. 47–48.

andar ēbgadīh mardōm mīrēnd tan ō zamīg gyān ō wād ēwēnag ō xwaršēd ruwān ō frawahr paywast kū dēwān ruwān murnjēnīdan nē tuwān bawād
And he [*Ohrmazd*] created humans in five parts: body, and life, and soul, and form and *Frawahr*. As the body belongs to the *gētīy*, and life is connected with wind — inhaling and exhaling of breadth — the soul is the one that together with the senses hears, sees, speaks and knows in the body. The form is that one which dwells in the sun station, (and) the *Frawahr* in the presence of Lord *Ohrmazd*. He fashioned (them) in this way because when humans die at the time of the onslaught of evil, the body joins the earth, life (joins) the wind, the form (joins) the sun, (and) the soul joins the *Frawahr*, where the demons cannot destroy the soul.

4.2. Second Conclusion

Considering the above, we might explain the notion behind the New Persian expression, جان به جان آفرین تسلیم کردن 'to surrender life to the creator of life'. In my view, surrendering life to the creator of life is not just a poetic expression for readiness to die, but continues the concept of the covenant between the deity and humans. The former is the creator and sole owner of *tan, gyān* and *ruwān* while the latter, namely humans, are only the possessors of *tan ud gyān*. Thus, جان به جان آفرین تسلیم کردن denotes the return of body and life to the rightful owner in a last act of dedication to the good religion of the Mazda-worshippers.

4.3. Third Conclusion

Most importantly, I would like to suggest that the covenant, if its existence and language are accepted, signifies the Zoroastrian discourse on martyrdom. It is very unlikely that the Zoroastrian priests and scholars of the Sasanian era were unaware of the concept of martyrdom as it is, for instance, reflected in the Christian martyr acts.[55] Yet, a comparable notion seemingly did not develop in Zoroastrian Middle Persian literature. Even Islam does not seem to have had an impact on Zoroastrianism in this respect. Instead, we find a rather complex discourse which suggests that devoting your body and life to a religious cause were accepted, indeed expected, forms of dedication. However, this discourse mostly avoids an explicit mention of death, blood, and impurity, replacing these terms with an abstract code of dedication and willingness to sacrifices one's own body and life.[56] It is in this context that the term *gyān-abespār* mildly relates to the covenant. I hesitate to propose that martyrdom was known in

55 On martyr acts in general, see BROCK's (2008, pp. 77–84) list of acts sorted according to the reign of individual Sasanian kings, and FRENSCHKOWSKI 2015, particularly p. 472. See also SAHNER 2018, who discusses Christian martyrs under Islam with useful references to Zoroastrianism and the Sasanian era.

56 The verb *kō(x)šīdan* 'strive, struggle, endeavour' seems to be related to the covenant as well. I will discuss this elsewhere.

Zoroastrianism when the religion itself has avoided to construe terminology for martyrdom.[57] FRUCHTMAN (2023, p. 249) has recently argued for a paradigm shift in the study of martyrdom based on her finding that 'Martyrs do not have to die in order to be martyrs'. One of the three correctives FRUCHTMAN offers in her argument is a political corrective, which she defines as 'a corrective relating to the operation of power'.[58] A similar case can be made for Zoroastrianism in late antiquity.

Despite the Zoroastrian aversion to death, the Iranian religion has been associated with three empires. All three had armies commanding their soldiers' loyalty and devotion. They all fought wars, engaging in the act of killing, thereby increasing evil in the world. The above passages could be viewed as justifications for engaging battles where supporters of the religion could die. In language reminiscent of Islamic views of *šehādat* 'martyrdom' the act of dying for the religion is justified by means of the soul's benefit, perhaps reunion with the deity. Admittedly, our sources are restrictive in what they allow us to read into them. But it is perceivable that the creation of the covenant, using legal terminology, has a political background, as managing the worldly matters was not an affair limited to the kings, and aspects of it would have been within the remit of the priestly scholars of the Sasanian era.[59] No matter how we interpret the above passages, it is evident that our understanding of the Sasanian era and Sasanian Zoroastrianism cannot be complete without in-depth readings of the Middle Persian translations of the *abestāg*.

Bibliography

ANKLESARIA, T.D. 1913 (ed.): *Dânâk-u Mainyô-i Khard: Pahlavi, Pazand and Sanskrit Texts*. Bombay.

BAILEY, H. 1943: *Zoroastrian problems in the ninth-century books*. Oxford.

BARTHOLOMAE, CH. 1904: *Altiranisches Wörterbuch*. Straßburg.

BOWKER, J. 1997 (ed.): *The Oxford dictionary of world religions*. Oxford.

BOYCE, M. 1975: *A history of Zoroastrianism: The early period*. Leiden.

—1977: *A Persian stronghold of Zoroastrianism*. Oxford (Persian Studies Series 12).

—1987: "Ayādgār ī Zarērān". In: *Encyclopædia Iranica*, vol. III, fasc. 2, pp. 128–129. New York.

BROCK, S.P. 2008: *The history of the Holy Mar Maʿin with a guide to the Persian martyr acts*. Piscataway, NJ (Persian Martyr Acts in Syriac: Text and Translation 1).

BUYANER, D. 2014: On a Pahlavi metonymic figure and its Indo-European roots. *Estudios Iranios y Turanios* 1, pp. 7–24.

57 For a discussion of martyrdom among Zoroastrians in modern Iran, which is in fact largely a borrowing from the majority religion of Islam, see STAUSBERG 2002 II, p. 218, and ROSE 2011, p. 187.

58 FRUCHTMAN 2023, p. 249.

59 On the latter point, see ZEINI 2018.

—2016: *Penitential sections of the Xorde Avesta (patits). Philological edition with commentary and glossary*. Wiesbaden (Iranica 22).
Choksy, J. 1989: *Purity and pollution in Zoroastrianism: Triumph over evil*. Austin.
Dhabhar, B.N. 1927: *Zand-i Khūrtak Avistāk*. Bombay (Pahlavi Text Series 6).
—1949: *Pahlavi Yasna and Visperad. Edited with an introduction and a glossary of select terms*. Bombay (Pahlavi Text Series 8).
—1963: *Translation of Zand-i Khūrtak Avistāk*. Bombay.
Dijkstra, J./J. Kroesen/Y. Kuiper 2010 (eds.): *Myths, martyrs, and modernity: Studies in the history of religions in honour of Jan N. Bremmer*. Leiden (Numen Book Series 127).
Dresden, M.J. 1966 (ed.): *Dēnkart. A Pahlavi text. Facsimile edition of the manuscript B of the K.R. Cama Oriental Institute Bombay*. Wiesbaden.
Francisco, H.R. 2016: "Corpse exposure in the acts of the Persian martyrs and its literary models". In: *Hugoye: Journal of Syriac Studies* 19(1), pp. 193–225.
Frenschkowski, M. 2015: "Christianity". In: M. Stausberg/Y. S.-D. Vevaina (eds.): *The Wiley Blackwell companion to Zoroastrianism*. Chichester, pp. 457–475. .
Fruchtman, D.Sh. 2023: *Living martyrs in late antiquity and beyond: Surviving martyrdom* (Routledge Studies in the Early Christian World). London.
Grenet, F. 2009: "The Pahlavi text māh ī frawardīn rōz ī hordād. A source of some passages of Bīrūnī's chronology". In: W. Sundermann/A. Hintze/F. de Blois (eds.): *Exegisti Monumenta. Festschrift in Honour of Nicholas Sims-Williams*. Wiesbaden (Iranica 17), pp 161–170.
Gropp, G. 1991: "Zādsprams Interpretation des Ahunavairyo-Gebetes". In: R. Emmerick/D. Weber (eds.): *Corolla Iranica: Papers in honour of Prof. Dr. David Neil MacKenzie on the occasion of his 65th birthday on April 8th, 1991*. Frankfurt, pp. 79–89.
Haruda, A./A.R. Ventresca Miller/J.L.A. Paijmans/A. Barlow/A. Tazhekeyev/S. Bilalov/Y. Hesse/M. Preick/T. King/R. Thomas/H. Härke/I. Arzhantseva. 2020: "The earliest domestic cat on the Silk Road". In: *Scientific Reports* 10(1). Available online: https://doi.org/10.1038/s41598-020-67798-6.
Herman, G. 2010: "Bury my coffin deep! Zoroastrian exhumation in Jewish and Christian sources". In: J. Roth/M. Schmelzer/Y. Francus (eds.): *Tiferet Leyisrael: Jubilee volume in honor of Israel Francus*. New York, pp. 31–50.
Hintze, A. 2007: *A Zoroastrian liturgy. The worship in seven chapters*. Wiesbaden (Iranica 12).
—2018: "Zoroastrian afterlife beliefs and funerary practices". In: Chr. Moreman (ed.): *The Routledge companion to death and dying*. London/New York, pp. 86–97.
Huyse, Ph. 1999: *Die dreisprachige Inschrift* Šābuhrs *I. an der Kaʿba-i Zardušt (ŠKZ)*. London (Corpus Inscriptionum Iranicarum part III, vol. I).
Jamasp-Asana, J.M. 1897 (ed.): *Pahlavi texts. Contained in the codex MK, copied in 1322 A.D. by the scribe Mehr-Âwân Kai-khûsrû*. Vol. I. Bombay.
—1913 (ed.): *The Pahlavi texts. Contained in the codex MK copied in 1322 A.C. by the scribe Mehr-Âwân Kaî-khûsrû*. Vol. II. Bombay.
Jamaspji Asa, H./M. Haug 1872: *The book of Arda Viraf*. London.
Kohlberg, E. 2012: "Shahīd". In: *Encyclopaedia of Islam, second edition*, Leiden. Available online: https://referenceworks.brillonline.com/entries/encyclopaedia-

of-islam-2/shahid-COM_1025?s.num=3&s.au=%22Kohlberg%2C+E.%22 (last accessed 21.12.2022).

KOTWAL, F./J. CHOKSY 2004: "To praise the souls of the deceased and the immortal spirits of the righteous ones: The staomi or stūm ritual's history and functions". In: M. STAUSBERG (ed.): *Zoroastrian rituals in context.* Leiden (Numen Book Series 102), pp. 389–401.

MACKENZIE, D.N. 1984: "Review of *Die Geschichte Zarēr's.* Ausführlich kommentiert von DAVOUD MONCHI-ZADEH, Acta Universitatis Upsaliensis, Uppsala 1981". In: *Indo-Iranian Journal* 27, pp. 155–163.

—1990: *A concise Pahlavi dictionary.* Oxford.

MACUCH, M. 1993: *Rechtskasuistik und Gerichtspraxis zu Beginn des siebenten Jahrhunderts in Iran: Die Rechtssammlung des Farroḫmard i Wahrāmān.* Wiesbaden (Iranica 1).

—2005: On Middle Persian legal terminology. In: C. CERETI/M. MAGGI (eds.): *Middle Iranian lexicography: Proceedings of the conference held in Rome, 9–11 April 2001.* Roma (Orientalia Romana), pp. 375–386.

—2007: "The Pahlavi model marriage contract in the light of Sasanian family law". In: M. MACUCH/M. MAGGI/W. SUNDERMANN (eds.): *Iranian languages and texts from Iran and Turan. Ronald E. Emmerick memorial volume.* Wiesbaden (Iranica 13), pp. 183–204.

—2008: "Anhang VI: Zur juristischen Terminologie der Berliner Pahlavi-Dokumente". In: *Berliner Pahlavi-Dokumente. Zeugnisse spätsassanidischer Brief- und Rechtskultur aus frühislamischer Zeit.* Wiesbaden (Iranica 15), pp. 249–266. .

—2009a: "Disseminating the Mazdayasnian religion. An edition of the Pahlavi Hērbedestān chapter 5". In: W. SUNDERMANN/A. HINTZE/F. DE BLOIS (eds.): *Exegisti monumenta. Festschrift in honour of Nicholas Sims-Williams.* Wiesbaden (Iranica 17), pp. 251–277.

—2009b: "The Hērbedestān as a legal source: A section on the inheritance of a convert to Zoroastrianism". In: C.A. BROMBERG/N. SIMS-WILLIAMS/U. SIMS-WILLIAMS (eds.): *Iranian and Zoroastrian Studies in Honor of Prods Oktor Skjærvø.* Bloomfield Hills (Bulletin of the Asia Institute 19), pp. 91–102.

—2015: "Substance and fruit in the Sasanian law of property and the Babylonian Talmud". In: M. GELLER (ed.): *The archaeology and material culture of the Babylonian Talmud.* Leiden (IJS Studies in Judaica 16), pp. 245–259.

MOAZAMI, M. 2005: "Evil animals in the Zoroastrian religion". In: *History of Religions* 44(4), pp. 300–317.

MONCHI-ZADEH, D. 1981: *Die Geschichte Zarēr's.* Uppsala (Studia Indoeuropaea Upsaliensia 4).

NAWABI, M. 1976 (ed.): *The Pahlavi codices K20 & K20b containing Ardāgh Vīrāz-Nāmagh, Bundahišn etc.* Shiraz (The Pahlavi Codices and Iranian Researches 48).

NYBERG, H.S. 1974: *A manual of Pahlavi. Ideograms, glossary, abbreviations, index, grammatical survey.* Vol. 2. Wiesbaden.

OMIDSALAR, M. 2020: "Cat I. In mythology and folklore". In: *Encyclopaedia Iranica Online*, Brill. Available online: https://iranicaonline.org/articles/cat-in-mythology-and-folklore-khot (last accessed 12.06.24).

PAKZAD, F. 2005: *Bundahišn. Zoroastrische Kosmogonie und Kosmologie.* Tehran (Ancient Iranian Studies Series 2).

ROSE, J. 2011: *Zoroastrianism: An introduction.* London.

SAHNER, CH. 2018. *Christian martyrs under Islam: Religious violence and the making of the Muslim world.* Princeton.

SHAKED, SH. 1994: *Dualism in Transformation: Varieties of Religion in Sasanian Iran.* London (Jordan Lectures in Comparative Religion XVI).

SHARMA, A. 2014: "Hinduism and conversion". In: L.R. RAMBO/CH.E. FARHADIAN (eds.): *The Oxford handbook of religious conversion.* Oxford, pp. , 429–443.

STAUSBERG, M. 2002: *Die Religion Zarathushtras. Geschichte - Gegenwart - Rituale.* Vol. 1 & 2. Stuttgart.

—2015: "Zoroastrians in modern Iran". In: M. STAUSBERG/Y.S.-D. VEVAINA (eds.): *The Wiley Blackwell companion to Zoroastrianism.* Chichester, pp. 173–190.

VAHMAN, F. 1986: *Ardā Wirāz Nāmag. The Iranian 'Divina Commedia'.* London.

VEVAINA, Y.S.-D. 2024: *Zoroastrian hermeneutics in late antiquity. Commentary on the Sūdgar Nask of Dēnkard Book 9.* Wiesbaden (Iranica 32).

WALKER, SH. 2020: "The last of the Zoroastrians: A funeral, a family, and a journey into a disappearing religion". In: *The Guardian.* Available online: https://www.theguardian.com/world/2020/aug/06/last-of-the-zoroastrians-parsis-mumbai-india-ancient-religion (last accessed 12.06.24).

WEBER, D. 2008a: *Berliner Pahlavi-Dokumente. Zeugnisse spätsassanidischer Brief- und Recht- skultur aus frühislamischer Zeit.* Mit Beiträgen von Myriam Krutzsch und Maria Macuch. Wiesbaden.

—2008b: "Villages and estates in the documents from the Pahlavi Archive: The geographical background". In: *Bulletin of the Asia Institute* 24, pp. 39–67 [Published in 2014].

—2019: "Two unknown documents from the 'Pahlavi Archive'". In: *Sasanika Papyrological Studies* 3, pp. 1–6.

YARSHATER, E. 1979: "Ta'ziyeh and pre-Islamic mourning rituals in Iran". In: P. CHELKOWSKI (ed.): *Ta'ziyeh: Ritual and drama in Iran.* New York (New York University Studies in Near Eastern Civilization 7), pp. 88–94.

ZEINI, A. 2018: "The king in the mirror of the Zand: Secrecy in Sasanian Iran". In: T. DARYAEE (ed.): *Sasanian Iran in the context of late anitquity: The Bahari lecture series at the University of Oxford.* Irvine (Ancient Iran Series VI), pp. 149–162.

ZEINI, A. 2020: *Zoroastrian scholasticism in late antiquity: The Pahlavi version of the Yasna Haptaŋhāiti.* Edinburgh (Edinburgh Studies in Ancient Persia 8).

Deciphering the Illegible:
Fes